Sexuality

Robert Glaisek, Sander L. Gilman Teaching Freud's Theory of Bisexuality, *1987.*

Other Works by the Same Author

MONOGRAPHS

Form und Funktion: Eine strukturelle Untersuchung der Romane Klabunds (1971)

The Parodic Sermon in European Perspective: Aspects of Liturgical Parody from the Middle Ages to the Twentieth Century (1974)

Bertolt Brecht's Berlin (1975)

Nietzschean Parody: An Introduction to Reading Nietzsche (1976)

The Face of Madness: Hugh W. Diamond and the Rise of Psychiatric Photography (1976)

Wahnsinn, Text und Kontext: Die historischen Wechselbeziehungen der Literatur, Kunst und Psychiatrie (1981)

On Blackness without Blacks: Essays on the Image of the Black in Germany (1982)

Seeing the Insane: A Cultural History of Psychiatric Illustration (1982)

Difference and Pathology: Stereotypes of Sexuality, Race, and Madness (1985)

Jewish Self-Hatred: Anti-Semitism and the Hidden Language of the Jews (1986)

Oscar Wilde's London (1987)

Disease and Representation: Images of Illness from Madness to AIDS (1988)

EDITIONS

Johannes Agricola, Die Sprichwörtersammlung (1971)

NS-Literaturtheorie (1971)

The City and Sense of Community (1976)

F. M. Klinger, Werke (1978 ff.)

Robert Blum: Aus dem literarischen Nachlass (1979)

Begegnungen mit Nietzsche (1981; third edition, 1987)

Introducing Psychoanalytic Theory (1982)

J. P. Eckermann: Aphorismen (1984)

Degeneration: The Dark Side of Progress (1985)

Conversations with Nietzsche: A Life in the Words of His Contemporaries (1987)

Friedrich Nietzsche's Writings on Rhetoric and Language (1989)

Sexuality
An Illustrated History

Representing the Sexual
in Medicine and Culture
from the Middle Ages to the Age of AIDS

Sander L. Gilman

WILEY

JOHN WILEY & SONS
NEW YORK · CHICHESTER · BRISBANE · TORONTO · SINGAPORE

For Marina

Library of Congress Cataloging in Publication Data:

Gilman, Sander L.
  Sexuality: an illustrated history/Sander L. Gilman.
    p. cm.
  Includes bibliographical references.
  ISBN 0-471-83792-X
  1. Sex (Biology) in art—History.   2. Sex in art—History.
  3. Sexually transmitted diseases in art—History.   I. Title.
  QP251.G46 1989
  306.7′022′2—dc20   89-37700
                                                        CIP

Printed in the United States of America

10 9 8 7 6 5 4 3 2 1

Preface

This volume has grown out of extensive work over the past five years, some of it supported by grants from the National Endowment for the Humanities as well as the Fund for Psychoanalysis of the American Psychoanalytic Society. The initial work was undertaken at the Wellcome Institute for the History of Medicine, London, which has continued to help supply materials and whose staff (including William Schupbach, William Bynum, Roy Porter, Vivian Nutten, and Christopher Lawrence) have been the sounding board for many of the ideas in the book. The volume was completed during my term as the Mellon Visiting Professor of Humanities at my alma mater, Tulane University, which provided me with all of the comforts of home. I am grateful to Francis Lawrence, the Provost of the University, for his hospitality.

In addition to the Wellcome Institute, many scientific and artistic collections supplied me with picture material, only a fraction of which is incorporated into the present volume. I am grateful to all of them and have listed them in the captions to the photographs.

It will be evident from the credits for this book that it could not have been undertaken without the major support of the Collection in the History of Science in Olin Library at Cornell University, Ithaca. The extraordinary Howard B. Adelmann collection in the history of embryology provided many of the sources for the volume. The staff of the collection, Margaret Rogers, Lillian Clark, and Magdalene Hagedorn, has been uniformly helpful and supportive, as have Cornell's photographic services. In addition, the reference librarians at the Olin Graduate Library have been (as always) the source of great encouragement. My research assistants, Howard Grier and Heather Munro Prescott, double- and triple-checked the material; Kate Bloodgood helped edit the manuscript and turn it into a real book. The index was prepared by Jane Marsh Dieckmann. Sections of this book have appeared in quite different form in *Social Research, Critical Inquiry, MLN*, and *October*.

SANDER L. GILMAN

Ithaca, New York
September 1989

v

Contents

CHAPTER ONE

Introduction: Representing Human Sexuality

Scientist not himself pornographer in the practice of his science, but the price of beauty and the elegance of the method of science = the dispossession of layman. Lewdness = climate of the anteroom of science. Pornography stands in mutual relation to science and Christianity and is reinforced by both.
—*Walker Percy*[1]

Man passes through the present with his eyes blindfolded. He is permitted merely to sense and guess at what he is actually experiencing. Only later when the cloth is untied can he glance at the past and find out *what* he has experienced and what meaning it has had.
—*Milan Kundera*[2]

How are our perceptions of human sexuality structured? Do these structures reflect only our personal fantasies, or do they also reflect a socially accepted and historically determined code of what is supposed to be perceived as "sexual"? Daniel Rancour-Laferriere concludes his sociobiological study of "the signs of the flesh" with the comment that "the flesh is semiotizable. It is not merely itself, but is capable of signifying something other than itself to interpreters. Sex is 'everything' when the flesh is highly semiotized, and it is practically nothing when the flesh is not semiotized."[3] When the flesh is given meaning, sexuality is given meaning. But, to expand upon Rancour-Laferriere's dictum, the flesh, our anatomy, is *always* given meaning. The flesh is never neutral, never meaningless, always part of a process that generates meaning.

And nowhere does the flesh have and has always had inherent meaning more than in the world of medicine, the world in which the normal as well as the pathological are both given meaning.[4] Indeed, the very term *semiotics*, which today rings with the

claims of literary scholarship, is inherently and historically a term describing medical interpretation. Semiotics, as the act of the interpretation of signs, bridges the worlds of the aesthetic and the medical. And it is to the historical reconstruction of some of these signs of the flesh that this book will be devoted. What is illustrated (through the study of icons, of the representations, visual and verbal, of sexuality from the broadest range of sources in our culture[5]) is what meaning sexuality has been given, what interpretations have been extrapolated from the "flesh," from our sexual anatomy, our genitalia, which comes to represent our internalized sense of ourselves as sexual beings.[6]

We naively assume that our perception of human biology is rooted in the absolute, objective nature of human anatomy, just as the infant truly believes that an object vanishes when it is held out of sight. We cannot easily understand that our sense of our bodies is shaped within our culturally determined perception of ourselves. For the body is "real," is it not? It is composed of muscles and tissue, of flesh and blood. All of these are "real," not merely the fantasies of the artist and certainly not merely social constructions. However, once a relatively detailed catalogue of icons of sexuality is compiled it becomes clear that the representation of human anatomy has evolved and that the pattern of meaning, its continuity or, indeed, discontinuity is the result of a society's construction of images representing sexuality and the body rather than any shift in the reality of human anatomy.[7] And it is these representations that reveal to us (in retrospect) how we have constructed the nature of our own bodies. Indeed, the very idea of seeing the naked or nude (the unclothed or revealed) body has its own mean-

1

ing, a meaning that shifts from place to place and time to time.[8] Robert Graves stresses this in his poem on the distinction between "the naked and the nude" in which the "naked" in his world view are placed within the contexts of the erotic and the medical gaze:

Lovers without reproach will gaze
On bodies naked and ablaze;
The Hippocratic eye will see
In nakedness, anatomy[9]

While the "nude" are seen "draping by a showman's trick / Their dishabille in rhetoric." For Graves, as well as for Western aesthetic theory, it is within the world of sexuality and science that the body is truly seen; the "mock-religious grin" of religion creates a self-consciousness that veils the body. This convention of modern British poetry can tell us much about the twentieth-century desire to "see" science as pure and distinct from religious models. As will be seen, this is an artifact of a "modern" image of the medical gaze that is strikingly different from the tradition that will be explored in this book.

But even as the fantasies about the body have shifted, human anatomy has remained constant. And this is the contradiction. At least for the period under study, the past thousand years, the human body has remained conservatively constant; we have not altered perceptibly in terms of our anatomy (even though we have been exposed to radical shifts in our environment). The perceived conservative nature of human sexual anatomy has especially been understood as remaining constant in its form and function. Havelock Ellis commented on the basic primitive form of the genitalia, a Victorian view that saw the genitalia as a reflection of the most primitive roots of *Homo sapiens sapiens*.[10] For the Victorians the genitalia, whose "conservative nature" is "immutable" across time, represented the primitive aspects still hidden within the human being. The genitalia became a "missing link" with the evolutionary past, which was understood as a period of untrammeled sexuality. No Victorian scientist made this claim about the anatomy of the brain. Indeed, much of the argument in Victorian science about the "progress" of the human being over time toward the perfection of the late nineteenth-century specimen was keyed to the development or growth of the brain and, by definition, the lack of development of the genitalia.[11] Such an attribution of meaning was able to be given to the very fact of the "immutability" of the genitalia because they are

never understood as neutral, even in the perception of their anatomical structure. The genitalia exist, they are "real," but we label them as having qualities apart from their physical reality, qualities such as "the primitive." We are therefore bound (or, indeed, enabled) by the anatomy that defines us just as we define our bodies in terms of our understanding of the body's function. This limits in subtle ways the free play of our fantasy. The contradictions between our physical selves and our need to see ourselves as rational beings absolutely in control of our bodies and their attendant forces lead us to the construction of boundaries that encompass and control aspects of ourselves that we wish to distance and regulate. Our ego (that mechanism that creates the cultural images of the self) in establishing the boundaries for the self generates the illusion that we know the body's contours, its boundaries, indeed, its anatomy. But our knowledge is always mediated by the images that we draw from the thought-collective to express our sense of the boundaries of the self. As with Havelock Ellis's image of the "primitive" genitalia, we "see" our anatomy, especially our sexual anatomy, in terms of our culture's presuppositions of what the body means.

Here I must take issue with one of Michel Foucault's basic theses in his history of sexuality, which sees "sexuality [not] as a kind of natural given which power tries to hold in check. . . . It is the name that can be given to a historical construct. . . . What is involved is the production of sexuality rather than the repression of sex."[12] Foucault's argument shifts the focus away from "sexuality" to a political apparatus that he calls "sexuality." The physicality of sexuality, its anatomical reality, serves historically as the focus for all of the constructs of ideas, myths, fantasies of sexuality. There are social constructs that can exist separately from aspects of the physical world. Sexuality does not happen to be one of them. And the genitalia represent not only the body, in physical terms, but also the parallel existence of powerful psychosexual drives. One must address the reality of the existence of the libido, of an intrinsic, if shapeless and unfocused force, within all human beings that provides the extraordinary power always associated with all of our constructs of sexuality. We, of course, can no more represent the "libido" through rational discourse than, to paraphrase Friedrich Nietzsche's discussion of the "birth of tragedy out of the spirit of music," the Dionysian can be represented in an unmediated form. Once such elemental forces are conceptualized, are represented, they become enmeshed in a symbolic discourse that speaks about them in a manner that violates their very nature by giving them form and structure. This form (the "ego") permits us to "understand," that is, create an illusion of control of sexuality, but in doing so we open ourselves to the process of socially constructing the meaning of our sexuality. We construct the idea of the sexual around our understanding of our genitalia. And we understand that construction not as symbolic but as absolute. To assure this illusion of the absolute, the idea of sexuality is as dynamic in its ability to transform itself as is the ego. We evolve a system of representation of the libido even prior to the formation of rational language. As Melanie Klein observes: "Identification is a stage preliminary not only to symbol formation, but at the same time to the evolution of speech and sublimation. The latter takes place by way of symbol formation, libidinal phantasies becoming fixated in sexual-symbolic fashion upon particular objects, activities, and interests."[13] Thus we find the link between the early libidinal phase and the formation of a symbolic, encoded language of images that reflect the underlying bipolar organization of the psyche. Thus paradigm shifts in our mental representations of the body can and do occur within our generation of symbolic representations of the world, even though we are still bounded by the anatomy that "represents" our sexuality for ourselves. But we must also understand, as Freud so ably did, the power of social contexts (as well as psychological development) to form and deform an individual's own sexuality, indeed even desire, into a wide spectrum of highly structured forms, some "pathological," some "normal," all, however, adaptive. The physical aspects of human anatomy in which the sexual drive is focused are those arenas in which the play of libidinal forces is found. Our definition of these "biological" arenas of sexuality remains wider than most. But the icon for all of these erotic areas remains the genitalia. In our study the genitalia are understood semiotically in the most extended sense, including both the primary and the secondary characteristics (breasts and buttocks) as well as the widest human potential to symbolically eroticize every possible aspect of the body and extend that eroticization to objects in the world.[14]

This is not to say that I am advocating a return to the repression model of sexuality as the only valid means of understanding the sexual. Such a model represents, as Martha Vicinus observes, "sexuality . . . as an independent force or energy disciplined by personal and social constraints. Sex is always something to be released or controlled;

if controlled, it is sublimated or deflected or distorted."[15] Sexuality exists within the self but as an intrinsic aspect of becoming a self. Each of us is a sexual being, but what that implies for each of us, in terms of our psychological, social, historical, national, class, and gender definitions can be very different.[16] And yet there seems to be a consensus among the writers and artists discussed in this book that sexuality is the most powerful force they must control in order to control themselves. Such a construction of sexuality reflects a culturally bound model of the "uncontrollability" of the sexual that is embedded in Western definitions of the sexual. It is clear that most of the views concerning sexuality reflected in this book are versions of this "energy-control (or hydraulic) model" of sexuality, because, as Vicinus quite correctly notes: "The male bias of the energy-control model reflects both the gender of the major theoreticians and the unchanging assumptions of a male-dominated society." We shall therefore be looking primarily at male writers, male artists, male scientists explaining human sexuality within their sense of themselves and their bodies. And as this icon, the image of the body held in check, rather than the body generating its sense of self, does dominate the discourse about human sexuality in general, it also forms one of the major axes of our investigation.

It is vital to understand that such a construction of the sense of self reflects our internalization of a biological reality. For the act of coitus creates within all of us a sense of the abandonment of the ego, a flight into the libidinal recesses of our inner self. The moment of orgasm represents the total abandonment of the highly ordered and controlled world of the superego. Such moments represent to us (as individuals) the potential for the loss of control of the totality of our existence. The sexual thus serves as the emblem of the potential for disorder within our highly ordered private worlds. Such disorder cannot be contained within the self. It must be expelled into the world. The projection of such disorder, a disorder exemplified by the sexual and concretized into our image of the genitalia, becomes the basis for our projections about sexuality, projections that take the form of the thought-collective's fantasies about the Other, whether the "sexual" or the "racial" Other.[17] It is the study of these projections within medicine and art that will form the basis for this study. What we are examining is not the realities of sexual difference but our fantasies about the sexuality of the dominant discourse. Thus those images of the genitalia are the forms, the socially and historically constructed icons, that represent not a "hydraulic" image of the sexual but an even more basic sense of the order and disorder, the internalized images of the "good" and the "bad" world of our preoedipal development.[18] It is the power of this early, non-gender-specific set of images that manifests itself within the icons of a gender-based image of the sexual. Seeing sexuality means seeing the most basic aspects of our hidden self projected into the world and thus placed within the illusion of control.

The range of the sexual is limited by the biological realities in the broadest sense because its central referent is the genitalia. But the genitalia are conceptualized as bipolar forms, as the "male" juxtaposed to the "female." Sexuality is not solely a social construct, not the representation of the cultural boundaries of sex, but the wide-ranging, multifaceted potential implicit within the body itself. The boundaries superimposed upon the body make us see the body in a similar antithetical manner— make us see the body as "healthy" or "pathological," "normal" or "deviant." This is a reflex of the earliest division of our symbolic representation of the world into its "good" and "bad" aspects, into those aspects that we believe ourselves to control and those aspects that seem beyond our authority. It is not merely the activities of the body that are so labeled but the body itself. Rather than being able to see our sexual activities on a spectrum of sexual continuity, in which all sexual actions are possible, "normal," we are constantly creating borders between our personal sexual identity and that of the Other. This Manichean perspective, which deals solely in radical dichotomies, leads to the division of the sexual world along the lines of the definition of the self and that of the sexual Other. Human sexuality as represented within the construction of the genitalia is perceived within this model. The restructuring of the continuum of sexual forms and identities into a polar model necessitates the suppression of the ambiguities implied by the idea of such a spectrum of sexual forms (which would include "hermaphroditic" forms as well as sexually neutral ones) and identities (which would include "sexually anorexic" as well as "polymorphously perverse" ones).[19] Gender as well as sexual identity becomes polarized along the bipolar model of the distinction between the two sexes. Everyone must be able to be placed within this bipolar model. The result is the constant restructuring of our understanding of ourselves and our bodies because the dynamic nature of the construction of these boundaries means that we are ever creating (and defending) them. The illusion is that these boundaries are permanent, unchanging,

static; the reality is that we are always at work creating and maintaining them.

In addition, the perception of there being a "male" and a "female" anatomical structure, a natural dichotomy, reifies the boundaries drawn between forms of acceptable and unacceptable sexual activities, between the "healthy" and the "diseased," between the "normal" and the "pathological." The perception of this dichotomy as "natural," ignoring the wide range of sexual forms and structures, creates an impression that sexual "intermediary forms," to use the turn-of-the-century formulation, were merely those structures that deviated from the central, bipolar model of sexual anatomy, and were pathological, rather than having a place within a more broadly defined spectrum of "normal" human sexual anatomy. Such a view of the *hermaphrodite* (a term taken in this context from the pathological anatomy of the nineteenth century but having its roots in the Greek paradigm of human sexuality as discussed in Chapter Two) reifies the "normality" of the "male/female" dichotomy. Thus the very juxtaposition of "male" and "female" is in itself taken separately from any other variable, a constructed opposition reflecting a particular understanding of the form and function of the genitalia. The genitalia can be understood as the core representation of the bipolar model of human sexuality, which is further echoed in sexualized categories such as "health" and "disease," "normal" and "abnormal," "natural" and "perverse."

The meanings ascribed to sexuality and thus to the genitalia are illustrated with particular power in the aspects of this study that deal with sexual pathology and disease. My intent within these sections is to plumb the meaning of specific representations of sexually related or transmitted categories of "illness" and relate them to the basic structures of understanding of the body. Some of these "diseases," such as masturbatory insanity, are social constructs centering about a sexual reality (masturbation); some, like syphilis and AIDS, have a demonstrable etiology, but are nonetheless subject to the social construction of their meaning. These images of disease are cast in icons, and they overtly link the visual representation of the sufferer with the context in which such images function. My interest is in understanding Western societies' iconographic references for such images, and through these references, the extraordinary power that such icons have to reflect (and to shape) society's response to individuals suffering with disease. I wish to illustrate the context in which these icons function, for both those producing the icons as well as those interpreting them. Inherent in examining the icon of the sufferer from those diseases labeled as *sexual*, a label that is perhaps the most stigmatizing of all designations of physical pathology, is an understanding of the boundaries that we necessarily draw between our fantasy about ourselves (as the epitome of the healthy) and the Other, the sexually polluting and polluted individual.[20] With some diseases these boundaries are more or less benign, reflecting the cultural importance any disease has at a point in history. Sexually related or transmitted diseases have always been viewed as morally significant. They always have functioned (and most probably always will) as the sign of the power of sexuality to destroy (as well as create). They are never neutral, and most, therefore, play a significant role in the shaping of our sense of our sexual body. The disease becomes one with the body, and as Susan Sontag has observed: "With the advent of Christianity, which imposed more moralized notions of disease, as everything else, a closer fit between disease and 'victim' gradually evolved. The idea of disease as punishment yielded the idea that a disease could be particularly appropriate and just punishment."[21] Sexually transmitted disease becomes in the course of the millennium that we are examining the sign of the power and destructive force of the sexual. The icon of the person suffering from sexually transmitted disease is not merely a peripheral subset of the image of sexuality in our culture; rather it delineates the border between our sense of our own personal control over our sexuality and the world of sexuality beyond all control. It is the space into which we project our deepest fears, not only about our vulnerability to disease but also about our marginal sense of control over the sexual being within each of us. Whether we suffer from such disease or whether we are only potential sufferers, the power of icons of sexually transmitted disease is extraordinary.

But our intent in examining icons of sexually transmitted disease in our history of icons of the genitalia is not solely one of dispassionate interest. For each of us has the potential of stigmatizing as well as being stigmatized. The construction of icons of the sufferer from disease is a dynamic process to which the sufferers, real and imagined, consistently respond. It is in our best interest that we learn to observe the processes through which such stigmatization is implemented. Not that we can eliminate this process, but we can at least be aware that such a process does occur regularly and with some historical consistency. For the individual this may well mean the ability to understand the power

of stigma as one of the mediated factors in the disease process and to counter this image as a means of dealing with the psychological ramifications of the illness. What is fascinating is that the icons of disease seem to have an existence independent of the reality of any given illness. This free-floating iconography of sexually related or transmitted disease (like that of sexuality in general) is an artifact of the tradition of representing illness in any society. The icons seem to have a life of their own, attaching themselves to various and sundry diseases (real or imagined). And yet there are clear, demonstrable structural patterns, all of which have the potential to be filled with various, indeed, even contradictory, meanings. What we are observing is the cultural tradition of restricting disease within a specific set of icons that thus forms a visual boundary for the idea (or fear) of disease. This boundary is another means of creating the order that we desperately need to understand the world and our place within it. Boundaries such as those between the sexes are paralleled, overlap, contradict, and confuse other sets of boundaries, such as that between the healthy and the diseased, which we generate to wrestle some sense of meaning from the inchoate world. When such sets of categories function simultaneously, they generate polyvocal meanings, either so contradictory as to be confusing or so powerful as to seem necessarily true.

In this study I examine the history of Western objectifications of human sexuality within their cultural setting. Our objects are taken from "high" art, the art of collectors and museums; "low" (i.e., mass as well as popular) art, the art of the streets, from advertising to pornography; and, centrally, medical illustration, specifically the history of the anatomical illustration of the genitalia. Indeed, these very categories, ranging from those of "scientific illustration" to "pornography," must be contextualized.[22] For any icon of the genitalia can be "understood" (i.e., categorized) once it is placed within a specific context and thus given the qualities ascribed to traditions of representation that are labeled as "neutral" (such as "medical illustration"), "positive" ("aesthetic"), or "negative" ("pornographic").[23] But how many schoolchildren have used *Webster's Unabridged Dictionary* as a source of sexual stimulation? (Is it therefore "pornographic"?)[24] How many adults have employed *Gray's Anatomy* for the same ends? These categories are themselves fantasies spun about representations of sexuality, placing icons of sexuality upon a ground of meaning that provides the limits to its interpretability.[25]

Such classification is problematic. Take, for example, the recent concern with the pornographic as a sign of the masculine exploitation of the female: "All heterosexual pornography . . . exhibits absolutely uncompromising woman-hating."[26] Such statements tend to confuse object and representation, depiction and enactment, reading the "pornographic" (i.e., sexually stimulating representations created for the male gaze) icon from the ground of just one of the potential communities of viewers. Indeed the limitations of such an interpretive community are evident because much of the recent literature in this area sees heterosexual "pornography" in a privileged position, ignoring, among many other things, the wide range of homosexual representations of sexuality as well as the pornographic literature written for women.[27] The problem of "objectification" in pornography is parallel to its presence within the medical and aesthetic representation of the genitalia. For "objectification" is the drawing of the illusionary "real" boundary between the world and the self. It is the same means of control that the self-labeled "healthy" observer has over the icon of the "diseased" Other. But it is played out within the carnivalesque world of icons, of the representations of reality. It may well be possible that men (and/or women) are desensitized through "pornography" (however defined) to view women (and/or men) as "objects." But the representation of the Other, in whatever medium that objectifies the Other, is determined solely by the interpretive community (or the thought-collective, as will be discussed later) in which an individual functions. And for most individuals, the boundary between representation and reality, between image and action is a real one. If one were to see a man on the street putting out his eyes, we might flee the sight or we might try to intercede, for we understand that in the real world those are our two options; in the theater we sit and watch Oedipus put out his eyes, because we are, at least subliminally, aware that we are in a theater and that we are watching representations of actions, not the actions themselves. This is how the catharsis of the work of art functions. And most normal viewers understand (or empathize) that the proper course of action is to observe that which we would normally flee from or attempt to halt. Not only is there no confusion between the "real" and the "representational" world, but the power of the representational world rests exactly on the boundary implied by the work of art, the boundary that draws the distinction between the "observed" and the "represented." So too in the images of sexuality that we have collected in this volume. Their power lies,

to no little extent, in the fact that they are images, that they provide a distance between the observer (or the creator) of the image and the realities of human sexuality, which are always more complex and multidimensional than the icons themselves.

The flight into the fantasy of representation, no matter what its form or source, means a flight from the realities of the world. There are indeed pathological cases in which the viewing of an image provides the contours for a path of action, as in the case of John Hinckley, the attempted assassin of Ronald Reagan, and the function of Martin Scorsese's film *Taxi Driver*, with all of its sexualized imagery, in structuring his paranoid delusion. Indeed, when a reporter for *Newsweek* interviewed him about whether there was any relationship between his fascination for the film and his destructive fantasies, he replied: "Yes, Yes, Yes. The line dividing Life and Art can be invisible."[28] But this is clearly the disease process using representations of reality to provide an inherently coherent delusional structure. It is not the manner in which most individuals respond to the world of images, sexualized or not, in which they exist.[29] For most people, the line between "image" and "reality" exists; it is indeed that border that gives the representation its very power. The argument about objectification, about the patterning of human sexual perception through images labeled pornographic, could be valid only if we lived in a "pornographic" world, a world in which all images were understood to be within this category.[30] But no such world can exist because the category of the "pornographic" is defined as that world of representations beyond the border of our (whoever "we" are) definition of the socially acceptable image of sexuality.[31] Thus pornography always exists as a category of depicting the sexual, but it is that category beyond the pale of socially acceptable representations of sexuality. These categories are mutually defining and infinitely mutable. This means that it is forbidden and taboo and therefore either reprehensible or stimulating. The pornographic is a category that we (in whatever thought-collective we contextualize ourselves) "know when we see it," to paraphrase the United States Supreme Court's ruling. But we know it because we are defining it out of our own perspectives and needs, and in defining it we acknowledge that it exists as a world of representations, not as a reality that shapes our relationship to the "real" world.

In addition there has been the argument that the real problem is the exploitation of those who are literally represented within contemporary pornography. It is not that we condone the physical or economic exploitation of women or men for sexual purposes, but no critique of such exploitation can be made solely by extrapolating social realities from those icons of sexuality that any given group or society labels *pornographic*. And indeed, such views have (and can) only arise with the introduction of mechanical means of reproduction, such as photography. For it is only at that moment that "real" pornographic images of "real" people could be produced. It is, of course, the illusion of the "realism" of the photograph that lies at the heart of the matter. In terms of representing reality, a photograph is no more "real" than an engraving. Although the problem of the exploitation of the Other in the contemporary pornography industry is one of concern, the basis of such concern cannot be extrapolated from photographs of the models' genitalia, only from a knowledge of their motivation or their working conditions.

This is, however, not to deny that there is, and evidently always has been, a category beyond the boundary that defines the self that could be labeled as *pornographic*. Pornography (however it is defined) has had a permanent niche in all epochs of European history, from the Roman wall murals at Pompeii to the videotapes sold on 42nd Street. And these images, for the most part, focus on the depiction of the genitalia.[32] But then so do the medical representations of sexuality. Pornography and medical illustration often reveal the same confusions, constructions, and fantasies as are found in all of the other icons of sexuality.[33] They are neither better nor worse as sources of understanding the social construction of the idea of the sexual. Only their context, their ground, is different. Medical representation reflects the discourse about sexuality within the public sphere of "science"; pornography reflects the discourse about sexuality within the hidden world of private fantasies. Each reflects the specific representational tradition of its (perhaps overlapping) thought-collective as well as the general cultural tradition of understanding human sexuality. One must be as aware, with them, of their context as of their public and/or private function. The icon itself is bound within a web of various potential viewers with different goals, but underlying all are basic paradigms of perception, ways of seeing the sexual.[34] A reconstruction of the "intent" of such images may provide the historian with a running definition that can separate the pornographic from the medical depiction of the genitalia at any given point in history and show how identical objects could (and did) have different social functions (think about *Webster's Dictionary*). But an examination of

such icons as concretizations of the interlocking group and personal fantasies about what the genitalia "mean" provides insight into the sense not of the object seen (the image) but of the body itself, of the observer as object of his or her own presuppositions about him- or herself.

We, therefore, shall define the "sexual" in a very general manner. We shall understand the *sexual* to encompass all those areas which a society and a cultural tradition, here those of Western Europe and the United States, have labeled as sexualized. The sexualized world subsumes within it the worlds of anatomy and reproduction, of pathology, and eroticizes the worlds of racial and gender differences as well as sexual preference and identity.[35] In examining this variety of icons of sexuality, a certain common ground can be shown to exist for all those boundaries drawn that were hoped to contain and control the sexual. In examining these interlocking resources a system of sexual iconography is revealed, a system that was formed by and formed the perception of human sexuality over the past thousand years.[36] Such a system of reference remains hidden because it is part of the assumptions of Western culture about the way the world must be perceived. The job of such a study is parallel to that of a self-conscious "bricoleur," the collector of bits and pieces, of rags and bones, of notions and icons, to employ Claude Lévi-Strauss's image of the "primitive" user of tools and myths. For the bricoleur, "his first practical step is retrospective. He has to turn back to an already existent set made up of tools and materials, to consider or reconsider what it contains and, finally and above all, to engage in a sort of a dialogue with it, and before choosing between them, to index the possible answers which the whole set can offer to his problem."[37] This is our task in this book. It cannot be to present an exhaustive catalogue of icons but rather to see which images provide for us, as participants as well as observers in the world of sexual image making, meaningful approaches to the complexities of the past.

The selected meanings attributed to human sexuality documented here are central to any understanding of the presuppositions of Western culture about both the physical and psychological natures of the human being. These models of human sexuality are important because they reveal the ideological implications of human biology over the course of history. The relationship between the codes of sexuality present in the biological and medical sciences and other, seemingly unrelated, models of human sexuality becomes evident once the ideological underpinnings of these systems are uncovered. The key is to make the invisible visible, just as the codes of human sexuality attempt to make the invisible (aspects of sexual anatomy and that most ineffable but powerful force, the human sexual drive) visible. It is not merely that such icons control, that they represent the use of systems of representation to wield power over the powerless, but more important that we need such systems to establish our illusion of control, of power over ourselves. Especially in the realm of human sexuality, the sense of being not completely (or, indeed, not at all) in control of ourselves is omnipresent. Once we understand how we structure our sense of our own sexuality so as to give us the illusion of control, we can understand the implications of these codifications of sexuality. In doing so, we are able to understand how sexuality was "seen" during any given period. Not merely represented but also comprehended. Here I differ with both Foucault as well as Niklas Luhmann's brilliant study of *Love as Passion* in that I cannot see a line drawn absolutely across the history of sexuality that divides one "ancient" or "primitive" period (whether the age of innocence or of barbarity) from our modern age, an age inherently different (better or worse) than that which has come before.[38] Indeed, depending on which semiotic systems are examined (for Foucault the written discourse about deviance; for Luhmann, the written discourse about love and passion), this line of the discontinuous history of sexuality can be found in the Enlightenment. In our history of the visualization of sexuality, it is evident that a similar line between the "primitive" understanding of the body that dominated the medieval (or post-Aristotelian) period of the history of human anatomy and the "modern" insights of the Renaissance anatomists would be equally possible—and equally specious. For bridging every chasm in understanding dividing extraordinary "leaps forward" of knowledge and insight about human sexuality from the "primitive" past are continuities of cultural attitudes toward the body that continue regardless of improved theories, better instrumentation, or more accurate information.

To undertake such a study means examining what Ludwik Fleck, the great Polish-Jewish sociologist of science, in an essay of 1947 described as the presuppositions of the thought-collective, the perceptual structures of any social unit.[39] This social ground of meaning, the context in which everything which is "looked at" is "seen" in order for it to be known, forms the basis for all interpretive meaning. Thus, in the present volume, we shall be "looking at" the history of sexuality from the standpoint of the paradigmatic structures that underlie the Western (read: Christian) understanding of human sexuality. Fleck asks the question of how we learn to see that which is unseen, unconceptualized for the first time. One of the visual examples he brings is directly germane to the topic of this book. He asks how the early modern anatomical figures (of the sort represented in the present volume in Plate 60) depicted the open body of the cadaver, a body into which they were gazing for the first time. He points out that there was a "wealth of comparisons with different known forms: bird's bill, plough, sword, stirrup, the letter S, etc." In the nineteenth century, when the body was seen and described in terms of its microscopic structures, the "comparison seemed to recall simple geometrical forms: rods, spheres, spirals." Extrapolating from those icons that were assumed to be understood, the thought-collective restructured the meaning of the object perceived (and, therefore, also the object received) in new iconographic terms. What is deemed to be essential in the iconographic description of the body was determined by the collective; as was that which was deemed to be variable. The general agreement on this division as well as its permanent mutability leads any group to both understand what it is seeing and to accept certain levels of change. Fleck's argument provides a context for understanding the basic structural permanence of the Western view of the body, while providing a wide range of variations, both in terms of individual understanding as well as shifts in group comprehension. In this volume I shall be employing Fleck's category of the thought-collective in a somewhat broader manner. I see thought-collectives existing through a wide range of socially organized categories, including economic and institutional ones, that bond (often overlapping) groups together when they construct icons of reality.

In a number of earlier books, especially my history of the depiction of insanity in the West, *Seeing the Insane* (1982), I have drawn upon the history of medical illustration to provide the documentation for the cultural matrix of medical knowledge.[40] The relationship between medical illustration and "higher" forms of aesthetic representation has shown the debt that "science" owes to the "humanities" and the parallel debt owed by the humanities to science for their shared iconography. Because this shared vocabulary of icons structures (as well as is structured by) medical knowledge, it is important to be able to document the preconceptions inherent in the visualization of medical knowledge. For in knowing the myths and errors (as well as the truths) inherent in the history of the medical representation of our shared human state we can begin to understand the preconceptions that operate today. Medicine is part of the general culture, but it has a rather central role. Hilary Putnam is thus not quite correct when he argues that medicine assumed the role of religion in the course of the nineteenth century.[41] Medicine had always (and in all cultures) had a central role, and it was a role often closely allied to religion. All cultures need some means of dealing with the illnesses that plague them. But medicine in turn is shaped by the cultural presuppositions of a given culture. And here Hilary Putnam was quite right. For in the "godless" age after the French Revolution, the necessarily perceived separation of religion and science altered the public perception of medicine. This close interrelationship between general cultural norms and medicine is nowhere more evident than in the history of the medical perception of human sexuality.[42] In her insightful essay on the illustrations of contemporary American textbooks on human sexuality, Carol A. Pollis points up the role that such "sensitive drawings" have in representing the sexual act in a manner that is comprehensible to the viewer, within the social norms of the thought-collective, and outside of the bounds of the social construction of the pornographic.[43] Medical illustration has its own special place in the modes of representing the body, but its claim is for "scientific" validity, the representation of the real. It is because scientific images of human sexuality are part of (and are shaped by and shape) the thought-collective's understanding of the "real" anatomical body—not the aesthetic body, not the pornographic body, not the erotic body but the "objective" body—that the study of the medical illustration of sexuality is of such importance. The focus of my study is to illuminate the tropological relationship among images from "science" and "art," from the realm of the world of "objectivity" and of "subjectivity." The thought-collective that represents the body is not limited to the realm of science; rather it contains all aspects of the body politic within it. For we may wish to objectify our understanding of the body by having recourse to a semiotic system that creates the illusion of distance (and, therefore, of control). With such systems we create the illusion of control that helps us bridge the inherent anxiety subconsciously present in our sense that the center will not hold, that our world, our sense of self is truly held together only by the constructions we generate to map our reality. Some semiotic systems project this sense of potential loss of control out into the world, finding

and labeling groups as the representation of all those forces of entropy we feel exist within ourselves. In all such systems, the body functions as the measure of control or loss of control, and human sexuality defines that potential for collapse within the semiotics of the body.

As in *Seeing the Insane*, I have related icons taken from the general culture, from the fine arts, from the spheres of popular and scientific illustration, to the broader traditions of imagining the body. It is not that I wish to show the "influence" of one system of representation on the others. On the contrary, I am never sure in what direction (if there is a direction) such "influence" would naturally move. Rather the juxtaposition of problems from the general culture, problems dealing with the shifting comprehension of reproduction, of parturition, of sexually transmitted diseases, with those systems of scientific codification of parallel aspects of human sexuality demonstrates that similar attempts at generating icons that control exist in both spheres.[44] The iconographies of the more limited arena of sexual anatomy as well as from the broader sphere of the icons of sexuality in the general culture provide the basic materials to unlock our hidden coding of human sexuality.

The center of my interest is the representation of the genitalia and those visual and cultural representations that come to represent the genitalia in any given time or place. The range of human sexual experience, its focus, its bounding, stands at the center of any discussion of the image making of gender. But it is little understood (though generally assumed) that our definitions of sexuality are also inherent in our conceptualization of "race." And in a strange reversal, both race and gender paradigms reappear within our attempts to visualize sexuality. Foucault noted that the discourse on sexuality became linked with the "thematics of the blood . . . beginning in the second half of the nineteenth century." For him "racism took shape at this point (racism in its modern, "biologizing," statist form): it was then that a whole politics of settlement, family, marriage, education . . . received their color and their justification from the mythical concern with protecting the purity of the blood and ensuring the triumph of the race."[45] Foucault is correct about the association; he is wrong about it being a late nineteenth-century phenomenon. It is an association that exists from the earliest images of human sexuality. In constructing all categories of difference, categories that postulate an absolute dichotomy between the observer and the observed, whether categories of "race" or "sexuality," the need to draw a boundary between the Other, the sexually, racially, biologically defined opposite, and the self is paramount. No space exists in such systems for ambiguity, and yet ambiguity is implicit in any system in which there is an attempt to draw absolute boundaries. On which side of the boundary does any given case fall? Such questions demand a resolution, and such resolutions lead to the construction of systems of classification. As Bernadette Bucher has observed: "It is precisely the interstices between classifications, where beings and things fail to fit into a preconceived order, that symbolic thinking freely develops through a medium of graphic images."[46] And it is here that our study can examine the visual associations between sexuality and race. It is not merely, as Foucault argues, that in late nineteenth-century Europe there was a link between the sexual health of the family and that of the race, but rather that there has been a constant historical association between these two models of control, sexuality and race.[47] In this present study our focus is on the systems of classification used to represent the genitalia and how these systems parallel other culturally generated systems through which the sexual is bound. Understanding the fantasies about the genitalia becomes a means of examining the underlying presuppositions about human sexuality, about the body, and about the body's function within other complex systems of representation, such as our fantasies about "race."

The fantasies about the genitalia are in no way separate from other systems of bodily representation as they relate to our construction of the idea of the physical nature of sexuality. The skin, the map upon which the idea of race is inscribed in the West, is also simultaneously the organ of touch.[48] Thus any study of the fantasies of the genitalia must encompass an understanding of that sense, touch, that relates most directly to human sexuality and that leads from its systems of the visual and verbal representation of ideology to other related systems, such as "race." The anatomy of the genitalia provides the potential for a wide range of fantasies about human sexuality, and one significant physical quality of the genitalia further is its incorporation into another circle of meaning, the meaning ascribed to touch and to the organ of touch, the skin. The related physiological aspects of the body, such as the qualities ascribed to the sense of touch, are also traditionally part of the thought-collective's understanding of sexual anatomy and sexuality.[49] Thus throughout this book there is a focus on the construction of the fantasy of sexualized touch with its implications for a more generalized understanding of the history of the senses. The physicality of touch, like the physicality of the genitalia themselves, provides a field of ambiguity for the play of interpretation. Much of the complexity of our cultural understanding of touch is rooted in the ambiguities inherent in the physiology of touch. This factor provides a matrix for an understanding of the representation of sexualized touch in its cultural context. The biological reality of touch, with its inherent ambiguities, permits an extraordinary latitude in the social and cultural construction of its representations.

Touch is at the same time the most complex and the most undifferentiated of the senses. Sight, hearing, smell, and taste all have specific, limited sensory organs, all of which have specific limited functions. The eye is placed at a specific point in the skull and it "sees," however we wish to construct the act of seeing. Touch seems to be an undifferentiated quality of the entire body, but it is, in fact, a multifunctional aspect of the skin.[50] Touch is indeed the complex response of sensors that judge pressure, temperature, and vibration. But the receptors are not clearly differentiated by function. Ruffini's corpuscle, for example, responds to pressure and warmth, whereas Meissner's corpuscle responds to pressure and vibration. Because of this complex factor, our response to "touch," that is, to the interrelationship of all of these sensations over the entire envelope of the skin (with, of course, great concentrations of certain receptors in specific areas), is much less focused than our response to the other senses. The physiology of touch, much more than that of the other senses, reinforces the potential for fantasy about its nature. Thus the necessity arises for our understanding the history of touch as part of the history of sexuality. For the representation of the genitalia within the world of the sexual is simultaneously a representation of other systems that are completely intertwined with it. The iconography of touch parallels, overlaps, and intersects with the iconography of sexuality, and both are influenced by the complex ambiguities that underlie their biological and psychological functions within the body.[51]

The examination of the representation of the genitalia within the related semantic fields of difference and the sensorium provides a greater contextualization for an understanding of the extraordinary power of the idea of sexuality to shape (and be shaped by) factors that build upon its libidinal forces. Barbara Duden has illustrated how necessary it is to see the body as both an anatomically fixed reality as well as a dynamic object being created and re-created constantly through the shifts in the perceptions of the thought-collective.[52] What she also shows, and I hope is also illustrated throughout this volume, is that the general patterns of representation, the "commonplaces" about the body that can be generated by examining the scientific and cultural sources of any given period concerning the body, must be measured against the way in which any given thinker or artist responds to such representations of his or her own body. Thus in the present study I have interleaved general overviews about aspects of the representation of human sexuality (and its related factors such as the history of the sexualized touch) with specific studies (of Leonardo, Goethe, Peter Altenberg, William James, and Manet) of how individuals who are aware (at least subliminally) of the models of sexuality of their world incorporate these icons into their own representation of sexuality, a sexuality that defines their own being. Following William Butler Yeats's dictum, the sexual icons that these figures produced were often opposite to their identity but identical with their desire.[53] They are therefore masked within the conventions of representing sexuality, masked in such a way as to need contextualization and interpretation. I believe that it is not solely the general setting of a society's construction of sexuality but the specific response and incorporation of such constructions into the world view of the individual, with all of his/her personal idiosyncrasies, which is of real interest in writing a history of the genitalia. In using a wide range of such "private" sources, what one accomplishes is to map the widest (and, perhaps, most superficial) terrain. These individual studies all depart from the analysis of a single central image (Leonardo's drawing of coitus, Goethe's "anatomical" sketches, James's vision of the masturbator and its visual analogue) and are thus different in quality than some of the broader overviews that provide a catalogue of images for the more detailed studies. Both types of studies are necessary in a study such as this because my intent is to capture both the thought-collective's perspective and how this perspective is adapted and altered by specific individuals. I am not merely trying to create a discourse that mechanically represents the most radical contours of the image of the sexual but rather trying to provide a series of sophisticated reworkings of this image in the context of specific creative artists' adaption of such iconographic traditions. There is a leveling effect that provides generalities but cannot account for individual differences in the construct of representations of human sexuality. In examining the texts on their own individual ground, one can better understand the subtle dynamics that underlie the culturally constructed structures of human perception within the confines of specific texts.[54]

My specific examples are all men, and this is not incidental to my argument. There is a general understanding in some circles that the "patriarchal" or "phallic," that is, dominant discourse about sexuality, deforms and constrains the woman, the universal Other in all systems of sexual representation. The creation of a homogeneous, ubiquitous "male gaze" tends to place more interest in the response of the female. Part of the covert argument of this book is that males, confronted with absolute boundaries concerning human sexuality, respond in ways as complex and differentiated as do females.[55] The myth of a homogeneous male response to the creation of categories of sexual difference is as fallacious as the fantasies of the complete powerlessness of the female in the face of the creation of such categories.[56] Indeed, if we look at the fantasies about the male genitalia as the baseline for the construction of the boundaries of all sexuality, and this is not an incorrect view given the sexual identity of most biologists and physicians over the past thousand years, it is not at all surprising that the male, simultaneously empowered and powerless, is as greatly influenced by these icons as is the woman. For, seeing oneself as both part of the world that generated icons and part of the world that is manipulated by images over which one seems to have no control creates a deep-seated antagonism, a double bind between the sense of control and the sense of domination.[57] It is "at once the prism through which and the prison out of which one views the world."[58] Thus the often confused and contradictory examples of male sexuality that form the subtext of this study reflect the confusions inherent in social constructions of icons of human sexuality.

From the Word to the Image: Biblical Icons of Sexuality in the Middle Ages and the Renaissance

OLD TESTAMENT IMAGES OF SEXUALITY AND WESTERN REPRESENTATIONS OF SEXUALITY

No single source of sexual images is more important within the modern Western tradition than the Bible.[1] It is not only that the theological implications of sexuality have their roots in the interpretation of scripture but also that the paradigms for the visual representation of human sexuality have their source in that central text of Western culture. Indeed, for the West, the biblical paradigm of sexuality, and the narratives in which it is incorporated, stands at the center of any understanding of the representation of the body. Our understanding of the body, at least from the Middle Ages to the present, is in terms of (or in spite of) those models of sexuality presented in the Bible.

The very concept of the "Bible" is ambiguous. We speak of a "biblical" tradition of representing sexuality in which one text—the "Old" Testament—is interpreted by a second text—the "New" Testament.[2] As St. Augustine stated in his manual for new converts to Christianity: "the New Testament is concealed in the Old; the Old Testament is revealed in the New."[3] And this Christian tradition is seemingly in opposition to the other major Western tradition of representing human sexuality, that of classical Greece and Rome. The tensions that result from such an interpretation of a "Jewish" text within a "Christian" hermeneutic tradition (which is itself in conflict with a "pagan" one) parallel the tensions in Western culture that result from the movement from the written text (coming out of a theological tradition that banned the representation of the human figure) to the visual representation of the body.

It was permitted to talk or write about the body, but it was forbidden to look at or depict it. Implicit in this Pauline ascetic reinterpretation of the body is the entire range of contrasts that the early Church needed to generate to establish its own authenticity. Central to this is the distinction between the "Christian" and the "Jew" that marks the very evolution of the gospels as they move from texts to be read within the Jewish tradition to texts (such as the story of Stephen) that reflect a tension between the early church and the synagogue. To no little extent, this dichotomy between the good and the bad, between the Christian and the Jew, is played out in the image of the body. Once the early Church moves into the cultural sphere of pagan Rome the distinction between black and white, between slave and freeman, between African and European, becomes part of the discourse about the body, a discourse understood in the early Church in theological terms. This tension that grew out of the conflicts within the early Christian Church lies at the source of all of our imaging of the body. The illusion is that there is a necessary tension between the traditions, the "newer" tradition coming as the fulfillment, culmination, or correction of the "older" one. The translation of Old Testamentary images of human sexuality into the representations stemming from the Pauline world of the New Testament seems radically to reinterpret the "meaning" of sexuality in the original text. The further transference of such complex, polar reinterpretations into the sphere of the visual seems to make explicit those aspects of human sexuality that remained covert in the Old Testament within its "new" incarnation in the Christian Church.

The power of human sexuality parallels only the power of God in the Old Testament. If God's plan is inherently if opaquely benevolent, then humankind's plan is random, driven by sexuality. From the creation of Adam and Eve and their expulsion from Paradise to David's seduction of Bathsheba, human malfaction seems to be rooted in the abuses of human sexuality.[4] The text is redolent of this split between God's divine nature and the sexual nature of humankind. The biblical model for human sexuality seems to be rooted in this Manichean division between good and evil symbolized by humankind's separation from God or man's division from woman or the "good" woman's from the prostitute. The telling of the Creation in Genesis is the recounting of antitheses, of the separation of the light from the dark, of the earth from the waters: "And God said, Let us make man in our image, after our likeness. . . . So God created man in his own image, in the image of God he created he him; male and female he created he them. And God blessed them, and God said unto them, Be fruitful, and multiply, and replenish the earth" (Genesis 1: 26–28). This dichotomy between the male and the female dominates biblical thought. It is at the root of all Western models of sexuality. And yet it is an opposition that is conceived of as complementary. In the *Sohar*, the central book of Jewish mysticism (and not uninfluenced by Greek and Christian thought), the inherent opposition between the masculine and the feminine is resolved in seeing them as "twins."[5] It is assumed that the biological forms of male and female are fixed at the moment of their creation. This presents the potential for sexuality without its necessary realization. In thinking about sexuality in terms of oppositions, built upon an understanding of human sexuality as the existence of two antithetical biological entities, what is necessarily excluded is the ambiguous, the boundary cases, and that exclusion will haunt Western representations of human sexuality from its beginning to the present. Human sexuality is "seen" in terms of overt or implied contrasts between antitheses.

The Old Testamentary view of human sexuality, in its Christian context, clearly moves away from the Platonic tradition, which sees the division into the two sexes as a factor that the human being is constantly striving to overcome. This Greek tradition is the hidden counterweight to the Christian view of the radical dichotomy of the sexes. In the *Symposium*, Plato has Aristophanes outline his view of the creation of the sexes and their central signifier.[6] Initially there were three sexes—the male, the female, and "a third which partook of the nature of both." Each of the beings was built like a ball, with four arms and four legs. This race, in its arrogance, attempted to capture Mount Olympus, and Zeus punished them by slicing each one in half. As a result the halves spent their time and energy looking for completion. "Now, when the work of bisection was complete it left each half with a desperate yearning for the other, and they ran together and flung their arms around each other's necks, and asked for nothing better than to be rolled into one." Zeus took pity on them and altered their anatomy to permit at least the semblance of a reunion of the fragmented segments:

> Zeus . . . moved their privates round to the front, for of course they had originally been on the outside—which was now the back—and they had begotten and conceived not upon each other, but, like the grasshoppers, upon the earth. So now, as I say, he moved their members round to the front and made them propagate among themselves, the male begetting upon the female—the idea being that if, in all these clippings and claspings, a man should chance upon a woman, conception would take place and the race would be continued, while if man should conjugate with man, he might at least obtain such satisfaction as would allow him to turn his attention and his energies to the everyday affairs of life.

Such a view can (and does) lead to an understanding of one of the levels of ambiguity possible within the construction of the image of human sexuality. Homosexuality (both male and female)—the third sex—has a place within Plato's (or, at least, Aristophanes's) depiction of human sexuality. The external marker of human sexuality is the genitalia. Zeus makes human sexuality, with all of its variations, possible through his displacement of the genitalia, from the rear to the front. This visual shift, which makes copulation merely a reflex of the desire to caress, creates the uniqueness of human sexuality. But the Platonic system, which attributes the origin of the three sexes to the spheres of the sun (male), earth (female), and moon (hermaphrodites, to use Plato's term[7]), still recognizes the existence of two "biological" types, the male and the female, even though it praises male homosexuality as "the most hopeful of the nation's youth, for theirs is the most virile constitution" (p. 191e). Ambiguity is reduced by Plato's exclusion of the true "hermaphrodite," the individual bearing the sexual signs of both male and female, from his categories. And yet the tension within a system of two divided sexes, each marked by a different biological form, a system that would permit all same-sex as well as cross-sex relationships, is quite different from that within a system that sees only the division of the sexes, as represented in Genesis, as the model for cross-sex sexual pairing.

The strict biblical dichotomy, excluding the shades of difference present within the Platonic model, stems from a need to generate categories that exclude all ambiguity. It is not merely that ambiguous forms of sexuality are thus labeled as *deviant*, but that the narrower biblical paradigm creates an absolute boundary based upon the biology of the difference, the structural form of the genitalia, which banishes any ambiguity into the pale of difference. All permitted sexuality is thus rooted in the signification of the biological sign, the different shapes, forms, and functions of the male and female genitalia. Form follows function, or so the ideology of Western sexuality would have it.[8] The Platonic model, which also sees the genitalia as the external marker of the underlying sexual drive, does not tie the potential of the sexual act to the representational limitations of seeing only two sexes. Pairing may be within the same sex as well as between sexes.

To understand this tension in the history of the representation of sexuality, we must begin with the paradigmatic images of sexuality within the Christian tradition. And it is no surprise that the most common image of human sexuality within the Christian reinterpretation of the Old Testament is the representation of the story of Eve and Adam.[9] (The uncomfortable feeling we have in reading their names in this order is indeed part of the story.) The creation of Eve out of the body of Adam is the creation of a boundary between man and woman, a boundary that by its nature is the destruction of all ambiguity in the creation of a polar opposite. The medieval biblical commentator Petrus Comestor even distances God from the scene, when he describes it as the angels removing "the woman made from the flesh of his flesh from the side of Adam."[10] The angel as midwife, taking Eve from Adam's side, distinguishes the representation from the actual act of vaginal childbirth, an act associated with Christ's birth in the New Testament. In a medieval Italian image of the creation, God the Father raises Eve from the side of the sleeping Adam using the sign of creation, the female sign, fingers clasped in an "o" shape, and the masculine (i.e., priest's) sign of blessing [PLATE 1]. It is the world complete, the final day of creation; all animals and plants have been created and are present. It is the image of creation within the totality of the universe, a universe complete even in the presence of its creator. The

PLATE 1. *Eve created from the side of Adam from the late fourteenth-century Florentine manuscript from* L'Ufiziolo Visconteo Landau-Finlay. *Florence: Bibliotece nazionale.*

PLATE 2. *Eve's creation masks the genitalia of both Eve and Adam in Baccio Bandinelli (1493–1560),* The Creation of Eve. *Florence: Galleria Pitti.*

boundary of the image is the boundary of all creation, and the asexual means of Eve's production stands at the center of the image, an image that prefigures the division of the masculine and the feminine. In the Renaissance image of the creation of Eve painted by Baccio Bandinelli (as well as, perhaps, by Andrea del Minga), the sign of the female is transferred to Eve, who clasps her hand in the form of her hidden genitalia[11] [PLATE 2]. In all of these images of creation, the genitalia are covered or masked because the genitalia signal the potential Fall from grace and its results, sexuality and death. The genitalia are present, however, not merely in their absence but also in the overt signs of sexuality, here, the gestures of the hand. The world of Adam and Eve—not Eve and Adam, because the female is seen as the offshoot of the male (unlike Plato's image of the splitting of the sexes)—is a sexualized world but also a world that places sexuality within a confined space in its totality.

Paradise after the creation is a world of untrammeled innocence, but an innocence that points toward the omnipresence of sexuality as signaled through the signs present at Eve's creation. Hieronymus Bosch presents an idealized world of the Paradise before the Fall with the genitalia visually present [PLATE 3]. The genitalia are not displaced within this icon; rather, they represent the ideal state before the eating from the tree of knowledge. They are the genitalia of the innocent and, therefore, can be observed by the viewer. The relationship of the image to the implied viewer of the image, a viewer self-consciously existing in the world after the Fall, determines the signification of the genitalia. Bosch creates a visual fiction and places the viewer back into the state of presumed innocence in the Garden, not as an observer existing in time after the Fall. Thus the presumed innocence of seeing the genitalia becomes an innocence shared by the now-pure observer returned to a prelapsarian perspective as well as by the pure figures in the Garden of Eden.

Although the genitalia of Bosch's figures seem to have the same physical shape and function in their role as markers of innocence, they are inherently different from the genitalia that mark the Fall (or its potential). Both St. Augustine and his twelfth-century commentator, Hugh of St. Victor, argued that intercourse did exist within the Garden of Eden, but innocently, in that it occurred under the control of human will. Only after the Fall did it come under the control of evil when the genitalia themselves become the mark of the satanic irrational dominance.[12] The idealized form of sexuality prefigures Bosch's image of the Fall, with its house of prostitution, the satanic irrational institutionalized. Lucas

PLATE 3. *The utopian world of Hieronymus Bosch*, God Presenting Eve to Adam, *detail from* Garden of Delights, *1486–87. Madrid: Prado.*

PLATE 4. *The utopian world of Lucas Cranach the Elder, Paradise, ca. 1530, with its intimations of sexuality. Vienna: Kunsthistorisches Museum.*

Cranach the Elder presents the entire story in dynamic form in 1530, from the creation of Eve and Adam to their expulsion from Paradise **[PLATE 4]**. There, too, the creation of Eve and the masking of the genitalia are linked. Likewise in Cranach's image of the "Golden Age," in the biblical sense, the world without sin is, however, a world of sexuality **[PLATE 5]**. In both images the yawning mouth of the cave functions as a representation of the vagina, the female principle of creation in the world.[13]

In Western art, the image of the Fall, of Adam and Eve, is paired with the image of the Christ Child and Mary, the New Adam and the New Eve, whose "pure" sexuality, represented in their deaths, redeems the fall from grace, which introduced uncontrolled sexuality and death into the world.[14] "Death," according to Paul, "reigned from Adam to Moses after the similitude of Adam's transgression, who is the figure of him that was to come" (Romans 5: 15). This is the central model of the Christian reading of the Old Testament. It is the idea of prefiguration, of the redemption of Adam's

fall in Christ. But the application of the model of polar opposites inherent in the model of sexuality also underlies the Christian retelling of the story of Genesis. Paul writes to the Corinthians that "the first man Adam was made a living soul; the last Adam was made a quickening spirit. . . . And as we have borne the image of the earthly, we shall also bear the image of the heavenly" (1 Corinthians 15: 45–48). This tradition is continued in the image of Mary as found in the earliest of the Greek Church fathers.[15] Justin Martyr, in the second century, contrasted the virgin Eve and the Virgin Mary:

He was made a man of the Virgin, that by the same way in which the disobedience which proceeded from the serpent took its rise, it might also receive its destruction. For Eve when a virgin and undefiled conceived the word of the serpent and brought forth disobedience and death. But Mary the Virgin, receiving Faith and Joy, when the angel Gabriel told her the good news that the spirit of the Lord should come upon her . . . answered, Be it unto me according to thy word.[16]

In a fifteenth-century image of the Fall, by Bertold Furtmeyr, the link between the Fall, the presence of death (the counterpart to the mortality introduced by sexuality and conception and birth), and Christ's redemption is clear [PLATE 6]. The tree from which Eve picks the forbidden fruit is the analogue to the other "tree," the crucifix. Or, as Irenaeus, in the second century, commented, it was by wood that we sinned, and it is by wood that we are saved.[17] The fruit, the emblem of fullness and the casing holding the seed, is almost an abstraction in this image of the Fall. In Jan van Eyck's image from the altarpiece in the Vijd Chapel in St. Bavo's Cathedral in Ghent (1426–32), it is "Adam's Apple," the exotic fruit, which is, at one and the same time, the mark of male sexual maturity, revealing, as does menstruation for the female, the male's Fall from grace[18] [PLATE 7]. Indeed, there is a tradition of Adam clutching his throat as if a piece of the forbidden fruit were lodged in it [PLATE 8]. Here, too, the downcast figures of Eve and Adam (created as counterimages to the images of Christ and Mary on the interior of the altar) signify their sexuality, their biological difference, through external signs, the genitalia, the sign pointed to by Adam's apple, remain hidden but present.

PLATE 5. *Lucas Cranach,* The Golden Age, *ca. 1530. Oslo: Nasjonalgalleriet.*

PLATE 6. *The creation and the redemption are both recalled in Bertold Furtmeyr,* Mors per Evam, vita per Mariam, *ca. 1481. Munich: Bayerische Staatsbibliothek.*

PLATE 7. *Adam's apple in Eve's hand in Jan van Eyck,* Adam and Eve, *Altarpiece of the Lamb, 1426–32. Ghent, Belgium: St. Bavo's Cathedral.*

PLATE 8. *Adam choking on the apple in the Medallion Master's Temptation, ca. 1415. Chantilly: Musée Condé.*

It is the sign of the Fall, the ambiguity in the Garden of Eden, which points toward the hidden sexuality of humankind.[19] For at the boundaries in the Garden of Eden is Evil, an evil not conceived of in the abstract, but as real within the visualizations of the Fall as the figure of God. Traditionally it is the snake (which hands the traditional apple or pomegranate or fig or grape) to Eve.[20] And it is indeed the snake that we find in the image by Furtmeyr. But in a series of images, beginning with the expulsion as represented on the eleventh-century doors of the Cathedral at Hildesheim, it is clear that the image of Evil, the boundary crosser, is reptilian **[PLATE 9]**. In Hugo van der Goes's image of the seduction (*ca.* 1467–74) **[PLATE 10]**, it is part human, part reptile. This tradition continues in Titian's image of the Fall, painted between 1571–72, which the pious and puritanical Philip II of Spain had overpainted to cover the exposed genitalia.[21] However, the reptile is now clearly a border crosser,

PLATE 9. *The wrath of God, driving Eve and Adam out of Paradise, with their genitalia covered, depicted on the early eleventh-century bronze doors of the Hildesheim Cathedral. Hildesheim: Archiv.*

PLATE 10. *The snake as a half-animal, half-human in Hugo van der Goes's mid-fifteenth century* The Fall of Man. *Vienna: Kunsthistorisches Museum.*

PLATE 11. *The masked genitalia of Titian's* The Fall (of Man), *ca. 1570, and the snake as half-animal, half-man. Madrid: Prado.*

half human, half animal **[PLATE 11]**. Baccio Bandinelli (and Andrea del Minga) give us the Renaissance counterpart to their *Creation of Eve*, with an androgynous (or perhaps, to use the Platonic term, hermaphroditic) half-human seducing Eve[22] **[PLATE 12]**. A creature both human and animal, both beautiful and repulsive, both aged and youthful. But, like Eve and Adam, it is sexless in its sexuality. In Bosch's *Last Judgement*, the image of sexuality and the reptile are linked **[PLATE 13]**. The house of prostitution that dominates the left fore-ground is crowned with a nude female encircled by a reptile and being led off by a reptilian bridegroom.[23] The image of the reptile and the purifying power of Christ occurs in an allegorical image by Bernardo Parentino of a female nude, holding her breast in the Roman image of the nursing mother, accompanied by a child, trampling a serpent underfoot before an altar **[PLATE 14]**. The secularization of this image is still very much within the Christian reworking of images of the serpent as sexual icon.

PLATE 12. *The snake as half-animal, half-man in Baccio Bandinelli's early sixteenth-century* The Expulsion from Paradise. *Florence: Galleria Pitti.*

PLATE 13. *Images of disease, death, and sexuality haunt Hieronymus Bosch's,* Last Judgement *(triptych), 1504. Vienna: Gemäldegalerie, Akademie der bildenden Künste.*

What can be observed in all of these images is that the covered genitalia of the female is paralleled by the uncovered breast, neither a breast marked by childbearing and nursing nor a breast redolent of old age. Eve's breasts are the breasts of the innocent.[24] The firm, rounded breasts come to signify the state of grace before the Fall. The icon of the "sagging breasts" is used to represent witches, demons, Death, the Devil. Indeed, in the representations of the native peoples of North America in the thirteen-volume *Grand Voyages* published by Theodor de Bry between 1590 and 1634, the shift from visually representing females with small, firm "classical" breasts to pendulous ones is a mark of the gradual bestialization of the Indian. They mark the difference between the Indian as understood as being in a state of perfect harmony with the world and the Indian as the barbaric savage in need of salvation. As Bernadette Bucher has argued, this is merely the displacement of the tale of the Fall, with the Indians as the new Adam and Eve, into a colonialist world in which the Indians, over the course of some forty years, come to have a quite different function. They move from representing the noble savage to representing the cannibal. But it is the female breast, the sign of succor and maternity, that signifies this shift in meaning.[25]

The tripartite relationship of Eve, Adam, and the serpent is understood as a "Judeo-Christian" (i.e., Christian interpretation of a Jewish text) version of the Platonic tripartite image of sexuality, which is usually repressed in the Adam–Eve and Christ–Mary dichotomies. As early as Philo's first-century treatise *On the Creation of the World*, there is an allegorical reading of the Creation and the Fall in terms of the Platonic tradition.[26] Philo's reading is exemplary for later paradigmatic Christian readings of the implications of human sexuality. Central to Philo's reading of Genesis is the idea of harmony and arrangement. The Creation is the ultimate proof of "the harmony with which the whole universal world is regulated" (p. 1). Adam's creation is the ultimate proof of this. Created directly by God, he, as "an imitation of a perfectly beautiful model must . . . be perfectly beautiful, for the word of God surpasses even that beauty which exists in nature" (p. 41). Adam is the most beautiful thing created. Woman was created from that beauty, and it was man's attraction to this narcissistic beauty that engendered sexuality:

> But when woman was also created, man perceiving a closely connected figure and a kindred formation to his own, rejoiced at the sight, and approached her and embraced her. And she, in like manner, beholding a creature greatly resembling herself, rejoiced also, and addressed him in reply with due modesty. And love being engendered, and, as it were, uniting two separate portions of one animal into one body, adapted them to each other with a view to the generation of a being similar to themselves. And this desire caused likewise pleasure to their bodies, which is the beginning of iniquities and transgressions, and it is owing to this that men have exchanged their previously immortal and happy existence for one which is mortal and full of misfortune. (p. 45)

This "Jewish" version of the Platonic myth of the creation of the sexes points toward the inherent division and attraction to the two sexes, which leads inexorably to the Fall, a Fall marked by "disease" and "corruption" (p. 46). It was the serpent, not Eve, however, that precipitated the Fall. The serpent represents Pleasure in Philo's allegory; Eve, the Senses; and Adam, Reason. It is the pleasure engendered by the sexuality present in the very creation of humankind that is embodied in the serpent. As Philo notes: "Now, the first approaches of the male to the female have a pleasure in them which brings on other pleasures also, and it is through this pleasure that the formation and generation of children is carried on. And what is generated by it appears to be attached to nothing rather than to it, since they rejoice in pleasure, and are impatient at pain which is its contrary" (p. 48). This is true of all animals, but they "pursue pleasure only in taste and in the acts of generation; but man aims at it by means of his other senses also, devoting himself to whatever sights or sounds can impart pleasure to his ears" (p. 48). Pleasure (whatever the gender of Philo's "man") is the domain of the woman: "the mind occupies the rank of the man, and the sensations that of the woman" (p. 49). But it is not any woman but the whore that pleasure is most like: "For we must altogether not be ignorant that pleasure, being like a courtesan or mistress, is eager to meet with a lover, and seeks for panders in order by their means to catch a lover" (p. 49). This is a Platonic reading of the Fall as it is based on the notion that the soul's initial nature, its positive role in participating in the transcendental world, was altered when Pleasure attached the soul's sensible part to the illusions of mere reality. The Senses undermined Reason. But it is in the sexually active female that this seeking after sexual pleasure is embodied. Eve becomes the prototypical harlot achieving her ends through the sensations.

A Christian counterreading begins with Augustine, in which the senses are represented by the serpent because they are common to brute creation as well as to the human race.[27] Thus the serpent is a transitory figure. Eve, in this reading, comes to represent the lower part of reason, *scientia*, which is concerned with the collection of sense impressions in order to form generalizations, and Adam represents *sapientia*, or higher reason. Eve is moved into the sphere of rationality, but, as with Philo, she remains associated (even if once removed) with the senses and the marginally unreflected physical world. Here the boundary is maintained, with Eve and Adam being paired against the boundary crosser—the serpent.

The images of creation and destruction are linked by the image of the reptile. It is the human as reptile who is different, whose genitalia are different. For the reptile's mode of reproduction is inherently different from the human being. This difference bridges the boundary, links the unlinkable. And such figures are always beyond the margin of acceptability. It is the ambiguity of sexual difference, pointed at by the ambiguity of the sexual intermediate figure, that is stressed here. Such intermediate figures hark back to Greco-Roman antiquity in its melding of human and animal. Like Herodotus's image of Africa, peopled by men with "dogs' heads" who share their wives, these are variations on the human form, literally cross-breeds.[28] They are a third sex, the amalgam of two otherwise unapproachable entities. They are Plato's hermaphrodites as the serpent.

Human sexuality is seen as divided into antagonistic but complementary male and female aspects at the moment of the Fall, just as it is in Plato's account of the division of each four-legged human into its two-legged segments. But one further prohibition is introduced in the Christian iconography of Old Testamentary sexuality, and that is the prohibition against same-sex relationships. With the image of the driving out from Eden comes the tradition of a world under the sway of the senses and of pleasure, of licentiousness and concupiscence. The narrative of Noah's nakedness exemplifies this.[29] Noah planted a vineyard after the flood, and "he drank of the wine and was drunken, and he was uncovered within his tent." It is the act of gazing at the father's genitalia that is prohibited, a displacement for same-sex contact. His son Ham gazed upon his father's nakedness and told his brothers, Shem and Japheth, who "took a garment, and laid it upon both their shoulders, and went backward, and covered the nakedness of their father; and their faces were backward, and they saw not their father's nakedness" (Genesis 9: 19–29). Ham is cursed by Noah, who damns him to be the "servant of servants . . . unto his brethren." Ham is the biblical figure traditionally understood as the progenitor of the "black" nation. *Blackness*, that is race, as an operative category, becomes a further means of drawing the boundaries between permitted and forbidden sexuality. Ham is condemned because he looked upon his father's nakedness. His gaze rested upon the genitalia of his father, upon the origin of his progeneration but also the mirror of his own sexual identity.

Blacks, the sons of Ham, are thus traditionally represented as emblems of hypersexuality. In the tradition of Romanesque Church ornament, these sons of Ham are represented as megaphallic figures, whose huge male members represent their ancestors' gazing upon Noah's nakedness. These phalluses are also false signs that the black is part of the human race because their exaggeration shows them to be counterfeits.[30] The association of the black

with concupiscence reaches back into the Middle Ages. The twelfth-century Jewish traveler Benjamin of Tudela wrote that "at Seba on the river Pishon . . . is a people . . . who like animals, eat of the herbs that grow on the banks of the Nile and in the fields. They go about naked and have not the intelligence of ordinary men. They cohabit with their sisters and anyone they can find. . . . And these are the black slaves, the sons of Ham."[31] For blacks, the sons of Ham, all sexual license is permitted because their nature was revealed (or formed) in the most heinous of all sexual acts, the same-sex gaze. This view permeated the medical literature of the Middle Ages. In Galen's account of the black, as reported in the work of the Arabic chronicler al-Mas'udi, the black's "large genitals" and "excessive emotionalism" defined the black as readily as did the color of the skin or the quality of the hair.[32] The physical quality of black sexuality and the uncontrolled nature of the emotions (for which the act of seeing the father's genitalia is the archetype) present the black as the genitalia *in nuce*, a walking phallus. But, as we shall see in the course of this study, it is not only the black male that represents the genitalia but also the black female. It is indeed blackness that comes to be the acceptable code for representing the unbridled force perceived as existing within oneself, a force that is externalized, given shape (and, needless to say, color) so as to differentiate it from the world in which the rational is believed to hold sway. The black, indeed the exotic in general, becomes the surrogate genitalia, the force out of control, for the fantasy of the Western European. And the act that set the black apart as the sexual outsider in the mythopoesis of the West was the observation of the phallus of the father, the condemned act that reveals the nature of the son and threatens the father's control. It is the sensory experience, the act of seeing (remember that Eve represents the sensory experience in the tripartite division of the Fall) the same sex that damns. Seeing the father's phallus is the same as being a female. Here all of the categories of differences merge in the image of the megaphallic black.

Michelangelo, on the Sistine ceiling, depicts the drunkenness of Noah and reveals his genitalia, so that we (all sharing the complex masculine gaze of the homosexual artist) seem to be placed in the position of Ham, the son who gazes upon his father's nakedness.[33] We are all revealed as voyeurs, as blacks, as deviants **[PLATE 15]**. But the genitalia of all three sons, including Ham, are also revealed to our gaze. The marker of the voyeuristic eye is

PLATE 15. *The origin of the myth of black hypersexuality in Ham's seeing of his father Noah's nakedness as represented in Michelangelo,* The Drunkenness of Noah, *1508–10. Ceiling, Rome: Sistine Chapel.*

PLATE 16. *Karel van Mander*, The Drunkenness of Noah, 1627. Bremen: Kunsthalle.

not only the genitalia but also the pointing hand of Ham, the icon of same-sex touching, which is the mark of Ham's sexual transgression. Likewise in Karel van Mander's seventeenth-century version of the same scene **[PLATE 16]**.

The image of touch, from Eve touching Adam through the agency of the apple or the serpent, through the seduction of Bathsheba or the healing touch of Christ's ministry that cleanses Mary Magdalene (but does not reach out beyond the tomb), haunts all of the representations of biblical images of sexuality. It is the touch that causes the spread of contagion, the contagion of sexuality as embodied in the image of sexual disease and its transmission (as will be discussed in Chapter Three), but it is also the image that is most closely associated with the body, the body as the organ of touch. But illness and pain—the Fall from grace as embodied in all aspects of human sexuality from the pain of childbirth through the suffering caused by sexually transmitted diseases—is not only to be understood as a representation of the realities of human sex-

uality. Rather, it is a series of complex metaphors for the image of the sexual as that force out of human control. Contagion becomes a metaphor for the universal nature of human sexuality, a universality that does not mitigate but rather heightens our anxiety about the boundaries we have tried to set between ourselves—healthy and in control of our own world, our own fates—and the Other, ever threatening, ever dangerous, ever out of control. All of this and more is embedded in the Western representations of sexuality. The hand, the emblem of touch and an icon of the senses—as well as the instrument of servitude, the sign of the slave—is also the mark of insubordination and inferiority. The representation of human sexuality is thus the means of drawing the boundary between those groups labeled as marginal, such as the black, and the male European observer, the creator of the world of images. It is a means of distancing and controlling, of defining one's own place in the complex universe of sexuality, in defining (negatively) the sexuality of the Other.

THE REPRESENTATION OF SEXUALITY
IN THE NEW TESTAMENT

The Old Testamentary boundaries of the taboo, the line between the permitted and the forbidden aspects of human sexuality, seem to be consciously reversed in images taken from the New Testament. Thus the representation of the touch, the direct experience through the senses, that characterizes Eve's sexuality is radically reversed in the representations of Christ's sexuality in the Western tradition.[34] In the representation of the sexuality of the infant Christ, in Hans Baldung Grien's 1511 image of Mary, Anne, and Joseph [PLATE 17], St. Anne's touching of the (uncircumcised) penis of the infant Christ, as Leo Steinberg has admirably shown, signifies the "earthly" as opposed to the "divine" nature of Christ.[35] The phallus in Christian iconography is the sign of the physical. Christ's double nature, as both the Godhead and man, not merely God masked as man but God as man, is revealed in the representations of Christ's sexuality. St. Thomas Aquinas saw the need for Christ's circumcision, the sign of his membership in the religious covenant of the Jews, not only as a sign of the reality of Christ's flesh but also as a sign of the "diminishing of fleshly concupiscence that thrives principally in those organs because of the intensity of venereal pleasure."[36] Circumcision, the surgical amputation of the foreskin of the male, comes to serve as the sign of the power of the senses overcoming the rational mind. The iconography of Christ's sexuality is thus unique, representing, as it does, the link between the material and the divine, an association only possible within Christ's body.

The representation of Christ's sexuality is the reversal of the image of Adam but also of Noah, who is the second figure of the Old Testament from which all of humankind must of necessity spring. Christ's Resurrection is the reversal of Adam's fall and Noah's nakedness. Because of the nature of medieval and Renaissance hermeneutics, there is an implicit simultaneity present in all images of Christ's life, in which all of the images reflect upon the final acts, the Crucifixion and the Resurrection. Thus the act of Christ's circumcision, celebrated in the Church calendar, points to the shedding of blood at the Crucifixion. However, the visual representation of the Christ whose circumcision is celebrated is as an uncircumcised male. The gentle touching of the Christ Child's penis is thus the visual antithesis to the seeing of Noah's nakedness. It is the innocence of the Christ Child that is traditionally opposed to the sexuality of Noah's debauchery. It is not merely

PLATE 17. *The most overt representation of the touching of Christ's penis in Hans Baldung Grien,* St. Anne, Joseph, Mary, and Child, *1511. Vienna: Graphische Sammlung Albertina.*

earthly sexuality but, perhaps equally important, the sexuality of innocence, the innocence attributed to sexuality before the Fall. For after the Fall, in all interpretations, the genitalia are understood as laboring in lust. In Sodoma's image of *The Holy Family* at the Villa Borghese (1525), the child Jesus touches his own genitalia, not only as a sign of ostentation, to use Steinberg's term, but also to indicate that his penis is uncircumcised [PLATE 18]. Thus Pope Innocent III, at the beginning of the thirteenth century, writes: "Everyone knows that intercourse, even between married persons, is never performed without the itch of the flesh, the heat of passion, and the stench of lust. Whence the seed conceived is fouled, smirched, corrupted, and the soul infused into it inherits the guilt of sin."[37] It is the itch, the sign of the sense of touch, which is the sign of the corruption of the genitalia. The genitalia are corrupt, and they show their corruption by their subservience to the most bestial of the senses—touch.

PLATE 18. *The Christ Child touches his own penis in Sodoma,* The Holy Family, ca. 1525. *Florence: Galleria Borghese.*

PLATE 19. *The Unicorn Tapestry, 1480–1500,* La Dame à la liicorne— le Toucher. *Paris: Cluny.*

The medieval fantasy of the sense of touch is built about this image of sexual corruption, even when it is not overtly connected with the representation of biblical versions of the Fall. In the well-known series of fifteenth-century tapestries at the Cluny representing the senses **[PLATE 19]**, usually called *The Lady with the Unicorn*, the tapestry representing the sense of touch centers on the lady grasping the horn of the unicorn[38] **[PLATE 20]**. The tradition of courtly love with its deified beloved, represented in this tapestry, has its roots in the medieval cult of Mary. Here the fantasy is of the surrogate touch of the pure beloved, for the unicorn can only be approached by a virgin. This secularization of the image of Mary is thus also sexualized but only within a highly symbolic iconographic system.

Retrospectively, we can imagine that this mode of caressing the horn, with its phallic form, could be read as a mode of touching the forbidden and hidden genitalia, the unspoken aspect of the image of the lover within the courtly love tradition of the high Middle Ages.[39] And indeed there are within this tapestry a series of iconic references that make such an interpretation likely. Of the four trees in the Edenic garden occupied by the maid and the unicorn, one is clearly the tree of knowledge, here represented by the tree with its stylized pineapples. More important, the monkey, which functions in the entire series as the lady's echo, the sign that the senses are shared by the lower animals with humans, is fondling not a unicorn horn but an apple, the sign of the Fall **[PLATE 21]**. It is this monkey, the sign of the animalistic senses unmitigated by reason and love, that is the parallel of the lady, for her actions are functions of her image as the representative of lower reason (*scientia*); its actions are functions of its animalistic nature reflecting its unmediated response to the world of the senses. The monkey is the parody of human activity, action without reason; it is the *turpissima bestie, simillima nostri,* "the most shameful beast, so similar to ourselves."[40] The monkey also signifies the sexual aspect of humankind. For women, as Iago says to Othello, are "hot as monkeys."[41] This romance of the senses places a boundary between the medieval fantasy about human sexuality understood within the paradigm of "courtly love" and the corruption of the animal.

PLATE 20. *The virgin's hand touches the unicorn's horn in this detail from The Unicorn Tapestry, 1480–1500, La Dame à la liicorne—le Toucher, detail: touch. Paris: Cluny.*

PLATE 21. *The monkey, the sign of lasciviousness, is chained in The Unicorn Tapestry, 1480–1500, La Dame à la liicorne—le Toucher, detail: the monkey. Paris: Cluny.*

PLATE 22. *Christ's hand touches his genitalia after he has been removed from the cross in Jan van Scorel,* Lamentation, *ca. 1535–40. Utrecht: Centraal Museum.*

In Baldung Grien's image of the infant Christ, we have the surrogate observer, here the sleeping Joseph, in the role of the masculine viewer of the act of sexualized touching, if a touching that is the admiration of human beauty rather than Eros. The same-sex gaze, the crime of Ham, is thus avoided. Only the women are awake, which makes even the gaze pure, that is, it is from one sex to the Other. The iconographic significance of his passive view places us, the observers, awake and aware, in the special position of the sexless seer. The surrogate observer here is unaware of the true significance of the act of touching, of the representation not only of Christ's humanity but also of the desire to touch the genitalia of the Other. And Christ becomes in the Renaissance the image of the Other who is, however, actually an extension of the self as observer.

The act of observing the touch echoes through many of the representations of the sexuality of Christ. In a typical representation, Jan van Scorel's early sixteenth-century (1535–40) representation of the lamentation, the central group of figures observe the crucified Christ, removed from the cross, whose left hand touches his genitalia [PLATE 22]. This touch would seem to violate the prohibition of standard authorities of the Church, such as Thomas Aquinas, of indulging in "lustful" behaviors, among which he lists masturbation.[42] Infants, including the representation of the infant Christ, are not included in this prohibition, simply because they have not yet reached the age of reason. But for the infant

Christ, the touching of his genitalia also prefigures this final self-touching, the physical agony of the Crucifixion symbolized by the touching after death. An absolute boundary is drawn in this image of the adult Christ between the act of self-pollution, forbidden to the viewer, and the iconographically significant one. The touch of the self can be polluting only for human beings, when the mortal hand touches the genitalia. The dead Christ, the embodiment of the transcendence of the material, can thus be represented as touching his genitalia in an act, as Steinberg notes, that places him beyond the mortal. And, one can add, places his mortal observers beyond the boundary that divides the act of "good" touching from that of "bad" touching.

Lucas Cranach the Elder uses this image in juxtaposition to the image of Mary as the Mother of Christ to create an anti-Adam and an anti-Eve.[43] The scourged Christ, who places his hand on his genitalia, and the pregnant Mary, sorrowing for her yet-to-be-born (but already crucified) son, form the most evident parallel to the vision of the Fall [PLATES 23–24]. The male as well as the female genitalia are represented in this set of images, but as exemplary images of purification, of birth and rebirth, rather than corruption and death. In Marten Jacobz van Veen Heemskerk's early sixteenth-century image of the Resurrected Christ, the emphasis of the viewer's sight, of the viewer's sensory response, is on the masked but evidently present erection of the adult Jesus [PLATE 25]. It is the Resurrection of the flesh, the *testimonium fortitudinis.*

PLATE 23. *Christ points toward his genitalia in Lucas Cranach the Elder,* Christ as Martyr, *ca. 1537. Berlin: Staatliche Museen.*

PLATE 24. *Mary, the mother of the suffering Christ, is depicted as she was before the nativity in Lucas Cranach the Elder,* Mary as Suffering Mother, *ca. 1520. Berlin: Staatliche Museen.*

PLATE 25. *The burial shroud covers the erect penis of Christ in Marten Jacobz van Veen Heemskerk,* Ecce Homo, *ca. 1525–30. Greenville, South Carolina: Bob Jones University.*

It is the sign of the strength of the Resurrection in overcoming the mortal. In Artemidorus's third-century *Interpretation of Dreams*, a text widely cited in the Renaissance, the penis is "the symbol of strength and physical vigor, because it is itself the cause of these qualities."[44] This parallel image to the image of the infant Jesus stresses the function of sexuality not as a mark of the Fall but as an indicator of the power of the Resurrection to purify and resurrect the flesh.

The iconography of same-sex touching in the touching of the self is linked to the sexualized gaze but also to the two aspects of the sense of touch, the pain of the Crucifixion and the pleasure of the touching of the genitalia.[45] (Both pain and pleasure, as aspects of sensory response, are associated with Eve in her role as the emblem of the sensorium.) Here the ambiguity of the touching (and therefore the representing) of the genitalia, with the linkage of pleasure and pain, becomes evident. The touching of the genitalia represents the touch of pleasure; the stigmata, the touch of pain. Each is an aspect of the human nature of Christ. Pleasure and pain are aspects of the body, of the sense of touch that recalls the Fall. This ambiguity is standard in medieval representations of touch.[46] This is a Christian reworking of the Platonic view as expressed in the *Phaedo* that pleasure and pain are as closely connected as if they were two bodies attached to the same head[47] (see Plate 80). This wholeness, without any of the negative associations to the Fall and the debased nature of human sexuality, echoes the image, found in the *Symposium*, of the entire body before its division into male and female segments. Pain and pleasure thus become analogues to the male and female aspects of human nature for Plato. Male and female, pleasure and pain are divided but closely, indeed necessarily, linked. In the iconography of the New Testament, they both serve as references to the debased nature of post-Edenic sexuality.

In the medieval and Renaissance understanding of the model character of the life of Christ, all aspects of Christ's life, from the pleasurable touching of the infant Christ's penis to the suffering mirrored by the crucified Christ, are inexorably interlinked. In the sixteenth century, St. Teresa of Avila evokes this sense of the link between the painful and the pleasurable (which assumes the form of the erotic) when she wrote:

> for an arrow is driven into the entrails to the very quick, and into the heart at times, so that the soul knows not what is the matter with it, not what it

wishes for. It understands clearly enough that it wishes for God, and that the arrow seems tempered with some herb which makes the soul hate itself for the love of our Lord, and willingly lose its life for Him. It is impossible to describe or explain the way in which God wounds the soul, nor the very grievous pain inflicted, which deprives it of all self-consciousness; yet this pain is so sweet, that there is no joy in the world which gives greater delight. As I have just said, the soul would wish to be always dying of this wound.[48]

The image of the arrow, with its representation of penetration and pain, is associated with Christ as the erotic metaphor for the *unio mystica*, the mystic union between the human and the Godhead. This is not solely the female mystic speaking, desiring to be pierced by the arrow that is Christ, for the central image of this passage was taken by St. Teresa from the works of St. John of the Cross. The image of painful penetration, of defloration, which ideologically should be a sexual reference to (and for) the female, has, of course, through the iconography of Christianity, been extended to Christ, the masculine representation of a Godhead in which masculine and feminine aspects are merged. It is the linking of the erotic, the sensual with the sense of pain and pleasure inherent in touch, which is inherent in the tradition of the representation of Christ crucified. This tradition is itself a religious reworking of the inherent relationship among pleasure, pain, and Eros that can be found even in Lucretius when he writes of touch as:

> the sense of the body: whether it be
> When something from without makes its way in,
> Or when a thing, which in the body had birth,
> Hurts it, or gives it pleasure issuing forth
> To perform the generative deeds of Venus.[49]

Indeed, it marks the return to a continuous understanding of touch such as that mirrored in Alain de Lille's *Anticlaudianus* of 1183, where touch is understood as that primary force that "the Mother of the Gods gave to Nature and with it the Knot of Love was tied tighter and bound their vows."[50] From the early Middle Ages, touch had been the sense of the "libido."[51] Touch is not a neutral sense for the Renaissance but is closely associated with brute sexuality rather than love in any of its forms. Marsilio Ficino, in his commentary on the *Symposium*, provides the link between the senses and desire. He sees the senses as able merely to generate qualities of objects (such as "cold, softness, hardness"). None of the senses provides the totality of human beauty, which demands a sense of the harmony of

PLATE 26. *A wide range of references to the sense of touch is present in Sebastiano del Piombo,* Holy Family with Saints and Donor, *ca. 1505–10. Paris: Musée du Louvre.*

the higher senses, of sight and hearing, and it is this that generates love (*amor*). The lower senses, such as touch, for Ficino, are the sources of "lust or madness."[52] Touch is the erotic sense, and Eros is the equivalent to the antithesis of rationality—madness. Both lust and madness are states beyond language.

Sebastiano del Piombo makes the link between the various aspects of touch overt in his image of the *Holy Family with Saints and Donor* (1505) **[PLATE 26]**. The infant Jesus touches his genitalia; Mary, in an almost medieval iconographic gesture, points at the thigh of the infant, just barely touching it; St. Agatha, protectress against diseases of the breasts, martyred by having her breasts amputated, touches her breast (her sign of identity with Christ's wounds); and St. Sebastian stands pierced, like the crucified Christ, his arrows being the sign of his identification with Christ.

But it is the passion of Christ, of the moment of suffering in which Christ laments that he has been

forsaken, that leads to his removal from the Cross (with the traditional touching of the genitalia), in preparation for the Resurrection, which is signified for the observer by the viewer's surrogate, Thomas's act of touching: "The other disciples therefore said unto him, We have seen the Lord. But he said unto them, Except I shall see in his hands the print of the nails, and put my finger into the print of the nails, and thrust my hand into his side, I will not believe" (John 19: 21). This placing of the finger into the body of Christ, as in Caravaggio's image of doubting St. Thomas (1602–03) **[PLATE 27]**, sees the touch as being proof of the Resurrection, the proof of the senses more than sight, a proof written on the skin in the stigmata of the Crucifixion. Christ's mortal shell, his Adamic nature, is represented in the touching of the body, a touching that reverses Adam's fall as well as Ham's gazing at his father's genitalia.

But the pure nature of Christ's sexuality stands in juxtaposition to yet another set of images of sex-

PLATE 27. *The importance of the sense of touch in opening the body in order to determine its nature can be seen in Caravaggio,* The Incredulity of St. Thomas, *ca. 1602–03. Potsdam–Sanssouci: Bildergalerie staatlicher Schlösser und Gärten.*

uality in the Middle Ages and the Renaissance. For Christ is not only the antithesis of Adam, whose fall he redeems; he is also the antithesis of the "perfidious" Jews who condemned him and whose nature he does not share. The image of the sexuality of Christ evoked until the Renaissance is an image that also delineates itself from the perverse sexuality of the Jews, a sexuality marked by the Jewish male's true secret sign, circumcision, as well as a mythic sign that marks the powerful myth of Jewish sexuality for the Christian world. Circumcision remains embedded in the Christian reading of the Old Testament as both the sign of the special covenant of the Jews with God (Genesis 17: 10–14) as well as a sign of their difference from the Christian (Colossians 3: 11). Circumcision was thus perceived simultaneously as both positive and negative. This is the reason for the strange juxtaposition between the celebration of the Feast of the Circumcision and the most evident fact that Christ is represented in Western art as uncircumcised. The outcast Jew (it

is the male Jew who represents the "Jew" iconographically, the female Jew is subsumed to the greater category represented by the male) becomes one with the disfigured, deviant male genitalia. This sign marks the Jew as inherently different, as his physical nature transgresses against the absolute boundary between male and female, a boundary represented by the radically different structure of their genitalia. The Jew is neither female nor entirely male; the form of his genitalia are proof enough of this. The iconographic Christ is thus not a Jew, and circumcision is a sign of the innate difference of the Jews. Indeed, throughout the history of the Jews in the West there has been a constant association of circumcision with castration, the making of the Jew by unmanning him, by feminizing him. But the Jew is neither male nor female, but a separate category. The touching of Christ's uncircumcised genitalia is thus also a sign of difference, differentiating the pure Pauline Christian (who has rejected circumcision and the Synagogue) from the

Jew (whose skin bears the scar of his rejection of Christ). Circumcision is viewed as a crime against the body as early as Origen, in the early Third Century, who understood "the disgrace which is felt by most people to attach to circumcision."[53] And Erasmus, in the sixteenth century, commented that circumcision ranked high among those Jewish customs to which "we cry shame."[54] Indeed, the images of the megaphallic sons of Ham carved on the Romanesque churches of Europe may represent not only blacks but Jews. In the churches at Frómista, Poiters, Arce, Savignac d'Auros, Santillana del Mar, Givresac, and Champagnolles these figures are clearly circumcised. The association between the Jew, the black, and the primitive in terms of the representation of the male member can be best seen in the church at Droiturier, where a circumcised megaphallic ape is represented.[55] For Western Christianity it is but one of a series of sexual markers that associated the Jew with the nature of the genitalia. One of the strongest of these myths was the legend of Jewish male menstruation.

The idea of male menstruation is part of a Christian tradition of seeing the Jew as inherently, biologically different, labeling the Jew as a figure outside of the dichotomy of the sexes, as a reptile in human clothing. Thomas de Cantimpré, the thirteenth-century anatomist, presented the first "scientific" statement of this phenomenon (calling upon St. Augustine as his authority).[56] Male Jews menstruated as a mark of the "Father's curse," their pathological difference. This image of the Jewish male as female was introduced to link the Jew with the corrupt nature of the woman (both marked as different by the same sign) and to stress the intransigence of the Jews. Thomas de Cantimpré recounts the nature of the Jews' attempt to cure themselves. They are told by one of their prophets that they would be rid of this curse by "Christiano sanguine," the blood of a Christian, when in fact it was "Christi sanguine," the blood of Christ in the sacrament, that was required. Thus the libel of blood guilt, the charge that Jews sacrifice Christian children to obtain their blood, is the result of the intransigence of the Jews in their rejection of the truth of Christianity and is intimately tied to the sign of Jewish male menstruation. The persistence of menstruation among Jewish males is thus not only a sign of the initial "curse of the Father" but of the inherent inability of the Jews to hear the truth of the Son. For it is the intrinsic "deafness" of the Jews that does not let them hear the truth that will cure them. This "deafness" to the truth of Christianity is embodied in the rejection of that divine "touch," baptism, which would necessarily prefigure the taking of communion. The belief in Jewish male menstruation continued through the seventeenth century. Heinrich Kornmann repeated it in Germany in 1614 as did Thomas Calvert in England in 1649.[57]

Franco da Piacenza, a Jewish convert to Christianity, repeated this view in his catalogue of "Jewish maladies," published in 1630 and translated into German by 1634.[58] He claimed that the males (as well as the females) of the tribe of Simeon menstruated four days a year! The sexuality of the Jews, polluting and polluted, is the sexuality that incorporates pain, the martyrdom of Christian children, and pleasure, but within the perversion of the Jews' sexuality. Jews are sexual border crossers; they possess, like the reptiles in the Garden of Eden, qualities ascribed to both poles of an absolute dichotomy and yet stand outside of the dichotomy as their own, deviant category. They are simultaneously males (and yet not "whole" males because they are circumcised) and females (but females only in the sense that they are not truly males). Christ is thus not a Jew because his sexuality is purifying, not corrupting. The touch of his own genitalia, a sign of the Jew's difference, becomes a sign of his purity.

This separation of the images of Christ (and his iconography of the skin and self-touch) from the image of the Jew was necessary for Renaissance Christianity. It was Martin Luther who in 1523 attacked the Church's position on this question in his pamphlet "That Jesus Christ Was Born a Jew." The differentiation of the Jews, the marginalized inhabitants of the ghettos established during the Renaissance, from Christ, the Godhead, was undertaken, among other ways, through the differentiation of the sexuality of Christ, as exemplified in the representation of the sexualized touch with its association of pain and transcendence, from the debasing feminizing sexuality of the Jewish male. The representation of the sexuality of Christ thus drew a clear boundary between acceptable and unacceptable touching, between healing and pathological touching.

It is within the narrative of the Resurrection that the image of the senses, especially the sense of touch, becomes one with the opening of the body. The resurrected Christ, who addressed Thomas and ordered him: "reach hither thy finger, and behold my hands; and reach hither thy hand, and thrust it into my side: and be not faithless, but believing" (John 20: 27) is the model for the piercing of Sebastian, whose arrows signify his martyrdom, as one can see in Caravaggio's image of doubting

PLATE 28. *The distancing effect of the forbidden touch is to be seen in Hans Holbein the Younger's early sixteenth-century* Noli me tangere. *London: Hampton Court Palace.*

Thomas.[59] Thomas's touch proves for him the truth of the Resurrection. But it is also the sign of entering the body, of placing the hand (the sign of the sense of touch) within the body of the ultimate Other, Christ. (A discussion of a further icon of touch in Caravaggio's oeuvre will be found in Chapter Five.) It is an opening of the body analogous to the penetration of the sexual act but also analogous to other modes of entering the body, such as that of the anatomist.

But it is the same Christ who would not be touched by Mary Magdalene, as in Hans Holbein the Younger's image **[PLATE 28]**: "Touch me not for I am not yet ascended to my Father" (John 20: 17)—*noli me tangere.* Christ, whose resurrected body could be touched, but whose corporeal body could not, is the central iconographic reference for this image. For Mary Magdalene's image remains constantly linked to the image of carnality, even after her conversion.[60] In the same image the Apostles John and Peter are depicted touching one another as they run to the now-empty sepulcher. Holbein provides for us a set of textual references that are clear and direct. Same-sex touching and self-touching, like cross-sex touching, can take place only under the most extraordinary circumstances, such as the intervention of the Godhead. The circumstances are circumscribed by the evocation of pain, of the Crucifixion that alters all relationships by bringing them into the realm of the Godhead.

PLATE 29. *Rembrandt places Bathsheba's body in the center of the viewer's gaze,* The Toilet of Bathsheba, *1632. New York: Metropolitan Museum of Art.*

Mary Magdalene, "one of the few complex, ambiguous saints," according to Moshe Barasch, becomes in the narrative of the New Testament its representation of carnal sexuality redeemed, the woman cleansed of sin, the prostitute rescued by Christ's purity. She is the "other" Mary, not Mary the Virgin—whose immaculate conception, usually represented by her "hearing" the words of the Holy Spirit and thus conceiving (the antithesis of the Jews who cannot hear the truth of God's message)—but Mary the prostitute. Indeed, the Byzantine tradition of depicting Christ risen has him meeting with the two Marys, who, according to St. John Chrysostomus, "grasp his feet, and by touching them, got proof of his resurrection."[61] The Western tradition has him meeting only with the redeemed prostitute, who is admonished *not* to touch him. The conversion of Mary Magdalene is understood as a New Testament reworking of a series of biblical models, most specifically the image of Bathsheba. Rembrandt's Bathsheba **[PLATE 29]** demurely covers her breast and yet gazes directly at the observer functioning as the surrogate for King David, who earlier was visible on a balcony of the palace in the background.[62] The black maid, the daughter of Ham, serves as a sign of sexual excess in her servitude as she combs Bathsheba's hair in preparation for seduction by David. This scene of seductiveness, signaled by the presence of the black and by the use of the woman's hair, can be contrasted with the shock registered in Charles Le Brun's portrait of Mary Magdalene's conversion **[PLATE 30]**. The jewel casket, so prominent in both images, represents the sexual seductiveness of each figure. It is the symbolic representation of the female genitalia. The clothed, repentant Mary Magdalene gazes toward heaven, her jewel casket fallen at her feet. The casket serves as an image of female sexuality, indicating the worldliness and venery of female sexuality. It is an image purified in the *Noli me tangere* and Crucifixion representations of Mary Magdalene in the unguent box, representing her preparation of Christ's mortal body at the tomb. Her shock is the shock of awareness of her perverse sexuality, but it is parallel to the shock of the female's awareness, the male gaze in images of Susanna seen in the bath by the Elders **[PLATE 31]**. Rembrandt's image covers both the genitalia and breasts, showing the viewer Susanna's gaze, a gaze as indicative of the revelation of the inner truth about human sexuality as the direct depiction of the genitalia would be.

PLATE 30. *Charles Le Brun's* Repentant Magdalene, 1656, *provides the moment of the prostitute's enlightenment. Paris: Musée du Louvre.*

PLATE 31. *Rembrandt,* Susanna Surprised by the Elders, ca. *1630. The Hague: Mauritshuis.*

PLATE 32. *The various episodes in the life of Mary Magdalene are represented in this thirteenth-century Italian altarpiece. Florence: Galleria dell'Accademia.*

Mary Magdalene is reclaimed, her sexuality purified by Christ's grace. She is the "woman in the city," the "sinner" who washed Christ's "feet with her tears, and did wipe them with the hairs of her head, and kissed his feet" (Luke 7: 37–48). Jesus forgives her. Following the Resurrection, she becomes an anchorite in the Egyptian desert, protected from the elements in her nakedness by her hair, and she is eventually raised into the company of the blessed after her death **[PLATE 32]**. Donatello illustrates this in a number of versions of the death of Mary Magdalene, with her long hair covering her nakedness[63] **[PLATE 33]**. Tilmann Riemenschneider presents the covering not merely as the extended hair of her head but as a pelt covering the entire body, except for one firm, idealized breast, a sign of her nurturing of those she succors in the desert as well as her restored innocence[64] **[PLATE**

PLATE 33. *Medallion of Mary Magdalene ascribed to the school of Donatello, ca. 1550, represents the hairiness of Mary as a coat of fur. London: Victoria and Albert Museum.*

34]. Such an image counteracts the tradition of depicting Eve and Adam after the fall as clothed in (or indeed, covered with) hair as representing the proverbial wild people. This visual sign of her blessedness, clearly associated with her act of wiping Christ's feet with her hair, creates a visual contrast to the seductiveness of Bathsheba's hair as well. Mary Magdalene becomes the image of the purified sexual being as part animal, in contrast to the half-animal, half-human figure representing the sexuality of the Edenic past. She is an image of purity, placed in juxtaposition to the sexuality of the Fall that has been redeemed by the Resurrection.

The medieval and early modern visual realizations of images of sexuality found in the New Testament are counterimages to their Old Testament parallels. They are attempts to create boundaries between the world and culture of their own time and the images generated by the Bible(s). The Bible serves as the depository for the range of the images I have discussed, as well as a range of further images of sexuality, ranging from Lot and his daughters to the beautiful black bride of the Song of Songs (who by the Middle Ages becomes a black witch seducing Solomon),[65] to the Pauline admonition that it is better to marry than to burn. These images encapsulate the Western understanding of the nature and complexity of sexuality within a strictly polar dichotomy of the sexes. But they are also riddled with contradictions about this very model. This sense of a dichotomy that is itself a model for the nature of the world (or vice versa) becomes the map of the world. The body is understood to be a microcosm of this world, and the systems, complex, contradictory, and overlapping, that map this world also map the body. What is central is the understanding of the sensorium, of how sexuality becomes related to a construction of the idea of the senses, and the vocabulary of visual images into which these abstractions are translated forms the basis for a long tradition of seeing human sexuality.

CHAPTER THREE

Sexuality, Difference, and Disease in the Science and Culture of the Middle Ages and the Renaissance

ANATOMIES AND THE BIBLE

Medieval anatomists, the scientists who began to open the body, saw the bodies they were examining in the terms dictated by visual images taken from their culture.[1] One major aspect of that culture, in all its complexity, was the image of the body in the representations of the Bible. Adam and Eve became the essential images for human sexuality, for its creation, for its Fall, and for its eventual resurrection. The translation into a single image (that of Eve and Adam) with their New Testament analogues, of the various ideologies of human sexuality should vanish once the shift is made from biblical models of sexuality to Renaissance ideals of a scientific understanding of the body. The Renaissance should be the age of empiricism rather than textuality.[2] Learning from the books of the classical anatomists was to be augmented if not replaced by learning from the ultimate book, the book of the body. But the anatomists of the Renaissance, like their medieval predecessors, built upon three major models of "seeing the body"—the body was the cosmos, the state, or the embodiment of the beautiful.[3] Male and female bodies served—within the visual interpretation of biblical narratives of the Garden, the Creation, and the Fall—as the map of the universe, the embodiment of the ideal (and degenerate) state, and the wellspring of the beautiful.[4] Thus the images of the body were, as Michel Foucault has noted, "within the truth" of the cultural presuppositions about sexuality. The "exterior" of the anatomists' discourse about the body matched the culturally determined discourse of the "interior," the theological presuppositions about the nature of the body (and the soul).[5]

Consider the full-length portraits of the male and the female, drawn by Johann Stephen of Calcar, from what is generally considered to be the first full-scale modern anatomical study based on actual opening of the body—Andreas Vesalius's *De humani corporis fabrica libri septem* (1543).[6] There the body is indeed anatomized, but the central metaphor for the *Fabrica* is the perfection of the body as the creation of God, a perfection that was, however, made mortal, which can become diseased because of the Fall. The opening plates of the textbook that accompanied the publication of this atlas, the *Epitome*, present the full-scale figures of the male and the female (probably after Titian) **[PLATES 35–36]** as the means by which Vesalius could create a scientific vocabulary for the surface features of the body. Vesalius's intent, in the *Epitome*, was to train the eye. Such figures, both male and female, had been incorporated in earlier sixteenth-century anatomies for precisely such a purpose. To do so he took the accepted images of Eve and Adam and presented them as the external manifestation of the unseen, the unknown, inner world of human sexuality represented in the *Fabrica* **[PLATES 37–38]**.

Vesalius's figures are not merely images of the external form of the human being on which to hang a series of labels. They represent the perfection of the human form, not its pathology. They are "beautiful" within the neoclassical tradition of Renaissance art. The breasts of the female are firm and small; the male is broad-shouldered, reflecting the idealized male form in Michelangelo's works. And yet there is a set of subtexts in these two "anatomical," full-length figures. First, the male is carrying a skull and is exposing his genitalia by extending his hand and arm, which given the intent to depict the surface

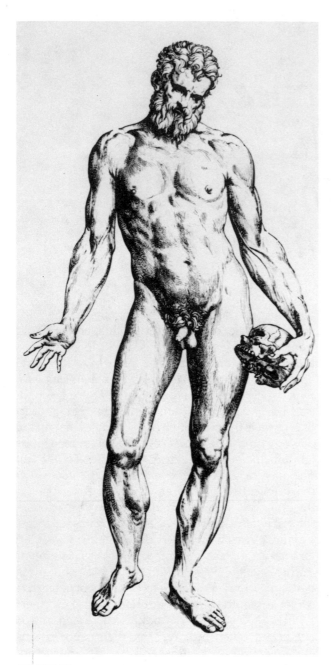

PLATE 36. *Eve covers her genitalia in Johann Stephen of Calcar, Eve, probably after Titian, from Andreas Vesalius,* Epitome *(Basel: Oporinus, 1543). Ithaca: Howard B. Adelmann Collection, Olin Library, Cornell University.*

PLATE 35. *The skull of Adam as held by Adam in Johann Stephen of Calcar, Adam, probably after Titian, from Andreas Vesalius,* Epitome *(Basel: Oporinus, 1543). Ithaca: Howard B. Adelmann Collection, Olin Library, Cornell University.*

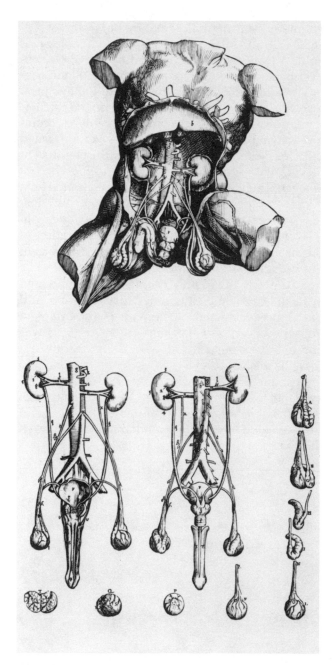

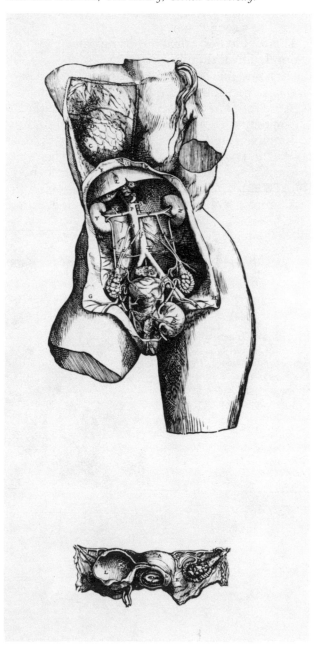

PLATE 38. *Composite plates of the female genitalia from the 1565 edition of Vesalius's anatomical atlas from John Bertrand Saunders and Charles O'Malley,* Illustrations from the Works of Andreas Vesalius *(Cleveland: World Publishing, 1950). Ithaca: Howard B. Adelmann Collection, Olin Library, Cornell University.*

PLATE 37. *Composite plates of the male genitalia from the 1565 edition of Vesalius's anatomical atlas from John Bertrand Saunders and Charles O'Malley,* Illustrations from the Works of Andreas Vesalius *(Cleveland: World Publishing, 1950). Ithaca: Howard B. Adelmann Collection, Olin Library, Cornell University.*

features of the body seems to be the only possible position. All of Vesalius's full-length "muscle" and "skeletal" figures are male, and all have their arms extended outward, usually with their palms toward the viewer in the *ostentatio vulnerum* position of the resurrected Christ. The female parallels the gesture of the outstretched hand and arm, but her hand covers her pudenda. Would it be too modern an interpretation to see the male figure as Adam, bearing his own skull, the sign of the Fall, and the female figure as Eve, whose sexuality was the ultimate cause of the Fall and like Adam's skull its sign, through the tumult of sexuality and the pain of childbirth? The male's exposed genitalia point toward his seduction; the female's covered, hidden, toward her seductiveness.

This would be a fanciful reading of an empirical, scientific illustration of the surface of the body in the first and most serious scholarly text of the Renaissance, had the contemporaries of Vesalius not seen these figures in exactly this manner. The Flemish anatomist Thomas Geminus, in his 1545 figures by John Herford based upon Vesalius's work, does not want the viewer to stop even momentarily to reconstruct the interpretation presented here[7] [PLATE 39]. The skull stands directly between the two figures, with the serpent coiling out of it. It is

not merely an anatomical feature but a sign of Adam's Fall and man's mortality. Adam no longer holds a skull, which is replaced by the apple, but Eve remains the same, covering her pudenda, signifying her sexuality. But this is a pre-Renaissance, medieval image that reflects not only on the exterior, the surface, of the body but on its internal composition and meaning. In the Lübeck version, dated 1485, of Bartholomaeus Anglicus's thirteenth-century *De proprietatibus rerum (On the Properties of Things)*, a medieval encyclopedia based on the long tradition of the universal overview of all knowledge, the "viscera man" stands, his hands extended in the *ostentatio vulnerum*, the traditional position of the risen Christ showing his wounds, whereas in the background, God the anatomist removes Eve from the side of Adam[8] [PLATE 40]. The body in all its internal complexity reflects the Creation (and the Fall) redeemed by Christ. It is important to note, however, that Bartholomaeus Anglicus was immensely popular throughout the sixteenth century, as his "medieval" work made the medical knowledge of the Greeks, Jews, and Arabs easily available to European readers. Thus, at the time of Vesalius, his was one of the major "books" that Vesalius (and Geminus) intended to rebut through their work.

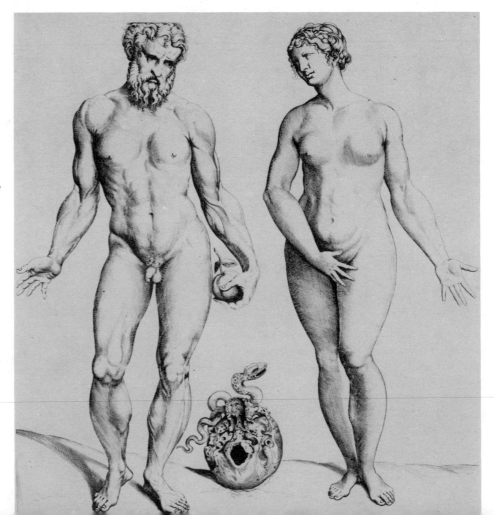

PLATE 39. *Thomas Geminus,* Comendiosa toitus anatomiae delineatio *(London: J. Herford, 1545), engraving of full-length male and female nudes. London: Wellcome Institute for the History of Medicine.*

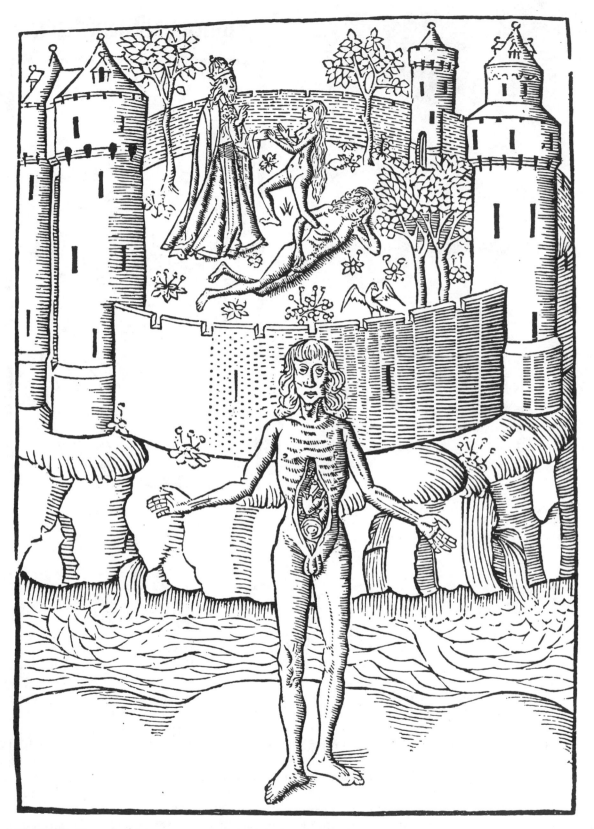

PLATE 40. *Illustration of the viscera man and the birth of Eve from Bartholomaeus Anglicus,* De proprietatibus rerum *(Lyons: Guilaume L. Roy, 1485). Ithaca: Howard B. Adelmann Collection, Olin Library, Cornell University.*

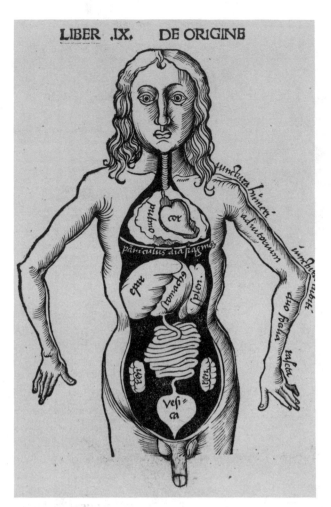

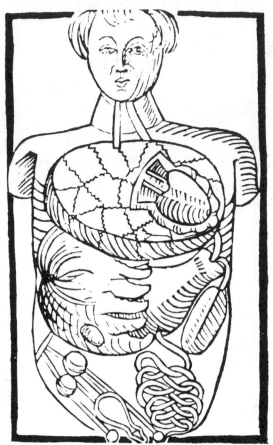

PLATE 41. *Woodcut of male anatomy from Gregor Reisch,* Margarita philosophica *(Freiburg im Breisgau: J. Schott, 1503). London: Wellcome Institute for the History of Medicine.*

PLATE 42. *The map of the body from Magnus Hundt,* Anthropologium *(Leipzig: Baccalarius Wolfgang Monacensen, 1501). Ithaca: Howard B. Adelmann Collection, Olin Library, Cornell University.*

Adam and Eve reappear in the anatomies of the Renaissance at the point where we least expect to see them given the claims of the anatomists for their new science. The model of the biblical concepts of sexuality, with all of its Greek and Jewish counterpoint, underlies what is actually seen in the opening of the body. The medieval understanding of anatomy was generally one derived from books, not from the body. Opening the body meant entering into oneself, with all of the theological complexity inherent in doing this. It was parallel to the questioning of doubting Thomas, which was answered by Thomas entering Christ's wounds. When the body was imagined to be opened, and this opening represented—as in the "viscera man" in Gregor

Reisch's 1503 overview of all knowledge, *Margarita philosophica* **[PLATE 41]**, or the hemisected male figure in Magnus Hundt's 1501 *Anthropologium* **[PLATE 42]**—an idealized map of the interior of the body was provided. It was a map understood within the iconographic language of the thought-collective. And this semiotic system drew heavily on biblical imagery, the imagery of Adam and of Christ. Hundt provides us with the interior of the body as well as the exterior, here representing the male. And this map reflected the ideas of human sexuality that the anatomist saw when he looked into the body. Male sexuality, the sexuality of Adam created in the direct image of God, was the baseline for any perception of human sexuality.

THE MAP OF THE BODY

The map of the body in the Middle Ages and the Renaissance was understood to be a map of overlapping and intertwined systems. Rooted in the work of the medieval Arabic anatomists, such as Avicenna, who first systematized the Galenic corpus, the body was conceived as having at least nine subsystems. There are representations of nine quite different modes of seeing the body: (1) arteries, (2) veins, (3) bones, (4) nerves, (5) muscles, (6) genitalia, (7) stomach, liver, and viscera, (8) womb, and (9) brain and eyes.[9] The sexual organs appear centrally in representations of the genitalia, the womb (usually with the attendant fetus), and the viscera, and are reflected in many of the other systems. The creation of these anatomical categories meant that the female genitalia, with all of their mysteries—their hidden anatomical structure, their role in conception and childbirth, their pathologies and anomalies (as perceived by the medieval and Renaissance observer)—were much more frequently represented in the anatomical texts of the period than were the male genitalia. The woman defined the male in many ways: she was the vessel through which he was able to define himself economically and socially, as she bore his heirs; she was the source of physical pleasure, through the ultimate cross-sexual touch, penetration; but she was also the potential source of disease and death, through her transmission through the act of coitus of certain diseases. It is not merely that women were the object of the sexual fascination of a male world but that the boundaries of human sexuality were set by the perceived dichotomy or polarity between the "male" and the "female." These boundaries became identical to other such bipolar means of structuring the world, for example the male became the unstated baseline definition of health, the woman, that of disease. The female was the Other, was that force that defined the self.[10] And the self was male. The self was the assumed presence, the reality against which the Other was constantly tested (and found lacking). It is this testing that is reflected in the multiple representations of female sexuality found in these sources.

The anatomical systems were not, however, merely mechanical representations of perceived anatomical realities but also had "meaning" because they were also understood as having references to broader systems, such as cosmology. These systems were understood as independent but intertwined. In early modern sets of ivory images of the body, used for teaching anatomy without the direct presence of the physical body, the systems are layered [PLATES 43–44]. The systems are basically those of the "viscera figures." Their complexity can be judged by the fact that the female figures are usually depicted with fetuses, centering their representation on their reproductive faculties. And this even in those figures in which the external genitalia are masked. The centrality of this image can be seen in the simple fact that of over fifty separate ivory anatomical figures extant only four represent a paired male and female. All of the rest are single gravid figures. The fetus comes, in these early anatomical representations, to signify the sexuality of the female as the reflex of her reproductive ability. The presence of the fetus also points toward the complex and often contradictory understanding of what was meant by conception. How, indeed, did the fetus get into the womb?

Two theories of conception dominate the Middle Ages and the Renaissance. The Aristotelian hylomorphic view sees the female as the depository of the male seed. Only the male possesses a seed that has "active virtue." The female provides a passive element with the menstruum; her seed has no active qualities. Galen of Pergamum, the second-century Greco-Roman physician, on the other hand, saw the female seed, formed in the ovarian vessels, as taking an active part in the formation of the fetus.[11] But the "seed" is not understood as the ovum, which was first described in 1827, but rather as the lubricant exuded during sexual arousal.[12] These secretions were understood as early as Aristotle's time, by his contemporary Herophilus of Alexandria, as female seminal fluid homologous to the sperm of the male. For Herophilus this semen arose in the "testis," that is, the ovaries, and traveled by tiny ducts to the neck of the bladder. Giles of Rome sees the female seed as having only one major role, as a lubricant that contributed to sexual pleasure.[13] Conception was tied to the visible fluids of the body, and the "sperm" of the female was understood as analogous to that of the male.

The body was understood as a system of signs, of meanings that reflected the image of the body as the map of the world. Sexuality in all its forms was understood as part of that complexity of intertwined systems. The "surface" meaning of the body (and the genitalia) was the homologue of the body with the other systems that explained the world. Typical of such systems of explanation were the signs of the zodiac (and the often parallel ideas of the humors). The body, like the universe, was divided into aspects, and each aspect was assigned to one of the signs. The sign that dominated the

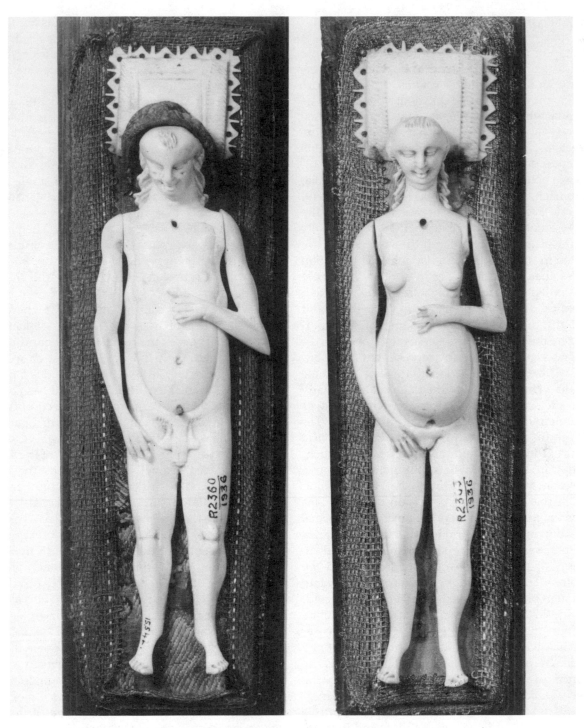

PLATE 43. *Late medieval ivory anatomical figures used for the teaching of anatomy. London: Wellcome Institute for the History of Medicine.*

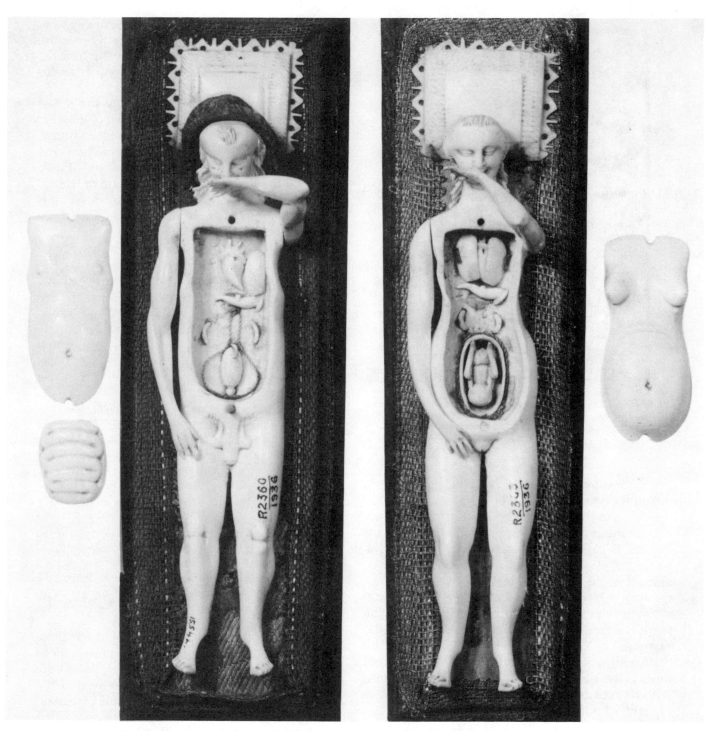

PLATE 44. *Uncovering the ivory miniatures reveals a fetus in the uterus of the female, as well as the intestines. London: Wellcome Institute for the History of Medicine.*

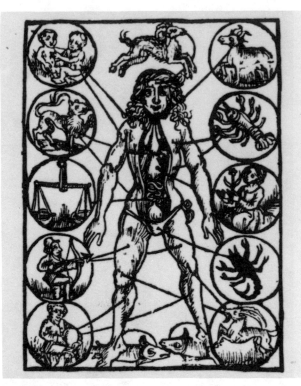

PLATE 45. *The zodiac man/woman with the genitalia masked but indicated by the sign of Scorpio, from Johannes Adelphus,* Mundini de omnibus humani corporis *(Strassbourg: M. Flach, 1513). Ithaca: Howard B. Adelmann Collection, Olin Library, Cornell University.*

heart, for example, was Leo, and the sign that controlled the sexual organs, in both males and females, was Scorpio **[PLATE 45]**. The figure of the scorpion is thus the hidden icon that signifies sexuality for the Middle Ages and the early modern period. The traditional classical Greek sign associated with male sexuality, the sign of the testicles, was the sign of Gemini, which by the Middle Ages becomes associated with the upper torso and the blood. The twins (Gemini) are traditionally associated with the castration of Chronos, as in Hesiod's account.[14] By the Middle Ages, it is Scorpio that dominates, and unites, the genitalia. The figure of the scorpion, with its broader iconographic implications, comes to signify both the male and female genitalia.

THE HOMOLOGOUS STRUCTURE OF THE GENITALIA

The parallelism between the male and the female, the image of their intertwined natures, is Platonic, and yet the aspects of the humors ascribed to the genitalia are antithetical. Richardus Anglicus, the early thirteenth-century anatomist, follows the classical Galenic tradition and describes the testes as "damp and warm," whereas the uterus is "dry

and cold."[15] The qualities of human sexuality, that is, the humors that dominate the idea of sexuality, achieve a singular importance in showing how the sexes are not only parallel but also counterimages of one another.

Nowhere is this image of reciprocity and difference stronger than in the understanding of the form and function of the genitalia.[16] In Galen's anatomy, the view is expressed directly. For Galen, and therefore for most of the anatomists of the Middle Ages and the Renaissance, the question of "heat," that is, of the dominance of specific humors, parallels the question of anatomy. Males are different from females in the nature of their "heat." The cooler version of man is woman. This reciprocity is to be found also in the structure of the genitalia. The female is but the inverse of the male. For one must only "turn outward the woman's [genitalia], turn inward, so to speak, and fold double the man's, and you will find the same in both in every respect."[17] Galen provides us with an image that then reverses this, so that his text reflects the parallel topology of the genitalia themselves:

> Think first please, of the man's [genitalia] turned in and extending inward between the rectum and the bladder. If this should happen, the scrotum would necessarily take the place of the uterus with the testes lying outside, next to it on either side.

And Galen provides the opposing image:

> Think too please, of the converse, the uterus turned outward and projecting. Would not the testes [ovaries] then necessarily be inside it? Would it not contain them like a scrotum? Would not the neck [cervix], hitherto concealed inside the body but now pendant, be made into the male member?

The homologous structure of male and female is paralleled by Galen's understanding of orgasm as the moment in which the male heat inflames the cold uterus and provides pleasure as well as the potential for conception. What happens in orgasm is that the woman develops an "itching" at the mouth of the womb because of the accumulation of excessive humorial material, and this itching is the physical sign for the desire for intercourse. Sexual pleasure in the male is the result of the release of semen, having likewise caused an itch that is pleasurable to relieve. It is this itching to which the medieval theologians referred when commenting on the Satanic nature of the sexual impulse, but it is an impulse understood as resting within the sensory structure of the female as explained by the action of the humors.

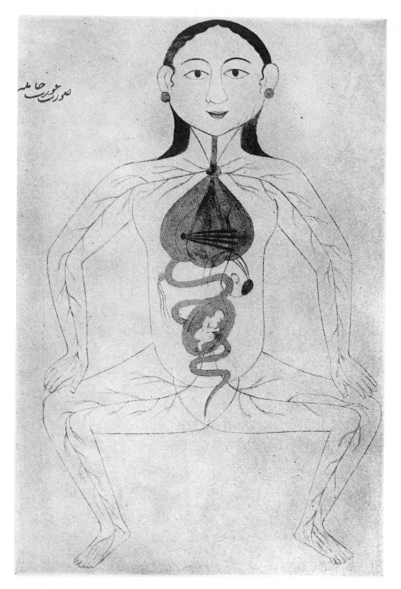

صورت عروق حامله

PLATE 46. *Arterial system of a pregnant woman, from Persian Ms. no. 1576. Oxford: Bodleian Library.*

It is in the arena of sexual pleasure that a basic distinction is made between the male and the female. The Montpellier anatomist, Gerard of Solo, 1330–1350, sees male and female sexual appetites as differentiated.[18] Females have a greater sexual appetite because they take pleasure from four factors during intercourse: reception of the male sperm, expulsion of their own sperm, motion of the uterus, and the "itch." It is the friction of the male member that causes the itch to be relieved. The male, on the other hand, takes pleasure only in the expenditure of sperm. The more often intercourse takes place, the more certain choleric vapors gather at the cervix, causing the itch that needs further intercourse to be relieved. Females therefore need intercourse more often (and exemplify this by their multiple orgasms). However, the male's experience of intercourse is more intensive because males are hotter than females, as Bernard de Gordon notes.[19] This disparity

is seen, however, as homologous, as the greater heat of the male is equivalent to the "itch" of the female. The male's experience is parallel to that of the female, but it is of "better" quality.

The power of the idea of the innate symmetry of the genitalia can be seen in one fascinating sidelight to the discovery of how the sexual organs function. Vesalius, in his discussion of the structure of the female reproductive system, simply assumes the validity of the Galenic idea of the analogy between the male and female reproductive systems, while attempting to counter much of Galen's discussion of the function of female sexual anatomy (as will be discussed later).[20] Semen existed, according to this theory, in both sexes, and the ovaries (called by Galen and the Arabic anatomists, such as Avicenna and Hali Abas, the female testes [**PLATE 46**]) emptied into the bladder by means of the "semen-carrying ducts."[21] These ducts, seen as visual analogues to the *ductus deferens*, served as the organs for the preparation of semen. As one can see in Vesalius's image of the female viscera (see Plate 38), the duct is a vessel that winds its way around the ovary, attached to the "testis" circumference rather than to the posterior of the male testis. And yet Vesalius, having described these tubes, could not comprehend that they could be the means by which the female semen entered the uterus. Vesalius, unlike Gabriele Fallopius in 1561, a full generation later, was so bound by the idea of analogy that he could not see the Fallopian tubes as anything but analogous to the male *ductus deferens*. Thus even though he opened the body, having dissected at least nine female corpses prior to the publication of the *Fabrica*, he could not see what was there apart from the powerful cultural image of the homologous nature of the genitalia that he held.[22]

THE FORM OF THE GENITALIA AND ITS MEANING

But the image of parallelism is undercut by a series of "differences" placed within the interrelation of the classical sexual theories by the anatomists of the Middle Ages. We can begin with the image of the uterus, all images of which relied on the physical opening of the body after death. The relative rarity of such actions led to the presumption of parallelism between human and other mammalian anatomy. The womb, from the time of the Egyptians, was "seen" as bicornate, that is, as possessing two branches.[23] Indeed, the hieroglyph for the uterus was a simplified version of the bicornate uterus of the cow. In the earliest Western illustration of the female uterus, a ninth-century illustrated Latin manuscript of the first-century Syracusan physician Moschion, the "horns" are quite clear. The uterus appears like an upturned amphora [PLATE 47]. The horns are understood by medieval anatomists, such as Jacopo Berengario da Carpi [PLATE 48], as aspects of both the reproductive system and the veins. In his anatomy he presents both an external version of "the entire uterus with its testicles and seminal vessels [which are] . . . similar to the mem-

bers of generation in men, but the male members are completed outside, since they thrust out on account of their heat. The members of women are diminished and retained within the body because of their lesser heat."[24]

We are also presented with the image of the uterus in situ [PLATE 49]. Da Carpi's image, the female placed on a pedestal in an idealized landscape, uncovering herself and thus revealing her inner nature, presents us with the mouth of the womb as a penislike structure. She is cloaked, but the cape is a secularized reference to the icon of Mary, the Protectress, the new Eve, who uses it to protect humankind. Beneath her cape the source of all humankind, the womb, is found. Da Carpi also provides a hemisected interior view, with the veins "through which flow the menses."[25] In 1536, J. Dryander provides a detailed image of the fabulous ducts and veins leading to the womb with the fetus placed within it. The fetus comes to signify the function and potential of the female, for the womb is the "home" of the fetus, even if, as is discussed in more detail in Chapter Six, it is not its origin. But this image is not that of a pregnant female. She exposes her bared, firm breasts, signifying her "pure" rather than her corrupt nature. It is the figure of Mary or the redeemed Mary Magdalene. Dryander's image of the long-haired, neoclassical female, spanned by two dryads, is provided with an accurate image of the external genitalia [PLATE 50]. When Vesalius comes to depict the womb removed from the female body, when he comes to look at the structure of the female reproductive system and the external genitalia as a system, he is able to give full force to his fantasy of homology. Vesalius has understood that the "bicornate" uterus belongs to the lower mammals, and he provides a comparative image of the uteruses of the dog and the cow [PLATE 51]; but his version of the human uterus, although lacking "horns," is the most penile of all. That is, it defines the difference between the human and the bestial in terms of the icon of male sexuality. When Vesalius strips away the horns from the uterus, he maintains the penile shape based on the model of homology.

PLATE 47. *The earliest image of the uterus (ninth century) from a European source. Brussels: Royal Library.*

posſit inquodqu/quaſ paſteſ diuider̅ e̅omnia mulier̅u traditio̅ e̅ inducaſ una que obſe̅-
ce tractata' altera q̅ de o̅mniƀ: obſetriciƀ: occurre̅t̅ confice̅t. hanc ipſū iter̅u diuidi

secundū natura̅ occurrenteſ cauſaſ et p̅ natura obſetricele r̅cao quida̅ muliebri
diffe̅rat q̅am. quod adipſa obſetrice e̅xerceatur queaſe̅t mulieriſ r̅catione cognoſcere.

Femina omniū mulie-
r̅u cauſarū docta etia̅ medicinali. exercitatione perita que poſſet univerſariū uel-
tudineſ competer̅t̅ curare latenſit̅ turbulenta nec uerboſa nec auara. ſed ſapienſ
&ſabria & taciturna. et uptirtuoſa. que ſua ſollicitudine. mulier̅eſ ſup̅ſtuentiƀ &

Princ̅pal̅
i aliiſ nominiƀ; dicta e̅ primu quide̅ abeo q̅d muliereſ paſtuſuo matreſ efficia̅t̅ g̅
e̅ta e̅ria appellatur. hoc e̅ in novſſima ſiquide̅ ut novſſima o̅mniƀ imp̅ſionſ
tacta autq̅ anniſ xiii. uacueſit apud virgineſ poſt mutationiſ etatiſ effec-
tū mulieriƀ; r̅p̅ſe̅rua greci etia delfiſ dicta e̅. e̅ quod frica reſ efficiatur o̅mneſ quia̅
una naſcantur.

Introduca̅ſ corteſ
intruſ q̅d e̅ ſub ſe habenſ. langao̅e et tuſſicu deſupnatura. V̅ oculiſ e̅

Nervoſa qq̅ e̅ compexto pulpiſ e̅tatū neruiſ e̅tatniſ duabuſ ſcilicet
e̅ tranciſſunt̅ una foriſ lenior e̅ et reliq̅ad no̅r et neruoſa. & pulpoſa
qu̅ibuſ rebuſ a ſeo̅mnia
ut̅recit̅ matriaſ tunice tenuiſſime. membraniſ & neruiſ V̅

SITIO FICURA e̅ MATRIX
Principaliter ſicut format̅
e̅ concurbitū medicinali ſingulaſ paſtuſ cognoſca̅t̅ et facilime intellegere poſſ
et ſingula uelute in pingere & exſingulſi paſtibuſ eiuſ ſingulaſ litterae adporſ
ubi ergo e̅ paſtū orificiuim dicitur quid e̅ conceptū pulpoſū et molle; poſt paſtū uero
calloſū et ſpatioſū e̅. ubi uero e̅ collū dicitur. ubi e̅ cerbiſ dicitur. omniſ horū concur̅
ſuſ caule dicitur. ubi uero p̅ conguſtiaſ rotunditate d̅lacere incipiunt. ubi e̅
umen dicuntur. ubi cute e̅. latera dicure̅. ubi uero rotunditaſ concluditur. et e̅
ibi funduſ appellatur. Intuſ uero ubi e̅ barſiſ grandiſ dicitur. Omniſq̅; In
ntaſ. illu̅ın medio q̅ e̅ nenter & ſinuſ dicitur.

Adparū eiciendum
haſ caracteneſ facis
Intenuſ et depan e̅
&ligaſ ad eoſ̅ a dextera

&a̅ ſoliberuenꞇ
cicuſ diſ ſoluiſ

FUNDUS

IA   TERA

META

CER   UIX
COL   LUM

ORI   FICIUM

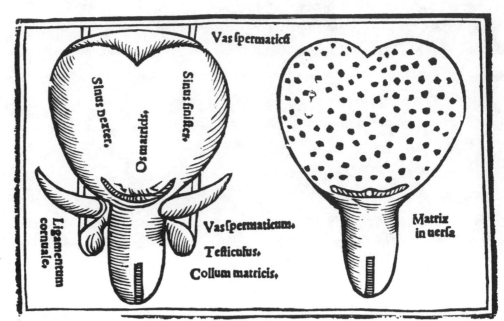

PLATE 48. *Image of the bi-cornate uterus from Jacopo Berengario da Carpi,* Isagogae breves *(Bonona: Benedictus Hector, 1522). Ithaca: Howard B. Adelmann Collection, Olin Library, Cornell University.*

The uterus is not only horned; it is also chambered.[26] The image that dominates the representation of the uterus is one of a seven-chambered womb, each chamber containing more or less "heat" depending on its relative position to the center. In Walter Ryff's handbook on pregnancy **[PLATE 52]** from 1569, the chambers of the uterus are quite distinctly outlined. And in a version of a fourteenth-century illustration from Mondino dei Luzzi that appeared in the *Anthropologium* of Magnus Hundt (1501) **[PLATE 53]**, the chambers are numbered 1 through 7. The child conceived in the farthest "left" chamber would be the most feminine, the one conceived in the farthest "right" chamber, the most masculine. Those conceived in the middle cell would be those of indeterminate sexuality, hermaphrodites. Vesalius, that great opponent of the Galenic views of the humors, taught during his first lectures on anatomy in 1540 that "if the right part of the uterus swells, then she has conceived a male, and if the left one swells, she has conceived a female. In the same way, the right testicle produces a male off-

PLATE 49. *Image of the uterus in situ from Jacopo Berengario da Carpi,* Isagogae breves *(Bonona: Benedictus Hector, 1522). Ithaca: Howard B. Adelmann Collection, Olin Library, Cornell University.*

spring, the left one a female."[27] For Vesalius there is no possibility (within the range of the normal) for the existence of hermaphrodites. Even though he subscribes to the image of the multichambered uterus and argues elsewhere in his lectures that this difference is due to the increase or decrease of bodily heat, the question of the homologous nature of the genitalia was never drawn into question. The parallel between the two sides of the uterus and the two testicles is an absolute one.

The genitalia were understood as homologous down to functional parallels. The sexual anatomy of the male, as described in detail by Aristotle, traced the testicular artery and vein, the *vas deferens* (the duct that carries the sperm away from the testis), the inner part of the urethra, as well as the *tunica vaginalis*, the inner sack of the scrotum. These were illustrated in the first representation of sexual anatomy, lost before the rise of medieval anatomy.[28] But, according to Galen, and reported to us as late

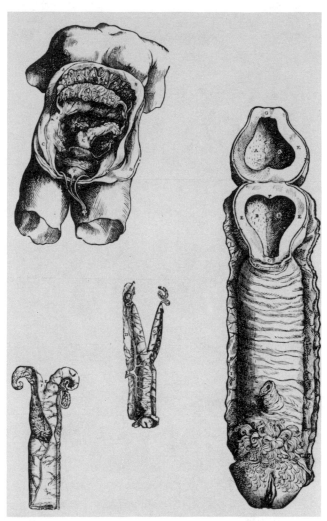

PLATE 51. *Composite plate from Andreas Vesalius,* De humani corporis fabrica libri sept *(Basel: Johannes Oporini, 1543), depicting the female torso, the bicornate uteruses of the cow and dog, and the penile representation of the human uterus. Ithaca: Howard B. Adelmann Collection, Olin Library, Cornell University.*

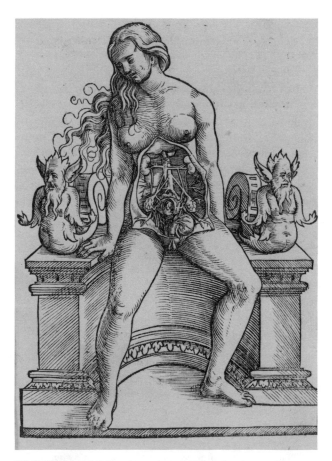

PLATE 50. *A full-length woodcut depicting female sexual anatomy from Johannes Dryander,* Anatomia capitis humani *(Marburg: E. Cervicornus, 1536). London: Wellcome Institute for the History of Medicine.*

Weiter aber / in natürlicher vnd vnna=

PLATE 52. *Woodcut of fetuses from Walter Hermann Ryff, Schwangerer Frauen Rosengarten (Frankfurt: C. Egenolff, 1569), depicting the seven-chambered uterus. London: Wellcome Institute for the History of Medicine.*

as Vesalius's student Baldasar Heseler, "the organs of procreation are the same in the male and the female. . . . For if you turn the scrotum, the testicles, and the penis inside out you will have all the genital organs of the female."[29] It was therefore not female sexual anatomy but that of the male that was the baseline for any representation of the genitalia. (This accounts for the greater number of representations of female sexual anatomy, as male sexual anatomy was understood to be "known.") Even though the internal sexual anatomy of the male was generally better understood than that of the female, some mysteries remained. Erections were understood as the inflation of the penis, either through the introduction of air in the *corpora cavernosa* or the existence of a "natural quality by which, when the living creature is moved to coitus, the penis is inflated and dilated."[30] The penis was also understood to contain two tubes, as will be discussed in more detail in Chapter Five, one that brought the urine and one that brought the semen from the spine.[31] For the image of a male organ that was simultaneously reproductive and excretory, whereas the female organ was one in which these functions were expressly differentiated, was impossible because of the power of homologous thinking. Popular broadsheets were widely circulated in the sixteenth century (for the information of the female and the fascination of the male) that represented the homologous "internal" nature of the female body and that made the invisible visible **[PLATE 54]**. The female is represented, with bared, firm breasts, but her genitalia are depicted as a rudimentary penis, her external genitalia paralleling the internal testicular structures. Da Carpi's image of the uterus in situ, with its long neck opening externalized, is here converted into a rudimentary penis.

PLATE 53. *The seven-chambered uterus from Magnus Hundt, Anthropologium (Leipzig: Baccalarius Wolfgang Monacensen, 1501). Ithaca: Howard B. Adelmann Collection, Olin Library, Cornell University.*

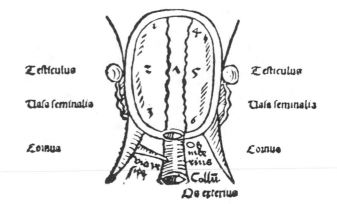

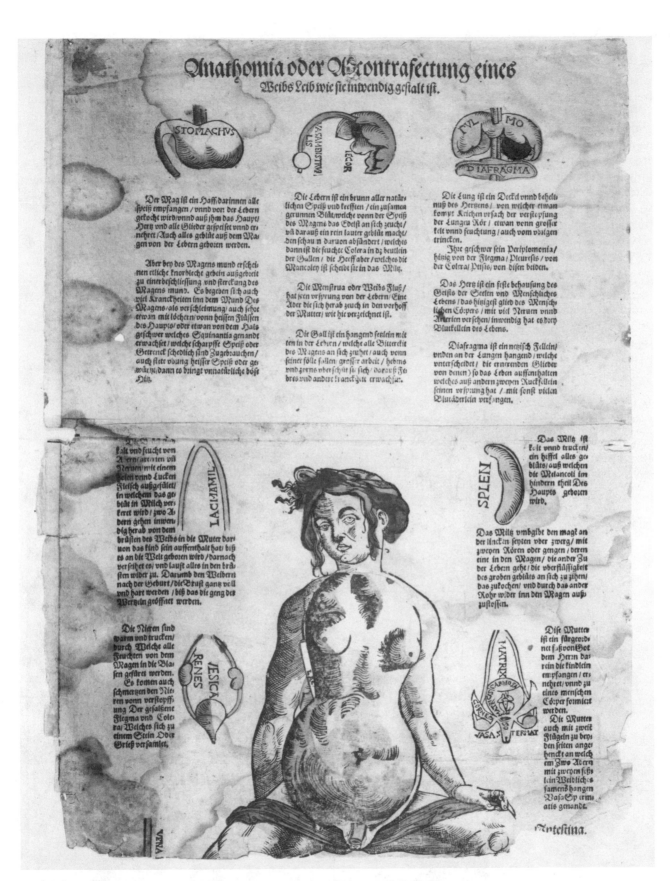

PLATE 54. *Anatomical fugitive sheets depicting the genitalia and intestines of a female.*
London: Wellcome Institute for the History of Medicine.

COITUS AND THE OBSERVER

The image of the homologous yet different genitalia speaks to the complexity of the boundary between the images of the masculine and the feminine. It is clear that the ideology of the female is tied to the image of coitus and childbirth.[32] Central to the masculine understanding of the hidden nature of female sexuality is the fetus, potentially the economic replication of the male or, at least, if a female child, a factor in expanding the father's economic power. Always upon gazing into the women in his fantasy, the male sees the fetus, the source of his benefit, as well as its antithesis, the source of his disease. For the icon of the woman is both simultaneously.

In the fifteenth-century Wellcome *Apocalypse* manuscript, there is a page representing a "disease woman," with the embryo presented in a flask-shaped womb. The page also contains versions of the "Rosengarten" fetuses.[33] Childbirth was considered a disease.[34] Not merely was childbirth both dangerous and painful but these associations indicated that it was a sign of the Fall from grace. Disease was a sign of the displeasure of God, a sign that was especially associated with the female and the female genitalia. Images of childbirth [PLATE 55], as in Reisch's 1503 handbook of all knowledge, show an idyllic scene parallel to the birthing of Christ. Likewise the images of coitus from the medical literature are benign. In a fourteenth-century

PLATE 55. *A woodcut of a childbirth scene from Gregor Reisch,* Margarita philosophica *(Freiburg im Breisgau: J. Schott, 1503). London: Wellcome Institute for the History of Medicine.*

PLATE 56. *Galen discusses the hidden nature of sexuality before two persons in bed. Fourteenth-century Galen Ms. Dresden: University Library.*

PLATE 57. *An image of coitus from the late medieval manuscript* Tacuinum sanitatis *of Ububchasym de Baldach. Ms. 4182. Rome: Biblioteca Casanatense.*

illustrated manuscript of Galen's works, the physician provides instruction on sexuality before the marriage bed. The position of the physician as the scientific observer of human sexuality, represented by the exposure of the genitalia, is analogous to the role played by the viewer in later "scientific" images of human sexuality **[PLATE 56]**. Likewise in Dryander's 1557 image, the image of coitus reflects the idyllic nature of the ideal pairing of the sexes. In the Roman manuscript of the illustrated late medieval manuscript of the *Tacuinum sanitatis*, originally written by Ububchasym de Baldach in twelfth-century Baghdad **[PLATE 57]**, the pairing of the ideal type, identical in nature, age, and color is represented. Male and female are parallel and without any overt stress. And the caption of the image refers to the perfect flow of the semen that results. It is, of course, an idealized image of the homologous nature of the female and the male, of the two sperm meeting to create the fetus. It is not sexuality that is represented here but conception; even though Dryander's text speaks of "love," his catalogue lists the problems of conception. Coitus is the joining of the male and female to create the fetus. And in the plate from the *Tacuinum sanitatis*, the one perfect exposed breast points toward the moment of conception and potential nursing. The itch described in such detail in both the theological as well as the medical literature is missing because of this fact.

And yet in one of Marcantonio Riamondi's sixteenth-century representations of the sexual positions, created as illustrations to Pietro Aretino's erotic sonnets, the nature of the "itch" is made manifest in the bedroom scene by the presence of a surrogate for the observer[35] **[PLATE 58]**. It is this opening of the iconographic equivalent of our own scopophilia, our own desire to see the sexual act represented by the presence of the observer within the work of art, which is analogous to the presence of the physician/observer in the Galenic text.[36] Our desire to touch is displaced in our act of looking. For in that act there can be no danger to the self, in terms of the potential for danger inherent in the icon of the female. The "itch" is not missing here. Sexuality is depicted as a type of physical exercise that will satisfy the physical demands of both parties. Rembrandt echoes this with only the viewer as observer in his 1646 representation of coitus **[PLATE 59]**. This observer of human sexuality is, however, also always a participant because he or she is using one of the senses, sight, to experience the sexual act. It is the role of the senses as the marker of the hidden force, the ape within, that signifies the presence of human sexuality in the observer as well as in the individuals observed. This homologue between the sensory stimulation of the participants and that of the observer is implied in the representations of coitus.

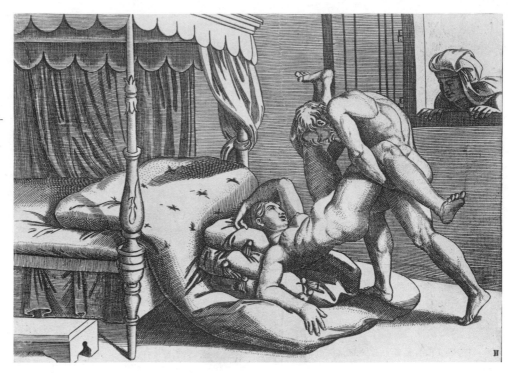

PLATE 58. *An image of coitus from Marcantonio Riamondi, I Modi, ca. 1534. Vienna: Graphische Sammlung Albertina.*

PLATE 59. *An image of coitus by Rembrandt,* Le Lit à la française (Ledekant), *1646. Hamburg: Kunsthalle.*

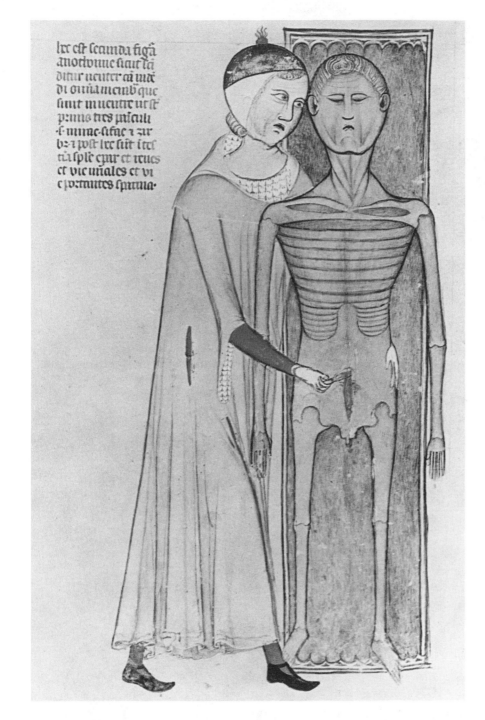

Illegibile manuscript text within the illustration:

lte est secunda figa
amortduine siait ta
ditur ucuter ca uia
di omia menib que
sunt in ucutte ur st
p: uia tres pisculi
f uma sitne z zir
b: z post lte sut i tet
ria sple cyar et reues
et uic uuales et ui
c p: muites spuua·

PLATE 60. *A 1345 image of the opening of the body from Guido da Vigevano,* Liber notabilium . . . ano-thomia. *Ms. 334, fol. 260v. Chantilly: Musée Condé.*

The image of the physician as observer of the act of sexuality, as the opener of the body, as the revealer of the hidden, is present throughout all of the various images of the act of autopsy throughout the Middle Ages[37] **[PLATE 60]**. Usually, the physician, like God in the Garden of Eden, stands upon his cathedra, whereas the physical act of opening the body is left to his assistant. It is on the famed opening title page to the *Fabrica*, attributed to Johann Stephen of Calcar, that Vesalius is himself depicted as opening the body **[PLATE 61]**. But the cosmological and pathological associations that the opening of the body have are placed center stage in this image. The body being opened is that of a woman. It is presented, using the most advanced techniques of Renaissance perspective, so that her abdomen is exposed, her firm, upright breast can be seen, her genitalia observed. Indeed, her position to the

PLATE 61. *Frontispiece from Andreas Vesalius,* De humani corporis fabrica libri sept *(Basel: Johannes Oporini, 1543). Ithaca: Howard B. Adelmann Collection, Olin Library, Cornell University.*

reader/observer of the frontispiece is exactly parallel to the exemplary figure of the nude woman that Albrecht Dürer uses to illustrate the means of creating perspective in his *Painter's Manual* of 1525.[38] The sole (but major) difference is that Dürer's model is posed with her genitalia covered, whereas Johann Stephen of Calcar exposes not only the genitalia but the entire female reproductive system. Vesalius discusses this dissection in the twenty-fourth figure of book five of the *Fabrica*:

> The peritoneum and the abdominal muscles have been opened and pulled to the sides. . . . Then we have resected all the intestines from the mesentary, but we have left the rectum in the body as well as the whole of the mesentery of which we have to some extent separated the membranes so that its nature is exposed to view. However, the present figure has been drawn for the special purpose of indicating the position of the uterus and bladder exactly as they occurred in this woman; we have not disturbed the uterus in any way, and none of the uterine membranes has been destroyed. Everything is seen intact just as it appears to the dissector immediately upon moving the intestines to one side in a moderately fat woman.[39]

This description is of the body of a prostitute who murdered one of her clients and who further attempted to escape her rightful execution by "falsely declaring herself pregnant." Thus it is not merely the opening of a body but the body of a prostitute, the source of pollution, who has claimed to be pregnant. She is a falsifier of her own sexuality. She marks the absolute nadir of female sexuality following the Fall. It is the opening of her body that permits insight into the true nature of female anatomy. It is the opening of the most degraded of women that permits insight into the hidden nature of all women. But Vesalius is also drawing on a conscious inversion of one of the most famous historical motifs representing the opening of the female body by the male, Nero's insistence on an autopsy of his mother's body in order to observe her uterus. Agrippina's death itself was at the behest of Nero, who feared her power over him. This icon is often found as a sign of the deviancy of opening the body, especially the female body. Vesalius reverses the implications of this image. It is not the male observer in his gaze into the female's body who is deviant but the female, the murdering prostitute who is being autopsied. She is the criminal and thus deserves her fate. Indeed Nero's oedipal gaze, with all of the intimation of postmortem incest, is replaced by the gaze of the scientist, the anatomist, who is not drawn away from his task by the cavorting of those icons of the sexual, the monkeys, placed within the image.

The *Fabrica* is aimed at correcting the errors of Galenic medicine, and Vesalius centers his critique of classical anatomy on the incorrect knowledge of the female reproductive system, the subject of three of the Galenic treatises, *Use of Parts*, *On Semen*, and *On Dissection of the Uterus*. Thus Vesalius, in the introductory image of the first "modern" study of human anatomy, is shown lecturing on that most hidden and misunderstood of subjects, the female sexual organs. Galen, writes Vesalius, never dissected a human uterus. He, Vesalius, will expose the errors of mere book learning through the act of opening the female book. Galen will be banished by the exposure of the secrets of the female.

Centrally placed in the foreground right of the frontispiece, dressed in the required ghetto garb of the Italian Jew, is Lazarus de Frigeis, whose eyes are turned to avoid looking at the autopsy. He was the scholar who introduced Vesalius to the works of Avicenna. Prominently placed at the lower left is a student whose attention is momentarily captured by the antics of a rhesus monkey. Jews, monkeys, and women play a central role in this image of the opening of the body. Each represents a version of the basic structure of the Christian male that dominates this scene. It is Vesalius who stands at the center, and male sexuality, not the perversions illustrated by Jews, monkeys, or women, that controls the scene. For male sexuality, unlike the hidden, destructive sexuality of the prostitute, the damaged or bisexual nature of the Jewish male, or the bestial sexuality of the monkey, is the baseline for the normal in Vesalius's world.

But over everything hangs Death, in the form of the huge articulated skeleton that dominates the scene. It is not merely a sign of the importance of osteology, the study of the human skeleton, to anatomy. The iron rod that supports the skeleton is paralleled by the iron rod that it is given to hold. It is the figure of Death domesticated into the ornament of the anatomy theater, the figure of Death whose scythe has been reduced to a pole. Vesalius takes the figure of Death from the tradition of the late medieval "Dance of Death," with Hans Holbein's version as its best-known representation, and domesticates it. Death becomes the anatomist's path into the body. Death and sexuality meet in the figure of the dead prostitute, for it is death as inherently related to female sexuality, as integral to it as the image of the life-giving fetus. For Eve's act, the seduction of Adam, let Death into the Garden.

PLATE 62. *The boundary-crossing serpent as the figure of death and disease in Hans Baldung Grien,* Eve, the Serpent and Death, *1515. Ottawa: National Gallery of Canada.*

Death thus has a traditional association with the sexual, specifically with the beautiful female. The tradition of the "beautiful girl and death," of the mutability of all human life, is echoed in this title page with its icons of deviant sexuality, the sexually active prostitute, the Jew with his reference to the legends of Jewish sexuality, the sexually "hot" monkey, and, most overtly, the opening of the hidden sexual anatomy of the female, Vesalius's intended purpose in depicting the autopsy. In Hans Baldung Grien's *Eve, the Serpent and Death*, the biblical associations hidden in this "scientific" motive are manifest[40] **[PLATE 62]**. The beautiful female, death, and the Edenic serpent circle the tree of life, Eve holding the "orange" firmly in her hand. This is the subtext of the Vesalius frontispiece. The original

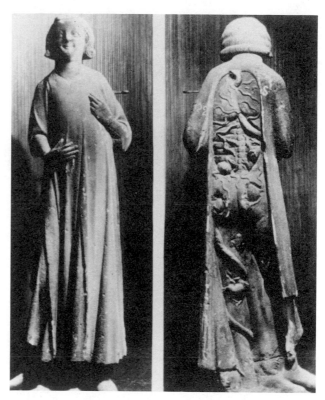

PLATE 64. *The fourteenth-century image of "Madam World" from the portal of the St. Sebaldus Church in Nuremberg displaying her overt beauty and her hidden corruption. Ithaca: Private collection.*

PLATE 63. *The figure of Death as a sign of the loss of feminine beauty through the process of aging in Hans Baldung Grien,* Three Ages of Woman and Death, *1510. Vienna: Kunsthistorisches Museum.*

fault of Eve opens the world for the Satanic control of human sexuality and resultant death. Thanatos, the death principle, is thus from the early modern period closely associated with the life force, with sexuality and conception. In Baldung Grien's *Three Ages of Woman and Death*, the stages of life are the stages of the woman's life, from infancy to old age **[PLATE 63]**. The various forms of the breasts are indicators of the life stages but also of the inherent fault, the necessary collapse of human life into pathological old age and eventual death. The innocence of the child, the beauty of the young woman only herald the eventual conquest of death. Female beauty, the sexually attractive female, is merely a mask for death and decay, for Eve, the murdering prostitute. In the High Middle Ages, as in the image of "Madam World" from the St. Sebaldus Church in Nuremberg as seen from the front and the obverse, the female was already understood as both seductive and physically corrupt **[PLATE 64]**. The beautiful, sexually beckoning figure is reversed to show the decomposition of death.

La diſſection des parties du corps
humain diuiſee en trois liures, faictz par Charles Eſtienne
docteur en Medecine: auec les figures & declaratiō des in-
ciſions, compoſees par Eſtienne de la Riuiere Chirurgien.

Imprime a Paris, chez Simon de Colines.
1546.

Auec priuilege du Roy.

PLATE 65. *The title page of Charles Estienne,* La dissection des parties du corps humain *(Paris: Simon de Colines, 1546). Ithaca: Howard B. Adelmann Collection, Olin Library, Cornell University.*

It is not only in the implications of Vesalius's title page but in a glance at other anatomies of his day that one can see the iconographic ambiguity of representing images of sexual difference and death on the title page of a textbook that both represents the "new science" and will serve as its surrogate where dissections will not (or cannot) take place. Étienne de la Rivière, the illustrator of the atlas compiled in 1545 by Charles Estienne, Vesalius's principal contemporary rival, strips everything else away on the title page of his anatomical atlas and gives us the secularized death, time, with his scythe (only hinted at in the *Fabrica*) prominently displayed[41] **[PLATE 65]**. For it is also time that the Fall introduces into the post-Edenic world, time that marks our eventual collapse and that mocks our human attempts, through reproduction, to make ourselves immortal.

Sexuality, difference, death are all linked on the title page of the *Fabrica*. Estienne, referring back to the full-page musclemen that Vesalius introduces and sets in the geography of a fantasy landscape continuous over the entire series of the muscle figures, brings his anatomical figures indoors and depicts them not in a utopian landscape but in a world redolent of human sexuality.[42] With the female figures, we find ourselves in a bedroom, the bedroom that iconographically refers us back to the world of the coitus images **[PLATE 66]**. It is a world in which the "reality" of sexuality and the female genitalia are hidden. The internal aspect of the female genitalia can only be viewed through the imposition of an implement, the speculum, which permits the observer the same access to the hidden nature of the female body as the viewer achieves in the engraving by Marcantonio Riamondi (see Plate 58) or in Rembrandt's image (see Plate 59) with its evocation of the male observer. We eventually come to the opening of the viscera.[43] The female is passively opened to view, but the observer, the student of anatomy, in books such as Estienne's and Vesalius's, can now see within the female body. When Estienne represents the male body the situation of the body is very different **[PLATE 67]**. He returns to Vesalius's idyllic, natural world. The male, his viscera piled before him, echoes the Vesalian male figures in all aspects. But unlike them, he holds his phallus, he is in control of his sexuality. He is in no way homologous to the female figures. Within the fantasy world of the anatomical atlas, his sexuality is public, external, as are his genitalia; the female's genitalia are private, hidden. Estienne makes manifest what Vesalius, by refusing to depict female figures of any type set into his dream landscape, only acknowledges by its absence.

En ce protraict/tu voy
la substance de la ma-
trice du tout coupée
& incisée : a fin de con-
gnoistre plus aperte-
ment le fond & les mé-
branes / renuersées d'i-
celle . Encor voy tu le
col de ladicte matrice
coupé par le milieu/
pour te monstrer les ri-
des & entrées d'iceluy.

PLATE 66. *The female reproductive system from Charles Estienne,* La dissection des parties du corps humain *(Paris: Simon de Colines, 1546). Ithaca: Howard B. Adelmann Collection, Olin Library, Cornell University.*

Le membre viril/
eſt en ceſte figure
deſnué de ſa peau:
cóme ſont auſſy les
teſticules : a fiu de
monſtrer plus aiſe⁹
ment les vaiſſeaux
ſpermatiques/les glá
dules/ & paraſtates/
auec le vaiſſeau que
lon nomme eiacula-
toire : pareillement
la communion du
dict membre/ auec
le droict inteſtin.

PLATE 67. *The male reproductive system from Charles Estienne,* La dissection des parties du corps humain *(Paris: Simon de Colines, 1546). Ithaca: Howard B. Adelmann Collection, Olin Library, Cornell University.*

DISEASE AND SEXUALITY

The set of "scientific" images of human sexuality that we now have, from the scorpion to the anatomical depiction of the genitalia, are all images of the "normal." They represent the healthy, with, of course, the intimations of disease and death always present. But there is a parallel set of images in which the image of the diseased, of the pathological, makes manifest the covert images of disease and difference present within the depiction of the normal. For the age of Vesalius and Estienne was also the age of the first great pandemic of sexually transmitted disease in modern times, the great outbreak of syphilis in the late fifteenth century, an outbreak that Martin Luther saw as one of the signs heralding the Last Judgment. The visual image of the syphilitic has its roots in the very first years after the beginning of the spread of an especially virulent form of syphilis, beginning when Charles VIII of France entered the besieged city of Naples on February 21, 1495. Spread by the retreating French armies, the "Mal de Naples," "Morbus Gallicus," "Malafranzcos," "French Pox," "Pudendagra," or "Franzosenkrankheit" soon appeared in the German states.[44] On August 1, 1496, the first visual representation of the syphilitic appeared, a broadside by Theodoricus Ulsenius, with an illustration by Albrecht Dürer [PLATE 68]. The broadside assigns the origin of the disease (for even then we were obsessed with finding

PLATE 68. *Albrecht Dürer's image of a syphilitic as fop (1496). Ithaca: Private collection.*

the origin of sexually transmitted diseases rather than discussing control) to the ill-fated appearance of Saturn and Jupiter in the sign of the Scorpion (the zodiacal sign that rules the genitalia) on St. Catherine's Day, September 25, 1484.[45] All of the authors of the period stressed the relationship between the stars and the genitalia:

> Furthermore, the condition here mostly affects the genitals initially, spreading from there to the whole body, and no other disease is found which spreads that way. But I guess that this is brought about by some affinity between the genitals and this disease. This may derive from some celestial effect, as the astrologers claim, arising from the conjunction of Saturn and Jupiter in the third aspect of Scorpio in the 23rd degree in 1484 as well as from a simultaneous configuration of other fixed stars which just happened to occur then. Over long stretches of time many diseases were seen to arise, as well as old ones to die out, as we clearly show later. Not only is the origin of this disease traced to the position of the stars, but the disease is fomented again and again especially by the sign of Scorpio, which rules the genitals.[46]

What strikes the viewer initially in Dürer's image is the representation of the isolated sufferer, re-vealing to the viewer the signs and symptoms of syphilis like the stigmata of a parodied Christ, the *ostentatio vulnerum*. This is a male figure echoing the position of the exemplum of masculinity, the suffering Christ. But it is the Christ who through his own acceptance of the physical state of Adam redeemed humankind. For, from the first appearance of the disease, it was seen as "caus[ed by] God, Who has sent it because He wants Mankind to shun the sin of fornication."[47] Jacques de Béthencourt, writing in 1527, cites the "theologians attribution to this disease a divine (super-celestial) cause; & to be a scourge of God for the punishment of the wicked" while noting that the disease is caused by "venereal contact (for at this time it is scarcely [spread] by any other method)."[48]

Christ is, of course, Adam redeemed, and it is not surprising that the medieval image of sexually transmitted disease prior to the syphilis epidemic of 1495 is closely associated with the image of the Fall. In a twelfth-century illustrated manuscript, the legend of the "fire-darting stones" is represented in order to explain the transmission of diseases such as gonorrhea, soft chancre or lymphogranu-loma inguinale **[PLATE 69]**. The removal of these

PLATE 69. *The illustration of "lapides infigeri," or the fire-darting stones, from an illustrated manuscript, Ashmole 1511. Oxford: Bodleian Library.*

stones from the sacred tree and their exchange between the sexes lead to the conflagration of sexually transmitted disease. The stones are substitutions for the apple, but it is clear that these Adam and Eve figures illustrate the image of the Fall as the origin of sexually transmitted diseases. It is not with the origin of syphilis that the iconography of sexual disease begins but with the iconography of the Fall from grace. Thus the early iconography of syphilis reflects the confusion not only with other existing forms of sexually transmitted disease but also with the image of those diseases, this iconography stemming from the Fall. The understanding was, on the one hand, that syphilis was a new disease, having its origin in the newly discovered lands of the New World; and yet, it had to be understood as a continuation of that age-old scourge of sexually transmitted diseases resulting from the Fall. The opening of the New World meant a disruption of the clear though already crumbling boundaries of nationality and class, in allowing the marginal and disaffected a place of their own. But the disease of the genitalia that was understood to be a punishment for crossing the boundary of class also had to be a disease that stemmed from the Fall.[49] The resulting confusion made it impossible conceptually to separate syphilis from the other sexually transmitted diseases. The Fall made all diseases of the genitalia equal.

In Dürer's image we have a social version of the fallen male, Adam after the Fall. Note the enormous, plumed hat, the abundant cloak, the broad-toed, slashed shoes, and the long, flowing hair. This is the Germans' caricature of the sufferer as a fop, as a Frenchman, as the outsider already associated in German myth with sexual excesses and deviancy. Even so, the victim of syphilis is portrayed here as the victim of the signs of the zodiac that determine his affliction.[50] The syphilitic is seen as isolated, visually recognizable by his signs and symptoms, and sexually deviant from this very first image.

But the image of the scorpion is not merely that of the genitalia.[51] For the scorpion is also the icon that symbolizes the "false church," the Synagogue, as opposed to the true Church. Indeed, in the Vatican Loggia, Raphael emblazons a scorpion on King David's standard. For the scorpion, according to Gregory the Great, was at once flattering and inoffensive (*blandus et innoxius*) but ready to wound from behind (*a posterioribus*). The scorpion attacks in contrast to its appearance; it is falsity, hypocrisy, and treason incarnate. The image of the genitalia as the independent force that is out of control of the rational mind, or under the control of Satan, is placed parallel to the image of the Jew. Thus every reference to the genitalia, whether in the anatomies or in the representation of the origin of sexually transmitted disease, is also a reference to the Jew as an image of the genitalia, to the Jew as the circumcised penis incarnate. Thus it is always the male Jew that is the focus of these representations, whether in the myth about male menstruation or in the anatomies. The association of the genitalia with the idea of the Jew is thus implicit in the use of the sign of Scorpio in the Renaissance and medieval anatomies. The scorpion is a syncretizing sign, meaning always more than one thing when it appears. But whether referring to the genitalia or to the Jews, it links all of its references by means of the common denominator of human sexuality.

The fact that women as well as men suffered equally from the new epidemic of syphilis is reflected in many of these early images of the sufferer. But there is always a shift that separates the active suffering of the male from the passive suffering of the female. The sense of isolation of the male sufferer can be seen in a reworking of one of the earliest images of the syphilitic. On the title page of a broadside on the new epidemic (1496) by the famed jurist and author of the *Ship of Fools*, Sebastian Brant **[PLATE 70]**, there is an image of a closed community of syphilitics, three male and one female.[52] They are being punished by the *flagellum Dei*, the whip of God, for their sexual transgressions. The arrows, like the arrows of St. Sebastian, also signify the martyrdom of the sufferer, suffering for Eve and Adam's fall. But the arrow, with all of its ambiguous but evocative force, also points toward the sensorium, the sense of touch. For it is in the act of sexual contact that the disease was acquired, and it is on the skin, the organ of the sense of touch, that the mark of the disease, the buboes and lesions, are found. Touch is the sense that is most closely associated with contagion, for it is the myth of physical proximity (well past the age of Pasteur) that underlies the sense of the transmission of illness. With sexually transmitted diseases such as syphilis, the touch is the hitherto permitted touch of the male and female genitalia, a touch that is made pathological through moving it into the realm of contacts that reach across the border created to separate the healthy from the diseased on the basis of the Judeo-Christian model that separated the male from the female.[53] In the parallel vignette, in Joseph Grünpeck's 1496 commentary on Brant, a visual interpretation of the image that introduces Brant's pamphlet, the image

⬥Ein hübscher Tractat von dem vrsprung des Bösen Franzos. das man nennet die Wylden wärtzen. Auch ein Regiment wie man sich regiren soll in diser zeyt.

of the male sufferer is brought forward and isolated[54] **[PLATE 71]**. This visual shift in emphasis creates the illusion that the male represents the exemplary sufferer, central in his suffering to any understanding of the nature of the disease. In this image the male sufferer is portrayed as the primary victim of the disease, rather than as its harbinger.

The single female in her uniqueness and nonexemplarity represents the source of the disease. She is the echo of the image of the beautiful woman and death, the seductive cause of the disease. It is the realization of the idea of temptation, as in Lucas van Leyden's *Temptation of St. Anthony* (1506)[55] **[PLATE 72]**. Her horned cap and her casket point toward her as the devil and the prostitute. She is both the snake from the Garden of Eden as well as Eve, at least Eve in her incarnation as the unrepentant Mary Magdalene. In Lucas Cranach's image of the prostitute and the peasant, the casket, here the peasant's pocketbook, points toward the exploitation of the crude and ugly peasant by the beautiful prostitute. The inequality of this pair, the coupling of the opposites of the scale of beauty, only points toward the innate corruption of what

PLATE 72. *The beautiful temptress in Lucas van Leyden,* Temptation of St. Anthony, *1506. Ithaca: Herbert F. Johnson Museum of Art.*

PLATE 73. *An engraving by J. B. Mauzaisse after a lost image by Lucas Cranach, "Peasant and Whore," depicts the "unequal lovers," unequal in all respects. Ithaca: Herbert F. Johnson Museum of Art.*

PLATE 74. *The icon representing the arranged marriage as a sexually transmitted disease from Andrea Alciatus,* Emblemes d'Alciat, de nouveau translates en françois vers pour vers iouxte les latins *(Lyons: Mace Bonhome, 1555). Ithaca: Private collection.*

seems to be beauty[56] **[PLATE 73]**. The prostitute bears only the superficial image of true beauty. Her beauty is the image of the potential for disease.

Sexually transmitted disease as the punishment of the transgression against the divine order through the Fall is represented in Andrea Alciatus's emblem of 1550 depicting the *flagellum Dei* (the arrows brandished by the infant Christ in the images from Brant and Grünpeck)[57] **[PLATE 74]**. Here it is sexuality that leads to disease and death, for the bound, copulating couple, with the female appearing to be

already dead, is admonished by the divine force on the throne. Alciatus's image is used in a specific social context to criticize the institution of *coemptio*, through which a father could purchase a husband for his daughter. Such a match (depicted in the wedding in the background) is like the tyrant Mezentius (depicted in the foreground) whom Virgil depicts as binding "the living and the dead [who] at his command, were coupled, face to face, and hand to hand, till choked with stench, in loath'd embraces tied, The ling'ring wretches pin'd away

PLATE 75. *The source of the disease that marks the face is to be found in the sexual fantasy of the male in Peter Breughel the Elder's late sixteenth-century* Syphilitic with Couple. *Ithaca: Private collection.*

and died."[58] Alciatus treats the "morbus Gallicus" together with the skin disease of *mentagra*, a type of herpes, which like syphilis leaves its mark upon the skin. Perverse sexuality thus links the social action, marriage, with the image of the transmission of disease. Peter Breughel makes this relationship between perverse sexuality and disease yet more direct in an image of a sexualized couple, in a forbidden sexual position, in the mind of a figure marked with the external sign of the syphilitic, the disfiguring buboes that are the mark of the disease in all of the early images **[PLATE 75]**. In Albrecht Dürer's 1496 broadside, the syphilitic is covered with the visible signs of his illness, with the "boils, ulcers and crusts" described in Theodoricus Ulsenius's Latin hexameters. The portrait by Hans Holbein the Younger, long believed to be a representation of Ulrich von Hutten, the German knight who not only suffered from syphilis but also wrote extensively

on the topic, presents the lesions as a clear marker of the sexuality of the young man **[PLATE 76]**. Disease is particularly marked in the face. And thus throughout Bosch's *Last Judgement* (see Plate 13), figures are marked with spots and nodules to indicate their degraded state.[59] And it is the face or mask of disease that signals sexuality. The female's beautiful mask, like the hidden source of pollution within the female, is matched by the exposed sores of the male. The face becomes the sign of the genitalia. The open, direct sign of masculine sexuality marks the male sufferer as the victim, whereas the hidden, masked image of female sexuality marks her as the wellspring of disease. This is an analogue to the perceived homologous relationship between the forms of the male and female genitalia. This sign of the buboes on the male is the accepted mark of sexually transmitted disease and is closely associated with the skin lesions of the leper.

PLATE 77. *The syphilitic as leper from Amico Aspertini's* Portrait of St Valerian and His Brother. *Reproduced from Karl Sudhoff,* Zehn Syphilis-Drucke aus den Jahren 1495–1498 *(Milan: Lier, 1924).*

In Amico Aspertini's image in the Oratoria of Saint Cecilia in Bologna, dated to 1506, of the decapitation of St. Valerian and his brother, the exemplary image of the syphilitic is that of the isolated male portrayed in the older, established iconographic tradition of the leper. He bears his signs of disease to the world, a disease given a specific sexual reference by the sign of the scorpion, the sign of the genitalia, on his banner **[PLATE 77]**. By the sixteenth century, leprosy, although still present, was no longer endemic in Western Europe. Although the disease had all but vanished, its iconography remained as part of the popular storehouse of images of disease and pollution and was immediately attached to the new disease of syphilis. Indeed, von

Hutten, who himself suffered from the disease, argued that the new disease of syphilis was merely another form of leprosy.[60] The leper's image, too, is of the isolated sufferer as the victim of forces, such as the signs of the heavens, over which he has no control. But his image is also closely connected with other images associated with the scorpion, such as that of the Jew. The icon of the scorpion brought two malevolent forces together, the Jews and sexuality, that through the fascination of European Christians with circumcision and its role in the central mystery of Christianity became interchangeable categories, and both were seen as the source of disease. Jews had long been associated with disease, including leprosy.[61] In 1321, in Aquitaine, the wells were believed to have been poisoned by a conspiracy between the lepers and the Jews. Disease was the means by which they accomplished their nefarious work.[62] This association is an ancient one. Manetho, an Egyptian historian of the second century, rewrites the Old Testament from the Egyptian point of view, so that the Exodus from Egypt merely became the gathering together and the driving out of the lepers from that nation. It is of little wonder that, when the fear of leprosy became transmuted into the fear of syphilis in the sixteenth century, it was the Jews who were often understood as being associated with the disease. But it was difficult to simply label the Jews as the cause of the disease because the origin in the stars or the New World was so much more powerful in its explanatory force. Jews had also long been characterized as healers, partially (as we have seen in the case of Vesalius) because of their association with the advanced knowledge of the Greeks and the Arabs, partially because of their magical association with the source of disease. (What corrupts should be able to cure.) The Jews came to be seen as the primary exploiters of the new disease of syphilis. Paracelsus in the 1520s condemns the "Jews" who "destroy, trick or seduce" the syphilitics into believing that they have a cure for the disease. The diseased are "as ill as they were before and are even more exploited and spoiled by the Jews who purge them, smear them, wash them, and perform all manners of monkey's tricks."[63] The close association of the Jews with this disease was possible not only because of the traditional characterization of Jews as physicians and as the source of disease but also because of the sexual nature of the disease itself. Who could cure sexually transmitted diseases better than those traditionally understood as sexually deviant?

It is a tradition that continues into the more recent past. During the eighteenth century, Voltaire, in his *Philosophical Dictionary*, provides the reader with a set of assumptions about the relationship between the Jews and the diseases of syphilis and leprosy. He begins his entry on leprosy with an essay on the origin of syphilis. He assumes that syphilis has its roots in the New World. In this same article, moving as if the association were self-evident, Voltaire provides a differential diagnosis between syphilis and leprosy. Leprosy was known to the ancients, whereas syphilis was not. But the primary sufferers were the Jews. "The Jews were more subject to [leprosy] than any other people living in hot climates, because they had neither linen, nor domestic baths. These people were so negligent of cleanliness and the decencies of life that their legislators were obliged to make a law to compel them even to wash their hands."[64] The shifts from one category of difference to another are effortless because the boundaries between the various categories of difference, including categories of "race" or "disease," are markers that delineate the boundaries between the observer and the object feared.

Such fear is not merely found represented by (and thus contained within) "vacant" constructions of disease, that is, images of disease for which there is no longer any active disease present in a society, such as the images of leprosy in the Renaissance. In a broadside prayer of about 1525, the image of the syphilitic is presented in the classic pose of melancholia[65] **[PLATE 78]**. The figure is that of the syphilitic as embodied by the prefiguration of Job "smote . . . with sore boils from the sole of his foot unto his crown" (Job 2: 7) by Satan. Job is portrayed in the iconographic position of the melancholic, elbow on knee, head on hand, a gesture of passive submission and reflection as well as despair.[66] Giovanni de Vigo, surgeon to Pope Julius II, in 1514 had labeled the disease as one directly caused by

PLATE 78. *The syphilitic as melancholic from a broadside "On the Pox Called Malafranzosa," ca. 1525. Reproduced from* Archiv für die Geschichte der Medizin 1 (1907).

copulation with an infected partner. He also described the course of the disease from the primary hard chancre to the later pain in the limbs and joints of such severity that the sufferer could not stand upright.[67] Thus the position of the sufferer marked the nature of the stage of his disease. As, indeed, did the signs written upon the skin. Shakespeare knew that the melancholic could well suffer from syphilis. His melancholy Jaques in *As You Like It*, for whom "all the world's a stage," was a "libertine / as sensual as the brutish sting itself." It was that the very genitalia themselves caused him to succumb to melancholy. And he is now covered with melancholy, says the Duke, as with "all the embossed sores and headed evils / That thou with license of free foot has caught."[68] But central to this image of the syphilitic as melancholic is also, as in the earlier images found in Brandt and Grünpeck, the image of cure. It is, however, a cure for melancholia. His friends come and play their instruments, attempting, as David did for Saul, to cure his melancholy madness through music. Indeed, the Renaissance physician Bartholomeus Montagnana saw the origin of syphilis in the accumulation of "melancholic blood."[69] It is the black blood, that fantasy fluid that haunted medieval humoral theory (the blackness within the body), that accumulated in Adam when he choked on the apple (see Plate 8), at least according to the medieval nun Hildegard of Bingen.[70] In a contemporary case study by Bernardus Tomitanus, we are given the course of a bout of syphilis that ends in melancholia: "He began to feel pain in all joints and to lose his hair, and became disfigured, thin, bluish, listless, moved with difficulty, was depressed, sighing, and incapable of any action."[71] The conflation of such images of existing "diseases," where there was a perceived cure, with the new disease of syphilis, provided a vocabulary of images through which to understand and, thus, limit a disease understood as boundariless. But the anonymous author of this broadside also located the other contemporary understanding of the source of the disease in another biblical prefiguration—he prays "that you [God] remember Abraham's prayer for Sodom and Gomorrah and save me from such a painful, horrible plague." Abraham's prayer was that if ten righteous men be found in these sinful cities, God would spare them. (They were not to be found [Genesis 18 and 19].)

Given the implications of the phrase "Sodom and Gomorrah" for the Renaissance, as will be discussed in detail in the next chapter, it is evident that the author is indicating the sexual source of the new pollution of syphilis. But it is the male, the Job figure, who represents the sufferer, the victim of the sexual pollution of the female.

It is not solely syphilis, as a sexually transmitted disease, that is associated with mental illness. Diseases of the mind are commonly associated with sexuality in the Middle Ages.[72] The very concept of "love illness" links the image of desire with that of disease in the medieval mind. Although Peter of Spain, in the thirteenth century, mentions a woman who fell into madness/mania because her lover never appeared, most medieval texts of the early Middle Ages see the male, very specifically the nobleman, as primarily at risk.[73] Thus the prescription, proposed by Avicenna (and following him a number of medieval physicians), the true cure for love sickness, is the purchase of a prostitute's favors.[74] By the seventeenth century, as in the work of Jacques Ferrand, it is the woman who becomes the exemplary sufferer from love sickness. The shift can be observed earlier in the work of Peter of Spain, later Pope John XXI, who, in a series of commentaries, observed that the origin of the love sickness was not in the mind but in the testicles (and both males and females possessed testes). As sexual physiology came to be seen as the source of love sickness (in analogy to physical illnesses such as gonorrhea), the social status of "love sickness" shifts, from the nobleman to the woman, from the top of the social ladder to its bottom, preserving the homology between the corporeal and social place of the disease. Syphilis, likewise, becomes in the sixteenth century the disease of the fop, of the courtier, in a world in which the rising middle class, embodied in the new Protestant world view, sees the upper classes as the source of all illness and pollution. The image of the sufferer from sexually transmitted disease is but a further reflex of the boundaries found throughout the Western tradition of seeing sexuality. This need to generate clearly differentiated boundaries is clearly heightened at times in which the "realities" of sexuality, such as the sudden onset of a sexually transmitted disease, exacerbate the fears always associated with human sexuality.

CHAPTER FOUR

Leonardo da Vinci's First Image of Human Sexuality

LEONARDO'S WORLD AND OURS

The images of human sexuality that dominated the Middle Ages and the Renaissance seem to us tangled and contradictory. They also appeared so to those who defined or were forced to define themselves in terms of their sexuality during this period. No one exemplifies the range of images and their inherent complexities more than Leonardo da Vinci, whose interest in anatomy and aesthetics typified one further strand present in the "seeing" of human sexuality during the early modern period, the extraordinary role that the production of works of art had in forcing both the layperson and the scientist to examine their understanding of the form of the body and the nature of human sexuality.[1]

On 9 April 1476 "Lionardo di Ser Piero da Vinci" was anonymously accused of having had carnal relations with the "soddomitare" Jacopo Saltarelli.[2] Tried for this crime with two others, Leonardo was released, evidently through the interposition of one of the leading families in Florence, the Tornabuoni, one of whose members was also accused.[3] The charge of homosexuality brought against Leonardo has traditionally led to detailed speculation about the roots of his homoeroticism and its significance for his aesthetic production. In this chapter, I shall be departing from quite another point than did Sigmund Freud. I shall be examining neither the nature nor the roots of Leonardo's sexual orientation but rather the question of what being gay in Renaissance Florence could have signified for Leonardo.[4] I shall not assume that homosexuality is a psychopathology but rather that any neurosis present in the homosexual is the result of the cultural conflict that arises between the individual's sense of self and society's image of the sexuality, against which this self-image is constantly measured. It is the presence of a society's construction of the Other—here the Other as defined by one of the salient markers of difference in the West, human sexuality—that shapes and focuses the image of the self.

It is important to contrast the internalized myths and their self-representation to the realities of daily life. Had Leonardo been publicly convicted of sodomy, he would most probably only have been fined about ten florins.[5] This was a very different world than that of Rome under Paul IV, where sodomy was one of the capital crimes punished by the Inquisition.[6] Indeed, many of the younger generation of artists and artisans in the circle in which Leonardo found himself were overtly gay, and little social ignominy seemed to result from the awareness of their sexual orientation. But in direct contrast to this social acceptance, homosexuality was marked by the culture in which Leonardo lived as a sign of the loss of control of an individual over those inner forces that human beings must harness. Homosexuality was understood as a form of "lust" and was condemned as part of a general condemnation of lustfulness, lustfulness as a sign of the absence of rational control over the self. And this view was embedded in the signifiers of culture, in the books and tracts in which, by their existence in the public sphere, was represented the society's mirage of difference. But it is a mirage of great importance because it denoted, as much by its status as by its acceptance, the importance of sexual difference as a marker of Otherness, a marker rebutted

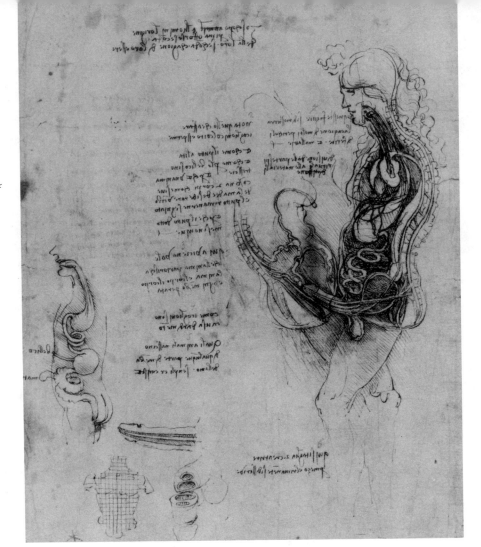

PLATE 79. *Leonardo's first image of sexuality and disease. Windsor: Queen's Collection.*

by social practice but reified by cultural (and theological) definitions of difference. Here the basic distinction is between practice, exemplified by daily reality, and theory, exemplified by the book. Thus the homosexual became one of the cultural signs of Otherness in the world of the book, an individual inherently different from the ideal state in which the body is dominated by the rational mind. It is within the cultural world of books, of images, the world of religious as well as secular texts written about homosexuality, which were available to Leonardo, that the image of the homosexual as deviant is present. And thus it is in the world of texts and images that we shall seek the source of Leonardo's internalization of the implications of that label applied to his sexual orientation. The double bind of the juxtaposition of Leonardo's sense of self and the greater culture's understanding of the homosexual is mirrored in Leonardo's images of sexual difference.[7]

The image that I shall be examining in this chapter, although not quite as well known a work as those images analyzed by Freud, the *Mona Lisa*, and the

Virgin and Child with St. Anne, is a work of immense power. Unlike Leonardo's great public works of art, this image was not created as a work for the public sphere but is rather from a more private source of images, from Leonardo's notebooks.[8] The image I shall be analyzing is, however, not unknown. It was the first page from Leonardo's anatomical drawings to be engraved and was circulated in a number of impressions as early as the late eighteenth century.[9] Indeed, Johann Friedrich Blumenbach, in one of the classic studies of Enlightenment racial biology, cites this engraving as existing in 1795[10] **[PLATE 79]**. All of the engraved versions of Leonardo's image of human sexuality reproduce only one set of figures, the hemisected figures in coition. And all of them tend to "improve" upon Leonardo's original. Indeed, it is one of these "improved" versions that led Sigmund Freud to his citation of a particularly damaging misreading of this very anatomical drawing by Rudolf Reitler in the notes to the 1919 revision of Freud's essay on Leonardo and to his embarrassed retraction of it in the 1923 version.[11]

LEONARDO'S REPRESENTATION OF HETEROSEXUALITY

The general principle for the elucidation of this early anatomical plate, created between 1493 and 1500, was stated in the first modern history of anatomical drawing, that of Ludwig Choulant, published in 1852.[12] Choulant, in his essay on Leonardo, stresses that in these early plates Leonardo was creating visual images out of his reading about anatomy. That is, he was transposing one type of representation, the verbal, into another, the visual. And indeed, in the historical literature on Leonardo's anatomical drawings, these very early drawings are all understood as attempts by Leonardo to translate the verbal imagery of the medieval and early Renaissance anatomists into his own repertoire of visual images. This baseline is of importance because it determines the relationship between text and image, both within the confines of the page taken from Leonardo's anatomical drawings and between these early drawings and the literary tradition in which they stand. Leonardo's primary source for his early anatomical drawings is the work of the fourteenth-century anatomist Mondino (Raimondo de' Luzzi).[13] The edition of Mondino that Leonardo evidently used was either the first printed Latin one, published in 1478 and unillustrated, or the 1493 Italian translation that appeared while Leonardo was beginning to record his study of human anatomy.[14] This need, therefore, to move from the printed word to the image will be the guideline for our examination of Leonardo's representations of human sexuality.

Let us begin by examining the hemisected coital figures that so confused Reitler and Freud. The sexual anatomy of these figures seems to be that of the medieval anatomist. The figures are joined completely, the "key and lock" fantasy of the structure of the genitalia that even certain contemporary biologists see as the source of the relationship between the shapes of male and female genitalia. "According to this theory females avoid having their eggs fertilized by the males of other species by evolving complicated genitalia that permit insemination only by the corresponding genitalia of males of their own species; the male has the 'key' to fit the female's 'lock.' "[15] This can also be stated in terms that would have appealed directly to Leonardo as the image of the genitalia as part of the *machina mundi*, the universal machine in which all of the segments have their proper fit.[16] The joining of the male and female in the image is complete, following the ideology of the key-and-lock metaphor—the cervix opens to receive the glans penis. A second level of implication is present in the key-and-lock

image of the genitalia in Leonardo's representation. For, not only does the structure of the "lock" preclude contact with anyone else except those who have the correct "key," but the key and lock are so structured that they complement each other exactly. This image of the inherent perfection of human anatomical structures is important to the understanding of the implications of the key-and-lock structure of the genitalia.

The representation of the penis reflects the fantasy existence of a second canal that transmits the animal spirit from the spinal cord to the embryo. Medieval anatomists, as has been noted, needed to create a boundary between the idea of urine, which was viewed as polluting (at least to the degree that it reflected pathology), and that of semen, the source of a new soul. It was a boundary between the material and the spiritual. In addition, the uterus residually reflects the medieval idea that it was divided into seven cells. The breasts are directly linked to the uterus, as in conception the retained menses are carried, by means of the epigastric veins, to the breast and there form milk. According to Kenneth Keele, the most widely read contemporary historian of science to deal with Leonardo's anatomical drawings, "Leonardo visualises conception arising from the act of coitus, according to the ideas of Plato and Hippocrates, in which the semen flowed from the spinal cord to the penis. Here [in the coital figure] the imagined nerves necessary for such transmission are displayed."[17] Now Leonardo is himself quite doubtful about the nuances of this model of coitus and conception. He questions the truths of Mondino's repetition of Avicenna's views on the nature of conception in the notes to this figure, wondering what role the testicles (the "first cause" of the sperm) played in relationship to the "second cause of the sperm," the spinal cord. All of these errors in anatomical representations and relationships can be traced back to specific literary sources; indeed, Leonardo provides them for us in his comments on this page.

Leonardo's source is the verbal image of human sexuality, but it is not only that found in the medieval anatomies. His primary source is Plato, who in his *Timaeus* saw the spinal marrow as containing " 'the universal seed stuff' of mortals."[18] Keele states quite directly that "the drawing of Leonardo follows Plato's description so literally that it is difficult to avoid the conclusion that Leonardo was illustrating what he read in the *Timaeus*." He repeats that this plate has figures that are "composed almost entirely of visualized structures as gleaned from the literature" and are "representations of the literature he had read in preparation for his own anatomical explorations." But Keele does not proceed quite far enough, for it is in *Timaeus* that the verbal source of the image that dominates all of the figures on this page is to be found.

It is the ideology of the function of the testicles, in Leonardo's question appended to the hemisected figures, "How are the testicles the cause of ardor?" which leads us back to the text, to Plato's *Timaeus*. It is not merely the question of the "primary" or "secondary" sources of sperm but rather the nature of the human sexual drive that is central. Plato observes:

> And the seed, having life, becoming endowed with respiration, produces in that part which it respires a lively desire of emission, and thus creates in us the love of procreation. Wherefore also in men the organ of generation becoming rebellious and masterful, like an animal disobedient to reason, maddened with the sting of lust, seeks to gain absolute sway, and the same is the case with the so-called womb or matrix of women. The animal within them is desirous of procreating children.[19]

It is the idea that the semen creates within the rational individual, for Plato both men and women, the "animal within" that dominates the image of human sexuality for Leonardo. We are helpless, manipulated by this "animal within," unable to act except to engage in intercourse. The human being, at that point, becomes the vessel that holds sexuality and that is dominated by it.

But for Leonardo, this is not all that is involved in the act of heterosexual coitus. For Leonardo appends one further note to the description of the hemisected figures: "By means of these figures, the cause of many ulcers and diseases will be demonstrated." Although both Mondino and, indeed, Plato speak of the diseases associated with the genitalia (either in terms of the ulcers that may result from the medication applied after a hernia operation or the repression of the semen with its resultant illness), Leonardo's choice of vocabulary ("per queste figure sidjmosstere / lacagiche dj moltj pericholj / dj ferite e mallattj") points to one very specific disease, the yet-unnamed syphilis. It is possible that this reference is the earliest recorded anatomical/medical reference to the new disease. Leonardo's reference appears at the very moment when the disease was first spreading throughout Italy and records the telltale signs of the illness, the genital ulcers that are its most prominent feature.[20]

The iconography of disease permeates the hemisected coital figures. Not the image of the hemisected figures themselves, for they exist in more primitive form in the anatomical illustration of the Middle Ages, but rather an iconographic feature that is almost lost to the contemporary observer. Let us again observe the figures. The virtual disappearance of the female figure was already commented on by Reitler. She is but womb and breasts. There is nothing about her that seems to point to pathology. But her breasts are pendulous. They are not flat, aged, and worn; they are rather the full breasts of the pregnant woman. The woman is seen here as but the potential container of the embryo. And pregnancy, as has been seen, is understood from the Middle Ages on as a potentially pathological situation.

The male figure is drawn with much more detail. What is striking in his representation in terms of the clearly drawn head and face is the cascade of hair that dominates. This is Leonardo's image of the male as the sufferer from syphilis, the fop of Dürer's later broadside illustration (see Plate 68). With the cascade of hair, Leonardo is pointing to the image of the syphilitic. It is the fop, the young male, who is at risk from the new disease with its evident sexual origin. He is paralleled to the other individual, the pregnant woman, who is represented as being at risk. Thus sexuality is not merely the release of the beast within; it is also the characterization of this "beast" as polluted and polluting. Coitus points toward defilement and illness.

These analogies to the hemisected image, as I have noted, are taken from the anatomy of the late Middle Ages. Yet the position of the act of coitus, upright, is unusual even for such hemisected figures. The very position of these figures also has iconographic significance. When Leonardo's corpus is examined, it is clear that there is a set of visual analogies to the upright position of the two figures. Leonardo's images of "pleasure and pain" and "virtue and envy" use the classical model of the self divided against itself as the image of irreconcilable differences **[PLATE 80]**. The Platonic antithesis between the masculine and the feminine, as has been seen, would fall into such a set of dichotomies for the Renaissance mind. But one other representation of sexuality from Leonardo's iconographic storehouse should be introduced here. For in the tradition of the representation of Leda and the swan, from Greco-Roman art through Leonardo, the sexual act is performed with two upright figures[21] **[PLATE 81]**. Thus the upright position points toward the existence of antithesis as well as the existence of a type of sexual contact that exemplifies the male as possessing the "beast within," Zeus in the form of the beast raping Leda. Leonardo's representation of this scene combines, in the sense of sensuality in the female, both attraction to and repellence by the aggressive male, a sensuality that also mirrors the "beast within."

PLATE 80. *Leonardo da Vinci,* Allegory of Virtue and Envy. *Oxford: Christ Church.*

PLATE 81. *A copy of the lost painting by Leonardo da Vinci of* Leda and the Swan, *1510–15. Rotterdam: Museum Boymans, van Beuningen.*

LEONARDO'S REPRESENTATION OF HOMOSEXUALITY

In terms of their historical suppression, the more interesting images are those on the left (Plate 79). Here, too, we have the translation of verbal images into visual ones. For we have an image here of what Leonardo calls in a reference to the hemisected figures the "material" (i.e., alimentary) parts as opposed to the "spiritual" (the thoracic) parts. Here we have a figure who represents only the "material" parts, the alimentary canal from the mouth to the anus. Leonardo's literary source for this image is Aristotle's essay on the parts of animals. In this image, Leonardo represents the jejunum as lying between the upper and lower stomachs, after which the gut becomes narrower and convoluted, ending in a straight portion running to the anus. This is the representation not of a human alimentary canal but that of a specific type of ruminant, those beasts that Aristotle calls "horned animals." The alimentary canal of these "horned animals" runs "in a straight line to the place where the residue is discharged . . . which is called the anus." And these parts have only one function, according to Aristotle, the "treating of food and . . . [the] dealing with the residue produced."[22] The human alimentary canal, which has but one true stomach and which ends with its sigmoid flexure leading to the rectum, is unrepresented.

The other figures on the left side of the page are of equal interest. The small torso, which is represented so that it can be easily enlarged, seems to represent a sexless figure, as does the more detailed hemisected figure of the alimentary canal. There are two figures of the penis, a transverse section (with testicles, the source of ardor) and a longitudinal section that represents the penile passages, one for the urine, the other for the animal spirit derived from the spinal cord.[23] The image of the penis, here erect and functioning quite independent of any external control, is represented as an autonomous force. This view that the genitalia, both male and female, can assume a life of their own has already been quoted from Plato. Leonardo subscribed to this view, at least for the male organ, as he observed in his notebooks:

This [the penis] disputes with the human intellect, and sometimes has an intellect of its own. And though the will of man may wish to stimulate it, it remains obstinate and goes its own way, sometimes moving on its own without the permission or intention of a man. Thus be he sleeping or waking it does what it desires. Often a man is asleep and it is awake, and many times a man is awake and it is asleep. Many times a man wants to use it, and it does not want to; many times it wants to and a man forbids it. Therefore it appears that this animal often has a soul and intellect separate from a man; and it appears that a man who is ashamed to name or show it is in the wrong, always being anxious to cover it up and hide what ought to adorn and show with solemnity like a minister of the human species.[24]

What is striking in the figures on the left-hand side of Leonardo's page is the visual relationship between the longitudinally represented penis and the anus of the alimentary figure. It is posed for entrance, at least visually. Here we can return to the ideology of the key-and-lock metaphor for the depiction of the genitalia. The vagina and uterus match perfectly to the form of the erect penis; but so do the rectum and anus, as represented by Leonardo.

The ambiguity of such a fantasy about the structure of the body, a fantasy that grows out of the ideologies associated with sexuality, presents a parallel case to Leonardo's image of heterosexuality. The idea of anal intercourse, here between a figure with a ruminant digestive system (and without any overt sexual signifier) and a penis without a body, returns us to the image of the bestial, the link between Plato and Aristotle, between the two texts translated into images by Leonardo. In the Church tradition, the term *bestial* is one of the encoded terms for homosexuality. Clement of Alexandria quotes Plato in this context: "It seems to me on this account that Plato in the *Phaedrus* deprecates pederasty, calling it 'bestial,' because those who give themselves up to [this] pleasure 'take the bit' and copulate in the manner of quadrupeds, striving to beget children [thus]."[25] For Leonardo the relationship between the anus and the penis is parallel in form (and therefore in function) to the relationship between the vagina and the penis. But the anus is clearly that of the "horned beast" of Aristotle's text.

The idea of homosexuality in the late Middle Ages is tied to the image of the bestial. Indeed, Leonardo himself, in a passage quoted from his notebooks (1488, *Fiore di virtù*), refers to the fact that the "bat, owing to unbridled lust, observes no universal rule in pairing, but males with males and females with females pair promiscuously, as it may happen."[26] This passage is indicative of one view of the nature of the animal. Homosexuality was understood as the result of unbridled lust and was therefore a quality ascribed to the beast.[27] Traditionally, the animals that served as the icons of homosexuality were the hare, the weasel, and the hyena, all of which were understood to be deviant within the animal kingdom.[28] But, by the Renaissance, all sexuality outside of the control of reason had become suspect in this model. Indeed, all sexuality outside the bounds of the sacrament of marriage and the intent of conception was lustful, and therefore bestial, according to the standard authorities such as Thomas Aquinas.[29] Indeed Aquinas lists homoerotic activity under the general category of "lust" because "it exceeds the order and mode of reason." Aquinas lists four categories of sexuality that are "lustful" and therefore sinful. They are ranked from the least serious to the most serious offense:

1. Masturbation
2. Intercourse in an unnatural position
3. Homosexuality
4. Bestiality

In the view of the Church all actions that were outside the bounds of marriage were forbidden if they did not directly lead to procreation, but some were worse than others. Homosexuality was linked with bestiality because it represented the activities of the base aspects of human lust. And bestiality was seen, because of its illicit nature, as one of the sources for the new, unnamed disease of the genitalia, syphilis.[30] This was viewed as the correct nature of the beast (such as the bat) but antithetical to the nature of human beings.

One further problem arises in examining this set of images, images that by their juxtaposition represent anal intercourse as a visual parallel to the heterosexuality of the hemisected figures. It is evident from Leonardo's notes that heterosexuality is associated with disease, with syphilis and pregnancy. What is not evident is that anatomists writing contemporaneously with Leonardo commented on the diseases of the anus and related them to "lustful" living. One of the most important Renaissance commentators on Mondino, Jacopo Berengario da Carpi, in his *Isagogae breves* (1522), observed that the "anus suffers all kinds of ills, which are hard to heal. . . . Sometimes a lascivious shamelessness of riotous living and burning lust in either sex by seeking low retreats or byways cause these ills."[31] This reference to anal intercourse, both heterosexual and homosexual, makes it evident that the anus could be pathologically influenced by "misuse." The anatomists whom Leonardo knew condemned anal intercourse on much the same ideological grounds as did the Church but also indicated that such acts led to disease. The parallels between Leonardo's sense of the nature of heterosexuality and his internalization of his culture's image of homosexuality,

as present in authoritative written texts, was not, however, limited to the written works of the anatomists.

It is in the text that had the central position in Leonardo's understanding of the culture of his own time, *The Divine Comedy*, the quintessentially Italian text by which Italian culture even in the Renaissance defined itself, that a vocabulary of verbal images (and their visual realizations) is provided that Leonardo could have drawn upon to comprehend the image of sexuality as bestial.[32] Twice in *The Divine Comedy*, Dante uses the term *sodomite*. The first time, in the *Inferno*, it is used as a term of political opprobrium, as Richard Kay has shown in his essay "The Sin of Brunetto Latini."[33] However, in the *Purgatorio*, Dante describes the lustful, those dominated by bestial forces, and he calls upon an image that is visually extraordinarily powerful. In Canto Twenty-Six, Dante makes reference to the poets Guido Guinicelli and Arneut Daniel as those consumed by the lust of the beast [PLATE 82]. What Dante first hears when he approaches them and those condemned with them is their muttering:

> There I see on either side each shade make haste, and one kiss the other without staying, satisfied with short greeting:
> even so within their dark battalions one ant rubs muzzle with another, perchance to spy out their way and their fortune.
> Soon as they break off the friendly greeting, ere the first step there speeds onward, each one strives to shout loudest;
> the new people, "Sodom and Gomorrah," and the other: "Pasiphaë enters the cow that the young bull may haste to her lust."[34]

Here two models of bestial lust (the lust of the antlike creatures), the heterosexual and the homosexual, cross. The rhetoric of "Sodom and Gomorrah" points toward the sins of the bestial in the form of the homosexual with a generally accepted biblical reference; the reference to Pasiphaë, the mother of the Minotaur, is perhaps less well known.[35] The legend is one of the standard repertoire of literary images of sexual transformation and perversion, having its best-known retelling in Ovid and Apuleius. Minos, king of Crete, calls upon Poseidon to send a bull from the sea for a sacrifice in order to confirm his right to rule. Pasiphaë, his wife, falls in love with the bull and contrives to have Daedalus disguise her as a cow to have carnal relations with the animal.

The alimentary figure, the figure with the viscera of the "horned beast," Leonardo's realization of Aristotle's anatomy of the beast, is the image of

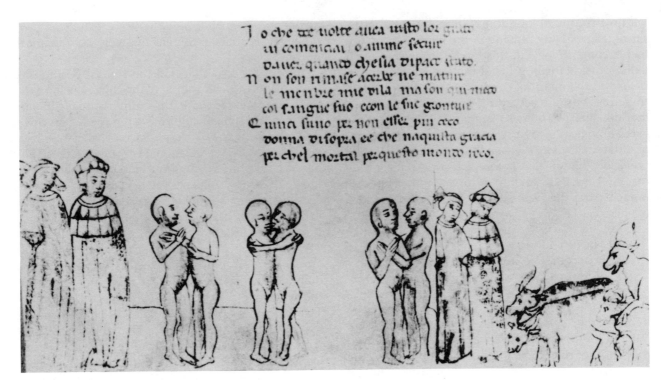

PLATE 82. *Illustration of the image of the "lustful" from a mid-fourteenth-century Italian manuscript of Dante's* Purgatorio *XXVI. Arsenal 8530. Paris: Bibliothèque nationale.*

the beast within.[36] This figure, Leonardo's "material" figure, however, seems sexless (Plate 79). Leonardo draws on it two labels: one is "umbilicus," which relates to the caecum; but from the gut stems an appendage unknown in anatomy and labeled with a term likewise unknown, "matron." This is indeed *metron*, Greek for "womb," placed outside of the figure for, like Pasiphaë, the figure is a reversed image. Such a reversal also has a long tradition in classical anatomical thought as we have seen in Galen's anatomy, as was discussed in Chapter Three. What prevents the inversion of the genitalia in most women is the absence of the excess heat of the male, that which drives the male to "lust." It is the wellspring of the bestial and is represented by the figure of the inverted woman, driven by the heat of the male, her uterus projecting like a penis. It is the man-woman, the sexual being simultaneously penis and uterus. It is Plato's hermaphrodite, but as pathology, not as the norm.

It is the woman, Pasiphaë, hiding within the image of the beast, who waits to assuage her lust; and it is the bestial within the human being that drives her to this action. It is an image with the bestial internalized, with the uterus, the sign of reproduction as a sign of the reversal of the roles of the sexes, externalized. The condemnation of the passive homosexual, the male as female, in Church law is reflected in this image.[37] The Church condemned any male taking the "female" role, condemned homosexuality as a reversal of the "natural order" of the world. The significance of the placement of the "horned" uterus, the organ of reproduction, outside of the body is Leonardo's sign of the "bestial" in his fantasy of role reversal within the traditionally accepted model of human sexuality.

The body itself becomes the vehicle for his critique of the irrational forces of sexuality, of the internalized sense of his own sexuality as condemned by the world in which he lives. This critique is a result of the double bind in which Leonardo finds himself between his sense of his own sexual identity, a sense reified by the attitudes of his peer group in Florence, and the mythic images of the homosexual present in the books that dominate his world, texts from the world of science as well as literature.

LEONARDO'S REJECTION OF SEXUALITY

Leonardo's bodies are transparent. We see the bestial forces within that move the individual in ways that are contrary to the teachings of the Church and the directives of the state. The result of the double bind that condemns both heterosexual as well as homosexual activity is finally mirrored in Leonardo's rejection of all sexuality as grotesque, as documented in the famed passage inscribed on one of the later anatomical plates:

> The sexual act and the members employed therein are so repulsive, that if it were not for the beauty of the faces and the adornments of the actors and the pent-up impulse, nature would lose the human species.[38]

It is not any specific form of sexuality but all sexuality that Leonardo condemns, repressing any sense of his own sexual identity, at least within the confines of the anatomical notebooks. Leonardo has internalized the negative image of sexuality that has salience for him. Accused of homosexuality, he converts the image of the condemned sexual act into the literal representation of bestiality. All sexuality is dangerous; it is sinful as the result of the Fall from grace in the Garden of Eden. It is the loss of consciousness and identity that leads to public humiliation, as he observes in a text written at about the same time as he created the plate representing coitus:

> Of Lust: And they will go wild after the things that are most beautiful to seek after, to possess and make use of their vilest parts; and afterwards, having returned with loss and penitence to their senses, they will be greatly amazed of themselves.[39]

For Leonardo, when he turns to his first attempts to represent human sexuality in a direct manner, it is within this internalized matrix that he understands his own Otherness. But this internalization is also ambiguous. For Leonardo condemns both homosexuality and heterosexuality as the conquest of the ugly, of the pathological, as the bestial, but he also equates them as natural, that is, as being sanctioned by his fantasy about the structure of human anatomy. The inherent ambiguity of this position is reflected in this first translation of images from texts into representations of sexuality. Here we have the moment of creative fantasy of Leonardo looking to the body of the Other and finding there his own body represented.

The complexities of human sexuality as understood and internalized by Leonardo can serve as a guidepost to how individuals respond to the myth-making about their own sexuality. It is not merely that human sexuality was misunderstood in the Middle Ages and the Renaissance, but that sexuality, one of the central markers of human identity, is always ideologically interpreted in Western society. Leonardo stood at what has generally been understood as the boundary between the "old" and the "new" manner of seeing the body, and yet his view, like that of Vesalius who came after him, was limited by the cultural presuppositions that dominated his age and that shaped his understanding not only of what he saw (and represented) but also of his own identity. In casting the history of the representation of human sexuality, it is important that we understand that these images are not merely neutral "snapshots" pasted in an album but keys to an understanding of how the artist understood his or her own sexuality.

CHAPTER FIVE

Icons of Sexuality in European Seventeenth-Century Art and Science

THE "NEWNESS" OF THE RENAISSANCE

The power of the Renaissance anatomists to reshape the understanding of the body was not merely a reflex of their new knowledge of human anatomy. It was also the self-conscious claim, a claim created by early Renaissance scholars such as Pico della Mirandola, that their science was inherently different from the ignorance and superstition that preceded them, that they constituted a true "Renaissance" of ancient learning. They claimed for themselves and their age an absolute discontinuity between the medieval understanding of the body and that of the Renaissance. As we have seen, the continuity of the understanding of human sexuality from the Middle Ages through the sixteenth century indicates that, no matter how self-consciously "new" their knowledge of sexuality was, it was also formed by the science and theology in (and against) which it developed. The synthesis of the new sexual anatomy and the preoccupations of the late sixteenth and seventeenth centuries with specific problems of disease led to complex variations of the problem of the representation of sexuality. It was during the seventeenth century that many of the Renaissance images of human sexuality, with their medieval subtexts, were refashioned—often with surprising results. This chapter will be devoted to examining a series of major questions that center on the reinterpretation of representations. Some of these questions—What is the nature of icons of popular sexuality? What are the related debates about the nature and implication of the fetus? Was there a development of a "Baroque" or manneristic mode of representing human sexuality and sexual pathology within the medicine and art of the seventeenth and early eighteenth centuries?—point toward the problem raised in the prior chapter about the implications of a hierarchical polarity of the sexes. The view that there are only two sexes and that the male is in every way (from structure to function) superior continues to dominate the discourse about human sexuality. The Other in this duality remains the female, and it is the female seen as the definition of difference who comes negatively to define the nature of male sexuality. The "female" becomes by extension the overarching label for all categories of sexual difference, whether labeled as *racial* or *geographic*. Thus we find a natural link between images of exotic sexuality and the idea of the female. This drawing of absolute boundaries between the sexes, of the elimination of categories (such as homosexuality) or the labeling of them as *marginal* provides a grid that is laid over the understanding of human sexuality in an absolute and reductive manner. Here science and art both capitulate—seeing sexuality within these specific boundaries.

SEXUAL ICONS, RACE, AND DIFFERENCE

The sexuality of the female is seen in terms of the meaning of her hidden sexual anatomy. Her hidden nature is further homologous to the hidden origin of sexually transmitted disease. But the image of male sexuality is not without its pathologization. The image of the sexualized Other in sixteenth-century Europe is closely associated with the icon of the circumcised Jew (as we have seen) given the centrality of Christianity in socially constructing the

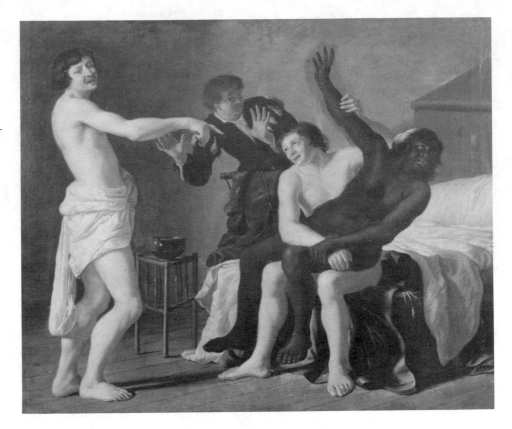

PLATE 83. *The image of sexual exploitation of the black woman in Christiaen van Couwenburgh,* The Rape of the Negress, *1632. Strasbourg: Musée des Beaux Arts.*

sexual. But in the course of the sixteenth and seventeenth centuries, with the further exploration of Africa and the Americas and the widespread introduction of black slavery into Europe and the Americas, the black female comes to hold a special place in their representation of sexuality. It was the focus, at least initially, on the black female as the image of exotic, seductive (and thus potentially dangerous) sexuality that served as the lightning rod for the evident fact that European, Christian males were sexually exploiting powerless, black females. Black female sexuality represented the colonialist fantasy of those dangers that could be overcome (unlike the threat posed by the specter of black male sexuality). In the extraordinary image of *The Rape of the Negress* by the minor Dutch painter Christiaen van Couwenburgh, painted in 1632, the Dutch Protestant involvement in the slave trade is reduced to the act of rape **[PLATE 83]**. The bed, that icon of coitus and exposure of the female genitalia, appears here as the scene of a gross indecency. The gestures of the three males point toward the ambiguity of the image. The black female attempts to ward off her attackers. The rapist touches his victim, holding her fast. His two companions gesture, the first, his genitalia masked only by a towel, in approbation, pointing at the scene; the second, clothed and not involved, with the traditional gesture

of Pontius Pilate, showing that his "hands are clean." But this image also points to the myth that it was the black male who strove to seduce the white female. The passive black woman is the object that can be overcome. She stands as the representation of white male dominance, paralleling the visually absent but strongly felt threat of the black male. Analogous to myths about aggressive Jewish male sexuality, the Jew as seducer (which likewise had its counterpart in the image of the "beautiful Jewess" as succubus), images of cross-"racial" sexuality, like images of cross-sexual contact, were forbidden but seductive. Touching the black or Jewish female was forbidden but attractive; the white, Christian female being touched by the black or Jewish male was taboo. This represented the same boundaries between the permitted and the forbidden act as did the taboo against same-sex touching. This formed the boundary between the permitted and the taboo sexual acts and reflected the necessary attractiveness of the different, which is attractive precisely because it is forbidden. The action of touching the Other was dared; but the Other could never of his or her own volition reach out across the boundary and touch.

In the sixteenth and seventeenth centuries, there was an added factor present in the boundaries created between "races," the close association of sexually transmitted diseases with leprosy, which was viewed as an African (as well as a Jewish) disease. Indeed, leprosy was understood as the source of the skin color of the black. This was coupled, in the medical literature, with a discussion of the sexual parts of the black female, which were seen to be deformed, inherently different from those of the white. Giovanni Morgagni discusses this linkage in detail in his 1717 essays on human anatomy.[1] The intense fear of sexually transmitted disease and its close association with other forms of illness, such as leprosy, led to the incorporation of images of black sexuality within the popular medical literature of the period.

It was assumed that the black, like the Jew, was inherently corrupt and corrupting, the sons and daughters of Ham. It was also assumed, following the exploration of Africa and the beginning of the slave trade during the sixteenth century, that the "reality" of black concupiscence was most manifest in acts of bestiality. It was sexual contact with animals (sodomy) that marked the sexuality of the black as inherently different and corrupt, giving rise to representations of black sexuality as bestial. Blacks were animals because they had sex with animals. Black sexuality was understood in terms of humorial theory. It was the excess heat of the tropical sun that drove Africans sexually mad. And it was heat that inherently differentiated the sexual drive of the male from that of the female in all peoples. Black sexuality thus represented an exaggerated form of normal male sexuality. Jean Bodin, in the seventeenth century, commented:

> They can only restrain themselves with great difficulty, and once launched on debauchery, they maintain the most execrable voluptuousness. Hence the intimate [sexual] relations between men and beasts that give birth to monsters in Africa.[2]

The monsters of Africa are, indeed, the border figures that confuse the basic seventeenth-century paradigm, the "great chain of being."[3] This postulated a hierarchy of the races, with the Europeans on the top and the blacks at the very bottom. (This "chain" had its analogies in perceived hierarchies of class as well as of gender.) Such "monsters" were monstrous precisely because they violated the boundaries implicit in the "chain of being."[4]

Africa is, of course, a place in the mind as well as a geographic locus.[5] Africa was the utopia or the distopia that defined a culture's sense of self. The existence of such sexual "monsters," halfway between human and ape, in equally exotic settings was assumed by the science of the day. William

Harvey's *De generatione animalium* (1651), on the generation of animals, is, along with his work describing the circulation of the blood, one of the major scientific works of the seventeenth century.[6] It is the first work on animal reproduction that argues for the gradual development of the fetus from the fertilized egg. In his discussion, Harvey concentrates on the reproductive system of the fowl. He rarely calls upon other species, and when he does it is on other oviparous animals such as reptiles. (It is Harvey's disciple Nicolaus Steno who in 1667 draws the evident conclusion that there is a homology among the genitalia of all of the vivipara, including the human.[7]) When Harvey turns to the human being it is in his discussion of the external female genitalia, where he comments on how, in the common fowl, there is an external protection of the genitalia, so that the genitalia are only exposed in estrus.[8] In animals with a tail, Harvey observes, parturition can take place only with the tail lifted up, "and even the human female is assisted in her labour by having the coccyx anointed and drawn outward with the finger." And then Harvey gives us the intermediate case:

> A surgeon, a trustworthy man, and with whom I am upon intimate terms, on his return from the East Indies informed me, in perfect sincerity, that some inland and mountainous parts of the island of Borneo are still inhabited by a race of caudate human beings (a circumstance of which we also read in Pausanias), one of whom, a virgin, who had only been captured with great difficulty, for they live in the woods, he himself had seen, with a tail, thick, fleshly, and a span in length, reflected between the buttocks, and covering the anus and pudenda: so regularly has nature willed to cover these parts.[9]

Certainly the animal, whatever it is, orangutan or "primitive," halfway between ape and human, is labeled by the nature of her external genitalia as nonhuman (and, therefore, as possessing a bestial sexuality). She in a real sense becomes the sign of her genitalia. The ape–human, neither fully human nor totally animal, is the parodic image of human sexuality because she has differently formed genitalia.

The exotic, but especially the black, became the representation of the monstrous because blacks could no longer be sexually differentiated from monkeys—their inherent, animalistic sexual drive led them to breed with animals. Buffon commented that "the interval which separates the monkey from the Negro is hard to understand."[10] The association of blacks with monkeys was readily made given the desired representation of the black (the potential

PLATE 84. *The chimpanzee as quasi-human with walking stick from Edward Tyson,* Orang-Outang, sive Homo Sylvestris; or, The Anatomy of a Pygmie Compared with That of a Monkey, an Ape, and a Man *(London: T. Bennett & D. Brown, 1699). Ithaca: Howard B. Adelmann Collection, Olin Library, Cornell University.*

slave) as animal and the existing representation of the monkey as the icon of parodied human activity and unbridled sexuality. It was the monsters in Africa, the monkeys who look and act like distorted humans, who provided the key to the European fantasy about black sexuality.

In 1699 Edward Tyson, the leading comparative anatomist of seventeenth-century Britain, published a major study of the anatomical distinctions between the various primates. *Orang-Outang, sive Homo Sylvestris; or, The Anatomy of a Pygmie Compared with That of a Monkey, an Ape, and a Man* states in its programmatic title Tyson's intent to destroy the seventeenth-century view that the blacks of Africa were merely types of (or crossbreed with) apes and monkeys. He produces, however, a set of icons that reflect the sixteenth- and seventeenth-century conviction that these primates were merely the next step down from the black **[PLATE 84]**. His chimpanzee, supporting himself on a walking stick, provides an image that is half-human, half-beast. But the covert intent of this image is to reveal the male chimpanzee's genitalia to the observer. We see the external genitalia of the primate, and, in a further plate, the inner structure of these genitalia are revealed **[PLATE 85]**. Tyson's intent is to contrast these anatomical images with the images of human anatomy. What he accomplishes is to provide an icon of the half-man, half-beast black as sexual object, the very view he wishes to undermine.

Let us for a moment seem to abandon the seventeenth-century's fascination with black sexuality as a marker of sexual difference and look at the work and reputation of one of the most important physicians of the sixteenth century, Ambrose Paré. Paré (1510–90) was one of the most serious medical scientists of his day.[11] An innovative surgeon, named "chirurgien du roy" in 1552, Paré's work was on the leading edge of medical knowledge during the sixteenth century, especially in the area of military medicine. He authored a wide range of texts dealing with subjects from war wounds to obstetrics. When his collected works appeared in 1575 they were widely read and translated because they were understood to reflect the height of knowledge of a wide range of medical fields of his day. In terms of his anatomical knowledge, he was very much a Vesalian. In his 1561 anatomical atlas, which is reprinted in the collected works, he expressly acknowledges his debt to Vesalius and to the illustrations in the *Fabrica*. Indeed, the two figures of the "parts of women and men" **[PLATES 86–87]** are versions of plates (see Plates 37–38) taken directly from Vesalius.[12]

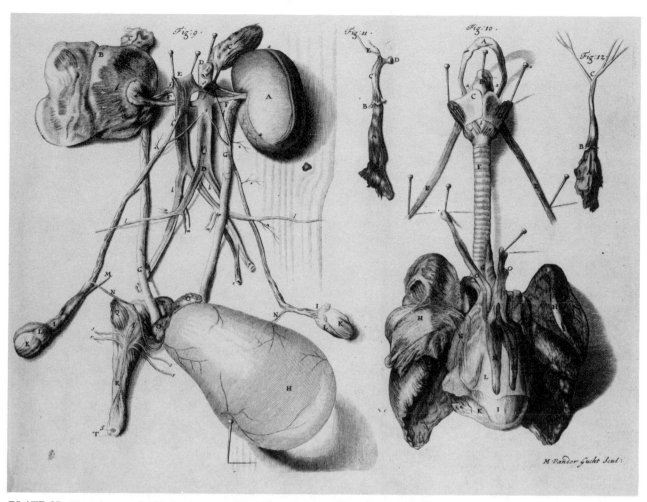

PLATE 85. *The urinary and reproductive parts of the chimpanzee from Edward Tyson,* Or-
ang-Outang, sive Homo Sylvestris; or, The Anatomy of a Pygmie Compared with
That of a Monkey, an Ape, and a Man *(London: T. Bennett & D. Brown, 1699). Ithaca:
Howard B. Adelmann Collection, Olin Library, Cornell University.*

The thirteenth Figure, shewing the parts of Women different from those in Men.

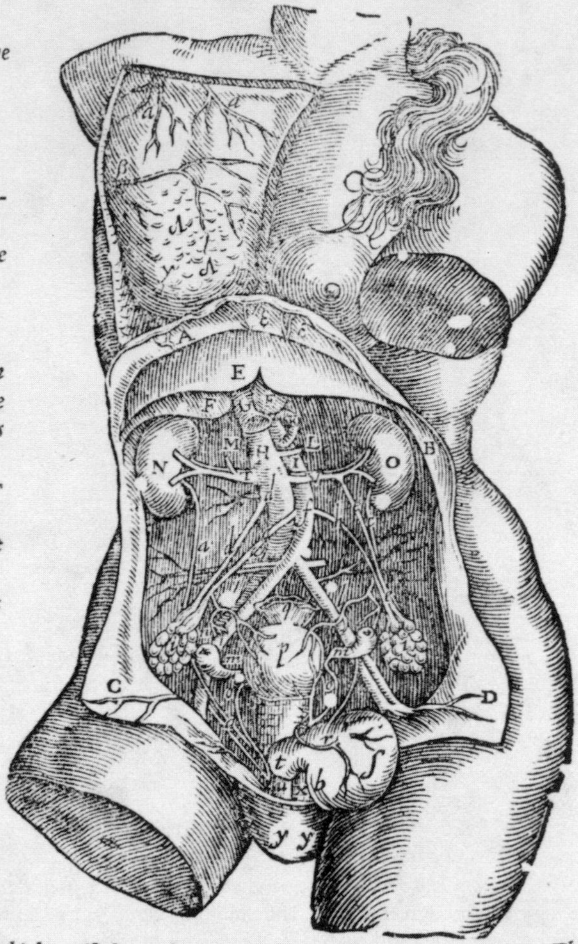

A B C D The Peritonæum reflected or turned backward, above and below.

E F The gibbous part of the Liver E, the cave or hollow part F.

G The trunk of the Gate Vein.

H The hollow Vein.

I The great Artery.

K The roots of the Cœliacal Artery which accompanieth the Gate Vein.

L M The fatty Vein going to the Coat of the Kidneys.

N O The fore-part of both the Kidneys.

T V The Emulgent Veins and Arteries.

a a The right Ureter at the lowest a, cut from apart which, near to b, sticketh yet to the bladder, because the bottom of the bladder is drawn to the left side.

c The left Ureter inserted into the Bladder near to r.

d d The Spermatick Vein which goeth to the left testicle marked with i.

e e The Spermatick Vein which goeth to the left testicle with i also.

f The trunk of the great Artery from whence the spermatical Arteries do proceed.

g h The spermatical Arteries.

i i The two testicles.

l l A branch which from the spermatick Vessels reacheth unto the bottom of the Womb.

m m The leading Vessel of the Seed which Fallopius calleth the Tuba or trumpet, because it is crooked and reflected.

n A branch of the spermatick Vessel compassing the leading Vessel. o o A Vessel like a Worm which passeth to the Womb, some call it Cremaster. p The bottom of the Womb, called Fundus Uteri. q A part of the right Gut. r ſ The bottom of the Bladder whereto is inserted the left Ureter, and a Vein led from the neck of the Womb near unto r. t the neck of the Bladder. u The same inserted into the Privity or Lap. x A part of the neck of the Womb above the Privity. y y Certain skinny Caruncles of the Privities, in the midst of which is the slit, and on both sides appear little hillocks.

The Figures belonging to the Dugs and Brests.

α α The Veins of the Dugs which come from those, which descending from the top of the shoulder, are offered to the Skin. β The Veins of the Dugs derived from those which through the arm-hole are led into the hand. γ The body of the Dug or Brest. δ δ The Kernels and fat between them. ε ε The Vessels of the Dugs descending from the lower part of the neck called Jugulum, under the Brest-bone.

From

PLATE 86. *The Vesalian torso of the female from Ambrose Paré,* The Works Translated out of Latin and Compared with the French by Th. Johnson. *(London: M. Clark for J. Clark, 1678). Ithaca: Howard B. Adelmann Collection, Olin Library, Cornell University.*

The Tenth Figure, wherein those things shewed in the former Figure, are more exactly set forth.

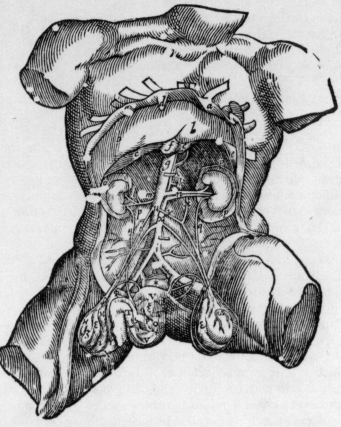

a a *A part of the Midriff, and of the* Peritonæum *with the ribs broken.*

bb cc *The convex or gibbous part of the liver marked with* bb, *the hollow or concavous part with* cc.

d e *The right and left ligaments of the Liver.*

f *The trunk of the gate-vein.*

g *The trunk of the hollow vein.*

h l *The fatty veins, both left and right.*

i *The ascent of the great Artery above the hollow vein, and the division thereof.*

k *The* Cœliacal *Artery.*

m n *The emulgent Vessels.*

oo pp *The fat tunicles or coats torn from both the Kidneys.*

qq *The Ureters that go unto the Bladder.*

t u *The right spermatical Vein which ariseth near to* u.

x y *The double original of the left spermatical Vein.*

x *From the Emulgent.*

y *From the hollow vein.*

α *The original of the spermatical Arteries.*

β *Certain branches from the sper-*
matick *Arteries which run unto the* Peritonæum. γ *The passage of the spermatical Vessels through the productions of the* Peritonæum, *which must be observed by such as use to cut for the Rupture.* δ *The spiry bodden* Hidie's *entrance into the testicle, it is called* Corpus varicosum pyramidale. ε *The* Parastatæ. ζ *The Stone or Testicle covered with his inmost coat.* η *The descendent of the leading Vessel called* Vas deferens. V V *The Bladder.* * *The right Gut.* ξ *The Glandules, called* Prostatæ, *into which the leading Vessels are inserted.* ρ *The muscle of the Bladder.* σ τ υ *Two bodies of the Yard,* σ *and* τ *and* υ *his Vessels.* φ χ *The coat of the Testicle.* ψ ω *The muscle of the Testicle* ψ, *his Vessels* ω.

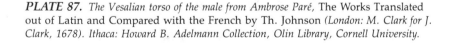

PLATE 87. *The Vesalian torso of the male from Ambrose Paré,* The Works Translated out of Latin and Compared with the French by Th. Johnson *(London: M. Clark for J. Clark, 1678). Ithaca: Howard B. Adelmann Collection, Olin Library, Cornell University.*

The visual world of Paré is, however, not solely that of the Renaissance anatomists taken from the "high" science of his day.[13] His view incorporates a further canon of images taken from the popular science of his day. For, as we have seen with the *Fabrica*, the boundary between high science and popular or theological views of sexuality is frangible. It is in one of the later segments of Paré's collected work, the reissue of his 1573 essay "Of Monsters and Prodigies," that a second level of meaning is given to the Vesalian images of sexuality.[14] Paré's study of teratology, the biological study of the production, development, anatomy, and classification of monsters, was originally written as an expansion of a chapter on obstetrics in one of his earlier works on human anatomy, published in 1543. It was expanded by drawing on the books and broadsides on wondrous births and miraculous occurrences that documented (and tried to explain) the various real and fantastic events that fascinated the sixteenth-century mind. Floods and eclipses were depicted and discussed, but central to this world of images (for all of these printed texts were richly illustrated) was the fascination with freaks and foreigners, with the misshapen and the exotic. Paré drew heavily on Conrad Lycosthenes's book of supernatural occurrences published in 1557, which was full of the widest range of "wonderful" events.[15] Because many of the physical anomalies described were "wonderous births," the overt association with human sexuality, or at least with conception and parturition, is clear. But many of the teratoid figures described were "monsters" precisely because of their highly sexualized nature. In the figures that Paré actually borrowed from Lycosthenes, this theme is dominant. It is especially hermaphroditism, the biological borderline between the male and the female **[PLATE 88]**, that plays a major role in defining the "monstrous" in these borrowings. Paré subscribed to the view that these "monsters" were the result of the absence of heat in the male that caused him to acquire female characteristics before birth.

But it is not merely in the physical anomalies and the teratoid births that one finds the roots of sexual fantasy about the self but in Paré's discussion of "monsters which take their cause and shape by imagination." Indeed, the question of the mind, the source of control, and its representation of the sexual are of equal importance to the biological source of physical anomalies. Here the central icon is one that is not taken from Conrad Lycosthenes **[PLATE 89]**. It is of a "Maid all hairy, and an Infant that was black by the imagination of their Parents." The "hairy maid" is the result, according to Paré, of the fact that "her Mother earnestly beheld in the very instant of receiving and conceiving the seed, the image of St. John covered with a Camels [*sic*] skin, hanging upon the posts of the bed."[16] The black child, Paré reports, was explained by Hippocrates, who "freed a certain Noble-woman from suspicion of adultery, who being white herself, and her husband also white, brought forth a child as black as an Ethiopian, because in copulation she strongly and continually had in her mind the picture of the Ethiope."[17] The image of the hairy woman and the black child is Paré's own composite—the hairy maid is the icon of Mary Magdalene in the Egyptian desert, and the little black boy is the sexualized monkey transmuted into a black child. For Paré's discussion of the powers of the imagination, of the control that the mind has over the shaping of the body, is a discussion of human sexuality and its foibles. It centers on the influence that female fantasy at the moment of conception can have on the form of the fetus. This is quite different from his earlier discussion of the hermaphrodites, which he sees as merely based on the influence of heat and cold. The creation of these monsters stems from the sexual fantasy of the female, as Marie-Helene Huet commented, as "the effect produced on pregnant women by lengthy contemplation of a desired object."[18]

The role of female fantasy in masking the woman's unbridled (but more superficial) sexuality, her adultery of the mind rather than of the body, leads the physician to see her as the source of sexual anomalies. She is Mary Magdalene, whose repentance comes from having led a sexually unbridled life. Her sign of redemption points to the reason she needed to be redeemed. Her companion, the little black boy, whose genitalia like hers are masked, is the sign of unbridled sexuality, the monkey. But these images are also the fearful sign (generated within the fantasy of the colonialist white male) of the white woman dreaming of the black sexual experience. The fear at the root of the image is that of the male's loss of control over his own sexuality, represented as "wild" and "primitive" in its projection into the world in the icon of the sexual difference of the black. This fantasy of the power of the black male is, of course, the counterimage to the reality, the real power we have seen in the picture by van Couwenburgh (see Plate 83).

Parallel to this image of black male sexual aggressiveness, the black as phallus, at least in Paré's text, is the case of the Queen of Ethiopia, who had a "daughter of a white complexion, by her husband Hidustes, being also an Ethiope, because in the embraces of her husband, by which she proved with child, she earnestly fixed her eye and mind

The Figure of Hermaphrodite Twins cleaving together with their backs.

Anno Dom. 1486. in the Palatinate, at the Village *Robach,* near *Heidelberg,* there were Twins, both Hermaphrodites, born with their backs sticking together.

The Effigies of an Hermaphrodite having four hands and feet.

The same day the *Venetians* and *Genoeses* entered into league, there was a Monster born in *Italy* having four arms and feet, and but one head; it lived a little after it was baptized. *James Ruef* a *Helvetian* Chirurgeon saith he saw the like, but which besides had the Privities of both sexes, whose figure I have therefore set forth, *Page* 590.

PLATE 88. *The image of the hermaphrodite from Ambrose Paré,* The Works Translated out of Latin and Compared with the French by Th. Johnson *(London: M. Clark for J. Clark, 1678). Ithaca: Howard B. Adelmann Collection, Olin Library, Cornell University.*

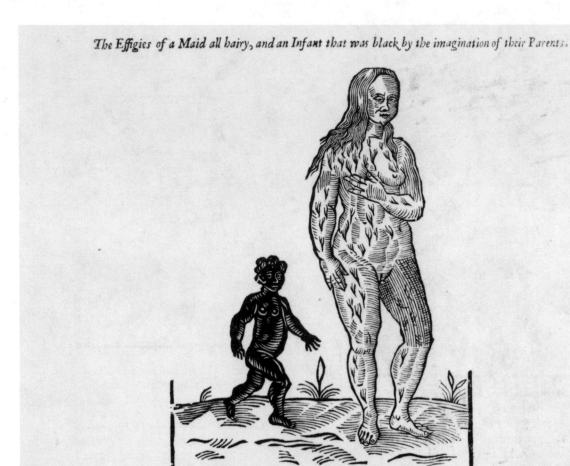

The Effigies of a Maid all hairy, and an Infant that was black by the imagination of their Parents.

PLATE 89. *The hairy woman and the black child from Ambrose Paré,* The Works Translated out of Latin and Compared with the French by Th. Johnson. *(London: M. Clark for J. Clark, 1678). Ithaca: Howard B. Adelmann Collection, Olin Library, Cornell University.*

upon the picture of the fair Andromeda standing opposite unto her." Blackness results from the black male's seduction (real or imagined) of the female white; whiteness from the sexuality of the black woman drawn to the beauty of whiteness.

The life of Paré's icon of black and female sexuality is quite extraordinary. For it reappears on the title page of the most famous sexual handbook in English history, *Aristotle's Master-piece*. First published in 1684, this text saw more than twenty editions in the eighteenth century alone.[19] Drawing on popular as well as medical literature on sexuality, *Aristotle's Master-piece* was the popular source for much contemporary knowledge of sexuality in late seventeenth- and eighteenth-century England. The first editions of this text bear a version of Paré's icon of deviant sexuality **[PLATE 90]**. The black child and hairy woman enter into the closed interior of the aged physician's world. He, the exemplary scientist, sits with his manuscript, and before his books, representing, as we shall see later in this chapter, not only masculine claims on sexual knowledge but specifically masculine knowledge about the nature of the dangerous and frightening aspects of female sexuality and its role in infecting the male with sexually transmitted diseases. For the image of the physician on the title page vignette is taken from the Renaissance portraits of the creator of the shepherd "Syphilis," the figure that gave the disease its present name. It is the portrait of Girolamo Fracastoro of Verona, who will be discussed later in this chapter. Beginning with a detailed, anatomically explicit exposition of "the parts of instruments of generation, both in men and women," these texts stressed the physical, not the psychological, reality of sex.[20] Sex, not love, was its topic. Its primary goal was to "display the secrets of generation," and it did so through images as well as words. The general thrust was moral, even though there was a considerable tradition of innuendo and bawdiness in versions of the book. The anatomical representation of the genitalia was based on the Galenic view of the homologous key-and-lock structures of the genitalia:

> Thus Nature does nothing in vain produce
> But fits each part for what's proper
> And tho' of different sexes form'd we be,
> Yet is there betwixt these that Unity,
> That we in nothing can a greater find,
> Unless the soul, that's to the Body join'd.[21]

This image of the balanced nature of the physical is contrasted to the origin of the teratoid malformation. The origin of the monster lies within the

PLATE 90. *The hairy woman and the black child as the frontispiece of* Aristotle's Compleat Master-piece . . . Displaying the Secrets of Nature in the Generation of Man, *twelfth ed. (London: The Booksellers [rep. in 1752]). Ithaca: Howard B. Adelmann Collection, Olin Library, Cornell University.*

sexual perversion of the woman: "Those monsters . . . not begotten by man but are the product of a Woman's unnatural lust and copulation with other creatures, shall perish as the brute Beasts by whom they were begotten, not having a reasonable soul."[22] The image of the black man and the white woman producing the black monster-child lurks behind this view. For having sexual relations with the black is analogous to having them with a monkey. It is the personification of the bestial, as found in Leonardo's

PLATE 91. *The woman, no longer hairy, and the black child as the frontispiece of* Aristotle's Master-piece: Displaying the Secrets of Nature in the Generation of Man *(London: The Booksellers, 1776). Ithaca: Howard B. Adelmann Collection, Olin Library, Cornell University.*

complex image, the bestial that reflects how sexuality was discussed and represented, as a force out of the control of the rational, of the human, and in the position of the animalistic, or the forces of evil. For here Paré's image of the sexual fantasy of the female as imagined sexual partner of the black male is exchanged for a male's fantasy of her as the actual sexual partner of the black male. The monster is the result of copulation, not of thinking about copulation. The black child and the sexually active woman, marked by her hairiness, Eve after the Fall, are exempla of a sexuality out of control.

But *Aristotle's Master-piece* echoes Paré in seeing the possibility of there being an imprinting of daily experiences on the fetus. Its anonymous author sees the future of the race as relying on the less than fully rational mind of the weaker vessel. And yet the woman is the same as or better than the male inverted:

> Thus the woman's secrets I have survey'd
> And let them see how curiously they're made
> And that, tho' they of different sexes be,
> Yet in whole they are the same as we.[23]

But the woman is not the same, for Eve is not *sapientia*, the rational faculty; she is the senses. She is thus the source of sexual dissimulation (as in the case cited from Hippocrates by Paré). It is this ability that could protect the women from the potential burden of bearing a black monster. For in the arms of her (black?) lover, she had but to think of her husband and the offspring would resemble him.

By the 1770s the frontispiece of *Aristotle's Compleat Master-piece* had begun to change. The black boy, with his hidden genitalia, and Mary remain, but Mary has shed her hair. She has become Eve before the Fall. The sign of her sexual deviancy is the presence in the image of the black child. The woman can "pass." She need only act like a "normal" female rather than a prostitute (to use Cesare Lombroso's categories, which we shall discuss in Chapter Ten) to be accepted within the world of the physician. But being visually "coupled" with the black child is sufficient to brand her as deviant. The icon of "enlightenment," the sun, shines over the scene [PLATE 91]. But the exemplary physician, Aristotle, still averts his eyes from these evolving signs of human sexual perversion. It is only at the beginning of the nineteenth century, when the little black boy vanishes, that Aristotle looks at the woman—with a double eye, his own and the Masonic sign for knowledge on the back of his chair. Now there seems to be no sign of her deviancy [PLATE 92]. The woman is now a Greek goddess admired by the scientific observer as the epitome of the beautiful.[24] But she is balanced in this tabulation of the "secrets of nature," the phrase written on the scroll, with the sign of mortality, the death's head and crossbones. The beauty of the female is, as we have seen, the sign of potential decay, a decay that not only is the result of human mortality but is due to the hidden implication of the "beauty" of the female. For beauty is merely the mask of corruption and infection. It is that which attracts the male and leads to his premature death. Deviancy and pollution remain central to the image taken from Paré, even in its seemingly altered form.

From the sixteenth century on, from Paré's construction of the icon of sexual deviance through the beginning of the nineteenth century, the significance of this image shifts. The debates about the abolition of black slavery that dominated British thought during the close of the eighteenth and the opening of the nineteenth century (slavery was abolished in Britain in 1811) made any use of the black as the image of sexuality unacceptable. The woman, who has already shed her overt mark of difference, her hairy coat, comes to represent the "beautiful" object, the object of the male's gaze and the cause of his eventual downfall. Paré's image of sexuality has moved from innate deviance, with its references to disease and bestiality, to death. This movement from Paré's initial icon of the deviant sexual to the representation of the female as the beautiful object does not represent, however, a shift in the inherent, phallic image of deviancy but in the representational function of the sign itself.

MODELS OF CONCEPTION
AND THE REPRESENTATION OF ANATOMY

The debate over the nature of conception reveals many of the implications inherent in the image of male and female sexuality in *Aristotle's Compleat Master-piece*. Harvey's epigenetic view, which is closest (but not identical with) our contemporary understanding of conception in no way dominated the seventeenth century.[25] The central discourse about sexuality that shaped the discussion of sexuality during the seventeenth century was whether the fetus was "preformed," that is, existed in its entirety in either the egg (ovism) or in the sperm (animalculism). Harvey's view, that the germ material acquired form gradually, beginning with the fertilized egg (epigenesis), was viewed as antiquated or simply wrongheaded.[26]

The debate about the nature of conception had its roots in antiquity. In Aeschylus's play *The Eumenides*, Apollo says:

Not the true parent is the woman's womb
That bears the child; she doth but nurse the seed
New-sown: the male is parent: she for him,
As stranger for a stranger, hoards the germ
Of life, unless the god its promise blight.[27]

Indeed, Plato and Empedocles saw the entire fetus present *in nuce* within the female seminal fluid as a tiny little homunculus that needed only the male semen to vitalize it. Paracelsus, on the contrary, held that this was exclusively true of the male's sperm: "let the sperm of a man by itself be putrefied in a gourd glass, sealed up, with the highest degree of putrefaction in horsedung, for the space of forty days, or so long until it begin to be alive, move, and stir, which may easily be seen. After this time it will be something like a man, yet transparent, and without a body. . . . It will become a true, and living infant, having all the members of an infant, which is born of a woman, but it will be far less."[28] The exception in the ancient world was Aristotle, who held, prefiguring Harvey in many ways, that the generative principle was present only in the combination of the male and the female, as Buffon stated: "The male semen is the sculptor, the menstrual blood is the block of marble, and the fetus is the figure which is fashioned out of this combination."[29] But by the end of the seventeenth century, preformation dominated all understanding of the nature of conception, and the real debate was between the ovists and the animalculists.[30] Although

William Harvey, in 1651, strongly advocated the epigenetic position, it was thinkers such as Marcello Malpighi whose preformist views carried the argument.[31] Harvey drew on the work of Hieronymus Fabricius of Aquapendente, who named the ovary (in the hen) but, rebelling against the facile Galenic parallels between animal and human anatomy, would not see its function in human reproduction[32] [PLATES 93–94]. Malpighi's science, that is, his close and accurate description of the development of the chicken embryo, should have made him into an epigeneticist, but the preformist blinders he wore precluded him from seeing the full implications of his own observations. For him, as well as for most of the biological and medical scientists of the time, fully formed human beings somehow preexisted within the egg or the sperm, needing only the vital force or specific context to enable them to become full-fledged human beings.

Following Anton van Leeuwenhoek's microscopic identification of the sperm in 1677, animalculism seemed to be established on the basis of perceived reality. For not only could the sperm be seen under the lens, but the scientific observer believed that the preformed fetus could be seen within the sperm. The microscope was the most advanced form of scientific observation of the time. Like the developments of all advanced scientific instrumentation from the Renaissance on, it was a means of heightening the perceptive ability of the highest and most rational of the senses, sight (and distancing of the object from the basest of the senses, touch). That which could be seen was real, and homunculi were seen.

Science gave the impetus to seeing the process of conception as merely the affirmation of existing form. It is perhaps predictably clear that the ovists, who understood the egg to contain the entire fetus, would see the influence of the female as predominant; the animalculists, the male. Some of the preformists, who saw the preexistence of the fetus within either egg or sperm, argued for a very specific type of "prenatal" influence. Chief among them was the Leyden physician Jan Swammerdam, who in his 1672 study of the structure of the uterus argued the theory of *emboîtement*—all organisms were divinely created at once, placed within one another, so that each original member of a species contained all future generations. "Even the foundation of original sin would have already been discovered [in embryology], since the entire human race would have been concealed in the loins of Adam and Eve, and to this could have been added

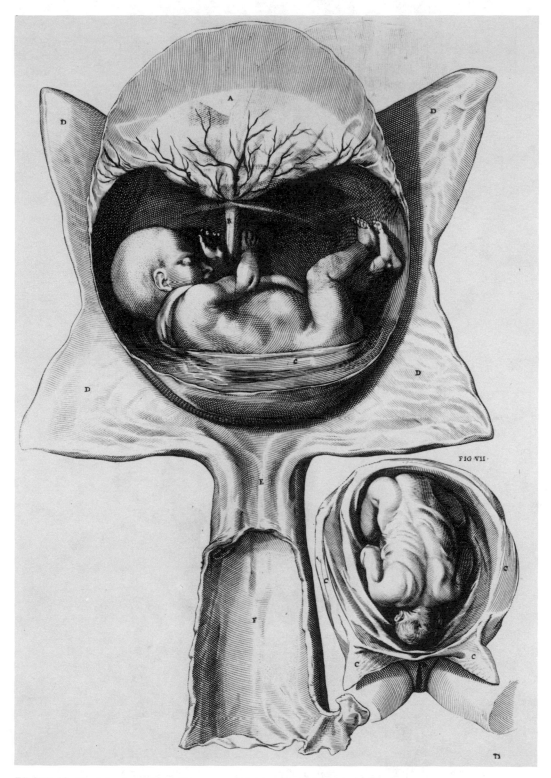

PLATE 93. *The fetus in situ from Hieronymus Fabricius,* De formato foetu *(Venice: Franciscus Bolzettam, 1600). Ithaca: Howard B. Adelmann Collection, Olin Library, Cornell University.*

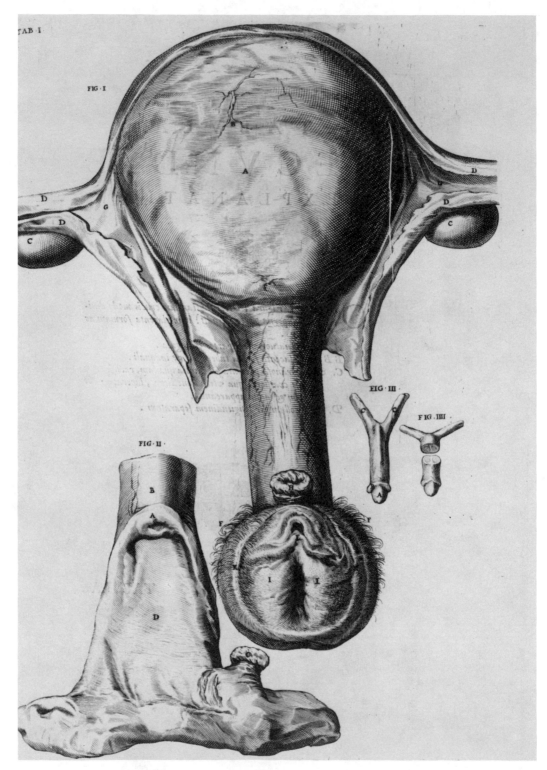

PLATE 94. *The female genitalia from Hieronymus Fabricius,* De formato foetu *(Venice: Franciscus Bolzettam, 1600). Ithaca: Howard B. Adelmann Collection, Olin Library, Cornell University.*

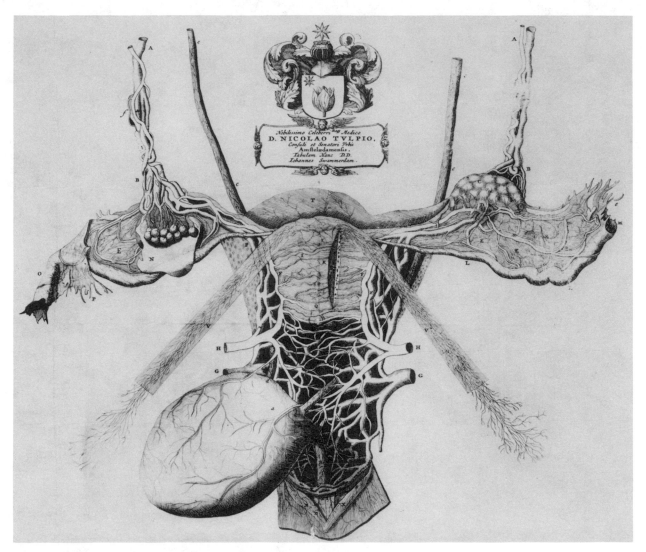

PLATE 95. *The female genitalia from Jan Swammerdam,* Miraculum naturae, sive uteri muliebris fabrica *(Rotterdam: C. Boutesteyn, 1679). London: Wellcome Institute for the History of Medicine.*

as a necessary consequence that when these eggs have been exhausted the end of mankind will be at hand"[33] **[PLATE 95]**. Swammerdam, contesting his contemporary Regnier de Graaf's discovery of the form and function of the human ovaries, saw them as more than merely the parallel to the ovaries of the hen.[34] The death not only of the individual but also of the species was sealed in the Graafian follicles, as the structure that de Graaf and Swammerdam described and that was eventually understood as containing the ovum came to be called. The finite number of ova was the major legacy of the Fall from grace.[35] Swammerdam, given all of this, should have been an ovist, believing that the

mortal, limited fetus is to be found in the egg, for indeed, was it not through Eve that the Fall was accomplished? But he also needed to hold to an understanding of the central role to be played by the male's seed. For St. Paul had argued (drawing a distinction between the views of the early Church and those of the Jews) that the descent is through the male, that the male parent supplied the seed, the female, the soil. Jews hold that descent is completely matriarchal. Swammerdam's theory of *emboîtement* articulated much of the ideological basis of the debate about conception. He returned the debate back to its theological underpinning but gave a quite different meaning to the genitalia.

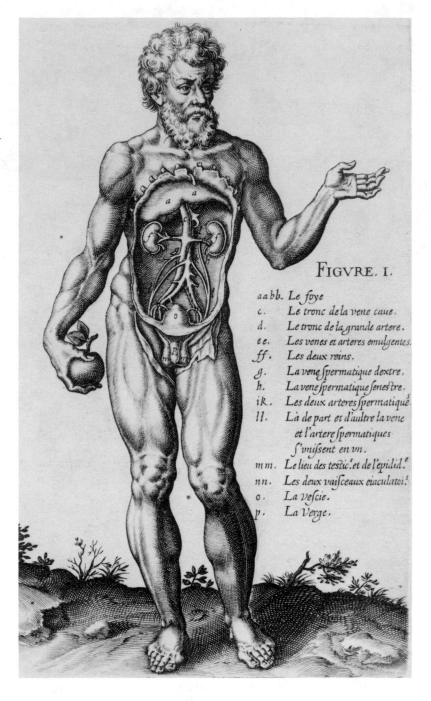

PLATE 96. *Adam's anatomy in an engraving attributed to Léonard Gaultier from Jourdain Guibelet,* Trois discours philosophiques *(Evreux: A. Le marie, 1603). London: Wellcome Institute for the History of Medicine.*

FIGVRE. I.

aabb. Le foye
c. Le tronc de la vene caue.
d. Le tronc de la grande artere.
ee. Les venes et arteres emulgentes.
ff. Les deux reins.
g. La vene spermatique dextre.
h. La vene spermatique senestre.
iK. Les deux arteres spermatiquē.
ll. Là de part et d'aultre la vene
et l'artere spermatiques
s'vnissent en vn.
mm. Le lieu des testic.̄ et de l'epidid.̄
nn. Les deux vaisceaux eiaculatoi.̄
o. La vescie.
p. La Verge.

It is therefore no wonder that, as late as the early seventeenth century, the conceit, present in a covert manner in Vesalius, of having the figures of Eve and Adam appear within the anatomical atlas continued. In Joudain Guibelet's 1603 atlas, Adam and Eve appear in engravings by L. Gaultier not as the representation of the external nature of the human being, a nature that could and would be redeemed by the soul, but as the viscera figures, specifically as the representations of their urogenital systems **[PLATES 96–97]**. The external sign of the Fall, the apple, reposes now in the hands of both figures, but as with the earlier tradition the external genitalia of Adam are exposed (and named), whereas those of Eve are covered, but covered with a branch taken from the tree of knowledge. The revelation of the nature of the male and the female at the moment of perfection (Adam's apple remains unbitten) pre-

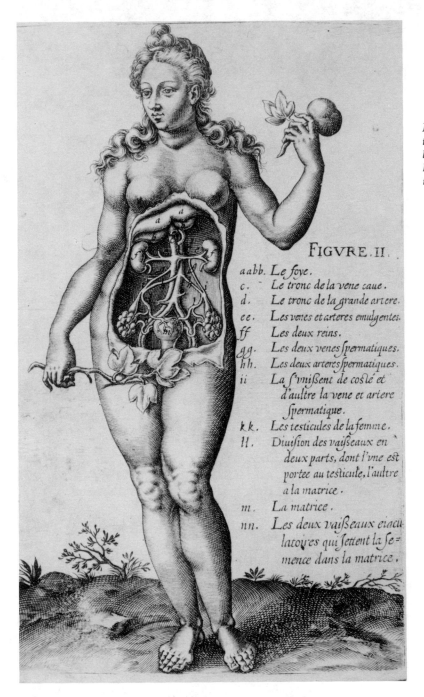

FIGVRE. II.

aabb. Le foye.
c. Le tronc de la vene caue.
d. Le tronc de la grande artere.
ee. Les venes et arteres emulgentes.
ff. Les deux reins.
gg. Les deux venes spermatiques.
hh. Les deux arteres spermatiques.
ii La s'vnißent de coslé et
    d'aultre la vene et artere
    spermatique.
kk. Les testicules de la femme.
ll. Diuision des vaißeaux en
    deux parts, dont l'vne est
    portee au testicule, l'aultre
    a la matrice.
m. La matrice.
nn. Les deux vaißeaux eiacu-
    latoires qui settent la se=
    mence dans la matrice.

PLATE 97. *Eve's anatomy in an engraving attributed to Léonard Gaultier from Jourdain Guibelet,* Trois discours philosophiques *(Evreux: A. Le marie, 1603). London: Wellcome Institute for the History of Medicine.*

sents the viewer with idealized types but types that place the female in the position of the seductress. The opening of the body reveals the perfection of God's creation at the moment before disease and death are introduced into the Garden. Because the viewers of this text were medical students, such a view presents to them the antithesis of their own experience, an experience of dissection of the bloated and putrefying corpses of criminals. Here we have the purity promised by God, which was never seen in the anatomical theaters of the Renaissance. Adam and Eve return the body to the Garden while foreshadowing the disease associated with human sexuality. But in a real sense the opening of these perfect anatomical figures, the origin of all of the finite number of preformed fetuses in the world, meant revealing the inner nature of the homunculus.

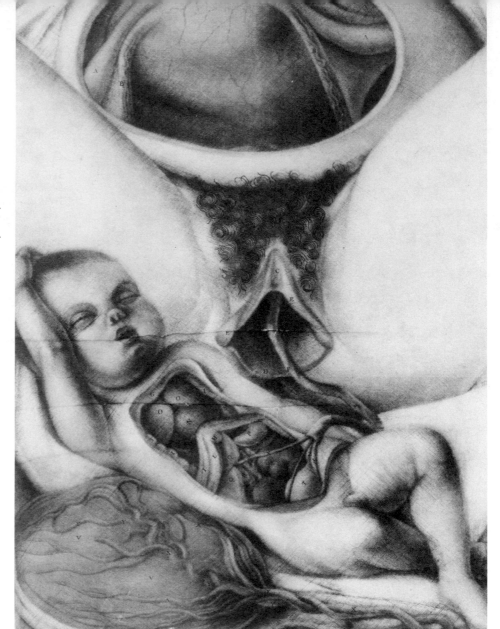

For the anatomical atlases of the age of mannerism presented at one and the same time images not only of perfection (and potential pathology) but also of the body as the microcosm. Nowhere is this clearer than in representations of the human body in the work of Jacques-Fabien Gautier d'Agoty (1710–81), who in the mid-eighteenth century articulated a version of the preformist doctrine in which he argued that the fetus, true and complete in all its parts, arose in the seminal vesicle of the male and was transferred to the female during coition[36] **[PLATE 98]**. Gautier (and later his son) provided a series of complex multicolored images of the fetus as found in the male semen. Later reproduced as colored prints, this was a series of simultaneous images, of the female and the male, in which all of the systems relate to the process of

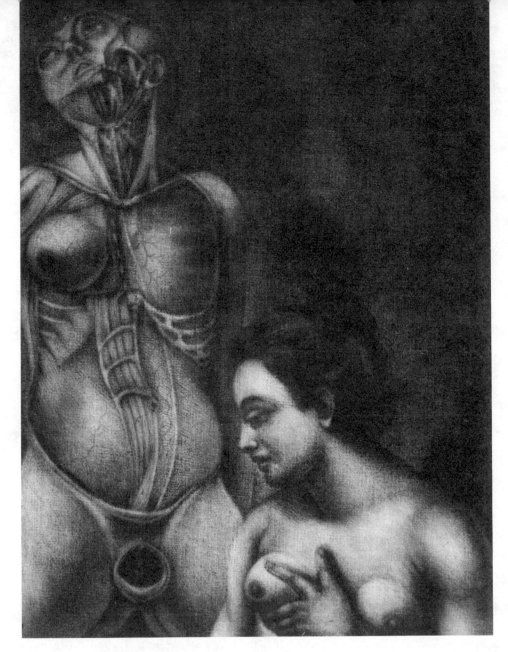

PLATE 99. *The breast and the vagina from Jacques-F. Gautier d'Agoty,* Anatomie des parties de la génération *(Paris: J. B. Bruned and Demonville, 1773). Ithaca: Howard B. Adelmann Collection, Olin Library, Cornell University.*

procreation. More than any other set of seventeenth- or early eighteenth-century images, these figures illustrated the process of preformist creation, from the homunculus through to the full-grown and reproducing adult. The use of four-color printing added a further dimension of verisimilitude to the representations **[PLATE 99]**. Suddenly the book was no longer only the world of black-and-white images, no matter how "realistic." It had become the source of "hyperreal" images that seemed to reflect further the sensory qualities ascribed to sexuality, the color and texture of skin and body. The female, holding her breast in the classic iconographic gesture of misericordia, becomes not only the female nursing but also the visual representation of the sensualized object of perception (an image that also has, however, pathological implications, as shall be discussed

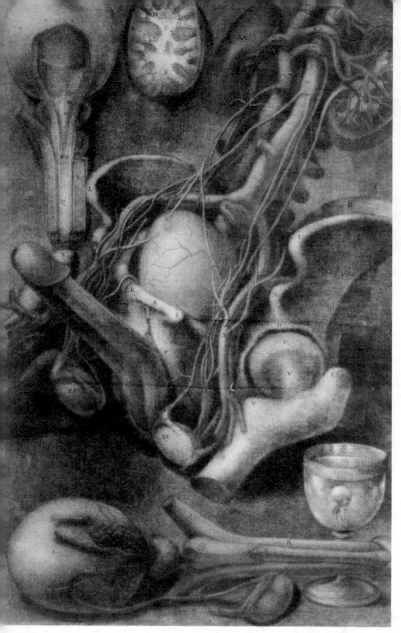

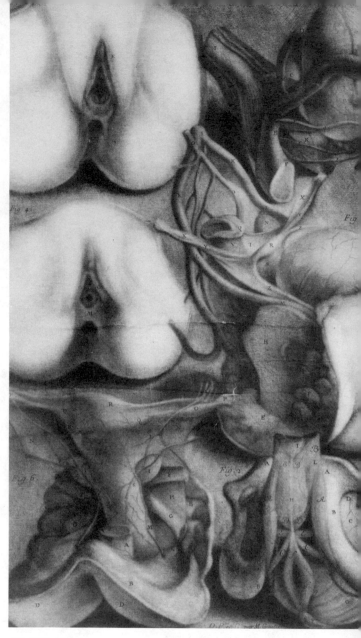

PLATE 100. *Male generative organs with homunculus in glass from Jacques-F. Gautier d'Agoty,* Anatomie générale des viscères en situation . . . *(Paris: Gautier, ca. 1752). London: Wellcome Institute for the History of Medicine.*

PLATE 101. *Female generative organs from Jacques-F. Gautier d'Agoty,* Anatomie générale des viscères en situation . . . *(Paris: Gautier, ca. 1752). London: Wellcome Institute for the History of Medicine.*

later in this chapter). The male is reduced to the erect phallus, whether in the plates representing the reproductive organs or those of the veins and arteries [**PLATE 100**]. What is striking is how the female also becomes reduced not to the Vesalian torso but to the position of the open genitalia, without legs or upper torso [**PLATE 101**]. This figure, the image of the "field" onto which the

homunculus is to be sown, becomes for the eighteenth century the central model of seeing and understanding the relationship between the masculine and the feminine. The rarity of the colored plate presents a greater awareness for the eighteenth-century "reader" or viewer of the function of sight in sensing the skin and the body [**PLATES 102–103**].

PLATE 102. *The vascular systems and deep muscles in an oil painting on canvas, by or after Jacques-F. Gautier d'Agoty, eighteenth century. London: Wellcome Institute for the History of Medicine.*

PLATE 103. *Gravidae in an oil painting on canvas, by or after Jacques-F. Gautier d'Agoty, eighteenth century. London: Wellcome Institute for the History of Medicine.*

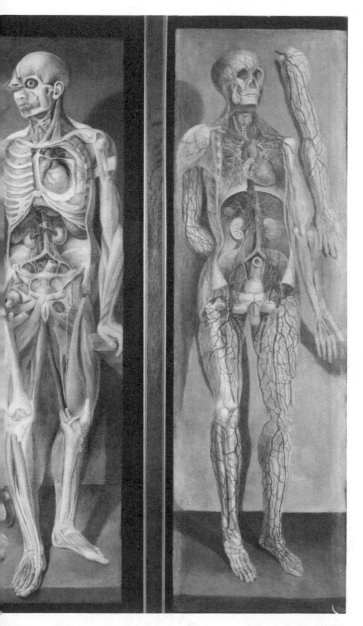

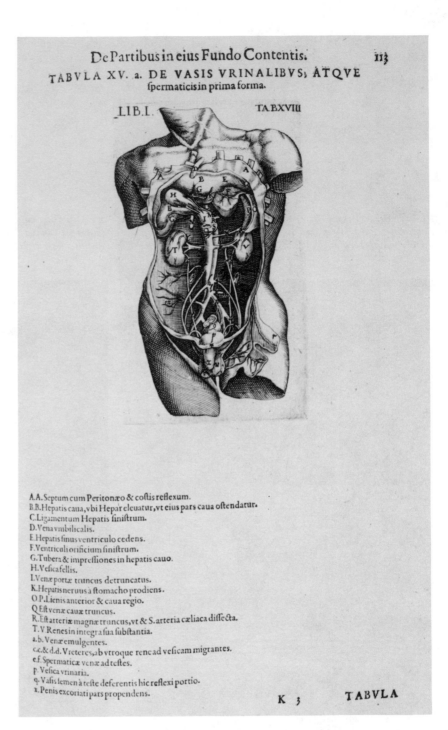

PLATE 104. *The Vesalian torso in quite a different context in an illustration by Robert Fludd and Johannes de Bry, from Robert Fludd,* Philosophia sacra *(Frankfurt: Officiana Bryana, 1626). Ithaca: Howard B. Adelmann Collection, Olin Library, Cornell University.*

If we refer not to Gautier and the mid-eighteenth century but to the opening decades of the seventeenth century and ask how the genitalia were represented within the anatomies, it is clear that the influence of Vesalius, as we have seen in the images taken from Guibelet, remained very powerful.[37] But although the images are related or, indeed, purloined from this sixteenth-century tradition, the context in which these images were read shifted radically. For the preformist–epigenesis debate, itself shaped by the new technology of the microscope, began to shift the implications of the relationship between the "seen" and the "unseen." The schematic representation of the genitalia pointed toward the hidden homunculus. And the homunculus pointed further toward the archaic past of the race, toward Eve, Adam, and the Garden of Eden. Indeed, in the work of one of the most speculative thinkers of the seventeenth century, the English Rosicrucian Robert Fludd, who proposed a Cabalistic Adam as

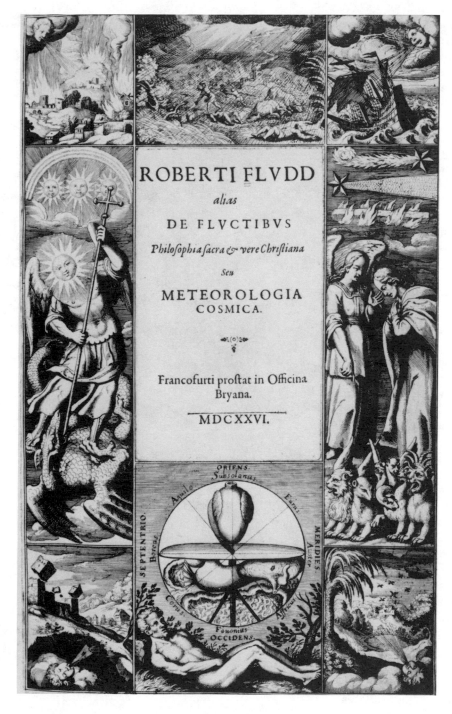

PLATE 105. *The title page illustrated by Robert Fludd and Johannes de Bry, from Robert Fludd,* Philosophia sacra *(Frankfurt: Officiana Bryana, 1626). Ithaca: Howard B. Adelmann Collection, Olin Library, Cornell University.*

the model for the universe, Vesalius's schematic image of the torso and the urogenital system reappears with great precision[38] **[PLATE 104]**. But these images are given a quite different set of meanings. The frontispiece to one of Fludd's major works, his *Philosophia sacra* of 1626, and further illustrations within it provide a rather different view **[PLATE 105]**. For Fludd, the human being is quite literally the microcosm, containing within him all of the universe and all of its history. Prior to the Creation, there existed a "divine hermaphrodite," composed of light and darkness. The Creation was the divine coition between these two aspects of the divine, between the heat and dryness of the male and the cold and dampness of the female. Adam and Eve were thus created to resemble these masculine and feminine principles that copulated to form the universe. First, the hermaphroditic divinity created Adam in its image. Adam was thus an androgynous being. Eve—the female part of the androgynous

Adam—was separated from him and given to him as a companion in the contemplative life. But Eve was inferior, her body dominated by cold and damp, and thus succumbed to the Devil's temptation. Fludd saw the original sin as double. First, it was an intellectual sin, a loss of innocence and the acquisition of the knowledge of good and evil. But it also led to a parody of the divine coition that created the world. And thus it led to the race of Cain. The title page of Fludd's work of the cosmography rests on Adam, the microcosmic man, an Adam represented in the position of the dead Christ, holding his hands between his legs. Above him lies the schematicized body of the human being, the heart, the source of knowledge, separated from the viscera, the source of emotions, and at the very bottom are the seminal vesicles. The natural history of the world, understood in terms of Fludd's "macrocosmic meteors," surrounds the image. Fludd is a mystic who sees the world very differently than Swammerdam with his microscope. And yet each sees the sexuality of the body as revealing the essence of the world. It is, however, a sexuality that is hidden within, within the nature of humankind, not overtly written in the external form. The title page of Fludd's *Utriusque cosmi historia*, his history of the macrocosm and the microcosm (1617) is explicit, placing Adam's phallus at the center of the universe [PLATE 106]. The outer circle of the chart represents the universe, and to this macrocosm is related the microcosm of man. At the center of all creation is the phallus, which links the Sun and the Moon; the traditional images, present in medieval paintings of the Crucifixion, represent the polar opposites between which Christ is sacrificed for the world.

The hidden, which had been the quality ascribed to the female, becomes in the course of the seventeenth century transcribed from a feminine to a human quality, but a quality still very much associated with human sexuality. Like Fludd, Adrian Spigelius and Julius Casserius in their 1627 anatomical atlas provide a catalogue of images taken directly or indirectly from the great anatomical atlases of the sixteenth century. The key-and-lock parallels of the penis and vagina are clearly made in their plates [PLATES 107–108]. The amputated torso of the female is seen as parallel to the amputated penis of the male. But their images of the reproductive systems in situ are quite different. Through the use of the torso, the female becomes her internal organs; her external genitalia remain hidden, are literally masked [PLATE 109]. The seemingly classical form of the figure, with firm breasts, is cloaked (as in da Carpi's sixteenth-century image [see Plate 49])

PLATE 106. *The title page from Robert Fludd,* Utriusque cosmi historia *(Oppenheim: Johannes de Bry, 1617). Ithaca: Howard B. Adelmann Collection, Olin Library, Cornell University.*

and placed in an idealized landscape. But the cloak, as we discussed in Chapter Three, is the secularized cape that Mary, the new Eve, uses to protect humankind in one of the most common religious representations of the Mother of God. Beneath her cape the field, the womb, upon which all humankind

PLATE 107. *The male generative organs from Adrian Spigelius and Julius Casserius,* De humani corporis fabrica *(Venice: E. Deuchinum, 1627). Ithaca: Howard B. Adelmann Collection, Olin Library, Cornell University.*

PLATE 108. *The female generative organs from Adrian Spigelius and Julius Casserius,* De humani corporis fabrica *(Venice: E. Deuchinum, 1627). Ithaca: Howard B. Adelmann Collection, Olin Library, Cornell University.*

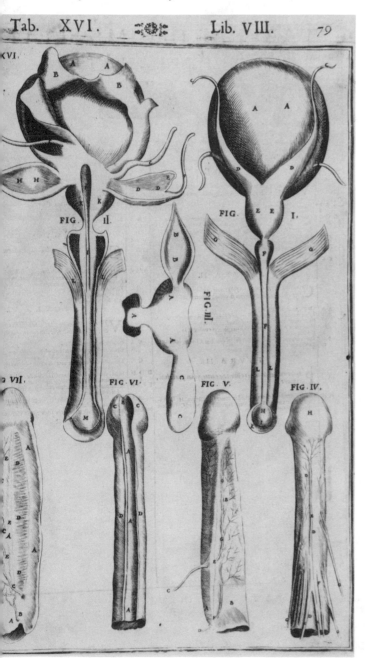

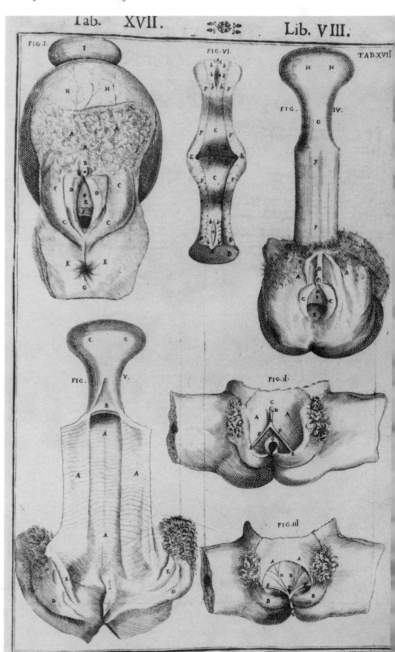

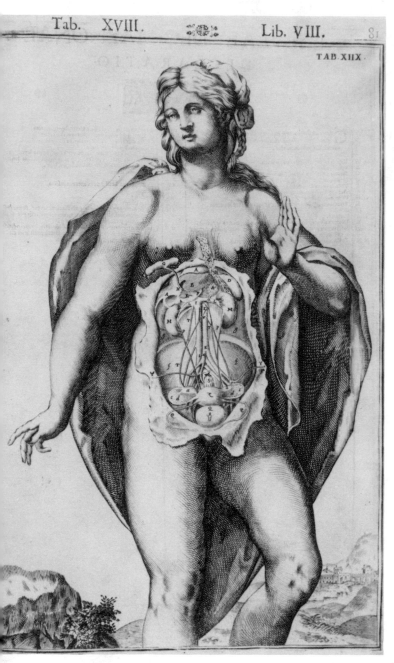

PLATE 109. *The female reproductive organs in situ from Adrian Spigelius and Julius Casserius,* De humani corporis fabrica *(Venice: E. Deuchinum, 1627). Ithaca: Howard B. Adelmann Collection, Olin Library, Cornell University.*

PLATE 110. *The male reproductive organs in situ from Adrian Spigelius and Julius Casserius,* De humani corporis fabrica *(Venice: E. Deuchinum, 1627). Ithaca: Howard B. Adelmann Collection, Olin Library, Cornell University.*

is grown, is to be found. Her position and very specifically the position of her hands are, however, those that we have found within the sixteenth-century anatomies of the male. They are not shielding the external genitalia; rather, they are raised in a partial exposure of the hand, as in the male figures based on the representation of the crucified Christ **[PLATE 110]**. The male, contrary to the traditions

of the sixteenth century, is placed supine, revealing the structure and form of the external genitalia. His hands are grasped in the manner of the female figures of the sixteenth-century anatomies, even though they are not covering his genitalia. This image is structured in a form that echoes the earlier images of female sexuality, such as that found in the work of Charles Estienne (see Plate 66). It is a

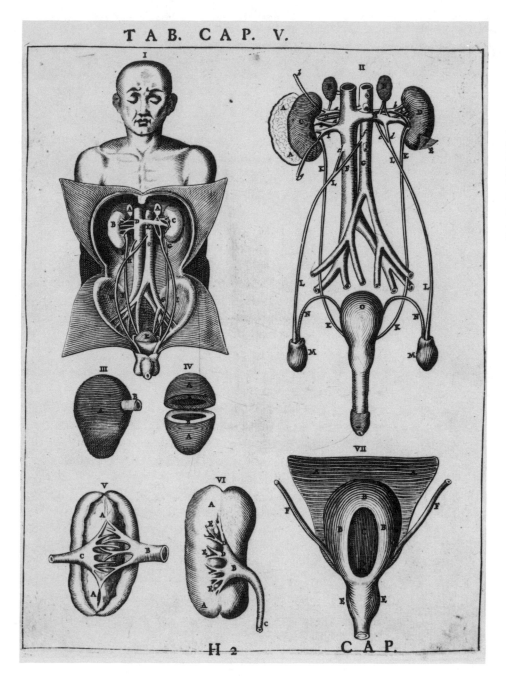

PLATE 111. The male generative organs in an engraving by Gerard Leonardo Blasio from Johann Vesling, Syntama anatomicum, commentarius (Amsterdam: Johann Jansson, 1659). Ithaca: Howard B. Adelmann Collection, Olin Library, Cornell University.

position of parturition. For it is the male within this system of representation who possesses the fetus.

Johann Vesling, in his 1659 systematic anatomical atlas, with illustrations by Gerard Leonardo Blasio, provided schematic images of "homunculi," that is, of models of the male and female that could be understood as the models for the fetuses hidden within **[PLATES 111–112]**. The technique creates a similar illusion as found in the flap images of the body (which will be discussed later in this chapter), with the torsos, especially in the image of the pregnant female, exposed to show the various layers of tissue. Indeed, the anatomical atlas, the atlas of the realities seen by the anatomists, becomes a cryptohandbook for the hidden world of the preformed embryo. The miniature images contained within the handbook could be seen as the hidden images of the homunculi. Central to these images was the question of the sexuality of the embryo. The connection between the genitalia and the process of conception placed the understanding of the genitalia at the center of the act of seeing the body.

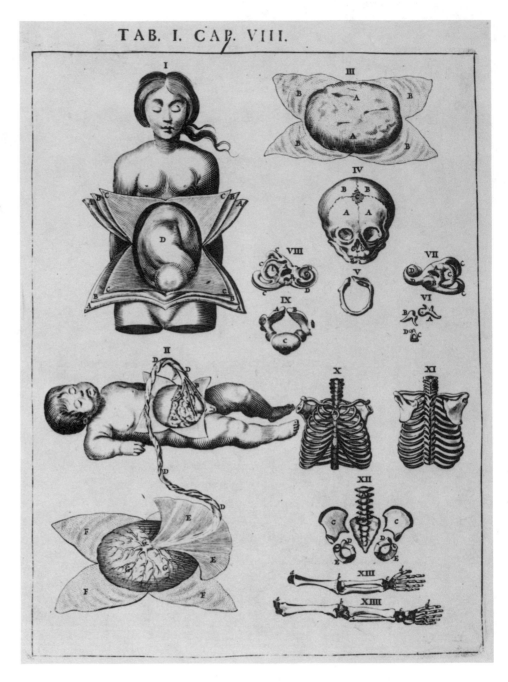

TAB. I. CAP. VIII.

PLATE 112. *The female generative organs in an engraving by Gerard Leonardo Blasio from Johann Vesling,* Syntama anatomicum, commentarius *(Amsterdam: Johann Jansson, 1659). Ithaca: Howard B. Adelmann Collection, Olin Library, Cornell University.*

The homunculi can be seen in the work of the remarkable Bartholin family of Copenhagen. Caspar Bartholin, the son, was the discoverer of Bartholin's gland, the lubricating gland near the vaginal opening.[39] Bartholin's discovery ended the classical speculation that the female sperm, the lubricating fluids, was analogous to the sperm of the male. Its origin was understood (incompletely, given our contemporary knowledge) to be from the vulvovaginal glands. These glands were not understood as analogous to the testes because the ovaries (the "female testes") already held that position in the conceptual structure of the genitalia. Thus the preformist view, which placed the fetus entirely within the powers of sexual generation of either the male or the female, also served as an answer to the collapse of the idea of homologous structures. For if one could not see the homologous structures in the genitalia, perhaps they were also lacking in the process of conception. The asymmetry of the structure of the genitalia served as visual proof of the potential for asymmetry in the origin of the fetus. There was no need to assume that male and female seed, now understood as inherently different, were necessary for conception, because the very structures of the genitalia from which they were generated were themselves inherently different. In Bartholin's anatomy, as well as that of his equally famous father, Thomas, these fetuses appear as fully formed homunculi attached to the placenta [PLATE 113]. The asymmetry of the structure of the genitalia reflects the hidden continuity of an older model of conception. All of these homunculi are male with the sole exception of the female figure on the top right, which reflects the older (and long abandoned) notion of the function of the seven-chambered uterus. These images repeat much of the iconography found in the figures of Spigelius's atlas. Indeed, the only difference is that the parts come to represent the whole. The male member is presented in an analogous position to that in the earlier text, and the female genitalia come to be represented in a schematic form that more or less reduces the external structure to an opening, a cave as in the images of the world before the Fall (see Plate 4). But implicit within these images are the underlying images of the power of the male genitalia. For all of these figures represent the erect and fully extended penis, a fiction given the realities of dissection. The erect male member is seen as the parallel to the vaginal opening, to the field, always open, always available, upon which the fetus is to be placed.

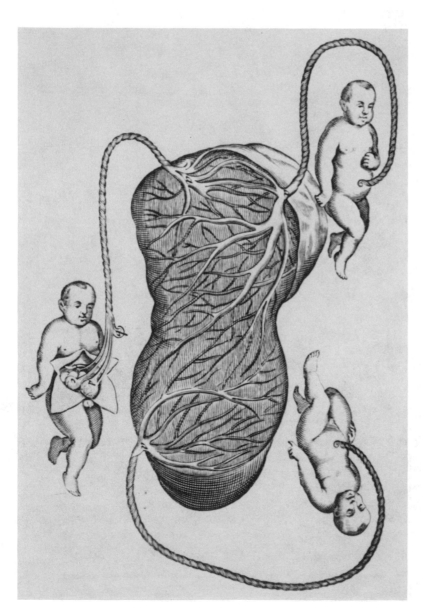

PLATE 113. *Homunculi and the placenta from Thomas Bartholin,* Anatome ex omnium veterum recentiorumque observationibus *(Amsterdam: Jacob Hackium, 1686). Ithaca: Howard B. Adelmann Collection, Olin Library, Cornell University.*

The male anatomist's readiness to open the female body is an analogy to the male's deep-seated desire to penetrate the female body. The sexual act, as depicted in the anatomies, is reenacted by the physician on the corpse of the woman, as can be seen on the title page of Thomas Bartholin's 1686 anatomy[40] **[PLATE 114]**. As with Vesalius, it is the female who is the object of investigation, and it is her lower body that is opened. The physician gesticulates toward the opening, his palm revealed, and the corpse itself points toward it, the hand in the position

PLATE 114. *The title page from Thomas Bartholin,* Anatome ex omnium veterum recentiorumque observationibus *(Amsterdam: Jacob Hackium, 1686). Ithaca: Howard B. Adelmann Collection, Olin Library, Cornell University.*

of that of the dead Christ. In Bauhinus's 1605 anatomy [PLATE 115], it is the male corpse itself that does the gazing.[41] In the anatomies of the seventeenth century, looking at the female body signifies the uncovering of the hidden as well as the opening of that which is forbidden. The hidden essence now lies within the male, not within the female. And one of the forms of the secrecy of the female body resides in the relative rarity of dissections of the female, as Frederich Hoffmann noted in 1694.[42] The "vein" man on the left of Bauhinus's title page,

engraved by Johannes de Bry, gazes quite intently at the pregnant woman, covering her genitalia and breasts in an icon of modesty. It is a modesty not of social convention but because she is but the vessel into which the homunculus was placed. Her nature, the nature of the field upon which the crop is sown, is depicted by her extended uterus; the male's nature by his hands, positioned so as to expose his genitalia, and his gaze, which is fixed on her.

In Spigelius's anatomy of 1627, the dichotomy between the male and the female is presented

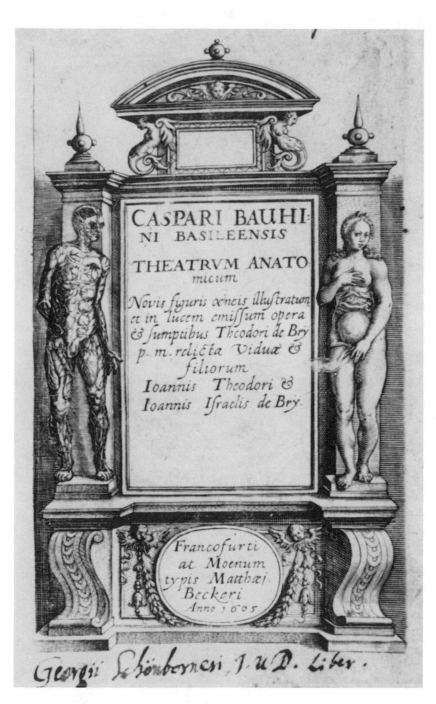

PLATE 115. *The title page illustrated by Johannes de Bry and Johannes Theodore from Caspar Bauhinus,* Theatrum anatomicum *(Frankfurt: Matthaei Beckeri, 1605). Ithaca: Howard B. Adelmann Collection, Olin Library, Cornell University.*

through a set of icons in which the female is portrayed as the superior. The superior figures on the page are the representatives of knowledge, and they are female, including Anatomia, the personification of the study of the body. Below them come the representations of the body, the muscle man and the bone man. The bone man expressly rests his arm on a spade, signifying death, the digging of the grave. Below them stand the representations of the animal drives, including that of sexuality, the monkey [PLATE 116]. Such a set of hierarchies points toward the finite nature of human existence, the bestiality of sexuality, and the tenuous grasp of reason. The shadow of the expulsion from Paradise is present in this image of systems.

The anatomies of the seventeenth century unveiled the body as a collection of systems, overt anatomical systems such as the veins and the womb but also covert systems such as those found in the

PLATE 116. *The title page from Adrian Spigelius and Julius Casserius,* De humani corporis fabrica *(Venice: E. Deuchinum, 1627). Ithaca: Howard B. Adelmann Collection, Olin Library, Cornell University.*

work of Robert Fludd. For circulating throughout the seventeenth century were images that functioned much like the ivory anatomical models discussed in Chapter Three (see Plates 43–44). These were paper models of the body that provided flaps that, once raised, revealed the hidden meaning of the body as well as its hidden structures. The motto of all of these is inscribed on the book represented in the first of them: "know thy self" [PLATE 117]. The best known are those by the German physician Johann Remmelin that present man and woman as the microcosm[43] [PLATES 118–121]. His foot is resting on Adam's skull (Plate 120), not merely the *memento mori*, because it is exemplified by the snake as well as the crucifix that accompanies it. His genitalia are the root of mankind and are covered by the fruitful plant. The Eve figure's genitalia are covered by the smoke that rises from the fire from which the phoenix is reborn. This image of spontaneous birth, the phoenix born out of its own ashes,

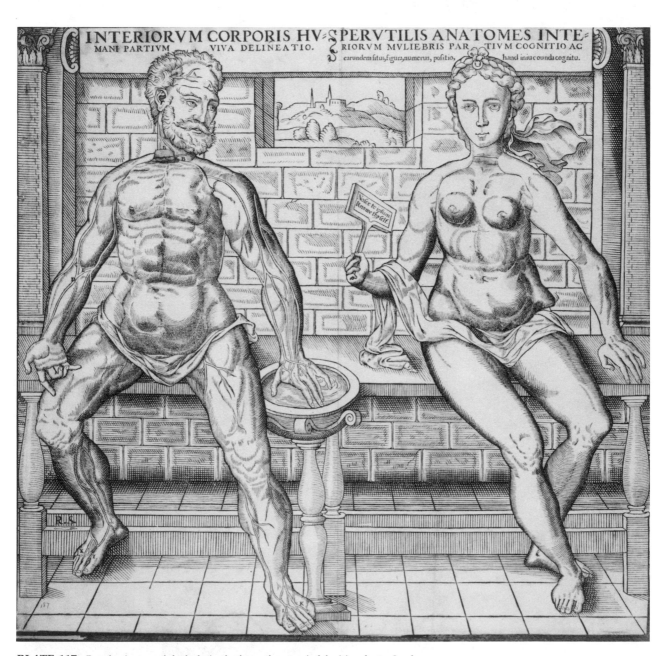

PLATE 117. *Popular images of the body in the form of anatomical fugitive sheets. London: Wellcome Institute for the History of Medicine.*

PLATE 118. *The male body reveals itself [primary level] from Johann Remmelin,* Catoptrum microcosmicum . . . *(Ulm: Sum pt. J. Gorlini, 1660). London: Wellcome Institute for the History of Medicine.*

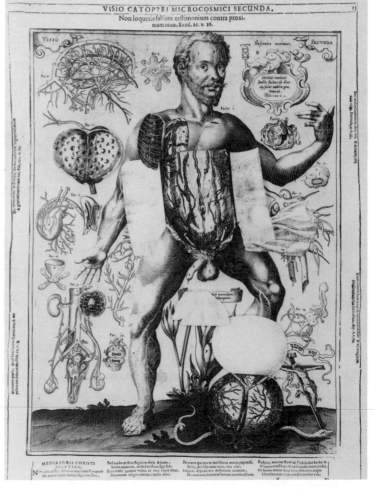

PLATE 119. *The secondary level of the male body from Johann Remmelin,* Catoptrum microcosmicum . . . *(Ulm: Sum pt. J. Gorlini, 1660). London: Wellcome Institute for the History of Medicine.*

PLATE 120. *The female body reveals itself [primary level] from Johann Remmelin,* Catoptrum microcosmicum . . . *(Ulm: Sum pt. J. Gorlini, 1660). London: Wellcome Institute for the History of Medicine.*

PLATE 121. *The secondary level of the female body from Johann Remmelin,* Catoptrum microcosmicum . . . *(Ulm: Sum pt. J. Gorlini, 1660). London: Wellcome Institute for the History of Medicine.*

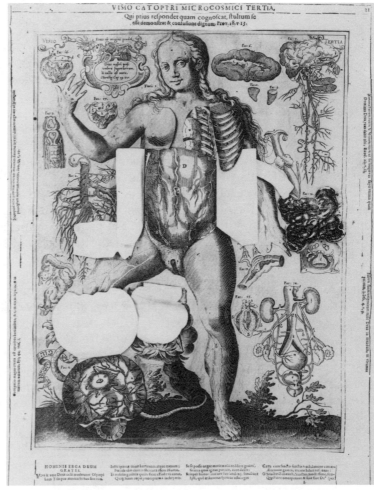

PLATE 122. *The title page from Johann Remmelin, Catoptrum microcosmicum . . . (Ulm: Sum pt. J. Gorlini, 1660). London: Wellcome Institute for the History of Medicine.*

as an analogy to the male providing the essential force for creation, points toward the female genitalia's function as the place of birth but not the origin of the fetus. There are fifteen flaps, some containing smaller flaps. The title page of Remmelin's atlas (1660) **[PLATE 122]** provides a purely theological context for his image. Christ and the devil confront one another at the top of the page, at the moment before Eve's creation, with the sleeping Adam between them. In the lower quadrants, the figures of knowledge, like those in *Aristotle's Master-piece*, are representations of aged men, with Adam's skull now functioning as their *memento mori*. But central to all this is the snake, which curls itself about the motto to the book, a quote from Ecclesiastes 10: 12 on the relationship between knowledge and honor. The serpent is evidently also the Edenic serpent. The boundaries created between male and female, between the "true" source of the fetus, the genitalia of the male, and its "mere" ground, the genitalia of the female, are absolute. Any violation of this boundary would be parallel

to the act of the seductive serpent and would lead to destruction.

These complex images are paralleled by an anonymous series of four images of the body and the genitalia, which are paralleled to the seasons and the ages of humankind **[PLATES 123–126]**. In the image of spring the figure of the half-formed homunculus is represented with children through the age of 14. That they are children is represented by the tiny, prepubescent genitalia of the upright, male figures. The image of summer has the womb of the female exposed; the male's genitalia are those of an adult, but the system that underlies it is that of the veins and arteries, as it is the blood that carries the heat to create the sexual urge. Autumn has the positions of the fetus within the uterus, and, so that there is no question what the origin of this fetus is, the male is presented with an erect and enlarged phallus, which opens to show its inner structure. Winter, of course, provides images of old age and death, with the female, however, bearing Adam's skull, the sign of seduction and collapse.

PLATE 123. *Engraving of the spring, an anatomical fugitive sheet showing seasons of the year and other scientific or moral matters; anon., n.d. [ca. 1620]. London: Wellcome Institute for the History of Medicine.*

PLATE 124. *Engraving of the summer, an anatomical fugitive sheet showing seasons of the year and other scientific or moral matters; anon., n.d. [ca. 1620]. London: Wellcome Institute for the History of Medicine.*

PLATE 125. *Engraving of the autumn, an anatomical fugitive sheet showing seasons of the year and other scientific or moral matters; anon., n.d. [ca. 1620]. London: Wellcome Institute for the History of Medicine.*

PLATE 126. *Engraving of the winter, an anatomical fugitive sheet showing seasons of the year and other scientific or moral matters; anon., n.d. [ca. 1620]. London: Wellcome Institute for the History of Medicine.*

PLATE 127. *Hidden oil painting by Sommonte on three layers of panel in box frame. The visible, outmost image is a still life of roses, n.d. [early nineteenth century], outside of first layer: roses. London: Wellcome Institute for the History of Medicine.*

The function of such images as icons of sexuality, of sexual development, of reproduction, becomes clear when they are understood within the tradition of the hidden erotic image of the sexual box within a sexual box. These images hung within the monk's cell or the scholar's study and were, at first glance, the representations of nature. A late eighteenth-century image may suffice to give one a sense of this process of revealing the unseen that existed in the popular culture quite parallel to these fugitive anatomical sheets **[PLATES 127–131]**. The opening panel is of the flowers of summer and is reversed to reveal the conflict between the aged and ugly female (death and winter) and the beautiful female (summer) accompanied by the male, phallus erect. The interior panel shows the fruits of autumn and is reversed to show a range of sexual positions; the final layer shows the sexual contact between a single couple. This set of erotic images places the figures not within the world of the bedroom, of coitus, but within the world of the neoclassical sexualized world, a world in which the phallus dominates as the sign of the sexual. The image of sexuality as part of a world of dynamic change, of growth and rebirth, is, of course, only hinted at in these images, which represent sexuality as a source of sensual enjoyment rather than reproduction. But here, too, the image of age, of the seasons, of the Fall from grace that introduced them, places the female at the center of images of altered and changing sexuality. It is the aged female who represents the Fall from grace, or at least, the shift from an aesthetic object to an unaesthetic one. But age, at least the aged female, has a second level of meaning—she is death incarnate, the source of disease. This potential may be hinted at in the representations of the male but is explicit in the representations of the female.

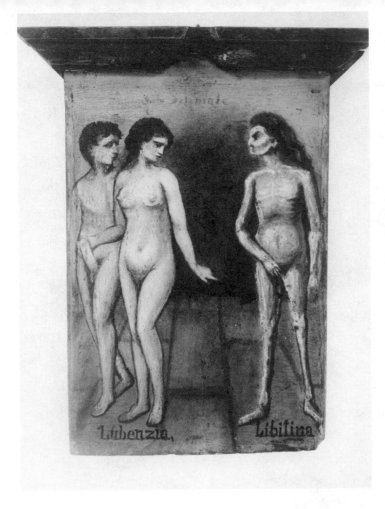

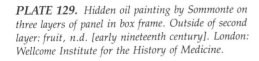

PLATE 128. *Hidden oil painting by Sommonte on three layers of panel in box frame. Inside of first layer: man, woman, death, n.d. [early nineteenth century]. London: Wellcome Institute for the History of Medicine.*

PLATE 129. *Hidden oil painting by Sommonte on three layers of panel in box frame. Outside of second layer: fruit, n.d. [early nineteenth century]. London: Wellcome Institute for the History of Medicine.*

PLATE 130. Hidden oil painting by Sommonte on three layers of panel in box frame. Inside of second layer: five erotic scenes, n.d. [early nineteenth century]. London: Wellcome Institute for the History of Medicine.

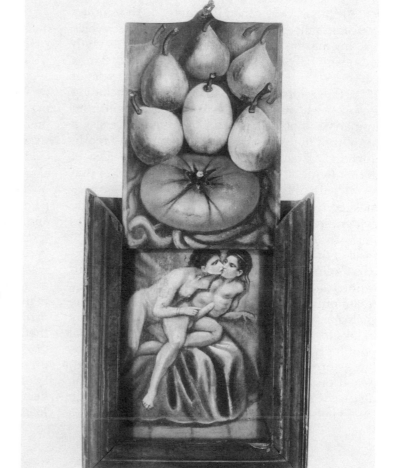

PLATE 131. Hidden oil painting by Sommonte on three layers of panel in box frame. Inside of second layer partly removed to show third layer, n.d. [early nineteenth century]. London: Wellcome Institute for the History of Medicine.

DISEASE, TEMPTATION, AND THE FACE OF THE MALE

By the seventeenth century, sexually transmitted diseases were ubiquitous but no longer as terrifying as at the perceived beginning of the epidemic.[44] People no longer died quickly from the disease. Indeed, it became recognized as a disease that would cause a lifetime of anguish rather than six months of torment and then the relief of death. Whether this was the result of the mutation of the syphilis spirochaeti and, therefore, a real change in the nature of the course of the disease, as has been argued, or whether European culture had become acclimated to the idea of syphilis and began to differentiate more closely its various forms cannot be judged. But the iconography of the disease also shifted during the course of the seventeenth century. "Syphilis," the eponymous Arcadian shepherd whose defiance of the gods caused him to be struck down with the disease that came to bear his name, had been created in a long Latin poem by the poet-physician Girolamo Fracastoro of Verona in 1530.[45] Drawing on the depiction of the plague in Lucretius, and prefiguring his own theory of contagion, Fracastoro created a mythic origin for the disease in the confrontation between man and the classical gods. Syphilis is a shepherd who chooses to offer sacrifices to his master, Alcithous, rather than the sun god. The scorned god afflicts the entire countryside, including Syphilis and his master, with a new disease. But this myth was eventually understood in terms of Fracastoro's "germ" theory. For in his essay *De contagione* of 1546 Fracastoro argued that disease, including syphilis, had its origins in the transmission from humans and objects of *seminaria* (literally *germs*), a term from the vocabulary of conception and reproduction.[46] Fracastoro's association of the idea of germs (with all of the sexual connotations of that term) with the sexual origin of the disease was masked by the mythology of his *Syphilis* but quite evident in the discussion on contagion. Central to Fracastoro's interest in the disease, indeed central to all of the discussions of the disease from its onset, was its cure. The primary cure during the sixteenth century, as in the seventeenth, was the mercury treatment. It is true that a rage for a new cure, the *guaiacum* wood (a tree—the iron tree—found only in the New World), appeared about 1517. The initial popularity of this treatment (with scholars such as Fracastoro and sufferers such as Ulrich von Hutten) rested on its benign nature. It was felt that if the disease was found in the New World then, through the belief in the existence of natural antidotes, a

PLATE 132. *The title page from Nicolaus Heinsius,* Schmachtende Venus, oder curieuser Trachtat vor spanischen Pocken. . . *(Frankfurt und Leipzig: C. Hülsse, 1700). Ithaca: Howard B. Adelmann Collection, Olin Library, Cornell University.*

quick and painless cure must also be found there. And the Fuggers, the great Augsburg trading family, which quickly created a monopoly for the wood, encouraged this view. Its only failing was that it was totally ineffectual. Part of the medieval pharmacy, it was mercury—a radical and dangerous therapy—that was proposed by the German physician Paracelsus as a cure for the new disease. It could indeed cure the disease in some cases but also could kill. Still, mercury came to be the cure of choice in the seventeenth century. On the title page of Nicolaus Heinsius's tractate on the cause and treatment of syphilis (1700), the mercury cure (portrayed as a type of punishment as well as cure) is represented by the vessel in which the patient was "cooked" in mercury vapors [PLATE 132]. The exemplary patient remains a male, and we see him in three stages, his face marred by the disease, first, being bled, then getting mercury treatment, and then on his deathbed. Johannes Sintelaer's image of 1709 presents the tortures of treatment even more graphically. And again the "leprous" male patient is to be found in the foreground, his rotting foot being chewed by a dog, itself a potent icon of disease, like a piece of dead meat [PLATE 133].

PLATE 133. *The martyrdom of mercury from Johannes Sintelaer,* The Scourge of Venus and Mercury, Represented in a Treatise of the Venereal Disease *(London: G. Harris, 1709). London: Wellcome Institute for the History of Medicine.*

PLATE 134. *The image of the shepherd Syphilis in Luca Giordano,* Allegory of Syphilis, *1664. Frankfurt: Staedelsches Kunstinstitut.*

Such images of the "realities" of treatment, the pain and the disfigurement of the disease and its cure, not portrayed in the early sixteenth century, greatly figure in the restructuring of the representation of syphilis as the exemplary sexually transmitted disease during the seventeenth century. In Luca Giordano's 1664 *Allegory of Syphilis*, one can judge the implications of the disease in the seventeenth century[47] **[PLATE 134]**. Central to this painting are two figures that make specific reference to the potential pathology inherent in human sexuality. The youth, the object of seduction, is at the center of the image, absolutely willing to yield to all temptation. Venus alights from her chariot, pressing her breast to eject a stream of her milk, and Bacchus's satyr pours his wine, both attempting to seduce him into the sweet life of idleness. Here the traditional figure of the Virgin Mary as *Maria lactans*, the nursing Mother of Christ and thus of all humankind, is made the emblem of excess and

nascent disease; the male Bacchus maintains his traditional role. This female figure is one that is closely connected to the anatomical representations of the female as found, for example, in Bartholin's anatomy (see Plate 114). It is the image of the female as simultaneously both mother and seductress.

The youth is protected by Minerva, whose shield repels Venus's sweet milk. Minerva, love's chief enemy, the rational mind, is present within the male, in the form of his *ratio*, shielding him, as long as he relies on it, from seduction and disease. Father Time, the other implacable foe of love, is present with his scythe, as the youth's other ally. For with the passage of time the object of his desire will fade, and she will reveal the ugliness beneath her beautiful mask. What is striking is the addition of a new, seventeenth-century figure—a homunculus floating within its globelike container that rests upon Time. This is not Cupid, who floats with his arrow above the scene, but a preformed fetus upon which Venus rests her knee. Here the associations in the preformist theories between conception and disease are explicitly made. The future is preformed, exists in its raw state, as do the forces, the senses, that drive the youth toward luxury. Venus relies on these prerational forces to overcome Time and the rational mind. But the rational mind is present in this world only in fully formed humans. It is indeed this factor that differentiates the homunculus from the human. The homunculus, like the monkey in the Middle Ages, serves as a sign of the link between Venus, the temptation of the senses, and the punishment inflicted when one capitulates to temptation—disease.

In the foreground, accompanied by a mangy dog, is a rudely dressed shepherd, who attempts to remove the youth's outer garments. He is Fracastoro's Syphilis the shepherd, bearing on his face the baleful consequences of imprudence. He is the representation not of the intense, quickly lethal form of syphilis to be found in the sixteenth-century images of the exemplary sufferer but rather the longer-term form of the disease that dominated seventeenth-century fantasy.[48] He is represented with a bone in his mouth, a visual reference to the caries

of the bones in tertiary syphilis. His hair has fallen out (syphilitic alopecia), and the bald spot is rimmed with sores; as Shakespeare notes in *A Midsummer's Night's Dream*, "some of your French crowns have no hair at all, and then you'll play barefaced."[49] His nose, its osseous structure destroyed, is a mere stump as seen in the images of the patient undergoing treatment in Heinsius and Sintelaer. And the dog is the traditional symbol of slothfulness, the "demon of acedia," the icon of melancholia.[50] Like other images of melancholia from the sixteenth century, the dog becomes associated with sexually transmitted disease. Syphilis is caused by luxurious indolence that leads to promiscuity and disease.

The image of sexually transmitted disease in Luca Giordano's image of lust and disease stood in a seventeenth-century manner of representing all of the dominant images of sexuality, from conception to disease, as interlinked within the same world. In an anonymous painting from the late 1580s after an engraving by Johann Sadeler, itself based on a lost work by Christoph Schwartz, presenting an image of the senses, seduction and disease are also linked **[PLATE 135]**. There Voluptas, wearing her horns, is seen playing a lute. Venus (and Cupid)

PLATE 135. *A Flemish copy after an engraving by Johann Sadeler based on a mid-seventeenth-century composition by Christoph Schwartz,* Warning against Venereal Disease. *Potsdam–Sanssouci: Bildergalerie staatliche Schlösser und Gärten.*

appear as statues in a fountain with Venus spurting water rather than milk from her breasts. This water eventually flows past the dog, the emblem of disease, who is seen fouling it, and the water is eventually drunk by Fracastoro's Syphilis, the shepherd. The figure accompanying the shepherd/hunter, the figure whose visage is already marked by the disease, is Ilceus, another victim of the disease, whose story, told at the climax of the second book of the poem, is used to illustrate the dangers of the mercury cure. Thus the viewer has two images of the disease, one associated with youthful male beauty, the other with the ravages of the disease on the face. Voluptas, in her medieval incarnation as the horned woman behind whose visage lurks sexually transmitted disease, age, and death, is a version of Kakia, the prostitute who attempts to persuade Hercules down the path of vice through her appeal to the pleasure of the senses in the traditional iconographic representation of the choice between sensual pleasure and duty that confronts every male. This legend has an extraordinary life in the Middle Ages and the Renaissance and becomes one of the standard means of representing the seductiveness (and potential danger) of female sexuality. For behind the temptress's beautiful mask is the origin of all disease and pollution, for Kakia is a prostitute, the source of disease. (The creation of the category of the *prostitute* provides a clearly differentiated boundary between the female as the source of children to carry on the economic well-being of the family and the female as the source of disease and the reason for profligacy, the expenditure of goods.) Kakia's horns, the horns of the bicornate uterus as well as those of the devil tempting St. Anthony, are here masked by her beauty[51] [PLATE 136]. It is the image of Voluptas, as a horned woman bearing Mary Magdalene's casket, which we have already seen in Lucas van Leyden's *Temptation of St. Anthony* (see Plate 72). Behind her beauty lurks death. Here the homologous nature of the two figures, Voluptas/Venus and Syphilis/Ilceus can be understood. For the beauty of the male will fade *because of* the beauty of the female; the seduction of the male will (in the present) lead to his downfall (through syphilis) just as it did in the past, in the Garden of Eden.

The figures in this image serve as a literal warning about the seductive power of the beautiful, for appended to the engraving on which this painting is based are three biblical references as well as a Latin poem. The biblical citations warn against the seductive woman whose husband is away (Proverbs 7) and admonishes the viewer (Proverbs 5: 15) to "drink waters only out of thine own cistern, and running waters out of thine own well." In the third citation, from Ecclesiastes 26, the good wife is contrasted with the bad: "An evil wife is a yoke shaken to and fro: he that hath hold of her is as though he held a scorpion" (26: 7). And the reader is warned what will happen if a "shameless daughter" is not kept "in straitly": "She will open her mouth, as a thirsty traveller when he hath found a fountain, and drink of every water near her: by every hedge will she sit down, and open her quiver against every arrow" (25: 12). These warnings against the promiscuity of women are translated into the danger with which such promiscuity threatens the male. The Latin poem that summarizes the image repeats this message, so that there is no misunderstanding possible:

Come here and join your limbs with me in a desirable embrace while my husband is absent, while there is no fear!
Let not the ways of the whore seduce you; but drink, alone the pure liquid from the proper source!
He who burns for Venus does the same as does he whom thirst compels to wet his mouth with whatever he finds first.[52]

The warning is spoken by the other figure in the image. Not Minerva but the image of the bearded scholar resting a book on his thigh in the position of the image of Aristotle in Raphael's famed *School of Athens*. This figure is patterned after the image of Girolamo Fracastoro as preserved in a series of sixteenth-century woodcuts (in his own works) and medallions. But we have seen this image elsewhere—it is the image of "Aristotle" on the various frontispieces of *Aristotle's Master-piece* (see Plates 90–92) as well as on the frontispiece of Bartholin's anatomy (see Plate 114). Not merely an aged, learned physician but Fracastoro himself, the creator of Syphilis, comes to represent the viewer in these images. A boundary is thus set absolutely between the knowledgeable healer and the victims, the creations of disease and those immune from it because of their position vis-à-vis the carriers of disease. The link between the image of Aristotle/Fracastoro and sexuality represents the boundary between the location of disease, among youth, among females, the sacrosanct line that is drawn between that world and the world of the aged, learned, male observer. This observer, because of his rationality, remains immune to temptation and thus to disease.

Temptation in the Sadeler/Schwartz image is

PLATE 136. *The icon of "The Choice of Hercules," engraved by Crispyn van de Passe the Elder taken from George Wither's* A Collection of Emblems, Ancient and Moderne *(London: R. Allot, 1635). Ithaca: Rare Book Collection, Olin Library, Cornell University.*

linked expressly to the senses. Voluptas sits next to a table covered with food and drink, playing her lute. Syphilis raises the water to his mouth with his hand, both tasting and feeling it. In the Luca Giordano painting, it is Bacchus, his childlike genitalia exposed, playing the lute, while one of his satyr helpers plays the tambourine. All of the temptations that could lead the youth astray are represented by the senses—the lute, for hearing; wine, for taste; Minerva's as well as Venus's breast, for

sight. But disease here is signified by the sense of touch represented by the shepherd, whose hand reaches for the youth's garment, as well as by the satyr's hand that grasps his arm. Touch is the exemplary sense associated with sexuality because it is the only sense in which there is an unmediated direct contact between the individual and the world. And it is exemplified by the organ of touch, by the skin, upon which the icons of sexually transmitted disease, the boils, lesions, and buboes, are inscribed.

TOUCH AND SEXUALITY

By the seventeenth century, the fantasy of "seeing" the sense of touch had already become a commonplace within the tradition of the visual representation of the senses. Following the Renaissance, the sexualization of the representation of touch, with its linkage of pain and pleasure, the material and the transcendental, becomes part of the standard repertoire of systematic images of the macrocosm (along with the seasons, the ages of man, etc.) in the fine arts.[53] Within the tradition of the emblem, touch, as part of the model of the five senses, becomes a standard aspect of the repertoire of icons. Touch, as we have seen in the Cluny tapestries (see Plate 19), is traditionally female and traditionally sexualized. In the Renaissance, touch and Eros are closely related. In two images by Agnolo Bronzino, from the first half of the sixteenth century, we see Venus holding Cupid's arrow.[54] In the first image (1546) Cupid moves to seduce her but does not touch her [PLATE 137]. In the second image, it has reached the point in his seduction where he is touching her [PLATE 138]. In the first image, sexuality is still held at bay, in the process of Cupid's seduction of Venus. In the background lurks a dark figure.[55] It is a male in the prime of life, his skin darkened. In the second image, in a pose redolent of pain and distress, he presses his hands to his head. His eyes are reddened, and we observe that he has lost some teeth. His fingers are swollen, and his hair, falling out in clumps, lies loose on his right shoulder and upper arm. It is the *morbus gallico*, Syphilis the shepherd, present in the background of the seduction of Venus. And it is a *black* Syphilis. For, at least in the Latin tradition, syphilis (like leprosy) was understood to turn one black, the syphilitic *rupia*. Francisco Lopez de Villalobos, court physician to Charles V, in his long poem on syphilis of 1498, observes that the "color of the skin becomes black" when one has the "Egyptian disease," the plague of boils recounted in the account of the Jews' escape from slavery.[56] Blackness marks the sufferer from disease, sets him outside of the world of purity and cleanliness.

In the second image, the one of direct contact, the erotic touch on the breast, Venus holds the apple, not merely the apple of the Hesperides but also the apple from the Tree of Knowledge. It marks the lascivious kiss and wanton embrace of mother and son, of Venus and Cupid. Present within the image, once the touch has occurred, are signs of vice and lechery. The mask of beauty, so familiar from the appearance of Kakia, but also the masks of age and disease, lie at the feet of the beautiful

PLATE 137. *The moment before the contagion spreads in Agnolo Bronzino,* Venus, Love and Jealousy, *1546. Budapest: Szépmüvészti Museum.*

creature with the clawed feet who offers pleasure in the form of the honeycomb—and at the left, the sting of the scorpion. In the second image, we have, in addition, Venus's cuckolded husband, the fire god Hephaistos. Immoderate, promiscuous, dangerous sexuality is linked to touch, disease, and deception in these two images. And the transition between the senses, images of sexually transmitted disease, and the images of race and sexual deviancy seen in other contexts, is found, and not only within Bronzino's work.

PLATE 138. *The moment of contagion in Agnolo Bronzino,* Venus, Cupid, Folly and Time, *ca. 1545. London: National Gallery.*

PLATE 139. *The black musician in Titian,* Venus and the Organ Player, *ca. 1550. Berlin: Staatliche Museen Preußischer Kultur/Dahlem: Gemäldegalerie.*

In Titian's *Venus and the Organ Player* (1550), of which there are many versions (some with organ, some with lute), the association between the world of the senses, sexuality, and touch adds a further dimension. It is evident that these pictures all serve as comments on the role of the various senses in the act of seduction.[57] For we again have Venus and Cupid in much the same iconographic position as in Bronzino, with Eros's hand on Venus's breast[58] **[PLATE 139]**. There are six versions of this painting, and in only one does Cupid rest his hand on (rather than near) Venus's breast. And in that one version the musician is clearly black. He also serves as the sign of promiscuous sexuality, in his role as the observer, the signifier that immodest sexuality is taking place. He is represented as playing the organ (with all of the puns associated with this phrase), but he also creates sound that reaches the body in immaterial form. What is represented is the incitement of the senses without direct, physical contact between the players. It is this translation of the sufferer from syphilis as black into the image of the black as the source of the sensuality that leads to

the representation of disease presented within Titian's image. The link of the sensual (with all of its intimation of disease and the exotic) becomes the manner of representing sexuality within the Italian sixteenth-century tradition.

Within the new tradition of the emblem books in the late sixteenth century, there is a radically altered association, that between the feminized touch and pain. Touch is most often represented by an image of the woman bitten or pierced by a wild animal. This is analogous to the wise and aged male's cutting open of the body of the dead prostitute (the source of the male's pain) that exemplifies the opening of the female body in the frontispieces to many of the anatomies of the period. The pleasure of the sense of touch, the sense of the sensual and the sexual, which is clearly part of the medieval representation of touch, is initially unrepresented in the northern world of Dutch Protestant emblems. In the sixteenth century, Hendrick Goltzius (1587) **[PLATE 140]** and Frans Floris (1561) **[PLATE 141]** helped establish this tradition in their representation of touch within their series of the five senses.[59]

PLATE 140. Hendrick Goltzius, Touch, *a copperplate engraving from a series of the five* senses, 1587. Ithaca: Private collection.

TACTVS SENSORIVM PER TOTVM CORPVS EXPANSVM EST AC PROINDE ETIAM EIVS ORGA

PLATE 141. *Frans Floris's image of Touch in an engraving (1561) by H. Cock. Ithaca: Private collection.*

(Note the abandoned boat in Floris's image. We shall see it again soon.) In 1611, Cesare Ripa, the great Italian emblemist, in what comes to be the major handbook of icons, discusses touch solely within the tradition of the painful[60] **[PLATE 142]**.

The animal bite—either falcon or snake—comes to represent for the early emblem tradition the sense of touch, even for artists as complex as Caravaggio, as has been discussed already in Chapter Two. With Caravaggio's image of the young boy being bitten

by a lizard **[PLATE 143]**, of course, the homoerotic aspects of the image are overt specifically because he works against the tradition of having the painful touch, the equivalent of penetration, exemplified by a female figure.[61] For Caravaggio, touch, at least touch as exemplified by pain (and, as we shall see, by sexuality), is male. But in all of these images and counterimages, pleasure, or at least sensual sexuality, seems to have vanished or been sublimated.

PLATE 142. *Cesare Ripa's image of Touch from an early French edition of his emblem book* Iconologie, ou, Explication nouvelle de plusieurs images, emblèmes, et autres figures hyerogliphiques *(Paris: Chez M. Guillemot, 1644). Ithaca: Rare Book Collection, Olin Library, Cornell University.*

PLATE 143. *The male responds to the painful touch in Caravaggio,* Boy Bitten by a Lizard, *1594. Florence: Fonazione Longhi.*

PLATE 144. *The erotic touch becomes domesticated in Dirck Hals,* The Five Senses, *1624. The Hague: Koninklijk Kabinet van Schilderijen.*

PLATE 145. *The image of the senses as a social event in Louis Finson,* Happy Party (Allegory of the Five Senses), *1737. Braunschweig: Herzog Anton Ulrich-Museum.*

PLATE 146. *Food as the context for the senses in David Teniers's mid-seventeenth-century* Merry Company at the Table. *Brussels: Musée des Beaux-Arts d'Ixelles.*

But although the emblem books place pain, the pain associated with penetration (and disease) in the forefront, the intimation of the erotic, the touching of the Other, is domesticated in the Northern Protestant tradition by Dutch genre painters such as in the 1624 painting by Dirck Hals **[PLATE 144]** as well as those by Louis Finson **[PLATE 145]** and David Teniers[62] **[PLATE 146]**. All of these images represent the world of the senses as social affairs, as parties in which the erotic is present but marginalized. In these three images, the representation of the erotic is literally reduced to a heterosexual kiss but not a heterosexual touch. The hand, the exemplary organ of touch, is never sexualized, which signifies that the body remains inviolate and untouched. In this world, all fear of disease and deviance is banished, and the sense of touch is placed within rigid boundaries. One may kiss, but one may not fondle. But touch also serves in this world of images as the common sense—all of the individuals represented are touching, if not one another, then objects within the world. And this universalization works to counter the sexual associations inherent in the representation of touch. What is missing is the heightened sense of the proximity of touch, an image that provides some of the hidden tension for these images. It is not merely that these individuals interact in a heterosexual world whose link is the seeing or hearing of the Other; they all interact through touching, but overtly not through the erotic touch. Touch in this Dutch Protestant tradition is desexualized, but in this desexualized form it points even more strongly toward the powerful tradition of the sexualized touch that it attempts to neutralize.[63] This is to be seen in a contemporary allegorical image of the senses, that of Hendrik van Balen **[PLATE 147]** in which Touch is represented in the traditional manner by the bird's bite (and the feel of the turtle's shell), but the response is clearly not pain but pleasure, the erotic present subliminally within the tradition of the painful.

At the very end of the sixteenth century, Crispyn van de Passe the Elder, in a more complex series relating the five senses to the four seasons, places

PLATE 147. *The social environment becomes the classical stage scene for the image of the senses in Hendrik van Balen's mid-seventeenth-century* Allegory of the Five Senses. *Karlsruhe: Staatliche Kunsthalle.*

the sense of touch equivalent to summer **[PLATE 148]**. Touch, in the emblem books always represented as a woman, her firm breasts bared, is about to be bitten by the falcon; she strokes the turtle that is part of the standard tactile image in the earlier emblematic tradition. To our right, a crude heterosexual seduction scene is taking place. The rude clothing of the two participants points toward a lustful Arcadian tryst.[64] (Sexuality is permitted in the "unreal" world of the Dutch iconographic emblem as it is banned from the "realism" of Dutch genre painting.) To our left, Christ is converting Peter, who walks toward him in the sea (which explains the abandoned boat in Floris's earlier emblem). Most important of the signs in the foreground are the figures of a lizard, the fabled salamander, and the scorpion at Touch's feet. The magical salamander is able to survive "the consuming flames of amorous fire."[65] The fire is both lust and disease.

And this is Caravaggio's reference. The youthful fear of penetration in his image is transferred to the young male, whose fear is of both the act of penetration and sexually transmitted disease.

The scorpion, as we have seen, is the zodiacal sign that rules the male as well as the female genitalia. The primary references of Touch are overtly sexual. For the lying, base nature of the scorpion's appearance denies its hidden, destructive potential. It is thus merely a woman (such as Kakia) in another form, carrying in its tail the sting of sexually transmitted disease, as in the citation appended to the image of syphilis cited earlier in this chapter from Ecclesiastes 26. But the scorpion is, as we discussed in Chapter Two, also the sign of the Synagogue (as opposed to the Church). With the visual reference to Simon's conversion to Peter, the Jew's conversion to a Christian, placed parallel to a scene of Arcadian or primitive sexuality, the double referent of the scorpion, this image evokes one of the hidden messages in the icon of touch, the difference of the Jews' sexuality (exemplified through the image of the circumcised penis) as a marker of their separateness from Christ. It is through a specific form of touching, through baptism, that conversion takes place and the damaged is made whole. Van de Passe's image makes reference to these iconographic traditions, with the image of the conversion of the Jew Simon to the apostle Peter and with the crude sexuality of the Arcadian woods. Even though the image of the touch remains central to his image, the restitution of human sexuality to its higher Christian form is the subtext of the image. But through this the erotic had to be connected with the religious. Thus the primary references of Touch in this image are sexual but ambiguous. For the male–male relationship of Christ and Peter is not exalted over the crude heterosexuality of Arcadia. The sign of the scorpion points toward the earthly nature of Christ's sexuality, which is, however, on a far superior plane to that of the gross heterosexual act of Arcadia, with its hidden motif of the illness of the shepherd Syphilis.

PLATE 148. *Crispyn van de Passe the Elder,* The Seasons and the Senses, *engraved in Cologne between 1594 and 1610. Ithaca: Private collection.*

PLATE 149. *The erotic touch becomes overt in Cornelius Drebbel,* Touch, *ca. 1596. Ith-aca: Private collection.*

By the close of the seventeenth century, the image of touch seems to have become one with the heterosexual erotic; the contradictory subtext of van de Passe's image on the superiority of male–male bonding had been suppressed as the image became secularized. The feminine figure of Touch in Cornelius Drebbel's engraving **[PLATE 149]** becomes the object of seduction, and in a seventeenth-century French moralizing engraving by Abraham Bosse, the act of touching is the predecessor of seduction **[PLATE 150]**. The placing of the icon of touch, the woman, in the bedchamber, with the bedclothes being drawn back, points toward a Richardsonian view of the role of the senses in the male's seduction of the female. It is the incorporation of the icon of coitus, the bed, with the act of seduction, exemplified by the touch. Indeed, the painting that adorns the back wall is of Amor and Psyche, a theme that becomes inherently entwined with the sexualization of the representation of touch in the following century. It is the image of the male's seduction (and penetration) of innocence. This fantasy is necessary to create a boundary between the pure (i.e., uninfected) object of desire and the sexually polluting female. The touch of the male, the sign of seduction, makes the female into the pure object; her seductive touch (as in the figure of Kakia) makes her into the diseased seductress—the succubus.

PLATE 150. *The erotic touch in the bedchamber as a seventeenth-century line engraving by Abraham Bosse,* Tactus, le Touche, *an allegory of the sense of touch (Paris: Tauermeier, n.d.). London: Wellcome Institute for the History of Medicine.*

PLATE 151. *The erotic touch as satire in Thomas Rowlandson's eighteenth-century* The Five Senses. *Ithaca: Private collection.*

Thomas Rowlandson, in the mid-eighteenth century [PLATE 151], ironically recognizes this domestication of the sense of touch in his satiric print of the five senses, in which *feeling*, with all of the multiple associations of that term, is abetted in its seduction of the female by the other senses. All of the senses are subordinate to feeling, and all aim toward the seduction of the female. The traditional feminization of Touch is thus made possible because of the implicit shift from the female touching to the female being touched. The touched female becomes the icon of the object of desire, a desire stimulated by and through the senses. And the male touching becomes the image of the touch that does not hurt, the touch without disease. The banishment of pain from these images is a banishment of both the projected pain of the male (the acquisition of sexually transmitted disease) and the pain associated with defloration (the only heterosexual coital act in which disease was viewed as impossible). But hidden within the seduction of the pure female through the sense of touch is a further indicator of the association of touch with inferior femininity. For Touch is a sign of the inferior senses, of the nonrational aspects of sexuality. It is also the source, for the male observer, of both pleasure and pain, both coitus and disease. Touch becomes the exemplary means of representing the complexities of sexuality, a sexuality written on the skin. For the potential of a disease that is exemplified by the state of the skin is linked to the organ of seduction—the skin. The image of touch thus becomes part of the repertoire of images that deal with the body and illness in the seventeenth and early eighteenth centuries.

CHAPTER SIX

The Representation of Sexuality during the Enlightenment

MONSTERS

During the closing decades of the seventeenth century, the representation of the sexual and the sexualized individual shifts within the group fantasy that truly thought it saw fully formed homunculi on the microscope slide. These tiny misshapen humans had the potential to become fully formed human beings, males and females, or to become monsters. And sexual monsters at that. Yet the visual patterns of the great anatomical atlases are present and shape the perception even of these monsters. Although one could interpret the images of human sexuality in the anatomical atlases of the late seventeenth and early eighteenth centuries as merely schematic presentations of the form of sexuality echoing the Vesalian manner of representation, they are also highly ornamental [PLATE 152]. Nowhere is this more clearly presented than in Frederik Ruysch's 1691 representation of the skeletons of the monstrous homunculi, engraved by Cornelis Huyberts, which so fascinated Paré and his contemporaries.[1] But their geographic location is not Africa, it is within the female. It is in the wilderness of feathered and besnaked fetuses, of the moles, calculi, and tumors that appear in his plates. It is an Africa of the spirit.

The association of "stones," primarily of the bladder, and misshapen fetuses is a common one for the sixteenth and seventeenth centuries. Edward Lhwyd in the late seventeenth century saw the formation of stones in the body as analogous to the existence of fossils in the earth—and monstrosities as the human parallel to the freakish skeletal forms of what we now understand to be prehistoric animals.[2] Stones and monsters, the products of the bladder and the uterus, the cause of seemingly identical and intense pain, are equated visually in this plate.[3] The sole pain the male can experience that is as intense as parturition is the horrid product of the stone, a stone that can only be "delivered" by opening the body.[4] The homology of cutting for stones (and other genitourinary diseases) and the act of childbirth was constantly made during the eighteenth century. Monsters are, likewise, the product of an anomaly, not an anomaly of the body but an anomaly of the spirit, which leads to the deformation of the preformed fetus. These monsters, the figures crossing all boundaries that define the human being, especially in terms of their ambiguous sexuality, are the result, to quote one of William Harvey's earliest opponents, the preformist Alexander Ross (1652), of growth "when the seed [the ovum] is faulty . . . and the blood [the menstruum] predominant."[5] It is the woman and her "field" that cause the birth of monsters. Their form, as we have seen in our discussion of Paré in Chapter Five, lies in the nature of the female and her fantasy.

It is not that Ruysch's interest in the monstrous is any different from that of his contemporaries but rather that he sees the anomaly of form, the wild variation from any stated aesthetic norm, as itself part of the plan of nature. Indeed, the mayfly grasped firmly in the skeletal hand of the fetus in the foreground is a standard icon of the fleetingness of life. This view is well documented in Ruysch's anatomical and surgical atlas of the 1720s. There the monstrous as ornament can be seen to run from

PLATE 152. *The world of the monstrous engraved by Cornelis Huyberts from Frederik Ruysch, Observationum anatomico–chirurgicarum centuria (Amsterdam: Henricum and Viduam Theodori Boom, 1691). Ithaca: Howard B. Adelmann Collection, Olin Library, Cornell University.*

the pathological, as in an image of the prolapsed uterus **[PLATE 153]** to the supposedly normal, as in the inner structure of the penis, represented as a multisectioned, erect phallus **[PLATE 154]**. The etiology of the monster, most often sought in the sexual fantasy of the female, is itself part of the potential variation of the human in all of the complexities of anatomy and pathology. The total plan of nature determines that the form of the fetus is shaped by the maternal "nest" or field on which it is sown. C. E. Eschenbach, as late as 1753, argued passionately that the source of these monstrosities lies in the "fantasy of the pregnant woman."[6] How the mechanism functioned was not as clear to him as it was to Ross a century before—what was clear was that traumatic events, such as the sexual "long-

ing" of the woman during pregnancy, could lead to the creation of monsters.

It is always the female whose "field" is viewed as the source of the monstrous. And it is the monstrous (and therefore) the female that reveals the hidden truths of nature (and the "normal"). William Hunter made the case for the scientific interest in the monstrous in 1784:

Even monsters, and all uncommon . . . animal productions, are useful in anatomical enquiries; as the mechanism, or texture, which is concealed in the ordinary fashion of parts, may be obvious in a preternatural composition. And it may be said, that nature, in thus varying and multiplying her productions, has hung out a train of lights that guide us through her labyrinth.[7]

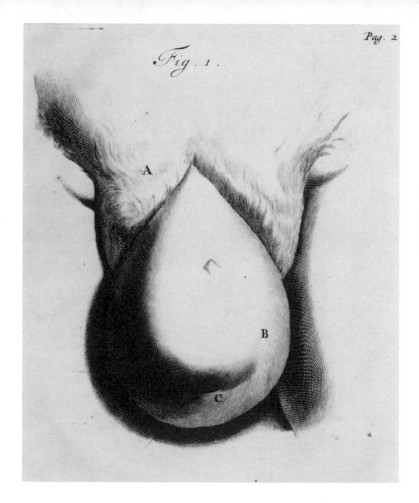

PLATE 153. *The prolapsed uterus from Frederik Ruysch,* Opera omnia anatomica–medica–chirurgica, *Vol. 3 (Amsterdam: Janssonio Waesbergios, 1721–[28?]). Ithaca: Howard B. Adelmann Collection, Olin Library, Cornell University.*

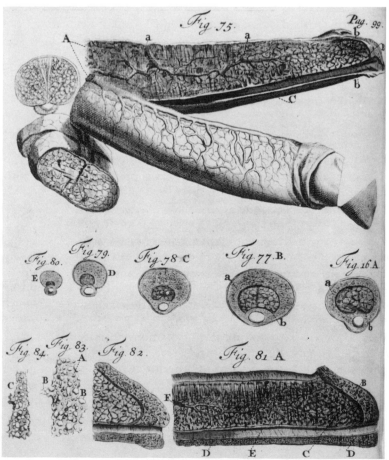

PLATE 154. *The penis anatomized from Frederik Ruysch,* Opera omnia anatomica–medica–chirurgica, *Vol. 1 (Amsterdam: Janssonio Waesbergios, 1721–[28?]). Ithaca: Howard B. Adelmann Collection, Olin Library, Cornell University.*

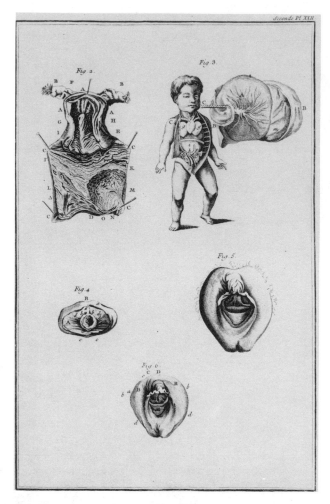

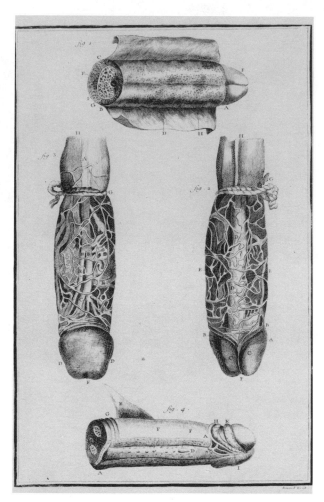

PLATE 155. *The female generative organs after Huber by Bernard from Denis Diderot and Jean-Baptiste le Rond d'Alembert,* Encyclopédie *(1751–80). London: Wellcome Institute for the History of Medicine.*

PLATE 156. *The penis after Heister, Morgagni, Du Verney, by Bernard from Denis Diderot and Jean-Baptiste le Rond d'Alembert,* Encyclopédie *(1751–80). London: Wellcome Institute for the History of Medicine.*

Nowhere was the ideology of the monstrous as a reflex of the representation of the sexual presented with more complexity than in the arch-Enlightener Denis Diderot's dialogue *D'Alembert's Dream* (1769). Diderot, co-editor with Jean-Baptiste le Rond d'Alembert, of the great eighteenth-century *Encyclopédie*, represents within this documentary tradition the "anatomy" of human sexuality, but it is a set of representations that echoes, as did the images found in Ruysch's anatomy, an ideology of sexuality that was complex and convoluted **[PLATES 155–156]**. Diderot used the existence of monstrosities as proof of his view of nature's self-creative dynamism: "All matter quick and bursting to birth."[8] In this fictive dialogue among the French Enlighteners, who are gathered to educate a woman, Mlle. de Lespinasse, the monster serves as proof of a

model of adaptive change, both within the fetus and within the species:

Imagine a long succession of generations born without arms; imagine their continual efforts and you will slowly see the two ends of this pair of pincers grow longer, longer still, cross over at the back, grow forward again, perhaps develop fingers at their ends, and create arms and hands once more. The original conformation of animals degenerates or is perfected by necessity and by the constant fulfillment of their normal functions.[9]

The monstrous, itself an anomaly of gradual development, can thus become normal over time. But its source lies in an error in the gradual development of the fetus in the womb. This faulty development is usually of the "fibers" that create the sensory organs. These, in turn, evolve from the basic sense, the sense of touch:

> The bundle is a pure sentient system; if it persisted in that form, it would be susceptible to all those kinds of impression that can be received by pure sentience, such as cold and heat, softness and roughness. These successive impressions—of different kinds, and each varying in intensity within its kind—might perhaps produce memory, self-consciousness, and a very limited power of reasoning. But that pure and simple sentience, that sense of touch, is diversified by the various organs that are produced by each of the fibers; one fiber, by forming an ear, gives rise to a particular sense for apprehending what we call noise, or sound; another forms the palate, thereby producing a second kind of touch, which we call taste; a third, by forming the nose and its lining, produces a third kind of touch, which we call smell; a fourth, by forming an eye, gives rise to a fourth kind of touch, which we call color. (p. 201)

The basic sense, touch, is the key to the formation of all of the other senses. Thus the monstrous becomes the malformation of this key sense. This presentation leads Mlle. de Lespinasse to respond to this information with the comment: "But, if I understand you correctly, the people who reject the possibility of a sixth sense or of a genuine hermaphrodite are being very stupid. How can they be certain that nature might not be able to make up a bundle including an additional fiber that would give rise to an organ we've never heard of?" The touchstone of the "monstrous" is the extension of the senses and the merger of the sexes into the figure of the hermaphrodite. And her instructor responds: "Or a bundle including both the fibers that characterize the two sexes" (pp. 202–3). Touch and hermaphroditism and the monstrous are linked in Diderot's comment as they are within the fantasies about sexuality in the eighteenth century. For both represent the inner nature of sexuality, sexuality in terms of its reproductive power but also sexuality as the anti-Rational force par excellence. To understand the monstrous means to understand the plan (and the meaning) behind the seemingly "bizarre" and "meaningless." Touch is the irrational sense that lies at the root of all experience (as we shall see), and the hermaphrodite is the form that combines the sexuality of both male and female, reconstituting the Platonic whole. The monstrous becomes then the uncanny reappearance of the underlying forces of nature, seen as "monstrous" only because they are misunderstood.

But to understand the wider implication of Diderot's (and the eighteenth-century's) association of the monstrous with the sensory and the sexual, we can turn to his essay on the nature of woman (1772). For Diderot, the true nature of the woman is captured by the shape of her reproductive system: "With a physical structure so much the opposite of our own, the cue that sets their sensuality in play is so delicate and its source so far removed that we cannot be surprised at its not reaching fulfillment or becoming lost on the way" (p. 310). It is the uterus that produces the monstrous and is itself a type of monster: "Woman bears within her an organ capable of the most terrible spasms, one that controls her completely and excites phantoms of every kind in her imagination" (p. 312). The uterus produces monsters through these hysterical phantoms, and the woman becomes—a monster herself. "Age comes on, beauty vanishes; the years of neglect, of ill humor, of boredom are upon her. And having prepared her to become a mother by means of a periodic indisposition, Nature now takes away that power by means of a long and dangerous illness" (p. 314). She becomes the ugly hag whose "only recourse is her religion." Thus the irrational forces of the womb, once exhausted, are replaced by the irrational forces of religious faith. The association that Diderot outlines in his work, the association among sexuality, the senses, the feminine, and the body is central to any understanding of the representation of sexuality during the eighteenth century.

One must add that this fantasy about the nature of female sexuality was countered in other scientific writing of the day. It was the great Swiss polymath Albrecht von Haller [PLATE 157] who, in his essay on the causes of monsters (1739), pointed out the self-evident—that numerous pregnant women experience such events and emotions without giving birth to monsters.[10] Haller was a preformist and saw the monstrous structures as preformed, just as all other structures were, in the most rudimentary states of the fetus. Although Haller began his career believing in the spermaticist preformation theory of his teacher Hermann Boerhaave, he abandoned it in the 1740s in favor of epigenesis[11] [PLATES 158–159]. Boerhaave believed in a form of "animalculist preformation," that is, that the rudiments of the embryo preexist in the animalcules found in the male semen, completely developing only in the uterus: "The father gives the embryo and first rudiments of life, the structure of the body being already created and prescribed in the animalcules

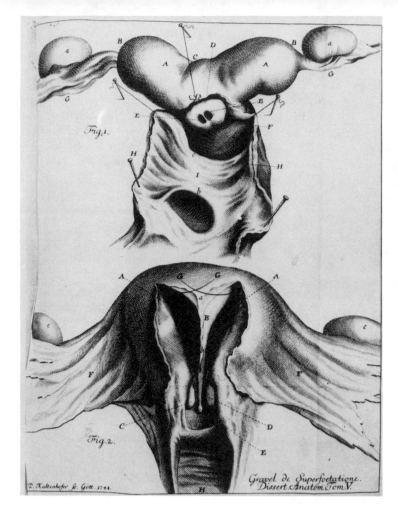

PLATE 157. *The female generative organs by D. Kaltenhofer engraved by Gött, 1748, from Albrecht von Haller, ed.,* Disputationum anatomicarum selectarum, *Vol. 5 (Göttingen: Abram Vandenhoeck, 1750). Ithaca: Howard B. Adelmann Collection, Olin Library, Cornell University.*

PLATE 158. *The male generative organs from Hermann Boerhaave,* Oecanomia animalis *(Amsterdam: Johann Noon, 1741). Ithaca: Howard B. Adelmann Collection, Olin Library, Cornell University.*

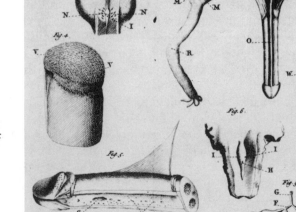

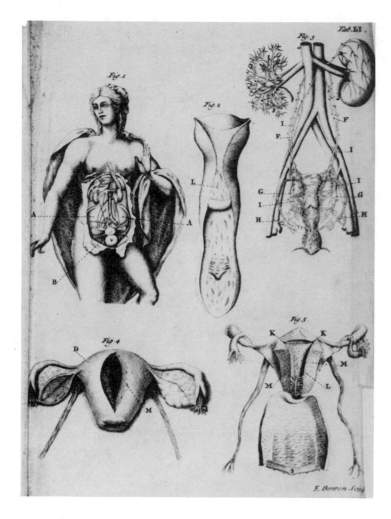

PLATE 159. *The female generative organs from Hermann Boerhaave,* Oecanomia animalis *(Amsterdam: Johann Noon, 1741). Ithaca: Howard B. Adelmann Collection, Olin Library, Cornell University.*

engendered in all animals. . . . The mother receives the living rudiments from the father, and retains and nourishes the same, maintaining therefore a dwelling place for the fetus."[12] But Boerhaave, like Swammerdam, believed not only that the embryo was preformed in the sperm; he also believed in the theory of *emboîtement*—the idea that all organisms were created at one time by God and encased within one another, so that each original member of a species contained all future generations.[13]

A decade later, Haller was converted from epigenesis back to preformation because of his own experiments on chicken embryos. Haller's new preformation theory, however, stated that the nascent embryo was encased in the egg, not the sperm. In his 1758 essay on the formation of the heart of a chicken, Haller wrote that all the changes in fetal development are based on forces of nature that operate mechanically. No single force is, however, responsible for development itself because this was preordained by God at the Creation.[14] Haller described his belief in *emboîtement* as an extension of his strong religious belief in the divine origin of life:

If the first rudiment of the fetus is in the mother, if it has been built in the egg, and has been completed to such a point that, it needs only to receive nourishment to grow from this, the greatest difficulty in building this most artistic structure from brute matter is solved. In this hypothesis, the Creator himself, for whom nothing is difficult, has built this structure: He has arranged at one time, or at least before the male force [of fecundation] approaches, the brute matter according to foreseen ends and according to a model preformed by his Wisdom.[15]

Haller, like Boerhaave before him, believed that "each particular generation of a new life is the result of causes established by God at the Creation. The material of future generations was organized in such a way that, through natural forces, also added to matter by God, development would proceed automatically at each instance of generation."[16] This view, although in line with the preformist view of the nature of the embryo, raised an interesting theological question—Why would God create an embryo that was not viable? Haller's major opponent, Caspar Friedrich Wolff, simply rejected any divine plan and therefore rejected all preformist ideas. For

Wolff "Monsters are not the immediate work of God, but of nature."[17] Haller's view, although widely circulated, did not have the power that the embodiment of sexuality in the form of the anomaly, the monster, held for the lay as well as the scientific mind of the eighteenth century.

Within the course of the seventeenth century, we move from a world in which the refusal to acknowledge any variation that would violate the borderline between the male and the female created a boundary between the perfect and the monstrous to a world in which the anomaly, especially the hermaphrodite, proved the existence of a stronger and a weaker sex. For the monstrous is the reflection of a faulty, a diseased, a corrupt sexuality—the sexuality of Eve. This is incorporated in the Baroque representation of the genitalia, as was elaborated in Jacques-Fabien Gautier d'Agoty's mid-eighteenth-century paintings and plates (see Plate 101). The bizarre and the grotesque fetus become a sign of the female genitalia because their faults are the source of such monsters. The female comes to represent, in the work of thinkers such as Diderot, the organized, rational world in collision with the forces of human sexuality and reproduction. And this battle, symbolized by the teratoid birth, was fought out within the female's body and mind. It was thus distanced from the nature if not the concern of the male. The debate between Haller and Wolff centers on this point—for the question of the monstrous raises the question of their origin. The view that has the monstrous rooted in the divine origin of humankind (Haller) comes into conflict with what comes to be the development model, that the monstrous is the result of a random (but never meaningless) error in the dynamic growth of the fetus. Is it Eve's curse and Adam's fall that are replicated by the life cycles of tiny, preformed males and females within the womb, or is it the error of individual evolution? The struggle between a hereditary/religious model and a dynamic/developmental one is cast in this debate.

MONSTERS AND THEIR ANATOMICAL ANALOGY

The monstrous becomes a paradigm for the search within the body itself for an understanding of the forces of sexuality that seem to shape human life and existence. But the conflict that underlies this search, the struggle between "religious" and "scientific" models of the body, is much more complex than can be seen at first glance. The Dutch physician Govard Bidloo's images of the exterior of the human

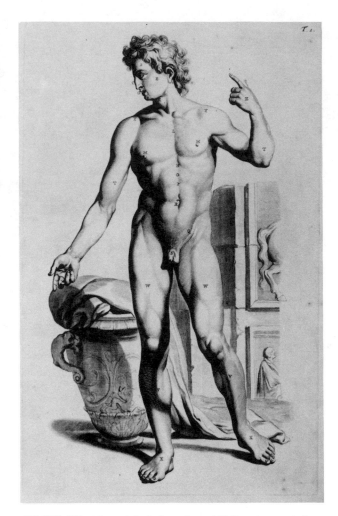

PLATE 160. *The male body from Govard Bidloo,* Anatomia humani corporis *(Amsterdam: Joannis a Someren, 1685). Ithaca: Howard B. Adelmann Collection, Olin Library, Cornell University.*

body, taken from his 1685 anatomy, appear to move radically away from the Eve and Adam images dominating the anatomies of the sixteenth and early seventeenth centuries[18] **[PLATES 160–161]**. Although not the first representations of the exterior of the genitalia that consciously avoid overt reference to the legend of the Fall, Bidloo's images of the female and male provide a sense of the relationship between symmetrical and asymmetrical views of the beautiful body. Drawn by the distinguished Dutch painter and engraver Gérard de Lairesse, they had a long and complex history.[19] It is clear that all of the schematic images of the internal genitalia to be found in earlier anatomical atlases are symmetrical; that is, they include their own representations of the genitalia reference to the homanner of representing the womb (and thus reproduction), points again to the preformist view of the relationship between the male and the female.

A subtext is also present in the question of representing the nude body, specifically the male nude body in the anatomies that follow Bidloo. When we examine the male nude figure in Johann Adam Delsenbach's 1733 anatomical atlas, its origin in the Adamic image is clear **[PLATE 162]**. The positioning of the muscle figure in a "natural" setting (as opposed to a "man-made" one) stresses the Adamic figure. The careful positioning of the leaves, so as to cover the genitalia, points (again) toward the Fall and the Tree of Knowledge. In a much more famous atlas (1747), the German anatomist Bernhard Siegfried Albinus (who studied under Bidloo) pre-

PLATE 161. *The female body from Govard Bidloo,* Anatomia humani corporis *(Amsterdam: Joannis a Someren, 1685). Ithaca: Howard B. Adelmann Collection, Olin Library, Cornell University.*

mologous form of the male and female genitalia. Bidloo's atlas begins with such a set of beautiful, homologous images, with Adam and Eve as classically secularized images. Eve/Mary's robe is no longer over her shoulders in the position of the robe of Mary the Protectress but draped so as to accent the line of the hips and the genitalia. The setting is a neoclassical Arcadian glade, with the tipped Greco-Roman vase representing the traditional image of the female genitalia as the container of the fetus. The male is posed in a rhetorical stance, speaking to an unseen audience, his vase upright (but his phallus is flaccid). His cloak is gathered together upon the vase. The contrast between the passive female and the active male, the use of the vase as an iconographic reference to the traditional

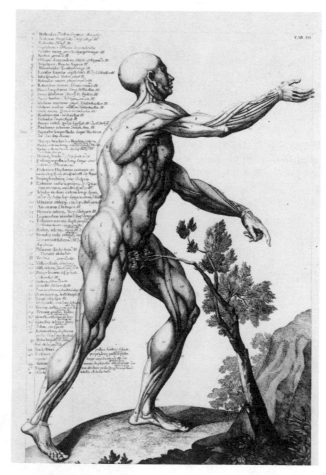

PLATE 162. *The muscles of the male body from Johann Adam Delsenbach,* Kurtzer Begriff der Anatomie . . . *(Nürnberg: L. Bieling, 1733). Ithaca: Howard B. Adelmann Collection, Olin Library, Cornell University.*

sents the "natural" setting for the muscle man but with the genitalia exposed [PLATE 163]. Albinus's artist/engraver Jan Wandelaer presented the idea of the body within a specifically "Enlightened" view. The movement between the two cannot be understood without some awareness of the reevaluation of the image of the nude, especially the male nude. For the religious revival of the seventeenth century brought forth, among many other Protestant cults, the Adamites, who stressed the inherent beauty of the body as the only true mirror of God's creation. In Bernard Picart's 1723 image of the Adamites, it is the visual exposure of the male genitalia that signifies the beauty of the body and the return to the stage of human purity before Adam's fall [PLATE 164].

It is in the "anatomical" rather than the aesthetic aspect of Bidloo's great atlas that the Baroque fascination with the asymmetrical, the monstrous, aspects of sexuality is to be found. It is masked by the use of a hyperrealistic manner of depiction. Bidloo's "realistic" image of the genitalia [PLATES 165–166] is, of course, a detailed image of the "reality" perceived during anatomical dissection. It is a stage beyond, though clearly related to, the still rather schematic images of the genitalia (1723) presented by Giovanni Morgagni, professor of anatomy at Padua, and the founder of the study of pathological anatomy.[20] Morgagni, who first identified

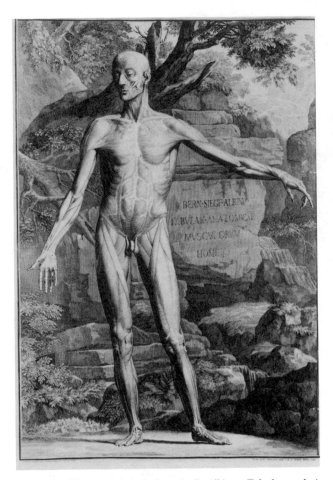

PLATE 163. *The male body from B. S. Albinus,* Tabulae sceleti et musculorum corporis humani *(Leiden: Verbeek, 1747). London: Wellcome Insitute for the History of Medicine.*

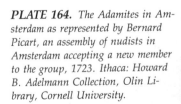

PLATE 164. *The Adamites in Amsterdam as represented by Bernard Picart, an assembly of nudists in Amsterdam accepting a new member to the group, 1723. Ithaca: Howard B. Adelmann Collection, Olin Library, Cornell University.*

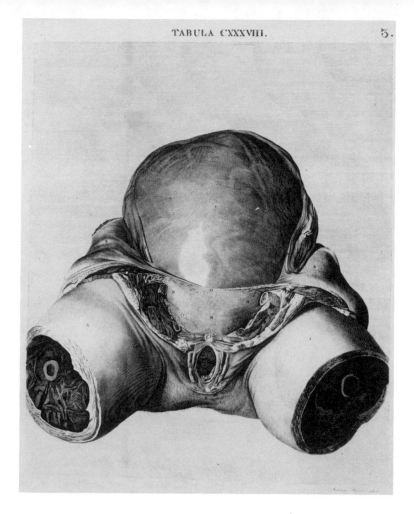

TABULA CXXXVIII.   5.

PLATE 165. *The female torso as flesh from Govard Bidloo,* Anatomia humani corporis *(Amsterdam: Joannis a Someren, 1685). Ithaca: Howard B. Adelmann Collection, Olin Library, Cornell University.*

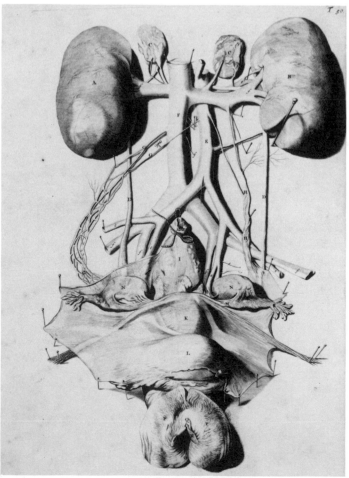

PLATE 166. *The reproductive organs and urinary tract of the female as the object of dissection from Govard Bidloo,* Anatomia humani corporis *(Amsterdam: Joannis a Someren, 1685). Ithaca: Howard B. Adelmann Collection, Olin Library, Cornell University.*

171

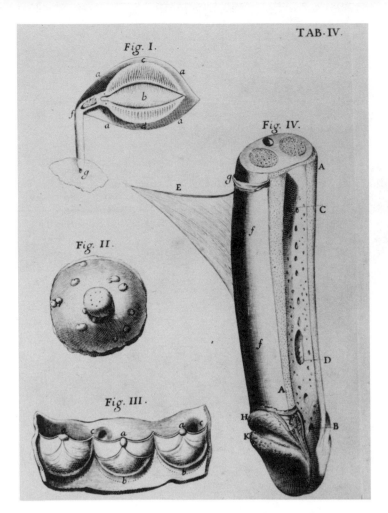

PLATE 167. *The penis anatomized from Giovanni Battista Morgagni,* Adveraria anatomica omnia *(Leiden: J. A. Langerak, 1723). Ithaca: Howard B. Adelmann Collection, Olin Libary, Cornell University.*

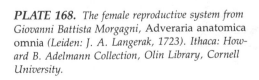

PLATE 168. *The female reproductive system from Giovanni Battista Morgagni,* Adveraria anatomica omnia *(Leiden: J. A. Langerak, 1723). Ithaca: Howard B. Adelmann Collection, Olin Library, Cornell University.*

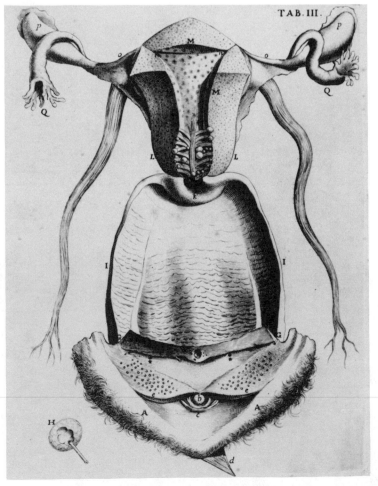

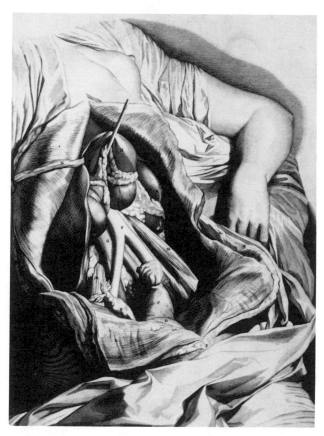

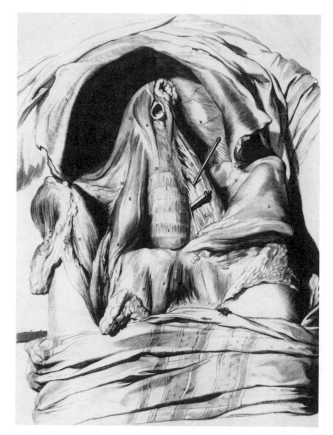

PLATE 169. *The anatomy lesson seen from the physician's point of view from William Cowper,* The Anatomy of Humane Bodies, *revised and published by Christianus Albinus, second edition (Leiden: J. A. Langerak, 1737). Ithaca: Howard B. Adelmann Collection, Olin Library, Cornell University.*

PLATE 170. *The fly crawling across the cover of the opened torso points toward the hidden genitalia, the source of corruption and death, in William Cowper,* The Anatomy of Humane Bodies, *revised and published by Christianus Albinus, second edition (Leiden: J. A. Langerak, 1737). Ithaca: Howard B. Adelmann Collection, Olin Library, Cornell University.*

the hydatids of the Fallopian tubes, the fringes that seem to reach out and envelop the ovaries, was still operating with a very schematicized understanding of the structure of sexual anatomy **[PLATES 167–168]**. What Bidloo alters in these images is the implied context, and in doing so, he reinterprets the meaning of the representations of the genitalia. Using the context not of the ideal schematic image as found in Vesalius but of the representation of the anatomical specimen, down to the nails holding the otherwise limp specimen and giving it form, Bidloo creates a sense of verisimilitude that is lacking in the schematic representations of the genitalia. But it is a verisimilitude rooted in the dichotomy between the aesthetic balance of the external form of humankind and the asymmetry present within the body. The conscious use of asymmetrical representation in the figures replaces any desire for an ideal schematic representation. It is a "Baroque" sense of the appropriateness of bizarre, asym-

metrical, fragmented form as a means of understanding the variety of nature. The torso is now exposed uterus and amputated legs, not a schema of the torso; the female genitalia, the reproductive system, and the uterus are neither amphora nor cups, neither field nor bed, but tissue. It is the image of the genitalia as tissue that reflects the radical disjuncture between the beautiful and the bizarre that we found in Ruysch's images of the monsters. This is the hidden field upon which the monsters grow. It is itself monstrous, as it is detached from the human.

With Bidloo, the shift from the fascination with systems to a fascination with form takes place. The power and importance of Bidloo's images cannot be underestimated. The British anatomist and surgeon William Cowper incorporated (without credit) Bidloo's plates in his 1698 anatomical atlas, with six additional plates by Cooke and Van Gucht **[PLATES 169–171]**. This led to a vituperative ex-

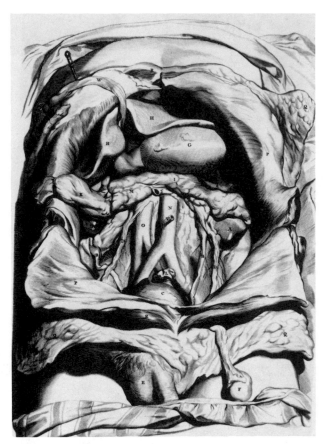

the asymmetrical structure, the monsters within. The form that represents the genitalia reflects the potential pathological nature of all human sexuality.

The model of the realistic (and, therefore, unusual) set by Bidloo (and to a lesser extent Cowper) appears as the standard in subsequent anatomical atlases of pregnancy, such as those of Albinus (1748). It is of no small importance that the "realistic" representation of the genitalia appears for the first time within those texts by "man midwives" who were attempting to create a new medical specialty, obstetrics, and a new medical discourse about the pathologies of female sexuality. The use of the "new"

PLATE 171. *The male reproductive system and viscera with the testicle removed but the scrotum unopened. From William Cowper,* The Anatomy of Humane Bodies, *revised and published by Christianus Albinus, second edition (Leiden: J. A. Langerak, 1737). Ithaca: Howard B. Adelmann Collection, Olin Library, Cornell University.*

change between the two men. This type of borrowing was common (as we have seen) to a greater or lesser extent in all of the late seventeenth-century anatomies. However, the power of Bidloo's manner of presenting the body, specifically the reproductive organs, created a new school of representing human sexuality. It is a movement that stresses the asymmetrical, ragged physical aspects of the body, and uses the representation of sexuality, within the idea of conception and of the genitalia, as its marker. Sexuality comes to represent the idea of meaningful but not symmetrical form, a form that exists within nature but is in no way shaped by the hand of the master sculptor, the great aesthetician, God. The Haller–Wolff debate is reflected thus in the understanding of the shape and function of the genitalia, which are represented as flesh, not spirit, as the seat of dynamic change, not the seat of Edenic origin. Bidloo's neoclassical figures, beautiful and well formed, which introduce the atlas, are the external, polished form that masks the "realities" of

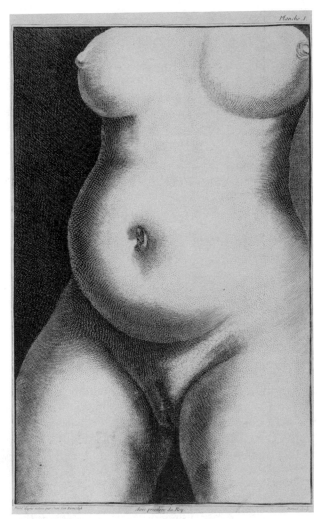

PLATE 172. *The female body as revealed in the midwife's handbook as redesigned for the "man mid-wife," the physician from C. N. Jenty,* Demonstration de la matrice d'une femme grosse et de son enfant à terme *(Paris: Charpentier, 1759). London: Wellcome Institute for the History of Medicine.*

manner of seeing, of the realism of the anatomical theater translated seemingly directly into the teaching handbook, gave these physicians a "modern" means of representation through which to claim the centrality of their new approach to the body. In the 1759 atlas by Charles Nicholas Jenty, the well-known device of the "flap" picture is employed to present a dissection of a "gravid uterus" in the new style. Jenty's images were (with one exception) drawn by the Dutch artist Jan van Rymsdyk, who was responsible for most of the "realistic" images in the obstetrical handbooks of the late eighteenth century[21] [PLATES 172–174].

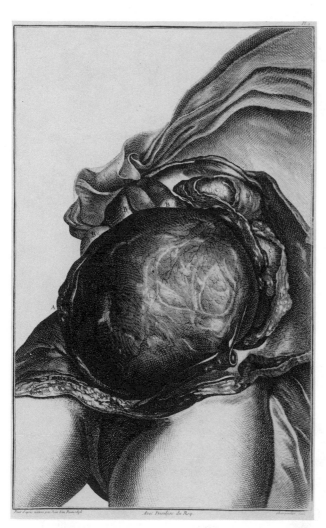

PLATE 173. *The gravid uterus revealed but the genitalia remaining in the shadows from C. N. Jenty,* Demonstration de la matrice d'une femme grosse et de son enfant à terme *(Paris: Charpentier, 1759). London: Wellcome Institute for the History of Medicine.*

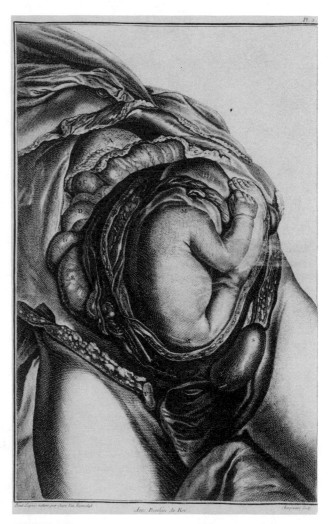

PLATE 174. *The fetus in situ from C. N. Jenty,* Demonstration de la matrice d'une femme grosse et de son enfant à terme *(Paris: Charpentier, 1759). London: Wellcome Institute for the History of Medicine.*

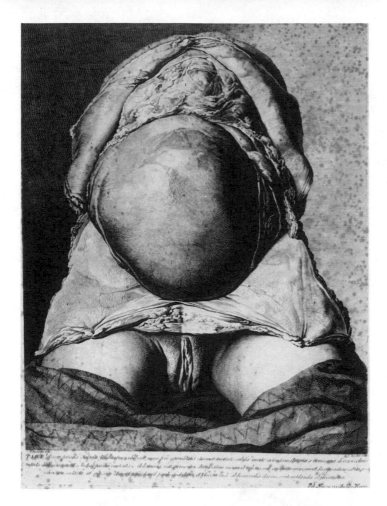

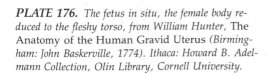

PLATE 175. *The female torso uncovered and the genitalia exposed but the legs discreetly covered, from William Hunter,* The Anatomy of the Human Gravid Uterus *(Birmingham: John Baskerville, 1774). Ithaca: Howard B. Adelmann Collection, Olin Library, Cornell University.*

PLATE 176. *The fetus in situ, the female body reduced to the fleshy torso, from William Hunter,* The Anatomy of the Human Gravid Uterus *(Birmingham: John Baskerville, 1774). Ithaca: Howard B. Adelmann Collection, Olin Library, Cornell University.*

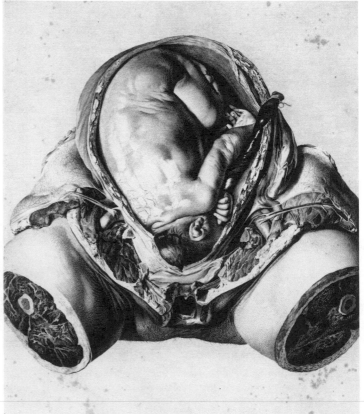

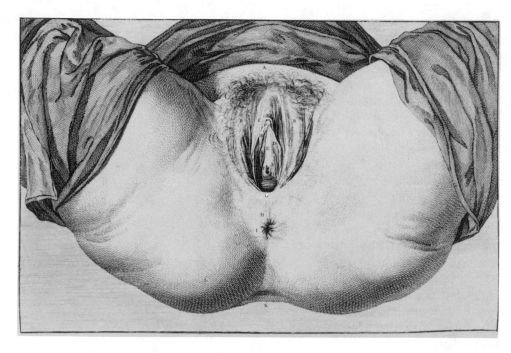

Without a doubt, the most famous of these post-Bidlooian images of the female are those found in William Hunter's 1774 *The Anatomy of the Human Gravid Uterus*, with plates by Jan van Rymsdyk **[PLATES 175–176]**. Rymsdyk had earlier also illustrated the midwife's handbook, *A Sett of Anatomical Tables* (1754), by Hunter's teacher, William Smellie[22] **[PLATE 177]**. Further examples of van Rymsdyk's work are to be found in Thomas Denman's *A Collection of Engravings, tending to illustrate the generation and parturition of animals, and of the human species* (1787) as well as Samuel Thomas von Soemmering's *Icones embryonicum humanorum* (1799). Engraved by (Sir) Robert Strange, these plates reappeared constantly in the medical literature of the eighteenth century, even as late as A. D. Burrowes's popular *The Modern Encyclopaedia* of 1816–20[23] **[PLATE 178]**.

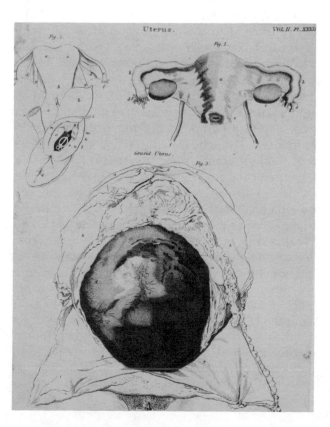

PLATE 178. *A standard reference book of the period, A. D. Burrowes,* The Modern Encyclopaedia; or a General Dictionary of Arts, Sciences, and Literature *(London: S. Richards, 1816–20 [?]) included a line engraving of the uterus as well as one of the gravid uterus by Campbell taken from the obstetrical atlases of the day. London: Wellcome Institute for the History of Medicine.*

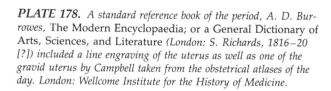

Beginning in 1750, Hunter had been involved in the dissection of the bodies of women who died at the end of their pregnancies. He dissected twelve bodies over a period of twenty-four years. But Hunter knew that he was creating more than a work of scholarship. He saw his atlas as a major addition to the aesthetics of the book as well as the practice of medicine. He had the volume published in Birmingham by John Baskerville, set in Baskerville's most stylish type, printed on the best paper. (It was one of only two medical books that Baskerville ever published.) Hunter's representations of the sexualized body, like the earlier eighteenth-century images, move from the exterior to the interior as if replicating an autopsy. The exterior images, however, those closest to the surface, present the body draped; as the image recedes into the interior, the drapery vanishes, and we are left with the image of the torso, so familiar from the anatomical atlases of the sixteenth century but with all of the "realism" of the eighteenth century.

But the height of realism is not to be found in two-dimensional, engraved representations of the genitalia intended for instructional purposes for the teaching of anatomy. William Hunter, as part of his great museum of anatomical specimens, began to collect wax casts of human genitalia[24] **[PLATE 179]**. The tradition of seeing the monstrous, the forces of sexual unreason, in the genitalia is reflected in the need to present the genitalia as three-dimensional. Here is the reality of the body, stripped, however, of the encumbrances of that flesh that is not of interest to the anatomist and devoid of all of the mutable aspects of the "real" body. It became a collection of representative aspects of human anatomy and pathology. When a specimen, in William Hunter's collections, was preserved for an anatomical museum, more often than not the specimen was seen as a pathological summary of the entire individual. Thus the skeleton of a giant or a dwarf represented "giantism" or "dwarfism," the head of a criminal, the act of execution that labeled him as *criminal*. Thus the collection also included the representation of the genitalia of the black as an indicator of the sense of the sexually monstrous **[PLATE 180]**. What is striking about Hunter's collection, however, is that it included the genitalia of the black female but not of the black male. By the eighteenth century, the representative function of the genitalia of the black female had already been established. In Chapter Ten, we discuss the representation of the genitalia of the black female and its signification in eighteenth- and nineteenth-century ideas of sexuality in more detail. Suffice it to say that Hunter's collection of anatomical and pathological casts of

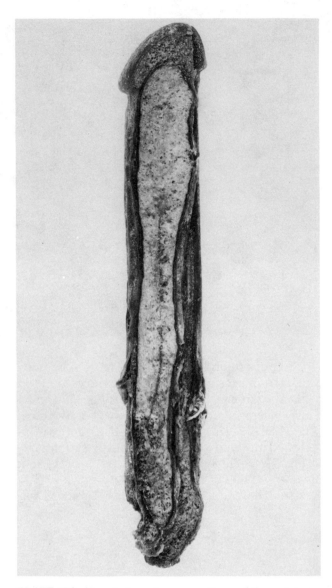

PLATE 179. *The arteries and cavernous tissues of the penis in a wax cast (Hunterian BB.21). Glasgow: Department of Anatomy of the University of Glasgow.*

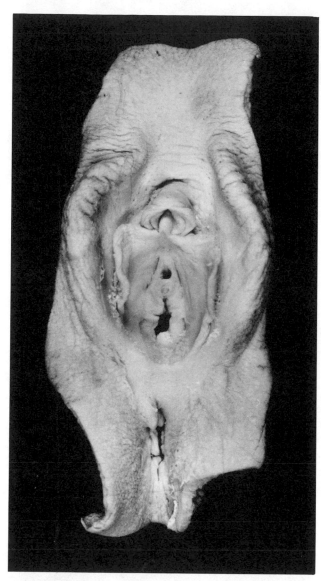

PLATE 180. *A wax cast of the external genitalia of an adult black woman (Hunterian CC. 16). Glasgow: Department of Anatomy of the University of Glasgow.*

the genitalia, founded for teaching purposes, became a three-dimensional syllogism to prove the difference between the normal and the abnormal, the acceptable and the deviant.

But it is the medium of the wax cast that is as important as the object cast in wax, for multicolored wax casting provided the most "realistic" possible anatomical figures. A long tradition of wax anatomical casting existed in Europe during the eighteenth century beginning with the specimens of the sixteenth-century Italian anatomist Lodovico Cigoli. In the mid-eighteenth century Albrecht von Haller had injected wax into the blood vessels to create the images he reproduced in his *Icones anatomicae* (1743–54), following a technique that had been developed by Frederik Ruysch.[25] It was a means of producing a mimetic set of observations, mimetic of the act of observation. One must see only "the pure things . . . that constantly happen the same way because they flow out of the nature of the thing itself." "Why do we err?" Haller asks. "We have seen [of something] many cases, and we conclude [that it must be so] for all without having seen all."[26] William Hunter, likewise, stressed the need for direct experience, even the illusion of direct experience through the mediated experience of the illustration:

> The art of engraving supplies us, upon many occasions, with what has been the great desideratum of the lovers of science, a universal language. Nay, it conveys clearer ideas of most natural objects, than words can express; makes stronger impressions upon the mind; and to every person conversant with the subject, gives an immediate comprehension of what it represents.[27]

The realism of the wax cast (and its replication in the engraving) created a new sense of the validity of representing the genitalia, both in terms of their anatomical structure (and function) as well as the dynamic processes (such as erection and conception) in which they were involved. The three-dimensional image of the genitalia became the "reality" against which the aesthetic nature of the anatomical image of the genitalia was measured. Contrast the purely "aesthetic" image of human sexuality to be found in the first publication in 1741 of the *Tabulae anatomicae* by the Italian Baroque master Pietro Berrettini da Cortona (1596–1669)[28] **[PLATES 181–182]**. Cortona's images, engraved by Ciamberlano, prefigure Bidloo's neoclassical images of the body to an extraordinary degree. They appeared to the eighteenth-century eye as extraordinary throwbacks to an age of the aesthetic image of the genitalia, genitalia that are so schematicized as to be placed in implicit contrast with the "realism" of Haller and Hunter.

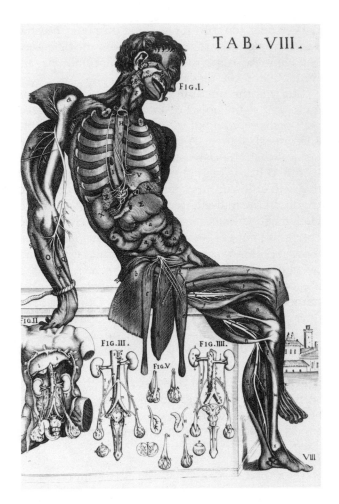

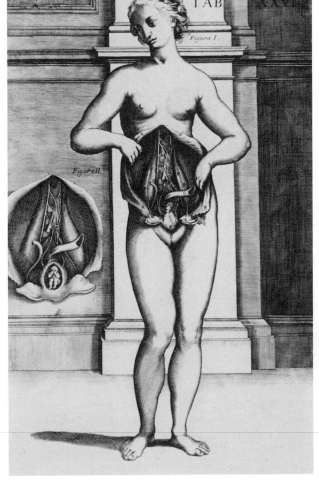

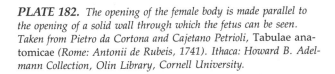

PLATE 181. *The "flayed man" with his reproductive parts from Pietro da Cartona and Cajetano Petrioli,* Tabulae anatomicae *(Rome: Antonii de Rubeis, 1741). Ithaca: Howard B. Adelmann Collection, Olin Library, Cornell University.*

PLATE 182. *The opening of the female body is made parallel to the opening of a solid wall through which the fetus can be seen. Taken from Pietro da Cortona and Cajetano Petrioli,* Tabulae anatomicae *(Rome: Antonii de Rubeis, 1741). Ithaca: Howard B. Adelmann Collection, Olin Library, Cornell University.*

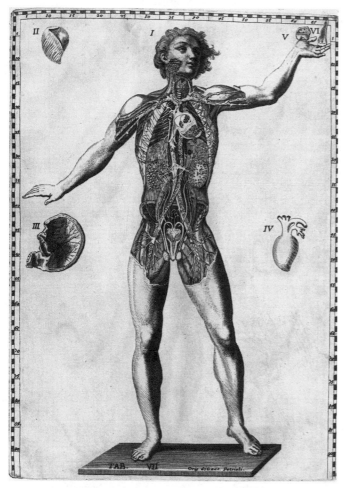

PLATE 183. *The male body from Bartholomeo Eustachi,* Otto tavole anatomiche *(Rome: Antonio de' Rossi, 1750). Ithaca: Howard B. Adelmann Collection, Olin Library, Cornell University.*

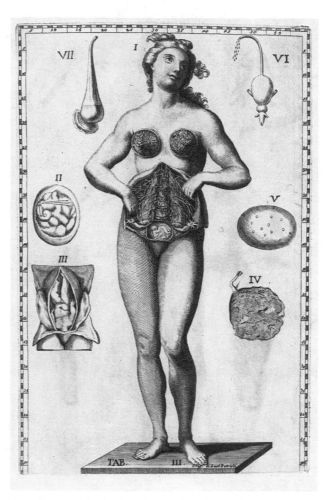

PLATE 184. *The female body from Bartholomeo Eustachi,* Otto tavole anatomiche *(Rome: Antonio de' Rossi, 1750). Ithaca: Howard B. Adelmann Collection, Olin Library, Cornell University.*

The realism of the wax casts of the genitalia incorporated both the aesthetic external form (as in Plate 188) as well as the "realistic" inner structure of the genitalia, representing both the erotic form and the "reality" of the flesh (including the monstrous, as in Plate 198). But this realism is only a misplaced aestheticism. For in another major sixteenth-century anatomical atlas, rediscovered in the course of the eighteenth century, one can find a direct line between the realism of the images of the genitalia in the Enlightenment and the techniques of early modern anatomical description. The anatomical works of Bartolomeo Eustachi, with engravings by Pier Matteo Pini, had been only partially published in 1552[29] **[PLATES 183–184]**. Thirty-nine plates, among them the images of the genitalia, were missing for about 150 years following Eustachi's death.[30] They were located by Giovanni Maria Lancisi, the chief physician to Pope Clement XI, and published by him in 1714. In 1744, Albinus, the professor of anatomy at Leiden, republished all of

the images in his edition of Eustachi, which he followed in 1747 by his own anatomical atlas. Eustachi's plates were literally Renaissance maps of the body—they lacked the numbered keys that explained the representations (as in Vesalius), but the readers were provided, on the margins of the image, with coordinates (latitude and longitude) that were keyed to explanations. Albinus replaced these with outline diagrams, schematic representations that carried the "meaning" of the images. But Albinus, whose work seems to be more "realistic" than the "schematic" representations of Eustachi (especially as seen through the eyes of the eighteenth-century anatomists) simply restructures Eustachi's images for his own purposes. It is Albinus's atlas, however, that forms the basis for what appears to the eighteenth-century viewer to be the ultimate realistic representation of the genitalia, the great wax anatomical models of La Specola in Florence designed by Clemente Susini and Francesco Calenzuoli from 1776 to 1780.[31]

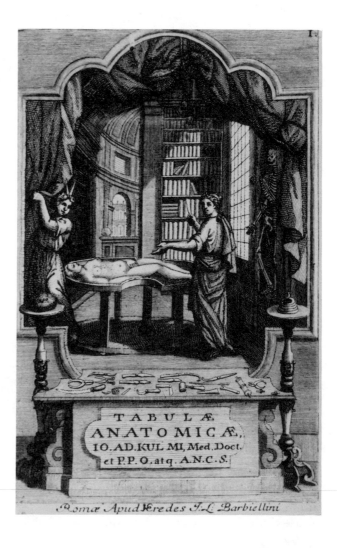

PLATE 185. *The title page of Bartolomeo Eustachi,* Otto tavole anatomiche *(Rome: Antonio de' Rossi, 1750). Ithaca: Howard B. Adelmann Collection, Olin Library, Cornell University.*

PLATE 186. *The title page of Johann Adam Kulmus,* Tabulae anatomicae *(Amsterdam/Rome: Laurentii Barbiellini, 1748). Ithaca: Howard B. Adelmann Collection, Olin Library, Cornell University.*

For all of its fabled realism, the work of the great wax sculptors of the eighteenth century is as highly aesthetic as anything that Pietro da Cortona or Bartolomeo Eustachi ever produced. When one turns to the representation of the sexualized body in the anatomical museum of the eighteenth century, museums (such as William Hunter's) that were initially created to train physicians far from the stench and horrors of the anatomical theater, one can quickly see that the image of the body, but very specifically of the genitalia, is "real," real in the sense that Haller and Hunter employ in their engravings but real only in the sense that they replicate another set of schematic (and therefore aesthetic) images, the images of the wax masters. For the source of the engraved image of the genitalia seems to have been the wax model of a dissection as often as the original cadaver itself. Indeed, in the representation of the anatomical theater, the scene of the opening of the body, in the anatomies of the eighteenth century a remarkable shift has occurred. Although there are images redolent of both Vesalius's title page engraving (and indeed of William Hogarth's image of *The Reward of Cruelty* of 1750–51) of the anatomical theater as a place of horror and dismemberment, such as the title page of Eustachi's anatomical atlas of 1750 **[PLATE 185]** with its dogs fighting over the scraps of flesh that fall from the table, there are also some very different images. In Johann Adam Kulmus's (1748) **[PLATE 186]** and Félix Vicq d'Azyr's (1786) **[PLATE 187]** anatomical atlases, one has an idealized anatomical theater, with the allegorical figure of Anatomia dominating the scene. This is a world without horror, without the stimulation of any of the senses except the rational sense of sight. It is a world in which the corpse is a waxworks figure, without putrefaction and stench.[32]

PLATE 188–196. *The wax anatomical figure of the female from the eighteenth-century anatomical collection at La Specola in Florence. On the surface, with pearls and coiffure, she is the epitome of the classical beauty. As her layers are removed, we move to the center of the male gaze, the fetus. All of this is done in the context of the torsos to be seen in the rear case, which reduce the female to the sum of her sexuality. Florence: Museo Zoologico della Specola.*

Hunter used the wax cast extensively in his own anatomical museum. But it was in the museums of Bologna, Florence, Rome, and Vienna that the anatomical figures, especially those representing childbirth and sexual pathology, were present in such a way as to dominate all Europe's understanding of the body **[PLATES 188–200]**. Although the first wax anatomical specimens seem to have been the creation of the sixteenth-century anatomists such as Volche Coiter in Altdorf and Lodovico Cigoli in Florence, the idea of creating entire bodies out of wax impressions was developed by the Bolognese anatomist Ercole Lelli in the mid-eighteenth century.[33] Reaching its height under the reign of Peter Leopold, the Grand Duke of Lorraine, the Hapsburg ruler of Tuscany in the mid-eighteenth century, Florence, specifically the Royal and Imperial Museum of Physics and Natural History (called La Specola because of its observatory), founded in 1775, became the center for the study and teaching of anatomy. The Florentine school, which modeled its wax specimens directly from cadavers, was founded about 1750 by the sculptor Giuseppe Ferrini and the obstetrician Giuseppe Galletti, a surgeon and sculptor himself. Among the great masters represented in the collection were Clemente Susini, Felice Fontana, Paolo Mascagni, and the Sicilian wax modeler Gaetano Giulio Zummo, who were responsible for much of the anatomical as well as religious art work in this medium.[34] And the tradition of wax molding, a technique that created (for the eighteenth-century eye) an absolutely "real" image, was applied to the creation of anatomical images. Prior to this use, this technique had been employed to create realistic relics in the form of mimetic human shapes for the bones of saints and martyrs.[35] The movement of the wax cast from the realm of religious art to the world of anatomical study is an important one, as it parallels the general secularization of the eighteenth century.[36] It is analogous to the core of the debate between Haller and Wolff, the relationship of the divine to the physical nature of humankind, to the source of the monstrous.

PLATE 189.

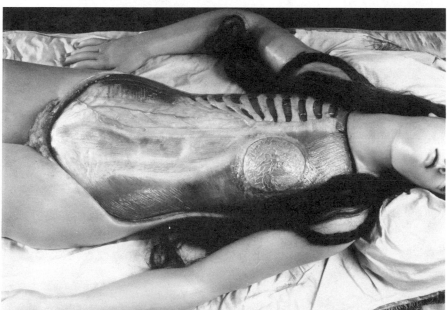

PLATE 190.

PLATE 191.

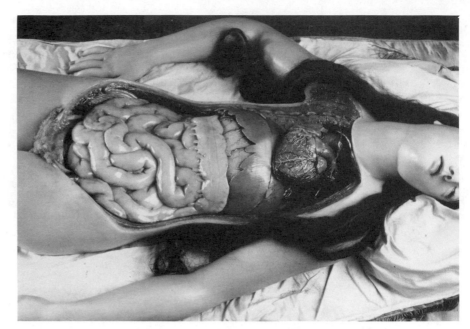

PLATE 192.

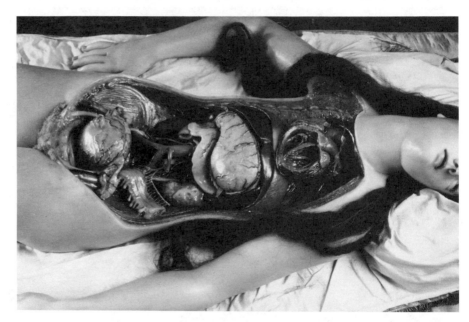

PLATE 193.

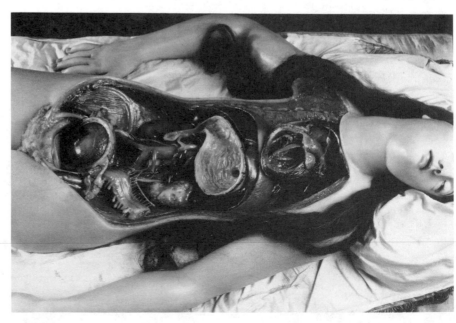

PLATE 194.

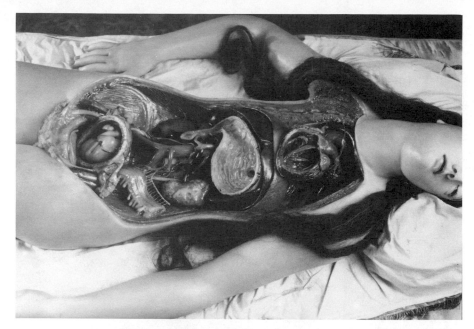

PLATE 195.

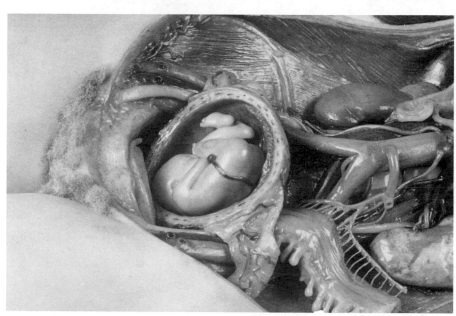

PLATE 196.

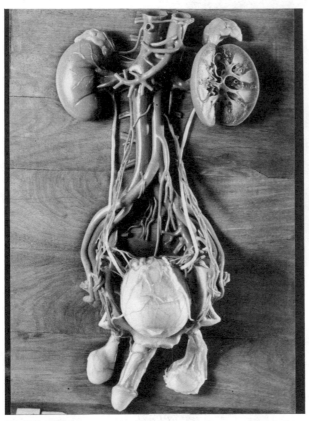

PLATE 197. *A wax model of the urogenital system of the male. Florence: Museo Zoologico della Specola.*

PLATE 198. *A wax model of a double monster with two chest cavities* (Cephalothoracopagus monosymmetros). *Vienna: Aus der Sammlung geburtshilflicher Wachspräparate, Josephinum.*

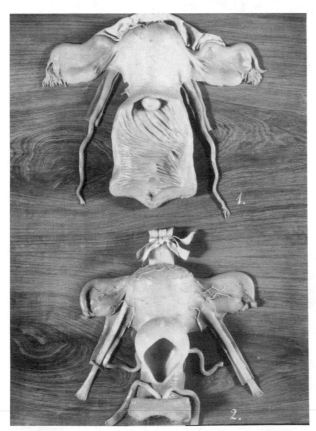

PLATE 199. *(1) A wax cast of the vagina (2) a wax cast of the uterus. Vienna: Aus der Sammlung anatomischer Wachspräparte, Josephinum.*

PLATE 200. *A hemisected view of the urogenital system of the male. Vienna: Aus der Sammlung anatomischer Wachspräparate, Josephinum.*

The anatomical museums were not solely the location of anatomical study; they were, as much as the great art museums of the eighteenth century, part of the sights to be seen on the Grand Tour. They were one of the sources of the sense of the "sublime," the emotion of overwhelming sensation to be had within nature but a nature captured within the aesthetic form of the wax cast, not to be found in the stinking cadavers of the anatomical theater. Goethe's father, Johann Caspar Goethe, who toured Italy in 1740, visited the exhibition of Zummo's representation of the plague in Florence and was struck by its extraordinary realism, down to a spiderweb "which one took for the real thing."[37] On his trip to Italy in 1775–76, the Marquis de Sade commented on these same wax casts in the Palazzo Torregiani in Florence:

> In one of these armoires one sees a sepulcher stuffed with a multitude of cadavers, exhibiting all of the various stages of decay, from the moment of death's advent to the total decomposition of the individual. This bizarre idea is the work of a Sicilian named Zummo. All are executed in wax with natural colors. The impression is so strong that the senses are overwhelmed. One inadvertently puts one's hand to one's nose in considering this gruesome detail, which is difficult to examine without being reminded of an ominous idea of destruction and because of this idea, being more comforted by the idea of a Creator. Next to this case is another in the same style, representing the sepulcher of a church, where the same gradations of dissolution can almost be observed. One notices above all a wretched, naked, fetching corpse which is thrown with the others and which, itself suffocated by the odor of the spectacle, falls into the confusion and dies like the others. This group represents a dreadful truth.[38]

De Sade's association between the deception of the senses (already mentioned by the elder Goethe), the sexualization of the body, and the image of the anatomical specimen is a powerful one. These are "real" bodies that escape the lower senses, such as smell, and are understood only by the highest sense, that of sight. Henry Wadsworth Longfellow, in the 1830s, saw these figures on his Grand Tour of the Continent and sensed both their reality and the unreality that one must ascribe to the medium of the wax sculpture:

> Zumbo [sic] . . . must have been a man of the most gloomy and saturnine imagination, and more akin to the worm than most of us, thus to have reveled night and day in the hideous mysteries of death, corruption, and the charnel house. It is strange how this representation haunts one. It is like a dream of the sepulcher, with its loathsome corpses, with "the blackening, the swelling, the bursting of the trunk,—the worm, the rat, and the tarantula at work." You breathe more freely as you step out into the bright sunshine and the crowded, busy streets next meet your eye, you are ready to ask, Is this indeed a representation of reality?[39]

The dream of the real, or perhaps the nightmare of death, of the body corrupt, of the body putrefied is "real" only because it tricks the highest sense, sight; it is "unreal," a false representation because it lacks the other senses, the senses that comprise the context for the sexual. Longfellow's vision was of the permanence of corruption, of the immutability of mutability, all images so contradictory that they lead to a questioning of the very body itself.

In death the body maintains its allure only through the visual representation of the anatomy, of the genitalia. Johann Wolfgang von Goethe, on his Grand Tour in 1787, visited the Piazzo Torregiani in Florence and likewise commented on the artificial "anatomical dissections" that "had the absolutely undecayed and colorful appearance of fresh preparations."[40] It is the purity of the images, images that are seen but not smelled; images of the body, the body opened and dissected, but the body immutable, that haunt Goethe's sight. For the genitalia, specifically the woman's genitalia, are consistently associated with wetness, disease, and with smell, the smell of putrefaction and death. In the often-cited chapter from Goethe's *Wilhelm Meister's Travels* (1829), in which Goethe describes the centrality that the wax anatomical models will have as the source of knowledge about the body in the utopian society that he envisions for the New World, it is precisely the immutability of the wax model that is stressed. It is the sense of the mutability of the body, its decay and pathology, that lies behind Goethe's sense of the sexualized body (and the genitalia), as we shall see in the next chapter. But Goethe also understands the close relationship between the depiction of the body as the ultimate work of God in religious art of the period and the wax anatomical casts. For the "expert" who makes the casts "was going in quest of bread, when the saints and martyrs whom he had been accustomed to carve no longer found a sale. I therefore induced him to master the art of skeleton-making, and to practice in life-size and on a smaller scale after nature."[41] Religion is closely associated, through the wax cast, with the erotic. As late as 1858, Nathaniel Hawthorne (on his Grand Tour) sensed the close relationship between the religious use of such wax sculptures and erotic imagery:

> And here, within a glass case, there is the representation of an undraped little boy in wax, very prettily modelled, and holding up a heart that looks like a bit of red sealing-wax. If I had found him anywhere else, I should have taken him for Cupid; but being in an oratory, I presume him to have some religious signification.[42]

It is not merely in the act of beholding the body that this sense of the sexuality of the wax model is embedded. For Goethe, in *Wilhelm Meister's Travels*, a text to which he makes express reference in his late essay on the need for wax anatomical models as the basis of the understanding of the body, sees the fascination with such models stemming from the need to understand the "inner parts" of the body, that metaphor for an understanding of the forces of sexuality present within his own body (and represented by the mysterious hidden genitalia of the female). For Wilhelm Meister is driven to seek an alternative to the opening of a "real body" when he is confronted with a chance to open a body that, for him, clearly represents beauty as well as unmediated sexuality. After a period of time as a student of anatomy, a period when there is a chronic shortage of cadavers, a suicide is brought in and made available (because of the act of suicide) for dissection. "An exceedingly beautiful girl, distracted by an unhappy love, had sought and found her death in the water." This Gretchen-like figure, who sought and found death out of love madness, for her lover was only under "a false suspicion," becomes the beautiful object that Meister is to autopsy in order to understand the body. He is to open her in order to comprehend the hidden inner workings of the body as a divinely created object. It is, however, not her genitalia, but her arm and hand that he is to dissect. Here (and as we shall see in the next chapter) the arm and hand become surrogates for the genitalia because they are the primary agent of touch, of the sense which is the most sexualized:

> Wilhelm, who as the first candidate was summoned forthwith, found in front of the seat indicated to him, up on a plain board neatly covered, a critical task; for when he took off the covering, there lay exposed to view the most beautiful female arm that probably had ever wound itself around a youth's neck. He held his instrument-case in his hand and did not trust himself to open it; he stood up, not venturing to sit down.

> Repugnance to still further deforming this glorious product of nature contended with the demand which the eager man of science had to make upon himself, and which all who sat around him took care to satisfy. (p. 299)

Meister's answer to his inability to cut into the flesh of this beautiful object is to flee to the aestheticism of the wax model, for there "building-up teaches more than pulling in pieces" (p. 301). His first task is to build the model of "a woman's arm." In moving from the anatomical theater to the wax-molding room, Goethe also moves from the real body, with all of its parts, with its association with sexuality and the emotional, to the world of art, with the abstract arm and hand amputated from the body and its function as the icon of Wilhelm's own sexuality.

The art of the wax cast is more accurate than dissection because it is more permanent than nature but also because in art we replicate that which we understand: "In what is new we see only the strangeness" (p. 305). The new becomes another category of the uncanny, the replication of the opening of the body to see—that source whence we came. Meister (and Goethe) see in the new science of seeing the body, in the collections of museums such as Florence (which he mentions at the close of this chapter), a means by which the mysteries of human sexuality, long preserved within the religious institutions of Europe, become cleansed, purified, and distanced through their transmogrification into "science"—the wax bodies of the martyrs become wax anatomical casts. Sexuality is distanced and controlled by being made part of science.

Goethe's use of the wax representation of the body as an answer to the liquefaction (and analogous decomposition) represented by human sexuality has its uncanny parallel in the fictional reconstruction of the Marquis de Sade's actual trip to Italy in his novel *Juliette* (1797)[43] **[PLATE 201]**. Using the device of a female protagonist, de Sade fictionally relives his trip to Italy as a woman's trip into the enjoyment of mutilation and pain. In the beginning of part four of the novel, Juliette finds herself (and her entourage) in Florence, where they visit Zummo's wax models that had been (in reality) earlier visited by the Marquis de Sade himself. De Sade literally quotes the passage from his journals cited before as Juliette's description of the wax casts. With, of course, one major shift—it is no longer the "religious" intimation of mortality, the *memento mori*, that is invoked by the sight of these models but rather the innate perversity of the observer, of the woman, Juliette. De Sade now concludes the para-

PLATE 201. *M. V. Acier's illustration for one of the Marquis de Sade's novels (1797) representing visually the genitalia as depicted verbally by the Marquis de Sade. Ithaca: Rare Book Collection, Cornell University.*

graph with the observation: "Let me say only that Nature probably impelled me to those crimes since even the mere recollection of them still thrills me to the core."[44] For it is the perversity, the monstrous nature of the female that is represented by the mimetic representation of death and decay.[45] And, as throughout the novel, Juliette's trip to Florence results in an orgy of torture and mutilation. The final scene in the chapter, the torture of a young girl, who is then buried alive with the decayed corpses of her parents, replicates with obsessive emphasis on the sense of touch the wax scene that Juliette had experienced without any sensory stimulation (except sight) in the museum.[46] It is touch that causes women to reveal themselves as the monsters they truly are, as the Marquis notes in a long footnote to this chapter:

> There is truly no limit to what one may obtain from women by causing them to discharge. Experience shows that one has only to make their cunts leak a few drops of fuck, and they are ready and eager for the most revolting atrocities; and if those women who have a native fondness for hideous crimes cared to reflect a little upon their emotions, they would admit the astonishingly powerful connection that exists between physical emotions and moral aberrations. The wiser for recognizing this, the sum of their pleasures would henceforth increase by leaps and bounds, since they would correctly situate the germs of voluptuousness in the disorders which they could from then on carry to whatever extreme their lust might demand. (p. 652)

The image of the female's genitalia as well as the source for this overwhelming, antirational force, human sexuality, with all of its potential for destruction (de Sade) as well as construction (Goethe) haunts the representation of the genitalia as the monstrous.

I have shown how the genitalia were understood as the projection of the monstrous force of the irrational within the male observer through juxtaposing the tradition of "realistically" representing the female torso and genitalia in obstetrical atlases (such as those of Hunter and Jenty) with the aestheticized "realistic" images of the body found in museums such as La Specola. We turn to Gustave Courbet's recently rediscovered painting *The Origin of the World* (1866) **[PLATE 202]** to judge how these traditions of the realistic representations of the female genitalia, with their origin in religious imagery and in the tradition of the wax anatomical cast (with the related tradition of realistic engraving that has its origin in the realism of the wax cast) impacted

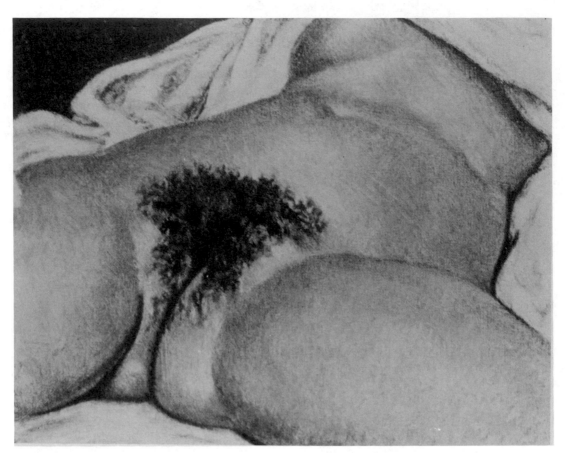

PLATE 202. *The image of the female genitalia as the Medusa by Gustave Courbet,* The Origin of the World, *as reproduced in Gerard Zwang's* Le sexe de la femme *(Paris: la Jeune Parque, 1967). Ithaca: Olin Library, Cornell University. The original has recently been rediscovered in Paris.*

upon the viewer. Commissioned by the "art" collector and Turkish ambassador to St. Petersburg, Khalil Bey, the work was initially received with extraordinary enthusiasm as a major, realistic work of art. Even Edmond de Goncourt, not the most enthusiastic supporter of Courbet, thought the belly "was as beautiful as the flesh of a Correggio."[47] It is art, not reality. But it is this painting that Maxime du Camp describes in his excoriation of the Paris Commune and his condemnation of Courbet as an agent and principal participant in the revolution:

> To please a Moslem who paid for his whims in gold, and who, for a time, enjoyed a certain notoriety in Paris because of his prodigalities, Courbet . . . painted a portrait of a woman which is difficult to describe. In the dressing room of this foreign personage one sees a small picture hidden under a green veil. When one draws aside the veil one remains stupefied to perceive a woman, life-size, seen from the front, moved and convulsed, remarkably executed, reproduced *con amore,* as the Italians say, providing the last word in realism. But, by some inconceivable forgetfulness, the artist, who copied his model from nature, had neglected to represent the feet, the legs, the thighs, the stomach, the hips, the chest, the hands, the arms, the shoulders, the neck, and the head.[48]

For Courbet is drawing, at least according to contemporaries such as Goncourt and du Camp, on the artistic tradition of representing the female genitalia, but we can also read in du Camp's "hysterical" description the continuation of the image of the monstrous, dissociated sense of human sexuality that was seen in the wax anatomical models, at least as interpreted by writers such as Goethe and de Sade. Courbet's image is an erotic one. It does not immediately evoke the associations with death and disease, with the anatomy theater, that

PLATE 203. *The female torso as seen by Philip Pearlstein,* Seated Female Nude on Black Chair, *1968. Troy, NY: Rensselaer Polytechnic Institute.*

are present in du Camp's outburst. The question of the context is here important. For du Camp sees Courbet as having crossed the line between the visual aesthetic representation of the erotic to the visual anatomical dissection of the sexual. Human sexuality becomes the monstrous, often represented by the monstrous child, the faulty product of conception. This image becomes one that the genitalia, and the hidden nature of the female genitalia, come to represent. It is both as the monstrous and the destructive, the irrational and the sublime. In one Viennese obstetrical wax model, the layer upon layer of tissue can be removed to reveal—a true monster, two bodies as one, like the Platonic ideal body, hidden within (see Plate 198). But the female genitalia come to represent this force within both the male (observer—in Courbet's image) and the female (subject—in Courbet's image). Gazing at the female's genitalia may well create a sense of anxiety about the potential castration of the male

as well as a heightened sense of the fantasy of the sexual touch.[49] But it also represents the power of male sexuality evoked by the image of the genitalia, separated from the body, presented as an independent (perhaps monstrous) force. By the mid-twentieth century, such images tend to lose their visceral response. Philip Pearlstein's *Seated Female Nude on Black Chair* (1968) **[PLATE 203]** presents just as amputated an image of the female torso, but lacking any of the medical associations of Courbet's piece, with its implicit quotation of the image of the gravid uterus, of the sexuality of conception and reproduction; it is neutral in its associations. Pearlstein's image of the female nude, without the identificatory force of physiognomy, is a study of the body, not explicitly of the genitalia. It is the power of the genitalia, masked and revealed, that is revealed in Courbet's image. In representing the hidden female genitalia, Courbet is also implying the existence of the visible, potent, and erect penis.

THE SENSIBILITY OF PENISES: ERECTIONS AND DISSECTIONS

Without a doubt the most important innovation in the understanding of the body, and by extension, the construction of the idea of the genitalia, is Albrecht von Haller's extraordinarily powerful (if not completely original) distinction (made in 1752) between the sensibility and the irritability of tissue.[50] Haller's often-cited definition runs in part: "I call that part of the human body irritable, which becomes shorter upon being touched. . . . I call that a sensible part of the human body which upon being touched transmits the impression of it to the soul; and in brutes, in whom the existence of a soul is not so clear, I call those parts sensible, the irritation of which occasions evident signs of pain and disquiet in the animal."[51] The genitalia are thus supposed "sensible" tissue because they relate the body to the "soul" of the animal. With this statement, Haller placed himself squarely in the debate between the animism of Georg Stahl, who argued that the body was entirely controlled and animated by the soul, and the materialism of J. O. de la Mettrie, who argued, as in the title of his 1748 treatise, that "Man [is but] a Machine."[52] The debate about sensibility as a sign of the nature of the human being, whether a creature created by God or a machine quite independent of rational control, centered quickly on the debate about the nature and implication of the male erection. Remembering the complex response of Leonardo da Vinci, who understood the erection as a sign of the irrational aspects of human sexuality, it should be of little surprise that when, in the eighteenth century, scientists return to the mind–body question (having disposed of Descartes's dualism), the male erection again becomes the centerpiece for an understanding of the irrational nature of the forces that act in the body. And as with the question of the origin of monsters, it is in the realm of sexual fantasy (here of the male) that the nature of the erection can be found. The mechanism of the erection had been well understood by the eighteenth century. In Philip Verheyen's *Anatomie* **[PLATE 204]**, there is a detailed description of the physiology of the erection. Verheyen ascribes the source of the erection to the effect of the "spirit" on the body, the effect of the "thought of the beloved." Verheyen is not completely sure, however, whether the erection is caused by the blockage of the veins from or the increased blood flow of arteries into the penis.[53]

The structure of the penis, with its two main distensible tubes, the corpora cavernosa, which

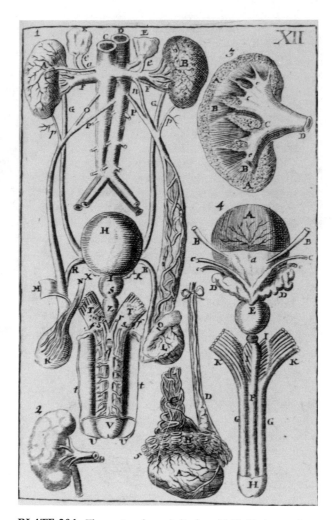

PLATE 204. *The erect male genitalia from Philip Verheyen,* Anatomie oder Zerlegung *(Leipzig: Fritschen, 1714). Ithaca: Howard B. Adelmann Collection, Olin Library, Cornell University.*

surmount a compressible tube, the corpus spongiosa, was seen, if not understood, in the late Middle Ages. The debate over the nature of the erection, whether the penis filled with air or blood, had been resolved by the Renaissance anatomists who understood the origin of the erection in the filling of the cavernosa with arterial blood, which, impeded in its exit from the penis by nervous or muscular mechanisms, stiffened the penis. So the major question left to the anatomists of the eighteenth century was the nature of the impetus for the nervous or muscular action.

The penis is represented within the eighteenth-century anatomical and medical treatises as erect; this is in striking contrast to the general anatomical atlases as well as the anatomical literature designed for the artists of the eighteenth century, such as

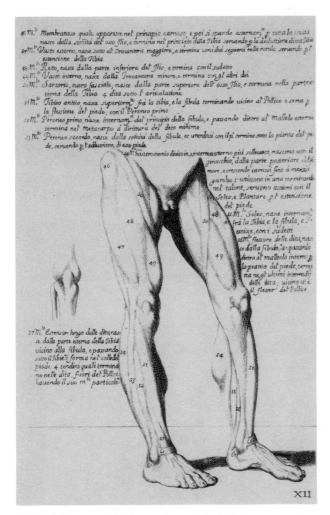

PLATE 205. *The flaccid penis from Carlo Cesi,* Cognitione de muscoli del corpo humano per il disegno *(Rome: Billy, [1730]). London: Wellcome Institute for the History of Medicine.*

Carlo Cesi's 1730 neoclassical anatomical atlas, in which the penis is flaccid [**PLATE 205**]. The distinction between the separate, dissected erect penis (as in Ruysch's anatomy [see Plate 154]) and other forms of pathologies should be stressed. As long as the penis is connected to the body, it remains "in control," that is, flaccid. Once the penis is separated from the body, it becomes the erect penis, the penis under the control of powerful but nonrational forces of human sexuality. It is the analogue to Courbet's image of the female genitalia. The missing body and the head serve as the normal context for the penis; once they are removed, the penis becomes pathological, taking on a life of its own, becoming erect, and therefore liable for infection and disease. In the images of disease (which will be discussed later) as well as in the studies of

the "normal" anatomy of the penis, the image of the erect penis signifies the potential for pathology. The opening of the penis, its dissection, becomes then an analogous action to the opening of the female body. It is the search for the origin of the loss of control, the search for the hidden power that takes control of the penis, a power that is often represented as the female genitalia but that is also the image of the erect penis.

Hermann Boerhaave commented that "the Muscles concerned in this Action, are not to be reckoned among the Class of vital or spontaneous Muscles, since of themelves they do not act in the most healthy Man; but they are rather in a Class *sui generis*, being under the influence of the Imagination. The Will has no influence either to suppress, excite, or diminish their Action."[54] The erection is caused neither by conscious action nor by spontaneous impulse. The debate that is engendered by Haller's understanding of "sensibility" begins to center about the nature of the penis, even though Haller gives only passing mention to the penis in his initial essay. The British anatomist Robert Whytt, in answering Haller in 1747, sees the "seed in the *vesiculae seminales*" or the lascivious sights and ideas as the source of the erection.[55] For Haller (answering Whytt in 1754), it is much the same, but Haller places his emphasis on the "external friction, or from venereal thoughts or dreams, a redundancy of good semen."[56] The mind serves as the origin of the erection, but it is not merely the mind as an abstract. Rather it is the play of the senses upon the penis as interpreted by the mind. The friction that Haller discusses, the direct touch, is thus analogous to the venereal thoughts or dreams, the products of sight and/or fantasy. But Haller does not merely stop there. He understands "voluptuous ideas [as] the most proper *stimulus* to put them [the constriction of the veins] in motion."[57] These ideas come from the conscious mind, over which we have control. Whytt disagrees, seeing their origin as that of the movement of the muscles of the heart: "As the erection of the *penis* often proceeds from lascivious thoughts, it must be ascribed, in these cases at least, to the mind, notwithstanding our being equally unconscious of her influence exerted here, as in producing the contraction of the heart."[58] Whytt describes the erection almost in terms familiar to us from Leonardo:

We cannot, by an effort of the will, either command or restrain the erection of the *penis*; and yet it is evidently owing to the mind; for sudden fear, or anything which

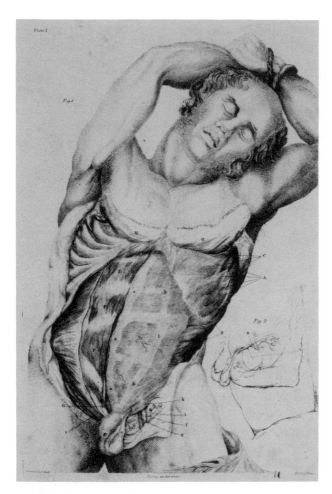

PLATE 206. *An engraving of the second stage of dissection: the torso of the flayed man and his genitalia from Sir Charles Bell,* A System of Dissections, Explaining the Anatomy of the Human Body *(Edinburgh: Mundell, 1798[–1800]). London: Wellcome Institute for the History of Medicine.*

terindicator of pleasure, fear, is an important one because it serves as the hallmark for the aesthetic discussion of the "sublime" during the eighteenth century. The force of the sublime, of the fearful on the penis, both as the image of the penis and on the male observer, can be judged in Sir Charles Bell's anatomical representation of the male reproductive system **[PLATE 206]**. Bell, a noted amateur artist, captures the flayed man, so popular from the Renaissance on, as the context for the depiction of the male genitalia. Bound, exposed, the male reveals his reproductive system "realistically" as well as schematically. But the flaccid penis and the bound figure refer us back to the world of the cultural reflection of this tradition, the world of de Sade and Courbet. It is in the image of the body tortured and mutilated rather than the phallic seeing eye that the observer finds him- or herself **[PLATE 207]**.

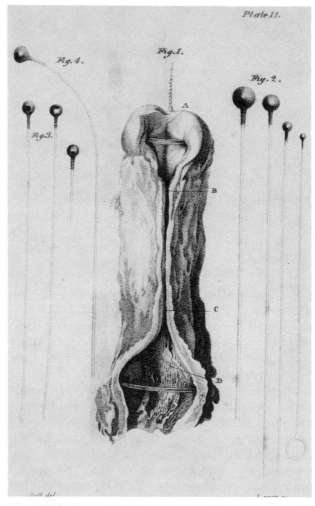

PLATE 207. *The penis dissected from Sir Charles Bell,* Letters concerning the Diseases of the Urethra *(Boston: W. Wells and T. B. Wait; Philadelphia: Edward Earle, 1811). London: Wellcome Institute for the History of Medicine.*

fixes our attention strongly and all at once, makes this member quickly subside, though it were ever so fully erected. The titillation, therefore, of the *vesiculae seminales* by the semen, lascivious thoughts, and other causes, only produce the erection of the *penis*, as they necessarily excite the mind to determine the blood in greater quantity into the cells.[59]

For Whytt, as for much of the eighteenth century, the assumption is that there is a place within the mind of which the conscious mind is not sensible.[60] Thus the erection is the proof of the existence of forces, such as sexuality, that are present but impervious to the effect of the conscious mind. The origin of fantasy, at least for Whytt, is in experience: "the remembrance or *idea* of things, formerly applied to different parts of the body, produce almost the same effect, as if they themselves were really present."[61] The example that Whytt brings as the coun-

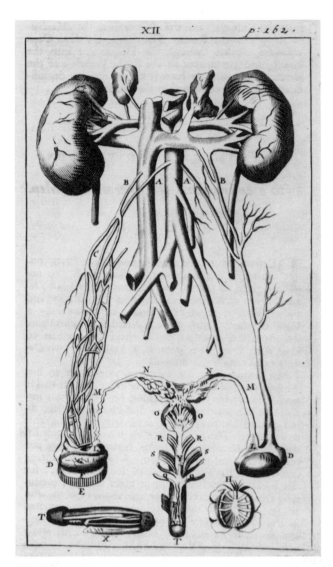

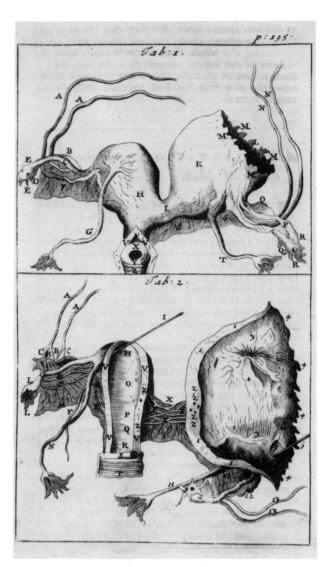

PLATE 208. *The male urogenital system from Pierre Dionis,* The Anatomie of Humane Bodies Improv'd *(London: H. Bonwicke, 1703). Ithaca: Howard B. Adelmann Collection, Olin Library, Cornell University.*

PLATE 209. *The female reproductive system from Pierre Dionis,* The Anatomie of Humane Bodies Improv'd *(London: H. Bonwicke, 1703). Ithaca: Howard B. Adelmann Collection, Olin Library, Cornell University.*

For the overall cultural context of these images is not solely that of the "neutral" world of the anatomist; the centrality that images of sexuality have for the eighteenth century moves them into the sphere of culture. And it must be understood that the "anatomists," especially artist-anatomists such as Sir Charles Bell, intended their work as much for the artist as for the physician. It is, therefore, as much in the aesthetic fantasies about sexuality, in Goethe and de Sade, that the context for the representations of human sexuality, such as those of the erect or the flaccid penis, is to be sought as much as in the debates within science, debates that mirror the general cultural discussions.

The discussion of the nature of the erection is

parallel to the discussion of the origin of monsters within the fantasy of the woman. For the womb is understood as an irritable tissue, just as is the penis, and is thus not under the control of the rational mind. It is under the domination of the fantasy of the female, a sexual fantasy that, as Paré had already elucidated, could alter the very nature and form of the child. It is the fantasy of the female that can "spoil" the preformed fetus. The penis is a "monster," a force out of the control and beyond the boundaries of rationality; the womb, likewise, is potentially a monster that can breed monsters. When we examine the images of human sexuality from anatomical atlases of the eighteenth century, in the works of Pierre Dionis (1703) **[PLATES 208–209]**,

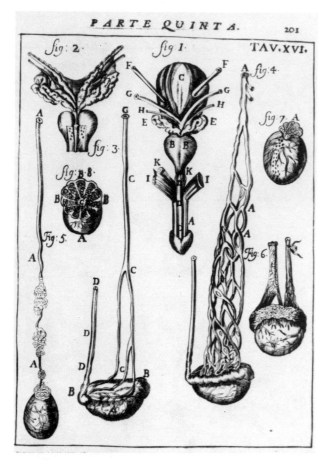

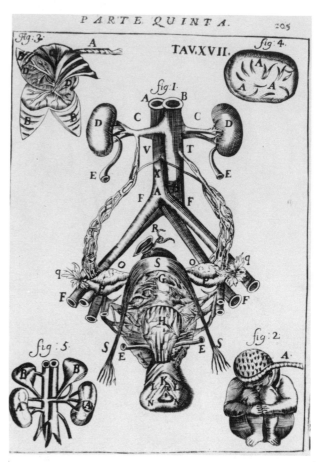

PLATE 210. *The male reproductive system from Alessandro Pascoli,* Il corpo-umani *(Venice: Presso Andrea Poletti, 1712). Ithaca: Howard B. Adelmann Collection, Olin Library, Cornell University.*

PLATE 211. *The female reproductive system with fetus from Alessandro Pascoli,* Il corpo-umani *(Venice: Presso Andrea Poletti, 1712). Ithaca: Howard B. Adelmann Collection, Olin Library, Cornell University.*

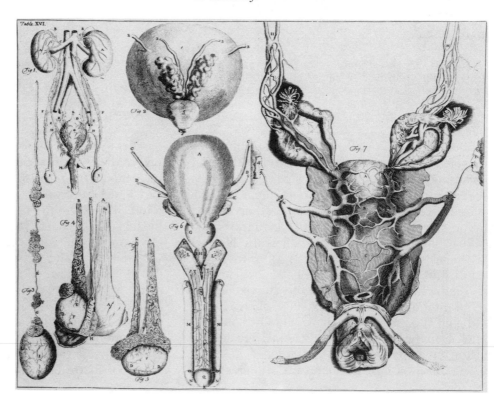

PLATE 212. *Etching of parts of the genitourinary systems of the male and female, after Eustachi, Cheselden, and De Graaf from R. James, A* Medical Dictionary *(London: T. Osborne and J. Roberts, 1743). London: Wellcome Institute for the History of Medicine.*

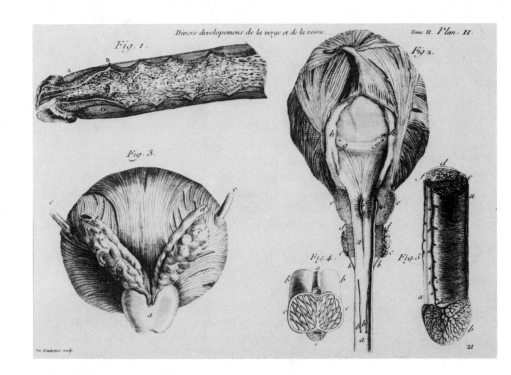

PLATE 213. *The penis from Guichard Joseph Duverney,* Oeuvres anatomiques, *Vol. 2 (Paris: Charles-Antoine Jombert, 1761). Ithaca: Howard B. Adelmann Collection, Olin Library, Cornell University.*

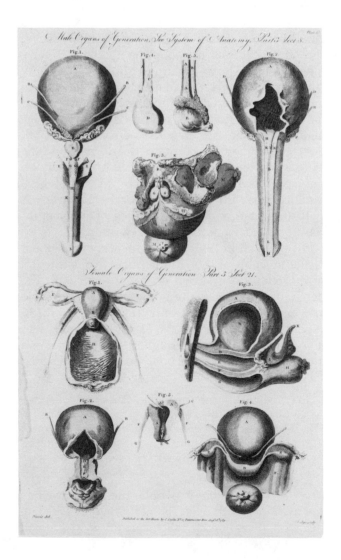

Alessandro Pascoli (1712) **[PLATES 210–211]**, R. James (1743) **[PLATE 212]**, Guichard Duverney (1761) **[PLATE 213]**, and W. H. Hall (1790) **[PLATE 214]**, we can see the gradual "realism" of the images but also the parallels between the opening of the penis and the opening of the womb. The development of these images of sexual difference is, however, cumulative, as one can see in the history of the clitoris and its representation.[62]

The very term *clitoris* makes direct reference to the image of the senses. It is closely related (either as source or influence) to the Greek "to tickle" (kleitoris = clitoris; klitorizein = to tickle). It is an organ of sensation, with seemingly no other function (unlike the penis). The clitoris was well described by the Renaissance anatomists. Matteo Realdo Colombo makes the claim in 1559 of first "discovering" the clitoris.[63] His discovery lies in his description of its erection in analogy to the penis. Francisco Plazzoni in 1620 seconded Colombo when he wrote:

> Therefore even the action of the clitoris, which is the woman's penis, will be erection. Wanton women themselves admit this erection, inasmuch as they affirm that something in their private parts stiffens and stands out when they are involved in lascivious activity.[64]

PLATE 214. *W. H. Hall,* The New Royal Encyclopaedia; or, Complete Modern Dictionary of Arts and Sciences, *second edition revised by T. A. Lloyd, n.d. [ca. 1790], pl. 10, line engraving with etching, male generative organs, by Lodge after Birnie, published 28 August 1789. London: Wellcome Institute for the History of Medicine.*

In 1708, Philip Verheyen sees the clitoris as an analogical structure to the penis. It is in "form and being parallel to the male organ."[65] According to Verheyen:

> Its "normal" size is equal to that of the uvula, but when it is erect, because of warmth and the "spirit of reproduction" it becomes thicker and longer. . . . Many write that this part in many persons becomes so large and long that it could be used in the stead of a male organ and they are incorrectly held to be hermaphrodites. (p. 223)

The hermaphrodite, the ultimate monster, doubling and connecting the genitalia, is the monster of reference when speaking of the relationship between the clitoris and the penis. De Sade (both in his journal as well as in *Juliette*) observes that in the same museum where the wax casts of death and decay were exhibited, Juliette/de Sade saw a "monster" with "its legs crossed, which is a pity, for the sculptor should have displayed what characterized its double sex and singular amenities: it is shown reclining upon a bed, exposing the most tempting ass in all the world."[66] The "lubricious reputation" of de Sade's hermaphrodite points to the border between the normal, the flaccid and small, and the pathological/deviant, the rigid clitoris that is like an erect penis.

In *Aristotle's Compleat Master-piece* (1752), the contrast between the clitoris and the penis is understood in terms of the senses. In the opening chapter entitled "Displaying the Secrets of Nature," there is a detailed account of the anatomical structures of the genitalia. The "Yard" is "the organ of Generation in Man" that "Nature has plac'd obvious to the Sight" (p. 11). The clitoris, on the other hand, is hidden and is the hidden source of sexual lust: "indeed resembles [the penis] in Form, suffers Erection, and Falling in the same manner and it both stirs up Lust, and gives delight in Copulation. . . . And, according to the Greatness or Smallness of this Part, they are more or less fond of Mens [sic] Embrace; so that it may properly be stil'd the Seat of Lust" (p. 15). It is touch, in the form of sexual contact, that stimulates the clitoris and therefore the larger, the more pleasure (according to this view). It is still the analogy to men's pleasure, to the size and form of the clitoris, that draws the line between the normal and the excessive. In *The Anatomical Dialogues; or, a Breviary of Anatomy . . . Chiefly Compiled for the Use of the Young Gentlemen in the Navy and Army*, compiled by "a Gentleman of the Faculty," "the use of the clitoris is to produce a titillation in coition, and it is said to be the chief seat of pleasure to women in that act, as the glans is in men."[67] However, if excessively abused it can become like the glans penis in form as well as function.

Sexuality, the sexuality of the Other, of the different, is marked by the most overt presentation of what the early modern anatomists argued was a normal, physiological action, the erection of the penis. The erection of the clitoris had to be understood as normal because the anatomists were constrained to argue in terms of the homologous structure of sensibility between the penis and the clitoris. The demand for parallel structures did not (as we have seen earlier) result in a demand for a parallel situation in which stimulation could take place. Women's sexuality was located in her body, in her response to (male) tactile stimulation; masculine sexuality had its location in the "soul" as well as in the body. Parallel physical reactions were needed but not parallel contexts for these erections.

The sexual contexts of the male and the female were understood as so very different that it became impossible for some anatomists to reconcile the parallel of the penis and the clitoris except by seeing clitoral erection as an abnormality. By the early nineteenth century, Johannes Müller could deny "the capacity for erection of the clitoris in the normal individual."[68] Certainly clitoral erections occurred, but they were the mark of the deviant. The hermaphrodite, the woman with a penis (even by analogy) was beyond the border of the normal, and the clitoris was the locus of stimulation that defined the monstrous. The sexual touch had pathological ramifications in the form of clitoral erections.

In one of the standard studies of nineteenth-century sexual anatomy, that written by Georg Ludwig Kobelt in 1844, there is an acknowledgment of the erection of the clitoris but a reconstruction of the realities of sexual anatomy to fit with the demands for an absolute homology between male and female sexual anatomy **[PLATES 215–216]**. When examining the clitoris, Kobelt demanded that it, in normal intercourse, ought to be brought down into the vaginal canal and ought to contact the penis:

> Every copulation movement has a value for both sexes simultaneously; the combined activity of both apparatuses must, under the progressive intensification of the need for stimulation, coincide at climax with ejaculation and the reception of the seed.[69]

The necessary analogy, even at the moment when the anatomy of the clitoris was generally well understood, demanded parallel structures and dynamic

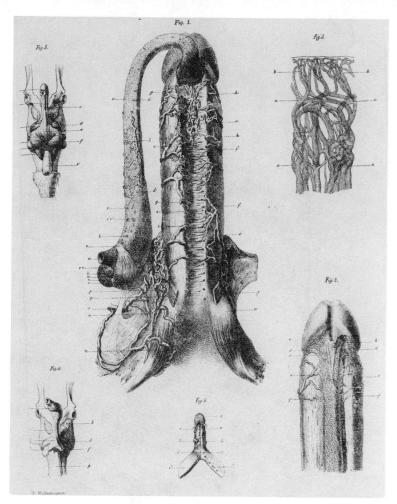

PLATE 215. *The penis as seen from below from Georg Kobelt*, Die männlichen und weiblichen Wollust-Organe der Menschen *(Emmerling: Freiburg i. Br., 1844). Ithaca: Howard B. Adelmann Collection, Olin Library, Cornell University.*

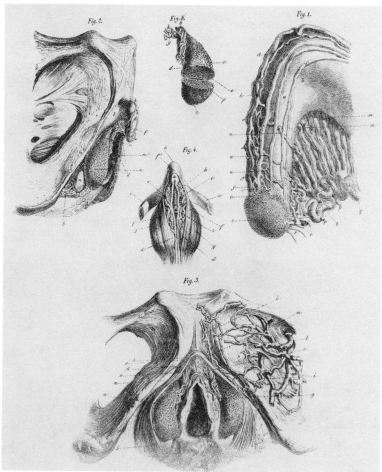

PLATE 216. *The clitoris from Georg Kobelt*, Die männlichen und weiblichen Wollust-Organe der Menschen *(Emmerling: Freiburg i. Br., 1844). Ithaca: Howard B. Adelmann Collection, Olin Library, Cornell University.*

PLATE 217. *Jean-Jacques Lequeu's early eighteenth-century image of the* Penis Strangulated by Paraphimosis. *Paris: Bibliothèque nationale.*

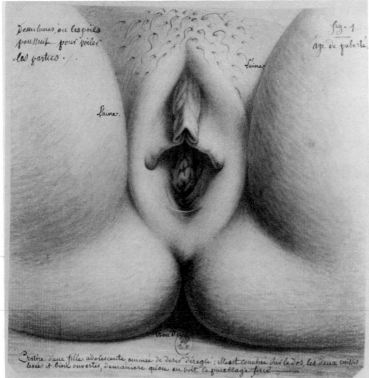

PLATE 218. *Jean-Jacques Lequeu's early eighteenth-century image of the* Vessel of an Adolescent Girl Inflamed with Unseemly Desire. *Paris: Bibliothèque nationale.*

action, or it became pathological. Kobelt demanded a dynamic parallelism equivalent to the constructed anatomical parallel that he saw between the forms of the male and the female genitalia. The subtext to Kobelt's anatomical description is the "naturalness" of sexual stimulation through coitus and the "unnaturalness" of masturbation, the manual manipulation of the clitoris purely for physical pleasure. The image that haunts late eighteenth- and early nineteenth-century discussions of the clitoris is the question of self-touch. The clitoris, recognized by medical (read: male) science from the sixteenth century on as the source of sexual stimulation, had to be understood as the source of direct sexual stimulation primarily during intercourse, in direct (hoped for) analogy to the penis. For once the image of the clitoris became loosened from that of heterosexual activity, once the clitoris took on a life of its own, as did the penis, it would become equally as dangerous as the penis. And its danger would lie in the realm of pathology. It would be cast in the form of images of disease that would haunt the "abused" penis and clitoris. For the passion inherently associated with the clitoris, once loosened from heterosexual activity, would, as in the dissected penis, threaten to become a disease as powerful as any sexual disease that afflicted the penis. It was an image of female sexuality out of control. Such images, even of the female genitalia, are projections of the sense of the animal within. Once projected into the world, it is associated with the anatomy of female sexuality, for it is only the female who has a sexual organ the sole function of which is pleasure. Pleasure and desire in the female become hallmarks of disease, but this disease is the projection of the sense of *dis-ease* with the irrationality of human sexuality felt by the male observer.

In the mid-eighteenth century, Jean-Jacques Lequeu, the architect, presents a set of "lascivious" images that reflect the juxtaposition of the disease of the clitoris, lustfulness, and the disease of the penis, physical ailment, such as sexually transmitted diseases or conditions such as paraphimosis, understood as resulting from such diseases.[70] As we have shown, such diseases are understood as originating with the female, the source of all sexually transmitted diseases and their sequelae [PLATES 217–218]. These are parallel images in Lequeu's world, the world in which penis and clitoris have assumed parallel status as potential sources for disease. But the female's disease is the product of her physiology; the male's disease, the result of her infection of him. Disease becomes a further locus of the monstrous in the eighteenth century.

THE FACE OF THE SUFFERER: PHYSIOGNOMY, DISEASE, AND THE GENITALIA

The monstrous takes various forms in the eighteenth century. One of the most striking is as the mask of disease, the deformed face of the sufferer from sexually transmitted diseases. Venereal disease, in the course of the eighteenth century, comes to be viewed as a ubiquitous problem in European society. But it is also understood as a disease that had a widely respected treatment in the application of mercury.[71] With the ability to localize the fear of the disease due to this alteration in the disease's image, the exemplary sufferer becomes even more localized as the disease of groups that are understood to be at risk—the prostitute, because of her profession, and the nobility, because of the bourgeois understanding of their innate decadence. Venereal disease, an eighteenth-century category that incorporated the 'gleet' (a whitish urethral discharge), the 'whites' (whitish vaginal discharge), gonorrhea, and syphilis was understood as a moral as well as a medical category. Copulation was permissible and did not necessarily lead to venereal disease unless excessive. As a moral failing, venereal disease presented society with the overt sign of the failings of the individual. The sign of these diseases was written on the skin.

The syphilitic skin lesion had an unabated signification for the eighteenth century as the public sign of those who were "seen" as at risk. When William Hogarth represents as the third plate of his series *Marriage à la Mode* (1745), the image of the *Luetic Viscount Visiting the Quack*, he presents a recognizable scene of the syphilitic seeking counsel from the physician[72] [PLATE 219]. The entire series depicts the mismatch between a member of the avaricious nobility and the rising bourgeoisie, which ends in disease and corruption. And it is cast within the eighteenth century's critical understanding of the signification of the syphilitic lesion. This becomes an exemplary image because Hogarth made direct reference to a well-known London quack, Dr. Misaubin of St. Martin's Lane, whose magnum opus lies open at the far right of the image. Misaubin was called "M. de la Pilule" for the pills that he dispensed to rid his patients of syphilis. So well known was this physician that Henry Fielding, in *Tom Jones*, could simply refer to his address as "To Dr. Misaubin, in the World."[73] Hogarth indicates the nature of the disease through the lesion on the face of the procuress as well as on the faces of all three of the figures who come to consult the doctor and through the pitted skull (with its indications of syphilis) on the table next to him.

PLATE 219. *A painting of the medicalized world of the syphilitic by William Hogarth,* The Luetic Viscount Visiting the Quack. *London: National Gallery.*

However, it is not only the disease that is written upon the face. For the treatment that was generally followed, mercury, also had a specific set of signs and symptoms that marked the individual as suffering from venereal disease. Constant salivation (as much as three or four pints a day), sore gums, loose teeth, and a strong metallic smell to the breath marked the individual undergoing mercury treatment. Literary references to the "stinking breath" of individuals became a shorthand manner of speaking about their social unacceptability because of their overt, public signs of sexual corruption.[74] In the most widely circulated British joke book of the eighteenth century, *Joe Miller's Jests*, jokes such as the following played upon the sexualized implications of the "stinking breath":

> The late Mrs. Oldfield being asked if she thought Sir W. Y. and Mrs. H—n, who had both stinking Breaths, were marry'd: I don't know, said she, whether they are marry'd; but I am sure there is a Wedding between them.[75]

The implication of this "joke" is that both of these lascivious individuals were being treated for syphilis; both are "wedded" by their common illness as well as their fornication. Both disease and cure were understood to stigmatize the venereal disease sufferer.

In Hogarth's context for the sign of the venereal disease sufferer, we find a room filled with the signs of the physician's role in curing or identifying sexual pathologies, from the phallic unicorn horn (i.e., narwhal tusk) with its magical properties for the cure of sexual dysfunction (as in the Cluny tapestry, see Plate 19) on one side of the curio cabinet to the pictures of the monstrous children, the sign of sexual ambiguity, over the door to the cabinet's right. One monster has both arms growing out of its head; the other simply has two heads. This later double figure, the sign of the hermaphrodite, is a sign that points to ambiguous sexuality, but it also has a more specific reference in this context. These images are present within the quack's office as signs of the "scientific" function of his craft. They refer back to the wax images of the monstrous that are found within the teaching collections of physicians such as William Hunter. The monstrous is also here a sign of the pathology of sexuality, of the idea of hereditary (not merely congenital) syphilis that was well understood by the eighteenth century. The eighteenth-century physician Antonio Sanchez saw hereditary syphilis as the potential cause of the destruction of the human race, as the disease could literally be passed from generation to generation.[76] Hogarth concludes his series on bad marriages with the Viscount (now an Earl) and his Countess dying

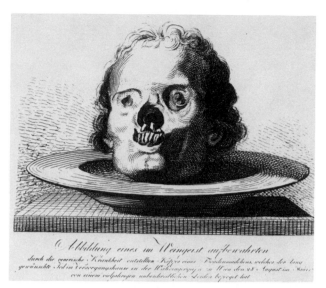

PLATE 220. *The head of a syphilitic prostitute preserved in wine spirit signified the hidden face of the polluted female in this eighteenth-century engraving. London: Wellcome Institute for the History of Medicine.*

of syphilis. Their young daughter, who grasps her dying mother, is marked, on her face, with an identical lesion to that of her father in this early image. Thus the sins of the parents are delivered unto the next generation. It was the potential of the new "fall," a fall seemingly implanted in the pollution of the female (and the destruction of the male), that dominated the idea of the syphilitic and the public sign of the syphilitic. The public sign of the syphilitic, the facial lesion, came to be the image of the fall of at least one class from its dominance in society. In a late eighteenth-century image of the decayed (but preserved) head of a prostitute who died of syphilis [PLATE 220], the skull is no longer a *memento mori* but a sign of danger, equivalent to the skull upon the poison bottle. But again it is an image that is experienced only through the sense of sight. This is the hidden face behind the procuress's sores (and beauty marks), for the beautiful leads to the diseased, the beauty mark to the syphilitic lesion.

The curio cabinet in Hogarth's image opens to reveal a parodic reproduction of the visual tradition of the seduction of the young woman by Death. Here it is a male muscular model being "kissed" by death, the male as the victim of the polluting female. The sign of the nature of the disease, the venereal infection, is also quite prominent on the faces of the young nobleman and the procuress and in the sore on the lip of the Viscount's bride. These marks may be seen as "beauty marks," as artificial representations of the actual lesions of the syphilitic. But Hogarth's contemporaries, such as the German philosopher G. C. Lichtenberg, saw the mark as

Il était jeune, beau ; et plein de Santé.

Il se débat contre la mort.

PLATE 221. *Hand-colored engraving of the young and healthy patient from Samuel Auguste André David Tissot, L'onanisme; ou dissertation physique sur les maladies produites par la masturbation, nouv. éd. annotée d'après les nouvelles observations des docteurs Gottlier, Vogel etc. (Paris: Chez les Marchands de nouveautés, 1836). London: Wellcome Institute for the History of Medicine.*

PLATE 222. *The same patient near death from the masturbation marked upon his skin from Samuel Auguste André David Tissot, L'onanisme; ou dissertation physique sur les maladies produites par la masturbation, nouv. éd. annotée d'après les nouvelles observations des docteurs Gottlier, Vogel etc. (Paris: Chez les Marchands de nouveautés, 1836). London: Wellcome Institute for the History of Medicine.*

the "stamp . . . [of] that type of disease which the linguistic usage of all nations has made a co-national of Monsieur le Docteur."[77] The sign of immoderate sexuality is on the face of all of the participants, from the procuress to the mistress, who appears to Lichtenberg as "small, childish, and in need of help." The question of the innocent female, here the victim of the procuress as well as the dissolute Viscount, is introduced to create a sense of the potential destruction of all elements of society through disease. But it also indicates that all women, no matter how innocent they appear, can be the source of the disease. Hogarth's work is filled with representations of syphilis as a sign of immoderate sexuality, and all of these representations are written on the face of the sufferer.

The image of venereal disease, particularly of the face of the male sufferer, is, at the close of the seventeenth century, transferred to yet a new disease associated with immoderate sexuality. In the course of the eighteenth century, self-touch becomes the central preoccupation of the culture of touch. With the rise of the fantasy of masturbatory disease, the medicalization of Christianity's prohibition against "self-abuse," the skin again becomes the slate on which is drawn the signs of decay. The hypothesis that masturbation was a cause, if not the prime cause, of disease was first promulgated in the anonymous English moral tractate *Onania; or, The Heinous Sin of Self-Pollution*, which appeared in 1700 in Holland.[78] Masturbation is a "disease" constructed to be analogous (in the eighteenth-century mind) with other forms of sexual pathologies such as homosexuality.[79] But it was not until the publication in 1758 of Samuel Auguste André David Tissot's *L'onanisme, ou dissertation physique sur les maladies produites par la masturbation* (translated into English in 1766 and German in 1785) that the idea of masturbation as a cause for a wide range of diseases, from dyspepsia to acne, became commonplace in the medical as well as the lay community **[PLATES 221–225]**.

Son corps est couvert de Pustules.

PLATE 223. *The pustules as the sign of disease on the skin of the masturbator from Samuel Auguste André David Tissot,* L'onanisme; ou dissertation physique sur les maladies produites par la masturbation, *nouv. éd. annotée d'après les nouvelles observations des docteurs Gottlier, Vogel etc. (Paris: Chez les Marchands de nouveautés, 1836). London: Wellcome Institute for the History of Medicine.*

M.lle Ch.as âgée de 15 ans.
(pleine santé)

PLATE 224. *Mlle. Ch_____ at the healthy age of 15 from Samuel Auguste André David Tissot,* L'onanisme; ou dissertation physique sur les maladies produites par la masturbation, *nouv. éd. annotée d'après les nouvelles observations des docteurs Gottlier, Vogel etc. (Paris: Chez les Marchands de nouveautés, 1836). London: Wellcome Institute for the History of Medicine.*

PLATE 225. *The same patient at the age of 16, during the final stage of her illness, from Samuel Auguste André David Tissot,* L'onanisme; ou dissertation physique sur les maladies produites par la masturbation, *nouv. éd. annotée d'après les nouvelles observations des docteurs Gottlier, Vogel etc. (Paris: Chez les Marchands de nouveautés, 1836). London: Wellcome Institute for the History of Medicine.*

By 1784, Germany's most respected educator, Christian Gotthilf Salzmann, had published for the broadest possible audience his essay *On the Secret Sins of Youth*. Salzmann even translated his views concerning the discourse about the dangers of sexuality into reality through the founding of an experimental school in which sexuality (with all of its dangers) was an item of the curriculum. In boarding schools throughout Europe, the cry went out: Masturbate and you will become ill, and that illness, in all its myriad forms, will be marked on your skin. The illness will be a public sign of your "secret vice." You will become marginalized and stigmatized. Your sexuality will become your burden. The understanding of juvenile dermatological outbreaks as the "corona veneris" (with all of its evocation of syphilitic lesions) becomes one of the salient signs of the masturbator **[PLATES 226–227]**. The transference of the sign of the syphilitic to the masturbator, like the confusion of masturbation and homosexuality, represents the establishment of an arbitrary boundary between "normal" and "deviant" sexuality.

The image of the disease written upon the skin incorporates the older tradition of the leper as part of the mythology of the new disease of the sense of touch, masturbatory insanity. The German playwright, Heinrich von Kleist, visiting an asylum in Würzburg in 1800, is horrified to see a masturbator "whom an unnatural sin had driven mad." Kleist describes him in considerable detail:

> An eighteen-year-old youth, who had shortly before been extremely handsome and still bore some signs of this, hung above the unclean opening with naked, pale, desiccated limbs; hollow chest; powerless, sunken head,—his dead white face, like that of a tubercular patient, became florid, lifeless, veined. His eyelids fell powerlessly over his dying, fading eyes; a few dry hairs, like those of an old man, covered his prematurely bald head; his dry, thirsty, parched tongue hung over his pale, shrunken lips; his hands, bound and sewn in restraints, lay behind his back. He could no longer move his tongue to speak, he had hardly the strength even for his piercing breaths. His brain-nerves were not mad but exhausted, completely powerless, no longer able to obey his soul. His entire life was nothing but a single, crippling, eternal swoon.[80]

This is a singular sign of the unnaturalness of masturbation. The representation, however, echoes the pathological images of the wax sculpture—the only sense that Kleist uses to record the image is sight. All of the other senses, from hearing to touch, are

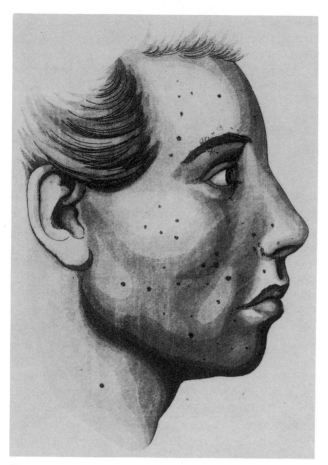

PLATE 226. *The "corona veneris" marks the face of the masturbator from Samuel La'mert,* Self-Preservation: A Medical Treatise on Nervous and Physical Debility, Spermatorrhoea, Impotence, and Sterility *(London: n.p. [ca. 1860]). London: Wellcome Institute for the History of Medicine.*

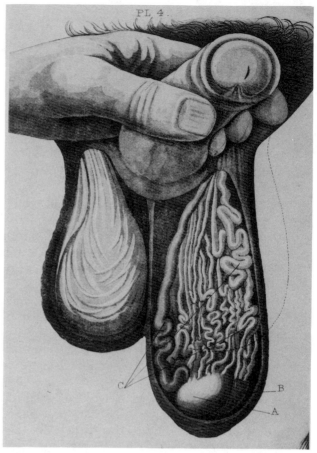

PLATE 227. *A line engraving of the "varicocele" showing dilated veins marks the hidden disease of the masturbator's genitalia signified by the "corona veneris" on his face from Samuel La'mert,* Self-Preservation: A Medical Treatise on Nervous and Physical Debility, Spermatorrhoea, Impotence, and Sterility *(London: n.p. [ca. 1860]). London: Wellcome Institute for the History of Medicine.*

removed from his recording of this image. For Kleist, the central figure in his panorama of the asylum is the youth, with whom he clearly identifies.

Kleist's patient actually existed. Anton Müller, who had functioned as the second medical officer in the Julius-Hospital after 1798, describes one of the patients present during the period from February 1798 to October 1801 (i.e., during the period Kleist would have visited the asylum): "A young man from Saxony, idiotic because of the sin of self-pollution, here not the cause but rather the result of the earlier manifestation of idiocy, brought him ever more to the level of the bestial."[81] But it is the visualization of the masturbator, the appearance of disease on the skin, that marks Kleist's understanding of the wages of sexual sin. Indeed, the visual image of the masturbator haunts the letters

reproduced in *Onania; or, The Heinous Sin of Self-Pollution* in the form of the remarks concerning the "Pimple on my privy parts" or my "Nose . . . full of red spots."[82] Such signs are a reflex of the erotic nature of the touch. The skin of the masturbator reveals the close relationship between the erotic self-touch and the representation of the sexual on the skin. The signs, like a witch's stigmata in the Middle Ages and Renaissance, point to the skin with all of its ambiguities as the source and the map of these signs of difference. The skin has become the map upon which these relationships are drawn. And thus the boundaries of difference, implicit in the Renaissance's iconography of Christ's sexuality and continuing through the Baroque, reappear within the medical discourse about sexuality in the eighteenth century.

It is within the philosophical as well as the medical discourse about the senses that a contemporary rationale for the sexualized nature of the skin (and its pathological implications) can be found. In the work of Denis Diderot, especially in *D'Alembert's Dream*, the sense of touch is the central sense, the sense that forms the basis for all of the other senses. And touch remains closely linked to sexuality as the sense that can lead to seduction and disease. It was therefore the sense that also served as the potential source for the sexually monstrous, for the hermaphrodite. For in the irrationality of touch, in its uncanny ability to seduce even the self, rested the core of the monstrous. But there is one further link that must be explored, for in the eighteenth century the monstrous, as it had been since the Middle Ages, was associated with the specter of other races, of human beings understood as inherently different from the observer as the female was from the male. The function of the sense of touch in the arena of the sexual connects it quite directly to the representation of race as a sexualized category in the anatomy of the eighteenth century, as we shall see.

These associations in the history of the sexualized touch refer back to the epistemological problem of perception raised by John Locke during the seventeenth century in regard to "Molyneux's question." Locke, in 1690, raised again the medieval question of whether we understand the world through "universals," concepts that exist separate from the world experienced through the senses or solely through our experience of the world as mediated by the senses.[83] This question had dominated Western epistemology from the Greeks and had been the source of the debates between the 'realists' and the 'nominalists' in the Middle Ages. It was not the senses and their information that provided a structure of the world for the individual but inherent, preformed ideas.[84] Locke's formulation of this problem centered on a question raised by his friend William Molyneux concerning what would happen when an individual, blind from birth, had his/her sight restored. Would that individual be able to relate the world experienced through touch to the world experienced by the newly acquired sense of sight? Locke argues against the conservative notion of innate ideas, seeing in all ideas responses to sensory impressions. But it is not merely chance that places the question of "universals" or "innate ideas" in the field between the sense of sight and that of touch. Touch, as the lowest sense, provides the ultimate proof for the centrality of the senses. If even the lowliest of the senses provided complex information that could be correlated with the sensory impressions of the highest sense, sight, through

the function of language (which is Locke's argument), then there existed some proof for the source of all "ideas" in experience.

Bishop Berkeley in 1709 argued that there were absolutely no shared "ideas," that the perceptions of each of the senses were equal and differentiated one from the other.[85] Kant, picking up on a paper by William Cheselden (which will be discussed in more detail later) that attempted to prove "Molyneux's question," best articulated the iconographic function of touch in the *Critique of Practical Reason* where he observed that "one might ask, like Cheselden's blind man: 'Which deceives me, sight or touch?' (Empiricism is based on touch, but rationalism on a necessity that can be seen.)"[86] Thus touch becomes closely associated with "empiricism," with a physically direct but unreflective knowledge of the world and, therefore, with the irrational. Sight is the icon of the rational but is a rationality acquired through a physical distance from the object perceived. This is the next step after Locke's use of sight and touch as the keystone to an understanding of innate ideas. Locke's use of sight and touch stems from the specific situation of a pathology, blindness, in which touch was believed to replace sight as the primary means of experiencing the world. For Kant, touch and sight become inherent antitheses, representing the two radically different ways of knowing the world for everyone, not just the impaired. One must understand that, in making this radical dichotomy, Kant also merged the two categories, the world understood exclusively through the senses and the world of innate ideas, and created the hybrid realm of what he calls a priori intuitions, "innate ideas" triggered by sensory impressions. The dichotomy between touch and sight exists even in such a world in which realities can exist "in themselves by our reason, and independently of the nature of our senses."[87] For one of the basic cases constantly used (from Burke to Lessing) to prove the relationship between the senses was that of William Cheselden's 1727 report of the couching of a blind boy for cataracts. The iconographic significance of the blind *boy*, that is, the blind male robbed of his major resource, the sense that provides his masculine rationality, becomes the centerpiece for Theodore Rombouts's *The Five Senses as Represented by the Ages of Man* [PLATE 228]. Greatly influenced by Caravaggio (see Plate 143), this representation of the senses as masculine draws the boundary among the senses in representing the sense of touch by a blind male as the last stage of life. Blindness is a sign of the loss of the rational, of the dominance of the unmediated. It is a state parallel to the sexual frenzy in its reduction of the male to the state of nature.

PLATE 228. *The senses as a masculine assemblage also representing the ages of man in Theodore Rombouts's early seventeenth-century image of* The Five Senses as Represented by the Ages of Man. *Rombouts studied with Rubens but was greatly influenced by Caravaggio, as can be seen in this image. Brussels: Institut Royal du Patrimoine Artistique.*

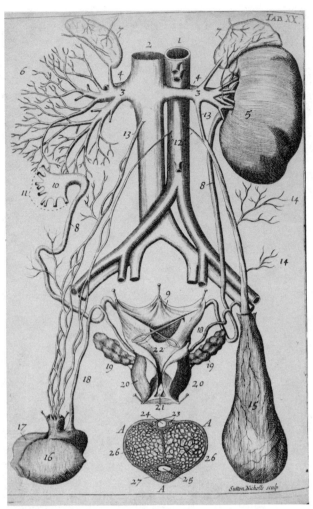

PLATE 229. *Urinary and genital parts of a man from William Cheselden,* The Anatomy of the Human Body *(London: N. Cliff, D. Jackson, & W. Innys, 1713). London: Wellcome Institute for the History of Medicine.*

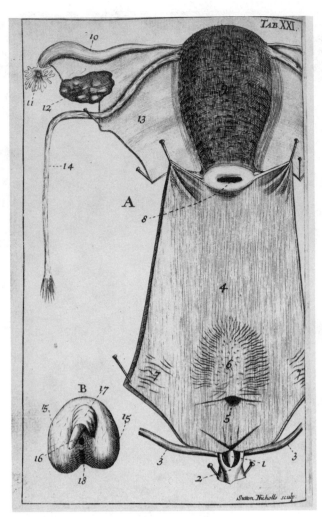

PLATE 230. *The genital parts of a woman from William Cheselden,* The Anatomy of the Human Body *(London: N. Cliff, D. Jackson, & W. Innys, 1713). London: Wellcome Institute for the History of Medicine.*

Cheselden's report tells of the boy's first response to seeing the color black, which he associated with the darkness of his period of blindness: "the first Time he saw Black, it gave him great Ineasiness, yet after a little Time he was reconcil'd to it; but some Months after, seeing by Accident a Negroe Woman, he was struck with great Horror at the sight."[88] The female, experienced by the child through the sense of touch, is associated with the source of anxiety, blackness, and "horror" arises. The false (in the view of the eighteenth century) association between the category of the "female" and that of the "black" heightens the sense of the distance created in constructing the image of seeing the black as differentiated from touching the woman. Cheselden's case stresses the seeming disparity

between the construction of a category through "touching" and that of one through sight. It is the incongruity of these two constructions that causes horror (and that enables Burke to cite this case as an example of the origin of the sublime). The problem of race and sexuality are again linked in the association of the skin and the sense of touch. When one turns to Cheselden's representation of the genitalia in his *The Anatomy of the Human Body* (1713), one is not surprised to find the traditional schematic images **[PLATE 229]**. The genitalia of the female are prepared, as in Bidloo's atlas, as an anatomical preparation, with the nails holding it quite present **[PLATE 230]**. But it is at the very end of Cheselden's atlas, as a sign of the anomalies of the body, of the monstrous, that Cheselden brings us an image that

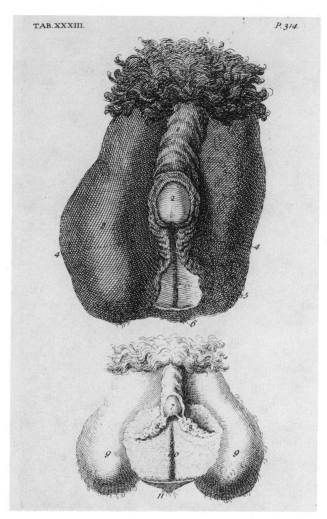

PLATE 231. An engraving of the genitalia of a black hermaphrodite from William Cheselden, The Anatomy of the Human Body *(London: C. Hitch & R. Dodsley, 1750). London: Wellcome Institute for the History of Medicine.*

is, like the wax images we have seen, quite striking in its "realism" **[PLATE 231]**. It is the image of the genitalia of a black hermaphrodite. The senses, sexuality, and race are linked in this image. It is an image of the genitalia that signifies the ambiguity of all of those categories that Cheselden takes as "real," sexual, and racial. But the image is also an image of the surface, of the skin, of the genitalia as the object of the erotic as well as the scientific touch. It is a part of a cadaver, an aspect that defines the nature of the different. For here, as in the midwife's handbooks of Smellie and Hunter, the part defines the whole. It is an object that bears the stigmata of difference, in its partial representation of the body. It is a removal of the part and its representation as the sign of the entire being.

With the secularization of the pleasurable touch in the eighteenth century as the erotic and seductive, pain, which still haunts the image of touch even into the eighteenth century, becomes domesticated. The close association of images of the painful touch (as a woman) and sexually transmitted disease seems to vanish. In Alexander Vanhacken's mezzotint of a painting by Jacopo Amigoni **[PLATE 232]**, the feminine Touch strokes the sharp end of the arrow, not the martyr's arrow but the arrow of Eros. The erotic touch, as in Jacques Louis David's *Cupid and Psyche* **[PLATE 233]** (1817) with Eros having shot his arrow, as symbolized by the bow, playfully links the erotic and the image of penetration. (The sense of the erotic touch is linked to the "shot rocket," in Hogarth's *Before and After* [1736] **[PLATES 234– 235]**.)

PLATE 232. A mezzotint, Feeling, *by Alexander Vanhacken after a lost early eighteenth-century painting by Jacopo Amigoni. London: Wellcome Institute for the History of Medicine.*

PLATE 233. *Jacques Louis David's postcoital image of* Cupid and Psyche, *1817. Leonard C. Hanna, Jr., bequest, Cleveland, OH: Cleveland Museum of Art.*

PLATE 234. *The act of seduction represented in William Hogarth's etching and engraving* Before, *1736. Ithaca: Herbert F. Johnson Museum of Art, Cornell University.*

PLATE 235. *Postcoital depression represented in William Hogarth's etching and engraving* After, *1736. Ithaca: Herbert F. Johnson Museum of Art, Cornell University.*

PLATE 236. *Moll Hacka-bout as the Jew's mistress, the second plate of William Hogarth's* A Harlot's Progress, *1731. Ithaca: Private collection.*

For Hogarth there is also one further image of sexual excess, and that is the icon of the marginal black in this world of sexual corruption. In two cycles, *A Rake's Progress* (1735) and *A Harlot's Progress* (1731), the figures of the black servants mark the high point of sexual activity.[89] They appear in the opposite sex to the central figure. It is the corruption of sexually transmitted disease, not of sexual deviancy, that is indicated by the icon of the black. In the second plate of *A Harlot's Progress*, we are shown Moll Hackabout as the mistress to a Jewish merchant, the first stage of her decline as a sexualized female **[PLATE 236]**. The prominent position of the monkey dressed in a doll's version of Moll's own clothing signifies her unbridled sexuality in a traditional iconographic manner, as has been discussed in Chapter Three. The Jew represents not only an eighteenth-century racial reinterpretation of the ancient topos of the sexual mismatch of age (wealth) and youth (the prostitute) (see Plate 73) but also a continuation of the image of the Jew as belonging to the world of the sexualized outsider. His wealth may create the illusion that he belongs to Hogarth's reference group, the world of the middle class, but his very association with Moll marks him as the sexualized Other. He attempts to cross the border between his pariah status and the accepted world of middle-class values, but the fact that he has a paid mistress marks him as as much an outsider as the members of the dissolute minor nobility in *Marriage à la Mode.* Present in this sexualized world

is another outsider, the young black male servant. In the third stage of Tom Rakewell's collapse, we find him in the notorious brothel, the Rose Tavern in Covent Garden[90] **[PLATE 237]**. The entire picture is full of references to illicit sexual activity, all portrayed negatively. Present is the figure of the young female black as servant. The black woman is the visualization of the female genitalia. For the slang term *black joke* referred to the female sexual organ.[91] And, indeed, in Hogarth's 1743 image, *The Discovery*, a black prostitute, her breasts exposed, is revealed to have occupied the bed of a would-be Lothario as an unacknowledged substitute for the lady who should have been present. Thus the meaning of the text, which Hogarth borrows from Ovid, is: "What was once white is now the opposite." The association of blackness and the female organ is a further elaboration of the concretization of images of sexually transmitted disease into the image of the female but here, not every female, only the marginal or deviant one, only the black female. Blackness becomes a sign for polluting and destructive sexuality, as the image of sexual license and its resulting disease.

Hidden within these images of erotic "play," however, is the original sense of foreboding inherent in the sexual during the seventeenth and early eighteenth centuries. With the mercury cure, the fear of disease was only mitigated, not eliminated. If we turn to the title page of Giuseppe Maria Bossi's 1793 monograph on syphilis, it is clear that the

PLATE 237. *The brothel represented in the third plate of William Hogarth's A Rake's Progress, 1735. Membership Purchase Fund, Ithaca: Herbert F. Johnson Museum of Art, Cornell University.*

syphilitic patient in this image is captured between Eros and Physis, sexuality and medicine. Cupid is here not benign but threatening **[PLATE 238]**. The physical proximate is the source of irrational empiricism, sexuality, as well as a deeper understanding of the aesthetic, through the realm of Kant's "rational" sense—sight.[92]

Of all the masks of the sexually monstrous during the eighteenth century, the mask of those driven mad by love is one of the most striking. If the sequence "masturbation–venereal excess–venereal disease–nervous disease–insanity" was the paradigm for the understanding of the course of one sexually related illness, then the sequence "love–sexual attraction–abandonment–insanity" is the paradigm for the eighteenth century's image of love madness.[93] It is written on the face not as pustules and lesions but as the physiognomy of madness.[94] Erotomania, a diagnostic category in J. É. D. Esquirol's early nineteenth-century nosology, has many prefigurations before the age of Enlightenment.[95] By the 1840s, and the publication of Alex-

PLATE 238. *The title page to G. M. Bossi,* Esposizione delle malattie veneree e della medicazione di esse *(Milan: Mon. S. Amb. Mag., 1793). London: Wellcome Institute for the History of Medicine.*

ander Morison's standard atlas of mental illness, the image of the erotomaniac had become fixed **[PLATE 239]**. Here is its Miss A. A., a domestic servant, who had fixated on a clergyman in her parish and was "generally disposed to kiss."[96] Abandoned by her middle-class beloved, she has selected an inappropriate object for her thwarted desires. Her disease is a disturbance that has its roots in those lower senses associated with sexuality, specifically touch. Within eight months in the hospital, she is cured **[PLATE 240]**. The contrast between the two plates provides a detailed representation of the physiognomy of the erotomaniac. Gone is the madwoman's gaze, which fixes the viewer with its intensity; gone is the fixed smile of the seductress. The restored Miss A. A.'s gaze no longer meets that of the observer; she no longer smiles, seductively or in any other way. She is no longer an erotomaniac.

In Goethe's description of the beautiful cadaver in *Wilhelm Meister's Travels*, we are presented with the result of love madness clouding a mind, the senseless suicide of a beautiful young woman, a theme that will loom large in our discussion of the "fallen" woman in Chapter Eight. Wilhelm cannot bring himself to touch her, to reduce her to an object of scientific interest, because of the cause of her suicide. Her erotomania was caused by her seduction and abandonment by her lover, a theme that haunts what is perhaps the best known popularization of images of madness during the late eighteenth century, Christian Heinrich Spiess's *Biographies of the Mentally Ill.*[97] Goethe cannot have Wilhelm replicate the cross-sexual touch, even of the cadaver, that brought her body into the anatomy theater.

Both in scientific as well as in popular representations of erotomania, the illness is written on the visage of the sufferer. The "source" of erotomania lies in the absence of the cross-sexual touch; this is parallel to the origin of masturbatory insanity in the self-touch. One of the central texts for this in the English tradition is to be found in the Scottish Enlightenment. Harley, the sentimental hero of Henry Mackenzie's novel *The Man of Feeling* (1771), is persuaded by an acquaintance to visit one "of those things called Sights, in London, which every stranger is supposed desirous to see,"[98] the asylum officially called the Bethlehem Royal Hospital but better known as Bedlam. They go to experience the world through sight, the highest and most rational of the senses. The path taken by this party through the asylum is marked by the inmates they hear. First they are led "to the dismal mansions of those who are in the most horrid state of incurable madness." Here "the clanking of chains, the wildness of their cries, and the imprecations that some of them uttered, formed a scene inexpressibly shocking." (The emotional impact is made by the movement down the hierarchy of the senses, from the seeing of the insane to touching them.)

Harley joins his companions in the women's wing, where he is drawn by the striking face of an erotomaniac to hear her tale of woe. He devotes half of a chapter to a recounting of the tale of this melancholic figure represented as different, as noble. Separated from her true love, who died on a voyage to the West Indies to seek his fortune, she was almost forced "to marry a rich miserly fellow, who was old enough to be her grandfather." She was reduced to madness. Harley, who converses with the poor mad girl, leaves "in astonishment and pity! . . . He put a couple of guineas into the man's

PLATE 239. Amatory Mania *from Alexander Morison,* The Physiognomy of Mental Diseases *(London: Longman, 1840). Ithaca: Private collection.*

PLATE 240. Amatory Mania, Recovered in About Eight Months *from Alexander Morison,* The Physiognomy of Mental Diseases *(London: Longman, 1840). Ithaca: Private collection.*

hand: 'Be kind to that unfortunate'—He burst into tears, and left them."

Mackenzie's image of Bedlam quite clearly stands within the traditional bounds of the understanding of madness in the eighteenth century. Madness is the product of a congenital inability to deal with the vicissitudes of life. But more than this, Mackenzie offers his reader a manner of seeing sexuality. The model that he employs is the theme of the "unequal lovers," a theme that has a long tradition in European art and letters, as we have already seen.[99] It is the pairing of the different, even when the different both stand outside the definition of the norm. The disproportionate relationship, the imbalance of life, forces the beautiful young woman (never the young man) into madness.[100] But it is an imbalance caused by the economics of sexuality, an economics already seen in Hogarth's *Marriage à la Mode*. In Hogarth's *A Rake's Progress* (1735), the moral (and sexual) dis-

solution of Rakewell's world is the direct result of his inherited (rather than earned) wealth.[101] Hogarth is certainly not offering the viewer an anticapitalist message—on the contrary, he sees earning a living as the highest goal. Living on acquired wealth, at least in the dissolution of London, leads to sexual adventures and eventual madness. This is part of the general Hogarthian association of disease and sexual license or excess. Rakewell's end in *A Rake's Progress* is an analogy to the diseased Viscount in *Marriage à la Mode* (see Plate 219). This is quite a different path from that taken by the protagonist in his *Harlot's Progress*, whose dissolute end is not of madness but of physical disease and decay, the sign of the difference between the "rewards" reaped by the sexually excessive female as opposed to the sexually excessive male. Such a view must be contrasted with the emblem of sexually transmitted disease, within the tradition of the *nupta contagio* which we have already seen from Andrea Alciatus (1550) (see Plate 74). There the critique of the image of the forced and ill-fitted marriage is, for the woman, like a case of sexually transmitted disease. Here this image is translated into "love madness." For Alciatus is criticizing the *coemptio*, the legal device through which a father can buy his daughter a husband (much as Petruchio purchases Kate in *The Taming of the Shrew*). Alciatus's "puella ingenua," pure girl, is very different from the Viscountess of Hogarth's *Marriage à la Mode*, who is, as a member of the socially ambitious bourgeoisie, really no better than her mercenary aristocratic husband. In the asylum visited by Harley, the beautiful woman's madness is the result of "love sickness"; her father's punishment is bankruptcy, the economic parallel to madness. Madness and wealth are linked in these two models in an overt manner. "Natural" actions—the earning of wages, the correct, fatherly attitude toward the daughter—are violated, and the result is an overturning of the world, a world that dissolves into madness or financial ruin. These are parallel signs of dissolution that link the basic economics of the worlds in which they are found with the representation of the "rational." Love madness is a somatic illness, its roots are in the physiology of the female, and its passage is marked upon the visage. Its emblem is the alteration of the mind as well as the body. The underlying fear of the male, however, surfaces within a subset of images of erotomania. For the erotomaniacs may not only flee into their madness; they may, like Sir Walter Scott's Lucy Ashton, in *The Bride of Lam-mermoor* (1819), go mad: "her head-gear dishevelled; her night-clothes torn and dabbled with blood,—her eyes glazed, her features convulsed into a wild paroxysm of insanity."[102] Having been forced to abandon her true love and marry for convenience, she sinks into a madness that results in her murdering her false bridegroom. This is the loss of control that frightens. It is the underlying text in all of the images of erotomania and may well be why Scott's novel, transmogrified into Donizetti's *Lucia di Lammermoor*, provided the model for images of the mad-woman for the rest of the nineteenth century. Lucy's madness, the source of her destruction of that male system of economy that forced her into an inappropriate marriage, is written on her face, a warning for all males about the power of thwarted sexuality. We see, of course, the projection of the controlled sexuality of the observer into the form of this boundary crosser, the erotomaniac, the female whose true sexual desire is denied. The face of the erotomaniac is the sign of the need to control one's own sexuality from within, rather than rely on the control (and denial) of sexuality through forces (such as those of the parent) external to oneself. Erotomania thus becomes the natural analogue to at least one sexually related disease, masturbation, a disease in which the internal forces cannot control one's sexuality and one is forced to rely on external, social forces, such as medicine. For what is inscribed through masturbation on the body, the signs of decay and pollution, is inscribed through love madness on the face.

CHAPTER SEVEN

Goethe's Touch

A POET'S HISTORY OF TOUCH

Throughout this book there has been an attempt to trace the relationship between the history of the senses, specifically the sense of touch, and the iconography of sexuality, as a means of understanding the basis for our communal fantasies about sexuality.[1] I have looked at how society represents the means by which we acquire knowledge of the world, specifically, how fantasies about the body, and more specifically about our sexuality, have been structured. In the eighteenth century, Immanuel Kant made axiomatic the Platonic view that we experience the world only through our senses. But the idea that the information processed by our senses is historically constructed, that our means of representing what information the senses transmit is structured by our presuppositions about the significance of aspects of the world, is relatively recent. There is a general assumption, however, on the part of many historians that the history of *all* of the senses could be written as part of the history of the *mentalité*, the historically created consciousness of any given culture. The earlier chapter on Leonardo and this chapter focus on the centrality of individual variations in shaping the generalized response of a culture to sexuality and the body. Here I will examine the response of another broadly creative individual, Johann Wolfgang von Goethe, not to a technical innovation that altered (or heightened) the cultural understanding of the senses but to a shift in the aesthetic and philosophical understanding of the senses. Goethe's response to the wax models of the body, discussed in Chapter Six, has already introduced us to some of the complexities of his manner of seeing sexuality and pathology.

With Goethe, the problem of the supposed discontinuity in the history of perception simply masked a radical refunctioning of the continuity of perception. Goethe's texts can be used to document the *mentalité* of the Germans of the eighteenth century confronted with new approaches to the senses and sexuality. His adaptation of the image of the sexual decodes the verbal and visual signs in his culture.

Central to our examination of how general patterns of the understanding of sexuality are shaped by individual needs and fears will be the paradox presented by Johann Wolfgang von Goethe and his use of the verbal representation of the image of touching in a series of poems written during a central period of his life, his trip to Rome in 1787–88. It was that period in his life when he (according to his own account) discovered the intensity of human sexuality and reflected that discovery in a series of poems that earned him in the Weimar court (where they were circulated) the nickname "Priapus."[2] To understand Goethe's construction of "touch" and its relationship to sexuality, we must also take into consideration the fact that the representation of touch is always in the realm of another sense, that of sight, whether it is the "seeing" of the text representing sexuality or the "seeing" of visual images of touch. Because we do not record our constructions of reality through touch but through sight, we need to link these two senses to write our history of the erotic touch. Thus the status afforded sight and touch, most often considered the highest and the lowest of the senses, is not random. These two senses are inexorably linked within their individual integration into "private" systems of representing the social construction of their history.

In addition to the relationship between seeing and touching, it is important to remember that there was a central splitting in the social construction of touch during the course of the eighteenth century. It is the separation of "good" touching and "bad" touching, of the touching of the opposite sex, with its erotic associations, and the touching of the self, with its associations of pain and disease. The iconography of masturbation, which has been discussed in detail in Chapter Six, and the erotic underlie this important shift in the understanding of the body. This division is represented in the image of touch, an iconography that incorporates not only the representation of the sense of touch but also the sign of the organ of touch—the skin. This seems evident in any discussion of the iconography of the other senses, for example, how closely the phenomenology of transcendentalism is linked to Emerson's caricature of the human being as a walking eye. However, the iconography of touch seems to be alienated from its sensory organ, the skin. Thus any critical history of the representation of the sense of touch must be closely linked to a history of the representation of the skin.

We know that the skin has been given meaning within other systems in eighteenth-century thought, such as physiognomy, that attribute specific meaning to aspects of the body. In such systems, specific qualities of skin are related to specific character traits. The skin thus is not only an organ of sensation but also serves as the canvas upon which touch and its cultural associations are represented. A person's character is written upon the skin as well as in the perception of the world through senses such as touch. The skin is understood simultaneously to be an organ of sensation, transmitting heat, cold, vibration, and pressure/pain to provide an aspect of our perception of the world as well as the blank page upon which the signs associated with these sensory impressions are written. Thus the "crude" individual will perceive the world in a "base" manner, according to physiognomists such as Johann Caspar Lavater, and this baseness will be reflected in the coarseness of the skin. This double function, the skin as organ of perception as well as the sign of the quality of perception, is crucial to our understanding of the ambiguities inherent in the social construction of touch.

In addition, there is a basic difference between the sense of touch and the other senses. Although we can "see" ourselves or "hear" ourselves, such an act is purely an act of reception, but when we touch ourselves, we respond both as the object "touched" and the subject "touching." And this is especially true in terms of our touching one area of greater sensitivity, such as the genitalia, with another, such as the hand. It is not merely the genitalia that are touched and stimulated but also the hand, so that the self-erotic touch is double-edged. The heightened quality of the self-touch is given a very specific negative evaluation within the Pauline tradition, a tradition that condemns out of hand the pleasurable aspects of the erotic. It is no wonder that the condemnation is understood, at least in the eighteenth century, to be written through pathological signs (i.e., pimples) on the skin of the masturbator, for it is the touch of skin upon skin that provides the stimulation.

Goethe's personal vision of the sexualized touch should be understood within the generalized construction of the erotic in the late eighteenth century, in which the desire to see becomes one with the desire to touch. Here I am arguing against what has become a dominant reading of the sexual implications of the erotic poetry Goethe wrote as a result of his first trip to Rome. K. R. Eissler has argued that Goethe had developed a neurotic relationship to women, a neurosis driven by his fear of sexually transmitted diseases, as well as his strong identification with his father.[3] According to Eissler, Goethe suffered from a form of premature ejaculation that was "cured" through his sexual relationship with a young waitress named Faustina, the daughter of Goethe's innkeeper, Agostino di Giovanni, during the first months of 1788. Eissler thus takes quite literally the function of poetry as an unmediated record of experience. His reading is an attempt to correct traditional German scholarship's "moral" image of Goethe, which stated that *if* such sexual adventures as recorded in Goethe's Italian poetry actually transpired, his partner was certainly his wife-to-be, Christiane Vulpius, who was disguised in his poetry as the young Italian girl, Faustina. Eissler based his correction on Antonio Valeri's neopositivistic claim to have discovered the identity of Goethe's Italian lover, a claim that rests on no contemporary documentation.[4] What I will show is that Eissler was quite correct in claiming that the poetry of the Roman period records an intense and meaningful sexual experience but that this experience is converted into the masked subtleties of poetic discourse, for reasons that I hope will become evident. Moreover, these subtleties can be documented through Goethe's visualization of the appropriate sexual object, his translation of the written word into images, much as Leonardo translates the axioms of Renaissance anatomy into his anatomical drawings. I agree with Eissler about the general fear of sexually transmitted disease that haunted Goethe as well as most of his contemporaries but draw rather different conclusions from this fact. Alternatives for sexual release, such as masturbation, were also understood as putting the individual at risk. But most important, all of these alternatives were associated by Goethe with his personal aesthetic reevaluation of the implication of the erotic nature of the senses of sight and touch, and this new association forms the basis for his "Roman Elegies."[5]

GOETHE'S ROMAN HOLIDAY

Sometime in January 1788, at least according to his text, a 38-year-old German poet found himself in bed with a Roman girl named Faustina, tapping out the meter of the poem he was composing on a supine spine:

> Happy now I can feel the classical climate inspire me,
> Past and present at last clearly, more vividly speak.
> Here I take their advice, perusing the works of the ancients
> With industrious care, pleasure that grows every day.
> But only through the nights by Amor I'm differently busied,
> If only half improved, doubly delighted instead.
> Also, am I not learning when at the shape of her bosom,
> Graceful lines I can glance, guide a light hand down her hips?
> Only thus I appreciate marble; reflecting, comparing,
> See with an eye that can feel, feel with an eye that can see.
> True, the loved one besides may claim a few hours of the daytime,
> But in nighttime hours too makes full amends for the loss.
> For not always we're kissing; often hold sensible converse.
> When she succumbs to sleep, pondering, long I lie still.
> Often too in her arms I've lain composing a poem,
> Gently with fingering hand count the hexameter's beat
> Out on her back; she breathes, so lovely and calm in her sleeping,
> That her breath to the inmost depth, glowing, transfuses my breast.
> Amor meanwhile refuels the lamp and remembers
> How his great triumvirs too likewise he once had obliged.[6]

"Sehe mit fühlendem Aug', fühle mit sehender Hand"[7] (See with an eye that can feel, feel with an eye that can see)—so goes the oft-cited conceit in Goethe's famed "Roman Elegies." The overt movement of this passage, the creation of the object of desire through the simultaneous acts of seeing and touching of the skin of the Other, is the objectification of the classic aesthetic scale of the senses, linking the highest, the realm of sight (and art), and the lowest, the realm of touch (and sexuality). The return of Eros in the form of an erection is linked by the text to the very act of the writing of poetry, an act that is represented as linking sight and touch. This neoclassical poem presents us with our text and our problem.

For Goethe stands at that moment in time, the eighteenth century, during which the abandonment of an absolute aesthetics of the senses makes Goethe's conceit possible as a conscious deconstruction of the established hierarchy of the senses. For Goethe, in an essay written in 1792, the senses had become building blocks of reality that "anyone will have the possibility of combining . . . according to his own manner and forming them to a whole that should be more or less pleasing . . . to the human mode of understanding in general."[8] This view underlies his ironic use of the hierarchy of the senses in his literary work. Earlier, in the confrontation between Faust and Mephistopheles in *Faust I*, Goethe had ironized the hierarchy of the senses:

> My friend, your senses will have more
> Gratification in this hour
> Than in a year's monotony.
> What the delicate spirits sing to you
> And the beautiful images that they bring to you
> Are no empty, idle wizardry.
> You'll have your sense of smell delighted,
> Your palate in due course excited,
> Your feelings rapt enchantingly.[9]

Mephistopheles uses the archaic hierarchy of the senses (beginning with the higher senses of hearing and sight and concluding with the excitement of touch [Gefühl with its double meaning of touch and feeling]) to seduce the pedantic Faust. With "Roman Elegies," Goethe establishes an overt relationship between touch (or at least its visual representation) and the act of touching, which by the eighteenth century had come to represent sexual seduction. But in a covert movement, he also reveals his abandonment of another eighteenth-century hierarchy, the scale that exists between the permissible sexual act and the forbidden one, between heterosexuality and homosexuality, a movement foreshadowed in his implicit critique of the hierarchy of the senses in *Faust* and its function in the intellectual (not physical) seduction of Faust by that minion of the Devil, Mephistopheles, whose defeat at the close of *Faust II* is the result of his own homoeroticism.

Touch becomes by the close of the eighteenth century (as we have seen in detail in Chapter Six) the sense that is associated again with the irrational, with the direct, unreflected, physically proximate comprehension of the world. And it is thus associated with the Pauline construction of the erotic as the overcoming of the irrational that dominates Western culture.[10] In the eighteenth century, one further factor was introduced, as was discussed. The association of the erotic and touch was linked to the production of representations of the world. For Locke's answer to "Molyneux's question," discussed in detail in Chapter Six, the question of what the nature of a blind man's senses of touch and sight would be once sight was restored, was to associate the world of the senses with the human ability to produce language, language that named that world perceived through the senses. If the blind man were told that the apprehension of the cube that he has had through touch was equivalent to that which he now has through sight, the common label *cube* would be sufficient (according to Locke) for him to make the association between the two discrete sensory impressions. Once the sensory impressions gathered through each sense were linked to a label, a word, the harmony of an integrated perception of the world was restored. Johann Gottfried Herder in his famed essay on the origin of language published in 1770 (and, indeed, later in the work of Jacob Grimm, one of the founders of modern linguistics) saw this labeling of sensory experiences as the very origin of language. For Herder, the experience of the world by unimpaired individuals provides an integrated impression of the world in which, however, following Aristotle, touch is the foundation of all senses. Touch is the common sense upon which the others are constructed. (It is still the lowest but now the most basic.) And it is upon this harmony of the senses built upon touch that language, the need to name, arises.[11] The physically proximate forms the basis for all language. In the eighteenth century language, touch, Eros, are all intertwined within the construction of the basis for all aesthetics, the psychology of perception.

Goethe's text thus provides one of the problems of speaking about seeing the sexualized touch, the protean nature of the construction of touch itself. This construction relies upon contemporary associations, values, and implications for its context. Goethe, in his "Roman Elegies," wished to undermine the accepted aesthetic hierarchy of the senses by seeing *and* touching and by writing about both, all acts that provide aesthetic as well as sensual stimulation.[12] These interrelated actions, he claims, enable him to understand the impact of the beautiful, which is exemplified by those white, marble statues of nude males that had become, through the German art critic and aesthetician Johann Joachim Winckelmann's mediation earlier in the century, the hallmark of the beautiful.[13] It is literally in the footsteps of Winckelmann that Goethe undertakes his trip to Italy. And it is no accident that the very first mention of Winckelmann in Goethe's account of that trip, his journal of the *Italian Journey*, begins with an account of Winckelmann's enthusiasm for a neoclassical forgery of a portrait of Ganymede, seen presenting Jupiter with a cup of wine and receiving a kiss in exchange.[14] Winckelmann's homoerotic aesthetics haunts Goethe's image of Italy, but at this point (in November 1786) only through the sense of sight, the act of seeing the representation of a homosexual encounter.

In "Roman Elegies," Goethe does undermine Kant's epistemology, in that seeing and touching not only reify the innate sense of the beautiful but construct it.[15] But let us for a moment ask ourselves who it is that Goethe is seeing and touching. We know from Lord Clark that the female form had been the definition of the beautiful since the Renaissance, and this topos seems to dominate Goethe's poetic representation of the interrelationship of the senses.[16] Given the centrality of Winckelmann's aesthetics for Goethe's trip to Italy, however, this perception of Goethe's equation of the female with the beautiful must be drawn into question. We are not that far historically from Schopenhauer's mid-nineteenth-century reworking of Kant's views on the relationship between the senses and knowledge in terms of gender, when Schopenhauer asks how anyone can be attracted (except through the sexual impulse's confusion of the senses) to that "undersized, narrow-shouldered, broad-hipped, and short-legged sex."[17] Women are unaesthetic beings, made the object of desire only through the impact of the biological drives on the senses. It is a view that, by the 1880s, becomes part of the credo of a homoerotic aesthetic. John Addington Symonds, in his *A Problem in Greek Ethics*, writes that "the male body exhibits a higher organization of the human form than the female." For Symonds, sexuality is overtly the source of all beauty: "men regard the female

PLATE 241. *From John Singer Sargent, secret notebooks dated from 1890–1915,* Reclining Male Nude, *a charcoal drawing on off-white paper. A gift of Mrs. Francis Ormond. Cambridge, MA: Fogg Art Museum, Harvard University.*

form as more essentially beautiful than the male. The contrary to this belief can be abundantly demonstrated. The male form is infinitely richer in a variety of lovely qualities, and is incomparably nobler in its capacities of energetic action."[18] The fascination with the perfect form of the male, as seen in the drawings of John Singer Sargent [PLATE 241], of the 1890s, places the position of a male as parallel aesthetic object to that of the female.[19] This view has its direct roots in Winckelmann's aesthetics as accepted and developed by Goethe. Is it really "woman" as the object of desire whom Goethe is seeing and touching, or is it a convention of high culture, of the language of the depiction of touch that dominates and masks the true object of desire?

THE CONTEXTS OF GOETHE'S TOUCH

The icon of touch (which was detailed in Chapter Five) is that of the woman, the woman in pain, the woman tortured. It is an image of the woman as the embodiment of the painful, the pain of childbirth represented by the bird or reptile, themselves not viviparous; the image of the woman as the source of the sexual pain of the male, of venereal disease. It is this image that dominates the idea of touch in the eighteenth century when the fantasy of "seeing" the sense of touch had already become a commonplace within the tradition of the visual representation of the senses. Following the Renaissance, the sexualization of the representation of touch, with its linkage of pain and pleasure, the material and the transcendental, becomes part of the repertoire of images in the fine arts and literature. Within the tradition of the emblem, touch, as part of the model of the five senses, becomes a standard aspect of the repertoire of icons. Touch, as we have seen in Goethe's poem, is female. Within the new tradition of the emblem books, the initial association is between the feminized touch and pain. The kiss, as Eissler noted in his appendix on Goethe's "Roman Elegies," became for Goethe (in his personal life as well as in his fictions) a means of sexual release that was not contaminated by the fear of disease.[20] In this world all fear is banished, and that means that the sense of touch is placed within rigid boundaries. It is, as in the world of the Dutch genre paintings discussed in Chapter Five, a world in which sexual contact is severely limited. There the kiss is permitted, but the touch of the hand is forbidden. The banishment of touch, its replacement with the chaste kiss, seems to make the touch of the "Roman Elegies" an even more radical act. Indeed, it is Goethe's Eros, "refueling the lamp" by touching the skin of the beloved, which mirrors the discussion of sensibility and the erection that dominated the eighteenth century's understanding of male sexuality. But the erection of the "Roman Elegies" draws upon a further set of representations of human sexuality.

Goethe's text in "Roman Elegies" seems, on the surface, to be a truly Lockeian one, one that creates the object of desire through the mediation of the higher as well as the lower senses. But when we turn to the social realities of his trip to Rome, we find a strange discontinuity between Goethe's fantasy about sexuality, seeing, touching, and writing, and his poetic representation. Language may be the result of our attempts to articulate our sensory impressions, but it also masks our comprehension and articulation of those impressions. In a strong letter to his patron, Karl August of Weimar, at the end of 1787, Goethe complains about the "uncertain" nature of the local female prostitutes, that is, that they may all be diseased and that he is avoiding them.[21] He also comments that the "unmarried women" are purer than anywhere else on his trip, and he is constantly confronted with the question "e che concluderemo" when he approaches them. Syphilis or marriage—not really a pleasant choice for a German tourist in Italy out for a sexual adventure.

His letter then takes a turn that may provide us with an interesting insight into his sexual seeing and touching, for he comments quite positively on the presence in Rome of male homosexuality, which, although it may not "reach the highest levels of sensuality," approaches the "most beautiful" manifestations known to him from Greek literature. That homosexual love could be understood as more beautiful, less bound to the realm of the lower senses than heterosexual love, must certainly color any reading of "Roman Elegies." This image of the male as the aesthetic object, an image that Goethe took from Winckelmann's self-consciously homoerotic aesthetics, is reified over half a century later in a conversation with Goethe's friend Friedrich von Müller in which Goethe observed that "aesthetically" the male is "far more beautiful, superior, more perfect than the woman."[22] But such love, Goethe goes on to remark, easily becomes "bestial, grossly material," that is, when it moves into the realm of the lower senses, of the sense of touch.

That Goethe wishes to avoid sexual contact with women during his trip to Italy is abundantly clear even in his poetry. And he makes no exceptions for this fear. Goethe stresses the ubiquitous nature of sexually transmitted diseases in his "Roman Elegies." He writes:

> Any kind of pleasure is a risk,
> Nowhere does one lay one's head safely in a woman's lap.
> Safe is no longer the marriage bed, nor adultery;
> Husband, wife and friend, one is injured in the other.[23]

Goethe's mention of sexually transmitted disease within "Roman Elegies" would have evoked for the eighteenth-century mind a very different tradition of seeing the skin, the organ of touch and the source of the erotic, in its function as the signs of the sexual pollution of the female. In Goethe's poem, as in all eighteenth- and nineteenth-century texts written from the male perspective, sexually transmitted diseases were the result of the female infecting the male. There was, as has been described in the earlier chapters, a tradition of representing the sexualized female with the crimes of her sexuality literally written on her skin. In an image of the head of an eighteenth-century German prostitute, dead of syphilis, we have an icon of decay that points toward the skin as the page upon which the perversions of the individual are inscribed (see Plate 220). These images are attempts to undermine the tradition of the female as the beautiful object, by claiming that the innate nature of their beauty is a mask for decay, a mortality rooted in their iconographic role as the object of desire.

The relationship between corruption, pollution,

and the female genitalia remains a powerful one for Goethe and remains associated with the sexual gaze, the act of looking at the sexual object. This remains constant even when he has his male characters observe not the act of coitus but urination. The sexual association of the image of the female genitalia with urination has a long textual history. Indeed, the first major text in the Western literary tradition that associates these two images relates them also to the figure of the exotic (and erotic) black woman. The author of *The Song of Songs* (7: 2) sings of the "navel that is like a round goblet, which wanteth not liquor" in describing his black beloved. The genitalia are both the organ of excretion as well as of erotic interest. Here the two images merge— after a masculine model in which the penis unifies both functions within a single anatomical structure, whereas in the more differentiated genitalia of the female, the functions are quite clearly separated. The masculine gaze unifies them and labels them as erotic. Inherent, however, in such a view is the link between the erotic aspects of the female genitalia and their excretory function. They become the projection of the male genitalia where the erotic image of the genitalia merely masks the sign of pollution. But it is with the further, post-Enlightenment association of urination and shame within a literary context that the fascination of the nineteenth-century male for the genitalia of the female is made overt. Goethe's *Wilhelm Meister's Apprenticeship* (1795–96) describes Wilhelm's seduction by the actress Marianne's overt unselfconsciousness:

> It seemed to him when he had here to remove her stays in order to reach the harpsicord, there to lay her skirt on the bed before he could set himself, when she herself with unembarrassed frankness would make no attempt to conceal from him many natural acts which people are accustomed to hide from others out of decency—it seemed to him, I say, that he became bound to her by invisible bonds.[24]

The act of observing the female's excretion destroys the social construction of "shame." The power of this passage from *Wilhelm Meister's Apprenticeship* can be judged in a report of William Wordsworth's response. He read the novel until "he came to the scene where the hero, in his mistress's bedroom, becomes sentimental over her dirty towels, etc., which struck him with such disgust that he flung the book out of his hand, would never look at it again, and declared that surely no English lady would ever read such a work."[25] It was clearly the "etc." that caused Wordsworth's agitation. For the observing of Marianne's act of exposure revealed the power that the perception of sexuality has on the male. It may be facile to point out that the observation of the act of a woman urinating stresses both the difference and the similarity of the Other. The woman urinates, an act associated by the male with the phallus, but the very act of urination as undertaken by the woman proves the absence of the phallus. This image of the "damaged" (and "damaging") genitalia of the female becomes associated with the act of urination, an act of excretion associated with pollution. The representation of female sexuality is thus linked for Goethe with the diseased and the fascinating, qualities that are linked within his imagination.

One further set of images must be evoked to place the image of the object of desire in its most limited context. For there is an unmentioned alternative to heterosexual and homosexual contact. It is masturbation. There is, of course, that moment in the mid-eighteenth century, not all that long before Goethe's visit to Rome, when touching the self becomes a central preoccupation of the culture of touch, as has been discussed in Chapter Six. The skin of the masturbator reveals the close relationship between the erotic self-touch and the representation of the sexual on the skin. It is only self-touch or the sexual pollution of the female that in the eighteenth century marks the individual. Homoeroticism, as we can see in Goethe's own comments, is associated with male beauty, not with a disease written on the skin. Mutual masturbation, the touching of the self in the touching of the Other, seems to be the alternative that is not overtly marked as diseased. Missing is the reciprocal relationship between the simultaneous touch of the self and the self being touched. The pathological signs of heterosexuality and autoeroticism point to the skin with all of its ambiguities as the source and the map of these signs of difference. Although not sanctioned in Western sexual practice, mutual masturbation is the one form of sexuality that is not associated with disease and its resulting mask of pathology. And it is inscribed in the text in the chiasmus of the oft-cited line "Sehe mit fühlendem Aug', fühle mit sehender Hand" (See with an eye that can feel, feel with an eye that can see), a line that turns upon itself in self-reflexive but not identical terms, parallel to the touching of the Other who is almost the self.

Can we read the image in "Roman Elegies" as an encoded one, one that in confusing the hierarchy of the senses also points toward the dissolution of the implied hierarchy of sexuality? Is it a covert form of resistance aimed against the cultural codification of the senses and the related, rigid scale of permitted sexual encounters? Is it possible that the destruction of the boundaries between the senses is paralleled by the blurring of the clear lines between the permissible and the forbidden object? It is clear from the grammatical references in Goethe's poem that the beloved is a female or is at least so addressed. But is it possible that this is an iconographic referent? Is it the image of Touch, whose emblematic presence masks the male lover? Is the act represented not coitus but rather mutual masturbation? It is one act in which the touch of the Other is, at one and the same time, the surrogate touching of the self. The perfection of form, the flawless nature of the skin, point toward an idealized lover, a lover unmarred by the icons of diseased skin. Neither the touch of the female nor the touch of the self could so be represented. Indeed, whose erection is re-created through the memory of the senses represented in the closing lines of the poem? The poet's erection or that of the object of desire?

It is not a question that can or should be answered from the text itself but one that demands a further context, one that would have been deemed aesthetically appropriate for Goethe's neoclassical sensibility. Much has been made of the intertextuality of Goethe's "Roman Elegies." Critics have pointed to Catullus and Propertius as the models for the "antique frankness" of the poems.[26] If we use the fiction present in Goethe's text as our guide, we come up with quite a different source. The limitations on our source are evident: it must present a fiction of a sexually active female who is associated with the representation of a hierarchy of the senses. If we turn to Xenophon's *Memorabilia*, a text that Goethe clearly knew, we find the oft-told fable of Hercules at the crossroads that points to the sexual ambiguity that seems to underlie the text. In this tale, the harlot Kakia (the origin of our Faustina?) attempts to move Hercules to a specific choice in life by seducing him through her representation of the senses:

> You shall taste all the sweets of life; and hardship you shall never know. First, of wars and worries you shall not think, but shall ever be considering what choice food or drink you can find, what sight or sound will delight you, what touch or smell; what young boy can give you most joy, what bed the softest slumbers; and how to come by all these pleasures with least trouble.[27]

Goethe's ironic list in *Faust I* parallels Xenophon's listing of the senses, without, of course, Xenophon's reference to homosexual love. But Kakia is the temptress whose mask of beauty hides the corruption and disease of heterosexual love. In George Wither's 1635 *Collection of Emblems*, Kakia is labeled *Vice*, and her mask of beauty reveals her inner corruption (see Plate 136). Kakia is thus an icon of precisely that heterosexuality that Goethe fears. For it is only heterosexuality (the seduction of Gretchen/ Helen's seduction of Faust) that tempts Faust; homosexuality is attributed, only at the very close of *Faust II*, to the minion of Satan. Sexuality, in *Faust*, becomes the boundary between those saved (Faust) and those eternally damned (Mephisto). In the Roman texts, in 1788, this radical boundary between sanctity and pollution is missing. And yet there is a haunting parallel to Xenophon's text in Goethe's poem dated to January 1788, written during his visit to Rome. The poem, printed with a retrospective commentary in his *Italian Journey*, is addressed to another fiction, this time, however, a masculine one, Cupid:

> Cupid, you free, self-willed boy,
> You asked to stay with me only an hour!
> How many days and nights have you stayed,
> And are now imperious, master of the house.
> I have been driven from my broad bed,
> Now I sit nights on the ground, tortured,
> Your petulance stokes flame upon flame in the fireplace,
> Burns the supplies for the winter and singes my arms.
>
> You have misplaced and warped my tool,
> I seek and have become as blind and mad.
> You roar so clumsily, I fear, the little soul
> Flees, to flee from you, and leaves the hut.[28]

May not this paean to the young and beautiful boy, the boy Cupid, the emblem of the erotic, be a tribute, masked within neoclassical conventions, to the beautiful boy whom Goethe also immortalizes in his "Roman Elegies"? Is Goethe's classical world in "Roman Elegies" that of Xenophon, with its beautiful young boy offered as part of Kakia's temptation of Hercules's senses? Goethe evokes, in this poem, the very confusion of the senses that seems to dominate his Roman experience. Blind and maddened by his beautiful young visitor, he can no longer trust his senses. Is the young visitor, Faustina/Cupid, wearing the mask of Touch, Goethe's homosexual lover? Is the answer to Eissler's question of what "cured" Goethe's sexual problem mutual masturbation with a beautiful boy, rather than coitus (and its associative fear of disease) with a beautiful young girl? Is the central question in the poem one of the shift of representation from the forbidden male as aesthetic object to the accepted image of the icon of touch?

PLATE 242.

PLATE 243.

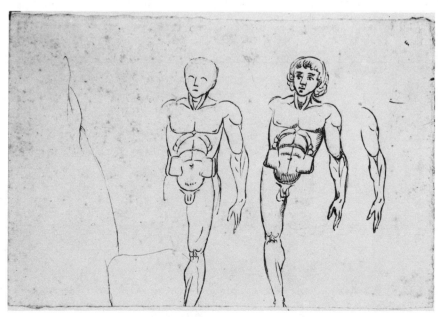

PLATE 244.

PLATE 242–244. *During his trip to Rome in 1787–88, Johann Wolfgang von Goethe made a number of sketches of the nude male, with prominent genitalia, in pencil and ink. Weimar: Nationale Forschungs- und Gedenkstätten der klassichen deutschen Literatur.*

The answers to such questions can probably never be given. It is clear, however, that in deconstructing the canon of the senses, Goethe, as well as many of the writers of the nineteenth century in his wake, also reworked their concept of the aesthetic in the light of their understanding of the role of aesthetics in determining the object of desire. Goethe's use of the beautiful young girl, Faustina, as an acceptable object of desire within the confines of the neoclassical poetic text does not transgress against the condemnation of homosexuality that dominated his culture. It is only within the confusion surrounding the accepted definition of the beautiful as the feminine that begins in the late eighteenth century as well as the battle over the destruction of the hierarchy of the senses, with its feminine iconography, that this literary image can be reinterpreted. With the "Roman Elegies," Goethe began to see the body differently. His motivation was a need to restructure the categories of perception, from sight to touch, that had dominated his age into new categories. This rethinking of the visual categories related to the sexual sphere can be most clearly seen in Goethe's sketchbooks from his trip to Italy. Missing from them is any possible image that could be the beloved Faustina. No lovely young women haunt the pages of his sketchbooks (unlike his subsequent sketchbooks from the period of 1788 to 1829, which are full of representations of women he knew intimately). Rather, his Roman sketchbook contains a number of "anatomical" (so writes the editor) drawings of young males.[29] And these images stress the male genitalia as the emblem of sexual identity [PLATES 242–244]. These sketches that represent the beautiful form of the male are the product of Goethe's seeing of the Other during his Italian journey. He sees the male as sexual object (in his art) and describes (in his poetry) the female as the representation of touch.

The confusion of categories made his initial sexual contact acceptable within that world of status, the aesthetics of the literary text, through which he defined his identity as a writer, but a writer in the wake of Winckelmann. He thus saw the function of poetic discourse, linked by the philosophy of his time to the representation of the senses, as a mode of resistance, a means through which he could recreate his most sensual movement in socially accepted terms. Winckelmann's homoerotic discourse was acceptable because he cast it within the language of aesthetic criticism, displacing his interest in the text onto the inanimate representations of the male. Goethe's clearly autobiographical mode would have made the poetic representation of homoeroticism too immediate. He thus undertook to represent his sensual experience within the highly structured conventions of "seeing" the sense of touch and seeing it with all of its complex interrelationships. It is through the reconstruction of the history of one of the senses, the sense of touch, within its cultural context, that the complexity of Goethe's undertaking can be appreciated. It is also within Goethe's text that his own, personal vision of the senses is articulated, a vision that draws on, refines, and makes its own, the historical consciousness of his time.

CHAPTER EIGHT

Icons of Sexuality during the Nineteenth and Early Twentieth Centuries

LOOKING AT THE ANATOMIES

There is no real break in the line between the world that inscribes itself through Goethe's late eighteenth-century representations of sexuality and the world of Victorian sexuality, neither in terms of the "realities" (i.e., recorded sexual practices) nor of the "fantasies" about human sexuality and the genitalia, as Peter Gay has shown in his study of bourgeois sexual practices.[1] And yet there are moments of heightened awareness in the latter half of the nineteenth century (the age of Victoria's maturity and of the German and Austrian reigns of Wilhelm II and Franz Josef II) that are captured in the images of the body. The sexualized body undergoes a substantial alteration during the course of the nineteenth century, if only in the disparity between the course of nineteenth-century medical visions of the body and the heightened visual spectatorship about the body that haunts the high arts of the nineteenth century.[2] But, unlike the sexual fantasies of the eighteenth century, which mix the prospects of pleasure and pain, the focus for the nineteenth century is either overtly or covertly on the pathological. Human sexuality, with its associations with disease, becomes the linchpin for any understanding of the body during the course of the nineteenth century, in a way that both continues and heightens the fascination with the body that was present through the Enlightenment. The movement that had become in the eighteenth century the translation of theological concepts of the corrupt body into medical categories dominates the understanding of the body by the late nineteenth century. And these secularized categories permeate all of the other cat-

egories of science, including the dominant "science" of the nineteenth century, the biology of race. Indeed, even thinkers such as Sigmund Freud who wished to generate developmental models of human sexuality resorted to complex models of sexual pathology to "explain" (and therefore, to represent) all sexuality.

The influence of the medical fascination with human sexuality on the representation of the body during the course of the nineteenth century radicalizes it in a manner that seems (on the surface) to distance it from the traditional representation of the body within the medical text—both anatomical and pathological—that documents the history of the seeing of the body from the Middle Ages on. Beginning in May 1827, when Karl Ernst von Baer first "saw" (observed and understood) the mammalian ovum "so clearly that a blind man could hardly deny it," the perception of the genitalia began to shift to the level of invisibility, to the microscopic, to the psychic, to that level in which the unseen became the "real," whereas the "seen" became merely the surface.[3] The final conquest of the invisible is to be found in Rudolf Virchow's groundbreaking study *Cellular Pathology* of 1858, which moved the focus of the physician's gaze from the individual to his/her component cells as the root of understanding the disease process.[4] Virchow's view exemplifies what Michel Foucault has called "the great myth of a pure Gaze that would be pure Language: a speaking eye,"[5] but a speaking eye that uses a microscope to see within the body and translate its report into visual as well as verbal icons. When we examine the development of the images from the very beginning of the century, as in Justus

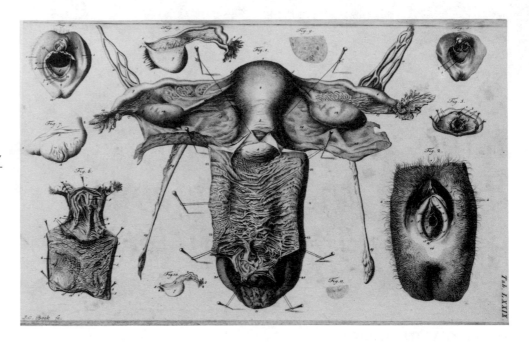

PLATE 245. *The female reproductive organs from Justus Christian von Loder,* Tabulae anatomicae *(Weimar: Landes–Industry–Comptoir, 1803). Ithaca: Howard B. Adelmann Collection, Olin Library, Cornell University.*

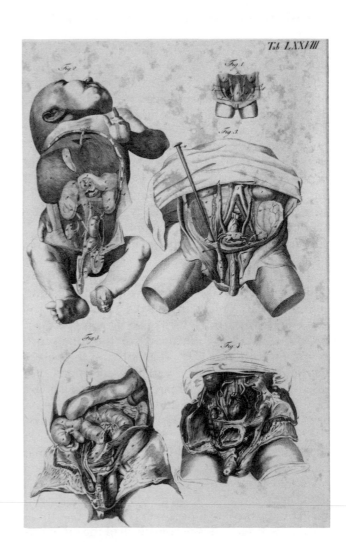

PLATE 246. *Fetal anatomy and reproductive anatomy seen as parallel structures from Justus Christian von Loder,* Tabulae anatomicae *(Weimar: Landes–Industry–Comptoir, 1803). Ithaca: Howard B. Adelmann Collection, Olin Library, Cornell University.*

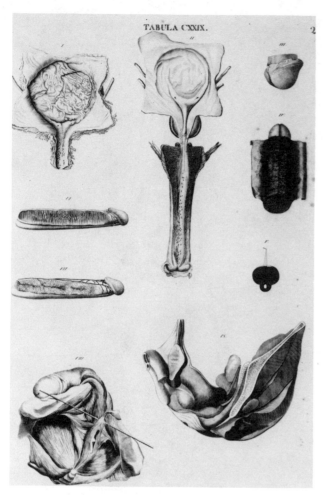

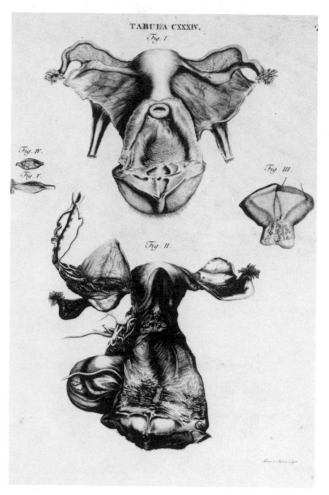

PLATE 247. *The male genitalia from Leopold Mark Antony and Caldani Floriani,* Icones anatomicae ex optimis neotericorum operibus *(Venice: J. Picotti, 1804). Ithaca: Howard B. Adelmann Collection, Olin Library, Cornell University.*

PLATE 248. *The female genitalia from Leopold Mark Antony and Caldani Floriani,* Icones anatomicae ex optimis neotericorum operibus *(Venice: J. Picotti, 1804). Ithaca: Howard B. Adelmann Collection, Olin Library, Cornell University.*

Christian von Loder's multivolumed anatomical atlas of 1803, the shift in the image of the body through to the dominance of Virchow in Berlin as well as the so-called second Viennese school by the end of the century is marked.[6] Loder's images **[PLATES 245–246]** are taken from the tradition of the mock-autopsy images that have their roots, as we have shown, in the portrayal of the body in the early eighteenth century. Often borrowed from earlier atlases, such as that of Jenty, these images present a solid image of the body (and thus the sexual organs) as palpable flesh. Even the images representing the systems, such as the circulatory systems of the uterus, are schematicized in such a manner as to be extrapolated from the more "realistic" images and are always directly related to these. Such schematic images can be seen, for example, in Leopold

Mark Antony and Caldani Floriani's atlas of 1804, where the schematic images are quite literally the restructured patterns of the more elaborate (and well-known) images of the genitalia taken from the earlier eighteenth-century atlases **[PLATES 247–248]**. This pattern, strongly reminiscent of the Renaissance layered images of the body, reveals the underlying relationships between aspects of the body—between the various systems into which the body is subdivided (muscular, circulatory, skeletal, etc.)—although in no way abandoning the complex image of the body part as experiment, autopsied flesh. Gerard Sandifort's atlas of 1804 thus represents the hemisected female figure in a manner that is uninterruptedly the same from the Renaissance through to the late eighteenth-century atlases **[PLATE 249]**.

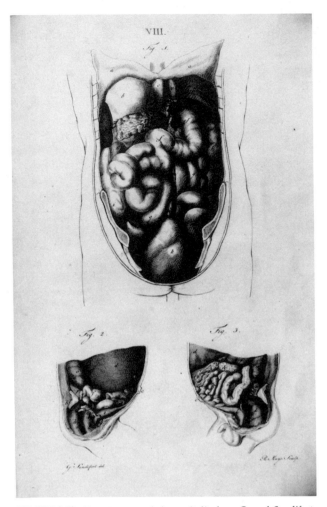

PLATE 249. *The viscera and the genitalia from Gerard Sandifort, Tabulae anatomicae (Rotterdam: S. and J. Luchtmans, 1804). Ithaca: Howard B. Adelmann Collection, Olin Library, Cornell University.*

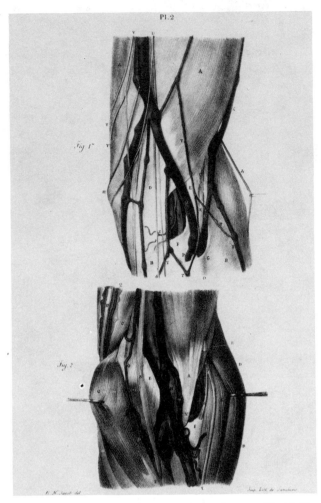

PLATE 250. *The image of the penis dissected engraved by N. H. Jacobs from Philippe Blawdin,* Traité d'anatomie topographique *(Paris: Auger Mequignon, 1826). Ithaca: Howard B. Adelmann Collection, Olin Library, Cornell University.*

As we move through the century the images retain their fleshy shape, as in Philippe Blawdin's 1826 anatomical atlas **[PLATE 250]**. The illusion of the autopsy, with its representation of the freshness of newly dissected flesh, is maintained, down to the hooks implanted in the muscular structure of the penis or the uterus that reveals, to the unseen eye, the inner structures quite evident in the illustrator's representation. By midcentury, in the historical space between von Baer and Virchow, the scientific gaze begins to reveal the hidden, not the hidden organs of sexuality but rather the microscopic structures that rest within or that form the basis for all development. Marc Jean Bourgery provides in his eight-volume anatomical atlas of 1844 a natural history of development ranging from the sperm and ovum **[PLATES 251–254]** to the fully developed

and normal genitalia. The patterns of development form the centerpiece for the movement from the microscopic to fully developed structures. The strong association between the idea of development, cast within nineteenth-century physiology as early as Lorenz Oken and the Romantics in the formula of "ontogeny recapitulating phylogeny" (the history of the development of the individual representing the history of the development of the entire range of life) and the "meaning" of the form and function of the genitalia cannot be understated.[7] But the movement from the microscopic to the fleshy is paralleled, indeed, overwhelmed by midcentury, by the movement from the fleshy to the microscopic. Heralded by the formulation by Virchow and by the pathological work undertaken in laboratories in Paris and Vienna, the focus of the new medicine, especially the new sexuality, was on that hidden within, the unseen motivators of disease and pathological change. This can be seen most clearly in one of the major works produced by the Vienna school, Karl Rokitansky's textbook of pathological anatomy, in which sexual anomalies (such as the bicornate uterus [PLATE 255]) are juxtaposed with cellular changes [PLATE 256] that are understood as underlying the disease process, here in Fallopian tube cysts. In both cases, the patient, the whole (if not intact) person, vanishes, to be replaced by ever-diminishing parts representing the disease process or the anatomy of the patient.[8] But central to the shift away from images of sexuality in the mid-nineteenth-century atlases, such as those by Marc Jean Bourgery, is the movement from the microscopic-but-normal to the microscopic-but-degenerate. The sense of these late nineteenth-century images of the sexual is that hidden within the cell, like a tiny time bomb awaiting detonation, lies the

source of all disease and decay. The hidden becomes, even for the anatomists, the source of danger. Although such attitudes have their roots as early as Vesalius, the image of the danger inherent in the hidden takes on new meaning in the age of Lister and Pasteur. Parallel to the sense of the hidden, of the secret sources of development, is the new sense of disease as rooted in the smallest aspects of the body. In the volumes concerning the sexual during the latter half of the nineteenth century, it is the cellular, the microscopic, that forms the centerpiece for all understanding of the body. It is not the visible, the sign upon the skin alone, but its roots, the maldevelopment of the cell, that are focused on. Indeed, it is the relationship between the visible sign, the form or malformation of sexuality, and its hidden roots that forms the paradigm for all of the fascination with the sexual and its "meaning" in the course of the nineteenth and early twentieth centuries.

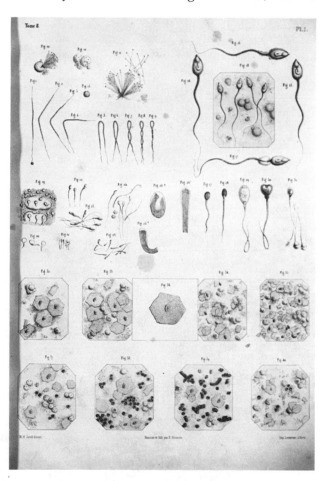

PLATE 251. *Spermatazoa in a lithograph by N. H. Jacobs from Marc Jean Bourgery,* Traité complet de l'anatomie de l'homme *(Paris: C. A. Delaunay, 1844). Ithaca: Howard B. Adelmann Collection, Olin Library, Cornell University.*

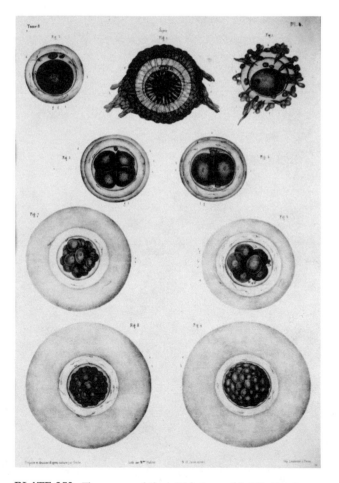

PLATE 252. *The ovum and the initial stages of fertilization in a lithograph by N. H. Jacobs from Marc Jean Bourgery,* Traité complet de l'anatomie de l'homme *(Paris: C. A. Delaunay, 1844). Ithaca: Howard B. Adelmann Collection, Olin Library, Cornell University.*

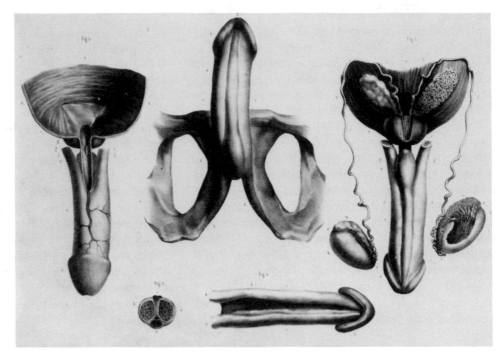

PLATE 253. *The erect penis in a lithograph by N. H. Jacobs from Marc Jean Bourgery*, Traité complet de l'anatomie de l'homme *(Paris: C. A. Delaunay, 1844). Ithaca: Howard B. Adelmann Collection, Olin Library, Cornell University.*

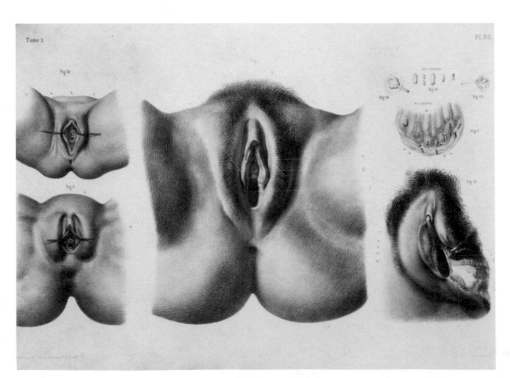

PLATE 254. *The female genitalia in a lithograph by N. H. Jacobs from Marc Jean Bourgery,* Traité complet de l'anatomie de l'homme *(Paris: C. A. Delaunay, 1844). Ithaca: Howard B. Adelmann Collection, Olin Library, Cornell University.*

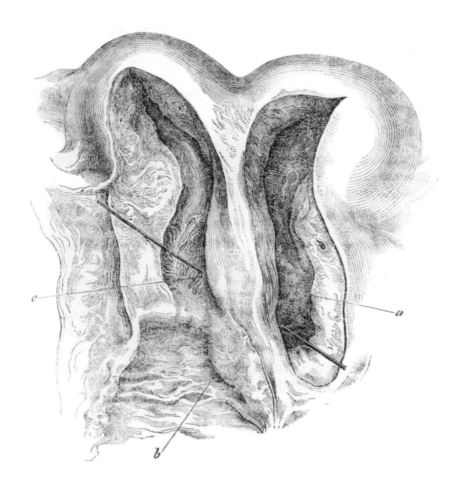

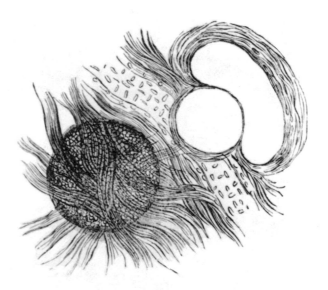

SEEING THE PROSTITUTE

Sexual disease begins to be seen differently during the course of the nineteenth century. The movement is from the overt sign to the hidden one, from signs of illness as the disease to the stigmata of disease that only hint at the true source, a source most often to be found in the history of the individual and his/her familial background. The power of such images of degeneration come to have direct political implications. Rudolf Virchow begins his *Cellular Pathology* with an extended metaphor of the body as the Hegelian fantasy of the well-organized state, with hierarchies of power represented by the levels of the organization of the body ranging from the cell, as the individual citizen, to the organ, to the body politic. Lurking within this body state from its conception are degenerate cells, the degenerate prostitutes of the body, who are the source for the potential destruction of the entire organism, whether body or state. This sense of the danger lurking within the body leads to an understanding of the public obligation to control sexuality as a source of pollution, much as it assumed in the course of the nineteenth century the obligation to control effluvia through the building of sewers. The icons of sexuality, which are continuous throughout the period

from the Renaissance to the twentieth century, accrue a complex set of further references, references not merely to the function of sexuality within society or morality but to sexuality as the force hidden within, either in the developmental history of the individual (after the model of ontogeny recapitulating phylogeny) or in the model of the pathology of the cell. It is that hidden within, the source of disease, that the image of sexual pathology, of the person with syphilis, mirrors. Thus in the first of the great nineteenth-century atlases of medicine, the dermatological atlas published by Jean-Louis Alibert in 1814, which demonstrated the "verisimilitude" of multicolored representations of disease, Alibert portrays a number of representations of male and female genitalia with syphilitic infections, but the faces of only the female syphilitics. The relationship between the hidden genitalia and the face, the public sign of the disease, is manifest [PLATES 257–259]. No faces of male syphilitics are represented. For it is the mask of female beauty, here revealed as the sign of corruption, that points toward her role as the source of disease. Alibert's syphilitics are in many ways the image of the Enlightenment syphilitic, but they are presented within the framework of the early nineteenth-century fascination with the hidden. The faces of the sufferers reveal their disease and are somber portraits, much in line with portraits of the patient, such as those by Théodore Géricault, that dominate the first half of the nineteenth century. The images of the genitalia, however, fall into the classification of the autopsy images, here the images of the treating room. Framed by the drapes that conceal the rest of the patient, the genitalia are emphasized and made anonymous by the drapes. The drapes serve as a curtain that has been raised to reveal the hidden nature of the disease, the presentation of genital signs and symptoms parallel to the facial ones seen in the portraits. The seeming anonymity of the genitalia is linked to the face, the icon of the individuality of the patient. Much as with the movement later in the century from the whole patient or person to the part, the movement within Alibert's atlas signifies the reduction of the anonymous male to his infected parts. The infected male is anonymous, faceless, for he is the incidental victim of the female's infection.

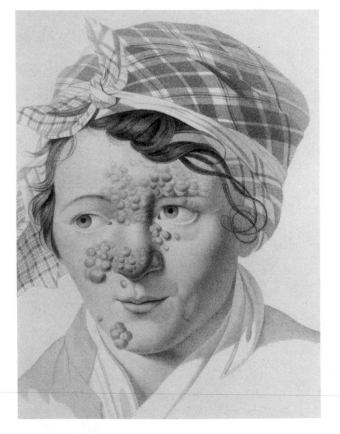

PLATE 257. *The face of the female syphilitic from Jean-Louis Alibert,* Description des maladies de la peau *(Paris: Barrois l'Aîné, 1814). London: Royal Society of Medicine.*

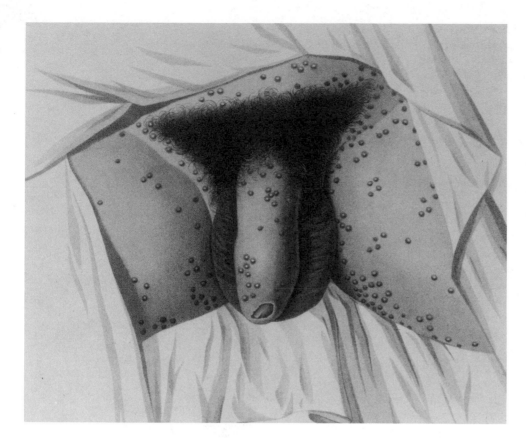

PLATE 258. *The genitalia of the male syphilitic from Jean-Louis Alibert,* Description des maladies de la peau *(Paris: Barrois l'Aîné, 1814). London: Royal Society of Medicine.*

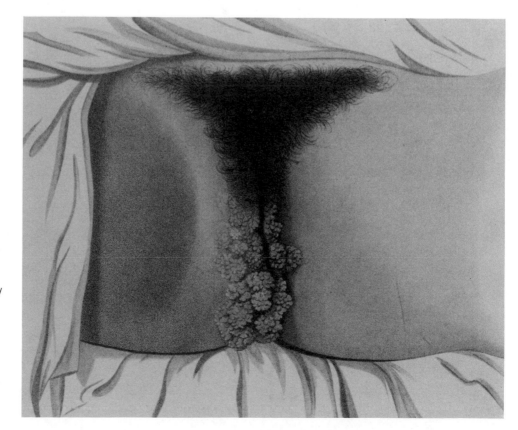

PLATE 259. *The genitalia of the female syphilitic from Jean-Louis Alibert,* Description des maladies de la peau *(Paris: Barrois l'Aîné, 1814). London: Royal Society of Medicine.*

The corrupt face of the female serves as a warning to the male of the potential pollution to be found in the genitalia. The male observer of the female (and the male physician gazing at Alibert's extremely expensive atlas) are assumed not to need any warning about the infectious potential of the male, for they are presumed not to be at risk from the same-sex touch. For the image of the syphilitic is closely tied to the image of heterosexual activity, to the cross-sexual touch.

It is important to understand that the corrupting touch is but the antithesis of the traditional healing touch. The image of the healing touch is always placed as the answer to the corrupting touch. In one form, it is the "King's/Queen's Touch" that frees the sufferer from the skin disease of scrofula. (Dr. Samuel Johnson, when only thirty months old, was the last person in England to be so "royally touched"—by Queen Anne. It did not help.) In another form, it is the physician's laying on of hands as the touch that cures (which Franz Kafka parodies in his 1919 tale of "The Country Doctor"). Such touches also cross boundaries, from the divine (as exemplified by the royal) to the common; from the healer to the sufferer. The power associated with the touch that cures is the same power associated with the touch that corrupts. Both scrofula (associated with the sexual as are all skin diseases, diseases of the organ of touch) and the healing of the open wound in the thigh of the country doctor's patient point toward the world of the sexual. All of these literary examples have as their model a secularized image of the healing Christ. Christ's touch heals, and it heals even those who are marked by those diseases that are sexual in nature (Matthew 9: 20) or those, such as leprosy, that serve as the model for sexually transmitted disease (Luke 5: 13). It is the very touch that heals. Not all aspects of the healing touch relate to the image of the sexual, but they all receive their power from the border drawn between the individual touched and the individual touching. Thus, as best expressed by Norbert Elias in *The Civilizing Process*, Western civilization evolved rigid etiquettes to regulate legitimate contiguity as a result of the fear of contagion of sexually transmitted disease as much as that of the plague.[9] (It is this double fear that haunts Boccaccio's little group of storytellers in the *Decameron*—who having fled the plague in fourteenth-century Florence now find themselves in a mixed-sex group unceasingly telling ribald tales to satisfy their sexual interest without exposing themselves to further risk of disease.) The need to control physical proximity associates itself with the healer as well as with the

PLATE 260. *The title page vignette of the nineteenth-century French translation of Fracastoro's poem* Syphilis *by Auguste Barthélémy,* Syphilis: Poème en deux chants *(Paris: Béchet junior et Labé & Bohaire, 1840). London: Wellcome Institute for the History of Medicine.*

patient. The healer, unless divinely protected, as Kafka's tale shows, can take on all of the attributes of the patient, including his/her uncleanliness. The rules for contact, as we have seen, may be clearly stated within a society, or, as in the case of the creation of images of sexual difference, may be embedded in the icons that a society generates to control the constantly slipping boundary between the "pure" and the "corrupt."

The portrait of the infected female overtly presents in the public image of the prostitute that which becomes a set element in the iconography of sexuality—moral decay as a sign of disease. It also is present within the repertoire of late nineteenth-century art.[10] Such an image appears in the vignette on the title page of the French translation (1840) of the Renaissance poem *Syphilis* **[PLATE 260]**.[11] This image stands in a long line of images of female beauty that mask decay, the decay represented in Alibert's atlas. Indeed, there is an entire vocabulary of images of prostitutes, a veritable salon of strumpets, within the high art of the late nineteenth century. Although, in Chapter Ten, I document how these images and other images of illicit or dangerous sexuality merge (in the work of Manet and Zola), in this chapter I sketch the visual history of the prostitute within the high art of the nineteenth century and relate it to the history of the sexualized touch that I have been tracing. The images I shall be discussing are all stages in the image of the "fallen" woman, a phrase itself of quintessentially Victorian provenance. They are in a way the Victorian parallel to Hogarth's *A Harlot's Progress*. Let us begin with Alfred Elmore's image *On the Brink*, exhibited at the Royal Academy in 1865[12] **[PLATE 261]**. Here we see the initial step before the seduction of the female. Alone, outside of the gambling salon in Bad Homburg, having lost her money, the potential object of seduction (Everywoman) is tempted by the man to whom she is indebted. Women, all women, were seen as potentially able to be seduced, as having a "warm fond heart" in which "a strange and sublime unselfishness, which men too commonly discover only to profit by" exists, or so writes W. R. Greg in the *Westminster Review* of 1850.[13] The well-dressed woman has come to the spa, has exposed herself to the exploitation of the male, and is caught between the light and darkness of her

PLATE 261. *The moment of seduction from Alfred Elmore,* On the Brink, 1865. *Cambridge: Fitzwilliam Museum, University of Cambridge.*

PLATE 262. *The dead prostitute in an engraving after Abraham Solomon, "Drowned! Drowned!" from* Art Journal *(March 1862). Ithaca: Olin Library, Cornell University.*

Engraved by] " DROWNED! DROWNED!" [J. and G. P. Nicholls.

future, a future mirrored in the representation of her face, half highlighted by the moonlight, half cast in shadow. She is at the moment of choice, a choice between the lily and the passionflower. According to *The Language of Flowers*, a standard handbook of Victorian culture, she is caught between the lily, signifying purity and sweetness, and the passionflower, representing strong feelings and susceptibility.[14] The gambling salon was the wrong locus for the female. As early as Hogarth's *The Lady's Last Stake* (1758–59), the seduction of the female might be seen as the result of being in the wrong place. Males can gamble; females cannot. Males can indulge their passions; females cannot. Sexuality is a game for the male; it is not for the female. But gambling is also here a metaphor, though a socially embedded one, for the process by which the seduction of the female takes place. Playing upon the innate biological nature of the female makes the seduction possible, but the metaphor of losing at gambling also points to the model of infection and disease. Alfred Elmore's picture shared this vocabulary of gambling. Gambling is a "fever" (*The Times*), the gambler is "infected by the fever of gambling" (*Illustrated London News*), the gambler is thus "feverish" (*Athenaeum*).[15] Gambling is a disease that infects and makes ill, the infiltration into the purity

of the female. Seduction thus has a course of illness: it begins with the signs and symptoms of disease, the fever of gambling, the result of the individual being out of place—much like the colonial explorer expecting to get malaria as a sign of being out of place—and leads inexorably to the next stages of the disease, prostitution and death.[16] The image of the gambler who stands at the moment of choosing between vice and virtue, who is gambling with life itself, is appropriate. Gambling is the sign of the moment before seduction and thus the male stands in proximity to, but not touching, the female. The sexualized touch is prepared but has not been consummated. Once it is (if it is, and that is the ambiguity of this image), the course is inevitable—at least for the female—for "seduction must, almost as a matter of course, lead to prostitution," as W. M. Sanger observed in 1859.[17]

The prostitute's end is suicide, "deserted to a life of misery, wretchedness, and poverty . . . terminated by self-destruction."[18] This is the penalty for permitting onself to be seduced by immoral men, to be infected, and thus to spread infection to—innocent men? This is the chain of argument that places the seducer and the prostitute beyond the boundary that defines polite sexuality, a sexuality, as in the case of Victoria's Prime Minister

William Gladstone's fascination with prostitutes, which led him to attempt their conversion at his own hearthside and undertake to have sexual contact with them simultaneously. The seducer and the prostitute are the defining borders of diseased sexuality. The seducer is parallel to the image of Bram Stoker's *Dracula* (1897). For in the act of seduction, he transforms the innocence of the female into a copy of himself, just as Dracula's victims become vampires. She becomes the prostitute as seductress, infecting other males as he had infected her with the disease of licentiousness (and, not incidentally, syphilis). Sexuality, disease, and death are linked in the act of seduction. In 1860, Abraham Solomon showed his image of the drowned prostitute who had been seduced and eventually committed suicide [PLATE 262]. As a contemporary reformist source noted, in this image, "the Deceiver recognizes the Deceived. . . . he, the tempter, the devil's agent. . . . Men, seducers, should learn from this picture and fallen women, look at this, and remember 'the wages of sin is death.' "[19] The sign of transmission of the disease of polluted (and polluting) sexuality, the sexualized touch, is as of this moment missing in Elmore's icon of seduction. In Thomas Hood's widely cited poem on the death of the prostitute, "The Bridge of Sighs" (1844), the sexualized touch, the source of disease, becomes the forgiving touch of the dead prostitute:

Take her up instantly,
Loving not loathing.
Touch her not scornfully;
Think of her mournfully,
Gently and humanly;
Not of the stains of her,
All that remains of her
Now is pure womanly. . . .[20]

Death purges the dead prostitute of her pollution, in Solomon's image (but also in a series of images of dead prostitutes in the nineteenth century from George Frederic Watt's *Found Drowned* [1848–50] through to the ubiquitous death mask of the "Beautiful Dead Woman from the Seine" that decorated many bourgeois parlors in France and Germany during the fin de siècle). The touching of the dead body is not merely a piteous gesture toward the "fallen," it is a permitted touching of the female, a not contagious, not infecting touching, a control over the dead woman's body, which as we shall see, will lead to a new twist in the image of human sexuality.

The moment of seduction is also documented in William Holman Hunt's *The Awakening Conscience* of 1853, exhibited at the Royal Academy in 1854[21] [PLATE 263]. But here it is the image of conscience overcoming seduction. The image is a literal reworking of Charles Le Brun's *Repentant Magdalene Renouncing All the Vanities of the World* (see Plate 30), a sign of the ability of the seduced (or potentially seduced) to escape. Everything in the image refers to the epiphany of awakening, from the bird escaping from the cat under the table to the sudden upright posture of the young woman, suddenly made aware of the implications of the sexualized touch, emblematic in the absolute centrality of the seducer's hand in juxtaposition to the clenched hands of the woman. Indeed, her hand reveals rings on every finger of her left hand but the third finger, signaling her precarious status outside of marriage. The very atmosphere of the space here is one that leads to the awareness—even the print of *Christ and the Woman Taken in Adultery* over

PLATE 263. *The seducer fails in William Holman Hunt,* The Awakening Conscience, *1853. London: Tate Gallery.*

PLATE 264. *An illustration for Alfred de Musset's* Garniani *(1883) by Achulle Deveria. Ithaca: Private collection.*

PLATE 265. *The redeemed prostitute from Dante Gabriel Rossetti,* Found, *begun in 1853. Wilmington: Delaware Art Museum.*

touch, the tradition of emblems of pain as emblems of sexuality. The male is reduced to the playful cherublike child, but the virgin's firm breasts here are indicative of the moment before seduction and corruption, before childbearing and disease.

Within all of these images of the painful touch (from the seventeenth through the nineteenth century) is hidden the male's fear of the female genitalia, which represent his own sense of the fragility of the self. One can interpret this in the light of Karen Horney's view that the male child is dominated by the "organic sensations . . . to *penetrate*. . . . On the one hand, a boy will automatically conclude that everyone else is made like himself; but on the other hand his phallic impulses surely bid him instinctively to search for the appropriate opening in the female body. . . . If we seriously accept Freud's dictum that the sexual theories formed by children are modeled on their own sexual constitution, it must surely mean in the present connection that the boy, urged on by his impulses to penetrate, pictures in fantasy a complementary female organ."[24] And yet there is a necessary caveat to Horney's position—for in the magical thinking that each of has about the body of the Other, we may well seek for complementarity, for the antithetical form of ourselves, but we project the sense of the contours and orifices of our own body onto the Other. The images of the painful touch, all crafted by males, depicting and representing the female, reflect the fear that males have in the opening of their body, of the fear of castration represented by the female organ. Because, as Horney argues in her paper, "The Denial of the Vagina," women relate to their bodies quite differently than do males; it is not at all surprising that the male, seeking after the missing orifice in his own body, and finding only a source of potential pain (either in the internalized representation of the castrated genitalia or the anus), understands penetration as painful and destructive.[25] (The masculinization of touch in Caravaggio's image [see Plate 143] represents this projection as the reflex of the closed nature of the male's body. The image of the "intact" genitalia is internalized at the stage of psychic development prior to gender definition. The male child knows that the Other must exist, but he creates the Other out of his internalized sense of his own body.) This, associated as it is with the fear, so evident in Bouguereau's image, of the innate inferiority of the size (and therefore potency) of the male child's genitalia in relationship either to the father's and, indeed, the mother's, leads to an anxiety about control. The male's image of the woman's genitalia reflects the

boundary that the male creates from his internalization and projection of the image of his own body. In Bouguereau's image, it is that of the child Eros, with his child's genitalia, attempting to penetrate the body of the young girl. Like Gulliver, he is the tiny lover of a Brobdingnag. Inherent in this image is the fearfulness of the woman's body, represented within the iconography of the nineteenth century in terms of the female as the source of sexually transmitted disease. This is quite a different image from that found in Moulin's erotic photograph that, because of its function as the necessary stimulant to the male's imagination (according to the theories of the erection still dominant in the nineteenth century), represses all fear of disease below the "beautiful" surface of the female's body as the object of desire. But still the noxious weeds that dominate the front of the marble block upon which Bouguereau's equally "beautiful" young girl sits point toward that hidden corruption. The sexualized touch leads to pathology, and pathology (whether social or physical) leads to death.

The resolution is, of course, clear. Prostitutes die. They die languishingly of tuberculosis, as in Verdi's *La Traviata* (1857), or as we shall see in the next chapter, horribly of smallpox. They commit suicide, as in Flaubert's *Madame Bovary*, whose eponymous central figure envied the love madness of Donizetti's *Lucia di Lammermoor* as a sign of her liberation from male domination. Their death is not merely the death of the woman that reduces the beloved to an object under the control of the lover, as in Oscar Wilde's image in "The Ballad of Reading Gaol" of each man killing the one he loves; it is the revelation of the female as the source of corruption through the ultimate sign of corruption--mortality. The woman infects the male (through love, through sex) and thus she herself must die, a death that both signifies this act of infection as well as expiating it. But all of these deaths are socially acceptable representations of the death by syphilis, by the disease that haunts the nightside of the male, of the flaneur, the seductive man of the city.[26] The slow, languishing death, the movement from the life of the whore to the ethereal beauty of death, is the sign of the interposition of the cleansing touch, the touch of the true lover, whether in Verdi's middle-class world or in Puccini's bohemian one. Ophelia's suicide, after her rejection by Hamlet (who ironically suggests that her sexual drives could be best harnessed in a "nunnery," an Elizabethan slang term for a brothel), was the inspiration for one of the most famous images of the beautiful dead woman in the Victorian age, John Everett Millais's

PLATE 268. *The woman mad with love as she commits suicide in John Everett Millais,*
Ophelia, *1852. London: Tate Gallery.*

Ophelia (1852) **[PLATE 268]**. Ophelia dies of her desire. Such a representation of desire, whether masked as the tubercular sexuality of Puccini's Mimi or the insanity of Millais's Ophelia, must end in the death of the female. For the sexually active female or indeed the female who desires sexual contact has transgressed the limits of the definition of the female as the distant, beautiful object. This image is not merely the glorification of the unapproachable beloved; it also mirrors the masculine fear of sexually transmitted disease that is projected onto the image of the beautiful woman. Women and death are related through the desire and the anxiety of the male. Madness, disease, and sexuality are all signs of the individual out of rational control, under the domination of the irrational. In placing the prostitute at the locus where these three forces intersect, the masculine gaze distances its own sense of vulnerability.

The death of the prostitute becomes the sign of the escape of the male from the anxiety about his own sexuality, a sexuality that is understood as at risk from all types of disease. In the long and detailed account of the death of a prostitute in the memoirs of the London physician Samuel Warren, published anonymously in 1830, the death of the prostitute is prefigured by a moment of recognition, a moment such as that captured in Rossetti's image:

"I am Dr. _____ ; you yourself sent for me! What is ailing you? You need not hide your face from me in this strange way!—Come"—
"There, then!—*Do you know me?*" she exclaimed, in a faint shriek, at the same time starting up suddenly in bed, and removing her hands from her face, which—her hair pressed away on each side by her hands—was turned towards me with an anguished, affrighted stare, her features white and wasted. . . . If the look did not petrify me, as the fabled head of Medusa, it shocked, or rather horrified me, beyond all expression, as I gazed at it . . . I gradually recognized the face as one known to me. The cold thrill that passed over me, the sickening sensations I then experienced, creep over me now that I am writing. "Why—am I right? *Eleanor!*"[27]

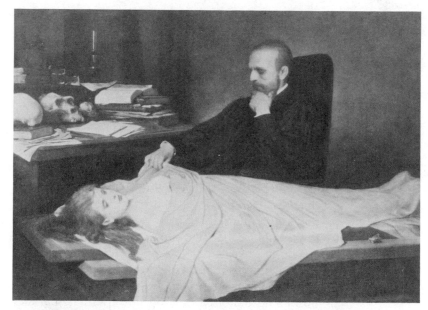

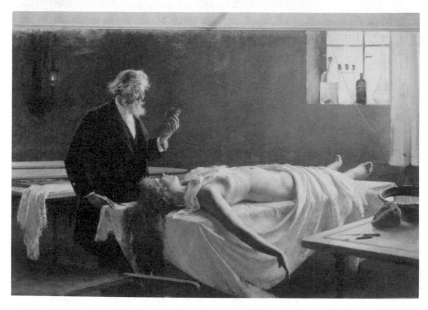

The death of Eleanor by the end of the essay is a transcendental one. Hers was no longer the face of the Medusa, the image of the female genitalia that haunted the nineteenth-century mind (as in the responses to Courbet's image of the genitalia [see Plate 202]). She dies "as if she was falling asleep" (p. 346) while sewing a sampler with the name of "Mary Magdalene" and her initials on it. But die she does. And her body becomes the corpse of the prostitute.

Moreover, that body becomes the object of study, the corpse to be opened by the physician. For one of the favorite images of late nineteenth-century

medical art is the unequal couple transmogrified into the image of the aged pathologist contemplating the exquisite body of the dead prostitute before he opens it. Both Gabriel Max's image of the anatomist (1869) **[PLATE 269]** and the later, even more striking image by Enrique Simonet (1890) **[PLATE 270]** present the moment when the body is opened.[28] What will be found in the body of these drowned women? Will it be the hidden truths of the nature of the woman, what women want, the answer to Freud's question to Marie Bonaparte?[29] Will it be the biological basis of difference, the cell with its degenerate or potentially infectious nature that parallels the image of the female and its potential for destroying the male? The face of the Medusa, with all of its castrating power?[30]

If we turn to the German expressionist Gottfried Benn's 1912 description of the autopsy of a beautiful drowned girl, we get an ironic, twentieth-century answer to this question:

The mouth of a girl, who had long lain in the reeds
looked so gnawed upon.
When they finally broke open her chest, the esophagus
was so full of holes.
Finally in a bower below the diaphragm
they found a nest of young rats.
One of the little sisters was dead.
The others were living off liver and kidneys,
drinking the cold blood, and had
here spent a beautiful youth.
And death came to them too beautiful and quickly
We threw them all into the water.
Oh, how their little snouts squeaked![31]

The physician/poet Benn ironically transfers the quality of the aesthetic ascribed to the beautiful dead prostitute to the dead and dying rats. What is found within the woman is the replication of herself: the source of disease, of plague, the harbor rats, nestled within the gut. The birthing of the rats is the act of opening the body, exposing the corruption hidden within. The physician's eye is always cast to examine and find the source of pathology. This is the role assigned to the physician by society. Here, again, it is the male physician (like Vesalius) opening the body of the woman.

KILLING PROSTITUTES

A century ago in Victorian England, there was another moment in which the opening of the woman's body became the object of intense interest of the community. It was the antithesis of the representation of the icon of the prostitute, for who could truly kill the prostitute but the prostitute herself, who could expiate her sins against the male but she herself? Not the physician, whose role was merely to examine and dissect the body condemned to death by its fall from grace. No one but Jack could remove the prostitute from the street, killing and dismembering. The model in which Jack and the prostitutes were understood to function was one taken from the popular medical discourse of the period: *Similia similibus curantur*, "like cures like," the motto of C. F. S. Hahnemann, the founder of homeopathic medicine. The scourge of the streets, the carrier of disease, can be eliminated only by

one who is equally corrupt and diseased. And that was Jack.

Jack, as he called himself, was evidently responsible for a series of murders that raised the anxiety level throughout London to a fever pitch in the cold, damp fall of 1888. The images of the murders in the *Illustrated Police News* provide an insight into how the murderer was seen and also how the "real" prostitute, not the icon of prostitution or of seduction, was portrayed in mass art [PLATES 271–282]. The murders ascribed to Jack the Ripper all took place in the East End of London, an area that had been the scene of heavy Eastern European Jewish immigration.[32] Who, within the fantasy of the thought-collective, can open the body, who besides the physician? No one but Jack, the emblem of human sexual perversion out of all control, out of all bounds. Jack becomes the sign of deviant human sexuality destroying life, the male parallel to the destructive prostitute. He is the representative of that inner force, hardly held under control, that has taken form, the form of Mr. Hyde. Indeed, an extraordinarily popular dramatic version of Robert Louis Stevenson's "Dr. Jekyll and Mr. Hyde" was playing in the West End while Jack (that not-so-hidden Mr. Hyde) terrorized the East End.

The images of the victims of "Jack"—ranging in number from four to twenty depending on which tabulation one follows—were portrayed as young women who had been slashed and mutilated.[33] But, because of the sensibilities of even the readers of the *Illustrated Police News*, the mutilation presented is the mutilation of the face (as in the image of Annie Chapman in Plate 274). The reality, at least that reality that terrified the London of 1888, was that the victims were butchered. The police photographs of the eviscerated prostitutes appeared only within "scientific" sources such as Professor Alexandre Lacassagne's 1889 study of sadism.[34] In the public eye, the prostitutes were their faces, the faces of the prostitute in death. These images are quite in contrast to those of the contemporary "Whitehall" murder where a decapitated torso was discovered and reconstructed from limbs found throughout the city (see Plates 271–77). The mutilated body was understood over the course of the further killings to be one of Jack's victims, even though it contrasted with the bodies of the prostitutes whom Jack killed. In the case of Jack, the bodies were opened and their viscera were removed. Such sexual disfigurement, along with the amputation of some of the victims' breasts, made it clear to both the police and the general public that Jack's actions were sexually motivated. And, indeed, most of the theories concerning Jack's identity assumed

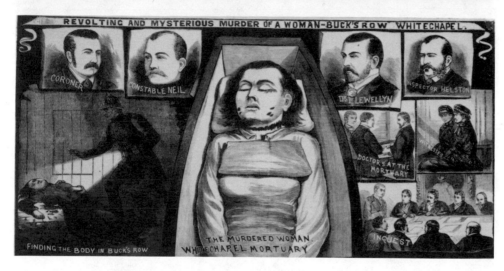

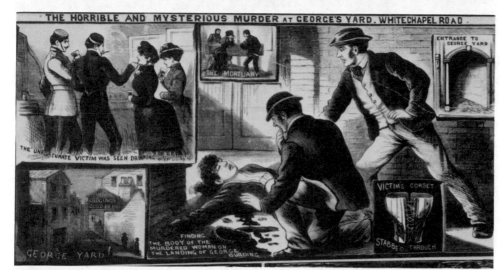

that he (or a close family member) had been infected with syphilis by a prostitute and were simply (if insanely) taking his revenge. But the vague contours of Jack the "victim" soon gave way to a very specific image of Jack.

What is striking is that the image of "Jack" is also set. He is (as one can see in Plate 273) the caricature of the Eastern Jew. Indeed, the official description of "Jack" was of a man "age 37, rather dark beard and moustache, dark jacket and trousers, black felt hat, spoke with a foreign accent."[35] There appeared scrawled on the wall in Goulston Street near where a blood-covered apron was discovered the cryptic message: "The Juwes are The men That

Will not be Blamed for nothing." The image of the Jews as sexually different, the Other even in the killing of the Other, led to the arrest of John Pizer, "Leather Apron," a Polish-Jewish shoemaker. Pizer was eventually cleared and released. But a high proportion of the 130 men arrested in the Ripper case were Jews. Sir Robert Anderson, the police officer officially in charge of the case, noted in his memoir that the police assumed that Jack was a Polish Jew.[36] When the body of Catherine Eddowes was found on 30 September outside the International Working Men's Educational Club by a Jew, a pogrom almost occurred in the East End, at least according to the *East London Observer* (15 October 1888): "On

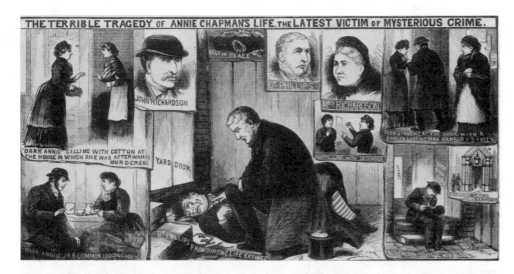

PLATE 275. *Annie Chapman's life as a prostitute represented as a reflex of her dead body.* From The Illustrated Police News. *Ithaca: Olin Library, Cornell University.*

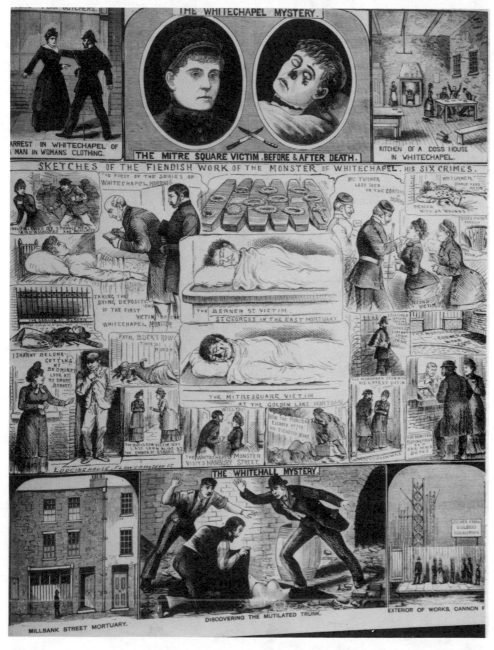

PLATE 276. *Jack the Ripper murdered Elizabeth Stride in Mitre Square and Catherine Eddowes in Berner Street on 30 September 1888. The prostitute becomes the torso of the anatomical atlases.* From The Illustrated Police News. *Ithaca: Olin Library, Cornell University.*

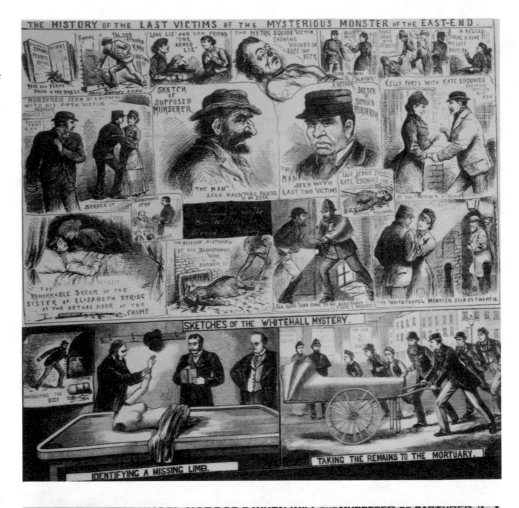

Saturday the crowds who assembled in the streets began to assume a very threatening attitude towards the Hebrew population of the District. It was repeatedly asserted that no Englishman could have perpetrated such a horrible crime as that of Hanbury Street, and that it must have been done by a JEW—and forthwith the crowds began to threaten and abuse such of the unfortunate Hebrews as they found in the streets" (see Plate 278). The powerful association between the working class, revolutionaries, and the Jews combine to create the visualization of Jack the Ripper as a Jewish worker, marked by his stigmata of degeneration as a killer of prostitutes. Here Jack had to intervene. In one of his rhyming missives sent to Sir Melville MacNaghten, the chief of the Criminal Investigation Division at Scotland Yard in 1889, he wrote:

I'm not a butcher, I'm not a Yid
Nor yet a foreign skipper,
But I'm your own light-hearted friend,
Yours truly, Jack the Ripper.[37]

When, during the 1890s, the German playwright Frank Wedekind visualized his Jack the Ripper killing the arch-whore Lulu, he represented him as a degenerate, working-class figure: "He is a square-built man, elastic in his movements, with a pale face, inflamed eyes, thick arched eyebrows, drooping moustache, sparse beard, matted sidewhiskers and fiery red hands with gnawed finger nails. His eyes are fixed on the ground. He is wearing a dark overcoat and a small round hat."[38] This primitive figure was quite in line with the views shared by the Italian forensic psychiatrist, Cesare Lombroso, and his French opponent, Alexandre Lacassagne, as to the representative image (if not origin) of the criminal but very specifically the sadist.[39] For the Germans, at least for liberals such as Wedekind, Jack was also seen as a member of the lumpenproletariat. But in Britain this image evoked a very specific aspect of the proletariat, that of London's East End, the Eastern Jew.

But why Eastern European Jews? The charge of ritual murder, the murder of Christian women by Polish Jews, appeared in the *Times* during this period. But this was but a subissue or perhaps a more limited analogy to the events in Whitechapel. Nor can we simply recall the history of British anti-Semitism, from the Norwich pogrom of 1144, caused by the charge of the ritual murder of a child, to the King's Road murders of 1771, which were laid at the feet of the Jews. The search for Jack the Ripper was the search for an appropriate murderer for the Whitechapel prostitutes. The murderer had to be representative of an image of sexuality that was

equally distanced and frightening. Thus the image of Jack the Ripper as the *shochet*, the ritual butcher, arose at a moment during which there was a public campaign against the "brutality" of the ritual slaughter of kosher meat.[40] But this image of the Jewish Jack rested on a long association of the image of the Jew with the image of the genitalia, as has been illustrated throughout this work. This mark of sexual difference was closely associated with the initial image of the syphilitic Jack, as shall be shown. The Jew remains the representation of the male as outsider, the act of circumcision marking the Jewish male as sexually apart, as anatomically different. The prostitute is, as has been shown, the embodiment of the degenerate and diseased female genitalia in the nineteenth century. From the standpoint of the normative perspective of the European middle class, it is natural that the Jew and the prostitute must be in conflict and that the one "opens up" the Other, as they are both seen as "dangers" to the economy, both fiscal and sexual, of the state.[41] This notion of the association of the Jew and the prostitute is also present in the image of "spending" semen (in an illicit manner) that dominates the literature on masturbation in the eighteenth and early nineteenth centuries. For the Jew and the prostitute are seen as negating factors, outsiders whose sexual images represent all of the dangers felt to be inherent in human sexuality. And consciously to destroy, indeed, to touch the polluting force of the Other, one must oneself be beyond the boundaries of acceptability.

The linkage between Jew and prostitute is much older than the 1880s, one that is related to the image of the black and the monkey in the second plate of Hogarth's *A Harlot's Progress* (see Plate 236). Here Moll Hackabout, the harlot, has become the mistress of a wealthy London Jew. The Jew has been cheated by the harlot; her lover is about to leave the scene. But her punishment is forthcoming. She will be dismissed by him and begin her slow slide downwards. Tom Brown, Hogarth's contemporary and the author of "A Letter to Madam _____ , kept by a Jew in Covent Garden," which may well have inspired the plate, concludes his letter on the sexuality of the Jew by asking the young woman "to be informed whether Aaron's bells make better music than ours."[42] It is this fascination with the sexual difference of the Jew, parallel to the sexual difference of the prostitute, which relates them even in death. Each possesses a sexuality that is different from the norm, a sexuality that is represented in the unique form of their genitalia. The nature of the Jew's anatomy has been discussed in this book; in Chapter Ten, we shall discuss in more detail the sexual anatomy of the prostitute.

PLATE 279. *Jack the Ripper as a well-shaved member of the working class, following the anti-Jewish riot in the East End. From* The Illustrated Police News. *Ithaca: Olin Library, Cornell University.*

PLATE 280. *The face of the prostitute. From* The Illustrated Police News. *Ithaca: Olin Library, Cornell University.*

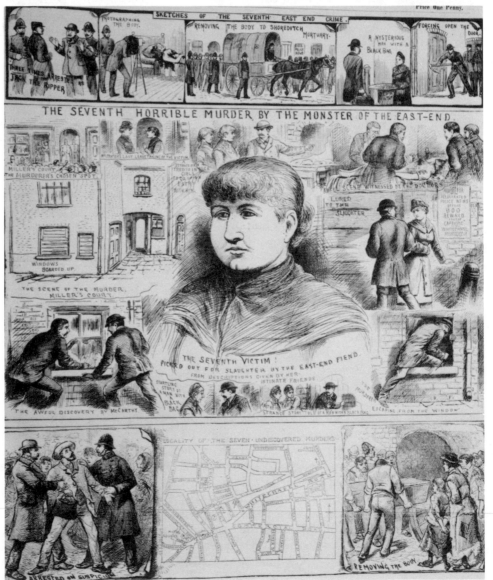

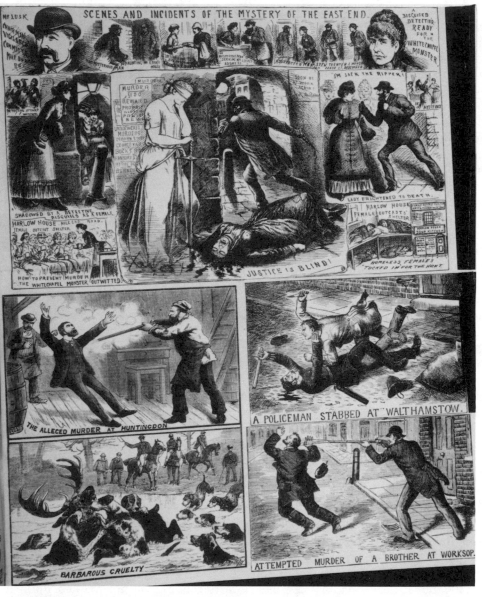

PLATE 281. *The bearded Jew in his kaftan flees the scene of the murders. From* The Illustrated Police News. *Ithaca: Olin Library, Cornell University.*

PLATE 282. *Jack the Ripper as a well-dressed Death as a physician, carrying his doctor's bag, about to open the prostitute's body. From* The Illustrated Police News. *Ithaca: Olin Library, Cornell University.*

The relationship between the Jew and the prostitute also has a social dimension. For both Jew and prostitute have but one interest, the conversion of sex into money or money into sex. "So then," Brown writes to the lady, " 'tis neither circumcision nor uncircumcision that avails any thing with you, but money, which belongs to all religions" (p. 200). The major relationship, as Tom Brown and Hogarth outline, is a financial one; Jews buy specific types of Christian women, using their financial ability as a means of sexual control. "I would never have imagined you . . . would have ever chosen a gallant out of that religion which clips and diminishes the current coin of love, or could ever be brought to like those people that lived two thousand years on types and figures" (p. 199).

By the end of the nineteenth century, this linkage had become a commonplace in all of Christian Europe. In 1892, an early nineteenth-century (1830s) pornographic "dialogue between a Jew and a Christian, a Whimsical Entertainment, lately performed in Duke's Palace," the "Adventures of Miss Lais Lovecock," reappeared in London. This dialogue represents the Jew and represents him in a very specific manner. First, the Jew speaks in dialect. By 1888, the British Jewish community had become completely acculturated. With Disraeli's terms as Prime Minister as well as the Prince of Wales (later King Edward VII) attending the wedding of Leopold de Rothschild on January 14, 1881, at a London synagogue, the boundary between the "native" Jew and the "foreign" Jew had to be drawn. This explains the use of dialect that in 1892 would point toward the Eastern Jew, toward Jack the Ripper, who could not command written English, at least about the "Juwes."[43] The text may well have reflected the image of the Jew in the 1830s, but it clearly had a very different set of associations after Jack the Ripper's appearance. The Jew, Isaac, describes his seduction of his father's Jewish (and, therefore, because all Jews are deviants in one way or another, hermaphroditic) maid who has a "clitoris, which was hard and shaped like a penis,"[44] while he seduces the Christian prostitute, Polly. (On the history of this icon, see the discussion of the image of the clitoris in Chapter Six.) She is described by him as having "little feet and ankles, I think of your pretty legs, and den I think of your snowy thighs, and den my fancy glowing hot got to de fountain of bliss, and dere I vill go immediately" (p. 66). She is the object of the Jew's desire, for his women (servant girls or whores) are as sexually marginal as he is himself. But it is only for money that Polly is willing to ring "Aaron's bells," for "nothing under three hundred a year" (p. 62). The prostitute is little more than a Jew herself. Both are on the margins of "polite" society. And, as we know, from the degeneration of Hogarth's Moll Hackabout following her relationship with the Jewish merchant, such sexuality in women leads to corruption and physical decay. The Jew, with all of his associations with disease, becomes the surrogate for all marginal males, males across the boundary from the (male) observer, males who, like women, can be the source of corruption, if not for the individual, then for the collective. This association of images of the deviant sexuality of the prostitute with marginal figures such as the Jew is illustrated in even more detail in Chapter Ten, where the association is between the black woman (representing the abstract stereotype of "blackness" as assuredly as the male Jew comes to represent "Jewishness") and the prostitute.

The association of the venality of the Jew with capital is retained even into the latter half of the twentieth century. In a series of comic books from the 1980s in which an anthropomorphized phallus plays the central role, the Jew is depicted as masturbating, committing an "unnatural" act (whereas all of the other phalluses are depicted having a potential female partner) while reading a financial journal[45] **[PLATE 283]**. What is striking in these comics is that all of the phalluses are circumcised. Here we have a problem within contemporary culture. In the post-World-War-II decades, circumcision became a commonplace—even among non-Jews—in the United States and Great Britain. How then to differentiate between the Jew and the non-Jew, between the "deviant" and the "normal"? We are faced with an analogous problem to why George Eliot's eponymous character Daniel Deronda did not know he was a Jew.[46] Did he never look at his penis? Here the hidden is not marked upon the skin, for the skin hides rather than reveals. It is the Jew within that surfaces: here, in seeing a financial journal as the source of power and therefore of sexual stimulation; in Eliot's novel with the "natural" sexual attraction between the crypto-Jew Deronda and the beautiful Jewess, Mirah Cohen. (Deronda never defines himself as sexually different, for his own body is the baseline that defines for him the sexually "normal." His circumcised penis is not a sign of difference, until he understands himself to be a Jew.)

The image of the Jew revealed in his sexuality seems to be an accepted manner of labeling the image of the deviant. Even his phallus does not know for sure until he performs a "perverse" act. Here the icon is a reversal of the traditional image of the phallus as the beast out of control. In this image it is the man, not his phallus, who is bestial

PLATE 283. *The masturbating Jew from Gray Joliffe and Peter Mayle,* Man's Best Friend *(London: Pan Books, 1984). Ithaca: Private collection.*

(read: Jewish). The perversion of the Jew (and thus the "humor" of this depiction of the phallus) lies in his sexualized relationship to capital. This, of course, echoes the oldest and most basic calumny against the Jew, his avarice, an avarice for the possession of "things," of "money," which signals his inability to understand (and produce) anything of transcended aesthetic value. The historical background to this is clear. For canon law forbade the taking of interest, seeing interest, according to Thomas Aquinas, as impossible, for money, not being alive, could not reproduce. Jews, in taking money, treated money as if it were alive, as if it were a sexualized object.[47] The Jew takes money as does the prostitute, as a substitute for higher values, for love and beauty. And thus the Jew becomes the representative of the deviant genitalia, the genitalia not under the control of the moral, rational conscience.

But the image of the Jew as prostitute is not merely that of the economic parallel between the sexuality of the Jew and that of the prostitute. For that relationship also reveals the nature of the sexuality of both Jew and prostitute as diseased, as polluting. Just as the first image of Jack the Ripper was that of the victim of the prostitute, the syphilitic male, so too were the Jews closely identified with sexually transmitted diseases. For the Jew was also closely related to the spread and incidence of syphilis. This charge appeared in various forms, as in the anti-Semitic tractate *England under the Jews* (1901) by Joseph Banister, in which there is a fixation on the spread of "blood and skin diseases."[48] Such

views had two readings. Banister's was the more typical. The Jews were the carriers of sexually transmitted diseases and transmitted them to the rest of the world. This view is to be found in Hitler's discussion of syphilis in *Mein Kampf*, and there he links it to the Jew, the prostitute, and the power of money:

> Particularly with regard to syphilis, the attitude of the nation and the state can only be designated as total capitulation. . . . The cause lies, primarily, in our prostitution of love. . . . This Jewification of our spiritual life and mammonization of our mating instinct will sooner or later destroy our entire offspring.[49]

Hitler's views, like those of Banister and the earlier British anti-Semites, also linked Jews with prostitutes. Jews were the arch-pimps; Jews ran the brothels; Jews infected their prostitutes and caused the weakening of the national fiber.[50]

Such a view of the Jew as the syphilitic was not limited to the anti-Semitic fringe of the turn of the century. It was a view that possessed such power over even "Jewish" writers such as Marcel Proust (whose uncomfortable relationship to his mother's Jewish identity haunted his life almost as much as did his gay identity). In Proust's *Remembrance of Things Past*, a series of novels written to recapture the world of the 1880s and 1890s, one of the central characters, Charles Swann, is a Jew who marries a courtesan. This link between Jew and prostitute is mirrored in Proust's manner of representing the sexuality of the Jew. For Proust, being Jewish is analogous to being gay—it is "an incurable disease."[51] But what marks this disease for all to see? Proust, who discusses the signs and symptoms of syphilis with a detailed clinical knowledge in the same volume, knows precisely what marks the sexuality of the Jew upon his physiognomy.[52] It is marked upon his face as "ethnic eczema."[53] This mark upon the face is Hitler's and Banister's sign of the Jew's sexual perversion. It is the infectious nature of that "incurable disease," the sexuality of the Jew, Proust's Jew fixated upon his courtesan. (This is an interesting reversal of one of the sub-themes of Zola's *Nana*, which will be discussed in Chapter Ten. There Nana is first the mistress of a Jew, whom she, quite easily reversing the role of Jack the Ripper, bankrupts and drives to suicide.) The Jew's sexuality, the sexuality of the polluter, is written on his face in the skin disease that announces the difference of the Jew. For Proust, all of his Jewish figures (including Swann and Bloch) are in some way diseased, and in every case, this image of disease links the racial with the sexual, much as Proust's image of the homosexual links class (or at least, the nobility) with homosexuality. (*Homosexuality* is a "scientific" label for a new "disease" coined by Karoly Benkert in 1869 at the very same moment in history that the new "scientific" term for Jew hating, *anti-Semitism*, was created by Wilhelm Marr.) The image of the infected and infecting Jew also had a strong political as well as personal dimension for Proust. For the ability to "see" the Jew who was trying to pass as a non-Jew within French society is one of the themes of the novels, a theme that, after the Dreyfus Affair, had overt political implications. Seeing the Jew was seeing the enemy within the body politic, was seeing the force for destruction. And Proust's "racial" as well as sexual identity was tied to his sense of the importance of class and society for the definition of the individual. Thus Proust's arch-Jew Swann was visibly marked by him as the heterosexual syphilitic, as that which he was not (at least in his fantasy about his own sexual identity).

The second model was to postulate exactly the opposite—that Jews had a statistically lower rate of syphilitic infection—because they had become immune to it through centuries of exposure. In the medical literature of the period, reaching across all of European medicine, it was assumed that Jews had a notably lower rate of infection. In a study of the incidence of tertiary lues in the Crimea undertaken between 1904 and 1929, the Jews had the lowest consistent rate of infection.[54] In an 18-year longitudinal study, H. Budel demonstrated the extraordinarily low rate of tertiary lues in Estonia dur-ing the prewar period.[55] All of these studies assumed that biological difference as well as the social difference of the Jews were at the root of their seeming "immunity."

Jewish scientists also had to explain the "statistical" fact of their immunity to syphilis. In a study of the rate of tertiary lues, the final stage of the syphilitic infection, undertaken during World War I, the Jewish physician Max Sichel responded to the general view of the relative lower incidence of infection among Jews as resulting from the sexual difference of the Jews. He responds—out of necessity—with a social argument. The Jews, according to Sichel, evidence lower incidence because of their early marriage and the patriarchal structure of the Jewish family but also because of their much lower rate of alcoholism. They were, therefore, according to the implicit argument, more rarely exposed to the infection of prostitutes whose attractiveness was always associated with the greater loss of sexual control in the male attributed to inebriety. The relationship between these two "social" diseases is made into a cause for the higher incidence among other Europeans. The Jews, because they are less likely to drink heavily, are less likely to be exposed to both the debilitating effects of alcohol (which increase the risk for tertiary lues) as well as the occasion for infection.[56] In 1927, H. Strauss looked at the incidences of syphilitic infection in his hospital in Berlin in order to demonstrate whether the Jews had a lower incidence but also to see (as in the infamous Tuskegee experiments among blacks in the United States[57]) whether they had "milder" forms of the disease because of their life-style or background. He found that Jews had indeed a much lower incidence of syphilis (while having an extraordinarily higher rate of hysteria) than the non-Jewish control. He proposes that the disease may well have a different course in Jews than in non-Jews.[58]

Both of these arguments saw the Jew as having a "special" relationship to syphilis (through the agency of the prostitute) and carried on the association between the Jew and the prostitute. But this special relationship could literally be seen on the Jew. Joseph Banister literally saw the Jews as bearing the stigmata of skin disease (as a model for discussing sexually transmitted disease): "If the gentle reader desires to know what kind of blood it is that flows in the Chosen People's veins, he cannot do better than take a gentle stroll through Hatton Garden, Maida Vale, Petticoat Lane, or any other London 'nosery.' I do not hesitate to say that in the course of an hour's peregrinations he will see more cases of lupus, trachoma, favus, eczema, and scurvy than he would come across in a week's wanderings in any quarter of the Metropolis."[59] Jews bear their diseased sexuality on their skin. Indeed, they bear the salient stigma of the black skin of the syphilitic.

The Jews are black, according to nineteenth-century racial science, because they are "a mongrel race which always retains this mongrel character."[60] That is Houston Stewart Chamberlain arguing against the "pure" nature of the Jewish race. Jews had "hybridized" with blacks in Alexandrian exile. They are, in an ironic review of Chamberlain's work by the father of modern Yiddish scholarship, Nathan Birnbaum, a "bastard" race the origin of which was caused by their incestuousness.[61] But the Jews were also seen as black. Adam Gurowski, a Polish noble, "took every light-colored mulatto for a Jew" when he first arrived in the United States in the 1850s.[62] Jews are black because they are different, because their sexuality is different, because their sexual pathology is written upon their skin. Gurowski's contemporary, Karl Marx, associates leprosy, Jews, and syphilis in his description of his archrival Ferdinand Lassalle (in 1861): "Lazarus the leper, is the prototype of the Jews and of Lazarus-Lassalle. But in our Lazarus, the leprosy lies in the brain. His illness was originally a badly cured case of syphilis."[63] Jews = lepers = syphilitics = prostitutes = blacks. This chain of association presents the ultimate rationale for the Jewish Jack the Ripper. For the diseased destroy the diseased, the corrupt the corrupt. They corrupt in their act of touching, of seducing, the pure and innocent, creating new polluters. But they are also able in their sexual frenzy to touch and kill the sexual pariahs, the prostitutes, who like Lulu at the close of Frank Wedekind's play (and Alban Berg's opera) go out to meet them, seeking their own death. Being unclean, being a version of the female genitalia (with their amputated genitalia), the male Jew is read (as Jack's Viennese contemporary Otto Weininger had read him) as really nothing but a type of female.[64] The pariah can thus touch and kill the pariah; the same destroy the same. Wedekind's Lulu dies not as a suicide but as the victim of the confrontation between two libidinal forces—the unbridled, degenerate sexuality of the male and the sexual chaos of the sexually emancipated female. But die she does, and Jack leaves the stage, having washed his hands, like Pontius Pilate, ready to kill again.

CHAPTER NINE

Representing the Sexual in the Fin de Siècle

TOUCH, CHILDREN, AND FREUD

During the fin de siècle, the sexualized touch is reformulated as a means of depicting corruption. Whether it is the disemboweling touch of Jack the Ripper or the seductive touch of the prostitutes he murders, the act of touching (either violently or erotically) comes to represent the fantasy of the transfer of infection (or, after C. F. S. Hahnemann's Victorian homeopathic motto that "like cures like," its eradication). As we have seen throughout this volume, the relationship between the "highest" and the "lowest" senses, between sight and touch, has consistently been eroticized. In the late nineteenth century, this eroticization of the high and low senses is paralleled by their medicalization. The erotic, because it is associated so very strongly with various forms of pathology, becomes even more oppressively a sign of disease.[1]

Although it is clear that all the senses can be (and have been) traditionally associated with the erotic, the pairing of sight and touch seems to have achieved a special status. This status maintains itself in the late nineteenth century, especially within the realm of the medical sciences. Sight and touch become the key to the understanding of sexual pathology. Sigmund Freud, in his *Introductory Lectures on Psychoanalysis*, observed the close relationship between the repression of sexuality (an act of touching) by young people confronted with their own sexuality and their heightened desire to undertake socially accepted acts, such as going to the theater (an act of seeing) as a displacement for that forbidden them.[2] This is a culturally mediated act of displacement, in which the forbidden stimulation from one sense is replaced by the permitted stimulation of another sense. It is important in the construction of the erotic nature of touch that the sense of sight, which replaces touch, has a higher value. It is more than a substitution of the act of seeing for the act of touching. It is the substitution of a perception of higher status for a perception deemed to be of lower status. It is not merely that seeing a play is acceptable but that seeing is a more highly prized stimulation than touch, at least within Western value systems. In the construction of the erotic implication of the senses, the sense of touch achieves "aesthetic" value only when it is related, in one way or another, to the higher sense of sight. That association mitigates the "crudity" associated with the erotic as perceived through the base sense of touch. It thus also makes the sight of the skin (but not its feel) beautiful.

This is Freud's understanding of the neurotic nature of the relationship among seeing, touching, and sexuality.[3] His discussion of the nature of the erotic touch, however, is rooted in his view of the evolution of human sexuality as part of human development. We all begin as sexually polymorphously perverse, able to take pleasure from the stimulation of every part of the body. This is a "primitive" status in which the erotic oral touch, the sucking of the breast, is our main means of interrelating with the world about us. In Freud's earliest developmental work, he identifies the "primitive" nature of the areas of heightened touch as the so-called erogenous zones. Freud sees the infant, like the scientific view of the fetus in the nineteenth century, undergoing a series of developmental "improvements" in its sense of touch from the most primitive, the use of the lips, to the most complex, the genitalia.[4] Self-touch becomes for Freud the sign of self-awareness for the infant, though he still is convinced of the deleterious effects of masturbation following childhood (or at least following the latency period). For Freud, masturbation is the cause of neurasthenia, one of whose many signs is the altered appearance of the skin.[5] Although Freud understands the erogenous zones as "normal," they have a specific chronological function that is absolute. Once the individual develops beyond the stage that is appropriate to the specific erogenous zone, its use becomes pathological. It is, of course, essentially the female who for Freud is the model for the necessary shift in the site of stimulation. Although all human beings undergo a shift from the anal to the oral to the genital areas as the site for sexual stimulation, the female has to undergo a further shift in puberty, from the clitoris to the vagina as the site of stimulation.[6] The anatomical reason for Freud's argument, stated in the most detail in the *Three Essays on the Theory of Sexuality* (1905), is the homologous relationship between the penis and the clitoris. (The background to this anatomical argument is outlined in Chapter Six.) It is in the act of self-touching, in Freud's discussion of female masturbation, that he finds the clue to the nature of the female child: "All my experience concerning masturbation in little girls has related to the clitoris and not the regions of external genitalia that are important in later sexual function."[7] For Freud, the self-touching of the female child is infantile; the self-touching of the male is not. For puberty in the male enhances his libido; in the female its proper form is the creation of a "fresh wave of repression." The female must learn to move from a quality of sexuality that is viewed as inherently masturbatory and therefore potentially pathological, clitoral stimulation, to vaginal orgasm: "When at last the sexual act is permitted and the clitoris itself becomes excited, it still retains a function: the task, namely, of transmitting the excitation to the adjacent female sexual parts, just as—to use a simile—pine shavings can be kindled in order to set a log of harder wood on fire."[8] The simile that Freud uses points to the touch of the Other, the stimulation of the sexual act, of the female by the male.

It is only vaginal stimulation that is "healthy" for the adult female: "When erotogenic susceptibility to stimulation has been successfully transferred by a woman from the clitoris to the vaginal orifice, it implies that she has adopted a new leading zone for the purposes of her later sexual activity."[9] The rejection of the self-touch, associated by Freud with clitoral stimulation, is a remnant of the view of the danger of masturbation, a danger attributed to both males and females in the medical literature of the nineteenth century. For Freud, the result of the persistent excitability of the clitoris is mental illness, neurosis, and hysteria. The homologous relationship between the sexual anatomy of the male and that of the female, the anatomical basis for Freud (and his contemporaries), is not powerful enough to destroy the boundary that he creates between the models of male and female sexuality, with their quite different development and potential pathology. And most important, clitoral orgasm's place is as an earlier, atavistic stage in sexual development. The sexuality of the female becomes a biological avatar of the primitive. Freud relied, as many a thinker of the late nineteenth century did, on the model of ontogeny recapitulating phylogeny. He wrote in his *Introductory Lectures on Psychoanalysis* (1916) that "each individual somehow recapitulates in an abbreviated form the entire development of the human race."[10] This argument reappears within Freud's understanding of the genitalia, with the stages of sexual development being the necessary stages of the movement from the more primitive to the civilized stage of sexuality. The appearance of the primitive in later stages of development was a clear sign of the pathological.

Freud's visual image of the child, taken from the Hungarian pediatrician S. Lindner's 1879 study of sucking, is of a primitive, libidinous individual **[PLATE 284]**. It is the image of the female as child. And Lindner's image is clearly a pathological one. He stresses the pleasure that the child receives from the act of sucking and touching, touching not only the genitalia but other highly sensitized parts of the body (*punctum voluptabile*) such as the nipple or navel. What is important about this image is the visual association made by Lindner between the masturbatory act, the representation of the female genitalia and the act of sucking (of consuming) the finger, the symbolic phallus. The image of the little girl is thus also the image of the Medusa, the pathological genitalia of the female, castrated and castrating, but it is also the hidden image of yet another set of mutilated genitalia, that of the male Jew, as we shall see. In the original essay, Lindner stresses it in order to prove that the act of compulsive sucking is an analogous pathological act to the act of masturbation. Freud's use of Lindner in the *Three Essays* brings into the discussion of the normal development of the child the image of the pathological self-touch, the fantasy of masturbatory disease, which we discussed in detail in Chapter Six. He "normalizes"

PLATE 284. *A six-year-old thumbsucker and masturbator, the daughter of a bookkeeper, from Freud's source, S. Lindner, "Das Saugen an den Fingern, Lippen etc. bei den Kindern (Ludeln.)," Jahrbuch für Kinderheilkunde und physische Erziehung 14 (1879). Ithaca: Olin Library, Cornell University.*

the erotic touch by displacing it onto the child's orality, but at its roots it remains a sign of pathological development, as he argues in the *Introductory Lectures.* Freud's visualization of this image of childhood sexuality has wider implications for his representation of the genitalia.

What must be noted is that Sigmund Freud, as a Viennese Jew of the late nineteenth century, was marked by the sign of his own sexual difference. He needed to document the universality of human sexuality and used the sexual touch to do so. According to European anti-Semitism, as has been discussed, Jews show their inherent difference through their damaged sexuality, and the sign of that is, in the popular mind, the fact that their males menstruate. Freud was reacting to much the

same sign, that of male menstruation, which characterized Jewish sexual difference in the Middle Ages. Freud's contemporary, the arch-racist Theodor Fritsch—whose *Antisemite's Catechism*, published in 1887, was the encyclopedia of German anti-Semitism—saw the sexuality of the Jew as inherently different from that of the German: "The Jew has a different sexuality than the Teuton; he will and cannot understand it. And if he attempts to understand it, then the destruction of the German soul can result."[11] The Jew was understood by fin-de-siècle medicine as being especially at risk for hysteria, with its roots in seduction and incest.[12] Freud's much-praised Parisian teacher, Jean Martin Charcot, among many others, stressed the "especially marked predisposition of the Jewish race for hysteria."[13] It is a hysteria that has its source in Jewish sexual selectivity, which European medicine understood in terms of late nineteenth-century eugenics as "inbreeding." Jews, both male and female, are hysterics because they indulge in perverted sexuality; the signs and symptoms are clearly marked on their physiognomy, written as it were on their skin. For the late nineteenth-century view associated the act of religious circumcision with the act of castration, the unmanning, the feminizing of the Jew in the act of making him a Jew.[14]

The feminization of the Jew (read: Jewish male) is a theme that, like the potential of the Jews for mental illness, haunts the pseudoscientific literature written against the Jews during the nineteenth century, the literature that was given the "scientific" label of *anti-Semitism* during that period. By the beginning of the twentieth century, the pseudoscientific literature of Jewish race hatred had become a genre in and of itself. Its most representative work, Otto Weininger's *Sex and Character*, is a work by a self-hating Jew that attempts to reveal the inner, destructive nature of both Jews and women. Published posthumously after the author's suicide in 1903, *Sex and Character* was seen, by thinkers as diverse as Freud and his American contemporary, the feminist theoretician Charlotte Perkins Gilman, as a major scientific contribution to the discussion of human psychology.[15] Weininger sought to create parallel categories of difference, showing that all Jews are merely women.[16] This was exemplified, for Weininger, by the Jew's discourse as a marker for difference, for Jews, like women, express their nature in their language. Women flirt or chatter, rather than talk (p. 195). For Weininger, it is the nature of the male Jew's discourse that also reveals his nature: "Just as the acuteness of Jews has nothing to do with true power of differentiating, so his shyness about singing or even about speaking in clear positive tones has nothing to do with real reserve. It is a kind of inverted pride; having no true sense of his own worth, he fears being made ridiculous by his singing or his speech" (p. 324). Here the image of the Jew as the feminized male, the castrated male, reappears. There was a basic cultural assumption at the turn of the century that the Jews were sexual perverts, and perversion took the form of a crime—incest. The incestuous touch was but the ultimate form of sexual selectivity, of "inbreeding." Popular medical knowledge of the period believed that "inbreeding" led to a weakening of the stock, to the appearance of specific illnesses, such as hysteria. This is the subtext of Freud and Breuer's *Studies on Hysteria* (1895), which accounts for why its Jewish authors suppress any mention of the religious identity of their patients in the published version of their cases, although it looms relatively importantly in their case notes.[17]

The feminizing "break of the voice," the inability to speak in a masculine manner, is also one of the standard stigmata of degeneration borne by the homosexual for late nineteenth-century medicine and popular culture. Homosexuality, by the close of the nineteenth century in the work of Richard Krafft-Ebing, Benjamin Tarnowski, Albert Moll, and others, was generally understood as being an innate, biological error that manifested itself not only in "perverted" acts but was written on the very body of the homosexual through the appearance of specific, visible signs.[18] And one of the most evident degenerative stigmata, cited in almost all case reports, is the quality of the voice. With the increased knowledge of the endocrinological system during the latter half of the nineteenth century, the biochemical link between the breaking of the voice and sexual change during puberty became known. The change of voice signaled the masculinization of the male; its absence signaled the breaking of the voice, the male's inability to assume anything but a "perverted" sexual identity. It is, however, also accepted within the fin-de-siècle nosological system describing homosexuality that those who become homosexuals, usually through the act of seduction, have some type of inborn predisposition to homosexuality that may well announce itself through the stigmata of degeneration. The tension between "nature" and "nurture," between these two models of homosexuality, also had its parallel in attitudes toward race during the same period and with much the same confused response on the part of those stereotyped. It is assumed that the stigmata are "real" signs of perversion, whether present or future, whether endogenous or exogenous. This assumption is internalized by those stereotyped and oftentimes in the most complex manner. One would imagine that the endogenous explanation for difference would have been rejected by those individuals so stigmatized. Not so.

Karl Heinrich Ulrichs, the first major advocate of homosexual emancipation during the 1860s, saw the homosexual as the "third sex," as a biological category of equal validity to the male and the female; likewise, some Jews, such as the early Zionists, by the 1890s began to accept the idea of racial difference as a means of establishing their own autonomy and separation.[19] Such a complex reading of categories of difference is reflected in the responses of highly acculturated German and Austrian Jews, such as Freud, who were caught between an acceptance of their own difference and a need to conceptualize it in such a way as to make it bearable. In Freud's own view on sexuality, these associations resurface, if in repressed and symbolic form. Thus Freud's concession, in the *Three Essays on the Theory of Sexuality* that the "erotic life [of men] alone has become accessible to research. That of women—partly owing to the stunting effect of civilized conditions and partly owing to their conventional secretiveness and insincerity—is still veiled in impenetrable obscurity."[20] This description of the innate nature of the woman and her relationship to "modern" civilization is merely a restating, in another context, of the traditional image of the Jew to be found in the medical (as well as popular) literature of the fin-de-siècle. Jews are unable to deal with modern civilization, it makes them mad because of their innate temperament; they are driven and they lie.[21] Thus the disease of being Jewish is analogous to the disease of being female. And this manifests itself in the rhetoric of the woman and the Jew. But the parallel of the discourse of women and men exists only as a reflex of the displacement of the genitalia. For inherent to the theory of castration that dominates Freud's image of the woman is the idea that the female genitalia represent the castrated male genitalia, for children "attribute to everyone, including females, the possession of a penis, such as the boy knows from his own body."[22] But children, at least Jewish male children, know something else from looking at their penis—that they are Jews. The male Jew's penis, according to the Jew self-conscious about the difference inscribed upon his body, generates fear of the Jew among Christians, for the penis is "castrated," circumcised. Thus anti-Semitism is the response to the Jew's body. Not an incorrect assumption given traditions such as that of Jewish male menstruation that represented the male Jew's genitalia as inherently different. Thus, according to Freud, the fear of the Medusa in Greek myth may be due to the fact that she is "a being who frightens and repels because she is castrated" and thus evokes the fear of castration in the male gaze. The Jew is also the Medusa, at least seen from the point of view of the self-conscious Jew, for the very sight of the Jew's body evokes a hostile reaction from the Christian world. The genitalia of the Jew are just as sinister as the genitalia of the woman because they both evoke fear in the "normal" beholder, that is, in the referent group. Freud thus displaces much of his anxiety about his own "racial" identity onto his image of the woman. But he must, in order to "save" a segment of the world of women from complete pathology, accept the view that there is a deviant subset of women (just as there is a deviant subset of Jews, the Eastern Jews in Vienna) in which this pathology is especially or specifically marked. Thus the feminized Jew becomes the representative type of Jew that Freud represses and projects as the sexualized, "degenerate" woman.

If the "degenerate," the greater category into which the nosologies of the nineteenth century placed the "pervert," was—according to Max Nordau, one of the very first supporters of Theodor Herzl's Zionism—the "morbid deviation from an original type," then the difference between the original type, the middle-class, heterosexual, Protestant male, and the outsider was a morbid one: the outsider was diseased.[23] Thus there is a general parallel drawn between the feminization of the Jew and the homosexual in the writings of assimilated Jews, Jews who did not seek to validate their difference from the majority during the late nineteenth century but did see themselves as potentially at risk as such morbid deviations from the norm. Nowhere is this illustrated with greater force than in an essay written in 1897 by the future foreign minister of the Weimar Republic, Walter Rathenau. Rathenau, who begins his essay by "confessing" to his identity as a Jew, condemns the Jews as a foreign body in the cultural as well as the political world of Germany: "Whoever wishes to hear its language can go any Sunday through the Thiergartenstrasse midday at twelve or evenings glance into the foyer of a Berlin theater. Unique Vision! In the midst of a German life, a separate, strange race. . . . On the sands of the Mark Brandenburg, an Asiatic horde."[24] As part of this category of difference, Rathenau sees the physical deformities of the Jewish male—his "soft weakness of form," his femininity (associated with his "oriental

ism")—as the biological result of his oppression. This was a restructuring of the charge that Jews were inherently feminine, rather than as a social reaction to their stigmatization. David Friedrich Strauss, the great critic of Christianity during the late nineteenth century and Friedrich Nietzsche's bête-noire, was able quite offhandedly to dismiss the "humbug" of the Resurrection as the result of the "fantastic," "oriental," "especially female" nature of the Jews.[25] The evils of Christianity lie in the mentality of their Jewish origin—a point that Nietzsche and many of the "Christian" critics of Christianity during the late nineteenth century ascribed.[26] It is the very biological (or "ontological") difference of the Jew that is the source of his feminized nature. This, of course, had to be modified by Jews such as Rathenau to provide a space where they were able to escape the stigma of feminization.

Male Jews are feminized and signal this feminization through their discourse. It is in the analogous category, that of voice, in which the biological assumptions of pathology and disease are linked. Such arguments are, as was Max Nordau's call in 1900 for all Jews to become "muscle Jews," an argument based upon nurture rather than nature.[27] The Jews' feminization comes as a result of society's oppression even though it has specific biological signs. With the use of the cracked voice of the Jew, Jewish thinkers may indicate the force that the persecution of the Jew had in forming the Jew's sexual identity. But the signs are the same—they are those of biological degeneration—no matter what the presumed cause. Jews are as marked by the signs of biological degeneracy as are the homosexuals, whatever the cause of their deviance. Both groups reveal their criminal perversion to us not only through their sexual activities but through their high or breaking voices. They are as such really no more than degenerate, masturbating women. (Indeed, the image of the masturbating Jew [see Plate 283] illustrates how protean these stereotypes are.) The Jews, with their "incestuous" sexuality, are frozen in an early (atavistic) stage of development, the same stage as the homosexual, the stage of narcissism. For the Jew, in committing "incest," loves his double and therefore loves himself; the homosexual, like the child, seeks after a love object and focuses on his own body.[28] This is like the image of the masturbating female child taken from Lindner, the child who is at an early stage of sexual development and who must transcend this, as she must transcend her fixation on clitoral orgasm to evolve into the "woman." If she does not , she will fixate on this early stage, as the male homosexual fixates, and she will become emotionally ill. Indeed, the sexuality of the Jew was like that of the masturbating female and the homosexual male—all become insane as a result of their sexual practices.

For Freud, the image of the child as sexual being (as found, for example, in his case of "Little Hans," a case that forms the basis for much of his discussion of childhood sexuality) is confused and amalgamated with that of the sexually active female.[29] And that figure serves in Freud's mental universe as the counterrepresentation to the feminized image of the male Jew that haunted the fin de siècle. In a widely quoted passage from the *Three Essays on the Theory of Sexuality* (1905), he comments that "children behave in the same kind of way as an averge uncultivated woman in whom the same polymorphous perverse disposition persists." This struggle with the polymorphous perverse is, for Freud, "a general and fundamental human characteristic."[30] It is class ("uncultivated"), not race, that Freud adds to gender and age as the three dominant markers of the sexually primitive, even though (or specifically because) the Jews (read: male Jews) have been accused of a primitive, undifferentiated, feminine (that is, "perverted") sexuality in the medical and pseudomedical literature beginning with the charge leveled in the Early Church, that the male Jew menstruated. Freud creates a new "universal," polymorphous sexuality, and applies it to a set of markers in none of which is he himself implicated.[31]

With the rise of psychoanalysis, Freud and his friend Wilhelm Fliess attempted to move the sign of male menstruation from being a sign of difference to one of universality.[32] Indeed, in his correspondence with Fliess, Freud noted his own periodic nasal bleeding as a proof of the universality of Fliess's theory of male and female periodicity. Just as the seventeenth-century convert to Christianity Franco da Piacenza tried to remove himself from the "curse of Eve" by claiming that only ancient Jews (and those of one of the "Lost Ten Tribes" at that) menstruated—not, of course, he and his contemporaries—so, too, do Freud and Fliess distance this charge from the Jews by making it universal. The public sign of Jewish identity (from the standpoint of the anti-Semitic society in which they live) is the nose (the icon of the anti-Semitic image of the "little Jew," "Herr Kohn," found on postcards and wall posters of the age) that "menstruates."[33] But its significance for Freud and Fliess, who are desperately trying to escape classification as "Jews" in the racial sense and therefore as inferior and different, is as a universal sign, a sign of the universal law of male periodicity that links all human beings, males and females. Thus for Freud every move

concerning the articulation of the nature of human sexuality responds to his desire to resist the charges of his own Jewish specificity by either projecting the sense of his own sexual difference onto other classes or by universalizing the attack on Jewish particularism, first articulated in the Early Church's rejection of circumcision and the particularism of the Jew's body.

Following Freud, the idea of the sexual touch within psychoanalysis again splits. On the one hand, Wilhelm Stekel sees masturbation as present in every developmental stage, including "latency." He correctly identifies the negative effects of masturbation as the internalization of the culture's attitude toward the touch of the self.[34] On the other hand, Sandor Rado (with his fascination of the pain/pleasure dichotomy) manages to posit a developmental system in which the "primitive" hedonistic world of touch is dominated and eventually replaced by the intellect.[35] This view is accepted by thinkers as different from Rado as Harry Stack Sullivan.[36] Sexuality, except for adult heterosexuality, becomes pathological. Although self-touch as a disease vanishes from somatic medicine (only to reappear as its antithesis, as sexual therapy with William H. Masters and Virginia E. Johnson in the 1960s[37]), it maintains itself within psychoanalysis in the concept of pathological masturbation.[38]

The neurological literature of the mid-twentieth century places the sensorium central to its concern.[39] The image of the human being thus generated places the sense of touch at a level of significance parallel to its importance within psychoanalysis. Wilder Penfield's 1952 image of the sensory homunculus **[PLATE 285]** presents an image of the (male) genitalia that dominates the representation of the individual. This creates a figure in which the male genitalia stand at the apogee of the sense of touch, representing the nature of neurological man's (not woman's) sexuality as the representation of the world of touch. Touch seems to be neutral in such an image, and yet there is a constant undertone, in the cultural context of neurological representations of sexuality, of the importance of sexual difference. It is the male's body that forms the baseline for the "normal" representation of the sensorium, not the body of the female. Penfield is abandoning the visual fixation, presented by the psychoanalysts, on the pathological image of the female body for his icon of the healthy, functioning one. The boundary between the "healthy" and the "diseased" is set even in this most "positivistic" of images.

The concepts of "good" touch and "bad" touch become buzzwords in discussions of incest and child abuse, the focus, in the 1980s, for our fears con-

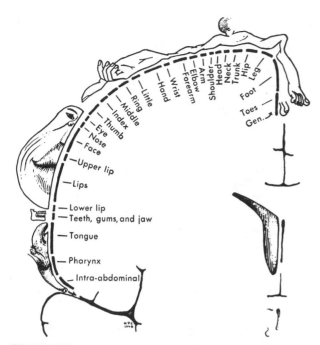

PLATE 285. *The sensory homunculus from Wilder Penfield, The Cerebral Cortex of Man (New York: Macmillan, 1952). The right side of the figure is laid upon a cross-section of the hemisphere, drawn somewhat in proportion to the extent of sensory cortex devoted to it. The length of the underlying block lines indicates more accurately the comparative extent of each representation. Ithaca: Olin Library, Cornell University.*

cerning childhood sexuality.[40] Indeed, a clinical study was undertaken in 1986 to determine when a child's touching of the parent's genitalia becomes "pathological" and finds (to its surprise) that "such activity is not uncommon on an 'incidental' basis even among 10-year-olds." The authors' double negative reveals their shock, for all such touching of the genitalia today falls under the suspicion of being "bad" or incestuous touching.[41] It is no longer the touching of the self or indeed even the cross-sexual touching of the individual beyond social boundaries (the seducer or the prostitute) that causes disease. Rather it is the touching across the boundary of age that places the child in the position of the taboo object. For we know what must happen if the child's genitalia are touched, even incidentally—permanent psychological harm. It is now the child who has become in the 1980s the new exemplary victim of the sexualized touch. Touch, especially the sexualized touch, remains dangerous in the 1980s, but with new objects and a heightened sense of the new boundaries in place between the "healthy" and the "diseased." In the late twentieth century, we have lost from view the antithetical position concerning child sexuality that haunted the fin de siècle, argued by Wilhelm Stekel in an oft-cited paper of 1895.[42] Stekel, in his essay on "coitus among children," argues that childhood

sexual contact is not as rare an occurrence as believed. He also illustrates that childhood sexual contact seems to have no deleterious effect on the emotional life of children. He cites in detail two cases—one of a physician and one of a jurist—who engaged in coitus with other children and adults while still children. He also makes further reference to other cases among children with whom he was working. It is evident that he labels as a universal of sexual practice (reflecting the late nineteenth-century Viennese social fantasy about the sexual potency of the child) the view that childhood coitus was widespread.[43] For Stekel, as opposed to Freud (even after his abandonment of the "seduction" theory[44]), sexual contact did not condemn the child to the life of a neurotic.

Neither the utopian view of Stekel nor the dis-topian view of contemporary attitudes toward child abuse is inherently correct. There is, however, an absolute boundary between these two positions, a labeling of one as *healthy* and the other as *diseased*. So is the sexual attractiveness of the child distanced from the observer. Such contact is labeled either as *taboo*, which emphasizes its illicit attractiveness, or as *normal*, flouting the cultural norms (including age) that are generated in all Western societies to create an absolute boundary between accessible and inaccessible sexual partners. The sexuality ascribed to the child is the fantasy of adult sexuality projected into the world. The adult desires to be the pure, the desirous, the uninhibited, the stereotype of the child—at least in the fantasy of the adult. It is the counterweight to our sense of the rigid limitations constructed for the place of sexuality in an adult world haunted by fears of sexually transmitted disease or the sense of the dissolution of the ego that such fears come to represent. The world of the social conventions of sexuality (our sexual superego), of whatever form, shapes our sense of self in each and every era. Thus we may well attribute the recent widespread, public interest in the dangers of child abuse, a danger that certainly existed to an equal degree a decade ago, to the increased sense of the vulnerability of the female as sexual object, a central theme of the women's movement of the 1970s. It is indeed women (and critical cross-dressers, to use Elaine Showalter's felicitous term[45]) who are at the forefront of the public discussion of child abuse. In many ways, they are projecting their internalized sense of victimization onto the child. They have excluded from consideration any potentially positive sexual relationship, such as described by Stekel and, indeed, advocated by a segment of the gay community. Sexuality has become the emblem of all that is fearful, and this fear is projected onto their image of the child. With their greater presence in the health sciences and the media during this period, women are for the first time directly shaping the fantasies about sexuality for the general thought-collective.[46] Thus the plurality of views at the turn of the century concerning the sexuality of the child, as exemplified by the sexual touch, has become a single voice labeling all such contact, whether in reality or in fantasy, pathological for both the adult and the child. What is clear is that the forms given the projections of sexuality are related to the stereotypical construction of the object, not to any "reality" that the object has in the world. Thus masculine projections concerning the sexuality of blacks or Jews are different from those concerning children because the boundaries between projections need to appear constant. What actually occurs is that certain fears about instability can best be articulated within shared fantasies about any given group. Thus the image of the child appears to stand apart from the images of other "outsiders," but the sense of "having been a child" (parallel to the fantasy for "pure women" to further the economic line) provides a category into which all of the anxieties about control, as epitomized by the sexual, can be placed or, indeed, as can be seen in such fictions as William Golding's *Lord of the Flies* (1954), negated.[47]

Such a fascination with the touch of the child has its roots in the nineteenth-century culture of touch. It is a fascination with the image of the self-polluting child (the pathological counterimage to the pure, almost noncorporeal child such as the eponymous protagonist in Frances Hodgson Burnett's *Little Lord Fauntleroy* [1886]) that haunts the representation of the touch of the child within the nineteenth century and against which Stekel argues. The sign of the child's self-touch points toward the corruptibility and corruption of the child but also toward the desired fantasy of the child as the icon of purity. In a world where the fear of sexually transmitted disease had become phobic (one can speak of the "syphilophobia" of the nineteenth century), the image of the pure, uninfected child becomes one of the central images representing the genitalia. The fear of syphilis was the concrete form assumed by the general fear of dissolution. The youthfulness of the child became the sign that resurrected the veiled memory of an age in which death and dissolution seemed remote. But this image also merged with the sense of the child as an inherently libidinal creature, the image that haunts Lindner's presentation of the sexuality of the child. The male's projection of the child as the genitalia

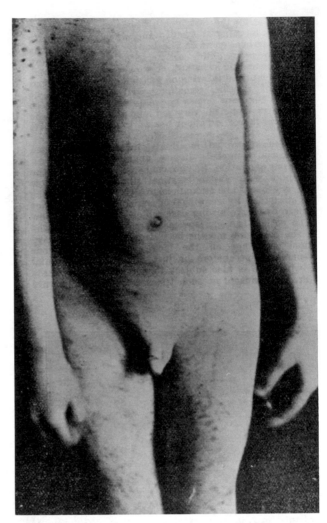

PLATE 286. *The skin of the hysterical child from T. D. Savill, "Hysterical Skin Symptoms and Eruptions,"* Lancet (20 January 1904). Ithaca: Olin Library, Cornell University.

incarnate points toward purity (i.e., lack of risk for infection and death) but also seductability (i.e., the child as the locus for the sexual touch).

In the nineteenth century, therefore, the image of the child is truly polyvocal—it is both the image of innate purity and latent corruption; of disease and health. The only means of distinguishing between them is by the nature of the skin. The corrupt child, the ill child, is marked upon the skin with the stigmata (and indeed Jean Martin Charcot introduces that very word for them) of his or her illness. The signs are the antithesis of Christ's stigmata, they are the *stigmata diaboli*, the signs of the devil that mark the body of the witch, and they point to the skin with all of its ambiguities as the source and the map of these signs of difference. But it is not only the sexual deviance of the prostitute

PLATE 290. *Hiram Powers,* The Greek Slave, *1846. Washington, DC: In the Collection of the Corcoran Gallery of Art, Gift of William Wilson.*

has a function in preserving the approachability of the child as well as the child's purity.[49] In the photographs of Wilhelm von Gloeden [PLATE 289], it is clear, however, that the image of the sexualized child is not solely that of the female child.[50] The nude or naked child, whether male or female, when placed in an "artistic" pose, becomes an object of desire, an object to be seen and about which the fantasies of touching (with all of its forbidden implications) can be spun. The child becomes its own sexual category, its purity and/or pollution standing in juxtaposition to adult sexuality, rather than to the sexuality of "male" or "female." The child becomes another marginal figure, standing apart from the traditional dichotomy of the two sexes. And as such, it is a danger as well as an attraction.

The image of the "pure" child draws on the aesthetics of position for its power. The unblemished skin of the child, placed in "aesthetic" position to stress its "beauty," also points toward the child's purity. Like the pure, white classical statues that Winckelmann and Goethe draw upon for their image of the pure sexual object (as discussed in Chapter Seven), the skin of the child represents the purity (and therefore the attractiveness) of the child as sexual object. In the nineteenth century, as in Hiram Powers's *The Greek Slave* of 1846 [PLATE 290], the association of the image of the nude marble statue with innate chastity had become a commonplace.[51] The complexity of the image of the "pure" child can be judged in the work and images collected by a late nineteenth-century contemporary of Lewis Carroll, the Viennese writer Peter Altenberg. In Altenberg's work, the sexual fantasies about the child, the Jew, and the black all intertwine.

PETER ALTENBERG'S BLACK CHILDREN

For a moment, let us remove ourselves to the German or Austrian zoological garden before World War I. If we cast our eye back into time, to turn-of-the-century Vienna, and we see with the eye of the Viennese of the period, we would be seeing a zoological garden quite different from that perceived if we found ourselves in our contemporary "zoo." We would be struck by the fact that animals were on display. And that "animal," in its accurate biological usage, would include specimens of the genus *Homo sapiens sapiens*. Indeed, the European zo-ological garden of the late nineteenth century provided "ethnological" exhibitions, representations of "exotic" cultures, eating what were viewed as appropriate foods, living in appropriate housing, and undertaking appropriate tasks for "primitives." Replaced in the 1910s by the film travelogue, the "ethnological" exhibition was a natural extension of the ethnological museum, placing living "exotics" within the daily experience of the European. Marcel Proust recounts such a visit in his *Remembrance of Things Past* when Mme. Blatin visited the zoo and "went up to one of these black fellows with 'Good morning, nigger . . .' . . . 'Me nigger,' he said angrily to Mme. Blatin, 'me nigger; you old cow!' "[52] The image of the zoological garden and that of the black are inexorably linked in the fin-de-siècle mind.

Vienna was certainly no exception to this. In the Prater, the major city park, imported exotics served as the focus for the fascination of the masses. Here were "noble" exotics whose presence countered the malignant "ignobility" of the local exotics, Eastern Jews, but as we shall see, they shared many of the same stereotyped sexual characteristics. It is important to understand that just as the Jews, especially the Eastern Jews, represented a specific type of perverse sexuality, in their case incest, within the stereotypes of fin-de-siècle perception, so too did the black represent another type of damaged sexuality. This sexuality, like that of the Jews, was presented within the systems of Western perception as a disease. This pathology, like that ascribed to the Eastern Jews, was one that articulated many of the fantasies of the publicly repressed sexual dis-course of the turn of the century. The signifier of black sexual pathology was tied to the form of the genitalia of the blacks. This is not to deny that the black was perceived as an attractive sexual object in fin-de-siècle Vienna. Magnus Hirschfeld reports in a rather jaundiced tone (quite unusual for this great sexual liberal) about the "queer predilection for Ashantis that for a while raged in Vienna" among the women of that city, who would "approach these negroes under different pretexts" for sexual en-counters.[53] The Ashantis exhibited in Budapest as well as Vienna became the sexual icon for the "royal and imperial" monarchy. But it is important to un-derstand that the Ashantis were simply represent-ative of the "black" as an abstraction, just as the "black" as an abstraction signified the diseased yet attractive Other for the Viennese. The attraction of the black was coupled with the sense of danger lurking within the pathological, as we shall see.

After an exhibition of a group of Ashantis in

1896, Peter Altenberg published his *Ashantee* (1897), a work that was then anthologized, but always in extract, in his later collections.[54] Altenberg was the master of the sketch, the creation of an intense, evocative literary image; in *Ashantee* he provided an interlocking series of such sketches, with, how-ever, an overall literary structure lacking in his other works. *Ashantee* is a record of Altenberg's inter-nalized fascination with the young Ashanti women and girls exhibited in the Prater. The structure that Altenberg superimposed upon the sketches included in the volume reveals the overt ideology of his public position as well as the hidden dimension of his perception of the black. On the surface, the book serves as a liberal protest against the exploitation of the blacks by the European public's taste for the exotic. But there is a powerful subtext that presents the author's association between his "seeing" of the black and his fantasy about human genitalia. The work opens with a long quotation from Meyer's Encyclopedia, placing the Ashantis into the eth-nology of Africa (pp. 3–4).

Following the general view of Friedrich Ratzel, the most influential geographer of the late nineteenth century, the anonymous author of the encyclopedia article begins by placing the Ashantis within the geography of the west coast of Africa, as the central determining qualifier for all of the following de-scription.[55] The author observes that the Ashantis are "true, woolly-headed blacks," whose priests have the function of exorcising evil spirits through "hysterical" dances. These two qualities, the "true" nature of the Ashantis as a race and the "hysterical" quality of their religion, begin Altenberg's text. The reader is presented with the black in the encyclo-pedia, a textual ethnological museum but one that exhibits the black within the context of scientific discourse rather than the sideshow of the Prater. In citing this passage as our opening into the text, Altenberg draws upon the scientific status of eth-nology, or at least upon the power of a "scientific" text to counter or undermine the popular tone of the Prater's exhibition of the black.

Yet the citation also begins to document, no matter how subtly, the analogy he will present between the black and the genitalia. Altenberg's opening vignette provides the expected liberal condemnation of the Ashanti exhibition in the Prater (pp. 5–13). In the zoological garden, there stands a cage in-habited by two exotic beasts from the Amazon, two pampas hares, sitting quite humanlike on their haunches nibbling the sweets tossed to them by the crowd. Next to this cage are the Ashantis, seen performing a native dance. We, the readers, find ourselves viewing the scene in the company of two employees of the zoo, who discuss the Ashantis, or at least one of the young Ashanti women, in much the same tone as they had spoken about the pampas hares. What is striking about the point of view created by the author for his figures is that it mirrors Peter Altenberg's own lifelong fascination with prepubescent females, for our narrative perspective throughout the work permits us to see only the young females present among the Ashantis. It excludes from our vision the males present.

The first vignette documents this exclusion and provides the reader with the appropriate liberal perspective: how horrible it is to have human beings exhibited and gawked at like pampas hares. This ideological message is completed in the closing sketch that frames the collection. The volume concludes with one of the employees commenting to the director of the zoo about someone who had just left the abandoned huts of the Ashantis in tears. The director's response is: "By the way, these huts have to be demolished tomorrow to make way for the tightrope walkers and a tethered balloon ride" (p. 72). Thus, on its surface, Altenberg's most sustained work serves as a condemnation of Viennese society for having turned the Ashanti into a source of amusement. This overtly ideological frame, however, contains within it a complex set of textual references to the sexual nature of the black, references that are the direct result of the observations by the narrative "I/eye" who is called "Peter A." These references are a hidden code that, once deciphered, reveal to us the function of the black within the fantasy world of Peter Altenberg but also within the world of the modernist text. Our first introduction to the consciousness of this "eye" is in the second vignette. The structure of this vignette is typical for all of the following sketches—a dialogue (with or without the other partner actually being present and responding) with one of the young females in the mock village of the Ashantis.

It is programmatically labeled "Dialogue" and begins with a discourse by "Peter A." on the nakedness of the young girls: "It is cold and very damp, Tioko. There are puddles everywhere. You all are naked. What are these thin linen things? You have cold hands, Tioko. I will warm them. You need at least cotton flannel, not this smooth cloth" (p. 14). Peter A.'s recourse is to the cross-sex touch, with all of its erotic implications, here masked as the healing touch, the touch that transforms the naked and cold child into the warm and clothed one. She responds by stressing the fact that it is

the exhibitioners who demand that the Ashantis appear "naked." Tioko observes that the Ashantis would never dress this way in Africa, nor would they live in huts that are only fit for dogs. "They want us to represent animals," she comments. The organizer of the exhibition told her that there are enough clothed females in Europe, and what they need is for them to be "naked." The word *naked* is Altenberg's label for the state of dress in which the Ashanti women are exhibited. It is clear that they are dressed in the traditional garment in which blacks were exhibited in Europe from the beginning of the nineteenth century, a garment that was thin enough to be quite revealing. But exactly what was the signification of the nakedness of the black female, a nakedness that Peter Altenberg deplores? The "Hottentot Venus," as will be shown in more detail in Chapter Ten, served as the emblem of black sexuality during the entire first half of the nineteenth century. She represented a sexuality inherently different from that of the European. There was an attempt to create an absolute distinction between the races based on a Western perception of her appearance.

The view that the races were inherently different rested to no little extent on the sexual difference of the black. By the late nineteenth century this fantasy of black sexual difference found a specific locus. For the idea of the sexual anomalies of the black female were linked with the fears of sexually transmitted disease. The genitalia of the black were perceived as analogous to those of the infected prostitute. Sexually transmitted illness and the pathology of the black genitalia were associated, and the fear (and fascination) accompanying the one became associated with the other. Thus by the time Peter Altenberg begins to write his *Ashantee*, the idea of black sexuality as a sign of pathology was well implanted in the consciousness of the European. The double sign of the unapproachability of the black woman—her difference as a member of an inherently different race—and her pathological character became a signifier for the European. As we shall see, its function within the structure of literary discourse assumed a most surprising dimension. By the late nineteenth century, seeing the black meant fantasizing about the human genitalia.

Following "Dialogue," the next paradigmatic sketch in Peter Altenberg's *Ashantee* is labeled "Culture" and presents the reader with an account of a dinner party in Vienna to which two of the Ashanti women were invited (pp. 28–29). The dinner party chitchat revolves about the fact that the guests perceive a real difference between the "childlike" nature of the black woman and the "adult" (although the word never falls) nature of Western women. Our eye in the tale, Peter A., comments quite directly that "blacks are children." Here is a further marker of difference, the roots of which can be found in classical antiquity. The Other is like the child, different from the mature and sensible adult. But in the fin de siècle the very idea of the analogy between "child" and "adult" assumes a sexual dimension. Indeed, when Josephine Baker appeared in Vienna in 1929, or at least tried to appear, for the city council found her costumes much too lascivious, she was glorified, totally without irony, by her supporters in Vienna as "that beautiful black child."[56] The implications of the child as sexual object become evident later in the course of the dinner party when the younger of the two Ashantis is given a "wonderful French doll," to which she begins to sing. The older of the two "suddenly bared her perfect upper body and began to nurse the doll from her magnificent breasts."

The audience to this spectacle is awed by the naturalness of her action, moving one of the guests to comment that this was one of the "holiest" moments in her life. The bared breast has a function as a sexual sign of physical maturity but is given here an association with "childishness," an association that is clearly contradictory. It has a quite different signification from, let us take a well-known example, the function of the iconography of the breasts in Theodor de Bry's illustrations of the early reports of the explorers of North America, where, as Bernadette Bucher has shown, the shift from the "classic," that is, firm, breasts to sagging breasts has major structural significance in representing the general shift in attitude toward the "exotic."[57] Here the sign of the breast is that of the "girl-woman": the child with the physical characteristics of the adult. The girl-child is suddenly revealed (and reveals herself) to be a woman. The image of the sexualized child is also the image of the infantilized black. Here the two images meet in Altenberg's fantasy. For the image of the black woman, whether the young girl in the Prater or Josephine Baker, is that she is innocent and pure as well as sexually seductive. She is the forbidden object of desire because of her age as well as her race. These qualities merge, and all black women become attractive children. The significance of the reference to the breast is that it visually refers to the maternal aspect of the feminine, with only a subordinate (though clearly motivating) cross-reference to the sexuality of the female. Altenberg can have it all ways—the black is the aesthetic object to be ad-

mired, the sexual object to be pursued, the idealized object to be worshiped.

The power of this association within the world of Peter Altenberg can be judged by the central sexually referential vignette, entitled "A Letter from Africa" (pp. 32–35). This, the eleventh vignette in the book, begins on a somber note. The brother of one of the young women has died in Accra, and this news is received by all with an act of communal mourning. This opening leads, however, to a further moment in the natural history of Altenberg's perception of the black. Suddenly it is nine at night:

> I enter the hut. On the ground lie Monabo, Akole, the wonderful one, and Akoschia. Not a pillow, not a blanket. Their perfect upper bodies are naked. The air is filled with the odor of pure, noble young bodies. I lightly touch the wonderful Akole.

The sexual overtones to this passage are unmistakable. What is striking is the association of the concept of racial purity, such as is mentioned in the selection from Meyer's Encyclopedia, and the "purity" ascribed to the "odor" of the black. Olfactory qualities had long been used to label the Other as different. Indeed, the mephitic odor of difference had been one of the central markers for the Jew in the biology of race in late nineteenth-century Germany.[58]

The function that the "pure" odor of the "noble young bodies" of the black women has is to reverse the association of odor and difference. Yet the deep structure associates the two within the system of sexual discourse in the late nineteenth century.[59] We have already remarked on Altenberg's use of the absence of "shame" as an indicator of the childlike "nobility" of the Ashanti. Cesare Lombroso provided a reading of the origin of this sense of shame in the "primitive." He remarked that in the Romance languages the term for *shame* is taken from the root *putere*, which he interprets as indicating that the origin of the sense of shame lies in the disgust for body smells. This he "proves" by observing that prostitutes show a "primitive pseudoshame," a fear of being repulsive to the male, because they are loath to having their genitalia inspected when they are menstruating. Altenberg's use of "pure odor" and absence of shame (the exposed upper bodies of the Ashantis serving as an icon of their unselfconsciousness) are signs of their sexual availability. But the association between odor and difference also points quite directly to the image of the source of pollution. The smell of the menses is equated with the stench of ordure, both human and animal, in the public health model of disease that still clung to the popular understanding of illness during the late nineteenth century.

Edwin Chadwick, the greatest of the early Victorian crusaders for public sanitation (who built upon the theoretical work of German writers such as E. B. C. Heberstreit) perceived disease as the result of putrefaction of effluvia. For Chadwick, "all smell is disease."[60] The link between public sanitation and the image of the corrupting female (and her excreta) is through the agency of smell. The next moment in the vignette makes the covert reference to the sexuality of the black overt. Peter A. is told by Akole, whom he has touched in her sleep, to go to Tioko. Monambo, awakened, turns to him and asks: "Sir, tomorrow can you bring us a 'piss-pot'? It is too cold to leave the hut at night. It must be blue outside and white inside. We will pay you what it costs. You could give Tioko one! What might it cost?!" Peter A. replies: "Monambo, I have never bought a 'piss-pot.' I don't know how much it will cost. Between 50 Kreuzer and 500 Gulden. Queens use golden ones." Monambo then repeats her first speech to him, and the vignette has Peter A. leaving the hut as dawn comes. Altenberg's fantasy of consummation with the black is cast in a literary mold. His seduction takes place within the safe confines of the text. But it is a fantasy of seduction that equates the black woman with her genitalia, which makes her into the representation of sexuality per se. Altenberg's literary encoding of this is uncomplicated. Without a doubt the most blatant sign is the conclusion of the vignette, the lover departing at the crack of dawn.

This theme, that of the *aube*, is part of the standard literary repertoire of seduction. It is an image whose associations are self-evident. Consummation has been accomplished, and the male leaves, walking into the new day. The act of coitus is part of the nightside of fantasy. It is associated with the image of touching the black girl-child within the sexual act, just as the narrator had "touched" her earlier at the moment he observed her "perfect upper body." But touching a black female child is not the same as touching a white female child. There is an absolute boundary between their natures, one spelled out quite directly in the scientific literature of the time.

Altenberg "sees" the black and fantasizes within his literary text about "touching" and "smelling" her. The function of the lower senses in representing the Other with his system of sexual fantasy points toward the function of these senses, rather than the higher, "aesthetic" ones, in defining the appropriate sexual object for him. His use of the image of the sexualized touch within the context of his own "exotic" status as a marginalized Jew in fin-de-siècle Vienna (as with Sigmund Freud's fantasy of the child) gave a special meaning to the sight and touch of the black. His views worked strongly against the dominant image of the senses as the means of differentiating among the various "races" of humankind. One major early nineteenth-century thinker, Lorenz Oken, used the senses as a means of differentiating among the various classes of his animal world.[61] Although Oken believed that all of the human "races" were related, he did see a hierarchy of human beings, the highest being the "Eye-Man, the White, the European" and the lowest being the "Skin-Man, the Black, the African."[62] Oken's view, which reflects an eighteenth-century understanding of embryological development, places the skin (which is the first of the sensory organs to evolve) at the nadir of development—thus the primitive basic nature of skin responses. The skin is the most primitive of all the sensory organs, its information the crudest. It is the source of irrational empiricism. Indeed, Havelock Ellis at the close of the nineteenth century can still speak with great authority of touch as "the least intellectual and the least aesthetic" of the senses.[63] Logically, if Eye-Men live by sight, by the aesthetic, it means that their world, the world of images and words, is a world of heightened acute visual sensitivity; the corollary should be that the Skin-Man should have a heightened physical response to tactile sensation. But the black, to whom Hegel denied any sense of the aesthetic, is denied even the status of the heightened sensibility of the skin. In the age of expanding colonies, the black became the primitive per se, and that primitivism is mirrored in the stultifying quality of his dominant sense, touch, as well as in the absence of any aesthetic sensibility. Thus Friedrich Nietzsche, writing in *The Genealogy of Morals* three-quarters of a century after Hegel, can comment (in line with the medical views of his age) that the history of the painful touch could be written through the examination of atavistic cases:

Perhaps in those days—the delicate may be comforted by this thought—pain did not hurt as much as it does now; at least that is the conclusion a doctor may arrive at who has treated Negroes (taken as representatives of prehistoric man—) for severe internal inflammation that would drive even the best constituted Europeans to distraction—in the case of Negroes they do *not* do so.[64]

Nietzsche's view places the black, the Skin-Man, in a position of insensitivity, for sensitivity (at least the word in German and English) is an aesthetic term, and the nineteenth century knew that blacks, like Jews, had no aesthetic sensibility. They could neither be "beautiful" objects upon which the sexual gaze was thrown nor could they be the creators of beauty. But is is not solely the black who is thus labeled. For by the close of the nineteenth century, Houston Stewart Chamberlain, in one of the most influential books of his time, *The Foundations of the Nineteenth Century*, wrote that Jews were really a "mongrel" race, having intermarried with blacks.[65] Blacks, like Jews, represented a hidden, different sexuality, a sexuality that defined the line between the self and the Other.[66] And thus Jews became interchangeable with blacks within the discourse of difference in late nineteenth-century German culture. The world of the desirable, the sensitivity and sensibility of the Romantic artist, of the German male, was not the world of the black and the Jew.

There is, of course, a revealing pendant to this anecdote, for Nietzsche's aphorism on the history of the senses is only tangentially about blacks. Its primary focus is on the biological changes in the "bluestocking," the educated, undersexed, upper-middle-class female with her pretensions to independent thought. He follows his bold statement about the innate primitiveness of the black's (as a surrogate for the Jew's) sensibility with a (parenthetical) comment:

> (The curve of human susceptibility to pain seems in fact to take an extraordinary and almost sudden drop as soon as one has passed the upper ten thousand or ten million of the top stratum of culture; and for my own part, I have no doubt that the combined suffering of all the animals ever subjected to the knife for scientific ends is utterly negligible compared with one painful night of a single hysterical bluestocking.) (p. 504)

The image of the educated, intelligent woman thus haunts the reading of the black. Here the "good" definition of the ego of the observer is bounded by the black, at one pole, and the female intellectual, at the other. Nietzsche's desire to abandon all such categorization falters at such moments, and the reader can suddenly see through his eyes, measure his own sensibility. For Nietzsche, the friend of such "bluestockings" as Malwida von Meysenbug and Lou Andreas-Salomé, knows that the biological model for human sensibility is not the answer. Quite the opposite, he feels it is culture that increases sensibility. For Nietzsche understood that "it is man who creates for himself the image of woman, and

woman forms herself according to this image."[67] Nietzsche comes, through his reading of Sigmund Freud's translation of John Stuart Mill's essay on the social and political status of women, to this awareness that the "nature" of woman is the response of the female to her "creation" by a phallic world. The cultural image of the woman is of one who does not suffer in childbirth but suffers in her avoidance of childbirth. The polar structuring principles, the need to create antithesis in order to structure the world, exist in this passage in an ironic reversal. The spectrum running from "Hottentot" to "European" that marks the movement toward "civilization" for the European intellectual of the nineteenth century is replaced with the spectrum "black–female intellectual," which is used to measure the distance "civilization" has created between the human being and his/her body. With Nietzsche's transvaluation, the polarity is ironized, but it still remains a polarity. And this polarity is rooted in the general need to see the world in antithesis. Even Nietzsche, who is extraordinarily aware of the power of categories and structures to manipulate human perception (even of the body) is unable to escape this trap. Cultural categories of difference function as the borders for his definition of his sense of his own sexuality. His body is placed beyond the culture of touch, in the inviolate world of the mind. This is, of course, the fantasy of being without the body, a fantasy that is defined by the creation of categories of sexual difference.

The culture of touch becomes one of the primary places where the boundary between the acceptable and the unacceptable is drawn. Blacks and Jews, with their less sensitive natures, repellent physicality, and diseased bodies were placed beyond the pale of the sexually desirable and, as a result, become the exotic sexual object par excellence. This fascination with the touching of the black, with the skin of the black, turns the figure of the black into the ideal sexual figure, the antithesis of the self, the self's alter ego. Adolf Hitler's condemnation of both Jew and black as sexual deviants, building upon Chamberlain's views, reveals a link between both constructions of race, a link that had become a commonplace by the 1920s. Jews and blacks were by their very "racial" designation sexualized figures. They mark the absolute boundary between the acceptable and the corrupt, between the healthy and the diseased.

In Altenberg's evocation of the black female child as the object of sexual desire, the dawn song serves as an extended metaphor for the postcoital depression of the male. But Altenberg has peppered his text with further sexual associations that lead the reader to expect the final "dawn song" rather than be startled by it. Central to them is Monambo's request for a "piss-pot." The sexual association of the image of the female genitalia with images of disease has been richly documented in this study. In the nineteenth century (as was discussed in Chapter Seven), there is an overt masculine fascination expressed in literature as well as practice with the urination of the female. The great French cultural historian of the nineteenth century, Jules Michelet, recorded in detail his observations of his wife's urination for the entire span of their marriage.[68] This fascination had a special place in the male's need to see and understand the hidden and different nature of the female genitalia as a means of understanding his own sexuality. The act of observing excretion destroys the illusion of "shame," just as the nakedness of the Ashantis and their request for a "piss-pot" remove the veil of social practice and bind the observer to the one designated as the exhibitionist. To summarize our discussion in Chapter Seven, it is important to note here that the observation of the act of a woman urinating stresses both the difference and the similarity of the Other. The woman urinates, an act associated by the male with the penis, but the very act of urination as undertaken by the woman proves the absence of the penis. This image of the "damaged" (and "damaging") genitalia of the female becomes associated with the black as the antithesis of self. The black becomes the genitalia as the sign of pathological difference. And at this level of analogy it is quite unimportant if the genitalia are male or female. Altenberg picks up this theme and links it to the fantasy of "seeing" the black, a black of "pure" race and "pure" sexuality. It results, however, in a seduction that takes place only within the text, only through the association of perceiving the black and fantasizing about his or her genitalia. The movement from talking about the act of urination to the fantasy of coitus is buried in a nest of ellipses in the text, ellipses that herald the introduction of the trope of the parting lovers.

Again, Altenberg uses a "liberal" overlay to rationalize his projection concerning the sexuality and genitalia of the black. Altenberg's use of the anglicized term *piss-pot* leads the reader back to a colonial world where, according to the women, piss-pots would not be used by blacks. The blacks need the piss-pot because they are being housed in kennels and clothed in thin, revealing garments. The covert association comes about through speaking about urination, for urination in the late nineteenth-century mind leads to a fantasy of the buttocks. In one of Havelock Ellis's case studies, which, as Phyllis Grosskurth has shown, are themselves fantasies on sexual themes, a "firsthand" account of this association between the act of urination and the buttocks is given:

> Florrie herself, who became so acute an analyst of her own experiences, pointed out the significant fact that in a woman there is invariably a mental association,—an association which has no existence in a man's mind,—between the nates and the act of urination. The little girl's drawers must be unfastened behind to permit of the act being accomplished and the grown woman must raise her clothes behind for the same act; even when, as is now so often the custom, she adopts the standing attitude in private, she usually raises the clothes behind, though, as the stream tends to take a forward direction, it would be more convenient to raise them in front. Thus, throughout life, in a woman's mind there is an association between urination and bared prominent nates. Custom, as Florrie emphasizes, compels a woman to bare and protrude the nates and sit for the purpose of urination, and when there is nothing to sit upon to squat, although, she adds, "as far as decency goes, it might be much more modest to turn one's back to any stray passerby, and raise the skirts in front, towards a protective bush; but this would be contrary to habit—and savour of a man!"[69]

Even when, as we have seen to be the case with Florrie, the practice of urination in the open without raising of the skirts is adopted, the prominence of the nates may still be asserted, for, as Florrie discovered, the act is best performed in this attitude when bending forward slightly and so protruding the nates. Present in Ellis's text are the associations of childhood, of exhibitionism, with the act of urination and the baring of the buttocks. The powerful association of the buttocks with the primitive, of the black in the nineteenth century, thus leads the reader back to Altenberg and the bodies of the young Ashanti women on display in the Prater, Havelock Ellis's case study of Flossie is a tale of the growth of a perversion. The analogy that Flossie sees among the image of the buttocks, the act of urination, and her eventual flagellist fetish document a representative course of associations for the fin-de-siècle perception of the sexual act. The distancing effect of presenting these analogies as the central focus for the image of the black stresses the strong historical associations of the black with the pathological, especially the sexually pathological. The fascination of fin-de-siècle writers such as Altenberg is the mirror image of the Victorian image of the sexualized being found in works such as George Gissing's *The Whirl-*

pool (1897). Bernard Meyer has commented that "when one of the characters is killed off by bad street drains, it is tempting to suspect that this annihilating instrument of public plumbing was a symbolic representation of the devouring female genital, an awful image of that cloacal anatomy that appears to have become for Gissing an emblem of all ugliness. The very streets of London appear to partake in the mephitic attributes of the women who roam them."[70]

It is the association of fantasies about pathology and excretion that Meyer associates, quite correctly, with the image of the genitalia. It is the reversal of this image, maintaining its association with pathology, that appears in the association of the excretory act with the genitalia among the moderns. It is the piss-pot that serves as a marker in the text of a shift from the accepted exoticism of the breasts of the black to the hidden sexuality of the black female. This, too, has a parallel in the text from Meyer's Encyclopedia cited at the very beginning of *Ashantee*. For the quotation stressed the fetishistic nature of the religion of the Ashantis and the "hysterical" dances of the priests. By 1896, the term *hysterical* had a specific female context that was used in analogy to the repressed sexuality of the clergy.[71] To describe the priests of the Ashanti as "hysterical" meant to classify them with the Bacchanti and other groups of "hysterical" females. The German makes this overt, because the masculine form of *priest* is used, excluding the female from this now feminized category, the fetishistic priest. The Ashanti females are thus portrayed as the antithesis of the hysteric. They are not hysterical even in their shared grief. They are users of objects in their nonfetishistic function; the piss-pot is to be used as a piss-pot. This places them in the antithetical category to the "hysterical" men who are the priests of the Ashanti. Altenberg has confused two categories that can quite easily be unraveled. The first is that of the adult, sexualized exotic, whether male or female. These are the priests, the male blacks who disappear from within the text and are banished to the margins, appearing only in the opening passage and our knowledge of the historical structure of the exhibition held in the Prater. The second is that of the child, the unconsciously sexualized exotic, the black as child, which he can approach in his fantasy. Manambo knows Altenberg's fantasy when she asks him to buy her a piss-pot and observes that she would most probably give one to Tioko. Altenberg approaches a fantasy of physical intimacy only hinted at in the description of Baudelaire's "Vénus noire." It is indeed a detailed fantasy of the difference

of the black based on the ethnologists' discussions of the inherent difference between black female sexual structure and that of the nonblack.

Again, it is in Friedrich Ratzel's ethnology that this sexual difference, perceived in the structure of the "Hottentot apron" (which will be discussed in detail in Chapter Ten), becomes one of the central markers for the polygenetic difference of the races. For Ratzel, this sexual anomaly is present in many of the African races and makes the woman into a "perfect monster."[72] For Altenberg, the difference perceived between the clothed, demure prepubescent Austrian "Mädel" such as the thirteen-year-old Hermine Rosen, whose character he praises [PLATE 291], and the bare-breasted "young Egyptian," whose photograph he described in a letter to Arthur Schnitzler as "my black friend Nahbaduh, . . . the last madness of my soul," is the fact of approachability [PLATE 292]. It is the difference between health and pathology. When Altenberg sees the black, it is as the approachable exotic, with the bared breast functioning as a signifier in analogy

Ihol meiner ägyptischen Träume !!! Peter Altenberg

PLATE 292. *The black female child as the image of the erotic, from the private photographic collection of Peter Altenberg. Vienna: Stadtbibliothek.*

to the beckoning genitalia. The image of the child-woman in fin-de-siècle Vienna became closely linked with sexual license through the distancing effects of projection. It is indeed the pure child as sexual object, the child free from the curse of adult sexuality (with all of its pathological associations for the nineteenth century), that is projected onto the exotic as sexual object. One must stress the importance of class as well as age as the matrix into which the projections of sexuality, the creation of the permissible object of desire, are made.[73] With Altenberg, the exotic is not solely class- and age-determined but also race-determined. Part of this is the patriarchal attitude of the West toward the black, mirrored in the liberalism of Peter A. as well as the conservatism of the entrepreneur in the Prater.

But there is a hidden agenda in Altenberg's projection. For there is yet another group viewed as a "pure" race, speaking a different tongue, whose males are portrayed as possessing feminine characteristics. It is, of course, the Jews. At the same time that Altenberg was publishing *Ashantee* (1897),

Walter Rathenau published his "Hear, O Israel," which was one of the most widely discussed self-critical texts of the day.[74] In it Rathenau described the Jews as a tribe much like the Ashantis, except stressing the negative aspects of such attitudes and behavior in the context of Western culture. Rathenau's views, which included the description of the male Jew as possessing all of the qualities usually ascribed to the woman (or indeed the homosexual), were part of the discourse on race that dominated the nineteenth century. The two major examples for theories of race in the nineteenth century were the blacks and the Jews. Altenberg identifies with the Ashanti as part of his distancing and projection of the conflicts he perceived in his own Jewish identity. Altenberg, who would convert to Catholicism three years after *Ashantee* was published, sees the young black female as the antithesis of the racial stereotype of the Jew. The Jew is a male who acts like a female, one who belongs to the category of the "hysteric" like the Ashanti male priests. The Jew belongs to a "pure" race, the sign of which is degenerative sexual selectivity. The Ashantis are females who act like children, who do not belong to the category of the hysteric. The Ashantis are a "pure" race who, however, permit the sexual attention of the outsider. This is Altenberg's reaction to the criticism of Jewish sexual selectivity. For nineteenth-century psychiatry saw all blacks as especially prone to hysteria, whether male or female. Like the Jews, the blacks were at risk because of the racial association.[75]

Altenberg has created an acceptable projection of his own internalization of the charges brought against the Jews because of their sexual selectivity. He has incorporated this into his own fantasy about the sexuality of the child and has thus created his own image of the accessible black child. Altenberg's fin-de-siècle fantasy of the black is not unique. His mentor, Karl Kraus, makes numerous references to the prejudiced attitudes of German and Austrian society toward the black but refers only to incidents concerning the depiction of black sexuality. Kraus's fascination is with the German and Austrian interest in black sexuality, but this focus reveals his own preoccupation with black sexuality. Austrian liberalism focuses on the question of an alternative, perhaps even utopian, sense of human sexuality as perceived within the sexual difference of the black. The sense of difference dominates this discourse, as it does the discourse of other writers, writers whose view of human nature stresses the biological aspects of human nature over the social conventions.

WILLIAM JAMES: MASTURBATION
IN THE NINETEENTH CENTURY

The relationship among childhood, race, and gender
is manifest during the nineteenth century. In Peter
Altenberg's representation of the sexuality of the
black child and the visual images that underlie it,
we have the projection of the sense of sexual difference with which one group (the Jews) are labeled
onto another group (the blacks). The ideological
implications of seeing the black as Skin-Man as the
representation of the genitalia are evident. The black
becomes, for the fin-de-siècle Jew, his surrogate as
the image of the primitive genitalia. When we turn
to the question of the internalization of the image
of self-touch, of how the turn-of-the-century mind
dealt with the complexities of seeing an action that
was understood to be pathological, the surrogate
is sought not in the wilds of colonialist Africa but
within the boundaries of the asylum. Let us turn
to a specific case in point, that of the American
philosopher and psychologist William James.

In Edinburgh during 1897, James delivered the
Gifford Lectures on Natural Religion.[76] James included ample discussion of the psychopathic aspects
of religious experience. It is, however, not so much
his discussion of this aspect of religion that is of
interest but his examples. In the segment of the
lectures entitled "The Sick Soul," James cites extensively from Tolstoy and Bunyan in describing
the nature of the melancholic mind. The conclusion
of this chapter in the printed version of the lectures
presents "the worst kind of melancholy," that
"which takes the form of panic fear."[77] To illustrate
this ultimate form of the sick soul he cites a lengthy
example:

> Whilst in this state of philosophic pessimism and gen-
> eral depression of spirits about my prospects, I went
> one evening into a dressing-room in the twilight to
> procure some article that was there; when suddenly
> there fell upon me without any warning, just as if it
> came out of the darkness, a horrible fear of my own
> existence. Simultaneously there arose in my mind the
> image of an epileptic patient whom I had seen in the
> asylum, a black-haired youth with greenish skin, en-
> tirely idiotic, who used to sit all day on one of the
> benches, or rather shelves against the wall, with his
> knees drawn up against his chin, and the coarse gray
> undershirt, which was his only garment, drawn over
> them inclosing his entire figure. he sat there like a
> sort of sculptured Egyptian cat or Peruvian mummy,
> moving nothing but his black eyes and looking ab-
> solutely non-human. This image and my fear entered
> into a species of combination with each other. That
> shape am I, I felt, potentially. Nothing that I possess

can defend me against that fate, if the hour for it
should strike for me as it struck for him. There was
such a horror of him, and such a perception of my
own merely momentary discrepancy from him, that
it was as if something hitherto solid within my breast
gave way entirely, and I became a mass of quivering
fear.

The passage continues chronicling how the author
was able, only after several months, to overcome
his anxiety. This "melancholia" had, according to
the writer, "a religious bearing," and he was able
to transcend it through clinging to scripture.

The source of the vision of the insane youth is
given by James in the following manner: "Here is
an excellent example, for permission to print which
I have to thank the sufferer. The original is in French,
and though the subject was evidently in a bad nervous condition at the time of which he writes, his
case has otherwise the merit of extreme simplicity.
I translate freely." His translation is indeed free,
for its author is none other than William James
himself. James's son recorded that his father stated
that the incident had actually happened to him, and
the son dated this vision to the spring of 1870.[78]

The vision of the madman has a specific function
in *The Varieties of Religious Experience*. Coming as
the final example in James's discussion of "the sick
soul," it serves for the author as his ultimate statement of "the fear of the universe" and "the real
core of the religious problem: Help! help!" James's
cry for help is focused in his presentation of his
own experience. But the use of the fictional mode
of expression and its form is not inherent in the
vision, usually equated with the "great dorsal collapse" of January 1870, but to James's models.[79] It
is vital to understand that James's fantasy came at
that moment in his own life when he was confronted
with a series of life choices as to his career path.
Again, there is a link between images of madness
(and, as we shall see, a madness understood as the
result of "self-abuse") and the question of career
choice and economic definition of the self.

Within the fictional structure surrounding the in-
vented quotation, there exist two clues to the origin
and nature of the models employed by the author.
The primary one is explicit. In a footnote to the
passage, William James refers to his own father's
work, *Society, the Redeemed Form of Man*, "for another
case of fear equally sudden." The elder James recorded his hallucinatory experience near Windsor
Castle when William was an infant. He experienced
his crisis after a "comfortable dinner" with his family:
"To all appearance it was a perfectly insane and

abject terror, without ostensible cause, and only to be accounted for, to my perplexed imagination, by some damned shape squatting invisible to me within the precincts of the room, and raying out from his fetid peronality influences fatal to life."[80] For the elder James the source of this vision is "the curse of mankind, that which keeps our manhood so little and so depraved . . . its sense of selfhood." This manifests itself in the fruitless search for truth, and the elder James's experience proved to him that "truth must reveal itself if it would be known. . . . For truth is God, the omniscient and omnipotent God, and who shall pretend to comprehend that great and adorable perfection?"

Although ignoring his father's Swedenborgian theology, William James makes use of the external structure of this experience when, shortly after the beginning of the twentieth century, he looks back to record his experience of some thirty years earlier. The general structures of the two passages are remarkably similar. The sense of anxiety appears suddenly, it is conceived of as a being, it destroys all sense of equilibrium, and it resolves itself in a form of religious awareness. But the specific nature of the vision is different. The amorphous "damned shape" takes on a definite form for the younger James in his vision of the madman.

How does James see the insane? And with what forces does he associate his own potential for insanity? He sees a solitary figure, without background or context, seated, his knees drawn up to his chin, an idiot, "looking absolutely non-human." James's portrait reflects a nineteenth-century understanding of how the insane are to be seen. For James's description is an almost literal portrait of one of the plates in Jean Étienne Dominique Esquirol's monumental *Des maladies mentales considérées sous les rapports médical, hygiénique et médico-légal* of 1838. This standard work contained the first atlas containing full-length portraits of the mentally ill. Plate 24 presents a figure seated on a low shelf, his knees drawn up to his chest, his coarse singlet drawn over his knees **[PLATE 293]**. His gaze is directed straight at the observer. In his text, Esquirol notes that this figure represents an idiot named Aba in the asylum at Bîcêtre. He can say only "ba ba ba" and is so simple that he cannot feed himself. He has no memory. And finally, "Aba is a masturbator."[81] James's vision of the insane is filtered through Esquirol's image of Aba. This explains, at least to a certain degree, why James creates a French source for his vision. It is not so much that James is describing Esquirol's plate but that he conceived of his vision in terms of a nineteenth-century under-

PLATE 293. *"Dementia" from J. É. D. Esquirol, from the atlas to his* Des maladies mentales *(Paris: Baillière, 1838). Ithaca: Private collection. This is the parallel image to that found in William James's representation of his own madness.*

standing and visualization of the insane as the result of the act of masturbation. What is central is that the image of Aba becomes James's representation of himself, of his own sexual identity and the fear created within him by that identity. Aba is a surrogate phallus, the controlling aspect of James's personality (within his own fantasy). He is dumb and immobile, and he is pathological. James's image of Aba is not only his representation of masturbatory insanity but also of himself as phallus. And the image of the phallus, to no one's surprise, is associated in his image with his image of his father.

When the final piece of information, James's contemporary account of his vision, is sought, the reader is stymied. For whereas it is evident that James underwent a period of severe depression in the winter of 1870, no reference is made during this period, neither in his diaries nor in his letters, to such a vision. One is led to the inescapable conclusion that James first recorded this vision during his writing of the Gifford lectures. At this point, he looked back at his earlier experience through the description in his father's text, which was not published until 1879, and through his scientific reading concerning the physiognomy of the insane. One might imagine that a scholar of James's reputation would avoid an overtly autobiographical presentation in a series of university lectures. But James's vision had an even more deeply personal bias that is revealed in his text.

In James's text, the existential anxiety that generated and is generated by the vision had a specific personal relationship. Why does James visualize a madman when his father sees nothing, only sensing the presence of evil? Taking into consideration the struggle between the elder Henry James and his sons, William and Henry, Jr., one might assume that the use of the structure of his father's vision may lead to a solution to the enigma of the vision.[82] James's use of the image of the madman provides the final clue. For James's vision, that which so frightened him, with which he so identified, portrayed a victim of masturbatory insanity. James's soul sickness of 1870 was indeed philosophical in its manifestation, but the evil "inherent in the universe's details" was of a personal nature. James's fear of madness was not an abstract fear, such as that portrayed by his father. It was a direct fear of receding into madness as a result of his own being.

The extensive entry in James's diary on February 1, 1870, describes his fear in a direct manner: "Hitherto I have tried to fire myself with the moral interest, as an aid in the accomplishing of certain utilitarian ends of attaining certain difficult but salutary habits. I tried to associate the feeling of Moral degradation with failure. . . . But in all this I was cultivating the moral . . . only as a means and more or less humbugging myself."[83] James's sense of inadequacy, his recently concluded medical studies, the success of his friends (such as Charles Peirce) could all be laid at the door of his personal life. James was confronted with a choice of what he was to do with the rest of his life.[84] Coloring this choice was James's inner sense of his own sexual inadequacy, an inadequacy stemming from the condemnation of masturbation as a sign of a "weak personality." Contemporary writers, such as Henry Maudsley, emphasized the relationship between diffuseness of character and masturbation: "The patient becomes offensively egotistic and impracticable; he is full of self-feeling and self-conceit;

insensible to the claims of others upon him and his duties to them: interested only in hypochondriacally watching his morbid sensations and attending his morbid feelings. His mental energy is sapped; and though he has extravagant pretensions, and often speaks of great projects engendered by his conceit, he never works systematically for any aim, but exhibits an incredible vacillation of conduct, and spends his days in indolent and suspicious self-brooding."[85] This eventually leads to masturbatory insanity.

In looking back at his experience of 1870, James structures his vision so as to incorporate the structure of his father's sense of dread. The conflict between father and son, the guilt felt in his personal life, his sense of inadequacy especially in regard to his father, all merge in the vision. In structuring it some thirty years after it occurred, James is able to externalize these feelings in his fiction recounting his earlier vision of his fear of masturbatory insanity. Here purgation is accomplished through the description of an earlier purgation.

Although James draws the root metaphor of masturbatory insanity, it is the psychological conflict between father and son present in the model of his father's own vision of doom that structures his text. The conflict between parent and child over career choice now understood in the concept of masturbatory insanity is played out by James in his representation of his own earlier experience. His image of the phallus is taken indirectly from his father's experience and is articulated within the realm of medical science, as the image of the disease resulting from deviant human sexuality. Aba is James's image of the phallus but the phallus both as the controlling aspect of the individual as well as the source of the repression of the sexual. Aba is both father and son, the theologian and the incipient physician. Aba is both the image of the disease of masturbatory insanity as well as the exorcism of that fear. In placing this vision between the pages of a book, James controls the image. In moving it from a remembered experience through a visual image taken from Esquirol to his own world of words, he assumes control of his fear, of his image of the phallus. He remembers his vision through the filter of these two modes of presenting experience.

The fantasies about human sexuality during the late nineteenth century link aspects of culture, society, and the body to the fears of disease during the age of Pasteur and Virchow, the age of the greatest public awareness of the modes of disease transmission as well as the historical implications of sexuality. From the representation of the body in the medical atlases of the period, with their ever receding image of the corporeal body and the ever more detailed look within, into the very membranes of the cell, through to the transferral of images of the opening of the body from the clinical to the criminal setting, more traditional images of sexuality become inexorably linked with pathology and disease. The culture of touch, both the self-touch and the touch of the Other, becomes linked to the cult of pathology. To deal with this powerful association of the body with disease, the hallmark of the late nineteenth-century's representations of the body, individuals such as Freud or Altenberg or James must find some device within the representations of sexuality to create an island of sanity for themselves, a place where they can deal with the affect inherent in their sense of their own pollution, their own disease. They find this in projecting their sense of themselves as the sum of their own genitalia, as a sexual being, as a being at risk, onto other groups. This process of projection creates even more involved images, as the dominant discourse about human sexuality becomes one with their sense of their own sexual fragility. The movement is an important one because such marginal figures give voice within culturally vital or scientifically accepted discourses to many of the images that haunt the sexual identity of the twentieth century.

CHAPTER TEN

Manet and Zola See Nana: *Representing Sexuality and Disease in the Fin de Siècle*

LOOKING AT *OLYMPIA* AND *NANA*

In our search for the meaning ascribed to the genitalia within the world of images of the fin de siècle, let us turn to one of the classic works of late nineteenth-century "modern" art, a work that presents the image of both the sexualized white woman and the sexualized black woman, two icons that, as we have seen, haunt the masculine representation of sexuality in the West. Édouard Manet's *Olympia*, painted in 1862–63, first shown in the salon of 1865, assumes a key position in documenting the merger of these two images **[PLATE 294]**. It can also serve as a case study for the complexity of those structures of perception that are generated in order to construct the idea of the sexual. This image building permeates all aspects of the thought-collective, from the world of medicine to that of the fine arts. Manet's work provides a grid upon which the broadest set of ideological and political associations concerning sexuality and race can be located. Their reification was in a single image, that of *Olympia*—initially greeted with horror and amazement as an image of the genitalia.

The conventional wisdom concerning Manet's painting states that the model, Victorine Meurend, is "obviously naked rather than conventionally nude,"[1] that her pose is heavily indebted to classical models such as Titian's 1538 *Venus of Urbino*, Goya's 1800 *Naked Maja*, Delacroix's 1847 *Odalisque*, as well as other works by Manet's contemporaries, such as Gustave Courbet.[2] George Needham has shown quite convincingly that Manet was also using a convention of early erotic photography in having the central figure directly confront the observer.[3] The

black female attendant, posed by a black model called Laura, has been seen as a reflex of both the classic black servant figure present in the visual arts of the eighteenth century as well as a representation of Baudelaire's "Vénus noire."[4]

Let us juxtapose *Olympia*, with all its aesthetic and artistic analogies and parallels, to a work by Manet which Georges Bataille, among others, has seen as a modern "genre scene," *Nana* of 1877[5] **[PLATE 295]**. Nana is, unlike Olympia, modern, a creature of present-day Paris, according to a contemporary.[6] But like Olympia, Nana was perceived as a sexualized female and is so represented. Yet in moving from a work with an evident aesthetic provenance, as understood by Manet's contemporaries, to one that was influenced by the former and yet was seen by its contemporaries as "modern," certain major shifts in the iconography of the sexualized woman take place, not the least of which is the seeming disappearance of the black female.

THE HOTTENTOT VENUS: AN ICON OF SEXUALITY

The figure of the black servant in turn-of-the-century Western European culture is ubiquitous. Richard Strauss knew this when he had Hugo von Hofmannsthal conclude their conscious evocation of the eighteenth century, *Der Rosenkavalier* (1911), with the mute return of the little black servant to reclaim Sophie's lost handkerchief.[7] But Hofmannsthal was also aware that one of the central implications of the black servant for the visual arts of the eighteenth

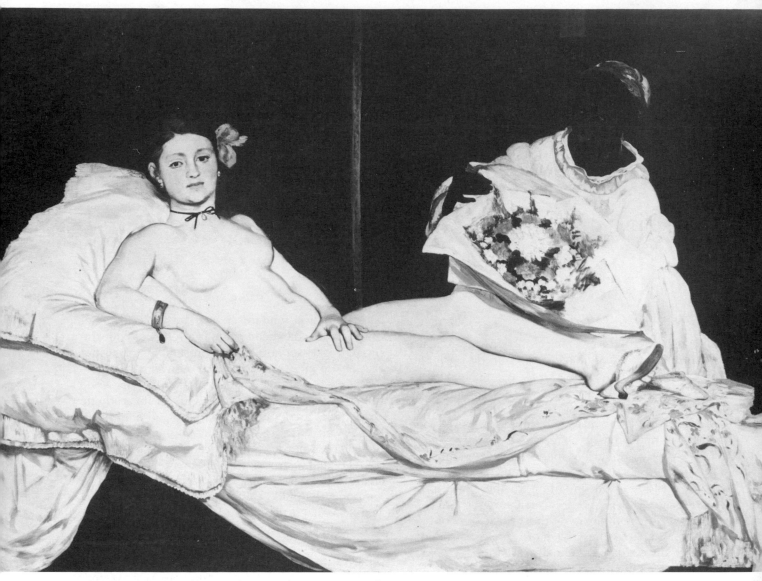

PLATE 294. *The prostitute unclothed and the black servant in Édouard Manet,* Olympia, *1862–63. Paris: Musée du Louvre.*

PLATE 295. *The prostitute clothed in Édouard Manet, Nana, 1877. Hamburg: Kunsthalle.*

PLATE 296. *The erotic representation of the black child in Franz von Bayros,* The Servant, *ca. 1890. Ithaca: Private collection.*

and nineteenth centuries was as a maker of the sexualization of the society in which he or she is found. For the reclaiming of the lost handkerchief marks the end of the opera but also the end of the relationship between Octavian, the Knight of the Rose, and the Marschallin, an illicit sexual relationship that had opened the opera, just as the figure of the black servant closed it.

Hofmannsthal and Strauss consciously drew on images of sexual license taken from eighteenth-century sources, such as the engravings of William Hogarth, discussed in Chapter Six. But the association of the black with concupiscence reaches back into the Middle Ages, as we have discussed in Chapter Two.[8] By the nineteenth century, as in *Olympia*, or more crudely in one of a series of fin-de-siècle Viennese erotic prints by Franz von Bayros entitled *The Servant*, the central female figure is associated with a black female in such a way as to imply a similarity between the sexuality of the image of the black and the white woman portrayed[9]

[PLATE 296]. In a contrastive image, Dante Gabriel Rossetti's *The Beloved, or The Bride* (1865) associates the unselfconscious innocence of the half-dressed young black serving girl with the sensuality of the "beloved" **[PLATE 297]**. The association of figures of the same sex stresses the special status of female sexuality. In *The Servant* the overt sexuality of the black child indicates the hidden sexuality of the white woman, a sexuality quite manifest in the other plates in the series. The relationship between the sexuality of the black woman and that of the sexualized woman enters a new dimension when the scientific discourse concerning the nature of black female sexuality is examined.

During the eighteenth century, Buffon had commented on the lascivious, apelike sexual appetite of the black, introducing a commonplace of early travel literature, such as that rebutted by Tyson in the seventeenth century, as has been discussed in Chapter Five, into a pseudoscientific context.[10] He stated that this animallike sexual appetite went so

PLATE 297. *The black child as the sign of the erotic in Dante Gabriel Rossetti,* The Beloved, *or* The Bride, *1865. London: Tate Gallery.*

far as to encourage black women to copulate with apes. The black female thus comes to serve as an icon for black sexuality in general. Buffon's view was based on a confusion of two applications of the "great chain of being" to the nature of the black. In this view of the nature of humanity, the black held the antithetical position to the white on a scale of humanity. Such a scale was employed during the nineteenth century to indicate the innate difference between the races. This polygenetic view was applied to all aspects of humanity, including sexuality and beauty. The antithesis of European sexual mores and beauty is the black, and the essential black, the lowest rung on the great chain of being, is the Hottentot. It is indeed in the physical appearance of the Hottentot that the central icon for sexual difference between the European and the black was found, a perceived difference in sexual physiology that puzzled even early monogenetic theoreticians such as Johann Friedrich Blumenbach.

The labeling of the black female as more primitive,

and therefore more sexually intensive, by writers such as Abbé Raynal in 1775, would have been dismissed as unscientific by the radical empiricists of late eighteenth- and early nineteenth-century Europe.[11] They would have demanded not generalizations based on perceived universals of difference but the examination of specific, detailed case studies to evolve a "scientific" paradigm. They would have needed a case study that placed both the sexuality and the beauty of the black in an antithetical position to those of the white. This paradigm had to be rooted in some type of unique and observable physical difference. It was found in the distinction drawn between the pathological and the healthy in the medical model. William Bynum's observation that nineteenth-century biology constantly needed to deal with the polygenetic argument is shown here again to have its validity.[12] For the polygenetic difference between the races is absorbed into the medical model.

The writer in whose work this alteration of the

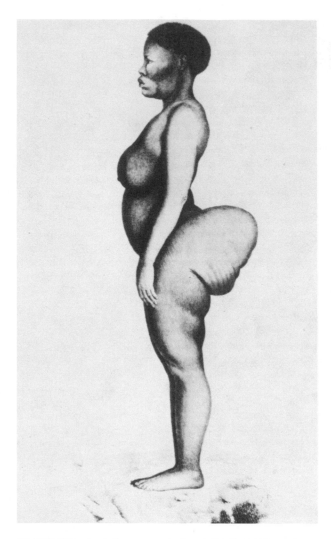

PLATE 298. *Sarah Bartmann, the famed "Hottentot Venus," from Geoffrey Saint-Hilaire and Fréderic Cuvier,* Histoire naturelle des mammifères avec des figures originales *(Paris: A. Belin, 1824). Ithaca: Olin Library, Cornell University.*

between her physiology and her physiognomy (her "hideous form" and her "horribly flattened nose"). His central proof is a discussion of the unique structure of the Hottentot female's sexual parts, the description of which he takes from the anatomical studies of his contemporary, Georges Cuvier.[14]

The black female looks different. Her physiognomy, her skin color, the form of her genitalia label her as inherently different. The nineteenth century perceived the black female as possessing not only a "primitive" sexual appetite but also the external signs of this temperament, "primitive" genitalia. Eighteenth-century travelers to southern Africa, such as Levaillant and Barrow, had described the so-called "Hottentot apron," a hypertrophy of the labia and nymphae caused by the manipulation of the genitalia and serving as a sign of beauty among certain tribes, such as the Hottentots and the Bushman as well as tribes in Basutoland and Dahomey.[15] In 1815 Sarah Bartmann, also called Saartje Baartman, or Saat-Jee, a twenty-five-year-old Hottentot female who had been exhibited in Europe for over five years as the "Hottentot Venus," died in Paris **[PLATE 298]**. An autopsy was performed on her, which was first written up by de Blainville in 1816 and then, in its most famous version, by Georges Cuvier in 1817.[16] Reprinted at least twice during the next decade, Cuvier's description reflected de Blainville's two intentions: the comparison of a female of the "lowest" human species with the highest ape, the orangutan, and the description of the anomalies of the Hottentot's "organ of generation." It is important to note that Sarah Bartmann was exhibited not to show her genitalia but rather to present to the European audience another anomaly that both they (and pathologists such as de Blainville and Cuvier) found riveting. This was the steatopygia, or protruding buttocks, the other physical characteristic of the Hottentot female that captured the eye of early travelers. As a nineteenth-century ballad commented:

> And what, in her is to be seen,
> Than other folks more rare,
> A rump she has (though strange it be),
> Large as a cauldron pot,
> And this is why men go to see
> This lovely Hottentot.[17]

The figure of Sarah Bartmann was reduced to her sexual parts, and the audience, which had paid to see her buttocks and fantasized about the uniqueness of her genitalia, could, after her death and dissection, examine both, for Cuvier presented

mode of discourse, but not the underlying ideology concerning the black female, took place was J. J. Virey. He was the author of the standard study of race published in the early nineteenth century. He also contributed a major essay (the only one on a specific racial group) to the widely cited *Dictionary of Medical Sciences* (1819).[13] In this essay, Virey summarized his (and his contemporaries') views on the sexual nature of the black female in terms of acceptable medical discourse. Their "voluptuousness" is "developed to a degree of lascivity unknown in our climate, for their sexual organs are much more developed than those of whites." Virey cites elsewhere the Hottentot woman as the epitome of this sexual lasciviousness and stresses the relationship

PLATE 299. *An engraving of a "Hottentot Venus" at The Ball of the Duchess du Barry, 1829. Ithaca: Olin Library, Cornell University.*

to "the Academy the genital organs of this woman prepared in a way so as to allow one to see the nature of the labia."[18] Her exhibition during 1810 in a London inflamed by the issue of abolition caused a public scandal because she was exhibited "to the public in a manner offensive to decency. She . . . does exhibit all the shape and frame of her body as if naked."[19] The state's objection was as much to her lewdness as to her status as an indentured black. In France her presentation was similar. In 1829, a nude Hottentot woman, also called "the Hottentot Venus," was the prize attraction at a ball given by the Duchess du Barry in Paris. A contemporary print emphasized her physical difference from the observers portrayed **[PLATE 299]**.

Sarah Bartmann's sexual parts, her genitalia and her buttocks, serve as the central image for the black female throughout the nineteenth century. And the model of de Blainville's and Cuvier's descriptions, which center on the detailed presentation of the sexual parts of the black, dominates all medical description of the black during the nineteenth century. To an extent, this reflects the general nineteenth-century understanding of female sexuality as pathological; that is, the female genitalia were of interest as examples of the various pathologies that could befall them but also because the female genitalia came to define the sum of the female for the nineteenth century. In the anatomical museums from the sixteenth to the nineteenth century (as discussed in Chapter Six), the part of the body

represented had iconographic significance.[20] Sarah Bartmann's genitalia and buttocks summarized her essence for the nineteenth-century observer, and, indeed, for the twentieth-century one, as they are still on display at the Musée de l'Homme in Paris **[PLATE 300]**.

Thus when one turns to the autopsies of Hottentot females in the nineteenth century, their description centers on the sexual parts. De Blainville (1816) and Cuvier (1817) set the tone, which is followed by A. W. Otto in 1824, Johannes Müller in 1834, W. H. Flower and James Murie in 1867, and Luschka, Koch, and Görtz in 1869[21] **[PLATE 301]**. These presentations of Hottentot or Bushman women all focus on the presentation of the genitalia and buttocks. W. H. Flower, the editor of the *Journal of Anatomy and Physiology*, included his dissection in the opening volume of that famed journal. His ideological intent was clear. He wished to provide data "relating to the unity or plurality of mankind." His description begins with a detailed presentation of the form and size of the buttocks and concludes with his portrayal of the "remarkable development of the labia minoria, or nymphae, which is so general a characteristic of the Hottentot and Bushman race." These were "sufficiently well marked to distinguish these parts at once from those of any of the ordinary varieties of the human species." The polygenetic argument is the ideological basis for all the dissections of these women. If their sexual parts could be shown to be inherently different, this would be a sufficient description of the autopsies of black males, from approximately the same period, what is striking is the absence of any discussion of the male genitalia whatsoever. For example, in Sir William Turner's three dissections of male blacks in 1878, 1879, and 1896, no mention is made at all of the genitalia.[24] For the uniqueness of the genitalia and buttocks of the black is associated with the female and is a sign of an anomalous female sexuality.

By midcentury the image of the genitalia of the Hottentot had assumed a certain set of implications. The central view is that these anomalies are inherent, biological variations rather than adaptations. In Theodor Billroth's standard handbook of gynecology, there is a detailed presentation of the "Hottentot apron" in the discussion of errors in development of the female genitalia. By 1877 it was a commonplace that the Hottentot's anomalous sexual form was similar to other errors in the development of the labia. The author of this section links this malformation with overdevelopment of the clitoris, which he sees as leading to those "excesses" that "are called 'lesbian love.' " The concupiscence of the black is thus association with the sexuality of the lesbian.[25]

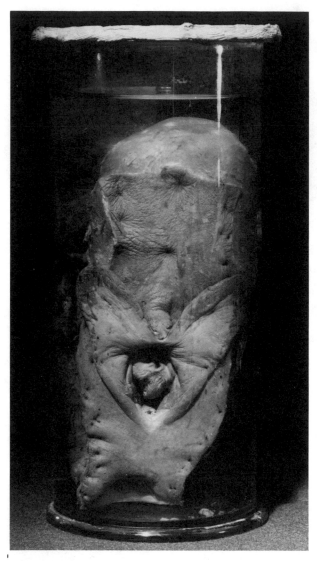

PLATE 300. *Cuvier's gift to the people of France, the preserved genitalia of the "Hottentot Venus." Paris: Musée de l'Homme.*

sign that the blacks were a separate (and, needless to say, lower) race, as different from the European as the proverbial orangutan.

Similar arguments had been made concerning the nature of blacks' (and not just Hottentots') genitalia but almost always concerning the female. Edward Turnipseed of South Carolina argued in 1868 that the hymen in black women "is not at the entrance to the vagina, as in the white woman, but from one-and-a-half to two inches from its entrance in the interior." From this he concluded that "this may be one of the anatomical marks of the nonunity of the races."[22] His views were seconded in 1877 by C. H. Fort, who presented another six cases of this seeming anomaly.[23] When one turns to the

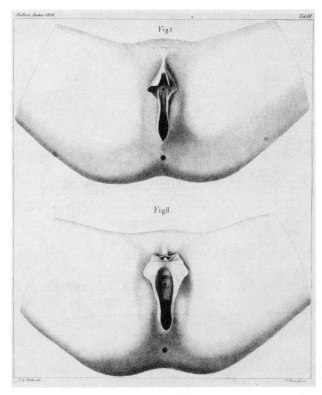

PLATE 301. *The genitalia of the "Hottentot Venus" from Johannes Müller, "Über die äusseren Geschlechtstheile der Buschmänninnen,"* Archiv für Anatomie, Physiologie und wissenschaftliche Medizin *(1834). Ithaca: Olin Library, Cornell University.*

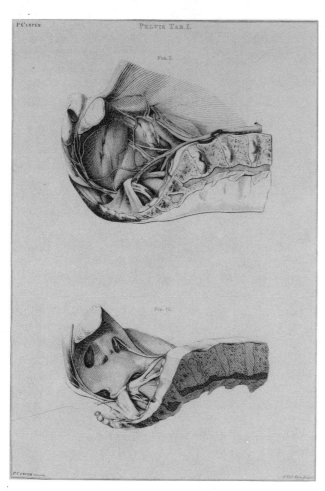

PLATE 302. *The pelvic angle as a sign of race from Pieter Camper,* Demonstrationum anatomicopathologicarum *(Amsterdam: J. Schreuder & P. Mortier, 1760–62). London: Wellcome Institute for the History of Medicine.*

More so, the idea of a congenital error incorporates the disease model applied to the deformation of the labia in the Hottentot. For the model of degeneracy presumes some acquired pathology in one generation that is the direct cause of the stigmata of degeneracy in the next. Surely, the best example for this is the concept of congenital syphilis as captured in the popular consciousness by Ibsen's drama of biological decay, *Ghosts*. Thus Billroth's congenital failure is presupposed to have some direct and explicable etiology, as well as a specific manifestation. Although this text is silent as to the etiology, one can see the link established between the ill, the bestial, and the freak (pathology, biology, and medicine) in seeing the Hottentot's genitalia.

An aside might be profitable to help explain both the association of the genitalia, a primary sexual characteristic, and the buttocks, a secondary sexual characteristic, in their role as the semantic signs of "primitive" sexual appetite and activity. Havelock Ellis, in the fourth volume of his *Studies in the Psychology of Sex* (1905), provided a detailed example of the great chain of being as applied to the perception of the sexualized Other.[26] Ellis believed that there is an absolute scale of beauty, one that is totally objective and ranges from the European to the black. Thus men of the lower races, according to Ellis, admire European women more than their own, and women of lower races attempt to whiten themselves with face powder. Ellis then proceeded to list the secondary sexual characteristics that comprise this ideal of beauty, rejecting the "naked sexual organs" as not "aesthetically beautiful" because it is "fundamentally necessary" that they "retain their primitive characteristics." Only people "in a low state of culture" perceive the "naked sexual organs as objects of attraction." The secondary sexual characteristics that Ellis then lists as the signs of a cultured (i.e., not primitive) perception of the body, the vocabulary of aesthetically pleasing signs, begins with the buttocks. This is, of course, a nineteenth-century fascination with the buttocks as a displacement for the genitalia. It is given the quality, by Ellis, of a higher regard for the beautiful. This view had been put forward as early as the mid-eighteenth century by Pieter Camper, whose work on the implications of the facial angle as a sign of racial inequality was paralleled by his work on the nature and meaning of pelvic structure **[PLATE 302]**. His discussion of the buttocks ranks the races by size of the female pelvis. This view was continued with Willem Vrolik's 1826 claim that a wide pelvis is a sign of racial superiority and was echoed by R. Verneau's 1875 study of the form of the pelvis among the various races.[27] Verneau uses the narrow pelvis of Sarah Bartmann to argue the primitive nature of the Hottentot's anatomical structure. **[PLATE 303]**.

Although Ellis accepts this ranking, he sees the steatopygia as "a simulation of the large pelvis of the higher races," having a compensatory function like face powder in emulating white skin. This view places the pelvis in an intermediary role, being both a secondary as well as a primary sexual sign. Darwin himself, who held similar views as to the objective nature of human beauty, saw the pelvis as a "primary rather than as a secondary character" and the buttocks of the Hottentot as a somewhat comic sign of the primitive, grotesque nature of the black female.[28]

When the nineteenth century saw the black female, it saw her in terms of her buttocks, and saw represented by the buttocks all the anomalies of her genitalia. In a midcentury erotic caricature of the "Hottentot Venus," she is observed through a

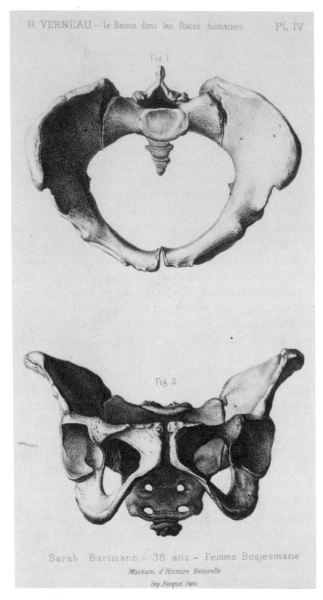

PLATE 303. *Sarah Bartmann's pelvis from René Verneau,* Le bassin dans les sexes et dans les races *(Paris: Baillière, 1875). Ithaca: Olin Library, Cornell University.*

out of all proportion. It was too big, but nevertheless it was fairly well shaped, with well-rounded cheeks meeting each other closely, her thighs were large, and she had a sturdy pair of legs, her skin was smooth and of a clear yellow tint."[30] The presence of exaggerated buttocks points to the other, hidden sexual signs, both physical and temperamental, of the black female. This association is a powerful one. Indeed, Freud, in his *Three Essays on Sexuality* (1905), echoes the view that female genitalia are more primitive than those of the male.[31] Female sexuality is tied to the image of the buttocks, and the quintessential buttocks are those of the Hottentot.

The centrality of this vocabulary in perceiving the sexualized woman can be seen in Edwin Long's painting of 1882 depicting *The Babylonian Marriage Market* **[PLATE 305]**. This painting was the most expensive work of contemporary art sold in nineteenth-century London. It also has a special place in documenting the perception of the sexualized female in terms of the great chain of aesthetic perception presented by Ellis. For Long's painting is based on a specific text from Herodotus, who described the marriage auction in Babylon in which

PLATE 304. *The "Hottentot Venus," a German caricature from the beginning of the nineteenth century from John Grand-Carteret,* Die Erotik in der französischen Karikatur *(Vienna: C. W. Stern, 1909). Ithaca: Private collection.*

telescope by a white male observer, who can see nothing but her buttocks[29] **[PLATE 304]**. This fascination with the uniqueness of the sexual parts of the black focuses on the buttocks over and over again. In a British pornographic novel, published in 1899, but set in a mythic, antebellum Southern United States, the male author indulges his flagellistic fantasy on the buttocks of a number of white women. When he describes the one black, a runaway slave, being whipped, the power of the image of the Hottentot's buttocks captures him: "She would have had a good figure, only that her bottom was

PLATE 305. *The scale of racial beauty in Edwin Long,* The Babylonian Marriage Market, *1882. London: Royal Holloway College Gallery.*

maidens were sold in order of comeliness. In the painting they are arranged in order of their attractiveness. Their physiognomies are clearly portrayed. Their features run from the most European and white (a fact emphasized by the light reflected from the mirror onto the figure at the far left) to the Negroid features (thick lips, broad nose, dark but not black skin) of the figure farthest to the observer's right. The latter figure fulfills all of Virey's categories for the appearance of the black. This is, however, the Victorian scale of acceptable sexualized women within marriage, portrayed from the most to the least attractive, according to contemporary British standards. The only black female present is the servant/slave shown on the auction block, positioned so as to present her buttocks to the viewer. Although there are black males in the audience and thus among the bidders, the only black female is associated with sexualized white women as a signifier of their sexual availability. Her position is her sign, and her presence in the painting is thus analogous to the figure of the black servant, Laura, in Manet's *Olympia*. Here it is not the perversities of human sexuality in a corrupt society that the black servants signify in Hogarth but rather the ascription of this perversity to one specific aspect of human society, the sexualized female, which the linkage between two female

figures, one black and one white, represents in the perception of late nineteenth-century Europe.

THE ICONOGRAPHY OF PROSTITUTION

The prostitute, as has been discussed in Chapter Eight, is the essential sexualized white female in the perception of the nineteenth century. She is perceived as the embodiment of sexuality, and all of that which is associated with sexuality, disease as well as passion.[32] Within the large and detailed literature concerning prostitution written during the nineteenth century, most of which is devoted to documenting the need for legal controls and which draws on the medical model as perceived by public health officials, there is a detailed analysis of the physiognomy and physiology of the prostitute. We can begin with the most widely read early nineteenth-century work on prostitution, that of A. J. B. Parent-Duchatelet, who provides a documentation of the anthropology of the prostitute in his 1836 study of prostitution in Paris.[33] Alain Corbin has shown how Parent-Duchatelet's use of the public health model reduces the prostitute to yet another source of pollution, similar to the sewers of Paris. Likewise in Parent-Duchatelet's discussion of the physiognomy of the prostitute, he believes himself

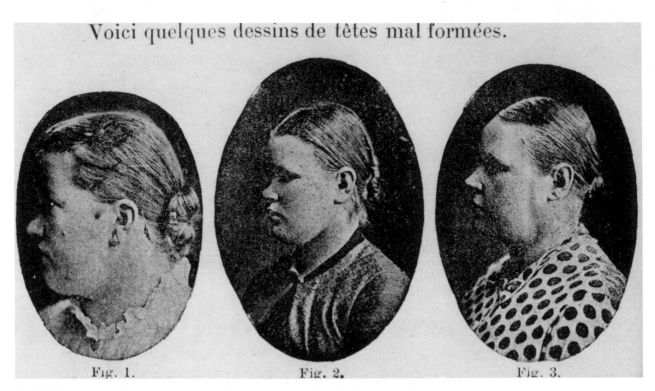

Voici quelques dessins de têtes mal formées.

Fig. 1.   Fig. 2.   Fig. 3.

PLATE 306. *"Anomalies of the Face and the Ear in Prostitutes," from Pauline Tarnowsky,* Étude anthropométrique sur les prostituées et les voleuses *(Paris: E. Lecrosnier et* Bébé, 1889). Ithaca: Private collection.

to be providing a descriptive presentation of the appearance of the prostitute. He presents his readers with a statistical description of the physical types of the prostitutes, the nature of their voices, the color of their hair and eyes, their physical anomalies, and their sexual profile in regard to childbearing and disease. Parent-Duchatelet's descriptions range from the detailed to the anecdotal. His discussion of the "embonpoint" of the prostitute begins his litany of their external signs. Prostitutes have a "peculiar plumpness" that is attributed to "the great number of hot baths which the major part of these women take." Or perhaps to their lassitude, rising at ten or eleven in the morning, "leading an animal life." They are fat as prisoners are fat, from simple confinement. As an English commentator noted, "the grossest and stoutest of these women are to be found amongst the lowest and most disgusting classes of prostitutes."[34] These are the Hottentots on the scale of the sexualized female. It is indeed the power of this image that Guy de Maupassant is able ironically to harness in his masterful short story "Boule-de-suif" ["Butterball"] (1880), the tale of a good-hearted prostitute whose physical form marks her as a member of the demimonde. Her ample personal charms should mark her as a hard-hearted, exploitative female. The reality as depicted

in the story turns this around, revealing her fellow but middle-class refugees as the exploiters and corrupters.

When Parent-Duchatelet turned to the sexual parts of the prostitutes, he provided two sets of information that merged to become part of the myth of the physical anthropology of the prostitute. The prostitute's sexual parts are in no way directly affected by their profession. He contradicts the "general opinion . . . that the genital parts in prostitutes must alter, and assume a particular disposition, as the inevitable consequence of their avocation." He cites one case of a woman of fifty-one "who had prostituted herself thirty-six years, but in whom, notwithstanding, the genital parts might have been mistaken for those of a virgin just arrived at puberty." Parent-Duchatelet thus rejected any Lamarckian adaptation, as well as any indication that the prostitute is inherently marked as a prostitute. This, of course, follows from his view that prostitution is an illness of a society, rather than that of an individual or group of individuals. Although he does not see the genitalia of the prostitute altering, he does observe that prostitutes were subject to specific pathologies of their genitalia. They are especially prone to tumors "of the great labia . . . which commence with a little pus and tumefy at each menstrual period." He identifies the central pathology of the prostitute in the following manner: "Nothing is more frequent in prostitutes than common abscesses in the thickness of the labia majora." Parent-Duchatelet's two views, first that there is no adaptation of the sexual organ, and second that the sexual organ is especially prone to labial tumors and abscesses, merge in the image of the prostitute as developing, through illness, an altered appearance of the genitalia.

From Parent-Duchatelet's description of the physical appearance of the prostitute (a catalogue that reappears in most nineteenth-century studies of prostitutes, such as Schrank's study of the prostitutes of Vienna), it is but a small step to the use of such catalogues of stigmata as a means of categorizing those women who have, as Freud states, "an aptitude for prostitution."[35] The major work of nineteenth-century physical anthropology, public health, and pathology to undertake this was written by Pauline Tarnowsky. Tarnowsky was one of a number of St. Petersburg female physicians in the late nineteenth century. She wrote in the tradition of her father, V. M. Tarnowsky, who was the author of the standard study of Russian prostitution, a study that appeared in both Russian and German and that assumed a central role in the late nineteenth-century discussions of the nature of the prostitute.[36] She followed his more general study with a detailed investigation of the physiognomy of the prostitute[37] [PLATE 306]. Her categories remain those of Parent-Duchatelet. She describes the excessive weight of prostitutes and their hair and eye color, provides anthropometric measurements of skull size and a catalogue of their family background (as with Parent-Duchatelet, most are the children of alcoholics), and discusses their fecundity (extremely low), as well as the signs of their degeneration. These signs deal with the abnormalities of the face: asymmetry of the face, misshapen noses, overdevelopment of the parietal region of the skull, and the appearance of the so-called Darwin's ear, the simplification of the convolutes of the ear shell and the absence of a lobe. All of these signs are the signs of the lower end of the scale of beauty, the end dominated by the Hottentot. All of the signs point to the "primitive" nature of the prostitute's physiognomy, for stigmata such as Darwin's ear are a sign of the atavistic female.

In a later paper, Tarnowsky provided a scale of the appearance of the prostitute in an analysis of the "physiognomy of the Russian prostitute"[38] [PLATE 307]. The upper end of the scale is the "Russian Helen." Here, classical aesthetics are introduced as the measure of the appearance of the sexualized female. A bit farther on is one who is "very handsome in spite of her hard expression." Indeed, the first fifteen on her scale "might pass on the street for beauties." But hidden even within these seeming beauties are the stigmata of criminal degeneration: black, thick hair; a strong jaw; a hard, spent glance. Some show the "wild eyes and perturbed countenance along with facial asymmetry" of the insane. Only the scientific observer can see the hidden faults and thus identify the true prostitute, for the prostitute uses superficial beauty as the bait for her clients. But when they age, their "strong jaws and cheek-bones, and their masculine aspect . . . hidden by adipose tissue, emerge, salient angles stand out, and the face grows virile, uglier than a man's; wrinkles deepen into the likeness of scars, and the countenance, once attractive, exhibits the full degenerate type which early grace had concealed." Change over time affects the physiognomy of the prostitute, just as it does her genitalia, which become more and more diseased as she ages. For Pauline Tarnowsky, the appearance of the prostitute and her sexual identity are preestablished in her heredity. What is most striking is that as she ages, the prostitute begins to appear more and more mannish. The linkage between the physical anomalies of the Hottentot and those of the lesbian appear in Billroth's *Handbook of Gynaecological Diseases*; here, the link is between two further models of sexual deviancy, the prostitute and the lesbian. Both are seen as possessing the physical signs that set them apart from the normal.

The paper in which Pauline Tarnowsky undertook her documentation of the appearance of the prostitute is repeated word for word in the major study of prostitution published in the late nineteenth century, Cesare Lombroso's study of the criminal woman, written together with his son-in-law, Guglielmo Ferrero, and published in 1893.[39] Lombroso accepts all of Tarnowsky's manner of seeing the prostitute and articulates one further subtext of central importance in the perception of the sexualized woman in the nineteenth century. It is a subtext that becomes apparent only when the plates in his study are examined. For two of the plates deal with the image of the Hottentot female, illustrating the steatopygia and "Hottentot apron" [PLATES 308-309]. Lombroso accepts Parent-Duchatelet's image of the fat prostitute and sees her as being similar to women living in asylums and Hottentots.

FISIONOMIE DI PROSTITUTE RUSSE.

PLATE 307. *The physiognomy of the Russian prostitute in the work of Pauline Tarnowsky: (25) is the "Russian Helen," (18) the "wild eyes of the insane," (20) "very handsome" from Archivio di psichiatria, scienze penali ed antropologia criminale 14 (1893). Ithaca: Private collection.*

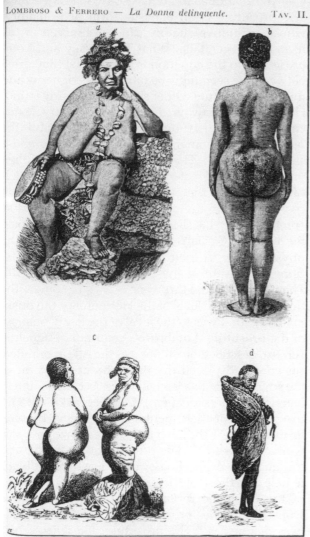

POLISARCIA IN ABISSINA.
CUSCINETTO POSTERIORE IN AFRICANE.

a) Ballerina o prostituta Abissina (Ploss), tipo di polisarcia africana. — *b)* Ottentotta con cuscinetto posteriore (Ploss). — *c¹)* Donna Bongo (Schweinfurth). — *c²)* Donna Koranna con cuscinetto posteriore e ipertrofia delle natiche e delle coscie (Ploss). — *d)* Donna selvaggia che porta un bambino sul dorso, come in tutti i popoli primitivi (Ploss).

PLATE 308. *Steatopygia in black females from Cesare Lombroso and Guglielmo Ferrero,* La donna deliquente: La prostituta e la donna normale *(Turin: L. Roux, 1893). Ithaca: Private collection.*

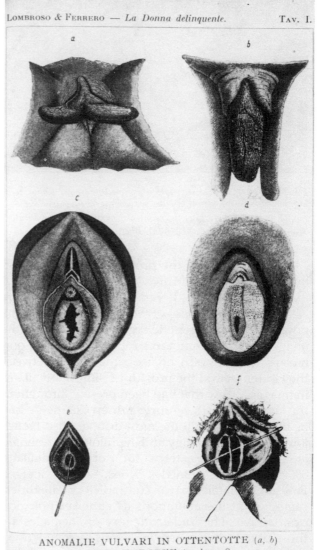

ANOMALIE VULVARI IN OTTENTOTTE (*a, b*)
ED IN EUROPEE (*c, d, e, f*).

a, b) Grembiule od ipertrofia delle piccole ninfe di Ottentotte (Blanchard). — *c)* Imene frangiato in vergine (Hoffmann). — *d)* Imene cribrato (Hoffmann). — *e)* Imene peduncolato (Miriewsky) o a campanilla.   *f)* Imene septato (Hoffmann).

PLATE 309. *"Sexual Anomalies in the Hottentot (a, b) and in the European Woman (c, d, e, f)" from Cesare Lombroso and Guglielmo Ferrero,* La donna deliquente: La prostituta e la donna normale *(Turin: L. Roux, 1893).*

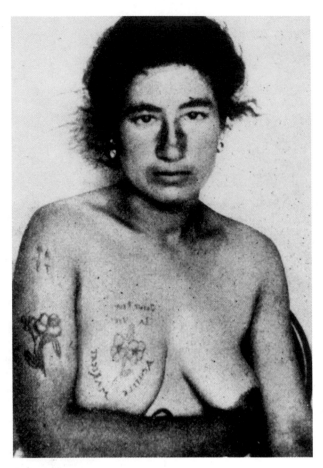

PLATE 310. *The atavistic, tattooed prostitute from I. Callari's study of Sicilian prostitution follows Lombroso's discussion of tattooing in his 1893 study of the criminal woman and the prostitute.* Archivio di psichiatria 24 (1903). Ithaca: Private collection.

The anomalies of the prostitute's labia are seen by him as atavistic throwbacks to the Hottentot, if not the chimpanzee. Lombroso sees the prostitute as an atavistic subclass of woman, and he uses the power of the polygenetic argument applied to the image of the Hottentot to support his views. Lombroso's text, in its offhand use of the analogy between the Hottentot and the prostitute, simply articulates in images a view that had been present throughout the late nineteenth century. Adrien Charpy's essay of 1870, published in the most distinguished French journal of dermatology and syphilology, presented an analysis of the external form of the genitalia of 800 prostitutes examined at Lyons.[40] Charpy merged Parent-Duchatelet's two contradictory categories, seeing all of the alterations as either pathological or adaptive. The initial category of anomalies are those of the labia, where he begins by commenting on the elongation of the labia majora in prostitutes, comparing this with the apron of the "disgusting" Hottentots. The image comes as a natural one to

Charpy, as it does to Lombroso two decades later. The prostitute is an atavistic form of humanity, whose "primitive" nature can be observed in the form of her genitalia. What Tarnowsky and Lombroso add to the equation is the parallel they draw between the seemingly beautiful physiognomy and this atavistic nature. Other signs were quickly found. Havelock Ellis saw as one of the secondary sexual characteristics that determine the beautiful the presence in a woman of a long second toe and a short fifth toe.[41] The French physician L. Julien presented clinical material concerning the antithetical case, the foot of the prostitute, which Lombroso in commenting on the paper immediately labeled as "prehensile."[42] I. Callari saw the tattoos that marked the body of Sicilian prostitutes as parallel to the physiognomy in their signification of the innate, primitive nature of the prostitute[43] **[PLATE 310]**. The ultimate of the throwbacks was, of course, the throwback to the level of the Hottentot or the Bushman, and that was to the level of the lasciviousness of the prostitute. Lombroso's coauthor, Guglielmo Ferrero, described prostitution as the rule in primitive societies and placed the Bushman at the nadir of the scale of primitive lasciviousness because adultery has no meaning for them, nor does virginity, and the poverty of their mental universe can be seen in the fact that they have but one word for "girl, woman, or wife."[44] The primitive is the black, and the qualities of blackness, or at least of the black female, are those of the prostitute. One major sign of the "atavistic resemblance" of the "primitive woman" and the "prostitute" is their "greater dullness of touch."[45] The prostitute, like Nietzsche's black, has a diminished sensory capacity. This sign of the inherent baseness of both the Hottentot and the prostitute is related to their inherent toleration of the cross-sexual touch. This association between the black and the prostitute becomes grotesquely evident when a student of Lombroso, Abele De Blasio, published a series of case studies on steatopygia in prostitutes, in which he perceives the prostitute as being quite literally the Hottentot[46] **[PLATE 311]**. Their lack of shame causes them to be unaware of the baseness of their own nature. Here the boundary between the "normal" woman and the "prostitute" is drawn absolutely as a means for the male to assure himself of his control over his own sexuality, the "beast within." The control of the woman's body becomes the projection of the male's own sense of lack of control over his own body. Thus the sexualized female is but a projection of his own anxiety about the "primitive" nature of his own sexuality.

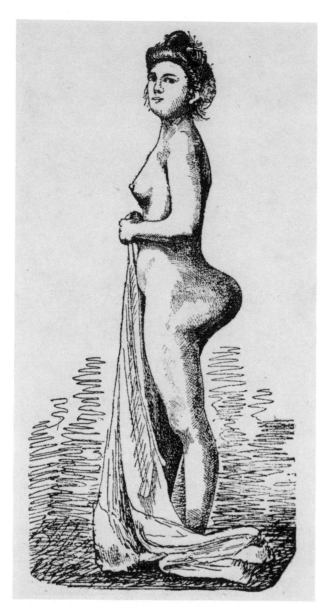

PLATE 311. *Abele De Blasio's image of "Steatopygia in an Italian Prostitute" in the* Archivio di psichiatria 26 (1905). Ithaca: Private collection.

The perception of the prostitute in the late nineteenth century has merged with the perception of the black. Both categories are those of outsiders, but what does this amalgamation imply in terms of the perception of both groups? It is a commonplace that the primitive was associated with unbridled sexuality. This was either condemned, as in Jefferson's discussions of the nature of the black in Virginia, or praised, as in the fictional supplement written by Diderot to Bougainville's voyages. However, it is exactly this type of uncontrolled sexuality that is postulated by historians such as J. J. Bachofen as the sign of the "Swamp," the earliest stage of

human history. Blacks, if both Hegel and Schopenhauer are to be believed, remained at this most primitive stage, and their presence in the contemporary world served as an indicator of how far humanity had come in establishing control over the world and itself. The loss of control was marked by a regression into this dark past, a degeneracy into the primitive expression of emotions, either in the form of madness or unbridled sexuality. Such a loss of control was, of course, viewed as pathological and thus fell into the domain of the medical model. For the medical model, especially as articulated in the public health reforms of the mid- and late nineteenth century, had as its central preoccupation the elimination of sexually transmitted disease through the institution of social controls. This is the intent of such writers as Parent-Duchatelet and Tarnowsky. The social controls that they wished to institute were well known in the late eighteenth and early nineteenth centuries but in quite a different context. For the laws applying to the control of slaves (such as the 1685 French *code noir* and its American analogues) had placed great emphasis on the control of the slave as sexual object, both in terms of permitted and forbidden sexual contacts as well as documentation as to the legal status of the offspring of slaves. The linkage that the late nineteenth century established between this earlier model of control and the later model of sexual control advocated by the public health authorities came about through the association of two bits of medical mythology. The primary marker of the black is skin color. There is a long history of perceiving this skin color as the result of some pathology. The favorite theory, which reappears with some frequency in the early nineteenth century, is that the skin color and attendant physiognomy of the black is the result of congenital leprosy.[47] It is not very surprising therefore to read in the late nineteenth century (after social conventions surrounding the abolition of slavery in Great Britain and France, as well as the trauma of the American Civil War, forbade the public association of at least skin color with illness) that syphilis was not introduced into Europe by Columbus's sailors but rather that it was a form of leprosy that had long been present in Africa and spread into Europe in the Middle Ages.[48] The association of the black, especially the black female, with the syphilophobia of the late nineteenth century was thus made manifest. Black females do not merely represent the sexualized female; they also represent the female as the source of corruption and disease. It is the black female as the emblem of illness who haunts the background of Manet's *Olympia*.

READING *NANA*

Manet's *Olympia* stands exactly midway between the glorification of the sexualized female and her condemnation. She is the antithesis of the fat prostitute. Indeed, she was perceived as "thin" by her contemporaries, much in the style of the actual prostitutes of the 1860s. But Laura, the black servant, is presented as plump, which can be best seen in Manet's initial oil sketch of her done in 1862–63. Her presence in both the sketch and final painting emphasizes her face, for it is the physiognomy of the black that points to her sexuality and that of the female presented to the viewer unclothed but with her genitalia demurely covered. The association is between these hidden genitalia and the signifier of the black. Both point to the potential for corruption of the male viewer by the female. This is made even more evident in that work that art historians have stressed as being heavily influenced by Manet's *Olympia*, his portrait *Nana*. Here the associations would have been quite clear to the contemporary viewer. First, the model for the painting was Henriette Hauser, called Citron, the mistress of the Prince of Orange. Second, Manet places in the background of the painting a Japanese crane, the French word for which ("grue") was a slang term for prostitute. The figure is labeled as a sexualized female.

Unlike the classical pose in *Olympia*, Nana is presented being admired by a well-dressed man-about-town (a flaneur). She is not naked but partially clothed, clothed however, in a corset that shapes her figure. What Manet can further draw upon is the entire vocabulary of signs associated by the late nineteenth century with the sexualized female. Nana is fulsome rather than thin. Here Manet uses the stigmata of fatness employed to characterize the prostitute. This convention becomes part of the visualization of the sexualized female, even though the reality of the idealized sexualized female is that of a "thin" female. Constantin Guy presents a fat, reclining prostitute in 1860, whereas Edgar Degas's *The Client* (1879) **[PLATE 312]**, one of his monotypes on this theme, presents the view with an entire brothel of fat prostitutes.[49] At the same time, Napoleon III's mistress, Marguerite Bellanger, set a vogue for slenderness.[50] She was described as "below average in size, slight, thin, almost skinny." This is certainly not Nana. Manet places her in a position vis-à-vis the viewer (but not the male observer in the painting) that emphasizes the line of her buttocks, the steatopygia of the prostitute.[51] Second, Nana is placed in such a way that the viewer (but again not the flaneur) can observe her ear. It is, to no one's surprise, Darwin's ear, a sign

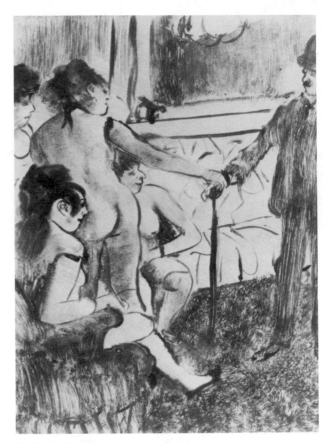

PLATE 312. *Edgar Degas's monotype of well-endowed prostitutes and* The Client, *ca. 1879. Paris: Musée du Louvre.*

of the atavistic female. Thus we know where the black servant is hidden in *Nana*. She is hidden within Nana. For even her seeming beauty is but a sign of the black hidden within. All her external stigmata point to the pathology within the sexualized female. And indeed, Manet's earlier (and much more controversial) work, the *Olympia*, a portrait understood as the icon of a prostitute, was simply dismissed by the art critic Victor Fournel as "cette Vénus hottentote" when it was first exhibited in the salon of 1865.[52]

Manet's *Nana* thus provides a further reading of his *Olympia*, a reading that stresses Manet's debt to the pathological model of sexuality present during the late nineteenth century. The black hidden within *Olympia* bursts forth in Pablo Picasso's 1901 version of the painting in which Olympia is presented as a sexualized black, with broad hips and revealed genitalia, gazing at the nude flaneur bearing her a gift of fruit, much as Laura bears a gift of flowers in Manet's original **[PLATE 313]**. But the artist, unlike in the works of Manet, is himself present in the work and is present as a sexualized observer of the sexualized female. Picasso owes part of his reading of *Olympia* to the polar image of the primitive female as sexual object, as found in the lower-class prostitutes painted by Van Gogh or the Tahitian maidens à la Diderot painted by Gauguin. Picasso saw the sexualized female as the visual analogue of the black. Indeed, in his most radical break with the Impressionist tradition, *Les demoiselles d'Avignon* (1907), he linked the inmates of a brothel in Barcelona with the black by using the theme of African masks to characterize their appearance. The figure of the male holding a skull in the early version of the painting is the artist as victim. Picasso's parody points toward the importance of seeing Manet's *Nana* in the context of the medical discourse concerning the sexualized female that dominated the late nineteenth century. For the portrait of Nana is embedded in a complex literary matrix that provides many of the signs needed to illustrate the function of the sexualized female as the sign of disease.

The figure of Nana first appeared in Émile Zola's 1877 novel *L'assommoir*, in which she was presented as the offspring of the alcoholic couple who are the central figures of the novel.[53] Her heredity assured the reader that she would eventually become a sexualized female, a prostitute, and, indeed, at the close of the novel she has run off with an older man, the owner of a button factory, and has begun her life as a sexualized female. Manet was taken by the figure of Nana (as was the French reading public) and his portrait of her symbolically reflected her sexual encounters presented during the novel. Zola then decided to build the next novel in his Rougon-Macquart cycle on the figure of Nana as a sexualized female. Thus in Zola's *Nana*, the reader is presented with Zola's reading of Manet's portrait of Nana. Indeed, Zola uses the portrait of the flaneur observing the half-dressed Nana as the centerpiece for a scene in the theater in which Nana seduces the simple Count Muffet.

Immediately before this meeting, Zola presents Nana's first success in the theater (or, as the theater director calls it, his "brothel"). She appears in a review, unable to sing or dance, and becomes the butt of laughter until in the second act of the review she appears unclothed on stage:

> Nana was in the nude: naked with a quiet audacity, certain of the omnipotence of her flesh. She was wrapped in a simple piece of gauze: her rounded shoulders, her Amazon's breasts of which the pink tips stood up rigidly like lances, her broad buttocks which rolled in a voluptuous swaying motion, and her fair, fat hips: her whole body was in evidence, and could be seen under the light tissue with its foamy whiteness.[54]

What Zola describes are the characteristics of the sexualized woman, the "primitive" hidden beneath the surface: "all of a sudden in the comely child

PLATE 313. *Pablo Picasso's black* Olympia, *1901. New York: Private collection.*

the woman arose, disturbing, bringing the mad surge of her sex, inviting the unknown element of desire. Nana was still smiling: but it was the smile of a man-eater." Nana's atavistic sexuality, the sexuality of the Amazon, is destructive. The sign of this is her fleshliness. And it is this sign that reappears when she is observed by Muffet in her dressing room, the scene that Zola found in Manet's painting:

> Then calmly, to reach her dressing-table, she walked in her drawers through that group of gentlemen, who made way for her. She had large buttocks, her drawers ballooned, and with breast well forward she bowed to them, giving her delicate smile. (p. 135)

Nana's childlike face is but a mask that conceals the hidden disease buried within, the corruption of sexuality. Thus Zola concludes the novel by revealing the horror beneath the mask. Nana dies of the pox. (This is a pun that works in French as well as in English and that was needed because of the rapidity of decay demanded by the moral implication of Zola's portrait. It would not do to have Nana die slowly over thirty years of tertiary syphilis. Smallpox, with its play on the pox, works quickly and gives the same visual icon of decay.) Nana's death reveals her true nature:

> Nana remained alone, her face looking up in the light from the candle. It was a charnel-house scene, a mass of tissue-fluids and blood, a shovelful of putrid flesh thrown there on a cushion. The pustules had invaded the entire face with the pocks touching each other; and, dissolving and subsiding with the greyish look of mud, there seemed to be already an earthy mouldiness on the shapeless muscosity, in which the features were no longer discernible. An eye, the left one, had completely subsided in a soft mass of purulence; the other, half-open, was sinking like a collapsing hole. The nose was still suppurating. A whole reddish crust was peeling off one cheek and invaded the mouth, distorting it into a loathsome grimace. And on that horrible and grotesque mask, the hair, that beautiful head of hair still preserving its blaze of sunlight, flowed down in a golden trickle. Venus was decomposing. It seems as though the virus she had absorbed from the gutters and from the tacitly permitted carrion of humanity, that baneful ferment with which she had poisoned a people, had now risen to her face and putrefied it. (pp. 464–65)

The decaying visage is the visible sign of the diseased genitalia through which the sexualized female corrupts an entire nation of warriors and leads them to the collapse at the battle of Sedan on September 1, 1870, and eventual Prussian victory over France. This image is an old one as we know; it is *Frau Welt*, "Madam World," who masks her corruption, the disease of being a woman, through her beauty (see Plate 64). But it is yet more, for Nana begins in death to revert to the blackness of the earth, to assume the horrible grotesque countenance perceived as belonging to the world of the black, the world of the "primitive," the world of disease. Nana is, like Olympia, in the words of Paul Valéry, "preeminently unclean."[55] And it is this uncleanliness, this disease, that forms the final link between two images of the woman, the black and the prostitute. For, just as the genitalia of the Hottentot were perceived as parallel to the diseased genitalia of the prostitute, so too the powerful idea of corruption links both images. Thus part of Nana's fall into corruption comes through her seduction by a lesbian, yet a further sign of her innate, physical degeneracy. She is corrupted and corrupts through sexuality.

The fear of miscegenation is a fear (and a word) from the late nineteenth-century vocabulary of sexuality. It is a fear not only of interracial sexuality but of its results, the decline of the population. For interracial marriages were seen as exactly parallel to the barrenness of the prostitute. If they produced children at all, these children were weak and doomed. Thus Havelock Ellis, drawing on his view of the objective nature of the beauty of humanity, states that "it is difficult to be sexually attracted to persons who are fundamentally unlike ourselves in racial constitution"[56] and cites Abel Herman to substantiate his views:

> Differences of race are irreducible and between two beings who love each other they cannot fail to produce exceptional and instructive reactions. In the first superficial ebullition of love, indeed, nothing notable may be manifested, but in a fairly short time the two lovers, innately hostile, in striving to approach each other strike against an invisible partition which separates them. Their sensibilities are divergent; everything in each shocks the other; even their anatomical conformation, even the language of their gestures; all is foreign.[57]

It is thus the inherent fear of the difference in the anatomy of the Other that lies behind the synthesis of images. The Other's pathology is revealed in her anatomy. It is in the similarity between the black and the prostitute as bearers of the stigmata of sexual difference and thus pathology that captured the late nineteenth century. Zola sees in the sexual corruption of the male the source of political impotence and provides a projection of what is basically an internal fear, the fear of loss of power, onto the world.[58] The loss of power for French intellectuals after the disastrous Franco–Prussian conflict was intimately connected to the image of the sexualized woman as the representative of disease. For it is solely the debilitating effects of "disease" that could explain the weakness of the French male and General Patrice MacMahon's capitulation at Sedan. Political weakness is the result of the seduction and corruption of the male by the polluted and polluting female. And this loss is represented through the image of the base and foreign female, the prostitute as Hottentot. Masculine sexuality is thus understood as being beyond the control of the male. The "white man's burden" thus becomes his sexuality and its control, and it is this that is transferred into the need to control the sexuality of the Other, the Other as sexualized female. For the colonial mentality that sees "natives" as needing control is easily transferred to the woman, but the woman as exemplified by the caste of the prostitute. This need for control was a projection of inner fears, and thus its articulation in visual images was in terms that were the polar opposite of the European male. The roots of this image of the sexualized female are to be found in the male observer, the progenitors of the vocabulary of images through which they believed themselves able to capture the essence of the Other. Thus when Sigmund Freud, in his essay on lay analysis (1926), discussed the ignorance of contemporary psychology concerning adult female sexuality, he refers to this lack of knowledge as the "dark continent" of psychology.[59] In using this English phrase, Freud ties the image of female sexuality to the image of contemporary colonialism and thus to the perceived relationship of the sexuality ascribed to the female to the exoticism and pathology of the Other. It is Freud's intent to explore this hidden "dark continent" to reveal the hidden truths about female sexuality, just as the anthropologist–explorers, such as Lombroso, were revealing further hidden truths about the nature of the black. Freud continues a discourse that relates the images of male discovery to the images of the female as the object of discovery. The line from the secrets possessed by the Hottentot Venus to twentieth-century psychoanalysis runs reasonably straight.

All of these images are part of an internalized search for the "authentic" projected onto the image of the sexuality of the black. Giacomo Leopardi stated it quite correctly in 1832: "In the present century, black people are believed to be totally different from whites in race and origin, yet totally equal to them with regard to human rights. In the sixteenth century, when blacks were thought to come from the same roots and to be of the same family as whites, it was held, most of all by Spanish theologians, that with regard to rights blacks were by nature and Divine Will greatly inferior to us. In both centuries, blacks have been bought and sold and made to work in chains under the whip. Such is ethics; and such is the extent to which moral beliefs have anything to do with actions."[60] Scientific ideology, whether liberal or conservative, employed the image of the black as a reflex of difference within the world of the literary text. The black, female genitalia as the embodiment of disease and corruption become the antithesis of the healthy genitalia of the male. The ideology of science and its image of the body can thus be formed by stereotypes as much as it forms them.

CHAPTER ELEVEN

The Image of AIDS: Representing Sexuality and Disease at the Turn of Another Century

ICONS WITHOUT END

The fantasies about sexual anatomy that create boundaries between each individual and the world are themselves not bounded. To conclude this book on the icons of human sexuality, I shall turn to the ongoing construction of the image of a disease powerfully associated with sexuality, AIDS, and use the history of that construction as a means of illustrating the ongoing protean nature of the iconography of sexuality. It is vital to understand the social construction of AIDS over the past years because the social implications of AIDS have directly affected the lives of so many individuals, individuals who have been stigmatized (and destroyed) by the "idea" of AIDS as well as its reality.

During the summer of 1986, many Americans read the *Newsweek* cover story on Gerald Friedland of Montefiore Medical Center entitled "The AIDS Doctor."[1] I begin my discussion of the construction of the image of people living with AIDS during 1986 and 1987 with this essay—which is in the style of the "new journalism," very personal and very informal—and examine its authors' desire to alter the dominant manifestation of the image of those living with AIDS and its inability to accomplish its intended goal. The opening sentence of the essay sets not only its tone but also its agenda: "One day in April 1985, Dr. Gerald H. Friedland found himself at the bedside of a young woman named Maria, letting her know as gently as he could that she was going to die." Disregarding the self-conscious echo of the opening of Dante's *Inferno*, we can read in this sentence what is clearly a desired shift in the image of people living with AIDS from that of the homosexual to that of the heterosexual, with all of its implications—the authors, Peter Goldman and Lucille Beachy, have introduced us to an exemplary person living with AIDS who is, however, a woman. Maria was not only female but she was a medical anomaly: "Nothing in her medical history marked her as a candidate for AIDS, not at first glance." She should have been a non-combatant in the AIDS invasion of North America. She was not one of the "4-H's": homosexuals, heroin addicts, hemophiliacs, and Haitians, the four categories labeled as being "at risk" for AIDS through the early 1980s.[2] She was an incidental victim, infected by her former husband, an IV drug user, who had subsequently died of AIDS.

The *Newsweek* cover story is part of a recent shift in the public image of the nature of the patient infected with AIDS. With over 22,000 cases in the United States, about one per million of the population, and a present case fatality rate of over 50 percent, it is not a trivial question to ask how these patients are (and have been) perceived.[3] To explore the iconography of the disease means to understand the overt level of meaning and also the complex confusions that permeate the image of people with AIDS. It means also to plumb how images of disease traditionally associated with sexuality, such as images of touch and images of race, have been refunctioned to provide an explanatory paradigm for this new disease. Roy Porter has summarized this need to know the context of AIDS as part of the "terrifying model of universal contagion." He notes the power of this model, the model of the polluting Other:

AIDS . . . is seen as a disease other people give you. Whether they do this innocently or deliberately, directly or indirectly, it comes from enemies within. Transmission takes place through terrifyingly tiny microorganisms. Their very minuteness bespeaks a certain invincibility (small is unstoppable). And if they are invisible, they must be everywhere. So it's *obvious* you're at risk of "catching" it from contaminated cutlery, from sitting next to someone in the bus, from lavatory seats, from shaking hands, from social kissing, from touching sufferers or even their clothes. It has seemed so not least to those medical staff who have refused to treat AIDS patients or even to admit them to their wards.[4]

The sexual touch is the touch of sexual contagion. (Remember that for the Victorians the term *contagion* was identical to venereal; thus when the laws attempting to regulate venereal diseases were promulgated in the 1860s, they were called the "Contagious Disease Acts.") The histories of the sexual touch, of the relationship between the genitalia and the idea of race, and of the images of the sufferer and the source of suffering have all been traced in this volume. The visualization of human sexuality has, in the image of the person with AIDS, reached its contemporary stage, but we shall see that the icons are old, familiar ones.

THE FIRST IMAGE OF PEOPLE WITH AIDS

The construction of the image of those living with AIDS has taken the past seven years to reach its present stage. In 1979, Alvin Friedman-Kien of New York University Medical Center identified a group of patients suffering from a rare dermatological disease, Kaposi's sarcoma, which has a striking visual presentation, bluish or purple-brown nodules that appear on the skin. The normal course of this disease is seldom fatal, but this group of young patients were dying within eight to twenty-four months after their diagnosis. Other physicians reported similar patterns during 1979.[5] By June 1981, 26 such cases were reported in the Centers for Disease Control's (CDC) *Morbidity and Mortality Weekly Report* (*MMWR*).[6] Parallel to this, five cases of *Pneumocystis* pneumonia, an illness caused by a ubiquitous protozoan parasite that usually manifests itself only in those individuals with depressed immune systems, appeared in Los Angeles. By the time of the report, two of these patients had died. Shortly thereafter, ten new cases of *Pneumocystis* pneumonia were diagnosed, and two of these patients also had Kaposi's sarcoma.[7]

The initial appearance of this pattern in the United States led the investigators at the CDC to try to comprehend its nature, to construct an icon of the patient.[8] The epidemiologists perceived a cluster of common attributes—these patients were living in large urban areas (New York, Miami, Los Angeles, and San Francisco), and they were all young men.

Here I wish to break the historical narrative—for it is clear that I have studiously avoided mentioning what by 1981 was central to the CDC's image of those living with AIDS—the patients' sexual orientation. As early as the 5 June 1981 report in the *MMWR*, the patients' sexual orientation as well as its "quality" had been noted: "Two of the five [patients] reported having frequent homosexual contacts with various partners" (p. 251). The centrality of sexual orientation as a factor can be further seen in the operational categorization of those living with AIDS during the first quarter of 1982 as suffering from G[ay] R[elated] I[mmune] D[eficiency] S[yndrome]. This label structured the idea of the patient suffering from AIDS in such a marked manner that the patient was not only stigmatized as a carrier of an infectious disease but also placed within a very specific historical category. For *AIDS*, a term officially coined in the fall of 1982, was understood as a specific subset of the greater category of sexually transmitted disease, a disease that homosexuals suffered from as a direct result of their sexual practices or related group-specific activities, for example, the use of drugs such as "poppers" (amyl or butyl nitrite).[9] The idea of the person afflicted with a sexually transmitted disease, one of the most potent in the repertory of icons of the stigmatized patient, became the paradigm through which those living with AIDS was understood and categorized. This idea persisted. Even though the *MMWR* began, in late 1982, to record the appearance of the disease among such groups as hemophiliacs and IV drug users, groups that could be defined by qualities other than sexual orientation, sexual orientation remained the salient characteristic used to exemplify the person living with AIDS.[10]

Indeed, the gratuitous appearance of the disease during the late 1970s linked two (at that time) unrelated social concerns: first, the perception of the increase of sexually transmitted diseases in society (following a long period of perceived decline), signaled in 1975 by the National Institute of Allergy and Infectious Diseases declaring research in sexually transmitted disease to be the number one priority of the institute; second, the growth of the public awareness of the homosexual emancipation movement, at least in large urban areas, following the "Stonewall" riot in Greenwich Village in 1969, in which there was a violent protest against police harassment of homosexuals.[11] From the beginning the person living with AIDS was seen as a male homosexual suffering a sexually transmitted disease and was seen as different from the perceived normal spectrum of patients—but different within very specific structures. We must stress that AIDS is caused by retroviruses, now labeled H[uman] I[mmunodeficiency] V[iruses], spread by direct contact with infected body fluids, including blood and semen. Sexual contact is not necessary to contract the illness.[12] It is a viral disease that can be transmitted sexually but also can be transmitted by other means. The ambiguity of this fact meant that the disease could have been categorized in many different ways—it was characterized, however, not as a viral disease, such as Hepatitis B, but as a sexually transmitted disease, such as syphilis.

THE IMAGE OF THOSE LIVING WITH AIDS

The early categorization of AIDS as a sexually transmitted disease (albeit in a very specific context) strongly marked the initial construction of the disease. Let me remind you of the icons we have seen in the complex history of the iconography of the syphilitic patient. This complex of icons provides the matrix for an understanding of the image of human sexuality as pathology associated with AIDS. Our images of people with AIDS are taken from a press sympathetic in general to the individuals living with AIDS. They are not taken from the papers and journals of the religious right, which have, since the nineteenth century, condemned such patients, as Allan Brandt observed, "as [suffering from] an affliction of those who wilfully violated the moral code [and suffering] . . . a punishment for sexual irresponsibility."[13] And yet the stigma of sexually transmitted disease still maintains itself even in these self-consciously supportive journals of public opinion.

It is important to understand that the association of the image of those individuals living with AIDS with the iconography of syphilis is not random. It is clear that the initial association rests on homosexuals and the perception that they suffer from a sexually transmitted disease. But it is also clear that the "taming" of syphilis and other related sexually transmitted diseases with the introduction of antibiotics in the late 1940s left our culture with a series of images of the mortally infected and infecting patient suffering from a morally repugnant disease but without a disease sufficiently powerful with which to associate these icons.

The twentieth-century iconography of syphilis is tied to a continuation of the images of the syphilitic that have been traced in detail throughout this volume. Standard images reappear, often in forms that are immediately "readable" because of the implicit tradition of representing syphilis and the syphilitic within Western culture.[14] Other images are added to the repertoire, images that, however, draw their power from older associations. In Louis Raemakers's 1916 Belgian poster [PLATE 314] representing the temptation of the female as the source of the disease, much of the traditional imagery of the seductress can be found. Standing among rows of graves, wearing a black cloak, and holding a skull that represents her genitalia, she is the essential *femme fatale*. But there is a striking fin-de-siècle addition to the image—for "la syphilis" is also the Medusa. Her tendril-like hair, her staring eyes, present the viewer with the reason for the male's seduction— not his sexuality but her vampirelike power to control the male's rationality. More traditional images of the syphilitic can also be found in the images from World War I. In Théophile-Alexandre Steinlen's 1916 French poster [PLATE 315], the traditional call to soldiers to remain strong for their country is forcefully made. The soldiers are admonished to resist the seductions of the street, where they risk exposure to an illness "as dangerous as war" and that leads to a "useless death without honor." The ambiguity of the pronoun (the *she* can be both the disease [*la syphilis*] as well as the *woman*) points toward the source of danger of another defeat as total as the one at the battle of Sedan against the Prussians in 1870, caused, at least in the popular mind, as we discussed in Chapter Ten, by the sexual corruption of the French male. This message is accompanied by an image of the seduction of the soldier paralleled by the image of the sick soldier posed in the traditional pose of melancholy. The association of disease and madness, of syphilis and mental collapse, is as strong in the early twentieth century as it is in the sixteenth century.

One can turn to the visual representation of syphilis during the 1940s to have a sense of the broad spectrum of icons associated with that disease, images that, as we have seen, have a long and complicated history. In the United States, a broad-based campaign aimed at soldiers stressed the mask of the seductress; the equation in this 1944 Office of War Information poster [PLATE 316] is between the wholesomeness of the female and her potential as the source of disease. Even though both males and females served in the armed services during World War I and World War II, the imagery of the syphilitic remained associated with the traditional images of the male victim and the female seductress.

PLATE 314. *A woman with spiderlike hair, wearing a black cloak, stands among rows of graves. She holds a skull in her hands in this powerful illustration of the evils of syphilis in Louis Raemakers's L'Hecatombe. La Syphillis, ca. 1916. Madison: University of Wisconsin Medical School Library Collection.*

PLATE 315. *The text of this poster by Théophile-Alexandre Steinlen, "Soldat, la patrie compte sur toi . . .," 1916, is written on a tombstone, and presents a dramatic appeal to French soldiers to keep strong their country and to resist those seductions in the street that risk exposure to an illness as "dangerous as war" leading to a "useless death without honor." New York: Private collection.*

Following the war, for the first time in 1945, the British Ministry of Health circulated a photographic display intended to inform the general public of the danger inherent in venereal diseases [PLATES 317–319]. What it also did was to provide a set of icons for the image of the sufferer. We have a set of miniature reproductions of this exhibition intended for the public health officer that provides a detailed description of the intent of the images. Icons of the healthy body are contrasted with icons of pathology, the entire healthy body with the infected genitalia. It is the sexual organs that are diseased, both in the transmission of the disease and in the drives that lead the individual to exposure to the disease. The "cause" is social rather than clinical—"boredom, excess drinking, the 'easy' girl-friend [or boy-friend], prostitution, and the disruption of war itself." The cure for temptation, for the drives, is self-control, clean living. But once infected, cures are available to assure the "future of our families." The analogous icons are those of the syphilitic man, woman, and child, with the letters "VD" superimposed on their faces like some great invisible mask, a shadow that is the hidden image of the disease, a disease that has an impact even upon unborn generations. These icons of syphilis carry through the visualization of the syphilitic that has been traced in detail in this study.[15]

313

The Venereal Diseases Photographic Display illustrated in miniature

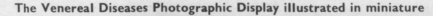

PANELS 1 to 6

introduce the Display, state its purpose and show, by contrasting the healthy and diseased man and woman ... the healthy and diseased family, how the choice between the two lies with every individual, so far as venereal diseases are concerned. (Female versions of Panels 2 and 3 are provided for substitution when the Display is shown to women.)

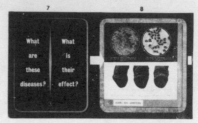

PANELS 7 to 16

answer the questions—What are these diseases? What is their effect?—with a series of medical photographs and diagrams showing the germs of V.D., the first symptoms on the sex organs, the parts of the body most vulnerable to mutilation and ulceration, the speed of attack, the three medical stages of syphilis as it spreads from the sex organs to the whole body, the results of syphilis and gonorrhœa in old age, and on the next generation. (Female versions of panels 8, 9, 10, 11 and 12 are provided for substitution when the Display is shown to women.)

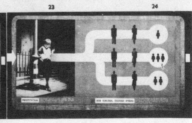

PANELS 17 to 27

show some of the root causes which lead, particularly in wartime, to the temptations of promiscuous sexual intercourse and consequently to the spread of venereal diseases—boredom, excess drinking, the "easy" girl-friend, prostitution and the disruption of war itself. Panel 26 deals with the almost non-existent risk of accidental infection. (Female versions of panels 17, 18, 19, 20, 21 and 22 are provided for substitution when the Display is shown to women.)

PANELS 28 to 32

suggest what everyone can do to reinforce self-control and so avoid the horrors of V.D.—by keeping mind and body in good health with exercise, reading, study and cheerful company; and by the thought of loved ones at home when temptation offers. (Female versions of Panels 29 and 30 are provided for substitution when the Display is shown to women.)

PLATE 317.

PANELS 33 to 36

stress the importance of *prompt* expert treatment for those who have been infected ; give a brief record of the scientists who have discovered how V.D. can be diagnosed, treated, and cured ; show the process and effects of treatment, and how, at recognised clinics, it is free and confidential. Panel 36 is left blank for the addition of local addresses of treatment centres by each exhibitor.

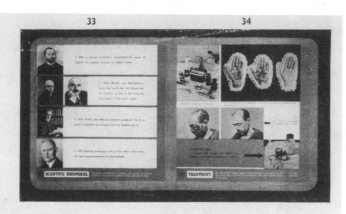

PANELS 37 to 40

warn against quack remedies and delay in beginning treatment, and against premature discontinuation, and conclude the display with an appeal for help from everyone by spreading knowledge of the diseases, by resisting temptation and by going for prompt treatment if infection has been risked. The final photographs show how health and fitness bring courage and cheerfulness now, and happiness for the future of our families.

NOTE: If, as a result of studying this leaflet, any organisation which has medical or nursing supervision for its staff wishes to book a set of this Venereal Diseases Photographic Display on free loan, please use the accompanying Order Form.

PLATE 318.

PLATES 317–319. *The British public health displays on syphilis from 1945, prepared by James Randal Hutchinson (ca. 1880–1955) in connection with his work in the Ministry of Health, 1919–47. London: Wellcome Institute for the History of Medicine.*

DOUBLE - CROWN & CROWN-FOLIO POSTERS

offered free to Local Authorities

(Above) " Confidential Treatment." Free textual poster with blank panel for local clinic details. Local Authorities must make their own arrangements for overprinting. Crown-folio size *only*, 15" × 10"—Key No. VD/CT/CF.

(Right) " VD is a great evil, etc." Textual poster printed in red, white and black, available FREE in two sizes : Double-crown, size 30" × 20" —Key No. VD/T/DC. Crown-folio, size 15" × 10"— Key No. VD/T/CF. →

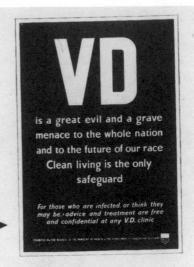

VD is a great evil and a grave menace to the whole nation and to the future of our race. Clean living is the only safeguard

For those who are infected, or think they may be, advice and treatment are free and confidential at any V.D. clinic

(Above) " VD—a shadow on health." Pictorial poster printed in red, grey, white and black, available FREE in two sizes: Double-crown, size 30" × 20" —Key No. VD/M/DC. Crown-folio, size 15" × 10" —Key No. VD/M/CF.

(Above) " VD—a shadow on happiness." Pictorial poster printed in red, grey, white and black, available FREE in two sizes : Double-crown, size 30" × 20" —Key No. VD/F/DC. Crown-folio, size 15" × 10" —Key No. VD/F/CF.

(Above) " VD—a shadow on his future." Pictorial poster printed in red, grey, white and black, available FREE in two sizes: Double-crown, size 30" × 20" —Key No. VD/B/DC. Crown-folio, size 15" × 10" —Key No. VD/B/CF.

ORDER FORM for the above Ministry of Health posters only.

To the Public Relations Division, Ministry of Health, Whitehall, S.W.1

Please send . . . . copies of Poster VD/CT/CF.
. . . . copies of Poster VD/T/DC.
. . . . copies of Poster VD/T/CF.
. . . . copies of Poster VD/M/DC.
. . . . copies of Poster VD/M/CF.
. . . . copies of Poster VD/F/DC.
. . . . copies of Poster VD/F/CF.
. . . . copies of Poster VD/B/DC.
. . . . copies of Poster VD/B/CF.

Posters to be sent to :

(Local Authority) . . . .

(Address) . . . .

. . . .

(Signature) . . . . (Date) . . . .

PLATE 319.

316

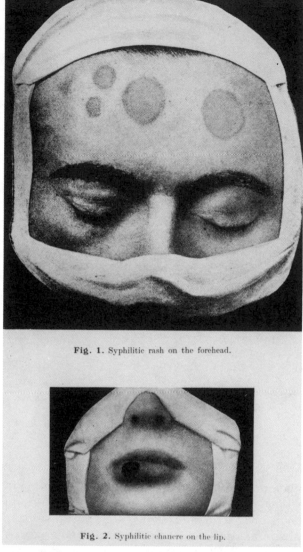

Fig. 1. Syphilitic rash on the forehead.

Fig. 2. Syphilitic chancre on the lip.

PLATE 320. *The face of the syphilitic from Norman Haire, ed.,* Encyclopaedia of Sexual Knowledge *(London: Francis Aldor, 1934). London: Wellcome Institute for the History of Medicine.*

A boundary is drawn between the infected and the source of infection, between the corrupt life-style of the diseased and the pure life of the innocent. Innocence is a quality of self-control, and thus the infant, infected in his or her mother's womb, is punishment of the mother, is corruption personified. The infant, too, bears the hidden shadow, the mask of corruption. Indeed, such images even haunt the popular sexual handbooks of the mid-twentieth century. In Norman Haire's sexual handbook of the 1930s, the syphilitic is represented by the lesions on the face of the sufferer **[PLATE 320]**. But such a pathognomonic representation is not limited to the face. Even the body of the syphilitic is represented within the received categories of perception. In the 1953 *Illustrated Guide to Sexual Happiness*, the dangers of syphilis are represented in a series of figures whose posture represents the disease. Among the positions reproduced is the traditional image of the melancholic, associated with syphilis from the first decade of its recorded appearance in Europe **[PLATE 321]**.

With the general introduction of antibiotics in the treatment of syphilis during the late 1940s, these extraordinarily powerful images were left without an equally devastating disease. From 1968 through the early 1970s, there was an attempt to associate such icons with genital herpes, but even though it was a sexually transmitted disease, its symptomatology was too trivial to warrant this association over the long run. AIDS was the perfect disease for such associations, even if it was not a typical sexually transmitted disease.

If we turn to an image of an individual living with AIDS that appeared in the *New York Times* of

PLATE 321. *The position of melancholy as a sign of syphilis from Lucia Radl,* Illustrated Guide to Sexual Happiness in Marriage *(London: William Heineman, 1953). London: Wellcome Institute for the History of Medicine.*

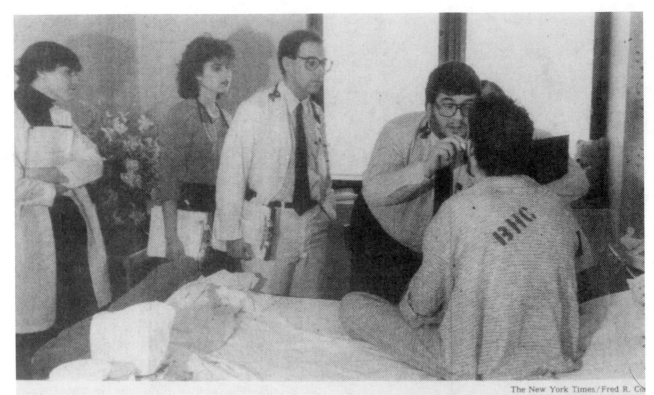

The New York Times/Fred R. Co

A group of doctors, above, examining a patient during rounds at **AIDS** clinic at Bellevue Hospital Cente

PLATE 322. *The AIDS patient being examined by his physicians, from the* New York Times, *23 December 1985. Ithaca: Olin Library, Cornell University.*

23 December 1985, we have the icon of the isolated patient in relationship to the act of healing (parallel to the icon found in the broadsides of Sebastian Brant and Joseph Grünpeck that appeared during the parallel period of the history of syphilis in Western Europe [see Plates 70–71]) **[PLATE 322]**. The physical sense of distance in this image is palpable; the observers are as far away from the patient as they can be without being in another room. Although this is a "typical" image of medical treatment, like many late nineteenth- and twentieth-century photographs of physicians at work, the ground provided for the observer of the icon is the tension communicated not by the treatment of the patient but by the implications associated with the patient's disease.[16] The *New York Times*, in 1985 (and subsequently), was full of articles on the anxiety of health workers treating people living with AIDS.[17] And this image corresponded, for the reader of the *Times*, to the anxiety of the general public concerning the transmission of the disease. By 1985, the significance of the single male patient for the readers of the *New York Times* was self-evident: this is the patient as homosexual male. The male is not only the sufferer

but also the cause of his own pollution. The combination of both sufferer and source of suffering in the image of the male combines both the male and female images traditionally associated with sexually transmitted diseases such as syphilis. The person living with AIDS is both the poor sufferer as well as the cause of his own suffering.

The association of AIDS with syphilis is a powerful one, even for the scientists who try to categorize the disease. During the summer of 1986, it became clear that there was an extraordinary increase in the number of syphilis cases being reported to New York City's Bureau of Sexually Transmitted Disease Control. The number of cases was reported to increase 105 percent over the six-month period beginning in February 1986. The increase in syphilis (as well as the increase in other sexually transmitted diseases) was indeed an artifact of the AIDS epidemic, a sign that many individuals who would not have reported (or even been completely aware of having) a sexually transmitted disease were turning to physicians. For Salvatore J. Catapano, a retired research technologist, as well as for two West German anesthesiologists, Klaus Dierig and

Urban Waldthaler, the artifact became a reality. They published a series of papers "documenting" their claim that AIDS was syphilis. This view postulated that AIDS was but a form of syphilis, one that could indeed respond to the specific cure for syphilis, penicillin. The argument rested on an inaccurate knowledge of syphilis. Catapano believed, for example, that in tertiary syphilis the composition of the semen is chemically altered and that this altered semen can produce syphilis in a sexual partner even without the presence of the syphilis spirochetes! What this view rested on was the powerful association of the "great masquerader," syphilis, with AIDS, AIDS as defined as a sexually transmitted disease. The essay reporting these findings in the public press, in a detailed report in the January 1988 *Atlantic*, was illustrated with a "scientific" image, a partial face staring at a test tube, the icon of "science," not the art of medicine and healing, but the hard science of research.[18] This image of AIDS and science becomes part of the repertoire of the idea of AIDS as it has been part of the idea of syphilis.[19]

Another set of images of people living with AIDS, such as a group of photographs taken from the Long Island newspaper *Newsday* on 4 August 1985, begins to show the attempt on the part of the "liberal" media to soften the image of the individual living with AIDS [PLATE 323]. The uppermost image is of the hemophiliac sufferer, a male, like the central figure in Brant's broadside, but like him within a mixed-sex group, the family, a potential source of more sufferers. But he is also, in analogy to the received image of the syphilitic, the source of infection for the group. His unmarred face serves as the image of the polluter within, an image reserved within the traditional iconography of syphilis for the female. The heterosexual male is seen here as both the victim (of a polluted blood supply) as well as the source of pollution (for his family). He is, as is the homosexual male, both the victim and the villain. But the next three images return to the association of the individual living with AIDS with the traditional iconography of sexually transmitted diseases and the resultant despair of contagion and death. They are marginal men, marginal sexually or "racially," presented visually as isolated, especially in the context of the first icon of the family, and are depicted within distinctive iconographic traditions of representing the sufferer from a sexually transmitted disease. These patients, as in Albrecht Dürer's Renaissance broadside depicting the syphilitic (see Plate 68) or Grünpeck's slightly later revision of the Brant icon (see Plate 71), show us their stigmata Kaposi's sarcoma.

The final image represents the individual living with AIDS as isolated, his very position echoing the classical iconographic position of melancholia, an association, as we have seen, already made with syphilis during the first decade after its first documented appearance. The sixteenth-century appearance of the traditional position of the melancholic as the icon of syphilis has numerous twentieth-century parallels (see Plates 315 and 321). The association of the image of the person living with AIDS with the traditional iconography of melancholy or depression is an extraordinarily powerful one, reappearing as the first illustration in a major update on AIDS in the popular scientific journal *Discover* in September 1986.[20] In an essay subtitled "still no reason for hysteria," which attempted to counter the evident fear that AIDS was becoming a danger to heterosexuals, John Langone's editorial intent was to combat the growing sense that AIDS was a potential danger for everyone [PLATE 324]. The iconography of depression, with its emphasis on the body, stresses the age-old association between the nature of the mind (here, the "mental illness" that is depicted as resulting from homosexuality) and the body (here, the icon of sexual deviance). The icon of the body becomes the message. The person living with AIDS remains the suffering, hopeless male, both the victim and the source of his own pollution. Those living with AIDS are represented iconographically as depressed males, with their sense of their marginality stressed even in those media that are not overtly condemnatory of their sexual identity. There is an additional dimension to the use of the icon of the melancholic in this image from *Discover*. For the tone of the essay is to condemn the "hysteria" about AIDS present within the American media because of what is labeled the "unfounded" fear of AIDS crossing into the non-IV-drug-using, heterosexual community. The image of the person living with AIDS is, on the most overt level, associated with the stigma of mental illness because the fear of impending death, the *memento mori*, is represented by the figure of the melancholic, a figure who has capitulated to despair. But the *Discover* icon not only draws the analogy with the despair of impending death but also, through a broader analogy extended to the general population, which now suffers from an "unwarranted" AIDS phobia, sees the person living with AIDS as the representation of the mental illness (read: fearful fantasy) of an entire nation. This association of AIDS with mental illness is a critique of the claim (which the *Discover* essay wishes to refute) that AIDS is a danger to the entire com-

The Burk Family

Patrick Burk, 28, of Cresson, Pa., has AIDS, as does his 1-year-old son, Dwight. His wife, Lauren, 24, has AIDS-Related Complex, an early stage of the illness. The virus was in a blood by-product that Patrick was injecting into himself weekly for hemophilia. He passed the virus on to his wife, who passed it on to her son when she was pregnant. They are seen here in the spring with their daughter, Nicole, who is healthy. Lauren works three days a week as a registered nurse, supporting the family. The three were diagnosed as having AIDS when their son became very ill. "At first I couldn't believe it," Lauren says. "And maybe I still cannot."

Photo by Frank Fournier / Contact

Alfredo Vega

A drifter and drug user born in New York to a poor Puerto Rican family, Vega, 25, says he got AIDS from his girlfriend, who has since died and who, he says, was a prostitute. Shown here amid medicine in a photo taken in April, he is dying and his body has turned brown in many places. "My family wanted me to stay with them, but my sister was afraid for her three children. So I went to sleep in the hallway for a week [in December]. Then my brother's wife called me. But my brother didn't want me. So I was staying at their place in the daytime and sleeping on the roof at night." He is living now in a Manhattan hotel.

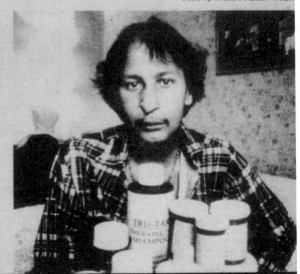

Photo by Alon Reininger / Contact

Victor Bender, Horacio Benegas

A fashion designer from Buenos Aires, Benegas, 36, in photo at right taken in April, is seriously ill with Kaposi's sarcoma, an AIDS-related disease. He lives in a three-story house with a terrace and a neatly tended garden owned by Victor Bender, 39, left, who also has Kaposi's sarcoma. Bender, shown at the Gay Men's Health Crisis Center in Manhattan, where he works on a hotline, is now staying at his mother's house because of the constant activity of crisis-center volunteers taking care of Benegas. "They are doing as much as they can," he says, "but it does not look good."

Photo by Ken Sawchuck   Photo by Alon Reininger / Contact

PLATE 323. *Four images of the AIDS patient from* Newsday, *4 August 1985. Ithaca: Olin Library, Cornell University.*

PLATE 324. *The AIDS patient as melancholic from* Discover, *September 1986. Ithaca: Olin Library, Cornell University.*

munity. The image of the person living with AIDS as a melancholic is only marginally related to the fact that one of the more frequent syndromes recently associated with AIDS in the press is "AIDS dementia." In such images, it is not the "reality" of mental illness, such as AIDS dementia, which is being represented but rather the stigma of mental illness, a stigma implied through the visual association of the representation of the person living with AIDS with one of the most powerful of all stigmatizing diseases—mental illness. Thus the boundary between the "normal" and the hysterically feared "abnormal" is drawn.

For the person with AIDS, the association with the icon of the sufferer, with the figure of Job, has yet even further ramifications. In a powerful, autobiographical essay entitled "Bearing Witness," George Whitmore sees himself as a person whose body and psyche the touch of AIDS has transformed:

My body. I hadn't looked at it much.

Before I left for New Hampshire, at the Passover seder with my lover Michael's family, we took turns reading the Haggadah in booklets illustrated with line drawings. When we reached the page with the plagues God brought down on the Egyptians, there was a locust, there was a dead fish with X's for eyes, there was the outline of a man with dots all over him, signifying boils. I stared at the cartoon of the man with the boils. I knew Michael, sitting next to me, was thinking the same thing. My body was like that now. I'd had three lesions 12 months before. Now there were three dozen.

One day in New Hampshire, in the shower, I looked at my body. It was as if I'd never seen it before.

A transformation had taken place and it was written on my skin.[21]

The internalization of the stigma of the polluting touch with all of its biblical associations reaches even into the self-representation of the person with AIDS. The depression of the sufferer is to no little degree the result of the internalization of the stigma associated with society's act of "representing" the person with AIDS.

TOWARD A GEOGRAPHY OF PEOPLE LIVING WITH AIDS

One aspect of the iconography of AIDS that points to the complexity of the construction of the image of AIDS patients is the "geography" of the disease. It is clear that we need to locate the origin of a disease because its source, always distant from ourselves in the fantasy land of our fears, gives us assurance that we are not at fault, that we have been invaded from without, that we have been polluted by some external agent. In the late fifteenth century, syphilis was initially understood as resulting from the malevolent influence of the zodiac. However, it quickly became associated with another major occurrence of the 1490s, Columbus's voyages of discovery to the Americas. Whether or not syphilis was actually imported by Columbus's sailors from the New World is not important. Syphilis was understood as society's punishment for transgressing against God-given boundaries of human endeavor. Syphilis was the divine scourge that punished Europe for the collapse of the rigid feudal class system, the rise of capitalism, and the desire to find new worlds to feed this new economic system. So Sebastian Brant labels it at the very end of the fifteenth century in *The Ship of Fools*.[22] In the nineteenth century, in an age of colonialism and black slavery, a counterargument arose, placing the origin of

321

PLATE 325. *AIDS as an American biological weapon. A drawing by D. Agaeva, from* Pravda, *1 November 1986. Ithaca: Olin Library, Cornell University.*

For the Soviets it is clear where the geographic origin of the disease lies—the HIV virus was man-made by the biological warfare specialists at Fort Detrick, Maryland, in conjunction with the scientists at the CDC **[PLATE 325]**. In the the Soviet view, AIDS is an American biological weapon gone berserk and destroying its creator.[26] Their image of AIDS, drawn for *Pravda* by D. Agaeva, reflects the complexity of national images of the AIDS patient. His cartoon represents an American general paying for a test tube of AIDS virus supplied to him by a venal-looking scientist. The test tube, as we have seen, represents the "science" associated with AIDS, here the "science" of biological warfare rather than the science of syphilology. Swimming about in the test tube, representing the power of the AIDS virus, are a multitude of tiny swastikas; the dead, the victims of AIDS, appear in the cartoon as concentration camp victims, their bare feet echoing the death camp photographs of bodies stacked like cordwood with only their feet showing. This attempt to place the blame for AIDS on the United States worked only until the spring of 1987, when the Soviets, in the climate of *glasnost*, admitted that they too had indigenous cases of the disease. But during 1985 and 1986, the Soviets were following an argument in the Marxist–Leninist image of the United States as fascist, degenerate, and therefore sick. Indeed, the "orthodox" Marxist–Leninist view was that homosexuality was a pathological reflex of the late forms of capitalism that would vanish once the Soviet state was created. Thus AIDS was defined as a Western disease, a reflection of bourgeois government and society.

In the United States, we have labeled AIDS an "African" or "Haitian" disease.[27] Whatever the reality of the presumed origin of the disease, this is, of course, very much in line with the white American sense that blacks have a basically different relationship to disease because of their inherent difference. This was true if the disease was mental illness, when blacks were assumed for over a century to have a much higher rate of mental disease because of their inability to cope with civilization.[28] But it is the Western fantasy about black sexuality that lies at the heart of the matter. Blacks, within the Western discourse on race, are sexual degenerates. "This animalism, this innate character of the African, will demonstrate itself more and more as he is allowed the liberty of his sway of ancestral sexual impulses," wrote William Lee Howard in 1903.[29] Thus blacks became the icon of the syphilitic. The disease was endemic among the black population. "The very irregular life that was led by the modern negro and the fact that the great majority had syph-

syphilis in Africa and predating Columbus.[23] As the need to locate the origin of the disease shifted with time and circumstance, so did the presumed locus of the disease.

AIDS presents a similar story in the 1980s. For the French, at least in 1981, it was clear that AIDS was an American disease. With the rise of American cultural models and practices among the homosexual community (the French homosexual community even adopted the Anglicism "gai"), it was initially believed that the disease was the result of the excessive use of contaminated "poppers" imported from North America.[24] Even today, the popular icon of the disease in Europe is as one born, along with jeans and rock, in the USA. This is nowhere clearer than in the German reception of the disease. In recent title stories on AIDS in the German weekly news magazine *Der Spiegel* (such as on 9 February 1987), the central images are taken from the American political cartoonists, even though the essay purports to be about AIDS in the Federal Republic.[25] In 1987–88, with the rise of a xenophobic right-wing political movement in France that (again) advocates "France for the French," graffiti began to appear on walls in Paris and Marseilles linking the immigrants from Africa, especially black Africa, with AIDS.

ilis, or had had syphilis, or would have syphilis, went toward establishing a very poor resistance to disease."[30] However, the very opposite was also assumed (as with the relationship between Jews and syphilis)—that American blacks had a greater immunity against syphilis because of the "African" origin of the disease. This led to the horrors of the Tuskegee syphilis experiment, in which black patients infected with syphilis were observed, without any medical intervention, until their deaths.[31] Blacks must be kept separate from whites, for blacks are a potential source of infection:

> The belief that the African was capable of living as hygienically and morally as the Caucasian was the great mistake. . . . Physicians know that this false idea sets in action three of the most powerful enemies of mankind: insanity, turberculosis, and syphilis. There is every prospect of checking and reducing these diseases in the white race, if this race is socially—in every aspect of the term—quarantined from the African.[32]

The image of the corrupt sexuality of the black, of a black whose "licentiousness left its slimy trail of sometimes ineradicable disease upon his physical being,"[33] is tied to the image of sexually transmitted disease. The icon is displaced, within the discourse on AIDS, onto the image of the African and the origin of AIDS.

The irony, of course, is that American blacks were indeed at special risk for AIDS because of the nature of treatment for sickle-cell disease, through transfusions. It was the polluted blood supply that placed American blacks, at least those suffering from such genetically transmitted diseases, in the forefront of those who were at risk.[34] But they were not understood as being in the same category as were the hemophiliacs. Blacks were deemed to be at risk because of their perceived sexual difference, their sexual practices, their hypersexuality, as well as their sociopathic use of drugs. Black sexuality, associated with icons of sexually transmitted disease, became a category of marginalization, as it had in the past.[35] What is interesting is that in the 1980s, after white America was made aware of the intolerable state of blacks in this country through the civil rights movement in the 1960s and 1970s, one could no longer as easily localize the source of disease among American blacks, as had been done in the Tuskegee experiment. Rather, the source of pollution was seen in foreign blacks, in black Africans (specifically in Rwanda, Uganda, and Zaire) and Haitians, thus assuaging American "liberal" sensibilities although still locating the origin of the disease within the paradigm of Western racist ideology.

Part of the construction of the image of those living with AIDS in the United States does incorporate the idea of geography—which included the search for the "African" or "Haitian" connection. Indeed, the recent withdrawal of the label of "risk group" from Haitians followed a period of severe persecution, both direct and indirect, of Haitians in the United States. Being Haitian in New York City meant that you were understood as having AIDS. The irony is that it seems evident, given the most recent epidemiology of the disease in Haiti, that the disease, limited to the large urban areas on the island, was a result of contact betweeen HIV seropositive North American tourists and Haitian men, who passed the disease to their female sexual partners and children.[36] In the United States, Haiti, like black Africa, was viewed as one of the original sources of the disease, specifically because it was to be found in Haiti in a heterosexual community. Heterosexual transmission was labeled by the investigators as a more primitive (or, to use the good nineteenth-century term, atavistic) stage of the development of AIDS. It was understood to be unlike the pattern of infection in the United States, where it existed only among marginal groups (which would include blacks).

It was only in the "higher" cultures, such as the United States, that the disease was limited to such specific groups that were immediately and visually identifiable. This creation of the boundary between the infected, labeled and literally seen as different, and the healthy, rested on the need to see a clear boundary existing between the heterosexual, non-IV-drug-using, white community and those at risk. The search for the origin of the disease in sub-Saharan Africa placed the origin (and the nature) of the disease beyond the boundaries of the normal. Thus in 1985 it was assumed that the origin of the disease was to be found in the transmutation of an "AIDS-causing virus in baboons, chimps and green monkeys found in Central Africa, because epidemiologists suspect that the human AIDS epidemic originated in that part of the world."[37] The disease somehow spread from Africa where "some Africans caught a mutated monkey virus some 15 years ago. Visitors eventually brought it to Haiti and to the United States."[38] The seemingly effortless tracing of the ancestry of the disease was, of course, merely an attempt to localize it within definable boundaries, to contain the idea of the disease.

The sexual association between black women and apes seemed to reach across the boundaries between the human and the primate, in a manner strangely reminiscent of eighteenth-century comments on the degenerate nature of black sexuality. Thus in the following citations from *Science*, there is the assumption that there is a close relationship between the black woman and the ape:

> [A report] suggests that strains of the virus causing AIDS in Africa are more closely related to the African green monkey virus than are the strains causing AIDS in the United States. . . . Serum samples taken from prostitutes in Senegal were found to have been infected with the monkey virus itself, rather than the closely related AIDS virus.[39]

The implication is that the disease, as it manifests itself in the African, has a more primitive, an atavistic quality. And its source is—the prostitute, the black female. "The first case of AIDS arose among African prostitutes," wrote *Time*,[40] seeing the origin of the disease within the genitalia of the black female. Female sexuality, the sexuality that may even cross the bounds between the bestial and the human, is the source of the disease. And it is within the female population of this atavistic world that the disease perpetuates itself. *The Boston Globe* sees "urban prostitutes constituting a major reservoir of AIDS virus in such African capitals as Nairobi, Kigali and Kinshasa."[41] The fascination with the origin of AIDS in Africa is also the fascination with the sexual difference of the black. *The Washington Post* provides a formulation for this fascination: "Why has AIDS exclusively afflicted heterosexuals in Africa rather than homosexuals? The simplest answer is that homosexuality is rare in the countries affected."[42] Black heterosexuality is as deviant, because it implies an interspecies sexuality (sodomy in its technical sense), as male homosexuality. Here the border between the cultures, the boundary that isolates the ideal middle-class, heterosexual reader of the American mass media, is absolute. Only in primitive climes, such as Africa, with their atavistic diseases, is AIDS a danger to the heterosexual community. Here, in the biologically different West, it is a disease that places only the homosexual at risk. "Few experts expect that AIDS will penetrate the heterosexual population in the West as rapidly or as persuasively as it has in Africa," writes *Time*, with the implication that sexuality in the West is inherently different from that in Africa. Or, as a scientist commented for *The Boston Globe*: "You hear about a 50-50 sex ratio in Africa and you sort of get a feeling that it can happen anywhere. . . . It might go to that in a very sexually active population. But I don't think that's even remotely going to happen in this country generally."[43] The fantasy is that in "this country" sexuality is inherently different, that disease is limited to the homosexual population and its "foreign"

black surrogates. As Anthony Pinching so cogently observed concerning the Western fantasies of a perverted and diseased black population that served as the necessary "originator" of AIDS: "Rumours have circulated about the use of anal intercourse as a common means of birth control in Africa; this idea represents a carry-over from the initial perceptions of AIDS as something intrinsically to do with homosexual behavior. The widespread acceptance of these alternative explanations seems to indicate a remarkable ignorance about the countries in question; more disturbingly they have shown that many observers are unwilling to accept the obvious, if unpleasant, conclusion that AIDS, or rather HIV, is heterosexually transmitted."[44] For the West, African heterosexuality is shaped by images of deviancy. Thus in Robert E. Gould's 1988 essay on AIDS in *Cosmopolitan*, black sexuality is labeled as a form of heterosexual rape, a violence that spreads AIDS:

> It has been said that in Africa heterosexual intercourse is a documented mode of transmission of the AIDS virus, the implication being that it is just a matter of time before the disease will spread throughout the world in this manner. As with so many other medical reports, I would recommend this one be viewed with strong skepticism. Cultural differences must be taken into account. . . . The data I gathered concerning heterosexual intercourse in Africa show marked differences from the way it is usually practiced in the United States. . . . Many men in Africa take their women in a brutal way, so that some heterosexual activity regarded as normal by them would be closer to rape by our standards and therefore be likely to cause vaginal laceration through which the AIDS virus could gain entry into the bloodstream.[45]

It makes little difference whether black sexuality is labeled as *homosexual* or *heterosexual*. The black remains the source of disease, the cause of which is the deviant sexuality inherent in his/her "nature."

The irony is that the search for the origin of the AIDS virus, a search that pointed the way for the reshaping of the Western definition of the sexuality of the blacks as the antithesis of "civilized" sexuality, was based on a faulty assumption. As Masanori Hayami of the University of Tokyo (part of a team headed by Masashi Fukasawa) has shown, it is most probable that the AIDS virus did not "jump" from the green monkey to the black prostitute but rather that the virus could well have infected a common ancestor of humans and monkeys at a much earlier point in the evolutionary chain.[46] The genetic material for the virus from humans and from the green monkeys simply differs too much for the transmission to have been a recent one.

Although heterosexual transmission may be understood as one of the primary means of the spread of the disease, another irony is that one of the minor means for the transmission of the HIV viruses in black Africa has its roots in the imposition (and acceptance) of models of Western medicine. The status of Western medicine and its association with inoculation is so high that no medical treatment, even by indigenous medical practitioners, is complete without an injection.[47] Due to the prohibitive cost of needles and syringes, blood is passed from patient to patient as the needle is used and reused. It is not the fantastic, perverted nature of black sexuality that is at the core of the transmission of the disease in Africa but the results of a wholesale importation of a Western model of medicine without sensitivity to local circumstances.

The geography of AIDS in North America, that is, the drawing of the boundaries of risk, has had yet another dimension. AIDS is perceived as an urban disease, a disease of cities, which have traditionally harbored disease and degeneration.[48] It is the plague of cities after the biblical icon of Sodom and Gomorrah. Righteous Abraham, who dwells in a tent, is contrasted in Genesis with the sinful dwellers in the city. And when the West represents the sexuality of black Africa, it is within this model. Thus *Newsweek* states: "The outbreak [of HIV infection] [was blamed] on the lawlessness of the area that is something of a smuggler's entrepot. 'Kashenye was like Sodom and Gomorrah; . . . there were wild parties, orgies."[49] "In [some] African countries, AIDS mostly afflicts city dwellers. Sheer numbers of people may be one reason, but some African leaders also contend that traditional values erode in the cities. This, they say, has led to greater sexual freedom and the spread of AIDS."[50] The image of Africa becomes linked with the image of the immoral city, as had been the image of the American black. "Sexual morality," wrote Charles Bacon in 1903, "as understood among us is generally wanting. In the North negroes live mostly in cities, and are mostly congregated in a few wards, often in very close proximity to the brothel quarters."[51]

Thus arises the seemingly natural association among three quite distinct groups of those perceived as city dwellers: homosexuals, IV drug users, and blacks, either city-dwelling Africans or Haitians. For we know where corruption lives—in the city. And purity lives where we fantasize that nature (and therefore goodness) dominates: on the farm and in the small town. This Rousseauian icon of

the city has joined with the image of those living with AIDS to give us an image of them as black, drug-using, homosexual, and urban—a geography of difference that is now part of the American iconography of the AIDS patient.

For some American blacks in the mid-1980s, fleeing from the association of AIDS with "blackness," the "geographic" projection of the disease into the world of Africa was not distanced enough. Returning to the age-old association of Jews with sexually transmitted diseases and calling upon the deepest wellsprings of Western anti-Semitism (in "Islamic" guise), Steve Cokely, an assistant to Mayor Eugene Sawyer of Chicago, held a series of speeches from 1986 to 1988 before the black religious group the Nation of Islam, claiming that "the AIDS epidemic is a result of doctors, especially Jewish ones, who inject AIDS into blacks."[52] He further alleged that "Jewish doctors routinely inject black children with infectious diseases."[53] The image of the corrupt and corrupting Jew places the black in the position of the victim and reverses the image of the pathogenic black as the source of AIDS. The power of this projection stems from the fact that Cokely (and the Nation of Islam) sees the black as the "African," displaced by slavery into North America but an African still. Thus images of the black African as the source of AIDS would not have been understood as a projection onto a distanced and exotic people by the members of the Nation of Islam. Rather it would speak directly to their primary self-image as "Africans." And the Jew—in the Western tradition (and, indeed, in the contemporary Islamic view[54])—is the source of all danger, the antithesis of the "healthy." It is, of course, merely a further projection, here on the part of an American black, of the source of AIDS as residing beyond the control of those now labeled as the exemplary victim.

THE BORDERS OF THE IMAGE

Now, the evident question that remains is what would have happened if AIDS had appeared in a much different context. What if it had first been identified among IV drug users or among hemophiliacs? Among hemophiliacs, it would have been seen as an iatrogenic illness, not the fault of the patient but of the system. And there the group stigma would have been less. Among IV drug users, AIDS would still have been stigmatized, as a disease of a marginal group, but it would have been seen as an artifact of a sociopathic act associated with a specific class and race. And it would, therefore, be limited in its perceived locus. For in 1981, it was not the yuppies with their drug of choice, cocaine, who would have been infected but the blacks of Harlem and the South Bronx, mainlining heroin with shared needles. But these were not the groups that defined the illness.

What did happen is that these two groups inherited the stigmatization of the sexually transmitted disease patient: the IV drug users continued to be defined through this paradigm as dangerous sociopaths and the hemophiliacs as a marginalized, genetically disordered minority. This stigmatization became so widespread that it permeated categories of social organization, such as childhood, which would seem to be generally immune to such stigmatization. In the 1985 Queens School Board Case, two community school boards sued the City Board of Education in order to exclude a seven-year-old child, diagnosed as having AIDS, from the school system. (At the time the case was brought, there were about seventy-eight children under the age of twelve in New York City who were diagnosed as having AIDS, and fifty-two had already died.) The child in question had most probably contracted the disease *in utero*.

The attorney for the local school board, Robert Sullivan, observed, concerning this child, that "in many instances children who have AIDS are the children . . . of parents who are not as responsible as we would like them to be. . . . They may be the children of an IV drug user or a victim of sexual abuse." They are, in short, "not in the best family setting a child should be in . . . not a recommended family setting."[55] Even the dying child, the exemplary innocent within our pantheon of images of disease (think of the death of Dickens's Little Nell or Harriet Beecher Stowe's Little Eva) has become infected with the unclean image of the sexually transmitted disease patient, as was the case with the syphilitic infant (see Plates 318–19). Nowhere is this often subconscious pollution of the image of the child clearer than in the caption to an Associated Press photograph of the central figure in a parallel court case, Ryan White, whose attempts to enter the Kokomo, Indiana, school system led to a massive boycott by parents of his schoolmates afraid of the potential for infection. In the *Ithaca Journal* of 1 May 1986 a photograph of Ryan White, as the caption stated, showed him and "his sister Andrea" . . . [meeting] cast members of 'Cats' at a star-studded gala in New York Tuesday night to raise money for AIDS research. Ryan . . . is a homophiliac [*sic*] who contracted AIDS through a blood transfusion." The conflation of the hemophiliac and the homosexual in the picture caption is an extraordinarily simple one given our construction of the image of the individual living with AIDS. Working against this conflation, many images of the child living with AIDS show the child in the family context. Such a juxtaposition contrasts radically with the imposed isolation of the homosexual or IV drug user living with AIDS. The presence of the family serves to signal the "normality" of the child and the low risk of transmission, in spite of the child's radical stigmatization. The media wish to maintain society's image of the pure, dying child. But such an iconographic device is rarely sufficient to overcome the stigma of AIDS.

The irrational reaction to the child living with AIDS has had disastrous effects for children and family alike. The hysteria crescendoed in the much publicized case of the Ray family in Arcadia, a small town in southern Florida. On 24 August 1987, their three hemophiliac sons, aged 8, 9, and 10, were admitted by court order to the local elementary school. They had been barred from the school the previous year following the finding that they tested positive for the HIV virus. The local community quickly organized a boycott of the school. The family's home was burned down on August 28, within a week of the admission of their children to school. Little sense of compassion, only fear of infection, was registered in the community. And yet the children were not ill but only had the potential to become ill. The irony is that this event took place the week before the September 7 Labor Day weekend, a period during which much of the United States sits before the television watching the annual telethon for "Jerry's kids," children suffering from muscular dystrophy. For the power of this annual telethon has been the appearance of the impaired children as the object of the viewer's sympathy and concern. One can imagine some of the same individuals who burned the Ray house in Arcadia sitting in their homes a week later, sympathetically watching the Jerry Lewis telethon.

To understand the need for the continuation of this stigmatization after it has become evident that AIDS is not solely a sexually transmitted disease, it is important to note that there is a powerful secondary effect to the stigma. It clearly defines the boundaries of pollution, limiting the risk of pollution to the homosexual (and those other groups now stigmatized) and thus confined the fears the heterosexual community had about its vulnerability to the spread of sexually transmitted disease. But recently we have seen the appearance of the disease among heterosexuals. If the disease remains attrib-

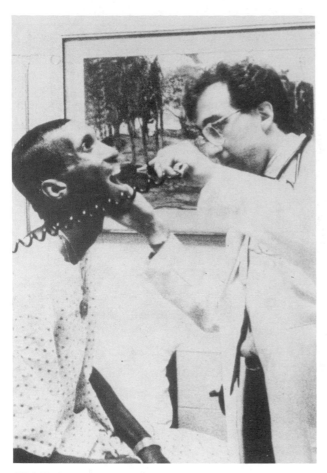

PLATE 326. *The AIDS paitent as black, male, and, by implication, gay, from* Newsweek, *21 July 1986). Ithaca: Olin Library, Cornell University.*

uted to individuals associated with categories traditionally perceived as being different, its locus remains strictly defined—it is "over there," not "over here." The more heterosexual transmission of AIDS becomes a "media" fact, the greater the need for heterosexuals to retain its image as being a disease of socially marginal groups.

There have been attempts in the media to make the public aware of the general risk run by all members of society, homosexual and heterosexual, of acquiring AIDS.[56] But the implied association of AIDS with homosexuality and sexually transmitted disease was more powerful than one can imagine. And this association was quite often captured in the image of the AIDS patient. In the *Newsweek* essay published in the summer of 1986, cited at the beginning of this chapter, there was the editorial intent stated to alter the image of individuals living with AIDS, in order to stress that all of the readers of this essay might be at risk. Accompanying this essay there are three images of people living with

AIDS. All of these are male and are represented in the traditional image of the male sufferer as isolated patient that dominates the early history of images of the syphilitic. And the first image, the first individual living with AIDS that the reader sees upon opening to this cover story, is not only male, but given the American mental geography of this disease in 1986, he is black **[PLATE 326]**. The black male homosexual (for the representation of any male with AIDS becomes a representative of the homosexual through the stigmatization associated with the disease) becomes the icon for the individual suffering from AIDS in a context in which the text of the story explicitly stresses the potential widespread heterosexual transmission of the disease. This contrast underlies the power of the essay but also points toward the power of the initial stereotyping of the individual living with AIDS as a marginal member of society.

By the spring of 1987, the public understanding of AIDS as a disease not limited to specific marginal groups had begun to grow. The statement of the Surgeon General of the United States, Everett Koop, in support of the general extension of information about condoms and the increased media attention to heterosexual transmission meant that by March 1987, a majority of those being tested in the public AIDS clinics in New York and San Francisco were heterosexuals. But even this awareness of the recategorization of AIDS from a disease of specific marginal groups to the "majority," to the heterosexual community, did not mitigate the need for strict boundaries to be maintained. In a cartoon of mid-March 1987, J. D. Crowe of the San Diego *Tribune* presents the source for the heterosexual transmission of AIDS in the form of a group of prostitutes represented as the threat of death **[PLATE 327]**. This image, so redolent of the icons of the female syphilitic present from the Enlightenment through the twentieth century, localizes the disease. This shift from the male sufferer to the female source of pollution clearly parallels the history of the iconography of syphilis. One can recall icons such as the famed Philippe Halsman photograph of Salvador Dali from 1944 with its evocation of death in the very presence of the woman's body **[PLATE 328]**. Here a new group is labeled as the source of disease, women, but not of course all women, only those who are beyond the social pale of respectability— only prostitutes are the source of disease. Even in the acknowledgment of the heterosexual transmission of the disease, the attempt is made to maintain clear and definite boundaries so as to limit the public's anxiety about their own potential risk.

PLATE 327. *The prostitute as the source of AIDS. A political cartoon by J. D. Crowe from the* San Diego Tribune, *March 14, 1987. Ithaca: Olin Library, Cornell University.*

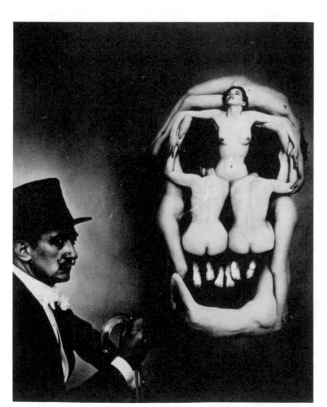

PLATE 328. *The face of death in the woman's body as represented by Salvador Dali,* In voluptate mors, *1944, photograph by Philippe Halsman. New York: Hastings Galleries.*

The study of the images, verbal or visual, popular or scientific, of the sufferer of a sexually transmitted or related disease reveals many of the often contradictory structures of our understanding of our own (as well as the Other's) sexuality. With society's attempt to categorize and limit AIDS still in its first decade, the construction of the image of the person living with AIDS can already be seen to be paralleling earlier models of sexuality that defined sexuality as a dangerous force out of human (i.e., rational) control and saw the genitalia as a weapon that could potentially be turned against the self. It is clear that the focus of Western fantasies at the turn of the twenty-first century, the present-day fin de siècle, are on this uncontrolled power of human sexuality. These fantasies that shape our understanding of our bodies revolve about the destructive aspects of the sexual. The control advocated for people with AIDS (including William Buckley's extraordinary post-Holocaust suggestion that they be tattooed) is, in fact, an extension of our need to see our own genitalia "under control." The icons that we use to represent the sexual, to "see" the genitalia, stem from our need constantly to construct and reconstruct the world. But we can only do so retrospectively. As the London psychoanalyst Joseph Sandler has noted:

> Essential to the representational world are the many organized schemata that the individual constructs during the course of his development and that form the background frame of reference to all current processes of perception, imagining, remembering, feeling and thinking. The representational world in all the different aspects of its organization is constantly influenced by stimuli arising from within and without the individual, and new schemata are constantly being created as new perceptual and conceptual solutions are being found. These schemata form the basis for future attempts at adaptation and problem solving, although they may in turn be modified by experience.[57]

This need to see the world retrospectively makes the reliance on extant models of representing sexuality a necessity in the thought-collective's comprehension of AIDS. A similar pattern has been traced in this volume in regard to the history of syphilis. Although the powerful iconography of the sexually transmitted disease patient haunts our contemporary Western understanding of AIDS, other images, such as those of depression, have begun to enter into the construction of the image of the person living with AIDS as it did the image of the syphilitic.

With the representation of AIDS, as with other images of sexuality, it is the translation of images of the inchoate into representations that seem, by their very stability, to mark the function and place of the individual in relationship to the ordered world in which he/she so deeply wishes to dwell. The icons that represent sexuality also reflect our attempts to control the sexual. From such images representing loss of control in the Other, we can begin to understand how such models of sexuality evoke the most deep-seated sense of the self's fragility. Necessary constraints are placed on our dealing with fantasies of the genitalia by our need to create a boundary for the nature of the sexual, our image of the Other as the container and transmitter of the sexual in all of its forms. But this act of projection, our need to distance and isolate those we designate as sexualized (and, therefore, dangerous) only reifies our sense of our own selves as sexual beings. This is especially destructive when we suddenly become the Other, when we are labeled as the sexualized being, the disease-bearing outsider. Those suffering from the very diseases about which such fantasies are spun are themselves not immune; they respond to the isolation and stigmatization that is the social boundary of their disease, not part of the disease itself. And one locus for Western society's fantasies about sexuality is the work of art, whether medical illustration, high art, or the illustrations in our popular weekly magazines. It is in this world of representations that we as a thought-collective temporarily banish our fear of sexuality, isolating it as surely as if we had placed it on a desert island. For the moment, we who produce and consume the icons of our civilization are freed from the fear of our own dissolution represented by our image of the sexualized body. And yet in this isolation, these icons remain alive and visible to all of us, proof that we (however we define ourselves) are still whole, healthy, in control of our sexuality, that we are not different, not diseased, not out of control.

Notes

NOTES FOR CHAPTER 1

[1] Walker Percy, *The Last Gentleman* (New York: Farrar, Straus and Giroux, 1966), p. 280.

[2] Milan Kundera, *Laughable Loves*, trans. Suzanne Rappaport (New York: Penguin, 1975), pp. 4–5.

[3] Daniel Rancour-Laferriere, *Signs of the Flesh: An Essay on the Evolution of Hominid Sexuality*. Approaches to Semiotics, 71 (Berlin: Mouton de Gruyter, 1985), p. 388. In this context see Roy F. Ellen, "Anatomical Classification and the Semiotics of the Body," in John Blacking, ed., *The Anthropology of the Body* (New York: Academic Press, 1977), pp. 343–73.

[4] See Earl E. Shelp, ed., *Sexuality and Medicine* (Norwell, MA: D. Reidel, 1987).

[5] I am using the term *icon* in the sense suggested by C. S. Peirce, *Collected Papers of Charles Sanders Peirce*, ed. Charles Hartshorne, Paul Weiss, and Arthur W. Burks, 8 vols. (Cambridge, MA: Harvard University Press, 1931–58), 2: 282. Peirce also argues that the properties of the sign that underlie its iconic nature are intrinsic, that is, whether or not the object actually exists (vol. 4, p. 447). Peirce argues, and I follow him in this, that therefore icons cannot represent particular individuals but only general classes of things (3: 434). Thus the very representation of a patient suffering from a disease, even if the patient and disease are "real," that is, existing separate from the icon in time and space, has iconic character, and it shall so be treated in the present volume. On the general background of these concepts of health and disease, see F. Kraupl Taylor, *The Concepts of Illness, Disease, and Morbus* (New York: Cambridge University Press, 1979), and D. Locker, *Symptoms and Illness: The Cognitive Organization of Disorder* (London: Tavistock, 1981).

[6] I refer here to the paradigm presented by Jacqueline Rose, *Sexuality in the Field of Vision* (London: Verso, 1986). See especially the first-rate essay on the visualization of sexuality by Arnold I. Davidson, "Sex and the Emergence of Sexuality," *Critical Inquiry* 14 (1987): 16–49 as well as Michel Feher, ed., *Fragments for a History of the Human Body*. 3 vols. (Cambridge: MIT Press, 1989).

[7] On the problems of writing a social history of sexuality rather than an ideological one, see Philippe Ariès and André Béjin, eds., *Western Sexuality: Practice and Precept in Past and Present Times* (New York: Basil Blackwell, 1985); David J. Pivar, *Purity Crusade: Sexual Morality and Social Control, 1868–1900* (Westport, CT: Greenwood Press, 1973); Charles Rosenberg, "Sexuality, Class, and Role in 19th-Century America," *American Quarterly* 25 (1973): 131–53 as well as his "The Bitter Fruit: Heredity, Disease, and Social Thought in Nineteenth-Century America," *Perspectives in American History* 7 (1974): 189–238; and Nancy Sahli, "Smashing: Women's Relationships Before the Fall," *Chrysalis* 8 (1979): 17–28.

[8] See Thomas McEvilley, "Who Told Thee Thou Was't Naked?" *Art Forum* 25 (1987): 102–8, and Judith Colton, "From Voltaire to Buffon: Further Observations on Nudity, Heroic and Otherwise," in Moshe Barasch and Lucy Freeman Sandler, eds., *Art the Ape of Nature: Studies in Honor of H. W. Janson* (New York: Harry N. Abrams, 1981), pp. 531–48. On the general theoretical background, see Robert Root-Bernstein, "Visual Thinking: The Art of Imagining Reality," *Transactions of the American Philosophical Society* 75 (1985): 50–67.

[9] Robert Graves, *Collected Poems* (London: Cassell, 1975), p. 189. Reprinted with permission of A. P. Watt Ltd. on behalf of the executors of the estate of Robert Graves.

[10] Havelock Ellis, *Studies in the Psychology of Sex*, vol. 4: Sexual Selection in Man (Philadelphia: F. A. Davis, 1920), pp. 152–85.

[11] The configuration of this argument is outlined by Anne Harrington, *Medicine, Mind, and the Double Brain* (Princeton, NJ: Princeton University Press, 1987).

[12] See Foucault's theoretical introduction that has been published as *The History of Sexuality. Volume 1: An Introduction*, trans. Robert Hurley (New York: Vintage, 1980), pp. 105, 114.

[13] Melanie Klein, "Early Analysis," *Love, Guilt, and Reparation, and Other Works 1921–1945* (London: Hogarth Press and the Institute of Psychoanalysis, 1975), p. 86.

[14] Compare the discussion in Allen S. Weiss, "An Eye for an I: On the Art of Fascination," *SubStance* 15 (1986): 87–95.

[15] Martha Vicinus, "Sexuality and Power," *Feminist Studies* 8 (1982): 136–37.

[16] See for example the work of Matthews M. Hamabata, "Ethnographic Boundaries: Culture, Class, and Sexuality in Tokyo," *Qualitative Sociology* 9 (1986): 354–71.

[17] See the best two studies of the relationship between sexual stereotyping and the actual shaping of political programs: Klaus Theweleit, *Male Fantasies*, trans. Stephan Conway, 2 vols. (Minneapolis: University of Minnesota Press, 1987), originally pub-

lished in 1977–78, and George L. Mosse, *Nationalism and Sexuality: Respectability and Abnormal Sexuality in Modern Europe* (New York: Howard Fertig, 1985).

[18] See the discussion of the function of our creation and internalization of the object in the introduction to my *Difference and Pathology: Stereotypes of Sexuality, Race, and Madness*, second edition (Ithaca: Cornell University Press, 1986), pp. 15–36.

[19] As an example of the pathologization of the ends of the spectrum, see Randy K. Hardman and David J. Gardner, "Sexual Anorexia: A Look at Inhibited Sexual Desire," *Journal of Sex Education and Therapy* 12 (1986): 55–59.

[20] On the idea of stigma as part of the historical process, see Howard M. Solomon, "Stigma and Western Culture: A Historical Approach," in S. C. Ainlay, G. Becker, and L. M. Coleman, eds., *The Dilemma of Difference: A Multidisciplinary View of Stigma* (New York: Plenum, 1986), pp. 59–76.

[21] Susan Sontag, *Illness as Metaphor* (New York: Farrar, Straus and Giroux, 1978), p. 43.

[22] Here I follow the direction outlined by Gayle Rubin in her comments recorded in Deidre English, Amber Hollibaugh, and Gayle Rubin, "Talking Sex: A Conversation on Sexuality and Feminism," *Socialist Review* 11 (1981): 43–62. Other such feminist positions are held by Ann Garry, "Pornography and Respect for Women," *Social Theory and Practice* 4 (1978): 395–421; and Paula Webster, "Pornography and Pleasure," *Heresies* 3 (1981): 48–51.

[23] See Peter Webb, "Erotic Art and Pornography," in Maurice Yaffé and Edward C. Nelson, eds., *The Influence of Pornography on Behaviour* (London: Academic Press, 1982).

[24] See the general discussion in Erving Goffman, *Gender Advertisements* (Cambridge, MA: Harvard University Press, 1979).

[25] See Leo Bersani, "Representation and Its Discontents," *Raritan* 1 (1981): 3–17; Annette Kuhn, *The Power of the Image: Essays on Representations and Sexuality* (London: Routledge, 1985).

[26] Marilyn Frye, *The Politics of Reality* (Trumansburg, NY: The Crossing Press, 1983), p. 136. Clearly the best known of such accusatory texts are Susan Brownmiller, *Against Our Will: Men, Women, and Rape* (New York: Simon and Schuster, 1975); Gloria Steinem, "Erotica and Pornography: A Clear and Present Difference," *Ms.* (November 1978); Susan Griffin, *Pornography and Silence: Culture's Revenge against Nature* (New York: Harper & Row, 1981); Laura Lederer, ed., *Take Back the Night: Women on Pornography* (New York: Morrow, 1980); and Andrea Dworkin, *Pornography: Men Possessing Women* (New York: Perigee Books, 1981).

[27] See David Fernbach, "Toward a Marxist Theory of Gay Liberation," *Socialist Revolution* 6 (1976): 29–41; Beatrice Faust, *Women, Sex, and Pornography* (New York: Macmillan, 1980); Lois Gould, "Porn for Women; Women for Porn," in her *Not Responsible for Personal Articles* (New York: Random House, 1978), pp. 126–30; as well as Claire D. Coles and Johanna M. Shamp, "Some Sexual, Personality, and Demographic Characteristics of Women Readers of Erotic Romances," *Archives of Sexual Behavior* 13 (1984): 187–209.

[28] See the discussion in Jay Martin, *Who Am I This Time? Uncovering the Fictive Personality* (New York: W. W. Norton, 1988), p. 53.

[29] See Ferrel Christensen, "Sexual Callousness Re-examined," *Journal of Communication* 36 (1986): 174–84; Nancy M. Henley, "Psychology and Gender," *Signs* 11 (1985): 101–19; Ilene Philipson, "The Repression of History and Gender: A Critical Perspective on the Feminist Sexuality Debate," *Signs* 10 (1984): 113–18; Maureen M. Killoran, "Sticks and Stones Can Break My Bones and Images Can Hurt Me: Feminists and the Pornography Debate," *International Journal of Women's Studies* 6 (1983): 443–56; Jerry Bergman, "The Influence of Pornography on Sexual

[30] Development," *Family Therapy* 9 (1982): 263–69.

[30] This is the view espoused by Susanne Kappeler, *The Pornography of Representation* (Minneapolis: University of Minnesota Press, 1986).

[31] Kenneth Yuen and William Ickes, " 'Prudes' and 'Pornophiles': Effects of Subject and Audience Attitudes on the Viewing and Rating of Pornographic Materials," *Journal of Social and Clinical Psychology* 2 (1984): 215–29.

[32] See Giuseppe Luigi Marini, *Il Gabinetto Segreto del Museo Nazionale di Napoli* (Turin: Ruggero Aprile, 1971), and Aline Rousselle, *Porneia: On Desire and the Body in Antiquity*, trans. Felicia Pheasant (New York: Basil Blackwell, 1988).

[33] A complex and well-reasoned case is made by Alan Soble, *Pornography: Marxism, Feminism and the Future of Sexuality* (New Haven, CT: Yale University Press, 1986), to which I am indebted. See also Murray S. Davis, *Smut: Erotic Reality/Obscene Ideology* (Chicago: The University of Chicago Press, 1983) and Walter Kendrick, *The Secret Museum: Pornography in Modern Culture* (New York: Viking, 1987).

[34] See in this context the discussion of the function of sexual images within a "folkloric" dimension by Thomas Hauschild, "Abwehrmagie und Geschlechtssymbolik im mittelmeerischen Volksglauben," *Baessler-Archiv* 28 (1980): 73–103.

[35] See Robert Young, "Sexual Difference," *The Oxford Literary Review* 8 (1986): 45–51.

[36] A counterreading of these models within feminist theory is offered by Jeri D. Wine, "Models of Human Functioning: A Feminist Perspective," *International Journal of Women's Studies* 8 (1985): 183–92. See also Regine Halter, "Widersprüchliche Erfahrungen mit dem männlichen Körper, auf den ein weiblicher Blick fallen soll," *Frauen und Film* 30 (1981): 45–51.

[37] Claude Lévi-Strauss, *The Savage Mind* (Chicago: The University of Chicago Press, 1966), p. 18.

[38] Niklas Luhmann's study is now available in English as *Love as Passion: The Codification of Intimacy*, trans. Jeremy Gaines and Doris L. Jones (Cambridge, MA: Harvard University Press, 1986).

[39] Ludwik Fleck, "To Look, to See, to Know" [1947], translated from the Polish in Robert S. Cohen and Thomas Schnelle, eds., *Cognition and Fact: Materials on Ludwik Fleck* (Dordrecht: D. Reidel, 1986), pp. 129–51.

[40] *Seeing the Insane* (New York: Brunner/Mazel, 1982); *Difference and Pathology*, second edition (Ithaca: Cornell University Press, 1986); *Disease and Representation* (Ithaca: Cornell University Press, 1988). On my work and its relationship to the history of "seeing," see Roy Porter, "Seeing the Past," *Past and Present* 118 (1988): 186–204.

[41] Hilary Putnam, *Reason, Truth and History* (Cambridge: Cambridge University Press, 1981), p. 185.

[42] See Owen Chadwick, *The Secularization of the European Mind in the Nineteenth Century* (Cambridge: Cambridge University Press, 1977).

[43] Carol A. Pollis, "Sensitive Drawings of Sexual Activity in Human Sexuality Textbooks: An Analysis of Communication and Bias," *Journal of Homosexuality* 13 (1986): 59–73.

[44] See the stimulating work of Anne Fausto-Sterling, *Myths of Gender: Biological Theories about Men and Women* (New York: Basic Books, 1985), and Emily Martin, *The Woman in the Body: A Cultural Analysis of Reproduction* (Boston: Beacon, 1987).

[45] Foucault, op. cit., 149.

[46] Bernadette J. Bucher, *Icon and Conquest: A Structural Analysis of the Illustrations of de Bry's 'Great Voyages'* (Chicago: University of Chicago Press, 1981), p. xiv.

[47] See Biddy Martin, "Feminism, Criticism and Foucault," *New German Critique* 27 (1982): 3–30. I am very grateful to my colleague Biddy Martin for having read this introduction and for having

provided me with a detailed critique of it.

[48] On the signification of touch, see E. Wyschograd, "Empathy and Sympathy as Tactile Encounters," *Journal of Medicine and Philosophy* 6 (1981): 25–43.

[49] The history of touch provides detailed documentation of cultural and personal fantasies about the senses and human perception. Much of the scholarly interest in the sense of touch during the past twenty years has, however, been in the biology of touch, rather than in its representation. Indeed, what should have been the major book on the social construction of touch, written by the anthropologist Ashley Montagu, seems, on its surface, to be more interested in describing the "real" physiology of touch with its importance for human development than the culture of touch [Ashley Montagu, *Touching: The Human Significance of the Skin* (New York: Columbia University Press, 1971)]. Writers as diverse as the anthropologist Desmond Morris and the historian of medicine Marielene Putscher, who otherwise write well on the cultural implications of touch, tend to return over and over again to the physiological "realities" for their understanding of the history of touch, as if these realities were unmediated by culture [Desmond Morris, *Intimate Behavior* (New York: Random House, 1971), and Marielene Putscher, ed., *Die fünf Sinne: Beiträge zu einer medizinischen Psychologie* (Munich: Heinz Moos, 1978)].

[50] On the nature of touch see the discussion in Vernon B. Mountcastle, ed., *Medical Physiology* (St. Louis: C. V. Mosby, 1968), 2: 1345–1675. On the cognitive approach to touch see William Schiff and Emerson Foulke, eds., *Tactual Perception: A Source Book* (Cambridge: Cambridge University Press, 1982).

[51] See Michel Serres, *Les cinq sens* (Paris: B. Grasset, 1985).

[52] Barbara Duden, *Geschichte unter der Haut: Ein Eisenacher Arzt und seine Patientinnen um 1730* (Stuttgart: Klett-Cotta, 1987).

[53] Richard Ellmann, *Yeats, The Man and the Masks* (New York: W. W. Norton, 1979), pp. 171–76.

[54] See Harry Berger, Jr., "Bodies and Texts," *Representations* 17 (1987): 144–66.

[55] See the argument of Rueben Fine, "The Forgotten Man: Understanding the Male Psyche," *Current Issues in Psychoanalytic Practice* 3 (1986): 1–368.

[56] Here I draw on the work of Jeffrey Weeks, *Sexuality and Its Discontents: Meanings, Myths and Modern Sexualities* (London and Boston: Routledge & Kegan Paul, 1985), and Gayle Rubin, "Thinking Sex: Notes for a Radical Theory of the Politics of Sexuality," in Carol S. Vance, ed., *Pleasure and Danger: Exploring Female Sexuality* (London and Boston: Routledge & Kegan Paul, 1984), pp. 267–319.

[57] See F. Gonzalez-Crussi, "On Male Genital Anatomy," in his *Notes of an Anatomist* (San Diego: Harcourt Brace Jovanovich, 1985), pp. 110–29.

[58] L. Zaphiropoulos, "Ethnocentricity and Psychoanalysis," *Contemporary Psychoanalysis* 23 (1987): 459.

NOTES FOR CHAPTER 2

[1] On the sources for this discussion of imagery, see Karl Künstle, ed., *Ikonographie der christlichen Kunst*, 2 vols. (Freiburg i. Br.: Herder, 1926–28); Engelbert Kirchbaum, ed., *Lexikon der christlichen Ikonographie*, 8 vols. (Rome: Herder, 1968–76); Gertrud Schiller, *Ikonographie der christlichen Kunst*, 3 vols. (Gütersloh: Gütersloher Verlagshaus G. Mohn, 1981–); Émile Mâle, *Religious Art in France, XIII Century: A Study of Medieval Iconography and Its Sources of Inspiration*, trans. Dora Nussey (London: J. M. Dent and Sons, Ltd., 1910); Guy de Tervarent, *Attributs et symboles dans l'art profane, 1450–1600: Dictionnaire d'un langage perdu*, Travaux d'Humanisme et Renaissance 29 (Geneva: Droz, 1958–59);

Fritz Saxl et al., *Verzeichnis astrologischer und mythologischer illustrierter Handschriften des lateinischen Mittelalters* (Heidelberg/London: C. Winter, 1915–66); and J. Danielou, *The Bible and the Liturgy* (Notre Dame, IN: University of Notre Dame Press, 1956).

[2] Here it is important to note that I am arguing quite counter to the generally accepted view that assumes the validity of the Christian expropriation of Jewish images. This view has been most forcefully presented in terms of the narrative nature of the "Old" Testament by Northrop Frye, *The Great Code: The Bible as Literature* (Toronto: Academic Press Canada, 1982). Compare Kenneth Burke, *The Rhetoric of Religion* (1961; rpt. Berkeley: University of California Press, 1970), and Frank Kermode, *The Genesis of Secrecy: On the Interpretation of Narrative* (Cambridge, MA: Harvard University Press, 1979). I am using the "King James" translation of the Bible in this study as it is the most generally available English translation. Where I differ in my reading of the Hebrew or Greek, it is noted.

[3] St. Augustine, *The First Catechetical Instruction*, trans. Joseph P. Christopher (Westminister, MD: Newman Bookshop, 1946).

[4] See Mieke Bal, "Sexuality, Sin, and Sorrow: The Emergence of Female Character (A Reading of Genesis 1–3)," in Susan Rubin Suleiman, ed., *The Female Body in Western Culture: Contemporary Perspectives* (Cambridge, MA: Harvard University Press, 1986), pp. 317–38.

[5] Ernst Müller, ed. and trans., *Der Sohar: Das heilige Buch der Kabbala* (Düsseldorf: Eugen Diedrich, 1982), pp. 140–42.

[6] All of the quotations are from Edith Hamilton and Huntington Cairns, eds., *The Collected Dialogues of Plato*, Bollingen Series 71 (New York: Pantheon, 1961), pp. 543–44. On the implications and background of Plato's views of sexuality, see Hartmut Buchner, *Eros und Sein: Erörterungen zu Platons Symposion* (Bonn: Bouvier, 1965).

[7] On the future history of this concept, see Joel Black, "The Aesthetics of Gender: Zeuxis Maidens and the Hermaphroditic Ideal," *New York Literary Forum* 8 (1981): 189–209.

[8] See here the discussion of "The Abominations of Leviticus" in Mary Douglas, *Purity and Danger: An Analysis of the Concepts of Pollution and Taboo* (London: Routledge & Kegan Paul, 1966), pp. 41–57.

[9] "No other story in the Old Testament has been so many times retold and represented in Christian art." James Snyder, "Jan van Eyck and Adam's Apple," *Art Bulletin* (December 1976): 511–15.

[10] Jacques Paul Minge, ed., *Patrologiae Cursus Completus. Series Latina.* 225 vols. (Paris: n.p., 1844–64), here 198, cap. xvii, 1070. Hereafter referred to as PL. See M.-Th. d'Alverny, "La femme dans la société occidentale," *Cahiers de civilisation médiévale X^e– XIIe siècle* 20 (1977): 105–29.

[11] In this context see Seymour Howard, "Fig Leaf, Pudica, Nudity and Other Revealing Concealments," *American Imago* 43 (1986): 289–302.

[12] Augustine: PL 44: col. 395; PL 44: cols. 407–8; Hugh of St. Victor, PL 176: cols. 314–18. On the general background see Norman Powell Williams, *The Ideas of the Fall and of Original Sin* (London: Longmans, Green & Co., 1927), and J. M. Evans, *Paradise Lost and the Genesis Tradition* (Oxford: Clarendon Press, 1968).

[13] Compare Cranach's image of the prostitute as discussed in M. J. Liebermann, "Ein 'Ungleiches Paar' Cranachs," *Acta Historiae Artium* 24 (1978): 233–36.

[14] On the image of Mary, see Marina Warner, *Alone of All Her Sex: The Myth and Cult of the Virgin Mary* (New York: Knopf, 1976).

[15] On the feminization of the image of Christ and its extension into the semantic sphere usually ascribed to Mary, see Caroline Walker Bynum, *Jesus as Mother: Studies in the Spirituality of the*

High Middle Ages (Berkeley: University of California Press, 1982).

[16] Justin Martyr, *Dialogue*, ch. 100 (in Jacques Paul Migne, ed., *Patrologiae Cursus Completus. Series Graeca.* 161 vols. [Paris: n.p., 1857–94], 6: 709–12). For a comprehensive treatment of the Mary–Eve comparison see Ernst Guldan, *Eva und Maria: Eine Antithese als Bildmotif* (Graz: Böhlau, 1966) as well as L. Cignelli, *Maria nuova Eva nella Patristica greca.* Collectio Assisiensis, vol. 3 (Assisi: Porziuncala, 1966). On the iconographic tradition that the Fall was a positive act, see Victor Y. Haines, "The Iconography of the *Felix Culpa*," *Floregium* 1 (1979): 151–85.

[17] Irenaeus, *Adversus haereses* V. xvi. 2; V. xvii. 4, 17, 19, cited in Adelin Rouseau, ed., *Contre les hérésies: Irenné de Lyon*, vol. 11 (Paris: Édition du Cerf, 1969).

[18] See Snyder, op. cit., on van Eyck. For further discussion of the image of the "Adam's apple," see Brooks W. Stoddard, "A Romanesque Master Carver at Airvault (Deux-Sèvres)," *Gesta* 20 (1981): 68.

[19] The best study of the visual tradition of Paradise is John Prest, *The Garden of Eden: The Botanic Garden and the Re-Creation of Paradise* (New Haven, CT: Yale University Press, 1981).

[20] See Jean-Paul Clébert, *Bestiaire fabuleux* (Paris: A. Michel, 1971), pp. 364–66.

[21] Harold E. Wethey, "Titian's Adam and Eve and Philip II," *Actas de XXIII Congreso Internacional de Historia del Arte. Granada 1973* (Granada: Universidad de Granada, Departmento de Historia de Arte, 1977), 2: 436–44.

[22] Roger Ward, "Some Late Drawings by Baccio Bandinelli," *Master Drawings* 19 (1981): 3–14.

[23] D. Bax, *Hieronymus Bosch and Lucas Cranach: Two Last Judgement Triptychs: Description and Exposition* (Amsterdam: North-Holland Publishing Company, 1983), pp. 42–46.

[24] On the feminization of the male in the iconographic tradition, see Leon Dewez and Albert Ierson, "La lactation de Saint-Bernard: Légende et iconographie," *Citeaux in de Nederlanden* 7 (1956): 165–89.

[25] See Bernadette J. Bucher, *La sauvage aux seins pendants* (Paris: Hermann, 1977), which is available in English as *Icon and Conquest: A Structural Analysis of the Illustrations of de Bry's 'Great Voyages'* (Chicago: University of Chicago Press, 1981). Bucher argues that the images in these texts reveal the "cultural and physical differences of other peoples." I will argue that these boundaries between the "civilized" and the "primitive" are means of creating a vocabulary of difference that will map the conflicted sense of sexuality present solely within Western culture. (See her essay, "The Savage European: A Structural Approach to European Iconography of the American Indian," *Studies in the Anthropology of Visual Communication* 2 [1975], p. 80.) A further source of iconography of the breast is to be found in Gustave-Jules Witkowski, *Les seins dans l'histoire* (Paris: A. Maloine, 1903) as well as his earlier *Tetoniana: Curiosités médicales, litteraires et artistiques sur les seins et l'allaitement* (Paris: A. Maloine, 1898).

[26] All references are to *The Works of Philo Judæus*, trans. C. D. Yonge (London: Bohn, 1854), 1: 1–53.

[27] A. Kent Hieatt, "Eve as Reason in a Tradition of Allegorical Interpretation of the Fall," *Journal of the Warburg and Courtauld Institutes* 43 (1980): 221–26.

[28] Herodotus, *History*, Book 4, chapters 171–94, trans. J. Enoch Powell (Oxford: Clarendon Press, 1949), 1: 341–48.

[29] P. Franke, "Bemerkungen zur frühchristlichen Noe-Ikonographie," *Revista di archeologia cristiana* 49 (1973): 174–82; J. Fink, *Noe der Gerechte in der frühchristlichen Kunst* (Münster-Köln; Böhlau, 1955); and J. P. Lewis, *A Study of the Interpretation of Noah and the Flood in Jewish and Christian Literature* (Leiden: E. J. Brill, 1968).

[30] Anthony Weir and James Jerman, *Images of Lust: Sexual Carvings on Medieval Churches* (London: B. T. Batsford, 1986), p. 98.

[31] Marcus Nathan Adler, trans., *The Itinerary of Benjamin of Tudela* (London: H. Frowde, 1907), p. 68.

[32] Al-Mas'udi, *Les prairies d'or*, trans. B. de Meynard (Paris: Imprimé nationale, 1861), 1: 162.

[33] For the general background, see Robert S. Liebert, *Michelangelo: A Psychoanalytic Study of His Life and Images* (New Haven: Yale University Press, 1983).

[34] On the history of the senses, see Michel Serres, *Les cinq sens* (Paris: Bernard Grasset, 1985).

[35] This section is an attempt to carry Leo Steinberg's argument further. I am using his argument, but, I hope, in a new context. See Leo Steinberg, *The Sexuality of Christ in Renaissance Art and in Modern Oblivion* (New York: Pantheon/October, 1983).

[36] *Summa theologiae* (Taurini: Marietti, 1952–76) III, q. 70, art. 3, resp. 1.

[37] Innocent III, *On the Misery of the Human Condition*, ed. Donald Roy Howard, trans. Margaret Mary Dietz (Indianapolis, IN: Bobbs-Merrill, 1969), p. 8.

[38] Phyllis Ackermann, "The Lady and the Unicorn," *Burlington Magazine* 66 (1935): 35–36; René Fédou, *Les hommes de loi lyonnais à la fin du Moyen Âge* (Paris: Les Belles-Lettres, 1964), pp. 347–49; *Le Musée de Cluny* (Paris: Édition des Musées nationaux, 1972), pp. 88–98.

[39] As early as the Cluny unicorn tapestries, the female comes to personify the senses, especially the sense of touch. This is true even in the earlier manuscript illustrations to Alain de Lille that Carl Nordenfalk, "Les cinq sens dans l'art du Moyen Âge," *Revue de l'Art* 34 (1976): 17–28, reproduces, in which it is clear that all of the other senses are represented by a gender-neutral figure (and the appropriate horse representing the sense), whereas the figure representing touch is clearly female.

[40] H. W. Janson, *Apes and Ape Lore in the Middle Ages and the Renaissance* (London: Warburg Institute, 1952).

[41] *Othello* 3: 3, 403.

[42] See Vern L. Bullough and James Brundage, eds., *Sexual Practices and the Medieval Church* (Buffalo, NY: Prometheus Books, 1982, for a discussion of Church law.

[43] See Marina Warner, op. cit., for more details of the representation of Mary.

[44] Artemidorus, *Oneiocritica*, trans. Robert J. White (Park Ridge, NJ: Noyes Press, 1975), I, 45, p. 38 ff.

[45] On the history of pain, see R. Janzen et al., eds., *Schmerz: Grundlagen, Pharmakologie, Therapie* (Stuttgart: Georg Thieme, 1972).

[46] For a detailed account of the representation of the senses, see Carl Nordenfalk, op. cit., note 39.

[47] Plato, op. cit., *Phaedo* 60b–c.

[48] *The Life of St. Teresa of Jesus*, trans. David Lewis (London: St. Anselm's Society, 1888), p. 233.

[49] Adapted from Lucretius, *Of the Nature of Things*, trans. W. E. Leonard (London: Dent, 1921), p. 61. See Ursula Schoenheim, "The Place of Touch in Epicurus and Lucretius" (M.A. thesis, Cornell, 1956).

[50] Alani de Insulis, *Opera omnia* (Patrologia Latina) (Paris: Sirou, 1855), cols. 522–23.

[51] See Lactantius, *Divinae institutiones* VI, 20, in his *Opera omnia* (Patralogia Latina) (Paris: Sirou, 1844), 1: col. 705.

[52] *Marsilio Ficino's Commentary on Plato's Symposium*, trans. Sears Reynolds Jayne, University of Missouri Studies, 19, no. 1 (Columbia, MO: University of Missouri, 1944), p. 130.

[53] Origen, *On First Principles*, trans. R. S. Buck (London: Routledge & Kegan Paul, 1955), IV, 3, 3, p. 293.

[54] Erasmus Desiderius, *Adages*, trans. Margaret Mann Philips (Cambridge: Cambridge University Press, 1967), pp. 335–36.

[55] Weir and Jerman, op. cit., p. 98.

[56] Thomas de Cantimpré, *Miraculorum et exemplorum memorabilum*

sui temporis libro duo (Duaci: Baltazris Belleri, 1605), pp. 305–6.

[57] See Heinrich Kornmann, *Opera curiosa I: Miracula vivorum* (1614; Frankfurt: Genschiana, 1694), pp. 128–29; Thomas Calvert, *The Blessed Jew of Marocco; or, A Blackmoor Made White Being a Demonstration of the True Messia out of the Law and Prophets by Rabbi Samuel* (York: Thomas Broad, 1649), pp. 20–21.

[58] On Franco de Piacenza, see Léon Poliakov, *The History of Anti-Semitism*, 3 vols., trans. Richard Howard (New York: Vanguard Press, 1965–75), 1: 143n.

[59] Howard Hibbard, *Caravaggio* (New York: Harper & Row, 1983), pp. 167–70.

[60] The only comprehensive discussion of the history of the "noli me tangere" theme in Western art is to be found in Moshe Barasch's study *Giotto and the Language of Gesture* (London: Cambridge University Press, 1987), pp. 139–82. See also Cornelia den Wildenberg-DeKroon, *Das Weltleben und die Bekehrung der Maria Magdalena im deutschen religiösen Drama und in der bildenden Kunst des Mittelalters* (Amsterdam: Rodopi, 1979) for a less detailed, comparative study. Edmund Leach's "Late Medieval Representations of Saint Mary Magdalene," *The Psychoanalytic Review* 75 (1988): 95–110, provides a detailed structuralist reading of a sixteenth-century altarpiece.

[61] Cited in Barasch, op. cit., p. 171.

[62] Amy Golahny, "Rembrandt's Early Bathsheba: The Raphael Connection," *Art Bulletin* 65 (1983): 671–75.

[63] Deborah Strom, "A New Chronology for Donatello's Wooden Sculpture," *Pantheon* 38 (September 1980): 239–48.

[64] Hartmut Krohm and Eike Oellermann, "Der ehemalige Münnerstädter Magdalenaltar von Tilmann Riemenschneider und seine Geschichte—Forschungsergebnisse zur monochromen Oberflächengestalt," *Zeitschrift des deutschen Vereins für Kunstwissenschaft* 34 (1980): 16–99.

[65] See Jean Devisse and Michel Mollat, *The Image of the Black in Western Art*, vol. 2, part 2: *Africans in the Christian Ordinance of the World*, trans. William Granger Ryan (New York: William Morrow, 1979) p. 44.

NOTES FOR CHAPTER 3

[1] On the history of medical illustration, see Robert Herrlinger and Marilene Putscher, *Geschichte der medizinischen Abbildung*, 2 vols. (Munich: Moos, 1967–72); John L. Thornton and Carole Reeves, *Medical Book Illustration: A Short History* (Cambridge/New York: The Oleander Press, 1983).

[2] On the question of medical authority in the sixteenth century, see C. B. Schmitt, "Aristotle among the Physicians," in A. Wear, R. K. French, and I. M. Lonie, eds., *The Medical Renaissance of the Sixteenth Century* (Cambridge: Cambridge University Press, 1985), pp. 1–15. On the knowledge of sexuality, see Thomas G. Benedek, "Beliefs about Human Sexual Function in the Middle Ages and Renaissance," in Douglas Radcliff-Umstead, ed., *Human Sexuality in the Middle Ages and Renaissance* (Pittsburgh: University of Pittsburgh Press, 1978), pp. 97–119.

[3] See the discussion in Leonard Barkan, "Elementated Man: Studies in the Metaphor of the Human Body" (Diss., Yale, 1971).

[4] See John Scarborough, "The Classical Background of the Vesalian Revolution," *Episteme* 2 (1968): 200–18, as well as William Brockbank, "Old Anatomical Theatres and What Took Place Therein," *Medical History* 12 (1968): 371–84.

[5] Michel Foucault, "The Order of Discourse," in Robert Young, ed., *Untying the Text: A Post-Structuralist Reader* (Boston and London: Routledge & Kegan Paul, 1981), pp. 48–78.

[6] On the images to be found in Vesalius, see M. H. Spielman, *The Iconography of Andreas Vesalius (André Vésal), Anatomist and Physician 1514–1564*. Wellcome Research Studies in Medical History 3 (London: John Bale, Sons & Danielsson, Ltd., 1925). On the tradition of the teaching atlas, see K. Bryn Thomas, "The Great Anatomical Atlases," *Proceedings of the Royal Society of Medicine* 67 (1974): 13–22.

[7] See F. N. L. Poynter, "Anatomie in England im 16. und 17. Jahrhundert," in Robert Herrlinger and Fridolf Kudlien, eds., *Frühe Anatomie: Eine Anthologie* (Stuttgart: Wissenschaftliche Verlagsgesellschaft, 1967), p. 202.

[8] See the discussion in Karl Sudhoff, *Tradition und Naturbeobachtung in den Illustrationen medizinischer Handschriften und Frühdrucke vornehmlich des 15. Jahrhunderts* (Leipzig: Johann Ambrosius Barth, 1907), pp. 41–43. On the background, see George W. Corner, *Anatomical Texts of the Earlier Middle Ages: A Study in the Transmission of Culture* (Washington: Carnegie Institution, 1927); Gernot Rath, "Pre-Vesalian Anatomy in the Light of Modern Research," *Bulletin of the History of Medicine* 35 (1961): 142–49; Gerhard Baader, "Zur Anatomie in Paris im 13. und 14. Jahrhundert," *Medizin-Historisches Journal* 3-4 (1968–69): 40–53.

[9] See the discussion in Peter Murray Jones, *Medieval Medical Miniatures* (London: The British Library, 1984), p. 39. See also Ynez Viole O'Neill, "The Fünfbilderserie Reconsidered," *Bulletin of the History of Medicine* 43 (1969): 236–45. A good bibliographic source for the history of medical illustration remains the catalogue prepared for the 1911 meeting of the German Obstetrical Society, *Ausstellung von Original-Werken zur Geschichte der medizinischen Abbildung: Aus der Sammlung von Gustav Klein in München* (Munich: Karl Kuhn, 1911).

[10] It is therefore not surprising that the literature on the anatomy of women has continued to be a separate category, even though the focus on female anatomy misrepresents the complex professional, self-, and counterdefinitions of the totality of human sexuality. This is as true in the histories of gynecology as well as in the more general histories of sexuality. See Gabriel Peillon, *Étude historique sur les organes génitaux de la femme: La fécundation et l'embryologénie humaines depuis les temps les plus reculés jusqu' à la Renaissance* (Paris: O. Berthier, 1891); Robert Müllerheim, *Die Wochenstube in der Kunst* (Stuttgart: Ferdinand Enke, 1904); Gustav Klein, "Geburtshilfliche und gynälogisch-anatomische Abbildungen des 15. und 16. Jahrhunderts," *Zentralblatt für Gynäkologie* 29 (1905): 845–47; E. Ingerslev, "Beiträge zur Lehre von dem Geburtsmechanismus: Eine obstetricische Studie," *Archiv für Geschichte der Medizin* 2 (1908): pp. 141–88; Douglas E. Cannell, "History of Obstetrics," in Elise Fitzpatrick, ed., *Maternity Nursing* (Philadelphia: Lippincott, 1971), 594–609; Harold Speert, *Iconographia Gyniatrica: A Pictorial History of Gynecology and Obstetrics* (Philadelphia: F. A. Davis, 1973); Stephen Kern, *Anatomy and Destiny: A Cultural History of the Human Body* (Indianapolis: Bobbs-Merrill, 1975); Jack R. Robertson, "History of Gynecological Urology," in his *Genitourinary Problems in Women* (Springfield, IL: Charles C. Thomas, 1978), pp. 6–13; Edward Shorter, *A History of Women's Bodies* (New York: Basic Books, 1982); Philippe Perrot, *Le travail des apparences ou les transformations du corps féminin XVIIIᵉ–XIXᵉ siècle* (Paris: Bernard Grasset, 1985); Susan Rubin Suleiman, ed., *The Female Body in Western Culture: Contemporary Perspectives* (Cambridge, MA: Harvard University Press, 1986).

[11] On Galen and anatomy, see Fridolf Kudlien, "Antike Anatomie und menschlicher Leichnam," *Hermes* 97–98 (1969–70): 78–94, and Anthony Preus, "Galen's Criticisms of Aristotle's Conception Theory," *Journal of the History of Biology* 10 (1977): 65–85.

[12] See Angus McLaren, *Reproductive Rituals: The Perception of Fertility in England from the Sixteenth Century to the Nineteenth Century* (London: Methuen, 1984).

[13] See M. Anthony Hewson, *Giles of Rome and the Medieval Theory*

of Conception: A Study of De formatione corporis humani in utero (London: The Athlone Press, 1975). See also Erna Lesky, *Die Zeugungs- und Vererbungslehre der Antike und ihre Nachwirkung* (Wiesbaden: Steiner, 1950), and Helen Rodnite Lemay, "Human Sexuality in Twelfth through Fifteenth Century Scientific Writings," in Vern Bullough and James Brundage, eds., *Sexual Practices and the Medieval Church* (Buffalo: Prometheus, 1980), pp. 187–205.

[14] Eberhard Hommel, "Zur Geschichte der Anatomie im alten Orient," *Archiv für Geschichte der Medizin* 11 (1919): 177–82.

[15] See Victor Tarrasch, *Die Anatomie des Richardus* (Diss., Berlin, 1898), pp. 47–48.

[16] See Thomas Laqueur, "Orgasm, Generation, and the Politics of Reproductive Biology," *Representations* 14 (1986): 1–41.

[17] Galen, *On the Usefulness of the Parts of the Body*, ed. and trans. Margaret May. 2 vols. (Ithaca, NY: Cornell University Press, 1968), 2: 628–29.

[18] Cited in Mary Frances Wack, "The Measure of Pleasure: Peter of Spain on Men, Women, and Lovesickness," *Viator* 17 (1986): 191.

[19] Bernard de Gordon, *Practica dicta Lilium medicine* (Lyons, 1574), chapter 20.

[20] Robert Herrlinger and Edith Feiner, "Why Did Vesalius Not Discover the Fallopian Tubes?" *Medical History* 8 (1964): 335–41.

[21] Wolfgang Gerlach, "Das Problem des 'weiblichen Samens' in der antiken und mittelalterlichen Medizin," *Sudhoffs Archiv* 30 (1977): 927–57.

[22] M. Saunders and C. D. O'Malley, *The Illustrations from the Works of Andreas Vesalius of Brussels* (Cleveland: World, 1950), p. 7.

[23] Kent R. Weeks, "The Anatomical Knowledge of the Ancient Egyptians and the Representation of the Human Figure in Egyptian Art" (Diss., Yale, 1970), p. 67. On the Jewish version of the analogy, see I. M. Lewinger, "The Structure of the Female Reproductive System in the Human and in Cattle (an Explanation of the Mishnah Niddah 2/5)," *Koroth* 4 (1968): lxxxviii (English summary). See also T. S. Chelvakumaran, "The Growth of Anatomy: A Historical Note," *Indian Journal of the History of Medicine* 11 (1966): 19–28.

[24] Jacopo Berengario da Carpi, *A Short Introduction to Anatomy (Isagogae breves)*, trans. L. R. Lind (Chicago: The University of Chicago Press, 1959), p. 80.

[25] On the iconography of blood, see Friedrich Leonhardt, "Zur Ikonographie der Blutschau," *Medizinhistorisches Journal* 17 (1982): 63–77.

[26] The most recent and detailed study is Robert Reisert, *Der siebenkammerige Uterus: Studien zur mittelalterlichen Wirkungsgeschichte und Entfaltung eines embryologischen Gebärmuttermodells.* Würzburger medizinhistorische Forschungen, 39 (Pattensen: Horst Wellm, 1986). See also Fridolf Kudlien, "The Seven Cells of the Uterus: The Doctrine and Its Roots," *Bulletin of the History of Medicine* 39 (1965): 415–23. In general, see Peter-Wilhelm Radtke, *Die geschichtliche Entwicklung der anatomischen Kenntnisse der weiblichen Geschlechtsorgans von den Anfängen bis zu Vesal* (Diss., Kiel, 1968). See also Ian Maclean, *The Renaissance Notion of Woman* (Cambridge: Cambridge University Press, 1980).

[27] Baldasar Heseler, *Andreas Vesalius' First Public Anatomy at Bologna 1540: An Eyewitness Report*, ed. and trans. Ruben Eriksson (Uppsala: Almqvist & Wiksells [1959]), p. 183.

[28] See Bernard Knight, *Discovering the Human Body: How Pioneers of Medicine Solved the Mysteries of the Body's Structure and Function* (New York: Lippincott & Crowell, 1980), p. 133.

[29] Baldasar Heseler, op. cit., p. 181.

[30] Jacopo Berengario da Carpi, op. cit., p. 72.

[31] Charles Singer, *The Evolution of Anatomy: A Short History of Anatomical and Physiological Discovery to Harvey* (New York: Alfred A. Knopf, 1926), p. 19, for a reconstructed diagram of the mammalian urogenital system according to Aristotle.

[32] On the visual representation of childbirth, see Volker Lehmann, *Die Geburt in der Kunst: Geburtshilfliche Motive in der darstellenden Kunst in Europa von der Antike bis zur Gegenwart* (Braunschweig: Braunschweiger Verlagsanstalt, 1978).

[33] See Franz Saxl, "A Spiritual Encyclopedia of the Later Middle Ages," *Journal of the Warburg Institute* 5 (1942): 82–142.

[34] See Bery Rowland's edition and translation of the *Medieval Woman's Guide to Health: The First English Gynecological Handbook* (Kent, OH: Kent State University Press, 1981).

[35] See Giorgio Lise, *L'incisione erotica del rinascimento* (Milan: Carlo Emilio Bestetti, 1975), for the entire series as well as the accompanying texts.

[36] See Andrew Samuels, "The Image of the Parents in Bed," *Journal of Analytic Psychology* 27 (1987): 323–39.

[37] The most extensive study of this topic remains G. Wolf-Heidegger and Anna Marie Cetto, *Die anatomische Sektion in bildlicher Darstellung* (Basel: S. Karger, 1967).

[38] On the complex relationship between perspective and sexuality in the Renaissance, see the brilliant essay by Donald Keith Hedrick, "The Ideology of Ornament: Alberti and the Erotics of Renaissance Urban Design," *Word and Image* 3 (1987): 111–37.

[39] Cited by C. D. O'Malley, *Andreas Vesalius of Brussels 1514–1564* (Berkeley: University of California Press, 1964), p. 143; from the *Fabrica* (1543), p. 376.

[40] On the nature of the serpent in the Garden, see A. Kent Hieatt, "Hans Baldung Grien's Ottawa *Eve* and Its Context," *Art Bulletin* 65 (1983): 290–304.

[41] See Gernot Rath, "Charles Estienne, Zeitgenosse und Konkurrent Vesals," in Robert Herrlinger and Fridolf Kudlien, eds., *Frühe Anatomie: Eine Anthologie*, op. cit., pp. 143–58. On other contemporary refunctioning of Vesalius's images, see M. D. Grmek, "Vidius et les illustrations anatomiques et chirurgicales de la Renaissance," *Sciences de la Renaissance, VIIIe Congrès international de Tours* (Paris: J. Vrin, 1973), pp. 176–85; W. S. C. Copeman, "The Evolution of Anatomy and Surgery under the Tudors," *Annals of the Royal College of Surgeons of England* 32 (1964): 1–21.

[42] See Martin Kemp, "A Drawing for the *Fabrica* and Some Thoughts upon the Vesalius Muscle-Men," *Medical History* 14 (1970): 277–88.

[43] On the parallels between "high" art and the anatomies, see Leo Steinberg's "The Line of Fate in Michelangelo's Painting," *Critical Inquiry* 6 (1980): 411–54, in which he discusses the self-representation of the artist in the face of the flayed skin held by St. Bartholomew in the *Last Judgement*. This is, of course, a standard means of presenting the unseen in the anatomical figures of the Renaissance, as in the 1556 anatomy of Juan Valverde di Hamusco. See A. W. Meyer and Sheldon K. Wirt, "The Amuscan Illustrations," *Bulletin of the History of Medicine* 14 (1943): 667–87 (on Valverde).

[44] The best introduction to the problems associated with the historiography of syphilis remains Ludwik Fleck, *Genesis and Development of a Scientific Fact*, trans. Fred Bradley and Thasseus J. Trenn (Chicago: The University of Chicago Press, 1979), pp. 1–145. On the general history of syphilis, see J. K. Proksch, *Die Geschichte der venerischen Krankheit.* 2 vols. (Bonn: Peter Hannstein, 1895), as well as Iwan Bloch, *Der Ursprung der Syphilis*, 2 vols. (Jena: Gustav Fischer, 1901–11). Proksch supports the "Unitarian" thesis; Bloch supports the "Columbian" thesis. Both summarize the extensive sixteenth-century literature on the subject as well.

[45] This may well have been an allegorical reading of the sexual

origin of the disease. For in a Dutch pamphlet printed in 1494, Paulus van Middelburg, a Dutch physician who worked mainly in Italy, noted explicitly that the disease was of sexual origin. See Karl Sudhoff, *Aus der Frühgeschichte der Syphilis* (Leipzig: J. A. Barth, 1912), pp. 159–61.

[46] Benedictus Rinius, "De morbo gallico, tractatus," in Aloysius Lusinus, ed., *De morbo gallico omnia quae extant . . .*, 2 vols. (Venice: Zilettus, 1566–67), 2: 17. Translations from Fleck, op. cit., p. 3.

[47] Antonius Musa Brassavola, "De morbo gallico, tractatus," in Lusinus, op. cit., 2: 672.

[48] Translation from Jacques de Béthencourt, *Nova poenitentialis quadragesima* (Paris, 1527), from Ralph H. Major, ed., *Classic Descriptions of Disease* (Springfield, IL: Charles C. Thomas, 1932), p. 64.

[49] There were some, such as Paracelsus, who rejected the association between the appearance of syphilis and the discovery of the New World as a means of rejecting the parallel between the cure found only in the New World, Guajac wood, and the origin of the disease in that selfsame world. He dated the epidemic to between 1470 and 1480, and faults the zodiac, the placement of Venus, and the "luxuria" that further the epidemic. His cure is the mastery of sexual desire. His association of this excess with the nobility, in the light of a rising middle-class identification of the noble as the corrupt, links control, a "middle-class" virtue in the sixteenth century, with the overcoming of disease. On the general background of this argument, see Walter Pagel, *Paracelsus: An Introduction to Philosophical Medicine in the Era of the Renaissance* (Basel: Karger, 1982), p. 24.

[50] Erwin Panofsky, "Homage to Fracastoro in a Germano-Flemish Composition of About 1590," *Nederlands Kunsthistorisch Jaarboek* 12 (1961): 1–33. On the more general problem of disease and art in the Renaissance, see Millard Meiss, *Painting in Florence and Siena after the Black Death* (Princeton: Princeton University Press, 1951).

[51] On the iconographic significance of the scorpion as a sign of perverse sexuality, see Luigi Aurigemma, *Le signe zodiacal du scorpion dans les traditions occidentales de l'antiquité gréco-latine à la Renaissance* (Paris: Mouton, 1976), pp. 57–61.

[52] Karl Sudhoff, *Zehn Syphilis-Drucke aus den Jahren 1495–1498* (Milan: R. Lier, 1924), p. xxii.

[53] See Elaine Pagels, *Adam, Eve and the Serpent* (New York: Random House, 1988).

[54] Ibid., p. 71.

[55] On these interlocked themes, see Aldred Scott Warthin, *The Physician of the Dance of Death* (New York: Paul Hoeber, 1931) and Jean Wirth, *La jeune fille et la mort: Recherches sur les thèmes macabres dans l'art germanique de la Renaissance*. Hautes Études Médiévales et Modernes, 36 (Geneva: Droz, 1979).

[56] M. J. Leibmann, "Ein 'ungleiches Paar' Cranachs," *Acta Historiae Artium* 24 (1978): 233–36.

[57] See Peter M. Daly, ed., *Andreas Alciatus* (Toronto: University of Toronto Press, 1985), for a full documentation of all of his emblems.

[58] John Dryden, trans., *The Works of Virgil* (Philadelphia: Claxton, Remsen and Haffelfinger, 1869), p. 117.

[59] D. Bax, *Hieronymus Bosch and Lucas Cranach: Two Last Judgement Triptychs—Description and Exposition* (Amsterdam: North-Holland Publishing Company, 1983), pp. 246–77. On the tradition of seeing leprosy as a sexually transmitted disease, see Saul N. Brody, *The Disease of the Soul: Leprosy in Medieval Literature* (Ithaca, NY: Cornell University Press, 1974).

[60] Ulrich von Hutten, *Über die Heilkraft des Guaiacum und die Franzosenseuche*, trans. Heinrich Oppenheimer (Berlin: August Hirschwald, 1902), p. 4. See J. W. van der Valk, *Bijdrage tot de kennis van de geschiednis der syphilis in ons land* (Amsterdam: Scheltema and Holkema, 1910), p. 17.

[61] On the general association of disease, heresy, and the Jews, see R. I. Moore, *The Formation of a Persecuting Society* (Oxford: Blackwell, 1986).

[62] On the Jews and leprosy, see Léon Poliakov, *The History of Anti-Semitism*, trans. Richard Howard (New York: Vanguard, 1965), 1: 9, 104.

[63] Theophrast von Hohenheim, gen. Paracelsus, *Sämtliche Werke*, ed. Karl Sudhoff. 21 vols. (Munich: Otto Wilhelm Barth, 1923), 7: 14–15. On the general background of this argument, see Walter Pagel, *Paracelsus: An Introduction*, op. cit., pp. 138–39.

[64] Voltaire, *Philosophical Dictionary*, 10 vols. (E. R. DuMont: Paris, 1901), 7: 114.

[65] Reproduced in the *Archiv für die Geschichte der Medizin* 1 (1907), Plate 8. On the general background of this image, see Stanley W. Jackson, *Melancholia and Depression from Hippocratic Times to Modern Times* (New Haven: Yale University Press, 1986), pp. 352–72.

[66] See Moshe Barasch, *Gestures of Despair in Medieval and Early Renaissance Art* (New York: New York University Press, 1976).

[67] Giovanni de Vigo, "The Fifth Boke: Of the French Pockes," in B. Traheron, trans., *The Most Excellent Works of Chirurgery* (London: Edwarde Whytchurche, 1543), fol. clx^r.

[68] *As You Like It*, Act 2, Scene 7, ll. 64–69.

[69] Bartholomeus Montagnana, "De morbo gallico, consilium," in Lusinus, op. cit., 2: 3.

[70] Hildegard of Bingen, *Causae et curae deutsch*, ed. and trans. Heinrich Schipperges (Salzburg: O. Müller, 1957).

[71] Bernardus Tomitanus, "De morbo gallico, libri duo," in Lusinus, op. cit., 2: 66.

[72] Mary Frances Wack, "The Measure of Pleasure," op. cit., pp. 173–96. See also the background in Denis de Rougemont, *Love in the Western World*, trans. Montgomery Belgion (New York: Harper & Row, 1956).

[73] Salvatore de Renzi, *Collectio salernitana*. 5 vols. (Naples: Filiatre-Sebezio, 1859), 5: 299–300.

[74] Avicenna, *Liber canonis* (Venice 1507, rpt., Hildesheim: Olms, 1964), bk. 3., fen. 1, tract 4, cap. 25.

NOTES FOR CHAPTER 4

[1] See Edward C. Streeter, "The Role of Certain Florentines in the History of Anatomy, Artistic and Practical," *The Johns Hopkins Hospital Bulletin* 27 (1916): 113–18; Charles Singer, "Notes on Renaissance Artists and Practical Anatomy," *Journal of the History of Medicine* 5 (1950): 156–62; A. Flocon, "Les artistes du XVIe siècle et la fabrique du corps humain," *Sciences de la Renaissance, VIIIe Congrès international de Tours* (Paris: J. Vrin, 1973), pp. 159–73.

[2] I will use the contemporary terms *gay* and *homosexual* to describe the internalized response as well as the social prejudice concerning same-sex erotic activity. Although there are certainly differences between the perceptions of same-sex eroticism in the Renaissance and contemporary ones, the opprobrium associated with the term *sodomite* would slant the rhetoric of my presentation. On the general background, see Margaret W. Ferguson et al., eds., *Rewriting the Renaissance: The Discourse of Sexual Difference in Early Modern Europe* (Chicago: The University of Chicago Press, 1986).

[3] There are numerous biographies of Leonardo that document this accusation. I rely here on the discussion of Giuseppina Fumagalli, *Eros di Leonardo* (Milano: Garzanti, 1952). Her view, stated against Freud's view of Leonardo, is used since she has taken the diametrically opposed position to the present analysis

concerning the interpretation of the anatomical drawings. Her discussion of this matter as well as the anatomical drawings are to be found on pp. 98–126. On the complex question of Freud's reading of Leonardo's image of sexuality, see Jacqueline Rose, "Sexuality in the Field of Vision," in her *Sexuality in the Field of Vision* (London: Verso, 1986), pp. 224–33.

[4] See Sigmund Freud, "Leonardo da Vinci and a Memory of His Childhood," *The Standard Edition of the Psychological Works of Sigmund Freud* (London: Hogarth, 1957), 11: 59–138. It is clear that I have attempted to cover some of the same ground as Meyer Shapiro did in his two seminal essays, "Two Slips of Leonardo and a Slip of Freud," *Psychoanalysis* 4 (1955–56): 3–8, and "Leonardo and Freud: An Art-Historical Study," *Journal of the History of Ideas* 27 (1956): 147–78, while trying to place the iconographic and historical reading within a psychological matrix. I have thus used K. R. Eissler, *Leonardo da Vinci: Psychoanalytic Notes on the Enigma* (New York: International Universities Press, 1961), which attempts to counter Schapiro, with some care, as Eissler's lack of understanding of the usefulness of Schapiro's method for a deeper reading of Leonardo is evident.

[5] I am grateful for the background of Leonardo's potential fine, had he been convicted of sodomy, to the work of Michael Rocke of the State University of New York at Binghamton, who is at present completing a dissertation on homosexuality in Renaissance Florence with the working title "Homosexuality in Late Medieval Florence."

[6] Ludwig Freiherr von Pastor, *The History of the Popes from the Close of the Middle Ages*, trans. Ralph Francis Kerr (London: Kegan Paul, 1924), 14: 238–39, 266–68. Compare this with James M. Saslow, *Ganymede in the Renaissance* (New Haven, CT: Yale University Press, 1986), in which the myth making about as well as the practice of homosexuality during the Renaissance, especially in Florence, is examined in great detail, as well as Guido Ruggiero, *The Boundaries of Eros: Sex Crime and Sexuality in Renaissance Venice* (New York: Oxford University Press, 1985), pp. 109–45.

[7] I am indebted to Mary Jacobus for making her chapter "Motherhood According to Kristeva" available to me in advance of the publication of her study *Reading Woman* (New York: Columbia University Press, 1986).

[8] Private, of course, only in the sense that diaries are private. Leonardo knew the representational value of these works even though he shielded them with his own "code," his mirror writing. He did will them to Francesco Melzi, who viewed them as one of the most valuable parts of Leonardo's estate. And these notebooks had immediate and constant value on the art market.

[9] All references to this plate and to the translations have been checked against Kenneth S. Keele and Carlo Pedretti, eds., *Leonardo da Vinci, Corpus of the Anatomical Studies in the Collection of Her Majesty the Queen at Windsor Castle*. 3 vols. (New York: Johnson Reprint/Harcourt Brace Jovanovich, 1979), hereafter referred to as *K/P*. I do not always agree with the translations in this edition, but it is the most accurate reproduction of all of the extant anatomical materials. On the general background, see Heidi Lenssen, *Art and Anatomy* (New York: J. J. Augustin, 1944); Mario Senaldi, *L'anatomia e la fisologia di Leonardo da Vinci*, vol. 8 (Milano: Il Museo nazionale della scienza e della tecnica, n.d.); Otto Baur, *Leonardo da Vinci, Anatomie, Physiognomik, Proportion und Bewegung* (Köln: Forschungsstelle des Instituts für Geschichte der Medizin der Universität zu Köln, 1984); Moriz Holl, *Ein Biologe aus der Wende des XV. Jahrhunderts, Leonardo da Vinci* (Graz: Leuschner & Lubensky, 1905). The literature on Leonardo's anatomical drawings is summarized in Heinz Ladendorf, *Leonardo da Vinci und die Wissenschaft: Eine Literaturübersicht*, 2 vols. (Cologne: Forschungsstelle des Instituts für Geschichte der Medizin

der Universität zu Köln, 1984).

[10] Charles D. O'Malley and J. B. de C. M. Saunders, eds., *Leonardo on the Human Body* (New York: Dover, 1983), p. 460.

[11] Rudolf Reitler, "Eine anatomisch-künstlerische Fehlleistung Leonardos da Vinci," *Internationale Zeitschrift für Psychoanalyse* 4 (1917): 205–7. The irony is that Reitler's misreading of Leonardo's image of coition is based on the same type of error of transmission as Freud's own misreading of Dmitri Mereschkowski's account of the childhood dream of Leonardo about the bird introducing its tail into the infant Leonardo's mouth. (See Freud's source, Dmitri Mereschkowski, *Leonardo da Vinci: Ein biographischer Roman aus der Wende des 15. Jahrhunderts*, trans. Carl von Goetschow [Leipzig: Schulz, 1903]. I am grateful to the Freud Museum, Hampstead, for granting me access to the volumes on Leonardo in Freud's London library.) Reitler used a version of Leonardo's image that had been "completed" and thus distorted in the nineteenth century; Freud used Mereschkowski's novel with its mistranslation of the bird's name. (Freud's primary source, in addition to the novel, seems to have been the German translation of Edmund Solmi's monograph on Leonardo [Edmund Solmi, *Leonardo da Vinci*, trans. Emmi Hirschberg, Berlin: E. Hofmann, 1908.] In his copy, Freud made a marginal note on the page where the dream is related with the same mistranslation of the bird's name as in Freud's later text.) Each of these confusions has a specific importance for the story that it tells. Freud's reliance on the novel about Leonardo's life was in no little part due to the confluence of two facts: Freud read the life of Leonardo the creative genius as outsider in Mereschkowski's account (which begins *in media res*) at the very point in his own life when Leonardo's biography begins (in middle age and at the sensed high point of his creativity), and Mereschkowski's novel was a world bestseller, giving its author a high status as a creative genius, a status sought after by Freud from the time of his contact with Wilhelm Fliess. Freud sees himself both as Leonardo and as the author of the novel about Leonardo and thus identifies completely with the validity of Mereschkowski's point of view (and the language of its representation). Reitler's perspective is a bit different. He sees the Leonardo anatomical drawing only through the eyes of the engraver, who, like Mereschkowski, has altered it for his/her own ends. But the alterations are not merely those of completion, for the engraver adds the feet of the figures and adds them incorrectly. Reitler falls into the trap of centering his analysis on these added features, and thus Freud, who quotes Reitler extensively in the notes to the 1919 edition, repeats Reitler's error. What is most interesting is that the anonymous engraver selects only the hemisected coitus figures from the sheet, ignoring the other figures as well as the commentary. This is, unbeknown to him, the source of Reitler's central error of interpretation. For once the hemisected figures are restored to their context within Leonardo's anatomical drawings, and once the central principle for their interpretation is elucidated, then the preselection of these hemisected coital figures as the central focus of Leonardo's earliest representation of human sexuality can be judged to be biased. One must examine the entire page, all of the figures in relationship to each other, as well as understand the implications of Leonardo's internalization of the idea of sexual difference in this first set of images of sexuality. Reitler's views are not unique. See Gabriel Peillon, *Étude historique sur les organes génitaux de la femme* (Paris: Berthier, 1891), pp. 131–73.

[12] Ludwig Choulant, *Geschichte und Bibliographie der anatomischen Abbildung nach ihrer Beziehung auf anatomische Wissenschaft und bildende Kunst* (Leipzig: Weiggel, 1852); translated and updated by M. Frank, *History and Bibliography of Anatomical Illustration* (Chicago: University of Chicago Press, 1945), pp. 23–27.

13 See Duilio Lucarelli, "L'anatomia dell'apparato genitale femminile nel trattato de Mondino de' Liucci," *Pagine de storia della medicina (Roma)* 10 (1966): 63–82.

14 Ernest Wickersheimer, *Anatomie de Mondino dei Luzzi et de Guido de Vigevano* (Paris: Droz, 1926), and Lino Sighinolfi and Giacinto Viola, eds., Mondino dei Luzzi, *Anatomia* (Bologna: L. Cappelli, 1930). The former is a reproduction of the first printed edition; the latter, of a manuscript version with a contemporary Italian translation. See also Charles Singer, ed. and trans., *The Fasciculo de Medicina Venice, 1493* (Florence: R. Leier and Co., 1925), 1: 75–79, for an English translation of the relevant passages from Mondino. See also his "Notes of Renaissance Artists and Practical Anatomy," *Journal of the History of Medicine* 5 (1950): 156–62, and G. Rath, "Prevesalian Anatomy in the Light of Modern Research," *Bulletin of the History of Medicine* 35 (1961): 142–48.

15 William G. Eberhard, *Sexual Selection and Animal Genitalia* (Cambridge, MA: Harvard University Press, 1985), pp. 19–20.

16 But even more specifically, the sexual imagery of the key and lock even haunts the description of the "cave of the lovers" in Gottfried von Strassburg's *Tristan*. See the clear reference to this in the text as translated by A. T. Hatto (Baltimore: Penguin, 1960), pp. 264–66.

17 Kenneth D. Keele, *Leonardo da Vinci's Elements of the Science of Man* (New York: Academic Press, 1983), here pp. 243–45. See also his general introduction in Kenneth Keele, *Leonardo da Vinci and the Art of Science* (Hove, East Sussex: Wayland Publishers, 1977).

18 Whether Leonardo read Plato directly or not cannot be shown, but the anatomical texts of his day extensively cite Plato in this regard. See the long passages from the *Timaeus* cited in Andrés de Laguna, translated in L. R. Lind, *Studies in Pre-Vesalian Anatomy: Biography, Translations, Documents* (Philadelphia: The American Philosophical Society, 1975), p. 280.

19 Edith Hamilton and Huntington Cairns, eds., *The Collected Dialogues of Plato*, Bollingen Series 71 (New York: Pantheon, 1961), p. 1210.

20 See Luigi Messedaglia, *Vita e costume della Rinascenza in Merlin Cocai* (Padua: Antenore, 1973), 2: 419–25. It is important to note that Leonardo's plate is undated, but even if the earliest date (1493) is taken, the potential for the knowledge of the disease was present. If a slightly later date is accepted (1495), such knowledge was a certainty.

21 The signification of this position for Leonardo and his contemporaries can be seen in the very fact that when Michelangelo chooses to portray his *Leda* after Leonardo, he places his figures in a much more conventional supine position. See the discussion of this in Robert S. Liebert, *Michelangelo: A Psychoanalytic Study of His Life and Images* (New Haven: Yale University Press, 1983), pp. 256–57, and Bernard Schultz, *Art and Anatomy in Renaissance Italy* (Ann Arbor, MI: UMI Research Press, 1985), pp. 69–109.

22 Aristotle, *Parts of Animals*, trans. A. L. Peck (Cambridge, MA: Harvard University Press, 1968), p. 297. Compare Kenneth Keele, "Leonardo da Vinci's Studies of the Alimentary Tract," *Journal of the History of Medicine and Allied Sciences* 27 (1972): 133 ff.

23 The actual anatomy of the penis contains two main distensible tubes, the corpora cavernosa, which surmount a compressible tube, the corpus spongiosa. The corpora cavernosa fills with arterial blood, and the corpus spongiosa enables the urethra to remain open in order to emit the seminal fluid. See the discussion in Bernard Knight, *Discovering the Human Body* (New York: Crowell, 1980), p. 137.

24 *K/P*, 72r. (See note 9.)

25 Cited in the best and most detailed study of early attitudes toward homosexuality, John Boswell, *Christianity, Social Tolerance and Homosexuality: Gay People in Western Europe from the Beginning of the Christian Era to the Fourteenth Century* (Chicago: The University of Chicago Press, 1980), p. 357.

26 Jean Paul Richter, ed., *The Literary Works of Leonardo da Vinci* (London: Oxford University Press, 1939), 2: 265.

27 The alternate view also existed. This view saw homosexuality, as well as all forms of sexuality that did not lead to conception, as a human fault, which could not exist among the lower animals. Matteo Ricci, in commenting on the widespread practice of homosexuality in sixteenth-century China, observed: "Even the wild animals only make their bonds between female and male, none of them overturn the nature heaven gave them." Cited by Jonathan D. Spence, *The Memory Palace of Matteo Ricci* (New York: Penguin, 1984), p. 229.

28 Boswell, op. cit., pp. 303–32.

29 It is clear that the views of homosexuality present in the Middle Ages and the Renaissance cannot be perfunctorily summarized. In addition to Boswell, I have relied on Vern L. Bullough and James Brundage, eds., *Sexual Practices and the Medieval Church* (Buffalo, NY: Prometheus, 1982), as well as Michael Goodich, *The Unmentionable Vice: Homosexuality in the Late Medieval Period* (Santa Barbara, CA; ABC-Clio, 1979), see especially pp. 28–30.

30 See J. K. Proksch, "Die venerischen Erkrankungen und deren Übertragbarkeit bei einigen warmblütigen Tieren," *Vierteljahrschrift für Dermatologie und Syphilis* 15 (1883): 309–53.

31 Jacopo Berengario da Carpi, *A Short Introduction to Anatomy*, trans. L. R. Lind (Chicago: University of Chicago Press, 1959), p. 76. His relationship to Leonardo's anatomical illustration has been described by A. Hyatt Mayor, *Artists and Anatomists* (New York: Artists' Limited Edition in Association with Metropolitan Museum of Art, 1984), pp. 90–93.

32 Guido Biagi, ed., *La Divina Commedia nella figurazione artistica e nel secolare commento*, 3 vols. (Turin: Unione Tipografico-Editore Torinese, 1924–39), and Peter Brieger, Millard Meiss, and Charles S. Singleton, eds., *Illuminated Manuscripts of the Divine Comedy*, 2 vols. (Princeton, NJ: Princeton University Press, 1969).

33 Richard Kay, "The Sin of Brunetto Latini," *Mediaeval Studies* 31 (1969): 262–86.

34 Thomas Okey, trans., and H. Oelsner, ed., *Dante's Purgatorio* (London: J. M. Dent, 1962), p. 325.

35 On the shift in the tradition of reading the "Sodom" passage from Genesis 19, see Boswell, op. cit., pp. 92–95.

36 This is a variation on a common Western conceit. See Otto Baur, *Bestiarum Humanum: Mensch-Tier-Vergleich in Kunst und Karikatur* (Munich: Heinz Moos, 1974).

37 Boswell, op. cit., pp. 234–35.

38 *K/P* 143r, pp. 115–16. On this passage Marie Bonaparte observes, in the introduction to her translations of Freud's essay on Leonardo (*Freud, Un souvenir d'enfance de Léonard de Vinci* [Paris: Gallimard, 1927], p. 30): "From the psychoanalytic point of view it is conceivable that this contiguity is not accidental and that there existed an unconscious connection between his undoubtedly extreme repression of infantile masturbation and his subsequent disgust of sexuality. This may even be true also of the fact that he was left-handed, or at least preferred the left hand for drawing, painting, and writing. For it is remarkable that the hands Leonardo drew on the page on which he set down his thoughts about the disgust prompted in him by the sexual act are *all right hands*."

39 Carlo Pedretti, *The Literary Works of Leonardo da Vinci: A Commentary to Jean Paul Richter's Edition*, 2 vols. (London: Phaidon, 1977), 2: 280.

NOTES FOR CHAPTER 5

1 Giovanni Battista Morgagni, *Adversaria anatomica omnia* (Leiden: J. A. Langervak, 1723), 2: 14.

[2] Jean Bodin, *La méthode de l'histoire*, ed. and trans. P. Mesnard (Paris: Société d'édition "Les Belles Lettres," 1941), p. 88. The English translation is taken from William B. Cohen, *The French Encounter with Africans: White Response to Blacks, 1530–1880* (Bloomington: Indiana University Press, 1980), esp. p. 20.

[3] The antiquity of this motif has been well documented by Arthur O. Lovejoy, *The Great Chain of Being: A Study in the History of an Idea* (Cambridge, MA: Harvard University Press, 1936), without, however, any sense of the political implications of the motif. See also W. F. Bynum, "The Great Chain of Being after Forty Years: An Appraisal," *History of Science* 13 (1975): 1–28; Stephen J. Gould, *Ontogeny and Phylogeny* (Cambridge, MA: Harvard University Press, 1982), esp. pp. 18, 201–2, 326–27. On the later political history of the use of this motif, see Nancy Stepan, *The Idea of Race in Science: Great Britain 1800–1960* (London: Macmillan, 1982), pp. 1–20.

[4] See Dennis Fletcher, ed., *The Monstrous* (Durham: Durham University Printing Unit, 1987).

[5] On the background, see John Block Friedman, *The Monstrous Races in Medieval Art and Thought* (Cambridge, MA: Harvard University Press, 1981).

[6] On the complex relationship between the history of gender and the history of embryology (specifically Harvey and Lazzaro Spallanzani), see Anne Fausto-Sterling, "Society Writes Biology/Biology Constructs Gender," *Daedalus* 116 (1987): 61–76.

[7] See F. J. Cole, *A History of Comparative Anatomy* (London: Macmillan, 1949), p. 387.

[8] All of the quotations from Harvey are from Robert Willis, ed. and trans., *The Works of William Harvey, M.D.* (London: The Sydenham Society, 1847). I am referring here only to Harvey's major work on generation, as that became the focus for his contemporaries. Harvey also authored smaller works on human sexuality: *On Parturition, On the Uterine Membranes and Humours,* and *On Conception.* See Walter Pagel, *William Harvey's Biological Ideas* (Basel and New York: S. Karger, 1967).

[9] Harvey, op. cit., p. 182.

[10] Cited in Paul Topinard, *Éléments d'anthropologie générale* (Paris: A. Delahaye et E. Lecrosnier, 1885), p. 43. Translation from Cohen, op. cit., p. 89.

[11] In general, see Janet Doe, *A Bibliography of the Works of Ambroise Paré: Premier Chirurgien and Conseiller du Roy* (Chicago: University of Chicago Press, 1937). See Stephen Greenblatt, *Shakespearean Negotiations* (Berkeley: University of California Press, 1988), pp. 66–93.

[12] In general, see Francis Joseph Cole, *A History of Comparative Anatomy* (London: Macmillan, 1949).

[13] Compare the work of Mondeville as represented in the text and plates in Marie-Christine Pouchelle, *Corps et chirurgie à l'apogée du Moyen Âge: Savoir et imaginaire du corps chez Henri de Mondeville, chirurgien de Philippe le Bel* (Paris: Flammarion, 1983).

[14] Ambroise Paré, *Deux Livres de Chirurgie* (Paris: André Wechel, 1573). The plates discussed are reproduced on pp. 404–8 (hermaphrodites) and p. 429 (black and woman). On the general background to this question, see K. Park and L. J. Daston, "Unnatural Conceptions: The Study of Monsters in Sixteenth- and Seventeenth-Century France and England," *Past and Present* 92 (1981): 20–54.

[15] Conrad Lycosthenes, *Prodigiorum ac ostentorum chronicon* (Basel: Henricum Petri, 1557). The image of the hairy Adam and Eve is to be found on p. 4; of the black male on pp. 7 and 231; of the hermaphrodites on pp. 118 and 163.

[16] I have used the major seventeenth-century English translation as the source of my quotes and my images from Paré: Ambroise Paré, *The Works Translated out of Latin and Compared with the French by Th. Johnson . . . Translated out of Andrian Spigelius* (London: M. Clark for J. Clark, 1678), p. 596. The quotes and images can

thus be understood as part of a major seventeenth- as well as a major sixteenth-century tradition. (There is no consequential difference between the original images and those of the later edition.) See the edition of *Des monstres et prodiges*, ed. J. Céard (Geneva: Droz, 1971) as well as Sir D'Arcy Power, "Archeologia medica: The Iconography of Ambroise Paré," *British Medical Journal* 2 (1929): 965.

[17] No such image is to be found in Lycosthenes, although a "realistic" portrait of a black male is used to discuss the question of the color of the black's skin and a very hairy Adam and Eve as wild-people introduce the book.

[18] Marie-Helene Huet, "Living Images: Monstrosity and Representation," *Representations* 4 (1983): 73.

[19] I am drawing here on the basic bibliographic and historical work undertaken by Roy Porter, " 'The Secrets of Generation Display'd': *Aristotle's Master-piece* in Eighteenth-Century England," in Robert P. Maccubbin, ed., *Eighteenth-Century Life: Unauthorized Sexual Behavior during the Enlightenment* 9 (1985): 1–22. See also Janet Blackman, "Popular Theories of Generation: The Evolution of *Aristotle's Works*. The Study of an Anachronism," in John Woodward and David Richards, eds., *Health Care and Popular Medicine in Nineteenth Century England* (London: Croom Helm, 1977), pp. 56–89; Paul-Gabriel Boucé, ed., *Sexuality in Eighteenth-Century Britain* (Manchester: Manchester University Press, 1982).

[20] The quote is taken from the twelfth edition of *Aristotle's Compleat Master-piece* (London, n.d. [late seventeenth century]), p. 11.

[21] Taken from the twenty-fourth edition (London, 1752), p. 21.

[22] Taken from the thirtieth edition (London, 1771), p. 91.

[23] Taken from the twelfth edition (London, early seventeenth century), p. 22.

[24] One must note, however, that Paré's image has not vanished; rather, it has been moved to illustrate the text. In the 1820 edition of *Aristotle's Compleat Master-piece* the image from Paré is to be found in its original form on p. 14.

[25] Harvey, op. cit., wrote: "Conception, according to the opinion of medical men, takes place in the following way: during intercourse the male and female dissolve in one voluptuous sensation, and inject their seminal fluids [*geniturae*] into the cavity of the uterus, where that which each contributes is mingled with that which the other supplies, the mixture having from both equally the faculty of action and the force of matter; and according to the predominance of this or that geniture does the progeny turn out male or female" (p. 294). The most detailed study of the idea of conception in the seventeenth century (with plates) is Pierre Darmon, *Le mythe de la procréation à l'âge baroque* (Paris: J.-J. Pauvert, 1977).

[26] See the discussion in F. J. Cole, *Early Theories of Sexual Generation* (Oxford: Clarendon Press, 1930).

[27] Whitney J. Oates and Eugene O'Neill, Jr., eds., *The Complete Greek Drama*, 2 vols. (New York: Random House, 1938), 1: 294.

[28] Cited in Cole, op. cit., p. 2. On the centrality of Paracelsus to the medicine of the seventeenth century, see F. Freudenberg, *Paracelsus und Fludd, die beiden grossen Okkultisten und Ärzte des 15. und 16. Jahrhunderts* (Berlin: H. Barsdorf, 1921); Allen Debus, *The Chemical Philosophy: Paracelsian Science and Medicine in the Sixteenth and Seventeenth Centuries*, 2 vols. (New York: Science History Publications, 1977), and Arlene Miller Guinsberg, "The Counterthrust to Sixteenth-Century Misogyny: The Work of Agrippa and Paracelsus," *Historical Reflections/Réflexions historiques* 8 (1981): 3–28.

[29] Cited in Cole, op. cit., p. 37.

[30] I am simplifying the question of the relationship between theories that traditionally see the embryo as preformed in the parent before conception and those that traditionally saw embryos as existing from the Creation. The reason for my simplification

is that contemporary theorists also confused these two categories. See J. S. Wilkie, "Preformation and Epigenesis: A New Historical Treatment," *History of Science* 6 (1967): 138–50, for a summary of the arguments.

[31] Even though Malpighi wrote: "By its very nature the uterus is a field for growing the seeds, that is to say the ova, sown upon it. Here the eggs are fostered, and here the parts of the living [fetus], when they have further unfolded, become manifest and are made strong. Yet although it has been cast off by the mother and sown, the egg is weak and powerless and so requires the energy of the semen to initiate growth." Howard B. Adelmann, *Marcello Malpighi and the Evolution of Embryology*, 5 vols. (Ithaca, NY: Cornell University Press, 1966), 2: 861.

[32] See Howard B. Adelmann, ed. and trans., *The Embryological Treatises of Hieronymus Fabricus of Aquapendente*, 2 vols. (Ithaca, NY: Cornell University Press, 1967).

[33] Jan Swammerdam, *Miraculum naturae, sive uteri muliebris fabrica* (Lugdundi Batavorum: T. Haak and S. Luchtmans, 1729). Translation from Adelmann, *Marcello Malpighi and the Evolution of Embryology*, op. cit., 2: 908. See also A. Schierbeek, *Jan Swammerdam (12 February 1637–17 February 1680): His Life and Works* (Amsterdam: Swets and Zeitlinger, 1967).

[34] See Regnier de Graaf, *On the Human Reproductive Organs*, trans. H. D. Jocelyn and B. P. Setchell, *Journal of Reproduction and Fertility*, Supplement No. 17 (Oxford: Blackwell Scientific Publications, 1972).

[35] In general, see Walter Pagel, "Religious Motives in the Medical Biology of the Seventeenth Century," *Bulletin of the History of Medicine* 3 (1935): 97–128; 213–31; 265–312.

[36] Hans Wolfgang Singer, "Der Vierfarbendruck in der Gefolgschaft Jacob Christoffel Le Blons, mit Oeuvre-Verzeichnissen der Familie Gautier-d'Agoty, J. Roberts, J. Ladmirals und C. Lasinsos," *Monatshefte für Kunstwissenschaft* 10 (1917): 177–99, 281–314; 11 (1918): 52–73.

[37] On the comparative medical illustration of the seventeenth century, see W. Artelt, "Bemerkungen zum Stil der anatomischen Abbildungen des 16. und 17. Jahrhunderts," *Acta des XV. Congreso internacional de Historia de la Medicina, Madrid-Alcalá* (Madrid: International Society for the History of Medicine, 1958), 1: 393–95.

[38] On Fludd, see especially Serge Hutin, *Robert Fludd (1474–1637): Alchimiste et philosophe rosicrucien* (Paris: Les Éditions de l'Omnium Littéraire, 1971); William Harold Huffman, "Robert Fludd: The End of an Era" (Diss., University of Missouri–Columbia, 1972); Frances Yates, *The Rosicrucian Enlightenment* (London: Routledge & Kegan Paul, 1972); Joscelyn Godwin, *Robert Fludd: Hermetic Philosopher and Surveyor of Two Worlds* (London: Thames and Hudson, 1979).

[39] See Julius Petersen, "Der Kreis der Bartholiner und die holländischen Medizin," *Janus* 14 (1909): 457–66; A. Thiset, "Les nobles Bartholins," *Janus* 21 (1916): 358–60; Harold Speert, "Caspar Bartholin and the vulvovaginal glands," *Medical History* 1 (1957): 355–58; Alain Bouchet, "De la découverte de la glande vulvovaginale à la bartholinite," *Presse médicale* 66 (1958): 337–38; Gustav Scherz, ed., *Briefe aus der Bartolinerzeit* (Copenhagen: Munksgaard, 1961).

[40] See Ernst Uhsemann, *Die Rechtfertigung der Anatomie im 17. Jahrhundert (unter besonderer Berücksichtigung der Praefationes Zeitgenössischer anatomischer Lehrbücher)* (Diss., Kiel, 1969).

[41] See Felix Haxler and Marie-Louise Portmann, "Johannes Bauhin d. J., seine soziale Bedeutung als behördlicher Arzt, Balneologe, und Botaniker," *Gesnerus* 20 (1963): 1–21, as well as their "Johannes Bauhin d. J. (1541–1613) und die Genfer 'Ordonnances sur l'éstat de la médecine, pharmacie et chirurgie' von 1569," *Gesnerus* 30 (1973): 99–104.

[42] See Jan Gerard De Lint, "Frederich Hoffmann's Man as a Machine," *Medical Life* 41 (1934): 164–76.

[43] I. A. Bowman, "Anatomical Illustrations with Superimposed Flaps," *The Bookman* 8 (1981): 3–7.

[44] On the general cultural setting of syphilis during the seventeenth century, see James Cleugh, *Secret Enemy: The Story of a Disease* (London: Thames and Hudson, 1954).

[45] Geoffrey Eatough, ed. and trans., *Fracastoro's Syphilis* (Liverpool: Francis Cairns, 1984). See also John E. Ziolokowski, "Epic Conventions in Fracastoro's Poem *Syphilis*," *Altro Polo* 1984: 57–73.

[46] See Hieronymous Fracastoro, *Drei Bücher von den Kontagien, den kontagiösen Krankheiten und deren Behandlung (1546)*, trans. and introduced by Viktor Fossel (Leipzig: Johann Ambrosius Barth, 1910), specifically the section on "syphilis" (pp. 67–70) in which he stresses the sexual origin of the disease.

[47] George Swarzenski, "Un quadro di Luca Giordana in Francoforte sul Meno," *Bollettino d'Arte* 2 (1922–23): 17–23. Swarenski shows that this painting is based on Otto van Veen's *Image of Indiscreet Youth* of about 1596, an image that has no specific references to venereal disease but only to the corruption of youth.

[48] See the discussion of Rembrandt's portrait of the syphilitic painter Gérard de Lairesse in the anonymous essay "Le nez de Gérard Lairesse," *Aesculape* 26 (1936): 239–45.

[49] *A Midsummer's Night's Dream*, 1, 2, 99. See Gregory Wayne Bentley, "Melancholy, Madness and Syphilis in *Hamlet*," *Hamlet Studies* 6 (1984): 75–80.

[50] Siegfried Wenzel, *The Sin of Sloth: Acedia in Medieval Thought and Literature* (Chapel Hill: University of North Carolina Press, 1967), p. 106.

[51] Erwin Panofsky, *Hercules am Scheideweg und andere antike Bildstoffe in der neueren Kunst*. Studien der Bibliothek Warburg, 18 (Leipzig/Berlin: B. G. Teubner, 1930).

[52] Cited from Erwin Panofsky, "Homage to Fracastoro in a Germano-Flemish Composition of About 1590," *Nederlands Kunsthistorisch Jaarboek* 12 (1961): 31–32.

[53] I am indebted to the presentation by Marielene Putscher, "Das Gefühl: Sinnengebrauch und Geschichte," in Marielene Putscher, ed., *Die Fünf Sinne: Beiträge zu einer medizinischen Psychologie* (Munich: Heinz Moos, 1978), pp. 147–59.

[54] See J. F. Conway, "Syphilis and Bronzino's London Allegory," *Journal of the Warburg and Courtauld Institutes* 49 (1986): 250–55.

[55] On the later history of this image, see Neil Hertz, "Medusa's Head: Male Hysteria under Political Pressure," *Representations* 4 (1983): 27–54.

[56] Francisco Lopez de Villalobos, *El somario de la medicina con un tratado sobre las pestiferas bubas*, ed. María Teresa Herrera (Salamanca: Ediciones del Instituto de Historia de la Medicina Española, 1973), pp. 159–61. See Yvonne David-Peyre, "Normativité et pathologie, au siècle d'Or," *Textes et Langages* 11 (1985): 5–22.

[57] See Otto Brendel, "The Interpretation of the Holkham *Venus*," *Art Bulletin* 28 (1946): 65–75. On the general question of the relationship between the senses and sexuality, see A. P. de Mirimonde, "La musique dans les allégories de l'amour," *Gazette des Beaux-Arts* 68 (1966): 265–90 and 69 (1967): 319–46.

[58] Charles Hope, "Problems of Interpretation in Titian's Erotic Paintings," *Tiziano e Venezia* (Venice: Neri Pozza, 1980), pp. 111–24.

[59] See the tabulation in Anton Pigler, *Barockthemen* (Budapest: Verlag der ungarischen Akademie der Wissenschaft, 1956), 1: 462–65.

[60] On the background, see W. Von Leyden, *Seventeenth Century Metaphysics* (London: Duckworth, 1968).

61 Caravaggio's work stands in contrast to the traditional image of the senses as a woman. The young boy who is represented recoiling from the bite of the lizard could easily be read as a homoerotic counterimage to this tradition, especially, in regard to the clearly sexual implications of the animal represented. On Caravaggio's use of the lizard, see J. Slatkes, "Caravaggio's Boy Bitten by a Lizard," *Print Review* 5 (1974): 148–53, and Jane Costello, "Caravaggio, Lizard, and Fruit," in Moshe Barasch and Lucy Freeman Sandler, eds., *The Ape of Nature: Studies in Honor of H. W. Janson* (New York: Harry N. Abrams, 1981), pp. 375–85. One could argue that the erotic is merely subsumed into the painful in Caravaggio's painting through the image of the act of penetration. See Donald Posner, "Caravaggio's Homo-Erotic Early Works," *Art Quarterly* 34 (1971): 301–24.

62 See the two essays on this topic: Herbert Rudolph, "'Vanitas': Die Bedeutung mitteralterlicher und humanistischer Bildinhalte in der niederländischen Malerei des 17. Jahrhunderts," in *Festschrift Wilhelm Pinder zum sechzigsten Geburtstage überreicht . . .* (Leipzig: Seemann, 1938), pp. 419–45 and Hans Kaufmann, "Die Fünfsinne in der niederländischen Malerei des 17. Jahrhunderts," *Kunstgeschichtliche Studien*, ed. Hans Tintelnot [Festschrift for Dagobert Frey] (Breslau: Gauverlag, 1943), pp. 133–57.

63 Svetlana Alpers, *The Art of Describing: Dutch Art in the Seventeenth Century* (Chicago: University of Chicago Press, 1983).

64 How very different from Louis Marin's reading of Poussin in his "Toward a Theory of Reading in the Visual Arts: Poussin's *The Arcadian Shepherds*," in Susan R. Suleiman and Inge Crosman, eds., *The Reader in the Text* (Princeton, NJ: Princeton University Press, 1980), pp. 293–324.

65 Herbert Friedmann, *A Bestiary for Saint Jerome: Animal Symbolism in European Religious Art* (Washington, DC: Smithsonian Institution Press, 1980), p. 269.

NOTES FOR CHAPTER 6

1 On Ruysch, his museum of anatomical specimens, and his images of sexuality, see F. J. Cole, *A History of Comparative Anatomy* (London: Macmillan, 1949), pp. 443–61. On the stereotypical function of such images, see Londa Schiebinger, "Skeletons in the Closet: The First Illustrations of the Female Skeleton in Eighteenth-Century Anatomy," in Catherine Gallagher and Thomas Laquer, eds., *The Making of the Modern Body: Sexuality and Society in the Nineteenth Century* (Berkeley: University of California Press, 1987), pp. 42–82. The fascination with monsters and wondrous births is as old as the earliest written records. See the Babylonian texts edited by Erle Leichty, *The Omen Series Summa Izbu*. Texts from Cuneiform Sources 4 (Locust Valley, NY: J. J. Augustin, 1968).

2 See J. Raven, *John Ray, Naturalist* (Cambridge: Cambridge University Press, 1942), pp. 436–37.

3 On the history of pain, see R. Janzen et al., *Schmerz: Grundlagen, Pharmakologie, Therapie* (Stuttgart: Georg Thieme, 1972).

4 "No malady entail'd upon human creatures, more frequently occurs; no disease carries along with it more excrutiating torture, nor a more formidable train of symptoms; neither is any cure attended in more barbarous circumstances, than that of freeing persons from the attack of the stony, petrifi'd substances found in the cavity of human bladders, by the only effectual means hitherto known, to wit, the operation of Lythotomy." [William Shaw], *A Dissertation on the Stone in the Bladder* (London: R. Gosling, 1738), p. 8.]

5 Alexander Ross, *Arcana microcosmi: or, The Hid Secrets of MAN'S Body Discovered* (London: Thomas Newcomb, 1652), p. 49. The best studies of these questions are Shirley A. Roe, *Matter, Life,*

and Generation: Eighteenth-Century Embryology and the Haller-Wolff Debate (Cambridge: Cambridge University Press, 1981) and François Duchesneau, *La physiologie des lumières: Empirisme, modèles et théories*. Archives Internationales d'Histoire des Idées, vol. 95 (The Hague: Martinus Nijhoff Publishers, 1982).

6 See Reinhold Schwarz, G. Wolte, and Emil Ehler, "Partus Monstrosi: C. E. Eschenbach (1753)," *Wissenschaftliche Zeitschrift der Universität Rostock* 17 (1968): 173–74.

7 William Hunter, *Two Introductory Lectures Delivered by Dr. William Hunter to His Last Course of Anatomical Lectures at His Theatre in Windmill Street* (London: Trustees of the Hunterian Museum, 1784), p. 4.

8 Lester G. Crocker, "Diderot and Eighteenth-Century French Transformism," in B. Glass, O. Temkin, and W. L. Straus, eds., *Forerunners of Darwin 1745–1859* (Baltimore: Johns Hopkins University Press, 1959), p. 120.

9 All of the quotations from Diderot are taken from Lester G. Crocker, ed. and trans., *Diderot's Selected Writings* (New York: Macmillan, 1966), here p. 199.

10 *Descriptio foetus bicipitis ad pectora connati ubi in causas monstrorum ex principiis anatomicis inquiritur* (Hannover: B. Nic. Foerster, 1739). See the discussion of Haller in E. Schwalbe, "Allgemeine Missbildungslehre," in his *Die Morphologie der Missbildungen des Menschen und der Tiere* (Jena: G. Fischer, 1906) and Shirley A. Roe, *Matter, Life, and Generation: Eighteenth-Century Embryology and the Haller-Wolff Debate* (Cambridge: Cambridge University Press, 1981), pp. 125–26.

11 On Boerhaave, see A. M. Luyendijk-Elshout, "Mechanicisme contra vitalisme de school van Hermann Boerhaave en de beginselen van het leven," *Tijdschrift voor de Geshiedenis der Geneeskunde, Natuurvetenschappen, Wiskunde en Techniek* 5 (1982): 16–26; M. J. Van Lieburg, "Het Rotterdamse handschrifft van Boerhaave's "Lectio publica de lue venera," *Tijdschr. Geschied. Geneeskd. Natuurwet. Wiskd. Tech.* 1 (1978): 83–87; W. L. Donnellan, "Medicine and Society in the Sixteenth and Seventeenth Centuries: Their Influence on the Life and Work of Hermann Boerhaave, 1668–1738 (Diss., Northwestern University, Evanston, 1981).

12 Quoted from Hermann Boerhaave, *Praelectiones academicae in proprias institutiones rei medicae*, edited and annotated by Albrecht von Haller (Göttingen: A. Vandenhoeck, 1739–44), v. 5, pt. 2 [1744], pp. 485, 487.

13 Hermann Boerhaave, *Sermo academicus De Comparando Certo in Physics, quem habuit in Academia Lugduni-Batavorum, quum Octavo Februarii, Anno 1715 Rectoratum Academie deponeret* (Lugduni Batavorum: Apud Petrum Van der Aa, 1715), p. 23.

14 *Sur la formation du coeur dans le poulet*, 2 vols. (Lausanne: M. M. Bosquet, 1758).

15 Quoted from Haller's *Elementa physiologiae corporis humanae*, 8 vols. (Lausanne: M. M. Bosquet; Bern; Societas Typographica, 1757–66), 8 (1766): 143. Translation from Shirley A. Roe, "Anatomia animata: The Newtonian Physiology of Albrecht von Haller," in Everett Mendelsohn, ed., *Transformation and Tradition in the Sciences: Essays in Honor of I. Bernard Cohen* (Cambridge University Press, 1984), p. 287.

16 Paraphrased from Haller by Roe, "Anatomia animata," op. cit., p. 287.

17 Caspar Friedrich Wolff, "Descriptio vituli bicipitis cui accedit commentatio de ortu monstrorum," *Novi Commentarii Academiae Scientiarum Imperialis Petropolitanae* 17 (1772): 567.

18 See Robert Herrlinger, "Bidloo's 'Anatomia'—Prototyp baroker Illustration?" *Gesnerus* 23–24 (1966–67): 40–47, and H. K. Schmutz, "Barocke und klassizistische Elemente in der anatomischen Abbildung," *Gesnerus* 35 (1978): 54–65. See also L. G. Audette, "Stylism in Anatomical Illustrations from the Sixteenth

to the Twentieth Centuries," *Journal of Biocommunication* 6 (1979): 34–37.

[19] See Paul Dumaitre, *La curieuse destinée des planches anatomiques de Gérard de Lairesse*. Nieuwe Nederlandse Bijdragen tot de Geschiedenis der Geneeskunde en der Natuurwetenschappen, 6 (Amsterdam: Rodopi, 1982).

[20] On Morgagni, see G. Ongaro and R. G. Mazzolini, "Morgagni sconosciuto: Le lezioni di anatomia e il diario medico-scientifico nel fondo morgagnano della Biblioteca Palatina di Parma," *Atti e memorie dell'Accademia Patavina di Scienze, Lettere, et Arti* 95 (1982–83): 19–32; D. Nardo, "Scienza e filologia nel primo Settecento padovano. Gli Studi classici di G. B. Morgagni, G. Poleni, G. Pontedera, L. Targa," *Quaderni Storia Univ. Padova* 14 (1981): 1–40; G. Ongaro, "I rapporti tra Giambattista Morgagni e Lazzaro Spallanzani," *Contributi* 5 (1981): 125–34; L. Stroppiana, "Metodologia Morgagnana," *Med. Secoli* 20 (1983): 3–10; J. Lindsten, "Sammanställde fal av korvuxenhet och bristand ovarifunktion hos flickor," *Lakartidiningen* 80 (1983): 2755; A. Gamba, "Un ritratto inedito di Giambattista Morgagni," *Acta Med. Hist. Patav.* 29 (1982–83): 67–74; G. Ongaro and R. G. Mazzolini, "Quasi tradens se totum: I manoscritto morgagnani della Biblioteca Palatina di Parma," *Annali dell'Instituto e Museo di Storia della Scienze di Firenze* 8 (1983): 101–5; L. Belloni, "Il Morgagni tra il Malpighi e il Cotugno," *Gesnerus* 39 (1982): 195–213; L. Premuda, "Fermenti illunistici nella prousione (1712) di G. B. Morgagni a Padova," *Morgagni* 4 (1971): 127–33; Entralgo P. Lain, "Ventura y riesgo del titulo de un libro," *Ascelpio* 22 (1970): 195–202; L. Bonuzzi, "Ricerche intorno all'influenze del pensiero di John Locke sull'impostazione scientifica di Giovan Battista Morgagni," *Acta Med. Hist. Patav.* 15 (1968–69): 63–86; and L. Belloni, "Contributo all'epistolario Boerhaave-Morgagni. L'Edizione della Epistolae anatomicae duae Leida 1728," *Physis* 13 (1971): 81–109.

[21] J. L. Thornton and Patricia C. Want, "Charles Nicholas Jenty and the Mezzotint Plates in His 'Demonstrations of a Pregnant Uterus,' 1757," *Journal of Audiovisual and Media Medicine* 1 (1978): 113–15.

[22] On the Rymsdyk illustrations, see J. W. Huffman, "Jan van Riemsdyk, Medical Illustrator Extraordinary," *Journal of the American Medical Association* 208 (1969): 121–24; J. W. Huffmann, "The Great Eighteenth Century Obstetric Atlases and Their Illustrators," *Obstetrics and Gynecology* 35 (1970): 971–76; J. L. Thornton and Patricia C. Want, "Artist versus Engraver in William Hunter's 'Anatomy of the Human Gravid Uterus,' 1774," *Medical and Biological Illustration* 24 (1974): 137–39; J. L. Thornton and Patricia C. Want, "William Hunter's 'The Anatomy of the Human Gravid Uterus,' 1774–1974," *Journal of Obstetrics and Gynecology of the British Commonwealth* 81 (1974): 1–10.

[23] On the popular reception of these scholarly images, see Ferdinand Wagenseil, "Eine anatomische Wandtafel aus dem 18. Jahrhundert," *Sudhoffs Archiv für Geschichte der Medizin* 49 (1965): 119–28.

[24] On the specimens in Hunter's museum, see John H. Teacher, ed., *Catalogue of the Anatomical and Pathological Preparations of Dr. William Hunter* (Glasgow: James MacLehose and Sons, 1900). For the discussion of Hunter's anatomical atlas (but not the museum specimens) as part of the visual representation of gender, I am indebted to L. J. Jordanova, "Gender, Generation and Science: William Hunter's Obstetrical Atlas," in W. F. Bynum and Roy Porter, eds., *William Hunter and the Eighteenth-Century Medical World* (Cambridge: Cambridge University Press, 1985), pp. 385–412. See also Jessie Dobson, "John Hunter's Practice," *Annals of the Royal College of Surgeons* (1966): 181–90.

[25] See F. J. Cole, *A History of Comparative Anatomy*, op. cit., p. 451.

[26] Albrecht von Haller, *Briefe über die wichtigsten Wahrheiten der Offenbarung* (Bern: Neue Buchhandlung, 1772), p. 45.

[27] William Hunter, *Anatomia uteri humani gravidi* (London: S. Baker and M. Leigh, 1774), preface.

[28] See Lüdike Duhme, *Die Tabulae Anatomicae des Pietro Berrettini da Cortona* (Diss., The University of Cologne, 1981) for an overview of the literature.

[29] Rumy Hilloowala, "Bartolomeo Eustachio: His Influence on Albinus and the Anatomical Models at La Specola," *Journal of the History of Medicine and Allied Sciences* 41 (1986): 442–62.

[30] On Eustachi, see the essays by L. Belloni, "Ancora sul manoscitto 'De dissensionibus, et controversiis anatomicis' di Bartolomeo Eustachi," *Physis* 23/4 (1981): 581–87; "Bartolomeo Eustachi, anatomico del cinquecento, al lume di recenti ricerche," *Archive Internationale d'Histoire de Science (Paris)* 29 (1979): 5–10; "Streitfragen zwischen Bartolomeo Eustachi und Gerolamo Mercuriali auf dem Gebiete der medizinischen Philologie," *Gesnerus* 33/34 (1976): 188–208; "Testimonianze dell'anatomico Bartolomeo Eustachi per la storia del 'compasso geometrico et militare' (Con un contributo al problema del luogo e della data di morte dell'Eustachi," *Physis* (1969) 11: 69–88; "Il manoscritto senese 'De dissensionibus, et controversiis anatomicis' di Bartolomeo Eustachi," *Physis* 14 (1972): 194–200.

[31] Rumy Hiloowala, "The Origin of the Wellcome Anatomical Waxes: Albinus and the Florentine Collection at La Specola," *Medical History* 28 (1984): 432–37. This essay convincingly details the parallels between the wax images and the earlier anatomical atlases. See also Linda A. Deer, "Italian Anatomical Waxes in the Wellcome Collection: The Missing Link," *Cereoplastica nella scienza e nell'arte serie: Atti del 1 congresso internazionale. Biblioteca della Revista di storia delle scienze mediche e naturali* 20 (1977): 281–96.

[32] One must add here one major caveat—one of the reasons that the wax model became so widely used was the limitation on the anatomist's acquisition of cadavers, a limitation that led to the "Resurrectionists" such as Burke and Hare in England and similar endeavors on the Continent. But it was not merely this inability to acquire cadavers but also the difference between the aesthetic response to a "real" body as opposed to a "wax" one that was at the core of the interest.

[33] L. Belloni, "Anatomica plastica: The Bologna Wax Models," *CIBA Symposium* 8 (1060): 84–87.

[34] François Cagnetta, "La vie et l'oeuvre de Gaetano Giulio Zummo," *Cereoplastica nella scienza e nell'arte serie: Atti del 1 congresso internazionale. Biblioteca della Revista di storia delle scienze mediche e naturali* 20 (1977): 489–501.

[35] On the religious background to this tradition, see the following two catalogues and their general historical introductions: Benedetto Lanza et al., *La cere anatomiche della Specola* (Florence: Arnaud Editore, 1979), on the Florentine collection, and, on the Viennese collection, Konrad Allmer and Marlene Jantsch, eds., *Katalog der josephinischen Sammlung anatomischer und geburtshilflicher Wachspräparate im Institut für Geschichte der Medizin an der Universität Wien* (Graz-Cologne: Hermann Böhlaus Nachf., 1965).

[36] On the backgrounds to this, see the opening chapter of Owen Chadwick, *The Secularization of the European Mind in the Nineteenth Century* (Cambridge: Cambridge University Press, 1977).

[37] Johann Caspar Goethe, *Viaggio in Italia (1740)*, ed. Arturo Farinelli, 2 vols. (Rome: Reale Accademia d'Italia, 1932–33), 1: 316–17.

[38] Marquis de Sade, *Voyage d'Italie*, eds. Gilbert Lely and Georges Daumas (Paris: Tschou, 1967), p. 152.

[39] Henry Wadsworth Longfellow, *Outre Mer: A Pilgrimage beyond the Sea* (London: C. Routledge, 1853), pp. 224–25.

[40] Johann Wolfgang Goethe, "Plastische Anatomie (1832)," in his *Werke* (Weimar: Hermann Böhlau, 1900), 49: 64–75. See also

Günter Martin, "Anatomia Plastica: Secrets of 18th-Century Wax Casts," *Austria Today* 11 (1977): 18.

[41] Johann Wolfgang Goethe, *Wilhelm Meister's Travels*, trans. Edward Bell (London: George Bell and Sons, 1882), pp. 301–2. This tradition continues in one of the great nineteenth-century novels of education influenced by Goethe's novel, Gottfried Keller's *Green Henry*. See the discussion in Laurence A. Rickels, *Aberrations of Mourning: Writing on German Crypts* (Detroit: Wayne State University Press, 1988), p. 185.

[42] Nathaniel Hawthorne, *Passages from the French and Italian Note-Books* (Boston/New York: Houghton, Mifflin and Co., 1871), p. 380.

[43] It is important to understand that the Marquis de Sade's fascination with the inflicting of pain, both in life as well as in his fictions, such as *Justine* (1791) [the first sections of *Juliette*] or *Eugénie de Franval* (1788), was understood in his time as criminal or perverse. The painful touch was not understood as the continuation of the pleasurable aspects of the erotic but as diametrically opposed to them. Here, too, the splitting of the senses of the painful and the pleasurable can be seen in the contemporary (but not the modern) reception of de Sade. One clear contemporary response to de Sade's fascination with the painful is chronicled in M. Heine, "L'affaire des bonbons cantharidés du Marquis de Sade," *Hippocrate* 1 (1933): 95–133. In this incident, de Sade was executed in absentia. For a more complete chronicle of his life and times, see Geoffrey Gorer, *The Life and Ideas of the Marquis de Sade* (London: Panther, 1964); John Richetti, "The Marquis de Sade and the French Libertine Tradition," in George Stade, ed., *European Writers: The Age of Reason and the Enlightenment* (New York: Scribner's, 1984), 4: 615–38; Jane Gallop, *Intersections: A Reading of Sade with Bataille, Blanchot, and Klossowski* (Lincoln: University of Nebraska Press, 1981), and Angela Carter, *The Sadeian Woman and the Ideology of Pornography* (New York: Pantheon, 1988).

[44] The Marquis de Sade, *Juliette*, trans. Austryn Wainhouse (New York: Grove, 1968), p. 613.

[45] On the continuity of such images of horror and decay, see Philippe Bordes, "Les arts après la Terreur: Topino-Lebrun, Hennequin et la peinture politique sous le Directoire," *Revue du Louvre et des Musées de France* 29 (1979): 199–212.

[46] "We disenterred the cadavers of Aglaia's two forebears, we buried them to the waist in two deep holes; facing them we placed the last of her line in a third hole, dug yet a little deeper, from which the head and shoulders emerged, and 'twas opposite that hideous sight we left her to perish slowly." *Juliette*, op. cit., p. 656. This is indeed a type of ecphrasis, the representation of works of art within the literary work.

[47] Edmond and Jules de Goncourt, *Journals: Mémoires de la vie littéraire* (Paris: Flammarion, 1956), 2: 996. I am indebted to Linda Nochlin's analysis of the reception of this painting in her essay "Courbet's *L'origine du monde*: The Original without an Original," *October* 37 (1986): 76–86. On the present location of this work, see Sarah Faunce and Linda Nochlin, eds., *Courbet Reconsidered* (The Brooklyn Museum, 1988), pp. 176–78.

[48] Maxime du Camp, *Les convulsions de Paris* (Paris: Hachette, 1889), 2: 189–90.

[49] See the interpretation of this passage in Neil Hertz, "Medusa's Head: Male Hysteria under Political Pressure," *Representations* 4 (1983): 27–54.

[50] On Haller's philosophy of physiology, see John Neubauer, "Albrecht von Haller's Philosophy of Physiology," *Studies on Voltaire and the 18th Century* 216 (1983): 320–22.

[51] Translation from Albrecht von Haller, "A Dissertation on the Sensible and Irritable Parts of Animals," trans. M. Tissot, *Bulletin of the History of Medicine* 4 (1936): 658–59.

[52] The most extensive discussion of this is to be found in François Duchesneau, *La physiologie des lumières: Empirisme, modèles et théories* (The Hague: Martinus Nijhoff, 1982); on Haller, see pp. 141–70.

[53] Philip Verheyn [sic], *Anatomie oder Zerlegung des menschlichen Leibes* (Leipzig: Thomas Fritsch, 1708), p. 200.

[54] Cited from the Anonymous, *Tabes dorsalis, or, The Cause of Consumption in Young Men and Women* (London: M. Copper, W. Reeve, C. Sympson, 1752), p. 14. I am indebted for this discussion to the essay by James Rogers, "Sensibility, Sympathy, Benevolence: Physiology and Moral Philosophy in *Tristram Shandy*," in L. J. Jordanova, *Languages of Nature: Critical Essays on Science and Literature* (London: Free Association Books, 1986), pp. 117–58.

[55] Robert Whytt, *An Essay on the Vital and Other Involuntary Motions of Animals* (Edinburgh: Hamilton, Balfour and Neill, 1751). For a more detailed discussion, see R. K. French, *Robert Whytt, The Soul, and Medicine* (London: The Wellcome Institute of the History of Medicine, 1969).

[56] Albrecht von Haller, *Dr. Albert Haller's Physiology* (London: G. Robinson, 1754), 2: 281.

[57] Albrecht von Haller, "Sensible and Irritable Parts," op. cit., p. 658.

[58] Whytt, 1751, op. cit., p. 301.

[59] Whytt, 1751, op. cit., p. 314.

[60] See Lancelot Law Whyte, *The Unconscious before Freud* (London: J. Friedmann, 1978).

[61] Whytt, 1751, op. cit., p. 252.

[62] On the general background, see Esther Fischer-Homberger, *Krankheit Frau und andere Arbeiten zur Medizingeschichte der Frau* (Bern: Hans Huber, 1979), and Susan Rubin Suleiman, ed., *The Female Body in Western Culture* (Cambridge, MA: Harvard University Press, 1986).

[63] Matteo Realdo Colombo, *De re anatomica* (Venice: Beuilaqua, 1559), p. 243. On this see Thomas Power Lowry, ed., *The Classic Clitoris: Historic Contributions to Scientific Sexuality* (Chicago: Nelson-Hall, 1978).

[64] F. Plazzoni, *De partibus generationis* (Patadij: Laur. Pasquati, 1620), Chap. 12, p. 147.

[65] Verheyen, op. cit., p. 223.

[66] De Sade, *Juliette*, op. cit., p. 614.

[67] A Gentleman of the Faculty, *The Anatomical Dialogues; or, a Breviary of Anatomy . . . Chiefly Compiled for the Use of the Young Gentlemen in the Navy and Army* (London: G. Robinson, 1778), p. 336.

[68] Johannes Müller, *Handbuch der Physiologie des Menschen* (Coldenz: J. Hölscher, 1836), vol. 2, section 7, p. 2.

[69] George Ludwig Kobelt, *Die männlichen und weiblichen Wollust-Organe des Menschen und einiger Saugethiere* (Freiburg i. Br.: Adolph Emmerling, 1844); translation from Lowry, op. cit., p. 50.

[70] See Philippe Duboy, *Lequeu: An Architectural Enigma*, trans. Francis Scarfe (Cambridge, MA: MIT Press, 1986); Mireille Gagebin, *L'irréprésentable ou les silences de l'oeuvre* (Paris: PUF, 1984).

[71] I am indebted to the discussion of William F. Bynum, "Treating the Wages of Sin: Venereal Disease and Specialism in Eighteenth-Century Britain," in William F. Bynum and Roy Porter, eds., *Medical Fringe and Medical Orthodoxy 1750–1850* (London: Croom Helm, 1987), pp. 5–28.

[72] In general, see the discussion by Ronald Paulson, *Hogarth's Graphic Works*, 2 vols. (New Haven: Yale University Press, 1970), 1: 271–72, with a number of interpretations of the relationship between the three figures. I have returned to Lichtenberg's view for my reading, as it was a contemporary interpretation of the image of the syphilitic. See also Hermann J. Real and Heinz J. Vienken, "The Syphilitic Lady," *The Scriblerian and the Kit Cats*

15 (1982): 52–54.

[73] Henry Fielding, *The History of Tom Jones* (New York: Modern Library, 1950), p. 234. Compare Roy Porter, "Mixed Feelings: The Enlightenment and Sexuality in Eighteenth-Century Britain," in Paul-Gabriel Bouce, ed., *Sexuality in Eighteenth-Century Britain* (Manchester: Manchester University Press, 1982), pp. 1–27.

[74] See John Andree, *Observations on the Theory and Cure of the Venereal Disease* (London: W. Davis, 1779), p. v.

[75] *Joe Miller's Jests; or the Wits Vade-Mecum* (London: T. Read, 1739), p. 5. The other joke on this theme runs: "A Lady being asked how she like a Gentleman's Singing, who had a very stinking Breath, the Words are good, said she, but the Air is intolerable" (p. 5).

[76] James Cleugh, *Secret Enemy: The Story of a Disease* (London: Thames and Hudson, 1954), p. 137.

[77] *Lichtenberg's Commentaries on Hogarth's Engravings*, trans. Innes and Gustav Herdan (London: Cresset Press, 1966), pp. 102–13.

[78] See René A. Spitz, "Authority and Masturbation: Some Remarks on a Bibliographical Investigation," *Yearbook of Psychoanalysis* 9 (1953): 113–45; Robert H. MacDonald, "The Frightful Consequences of Onanism: Notes on the History of a Delusion," *Journal of the History of Ideas* 28 (1967): 423–31; E. H. Hare, "Masturbatory Insanity: The History of an Idea," *Journal of Mental Science* 108 (1962): 1–25; H. T. Engelhardt, Jr., "The Disease of Masturbation: Values and the Concept of Disease," *Bulletin of the History of Medicine* 48 (1974): 234–48. Of use is Karl-Felix Jacobs, *Die Entstehung der Onanie-Literatur im 17. und 18. Jahrhundert* (Diss., Munich, 1963), and R. P. Neuman, "Masturbation, Madness, and the Modern Concepts of Childhood and Adolescence," *Journal of Social History* 8 (1975): 1–26. None of these studies treats the eighteenth-century literature on masturbation printed in German. On the more general background, see Jean-Paul Aron and Roger Kempf, *La pénis et la démoralisation de l'occident* (Paris: Grasset & Fasquelle, 1978), which attempts to place this question into the general problem of the nature of class development.

[79] See Vern L. Bullough and Martha Voght, "Homosexuality and Its Confusion with the 'Secret Sin' in Pre-Freudian America," *Journal of the History of Medicine and Allied Sciences* 28 (1973): 143–55.

[80] Cited in my essay "Seeing the Insane: Mackenzie, Kleist, William James," *MLN* 93 (1978): 875.

[81] Anton Müller, *Die Irren-Anstalt in dem Königlichen Julius-Hospital zu Würzburg und die sechs und zwanzigjährigen ärtzlichen Dienstverrichtungen an derselben* (Würzburg: Stahel, 1824), p. 167.

[82] *Onania; or, The Heinous Sin of Self-Pollution*, sixteenth edition (London: J. Isted, 1737), pp. 31 and 26.

[83] On the general background, see Michael J. Morgan, *Molyneux's Question: Vision, Touch and the Philosophy of Perception* (Cambridge: Cambridge University Press, 1977), and Ralph M. Davis, "Some Philosophical Problems of the Sense of Touch (Diss., University of Oregon, 1967).

[84] See W. Von Leyden, *Seventeenth Century Metaphysics* (London: Duckworth, 1968).

[85] Bishop Berkeley, *A New Theory of Vision*, ed. A. D. Lindsay (London: Dent, 1910), sections 79, 122, 126.

[86] Immanuel Kant, *Critique of Practical Reason*, trans. L. W. Beck (Indianapolis and New York: Liberal Arts Press, 1956), p. 14.

[87] Immanuel Kant, *Critique of Pure Reason*, trans. F. M. Müller (London: Macmillan, 1881), p. B44.

[88] William Cheselden, "An Account of some Observations made by a young Gentleman, who was born blind, or lost his sight so early, that he had no Remembrance of ever having seen, and was couched between 13 and 14 Years of Age," *Philosophical Transactions of the Royal Society* 35 (1727–28): 447–48. For a detailed discussion of the idea of race and perception, see Sander L.

Gilman, *On Blackness without Blacks: Essays on The Image of the Black in Germany* (Boston: G. K. Hall, 1982), pp. 19–34.

[89] See David Dabydeen, *Hogarth's Blacks: Images of Blacks in Eighteenth Century English Art* (Kingston-upon-Thames: Dangaroo, 1985).

[90] See the various works on Hogarth by Ronald Paulson as well as R. E. Taggert, "A Tavern Scene: An Evening at the Rose," *Art Quarterly* 19 (1956): 320–23.

[91] Francis Grose, *A Classical Dictionary of the Vulgar Tongue*, ed. Eric Partridge (London: 1931), p. 39.

[92] Immanuel Kant, *Critique of Practical Reason*, op. cit., p. 14.

[93] On the image of masturbation, see Richard Hunter and Ida Macalpine, eds., *Three Hundred Years of Psychiatry 1535–1860* (London: Oxford University Press, 1970), p. 349.

[94] For a detailed discussion of this, see my *Seeing the Insane* (New York: Brunner/Mazel–Wiley, 1982).

[95] J. É D. Esquirol, *Des maladies mentales considérées sous les rapports médical, hygiénique et médico-légal* (Paris: J. B. Baillière, 1838). One of the most interesting pre-Enlightenment discussions of "Amorous Consumption" that discusses it in terms of its signs and symptoms is Gideon Harvey, *Morbus anglicus, or a Theoretick and Practical Discourse of Consumptions, and Hypochondriak Melancholy* (London: Thackery, [1672]), pp. 29–32.

[96] Alexander Morison, *The Physiognomy of Mental Diseases* (London: Longman, 1840), p. 79.

[97] Christian Heinrich Spiess, *Biographieen der Wahnsinningen*, 2 vols. (Leipzig: Voss, 1795–96).

[98] All references to the novel are to the edition edited by Brian Vickers (of Henry Mackenzie), *The Man of Feeling* (London: Oxford University Press, 1931) but also of interest is W. F. Wright, *Sensibility in English Prose Fiction, 1760–1814: A Reinterpretation*, Illinois Studies in Language and Literature, xxii, 3–4 (Urbana: University of Illinois Press, 1937) and the essay by A. M. Kinghorn, "Literary Aesthetics and the Sympathetic Emotions—A Main Trend in Eighteenth-Century Scottish Criticism," *Studies in Scottish Literature* 1 (1963): 35–47. More generally on the present topic, the following studies are of interest: Max Byrd, *Visits to Bedlam: Madness and Literature in the Eighteenth Century* (Columbia, SC: University of South Carolina Press, 1974); Michael V. DePorte, *Nightmares and Hobbyhorses: Swift, Sterne and Augustan Ideas of Madness* (San Marino, CA: Huntington Library, 1974); Mervyn James Jannetta, "The Predominant Passion and Its Force: Propensity, Volition and Motive in the Works of Swift and Pope" (Diss., York, 1975). On the general background, see Roy Porter, *Mind-Forg'd Manacles: A History of Madness in England from the Restoration to the Regency* (Cambridge, MA: Harvard University Press, 1987).

[99] See Alison G. Stewart, *Unequal Lovers: A Study of Unequal Couples in Northern Art* (New York: Abaris Books, 1977).

[100] See the discussion in Elaine Showalter's *The Female Malady: Women, Madness, and English Culture, 1830–1980* (New York: Pantheon, 1985), pp. 14–15.

[101] A detailed description of the plate can be found in Ronald Paulson, *Hogarth's Graphic Works*, revised edition (New Haven: Yale University Press, 1970), 1: 169–70.

[102] Sir Walter Scott, *The Bride of Lammermoor* (London: J. M. Dent, 1964), p. 323.

NOTES FOR CHAPTER 7

[1] See especially Michel Serres, *Les cinq sens* (Paris: B. Grasset, 1985). On the history of the sense of smell, see Alain Corbin, *Le miasme et le jonquille: L'ordorat et l'imaginaire social XVIIIe-XIXe siècles* (Paris: Aubier Montaigne, 1982), as well as the brilliant novelistic treatment of this question in Patrick Süskind, *Das*

Parfum: Die Geschichte eines Mörders (Zurich: Diogenes, 1985).

2 See Leif Ludwig Albertson, "Die Anerkennung des Sexuellen vor und bei Goethe: Was war an den *Römischen Elegien* so aufregend?" *Text und Kritik* 9 (1981): 331–42; Hans Rudolf Vaget, "Das Schreibakt und der Liebesakt: Zur Deutung von Goethes Gedicht 'Das Tagebuch,'" *Goethe Yearbook* 1 (1982): 112–37; Klaus Oettinger, "Verrucht, aber schön . . . Zum Skandal um Goethes *Römische Elegien*," *Deutschunterricht* 35 (1983): 18–30; Heidi Glockhammer, "Fama and Amor: The Function of Eroticism in Goethe's *Römische Elegien*," *Eighteenth-Century Studies* 19 (1985–86): 235–53.

3 K. R. Eissler, *Goethe: A Psychoanlytic Study* (Detroit: Wayne State University Press, 1963), 2: 1012, 1020, 1034, and especially his Appendix O, pp. 1266–72.

4 Antonio Valeri ("Carletta"), *Goethe a Roma* (Rome: Editrice Dante Alighieri, 1899).

5 As in the approach of Rainer Nägele, *Reading after Freud* (New York: Columbia University Press, 1987), pp. 23–46. See also Nägele's first-rate critique of Eissler in the same volume, pp. 1–22.

6 The translation is by Michael Hamburger from Stephen Spender, ed., *Great Writings of Goethe* (New York: Mentor, 1958), pp. 228–29. On the general problem of the literary representation of the senses, see Jean Pierre Richard, *Littérature et sensation* (Paris: Édition du Seuil, 1954).

7 All of the German references to Goethe are to the so-called "Hamburger Ausgabe," edited by Erich Trunz unless otherwise noted (reprint: Munich: C. H. Beck, 1981), here 1: 160.

8 Goethe, op. cit., 13: 20.

9 Spender, op. cit., 99; Goethe, 3: 50 (lines 1436–46). Compare the discussion of language and aesthetics in Benjamin Bennett, *Goethe's Theory of Poetry: Faust and the Regeneration of Language* (Ithaca, NY: Cornell University Press, 1986).

10 See Michel Foucault, *The History of Sexuality*, trans. Robert Hurley, vol. 1: *An Introduction* (New York: Vintage, 1980).

11 Johann Gottfried Herder, *Über den Ursprung der Sprache*, ed. Claus Träger (Berlin: Deutsche Akademie der Wissenschaften zu Berlin, 1959), pp. 49–52.

12 See the discussion of the texts in Norbert Miller's excellent introduction, "Der Dichter als Landschaftsmaler: Zu Goethes Umgang mit der Wahrnehmung," to Michael Ruetz, *Goethes Italienische Reise* (Munich: Hanser, 1985), pp. 9–19. This essay stresses the question of the perceptual shift within Goethe's work following his trip to Italy. Of the older literature, the following works were of value: C. H. Herford, "The Influence of Goethe's Italian Journey upon His Style," *Modern Quarterly of Language and Literature* 1 (1898): 29–42; M. D. Henkel, "Wat zag Goethe in Italië?" *Nieuwe gids* 42 (1927) 1: 691–706, 2: 1–17, 143–58; Giulio Monti, "Goethe e l'Italia," *Emporium* 75 (1932): 195–210; René Michéa, *Le "Voyage en Italie" de Goethe* (Paris: Aubier, 1945); Elizabeth M. Wilkinson, "Goethe's Conception of Form," *Proceedings of the British Academy* 37 (1951): 175–97; Alois Lun, ed., *Incontri italo-tedeschi* (Rome: Gopa, 1955), pp. 20–62; Elizabeth M. Wilkinson, "Sexual Attitudes in Goethe's Life and Works," in her *Goethe Revisited: A Collection of Essays* (London: Calder, 1984), pp. 170–84; Glockhammer, op. cit.

13 It is not that Winckelmann exclusively claimed the male as the epitome of beauty. Contrary to what much of the critical literature on Winckelmann states, he does not exclusively praise the ideal of male beauty. What he does is to place, in good Enlightenment manner, the ideal of male beauty on the same plane as that of female beauty. As one can see, however, from the contemporary reception of his views, Winckelmann's public homosexual identity caused this reorientation to be read as a praise of the ideal of the male over that of the female. Winckelmann's own views were quite parallel to those of Wieland, who argued that there was no absolute hierarchy of beauty. I will, however, use the contemporary reading of Winckelmann's views as a "homoerotic" aesthetics in this essay, as my use refers to the reception of Winckelmann's aesthetics rather than to Winckelmann's actual program. See Dennis Sweet, "The Personal, the Political, and the Aesthetic: Johann Joachim Winckelmann's German Enlightenment Life," in Kent Gerard, ed., *The Pursuit of Sodomy in Early Modern Europe: Male Homosexuality from the Renaissance through the Enlightenment* (New York: Haworth, forthcoming), as well as the general introduction in John Gage, ed. and trans., *Goethe on Art* (Berkeley: University of California Press, 1980).

14 Goethe, op. cit., 11: 139.

15 See the discussion by Jeffrey Barnouw, "Goethe and Helmholtz: Science and Sensation," in Frederick Amrine et al., eds., *Goethe and the Sciences: A Reappraisal* (Dordrecht: D. Reidel, 1987), pp. 45–82, for an excellent summary of Goethe's theories of sensation.

16 Kenneth Clark, *The Nude: A Study of Ideal Art* (London: John Murray, 1956) as well as his *Feminine Beauty* (New York: Rizzoli, 1980).

17 *Selected Essays of Arthur Schopenhauer*, trans. Ernest Belfort Bax (London: George Bell and Sons, 1891), p. 344.

18 Both quotations are taken from Phyllis Grosskurth, *The Woeful Victorian: A Biography of John Addington Symonds* (New York: Holt, Rinehart & Winston, 1964), p. 276.

19 Trevor J. Fairbrother, "A Private Album: John Singer Sargent's Drawings of Nude Male Models," *Arts Magazine* 56 (1981): 70–78.

20 Eissler, op. cit., 2: 1012.

21 *Goethes Briefe. Weimarer Ausgabe*, vol. 8: *August 1786–Juni 1778* (Weimar: Hermann Böhlau, 1890), pp. 314–15.

22 *Goethes Gespräche*, ed. Wolfgang Herwig, vol. 3: *1825–1832* (Zürich: Artemis, 1972), p. 603.

23 I quote the translation from K. R. Eissler, *Goethe*, op. cit., 2: 1269.

24 Johann Wolfgang Goethe, *Wilhelm Meister's Apprenticeship*, trans. Thomas Carlyle (Boston: S. E. Cassino, 1884), p. 60.

25 John Ritchie Findlay, *Personal Recollections of Thomas De Quincey* (Edinburgh: A. & C. Black, 1886), p. 36.

26 Henry Hatfield, *Goethe: A Critical Introduction* (New York: New Directions, 1963), pp. 77–78.

27 Adapted from the English translation by E. C. Marchant in Xenophon, *Memorabilia and Oeconomicus* (Cambridge, MA: Harvard University Press, 1965), p. 97. My reading is in the light of J. F. Kermode's "The Banquet of Sense," *Bulletin of the John Rylands Library* 44 (1961–62): 68–99. The most comprehensive study of this motif remains Erwin Panofsky, *Herkules am Scheideweg und andere antike Bildstoffe in der neueren Kunst*, Studien der Bibliothek Warburg, 18 (Leipzig/Berlin: B. G. Teubner, 1930).

28 Goethe, op. cit., 11: 478; my translation.

29 See Gerhard Femmel, ed., *Corpus der Goethezeichnungen*, 7 vols. (Leipzig: VEB E. A. Seemann, 1965), 3: drawings 221–32.

NOTES FOR CHAPTER 8

1 Peter Gay, *The Bourgeois Experience, Victoria to Freud*, vol. 1: *The Education of the Senses* (New York: Oxford University Press, 1984).

2 This is documented in detail by Alan Rusbridger, *A Concise History of the Sexual Manual 1886–1986* (London/Boston: Faber and Faber, 1986).

3 J. G. Bearn, "The Mammalian Ovary: The Development of Ideas on Its Functional Anatomy," *Middlesex Hospital Journal* 66 (1966): 244–49.

4 Rudolf Virchow, *Die Cellularpathologie* (Berlin: A. Hirchwald, 1858).

5 Michel Foucault, *The Birth of the Clinic: An Archeology of Medical Perception*, trans. A. M. Sheridan Smith (New York: Vintage, 1975), p. 114.

6 See the general background in Russell C. Maulitz, *Morbid Appearances: The Anatomy of Pathology in the Early Nineteenth Century* (Cambridge: Cambridge University Press, 1987).

7 Stephen J. Gould, *Ontogeny and Phylogeny* (Cambridge, MA: Belknap Press, 1977).

8 On the background to Rokitansky, see Erna Lesky, *Die Wiener medizinische Schule im 19. Jahrhundert* (Graz: Böhlau, 1965).

9 Norbert Elias, *The Civilizing Process*, 3 vols. (New York: Pantheon, 1976). This first appeared in 1939.

10 See, in this regard, the brilliant discussion by T. J. Clark, *The Painting of Modern Life: Paris in the Art of Manet and His Followers* (Princeton, NJ: Princeton University Press, 1984), pp. 79–146, which, however, does not discuss the question of sexuality and disease in any detail. See also the fascinating study by Bram Dijkstra, *Idols of Perversity: Fantasies of Feminine Evil in fin-de-siècle Culture* (New York: Oxford University Press, 1987).

11 August Barthelemy, trans., *Syphilis: Poème en deux chants* (Paris: Bechet junior et Labe & Bohaire, 1840). This is a translation of a section of Fracastoro's Latin poem on the nature and origin of syphilis. The French edition was in print well past midcentury.

12 I am here indebted to Lynda Nead, "Seduction, Prostitution, Suicide: *On the Brink* by Alfred Elmore," *Art History* 5 (1982): 309–22. On the general history of prostitution in Great Britain during the nineteenth century, see Judith R. Walkowitz, *Prostitution and Victorian Society: Women, Class, and the State* (Cambridge: Cambridge University Press, 1980).

13 W. R. Greg, "Prostitution," *Westminster Review* 53 (1850): 456.

14 *The Language of Flowers* (London: Milner and Co., 1849), pp. 19, 22.

15 Cited by Nead, op. cit., p. 316.

16 The image of the dead woman is a basic trope within the art and literature of the nineteenth century. See Elisabeth Bronfen, "Die schöne Leiche: Weiblicher Tod als motivischer Konstante von der Mitte des 18. Jahrhunderts bis in die Moderne," in Renate Berger and Inge Stephan, eds., *Weiblichkeit und Tod in der Literatur* (Cologne: Böhlau, 1987), pp. 87–115. On the general background of the fascination with and representation of death in the West, see Philippe Ariès, *The Hour of Our Death*, trans. Helen Weaver (New York: Knopf/Random House, 1981) as well as Mario Praz, *The Romantic Agony*, trans. Angus Davidson (Cleveland: World, 1956), and John McManners, *Death and the Enlightenment: Changing Attitudes to Death among Christians and Unbelievers in Eighteenth-Century France* (Oxford: Clarendon Press, 1981).

17 William W. Sanger, *The History of Prostitution; Its Extent, Causes, and Effects throughout the World* (New York: Medical Publishing Company, 1927), p. 322.

18 William Tait, *Magdalenism: An Inquiry into the Extent, Causes, and Consquences of Prostitution in Edinburgh* (Edinburgh: P. Rickard, 1840), p. 96. Compare Margaret Higonnet, "Speaking Silences: Women's Suicide," in Susan Rubin Suleiman, ed., *The Female Body in Western Culture: Contemporary Perspectives* (Cambridge, MA: Harvard University Press, 1986), pp. 68–83.

19 "Drowned! Drowned!," *The Magdalen's Friend, and Female Homes' Intelligencer* 1 (1860): 71. On the Continental background to the image of the female suicide, see Aaron Sheon, "Octave Tassert's 'Le suicide': Early Realism and the Plight of Women," *Arts Magazine* 76 (May 1981): 142–51, as well as Judith Wechler, *A Human Comedy: Physiognomy and Caricature in Nineteenth-Century Paris* (Chicago: University of Chicago Press, 1982).

20 Thomas Hood, "The Bridge of Sighs," *The Complete Poetical Works of Thomas Hood* (New York: G. P. Putnam, 1869), 1: 27. On the literary image of the prostitute, see Martin Seymour-Smith, *Fallen Women: A Sceptical Enquiry into the Treatment of Prostitutes, Their Clients, and Their Pimps, in Literature* (London: Nelson, 1969).

21 I am indebted for my discussion of Hunt and Rossetti to the extraordinary essay by Linda Nochlin, "Lost and *Found*: Once More the Fallen Woman," *Art Bulletin* 62 (1978): 139–53. See also Carol A. Bock, "D. G. Rossetti's *Found* and *The Blessed Damozel* as Explorations in Victorian Psychosexuality," *Journal of Pre-Raphaelite Studies* 1 (1981): 83–90, and G. L. Hersey, "Rossetti's "Jenny": A Realist Altarpiece," *Yale Review* 69 (1979): 7–32.

22 Cited in Virginia Surtess, *The Paintings and Drawings of Dante Gabriel Rossetti (1828–1882): A Catalogue Raisonné* (Oxford: Clarendon Press, 1971), 1: 28.

23 See, for example, William Hauptman, "Ingres and Photographic Vision," *History of Photography* 1 (1977): 117–27, on the relationship between "erotic" photographs and high art representations of the nude.

24 Karen Horney, "The Dread of Women: Observations on a Specific Difference in the Dread Felt by Men and by Women Respectively for the Opposite Sex," in her *Feminine Psychology*, ed. Harold Kelman (New York: W. W. Norton, 1967), pp. 133–46.

25 Karen Horney, "The Denial of the Vagina: A Contribution to the Problem of the Genital Anxieties Specific to Women," in her *Feminine Psychology*, op. cit., pp. 147–62.

26 The best discussion is that of Elaine Showalter, "Syphilis, Sexuality, and the Fiction of the fin-de-siècle," in Ruth Bernard Yeazell, ed., *Sex, Politics, and Science in the Nineteenth-Century Novel* (Baltimore: Johns Hopkins University Press, 1986), pp. 88–115. Compare also Patrick Wald Lasowski, *Syphilis: Essai sur la littérature française au XIXe siècle* (Paris: Gallimard, 1981).

27 Samuel Warren, *Passages from the Diary of a Late Physician* (Edinburgh and London: William Blackwood and Sons, 1858), p. 213.

28 The aesthetic tradition is an older one but one that is usually associated with the opening of the criminal's body. See the extraordinarily complex reading by Francis Barker, *The Tremulous Private Body* (London and New York: Methuen, 1984), pp. 73–87.

29 Ernest Jones, *Sigmund Freud: Life and Work* (New York: Basic Books, 1953–57), 2: 468. See Noel Montgrain, "On the Vicissitudes of Female Sexuality: The Difficult Path from 'Anatomical Destiny' to Psychic Representation," *International Journal of Psycho-Analysis* 64 (1983): 169–86.

30 See Sigmund Freud's essay, "Medusa's Head," *The Standard Edition of the Complete Psychological Works of Sigmund Freud*, trans. James Strachey (London: Hogarth, 1953–74), here 18: 273–74. See Annemarie Taeger, *Die Kunst, Medusa zu töten: Zum Bild der Frau in der Literatur der Jahrhundertwende* (Bielefeld: Aisthesis, 1988).

31 Gottfried Benn, *Sämtliche Werke* (Stuttgart: Klett-Cotta, 1986), 1: 11. Translation mine.

32 The fantasy of a "Jewish" Jack the Ripper dies very hard. Robin Odell, *Jack the Ripper in Fact and Fiction* (London: George C. Harrap, 1965), proposed again that Jack was a *shochet*, a ritual slaughterer. This theme has reappeared in the recent volume by Martin Fido, *The Crimes, Detection and Death of Jack the Ripper* (London: Weidenfeld and Nicolson, 1987), which argues that a Jewish tailor named David Cohen was "Jack."

33 The Whitechapel murders most probably included Emma Smith (2 April 1888), Martha Tabram (7 August 1888), Mary Ann Nichols

(31 August 1888), and Annie Chapman (8 September 1888). Elizabeth Stride and Catherine Eddowes were both murdered on 30 September 1888. On the Whitechapel murders, see Tom A. Cullen, *When London Walked in Terror* (Boston: Houghton Mifflin, 1965); Wolf Von Eckardt, Sander L. Gilman, and J. E. Chamberlin, *Oscar Wilde's London* (New York: Doubleday, 1987); Colin Wilson and Robin Odell, *Jack the Ripper: Summing Up and Verdict* (London: Bantam, 1987); and Deborah Cameron and Elizabeth Frazer, *The Lust of Kill: A Feminist Investigation of Sexual Murder* (Oxford: Polity Press, 1987).

[34] Alexandre Lacassagne, *Vacher l'eventreur et les crimes sadiques* (Lyons: A. Storck, 1889).

[35] Cited in Christopher Frayling, "The House That Jack Built: Some Stereotypes of the Rapist in the History of Popular Culture," in Sylvana Tomaselli and Roy Porter, eds., *Rape* (Oxford: Basil Blackwell, 1986), p. 183.

[36] Robert Anderson, *The Lighter Side of My Official Life* (London: Hodder and Stroughton, 1910), p. 32.

[37] Cited in Alexander Kelley and Colin Wilson, *Jack the Ripper: A Bibliography and Review of the Literature* (London: Association of Assistant Librarians, 1973), p. 14.

[38] Frank Wedekind, *Five Tragedies of Sex*, trans. Frances Fawcett and Stephen Spender (New York: Theatre Arts Books, n.d.), p. 298. It is clear that the anti-Semitic press in Germany during 1894 saw "Jack" as a Jew. See Peter Pulzer, *The Rise of Political Anti-Semitism in Germany and Austria* (London: Peter Halban, 1988), p. 6.

[39] Cesare Lombroso and Guglielmo Ferrero, *La donna deliquente: La prostituta e la donna normale* (Torino: Roux, 1893), and Alexandre Lacassagne, *L'homme criminel comparé á l'homme primitif* (Lyons: Association typographique, 1882).

[40] Frayling, op. cit., p. 196.

[41] See the discussion by Alain Corbin, "Commercial Sexuality in Nineteenth-Century France: A System of Images and Regulations," *Representations* 14 (1986): 209–19.

[42] Tom Brown, *Amusements Serious and Comical and Other Works*, ed. Arthur L. Hayward (London: George Routledge and Sons, Ltd., 1927), p. 200.

[43] On the background to this concept, see my *Jewish Self-Hatred: Anti-Semitism and the Hidden Language of the Jews* (Baltimore: Johns Hopkins University Press, 1985).

[44] *The Bagnio Miscellany Containing the Adventures of Miss Lais Lovecock . . .* (London: Printed for the Bibliopolists, 1892), here pp. 54–55.

[45] Gray Joliffe and Peter Mayle, *Man's Best Friend* (London: Pan Books, 1984).

[46] Mary Wilson Carpenter, " 'A Bit of Her Flesh': Circumcision and 'The Signification of the Phallus' in *Daniel Deronda*," *Genders* 1 (1988): 1–23.

[47] See Benjamin Nelson, *The Idea of Usury: From Tribal Brotherhood to Universal Otherhood* (Princeton, NJ: Princeton University Press, 1949), and John Thomas Noonan, *The Scholastic Analysis of Usury* (Cambridge, MA: Harvard University Press, 1857).

[48] Joseph Banister, *England under the Jews* (London: [J. Banister], 1907 [3rd edition]), p. 61. For a more detailed account of Banister and the idea of the diseased Jew, see Colin Holmes, *Anti-Semitism in British Society, 1876–1939* (New York: Holmes & Meier, 1979), pp. 36–48. The parallel concern in Germany about Jews and skin diseases centers about the "Judenzopf." See Wolf Derblich, *De plica polonica* (Diss., Bratislava, 1815) that traces this concern back to the thirteenth century.

[49] Adolph Hitler, *Mein Kampf*, trans. Ralph Manheim (Boston: Houghton Mifflin Company, 1943), p. 247.

[50] Holmes, op. cit., pp. 44–45. Compare Edward J. Bristow, *Prostitution and Prejudice: The Jewish Fight against White Slavery,*

1870–1939 (Oxford: Clarendon, 1982).

[51] The discussion of the images of the Jew and the homosexual is to be found in "Cities of the Plain," in Marcel Proust, *Remembrance of Things Past*, trans. C. K. Scott Moncrieff and Terence Kilmartin (Harmondsworth: Penguin, 1986), 2: 639.

[52] On syphilis and Charcot, see Proust, op. cit., 2: 1086.

[53] Proust, op. cit., 1: 326.

[54] N. Balaban and A. Molotschek, "Progressive Paralyse bei den Bevölkerungen der Krim," *Allgemeine Zeitschrift für Psychiatrie* 94 (1931): 373–83.

[55] H. Budul, "Beitrag zur vergleichenden Rassenpsychiatrie," *Monatsschrift für Psychiatrie und Neurologie* 37 (1915): 199–204.

[56] Max Sichel, "Die Paralyse der Juden in sexuologischer Beleuchtung," *Zeitschrift für Sexualwissenschaft* 7 (1919–20): 98–1104.

[57] James H. Jones, *Bad Blood: The Tuskegee Syphilis Experiment— A Tragedy of Race and Medicine* (New York: The Free Press, 1981).

[58] H. Strauß, "Erkrankungen durch Alkohol und Syphilis bei den Juden," *Zeitschrift für Demographie und Statistik der Juden* 4 (1927): 33–39.

[59] Banister, op. cit., p. 61.

[60] Houston Stewart Chamberlain, *Foundations of the Nineteenth Century*, trans. John Lees, 2 vols. (London: John Lane, 1910), 1: 388–89.

[61] Nathan Birnbaum, "Über Houston Stewart Chamberlain," in his *Ausgewählte Schriften zur jüdischen Frage*, vol. 2 (Czernowitz: Verlag der Buchhandlung Dr. Birnbaum & Dr. Kohut, 1910), p. 201.

[62] Adam G. de Gurowski, *America and Europe* (New York: D. Appelton, 1857), p. 177.

[63] Saul K. Padover, ed. and trans., *The Letters of Karl Marx* (Englewood Cliffs, NJ: Prentice-Hall, 1979), p. 459.

[64] Otto Weininger, *Geschlecht und Charakter* (Vienna: Braumüller, 1903).

NOTES FOR CHAPTER 9

[1] In this context, see Alain Corbin, *Les filles de noce: Misère sexuelle et prostitution aux 19ᵉ et 20ᵉ siècles* (Paris: Aubier, 1978). On the evolving clinical concepts of sexually transmitted disease, see John Thorne Crissey and Lawrence Charles Parish, *The Dermatology and Syphilology of the Nineteenth Century* (New York: Praeger, 1981).

[2] Sigmund Freud, *The Standard Edition of the Complete Psychological Works of Sigmund Freud*, trans. James Strachey (London: Hogarth, 1953–74) 15: 225–26; 16: 369–70.

[3] On the general question of Freud's understanding of female sexuality, see Mary Jane Sherfy, *The Nature and Evolution of Female Sexuality* (New York: Random House, 1972), pp. 21–29.

[4] S. Lindner, "Das Saugen an den Fingern, Lippen etc. bei den Kindern (Ludeln.)," *Jahrbuch für Kinderheilkunde und Physische Erziehung* 14 (1879): 68–91. See M. B. Macmillan, "Freud and Lindner on Pleasure Sucking," *Storia e critica delle psicologia* 1 (1980): 111–16, and Arnold I. Davidson, "Sex and the Emergence of Sexuality," *Critical Inquiry* 14 (1987): 16–48.

[5] See my *Difference and Pathology: Stereotypes of Sex, Race, and Madness*, second edition (Ithaca, NY: Cornell University Press, 1986), p. 200.

[6] A mid-twentieth-century analogy to the fantasy about vaginal orgasm is the discovery of the "G" spot. See Heli Alzate and Zwi Hoch, "The 'G Spot' and 'Female Ejaculation': A Current Appraisal," *Journal of Sex and Marital Therapy* 12 (1986): 211–20.

[7] *Standard Edition*, op. cit., 7: 220. See Stephen Jay Gould, "Freudian Slip," *Natural History* 96 (1987): 14–21.

[8] *Standard Edition*, op. cit., 7: 221.

[9] Ibid.

[10] *Standard Edition*, op. cit., 15: 199. See Stephen Jay Gould, "Freud's Phylogenetic Fantasy," *Natural History* 96 (1987): 10–19.

[11] Theodor Fritsch, *Handbuch der Judenfrage* (Leipzig: Hammer, 1935), p. 409.

[12] See my essay, "The Madness of the Jews," in my *Difference and Pathology*, op. cit., pp. 150–62, as well as Jan Goldstein, "The Wandering Jew and the Problem of Psychiatric Anti-Semitism in Fin-de-Siècle France," *Journal of Contemporary History* 20 (1985): 521–52.

[13] Cited in his summary of the nineteenth-century medical literature on Jews and hysteria by Alexander Pilcz, *Beitrag zur vergleichenden Rassen-Psychiatrie* (Leipzig: Franz Deuticke, 1906), p. 18.

[14] See my discussion of this in *Difference and Pathology*, op. cit., pp. 33–35.

[15] Charlotte Perkins Gilman, "Review of Dr. Weininger's *Sex and Character*," *Critic* 12 (1906): 414.

[16] All citations are from the English translation, Otto Weininger, *Sex and Character* (London: William Heinemann, 1906).

[17] See Breuer's case notes to the case of "Anna O." in Albrecht Hirschmüller, *Physiologie und Psychoanalyse in Leben und Werk Josef Breuers* (Bern: Hans Huber, 1978).

[18] On the medical literature, see, for example, the case studies of homosexuality reported in Richard Krafft-Ebing, *Psychopathia Sexualis mit besonderer Berücksichtigung der conträren sexualempfindung: Eine klinisch-forensische Studien* (Stuttgart: Ferdinand Enke, 1893), which regularly record the nature of the patient's voice. For an overview of the problem of the signs and symptoms of degeneration, see *Degeneration: The Dark Side of Progress*, ed. J. E. Chamberlin and Sander L. Gilman (New York: Columbia University Press, 1985).

[19] See Hubert Kennedy, *Ulrichs: The Life and Works of Karl Heinrich Ulrichs, Pioneer of the Modern Gay Movement* (Boston: Alyson, 1988).

[20] *Standard Edition*, op. cit., 7: 151.

[21] See the general discussion of this image in my *Jewish Self-Hatred: Anti-Semitism and the Hidden Language of the Jew* (Baltimore: Johns Hopkins University Press, 1986).

[22] *Standard Edition*, op. cit., 9: 215.

[23] Cited from the English translation, Max Nordau, *Degeneration* (New York: Appleton, 1895), p. 16.

[24] See his essay "Höre, Israel!" *Die Zukunft* (6 March 1897): 454–62.

[25] David Friedrich Strauss, *Der alte und der neue Glaube: Ein Bekenntnis* (Leipzig: G. Hirzel, 1872), p. 71.

[26] See my essay "Nietzsche, Heine, and the Otherness of the Jew," in Timothy Sellner et al., eds., *Nietzsche and the Judaeo-Christian Tradition* (Chapel Hill: University of North Carolina Press, 1985), pp. 206–25.

[27] Max Nordau, *Zionistische Schriften* (Cologne: Jüdischer Verlag, 1909), pp. 379–81.

[28] *Standard Edition*, op. cit., 12:. 1–79.

[29] On "Little Hans" and masturbation, see Peter Gay, *Freud: A Life for Our Time* (New York: W. W. Norton, 1988), pp. 255–61.

[30] *Standard Edition*, op. cit., 7: 191. See Stephen Kern, "The Discovery of Child Sexuality: Freud and the Emergence of Child Psychology" (Diss., Columbia, 1972) for the background on the pathologization of childhood sexuality.

[31] This is detailed to a much greater extent in my essay "Freud and the Prostitute: Male Stereotypes of Female Sexuality in Fin-de-Siècle Vienna," *Journal of the American Academy of Psychoanalysis* 9 (1981): 337–60.

[32] See my essay "The Struggle of Psychiatry with Psychoanalysis: Who Won?" *Critical Inquiry* 13 (1987): 293–313, for the details.

[33] Dietz Bering, *Der Name als Stigma: Antisemitismus in deutschen Alltag 1812–1933* (Stuttgart: Klett-Cotta, 1987).

[34] Wilhelm Stekel, *Auto-Eroticism: A Psychiatric Study of Onanism and Neurosis*, trans. James S. Van Teslaar (New York: Liveright, 1950).

[35] Sandor Rado, *Adaptational Psychodynamics: Motivation and Control* (New York: Science House, 1969), pp. 12–37, 72–79, and his discussion of "The Problem of Melancholia (1927)" in his *Psychoanalysis of Behavior: Collected Papers* (New York: Grune & Stratton, 1956), pp. 47–63.

[36] Harry Stack Sullivan, *Conceptions of Modern Psychiatry* (New York: W. W. Norton, 1940), pp. 24–69.

[37] See William H. Masters and Virginia E. Johnson, *Human Sexual Response* (Boston: Little, Brown, 1966), and *Human Sexual Inadequacy* (Boston: Little, Brown, 1970).

[38] See, for example, the discussion throughout Peter Blos, *On Adolescence: A Psychoanalytic Interpretation* (New York: The Free Press, 1962), as well as G. W. Grumet, "Pathological Masturbation with Drastic Consequences: Case Report," *Journal of Clinical Psychiatry* 46 (1985): 537–39, in which the psychoanalytic model is adapted into a clinical setting.

[39] See Wilder Penfield, *The Cerebral Cortex of Man* (New York: Macmillan, 1952).

[40] For example, see the literature collected by Margo Hittelman, "Sexual Abuse: Teaching about Touching," *School Library Journal* 31 (1985): 34–41. See also Janie Hart-Rossi, *Protect Your Child from Sexual Abuse, A Parent's Guide: A Book to Teach Children How to Resist Uncomfortable Touch* (Seattle, WA: Parenting Press, 1984), and *Touching*, by the Coalition for Child Advocacy (Bellingham, WA: Whatcom County Opportunity Council, 1985).

[41] Alvin Rosenfeld, Robert Bailey, Bryna Siegel, and Gwyn Bailey, "Determining Incestuous Contact between Parent and Child: Frequency of Children Touching Parents' Genitals in a Nonclinical Population," *Journal of the American Academy of Child Psychiatry* 25 (1986): 481–84.

[42] Wilhelm Stekel, "Über Coitus im Kindesalter," *Wiener medizinischen Blätter* 18 (1895): 247–49.

[43] See my *Difference and Pathology*, op. cit., pp. 44–48.

[44] See the general debate about the views concerning the seduction theory put forth by Jeffrey Moussaieff Masson, *The Assault on Truth: Freud's Suppression of the Seduction Theory* (New York: Farrar, Straus and Giroux, 1984).

[45] Elaine Showalter, "Critical Cross-Dressing: Male Feminists and the Woman of the Year," *Raritan: A Quarterly Review* 3 (1983): 130–49.

[46] Kay Mills, *A Place in the News: From the Women's Page to the Front Page* (New York: Dodd, Mead, 1988).

[47] P. Michel-Michot, "The Myth of Innocence," *Revue des langues vivantes* 28 (1962): 510–20.

[48] T. D. Savill, "Hysterical Skin Symptoms and Eruptions," *Lancet* (20 January 1904): 273–78. On the context for this image, see K. Codell Carter, "Infantile Hysteria and Infantile Sexuality in Late Nineteenth-Century German-Language Medical Literature," *Medical History* 27 (1983): 186–96.

[49] See in detail Morton N. Cohen, *Lewis Carroll, Photographer of Children: Four Nude Studies* (New York: Crown, 1978). Contrast this study with Ronald Peasall, *Tell Me, Pretty Maiden: The Victorian and Edwardian Nude* (Exeter: Webb & Bower, 1981).

[50] See Baron Wilhelm von Gloeden, *Photographs of the Classic Male Nude* (New York: Camera/Graphic Press, 1975), and Italo Mussa, "Wilhelm von Gloeden," *Flash Art* 109 (1982): 64–65; Brandt Aymar, *The Young Male Figure in Paintings, Sculptures, and Drawings from Ancient Egypt to the Present* (New York: Crown,

1976), and David Martocci, *The Male Nude: Catalogue and Exhibition* (Williamstown, MA: Sterling and Francine Clark Art Institute, 1980).

[51] Vivien M. Green, "Hiram Powers's *Greek Slave*: Emblem of Freedom," *American Art Journal* 14 (1982): 31–39.

[52] Marcel Proust, *Remembrance of Things Past*, trans. C. K. Scott Moncrieff and Terence Kilmartin (Harmondsworth: Penguin, 1986), 1: 577.

[53] Magnus Hirschfeld, *The Sexual History of the World War* (New York: Cadillac, 1941), p. 47.

[54] Peter Altenberg, *Ashantee* (Berlin: S. Fischer, 1897). All citations are to this edition. On Altenberg, the best overviews are Camillo Schaefer, *Peter Altenberg: Ein biographischer Essay. Friebord*, Sonderreihe nr. 10 (Vienna: Friebord, 1980), and Hans Christian Kosler, ed., *Peter Altenberg: Leben und Werke in Texten und Bildern* (Munich: Matthes and Seitz, 1981).

[55] Friedrich Ratzel, *The History of Mankind*, trans. A. J. Butler (London: Macmillan, 1898), 2: 352–57; 3: 125–43. On the importance of the anthropological literature of the nineteenth century as a source for the image of the Other, see Paul Weideger, *History's Mistress: A New Interpretation of a Nineteenth-Century Ethnological Classic* (New York: Pelican, 1986).

[56] *Die Fackel*, 806–9 (May 1929): 46 ff.

[57] Bernadette Bucher, *La sauvage aux seins pendants* (Paris: Hermann, 1977), which is available in English as *Icon and Conquest: A Structural Analysis of the Illustrations of de Bry's 'Great Voyages'* (Chicago: University of Chicago Press, 1981).

[58] Gustav Jaeger, *Die Entdeckung der Seele* (Leipzig: Ernst Günther, 1880), pp. 106–9.

[59] Iwan Bloch, *Das Sexualleben unserer Zeit in seinen Beziehung zur modernen Kultur* (Berlin: Louis Marcus, 1907). Typical for the resonance of this theme in the philosophical literature of the period is Paul Ree, *Der Ursprung der moralischen Empfindungen* (Chemnitz: Ernst Schmeitzer, 1877), pp. 74–77.

[60] John M. Eyler, *Victorian Social Medicine: The Ideas and Methods of William Farr* (Baltimore: Johns Hopkins University Press, 1979), p. 100.

[61] See the discussion by Stephen Jay Gould, *The Flamingo's Smile: Reflections in Natural History* (New York: W. W. Norton, 1985), pp. 200–9.

[62] Lorenz Oken, *Elements of Physiophilosophy* (London: The Ray Society, 1847), p. 651.

[63] Havelock Ellis, *Studies in the Psychology of Sex: Sexual Selection in Man* (Philadelphia: F. A. Davis, 1926), p. 6.

[64] *Basic Writings of Nietzsche*, ed. and trans. Walter Kaufmann (New York: Modern Library, 1968), p. 504.

[65] Houston Stewart Chamberlain, *Foundations of the Nineteenth Century*, trans. John Lees, 2 vols. (London: John Lane, 1910), 1: 388–89.

[66] On the iconographic function of black sexuality attraction, see Iwan Bloch, *Beiträge zur Aetiologie der Psychopathia Sexualis* (Dresden: H. R. Dohrn, 1903), 2: 261–62.

[67] Friedrich Nietzsche, *The Gay Science*, trans. Walter Kaufmann (New York: Random House, 1974), p. 126.

[68] Jules Michelet, *Journal*, 4 vols. (Paris: Gallimard, 1959–76).

[69] Havelock Ellis, *Studies in the Psychology of Sex* (Philadelphia: F. A. Davis, 1928), 7: 171–72. See Phyllis Grosskurth, *Havelock Ellis: A Biography* (New York: Knopf, 1980).

[70] Bernard C. Meyer, "Some Observations on the Rescue of Fallen Women," *Psychoanalytic Quarterly* 53 (1984): 224. Compare the discussion in Nina Auerbach, *Woman and the Demon: The Life of a Victorian Myth* (Cambridge, MA: Harvard University Press, 1982), pp. 150–84.

[71] Jan Goldstein, "The Hysteria Diagnosis and the Politics of Anticlericalism in Late Nineteenth-Century France," *Journal of Modern History* 54 (1982): 209–39, as well as her broader study *Console and Classify: The French Psychiatric Profession in the Nineteenth Century* (Cambridge: Cambridge University Press, 1987).

[72] Ratzel, *History of Mankind*, op. cit., 2: 283.

[73] See my essay "Freud and the Prostitute: Male Sterotypes of Female Sexuality in Fin-de-Siècle Vienna," *Journal of the American Academy of Psychoanalysis* 9 (1981): 337–60.

[74] Walter Rathenau, "Höre, Israel!" *Die Zukunft* 18 (1897): 454–62. On the iconography of the "feminine male," see James D. Steakley, "Iconography of a Scandal: Political Cartoons and the Eulenberg Affair," *Studies in Visual Communication* 9 (1983): 20–51.

[75] Alexander Pilcz, *Beitrag zur vergleichenden Rassen-Psychiatrie*, op. cit., pp. 40–41, gives a detailed summary of the entire late nineteenth-century literature on race and hysteria. For a psychoanalytic parallel, see Arrah B. Evarts, "*Dementia praecox* in the Colored Race," *Psychoanalytic Review* 7 (1913–14): 388–403.

[76] The standard biography of James is Ralph Barton Perry, *The Thought and Character of William James, I: Inheritance and Vocation* (Boston: Little, Brown, 1935), pp. 320–23. Perry is extremely careful not to assume the literal dating of this passage to the winter of 1870. Quite independently of this chapter, Cushing Strout, "William James and the Twice-Born Sick Soul," in his *The Veracious Imagination: Essays in American History, Literature and Biography* (Middletown, CT: Wesleyan University Press, 1981), pp. 199–222, sought a "French" source for James's representation of his illness. Also of interest is Maurice Le Breton, *La personnalité de William James* (Bordeaux: Imprimerie de l'Université, 1928), especially pp. 238–44.

[77] All quotations from the text are from William James, *The Varieties of Religious Experience* (New York: Collier, 1961), pp. 137–39. This is the most accessible edition. In the first edition, this passage is found on pp. 160–61. The question of James's linking of his own experience to older examples of melancholy (primary affective disorder) is tenuous. See Bridget Gellert Lyons, *Voices of Melancholy: Studies in Literary Treatments of Melancholy in Renaissance England* (London: Routledge & Kegan Paul, 1971) for comparative examples.

[78] Gay Wilson Allen, *William James: A Biography* (New York: Viking, 1967), pp. 164–67. See also Don S. Browning, *Pluralism and Personality: William James and Some Contemporary Cultures of Psychology* (Lewisburg, PA: Bucknell University Press, 1980); Daniel W. Bjork, *The Compromised Scientist: William James and the Development of American Psychology* (New York: Columbia University Press, 1983); and Gerald E. Meyers, *William James: His Life and Thought* (New Haven, CT: Yale University Press, 1986).

[79] Cited from James's diaries by Allen, op. cit., p. 164.

[80] Henry James, *Society, the Redeemed Form of Man* (Boston: Houghton, Osgood & Co., 1879), pp. 44–49. See also Frederic Harold Young, *The Philosophy of Henry James, Sr.* (New York: Bookman Associates, 1951).

[81] J. É. D. Esquirol, *Des maladies mentales considérées sous les rapports médical, hygiénique et médico-légal* (Paris: J. B. Baillière, 1838), 2: 93–94.

[82] The standard study has been C. Hartley Grattan, *The Three Jameses: A Family of Minds* (London: Longmans, Green and Co., 1932), especially pp. 122–25. See also Howard Feinstein, *Becoming William James* (Ithaca, NY: Cornell University Press, 1984).

[83] Cited by Perry, op. cit., p. 165.

[84] On the relationship between the sense of self and the economic definition of the self in the nineteenth century, see Ben Barker-Benfield, "The Spermatic Economy: A Nineteenth-Century View of Sexuality," *Feminist Studies* 1 (1972): 45–74.

[85] Henry Maudsley, *Body and Mind* (London: Macmillan, 1873), pp. 86–87.

NOTES FOR CHAPTER 10

[1] George Hamilton, *Manet and His Critics* (New Haven: Yale University Press, 1954), pp. 67–68. See John Berger, *Ways of Seeing* (London: Penguin, 1972), p. 54. A reworking of this formulation is taken from Kenneth Clarke's *The Nude: A Study of Ideal Art* (London: John Murray, 1956), p. 1. I am ignoring here the peculiar position of George Mauner, *Manet: Peintre-Philosophe: A Study of the Painter's Themes* (University Park: Pennsylvania University Press, 1975) that "we may conclude that Manet makes no comment at all with this painting, if by comment we understand judgment or criticism" (p. 99).

[2] For my discussion of *Olympia*, I draw on Theodore Reff, *Manet: Olympia* (London: Allen Lane, 1976), and for my discussion of *Nana*, on Werner Hofmann, *Nana: Mythos und Wirklichkeit* (Cologne: Dumont Schauberg, 1973). Neither of these studies examines the medical analogies. See also Eunice Lipton, "Manet: A Radicalized Female Imagery," *Artforum* 13 (1975): 48–53.

[3] George Needham, "Manet, Olympia and Pornographic Photography," in Thomas Hess and Linda Nochlin, eds., *Woman as Sex Object* (New York: Newsweek, 1972), pp. 81–89.

[4] P. Rebeyrol, "Baudelaire et Manet," *Les Temps Modernes* 5 (1949): 707–25.

[5] Georges Bataille, *Manet*, trans. A. Wainhouse and James Emmons (New York: Skira, 1956), p. 113.

[6] Edmund Bazire's 1884 view of *Nana* is cited by Anne Coffin Hanson, *Manet and the Modern Tradition* (New Haven, CT: Yale University Press, 1977), p. 130.

[7] See my *On Blackness without Blacks: Essays on the Image of the Black in Germany* (Boston: G. H. Hall, 1982). On the image of the black, see Ladislas Bugner, ed., *L'image du noir dans l'art occidental* (Paris: Bibliothèque des Arts, 1976 ff.). The fourth volume, not yet published, will cover the post-Renaissance period. In the course of the nineteenth century, the female Hottentot becomes the black female *in nuce*, and the prostitute becomes representative of the sexualized woman. Both of these categories represent the creation of classes that represent very specific qualities. Although the number of terms for the various categories of the prostitute expanded substantially during the nineteenth century, all were used to label the sexualized woman. Likewise, whereas many groups of African blacks were known in the nineteenth century, the Hottentot remained representative for the essence of the black, especially the black female. Both concepts fulfilled an iconographic function in the perception and representation of the world. How these two concepts were associated provides a case study for the investigation of patterns of conventions, without any limitation on the "value" of one system over another. One must also note the fascination with the primitive during this period and the association of blacks with the idea of the primitive forms that represented (to the nineteenth-century eye) the idealized form of the primitive female. See Mario Petrocchi, "La femme dans l'art préhistorique: Interprétation historique et médicale," *Medicina nei secoli* 3 (1966): 72–82.

[8] One might add that it also reaches deep into the twentieth century. See Elizabeth Lunbeck, " 'A New Generation of Women': Progressive Psychiatrists and the Hypersexual Female," *Feminist Studies* 13 (1987): 513–43.

[9] See Ludwig von Braun, ed., *The Amorous Drawings of the Marquis von Bayros* (New York: Cythera Press, 1968).

[10] See John Herbert Eddy, Jr., "Buffon, Organic Change, and the Races of Man" (Diss., Oklahoma, 1977), p. 109, as well as Paul Alfred Erickson, "The Origins of Physical Anthropology" (Diss., Connecticut, 1974), and Werner Krauss, *Zur Anthropologie des 18. Jahrhunderts: Die Frühgeschichte der Menschheit im Blickpunkt der Aufklärung*, ed. Hans Kortum and Christa Gohrisch (Munich: Hanser, 1979). See also George W. Stocking, Jr., *Race, Culture and Evolution: Essays in the History of Anthropology* (Chicago: University of Chicago Press, 1982).

[11] Guillaume Thomas Raynal, *Histoire philosophique et politique des établissements et du commerce des Européens dans les deux Indes* (Geneva: Chez les libraires associés, 1775), 2: 406–7.

[12] William F. Bynum, "The Great Chain of Being after Forty Years: An Appraisal," *History of Science* 13 (1975): 1–28, and his dissertation "Time's Noblest Offspring: The Problem of Man in British Natural Historical Sciences" (Diss., Cambridge, 1974).

[13] *Dictionnaire des sciences médicales* (Paris: C. L. F. Panckoucke, 1819), 35: 398–403.

[14] J. J. Virey, *Histoire naturelle du genre humain* (Paris: Crochard, 1824), 2: 151.

[15] George M. Gould and Walter L. Pyle, *Anomalies and Curiosities of Medicine* (Philadelphia: W. B. Saunders, 1901), p. 307, and Eugen Holländer, *Äskulap und Venus: Eine Kultur- und Sittengeschichte im Spiegel des Arztes* (Berlin: Propyläen, 1928). Much material on the indebtedness of the early pathologists to the reports of travelers to Africa can be found in the accounts of the autopsies presented below. One indication of the power that the image of the Hottentot still possessed in the late nineteenth century is to be found in George Eliot's *Daniel Deronda* (1876). On its surface, the novel is a hymn to racial harmony and an attack on British middle-class bigotry. Eliot's liberal agenda is nowhere better articulated than in the ironic debate concerning the nature of the black in which the eponymous hero of the novel defends black sexuality (p. 376). This position is attributed to the hero not a half-dozen pages after the authorial voice of the narrator introduced the description of this very figure with the comparison: "And one man differs from another, as we all differ from the Bosjesman" (p. 370). Eliot's comment is quite in keeping with the underlying understanding of race in the novel. For just as Deronda is fated to marry a Jewess and thus avoid the taint of race mixing, so too is the Bushman, a Hottentot surrogate in the nineteenth century, isolated from the rest of humanity. That a polygenetic view of race and liberal ideology can be held simultaneously is evident as far back as Voltaire. But the Jew is here contrasted to the Hottentot, and, as has been seen, it is the Hottentot who serves as the icon of pathologically corrupted sexuality. Can Eliot be drawing a line between outsiders such as the Jew and the sexualized female in Western society and the Hottentot? The Hottentot comes to serve as the sexualized Other onto whom Eliot projects the opprobrium with which she herself was labeled. For Eliot, the Hottentot remains beyond the pale, showing that even in the most Whiggish text the Hottentot remains the essential Other. George Eliot, *Daniel Deronda*, ed. Barbara Hardy (Harmondsworth: Penguin, 1967).

[16] De Blainville, "Sur une femme de la race hottentote," *Bulletin des sciences par la société philomatique de Paris* (1816), pp. 183–90. This early version of the autopsy seems to be unknown to William B. Cohen, *The French Encounter with Africans: White Response to Blacks, 1530–1880* (Bloomington: Indiana University Press, 1980), esp. pp. 239–45, for his discussion of Cuvier. See also Stephen Jay Gould, "The Hottentot Venus," in his *The Flamingo's Smile: Reflections in Natural History* (New York: W. W. Norton, 1985), pp. 291–305.

[17] Cited from Leslie Fielder, *Freaks: Myths and Images of the Secret Self* (New York: Simon & Schuster, 1978), p. 146.

[18] Georges Cuvier, "Extraits d'observations faites sur le cadavre d'une femme connue á Paris et a Londres sous le nom de Venus Hottentote," *Memoires du Musée d'histoire naturelle* 3 (1817): 259–74. Reprinted with plates by Géoffrey Saint-Hilaire and Frederic Cuvier, *Histoire naturelle des mammifères avec des figures originales*

(Paris: A. Belin, 1824), 1: 1 ff. The substance of the autopsy is reprinted again by Flourens in the *Journal complementaire du dictionnaire des sciences médicales* 4 (1819): 145–49, and by Jules Cloquet, *Manuel d'anatomie de l'homme descriptive du corps humain* (Paris: Bechet jeune, 1825), Plate 278. Cuvier's presentation of the "Hottentot Venus" forms the major signifier for the image of the Hottentot as sexual primitive in the nineteenth century.

[19] Quoted from the public record by Paul Edwards and James Walvin, eds., *Black Personalities in the Era of the Slave Trade* (London: Macmillan, 1983), pp. 171–83. A print of the 1829 ball in Paris with the nude "Hottentot Venus" is reproduced in Richard Toellner, ed., *Illustrierte Geschichte der Medizin* (Salzburg: Andreas and Andreas, 1981), 4: 1319. (This is a German reworking of Jacques Vie et al., *Histoire de la médecine* (Paris: Albin Michel-Laffont-Tchon, 1979). On the showing of the "Hottentot Venus," see Percival R. Kirby, "The Hottentot Venus," *Africana Notes and News* 6 (1949): 55–62, and his "More about the Hottentot Venus," *Africana Notes and News* 10 (1953): 124–34; Richard D. Altick, *The Shows of London* (Cambridge, MA: Belknap Press of Harvard University, 1978), p. 269; and Bernth Lindfors, " 'The Hottentot Venus' and Other African Attractions in Nineteenth-Century England," *Australasian Drama Studies* 1 (1983): 83–104.

[20] See Barbara J. Babiger, "The *Kunst- und Wunderkammern*: A *catalogue raisonné* of Collecting in Germany, France and England, 1565–1750" (Diss., University of Pittsburgh, 1970) as well as Walker D. Greer, "John Hunter: Order Out of Variety," *Annals of the Royal College of Surgeons of England* 28 (1961): 238–51.

[21] Adolf Wilhelm Otto, *Seltene Beobachtungen zur Anatomie, Physiologie und Pathologie gehörig* (Breslau: Wilibald Holäafer, 1816), p. 135; Johannes Müller, "Über die äusseren Geschlechtstheile der Buschmänninnen," *Archiv für Anatomie, Physiologie und wissenschaftliche Medizin* (1834), pp. 319–45; W. H. Flower and James Murie, "Account of the Dissection of a Bushwoman," *Journal of Anatomy and Physiology* 1 (1867): 189–208; Hubert von Luschka, A. Koch, and E. Görtz, "Die äusseren Geschlechtstheile eines Buschweibes," *Monatsschrift für Geburtskunde* 32 (1868): 343–50. The popularity of these accounts can be seen by their republication (in extract) in *The Anthropological Review* (London) 5 (1867): 316–24, and 8 (1870): 89–318, which was aimed at a lay audience. These extracts also stress the sexual anomalies described.

[22] *Richmond and Louisville Medical Journal* for May 1868, p. 194, cited by Edward Turnipseed, "Some Facts in Regard to the Anatomical Differences between the Negro and White Races," *American Journal of Obstetrics* 10 (1877): 32–33. On the "external genital organs," see also R. W. Schufeldt, "Comparative Anatomical Characters of the Negro," *The Medical Brief* 32 (1904): 26–28.

[23] C. H. Fort, "Some Corroborative Facts in Regard to the Anatomical Difference between the Negro and White Races," *American Journal of Obstetrics* 10 (1877): 258–59. Paul Broca was influenced by similar American material that he cites from the *New York City Medical Record* of 15 September 1868 concerning the position of the hymen, *Bulletins de la société d'anthropologie de Paris* 4 (1869): 443–44. Broca, like Cuvier before him, supported a polygenetic view of the human races.

[24] William Turner, "Notes on the Dissection of a Negro," *Journal of Anatomy and Physiology* 13 (1878): 382–86; "Notes on the Dissection of a Second Negro," 14 (1879): 244–48; "Notes on the Dissection of a Third Negro," 31 (1896): 624–26. This was not merely a British anomaly. Jefferies Wyman reports the dissection of a black suicide victim in the *Proceedings of the Boston Society of Natural History* on 2 April 1862 and 16 December 1863 and does not refer to the genitalia of the male Hottentot at all. *Anthropological Review* 3 (1865): 330–35.

[25] H. Hildebrandt, *Die Krankheiten der äusseren weiblichen Genitalien.*

In Theodor Billroth, ed., *Handbuch der Frauenkrankheiten III* (Stuttgart: Enke, 1877), pp. 11–12. See also Thomas Power Lowry, ed., *The Classic Clitoris: Historic Contributions to Scientific Sexuality* (Chicago: Nelson-Hall, 1978).

[26] Havelock Ellis, *Studies in the Psychology of Sex, 4: Sexual Selection in Man* (Philadelphia: F. A. Davis, 1920), pp. 152–85.

[27] Willem Vrolik, *Considerations sur la diversité du bassin des différentes races humaines* (Amsterdam: Van der Post, 1826); R. Verneau, *Le bassin dans les sexes et dans les races* (Paris: Baillière, 1875), pp. 126–29.

[28] Charles Darwin, *The Descent of Man and Selection in Relation to Sex* (Princeton: Princeton University Press, 1981), 2: 317 on the pelvis, and 2: 345–46 on the Hottentot.

[29] John Grand-Carteret, *Die Erotik in der französischen Karikatur*, trans. Cary von Karwarth and Adolf Neumann (from the manuscript), Gesellschaft Österreichischer Bibliophilen XVI (Vienna: C. W. Stern, 1909), p. 195.

[30] *The Memories of Dolly Morton: The Story of a Woman's Part in the Struggle to Free the Slaves: An Account of the Whippings, Rapes, and Violences That Preceded the Civil War in America with Curious Anthropological Observations on the Radical Diversities in the Conformation of the Female Bottom and the Way Different Women Endure Chastisement* (Paris: Charles Carrington, 1899), p. 207.

[31] Sigmund Freud, *The Standard Edition of the Complete Psychological Works of Sigmund Freud*, trans. James Strachey (London: Hogarth, 1953–74), here 7: 186–87, especially the footnote added in 1920 concerning the "genital apparatus" of the female.

[32] The best study of the image of the prostitute is Alain Corbin, *Les filles de noce: Misère sexuelle et prostitution aux 19ᵉ et 20ᵉ siècles* (Paris: Ambier, 1978). On the black prostitute, see Khalid Kistainy, *The Prostitute in Progressive Literature* (New York: Schocken, 1982), pp. 74–84.

[33] A. J. B. Parent-Duchatelet, *De la prostitution dans la ville de Paris* (Paris: Baillière, 1836) 1: 193–244.

[34] *On Prostitution in the City of Paris* (London: T. Burgess, 1840), p. 38. It is of interest that it is exactly the passages on the physiognomy and appearance of the prostitute that this anonymous translator presents to an English audience as the essence of Parent-Duchatelet's work.

[35] Freud, *Standard Edition*, op. cit., 7: 191.

[36] V. M. Tarnowsky, *Prostitutsija i abolitsioniszm* (Petersburg: n.p., 1888); *Prostitution und Abolitionismus* (Hamburg: Voss, 1890). A contemporary introduction to the historiographical problems of syphilis using Russian materials is to be found in Laura Engelstein's "Syphilis, Historical and Actual: Cultural Geography of a Disease," *Reviews of Infectious Diseases* 8 (1986): 1036–48 as well as her "Morality and the Wooden Spoon: Russian Doctors View Syphilis, Social Class, and Sexual Behavior, 1890–1905," *Representations* 14 (1986): 169–208.

[37] Pauline Tarnowsky, *Étude anthropométrique sur les prostituées et les voleuses* (Paris: E. Lecrosnier et Bébe, 1889).

[38] Pauline Tarnowsky, "Fisiomie di prostitute russe," *Archivio di Psichiatria, scienze penali ed antropologia criminale* 14 (1893): 141–42.

[39] Cesare Lombroso and Guglielmo Ferrero, *La donna deliquente: La prostituta e la donna normale* (Torino: Roux, 1893) on the photographs of the Russian prostitutes, pp. 349–50; on the fat of the prostitute, pp. 361–62; and on the labia of the Hottentots, p. 38.

[40] Adrien Charpy, "Des organes génitaux externes chez les prostituées," *Annales des Dermatologie* 3 (1870–71): 271–79.

[41] Ellis, *Psychology of Sex*, op. cit., 4: 164.

[42] *Congrès international d'anthropologie criminelle* (1896) (Geneva: Georg et Co., 1897), pp. 348–49.

[43] I. Callari, "Prostituzione e prostituta in Sicilia," *Archivio di*

Psichiatria 24 (1903): 1193–1206.

[44] Guglielmo Ferrero [Guillaume Ferrero], "L'atavisme de la prostitution," *Revue scientifique* (Paris) 1892, pp. 136–41.

[45] Lombroso and Ferrero, *La donna deliquente*, op. cit., p. 111.

[46] Abele De Blasio, "Steatopigia in prostitute," *Archivio di psichiatria* 26 (1905): 257–64.

[47] See Winthrop Jordan, *White over Black: American Attitudes toward the Negro, 1550–1812* (New York: W. W. Norton, 1977), pp. 3–43.

[48] Iwan Bloch, *Der Ursprung der Syphilis*, 2 vols. (Jena: Gustav Fischer, 1901–11).

[49] On Degas, see Eunice Lipton, *Looking into Degas: Uneasy Images of Women and Modern Life* (Berkeley, CA: University of California Press, 1986), pp. 151–86, and Charles Bernheimer, "Degas's Brothels: Voyeurism and Ideology," *Representations* 20 (1987), 158–87.

[50] Reff, *Manet: Olympia*, op. cit., pp. 57–58, also p. 118.

[51] The close relationship between "the extension of the labia in Hottentot culture" and the "corseting and lacing common in the West during the later nineteenth and early twentieth centuries" has been commented on by Leslie Fielder, op. cit., p. 251.

[52] Cited in the notes to T. J. Clark, *The Painting of Modern Life: Paris in the Art of Manet and His Followers* (Princeton, NJ: Princeton University Press, 1984), p. 287.

[53] See Auriant, *La véritable histoire de "Nana"* (Paris: Mercure de France, 1942) as well as Adeline R. Tintner, "What Zola's *Nana* Owes to Manet's *Nana*," *Iris* 2 (1983): 15–16. See also Demetra Palamari, "The Shark Who Swallowed His Epoch: Family, Nature and Society in the Novels of Emile Zola," in Virginia Tufts and Barbara Meyerhoff, eds., *Changing Images of the Family* (New Haven, CT: Yale University Press, 1978), pp. 155–72, and Robert A. Nye, *Crime, Madness, and Politics in Modern France: The Medical Concept of National Decline* (Princeton, NJ: Princeton University Press, 1984).

[54] All the quotations are from Charles Duff's translation of *Nana* (London: Heineman, 1953), here p. 27. The position described by Zola mirrors Manet's image of Nana. It emphasizes her state of semiundress (echoing the image of the half-dressed "Hottentot Venus"). In Manet's image, she is in addition corseted, and the corset stresses her artificially narrowed waist and the resultant emphasis on the buttocks. Both Manet's and Zola's images recall the bustle that Nana would have worn once dressed. (Nana is, for Zola, a historical character, existing at a very specific time in French history, in the decade leading up to the Franco-Prussian War of 1872.) The bustle (or *tounure*) was the height of fashion between 1865 and 1876 (and again in the mid-1880s). Worn with a tightly laced bodice, the bustle created the illusion of the female as the image of the primitive and the erotic, while maintaining her within the acceptable limits of middle-class fashion. Both the woman wearing a bustle and her audience knew the inherent artificiality of the bustle as a representation of the protruding buttocks but were also aware of the implications of this sign. The "bum rolls" of the seventeenth century and the "cork rumps" of the eighteenth century had already established this association. But the bustle of the late nineteenth century, stretching out at the rear of the dress like a shelf, directly echoed the primitive sexuality of the Hottentot. Thus the dress implied by Nana's state of semiundress and by her undergarments, in Manet's painting and in Zola's description, also point to the primitive hidden within. See David Kunzle, *Fashion and Fetishism: A Social History of the Corset, Tight-Lacing and Other Forms of Body Sculpture in the West* (Totowa, NJ: Rowman and Littlefield, 1982).

[55] Cited by Bataille, *Manet*, op. cit., p. 65.

[56] Ellis, *Psychology of Sex*, op. cit., 4: 176.

[57] Abel Hermant, *Confession d'un enfant d'hier*, cited by Ellis, op. cit. Parallel views can be found throughout the late nineteenth century. See the discussion of sexuality between the races in Iwan Bloch, *Beiträge zur Ätiologie der Psychopathia sexualis* (Dresden: H. R. Dohrn, 1903), vol. 2, pp. 260–63, where sexual contact between "races" is labeled as pathological (sadistic).

[58] Joachim Hohmann, ed., *Schon auf den ersten Blick: Lesebuch zur Geschichte unserer Feindbilder* (Darmstadt: Luchterhand, 1981).

[59] Freud, *Standard Edition*, op. cit., 25: 212. See also Renate Schliesier, *Konstruktion der Weiblichkeit bei Sigmund Freud* (Frankfurt: Europäische Verlagsantalt, 1981), pp. 35–39.

[60] Giacomo Leopardi, *Pensieri*, trans. W. S. Di Piero (Baton Rouge: Louisiana State University Press, 1981), p. 111.

NOTES FOR CHAPTER 11

[1] *Newsweek*, 21 July 1986. On the general background of the image of the AIDS patient, see Caspar G. Schmidt, "The Group-Fantasy Origins of AIDS," *Journal of Psychohistory* 12 (1884): 37–78; Dennis Altman, *AIDS in the Mind of America: The Social, Political, and Psychological Impact of a New Epidemic* (New York: Anchor/Doubleday, 1986); David Black, *The Plague Years: A Chronicle of AIDS, the Epidemic of Our Times* (New York: Simon & Schuster/London: Picador, 1986); Graham Hancock and Enver Carim, *AIDS: The Deadly Epidemic* (London: Gollanz, 1986); Richard Liebmann-Smith, *The Question of AIDS* (New York: The New York Academy of Sciences, 1985); Eve K. Nicols, *Mobilizing against AIDS: The Unfinished Story of a Virus* (Cambridge, MA: Harvard University Press, 1986); Lon G. Nungasser, *Epidemic of Courage: Facing AIDS in America* (New York: St. Martin's, 1986); Earl E. Shelp, Ronald H. Sunderland, and Peter W. H. Mansell, *AIDS: Personal Stories in Pastoral Perspective* (New York: Pilgrim Press, 1986); Barbara Peabody, *The Screaming Room: A Mother's Journal of Her Son's Struggle with AIDS/A True Story of Love, Dedication and Courage* (San Diego, CA: Oak Tree, 1986); Randy Shilts, *And the Band Played On: Politics, People, and the AIDS Epidemic* (New York: St. Martin's, 1987), and Mirko D. Grmek, *Histoire du sida* (Paris: Payot, 1989). More important, see George L. Mosse's brilliant study *Nationalism and Sexuality: Respectability and Abnormal Sexuality in Modern Europe* (New York: Howard Fertig, 1985), for a sense of the cultural context of much of this literature.

[2] Michael S. Gottlieb and Jerome E. Groopman, eds., *Acquired Immune Deficiency Syndrome: Proceedings of a Schering Corporation–UCLA Symposium* (held in Park City, Utah, 5–10 February 1984) (New York: Liss, 1984).

[3] See H. Schwartz, "AIDS in the Media," in the Twentieth Century Fund's *Science in the Streets* (New York: Priority Press, 1984), pp. 30 ff. as well as Andrea J. Baker, "The Portrait of AIDS in the Media: An Analysis of the *New York Times*," in Douglas A. Feldman and Thomas M. Johnson, eds., *The Social Dimension of AIDS: Method and Theory* (New York: Praeger, 1986), pp. 179–97. See also Simon Watney, *Policing Desire: Pornography, AIDS, and the Media* (Minneapolis: University of Minnesota Press, 1987), and Paula A. Treichler, "AIDS, Homophobia, and Biomedical Discourse: An Epidemic of Signification," *October* 43 1987): 31–70.

[4] Roy Porter, "Ever since Eve: The Fear of Contagion," *The Times Literary Supplement* (27 May–2 June 1988): 582.

[5] A detailed chronology of the scientific findings about AIDS has now been worked out between Robert C. Gallo and Luc Montagnier, scientists who were both involved in many of the initial discoveries concerning the disease. It details the disease from 1981 to 1985. See *The Chronicle of Higher Education* (8 April 1987), p. 8, for that chronology.

[6] A. Friedman-Kien et al., "Kaposi's Sarcoma and *Pneumocystis*

Pneumonia among Homosexual Men—New York City and California," *Morbidity and Mortality Weekly Report* 30 (1981): 305–8.

[7] M. S. Gottlieb et al., "*Pneumocystis* Pneumonia—Los Angeles," *Morbidity and Mortality Weekly Report* 30 (1981): 250–52 as well as S. M. Friedman et al., "Follow-Up on Kaposi's Sarcoma and *Pneumocystis* Pneumonia," *Morbidity and Mortality Weekly Report* 30 (1981): 409–10.

[8] See the initial editorial by J. A. Sonnabend, "The Etiology of AIDS," in *AIDS Research* 1 (1983/4): 1–12.

[9] See Liebmann-Smith, op. cit., pp. 84–86, and M. M. Lederman, "Transmission of the Acquired Immunodeficiency Syndrome through Heterosexual Activity," *Annals of Internal Medicine* 104 (1986): 115–17.

[10] See Jacques Liebowitch, *A Strange Virus of Unknown Origin*, trans. Richard Howard (New York: Ballantine, 1985), pp. 3–9, as well as J. W. Curran, W. M. Morgan, E. T. Starcher, A. M. Hardy, and H. W. Jaffe, "Epidemiological Trends of AIDS in the United States," *Cancer Research* 45 (1985): 4602s–4s.

[11] June E. Osborn, "The AIDS Epidemic: An Overview of the Science," *Issues in Science and Technology* 2 (1986): 56–65.

[12] J. Seale, "AIDS and Hepatitis B Cannot Be Venereal Diseases," *Journal of the Canadian Medical Association* 130 (1984): 109–10. See further, L. D. Grouse's editorial "HTLV-III Transmission," *Journal of the American Medical Association* 254 (1985): 2130–31. It is not, as Helen Mathews Smith notes, that "syphilis presents a paradigm for our latest venereal epidemic" but rather that AIDS is not a sexually transmitted disease but has been so categorized. (Helen Mathews Smith, "AIDS: Lessons from History," *MD Magazine* 30 [1986]: 43–51.)

[13] Allan Brandt, *No Magic Bullet: A Social History of Venereal Disease in the United States since 1880* (New York: Oxford University Press, 1985), p. 134. See also his informative essay, "The Syphilis Epidemic and Its Relation to AIDS," *Science* 239 (1988): 375–80.

[14] In this context, see Suzanne White, "*Mom and Dad* (1944): Venereal Disease Exploitation," *Bulletin of the History of Medicine* 62 (1988): 252–70.

[15] On the image of the prostitute in the twentieth century, see Pierre L. Horne and Mary Beth Pringle, eds., *The Image of the Prostitute in Modern Literature* (New York: F. Ungar, 1984).

[16] Compare Daniel M. Fox and Christopher J. Lawrence, *Photographing Medicine: Images and Power in Britain and America since 1840* (New York: Greenwood Press, 1988).

[17] A. Zuger and S. H. Miles, "Physicians, AIDS, and Occupational Risk: Historic Traditions and Ethical Obligations," *Journal of the American Medical Association* [*JAMA*] 258 (1987): 1924–28.

[18] Katie Leishman, "Public Health: AIDS and Syphilis," *The Atlantic* 261 (January 1988): 17–26.

[19] On the complexity of the categorization of sexually transmitted diseases, see J. D. Oriel and M. A. Waugh, "Sexually Transmitted Diseases Today," *Journal of the Royal Society of Medicine* 81 (1988): 312–14.

[20] John Langone, "AIDS Update: Still No Reason for Hysteria," *Discover* 7 (September 1986): 28–47. See also his book, *AIDS: The Facts* (Boston: Little, Brown, 1988). This view has surfaced again within the spectrum of the "woman's magazine," when Dr. Robert E. Gould, in an essay entitled "Reassuring News about AIDS: A Doctor Tells Why You May Not Be at Risk," in the mass circulation periodical *Cosmopolitan* (January 1988): 146 ff., argued that there was a natural firebreak for the spread of the disease, as AIDS was limited to two clearly defined groups, homosexuals and IV drug users. Heterosexuals, according to this argument, were in no way at risk. This argument assumes of course the existence of real, impermeable barriers between social groups; it reifies the fantasy of the borderline between the "normal" and the "deviant," between the "healthy" and

the "diseased." In reality, it is impossible to know whether one's sexual partner is bisexual or mainlining drugs because there is no true barrier that exists between these socially constructed categories.

[21] Cited from the selection from George Whitmore's book *Someone Was Here: Profiles in the AIDS Epidemic* (New York: New American Library, 1988) as published in *The New York Times Magazine* (31 January 1988), p. 16. This passage was not included in the final version of the book.

[22] See Edwin H. Zeydel's translation of *The Ship of Fools* (New York: Dover, 1962), pp. 220–23. Brant's is the first German text to indicate the source of the disease in the New World. See the discussion in Chapter Three.

[23] On the meaning of Africa in this context, see Oliver Ransford, *"Bid the Sickness Cease": Disease in the History of Black Africa* (London: John Murray, 1983).

[24] Liebowitch, *Strange Virus*, op. cit., p. 5.

[25] See the comparative essay by John Borneman, "AIDS in the Two Berlins," *October* 43 (1987): 223–36.

[26] J. Seale, "AIDS Virus Infection: A Soviet View of Its Origin," *Journal of the Royal Society of Medicine* 79 (1986): 494–95.

[27] Liebowitch, *Strange Virus*, op. cit., pp. 77–80.

[28] Sander L. Gilman, *Difference and Pathology: Stereotypes of Sexuality, Race, and Madness*, second edition (Ithaca, NY: Cornell University Press, 1986), pp. 131–49.

[29] William Lee Howard, "The Negro as a Distinct Ethnic Factor in Civilization," *Medicine* 9 (1903): 423.

[30] C. M. Brady, "The Negro as Patient," *New Orleans Medical and Surgical Journal* 56 (1903–4): 41.

[31] James H. Jones, *Bad Blood: The Tuskegee Syphilis Experiment— A Tragedy of Race and Medicine* (New York: The Free Press, 1981).

[32] Howard, op. cit., p. 424.

[33] J. F. Miller, "The Effects of Emancipation upon the Mental and Physical Health of the Negro of the South," *North Carolina Medical Journal* 38 (1896): 290.

[34] S. Piomelli, "Chronic Transfusions in Patients with Sickle Cell Disease: Indications and Problems," *American Journal of Pediatric Hematology and Oncology* 7 (1985): 51–55.

[35] Gilman, *Difference and Pathology*, op. cit., pp. 76–108.

[36] On the Haitian question, see J. W. Pape et al., "The Acquired Immunodeficiency Syndrome in Haiti," *Annals of Internal Medicine* 103 (1985): 774–78. On the "African" connection, see the exchange of letters in the *British Medical Journal* [*Clinical Research*] 290 (1985): 1284–85, 932, 1006; 291 (1986): 216.

[37] "Monkeys Possible Source of Human AIDS," *Science News* 127 (20 April 1985): 245. See the discussion in Margaret Cerulo and Evelynn Hammonds, "AIDS and Africa: The Western Imagination and the Dark Continent," *Radical America* 21 (1988): 21. I am grateful to my student Bryn Austin whose library work provided material for this segment.

[38] "Tracking AIDS to the Ends of the Earth," *Esquire* 106 (December 1986): 212.

[39] "Africa Begins to Face Up to AIDS," *Science* 230 (6 December 1985): 1141.

[40] "In the Grip of the Scourge," *Time* 129 (16 February 1987): 58.

[41] "Study Links AIDS in Eastern Africa to Primarily Heterosexual Behavior," *The Boston Globe* (13 February 1986): 26.

[42] "Alarming Increase of AIDS among Heterosexuals in Some African Nations," *The Washington Post* (16 August 1985): A6.

[43] *The Boston Globe*, op. cit. (13 February 1986): 26.

[44] Anthony J. Pinching, "AIDS and Africa: Lesons for Us All," *Journal of the Royal Society of Medicine* 79 (1986): 501–3.

[45] Robert E. Gould, op. cit., 147.

[46] See Masashi Fukasawa, Tomoyuki Miura, Akira Hasegawa, Shigeru Morikawa, Hajime Tsujimoto, Keizaburo Miki, Takashi

Kitamura, and Masanori Hayami, "Sequence of Simian Immunodeficiency Virus from African Green Monkey, a New Member of the HIV/SIV Group," *Nature* 333 (1988): 457–61.

[47] John R. Seale and Zhores A. Medvedev, "Origin and Transmission of AIDS: Multi-Use Hypodermics and the Threat to the Soviet Union: Discussion Paper," *Journal of the Royal Society of Medicine* 80 (1987): 301–4.

[48] On theories of degeneration and the city, see Sander L. Gilman and J. Edward Chamberlin, eds., *Degeneration: The Dark Side of Progress* (New York: Columbia University Press, 1985).

[49] "Africa in the Plague Years," *Newsweek* (24 November 1986): 46.

[50] "AIDS: The Plague That Knows No Bounds," *Reader's Digest* 130 (1987): 52.

[51] Charles S. Bacon, "The Race Problem," *Medicine* 9 (1903): 339.

[52] Ann Marie Lipinski and Dean Baquet, "Sawyer Aide's Ethnic Slurs Stir Uproar," *Chicago Tribune* (1 May 1988): 1. See Anthony Lewis, "A Dangerous Poison," *New York Times* (31 July 1988): E: 25.

[53] Cheryl Deval, "Sawyer Won't Fire Aide over Ethnic Slurs," *Chicago Tribune* (5 May 1988): 1.

[54] See Bernard Lewis, *Semites and Anti-Semites: An Inquiry into Conflict and Prejudice* (New York: Norton, 1986).

[55] Dorothy Nelkin and Stephen Hilgartner, "Disputed Dimensions of Risk: A Public School Controversy over AIDS," *Milbank Memorial Fund Quarterly* 64, Supplement 1 (1986): 118–42. Compare K. M. Shannon and A. J. Amman, "Acquired Immune Deficiency Syndrome in Childhood," *Journal of Pediatrics* 106 (1985): 332–42.

[56] The hostile reception of the book by William H. Masters, Virginia E. Johnson, and Robert E. Kolodny, *Crisis: Heterosexual Behavior in the Age of AIDS* (New York: Grove, 1988), is an excellent indication of what happens when the view of risk is confused with the existing status of infection. Although overstating their case in a most liberal interpretation of the ambiguities of the existing data, the extraordinary hostility to their message is clearly because they are stating the self-evident, that there are no natural barriers for the spread of the disease, no inherent boundaries for it. What is clear is that there is a potential for the disease to spread beyond the existing patient population. Masters and Johnson's error was to claim that that potential was already actualized, a claim without any substantial evidence in the spring of 1988. On the background of this debate about male-to-female transmission of AIDS, see the exchange of letters in *Journal of the American Medical Association* 258 (18 December 1987): 3386–89.

[57] Joseph Sandler, *From Safety to Superego* (New York: Guilford Press, 1987), p. 123.

List of Plates

23. Christ points toward his genitalia in Lucas Cranach the Elder, *Christ as Martyr*, *ca*. 1537. Berlin: Staatliche Museen.

24. Mary, the mother of the suffering Christ, is depicted as she was before the nativity in Lucas Cranach the Elder, *Mary as Suffering Mother*, *ca*. 1520. Berlin: Staatliche Museen.

25. The burial shroud covers the erect penis of Christ in Marten Jacobz van Veen Heemskerk, *Ecce Homo*, *ca*. 1525–30. Greenville, South Carolina: Bob Jones University.

26. A wide range of references to the sense of touch is present in Sebastiano del Piombo, *Holy Family with Saints and Donor*, *ca*. 1505–10. Paris: Musée du Louvre.

27. The importance of the sense of touch in opening the body in order to determine its nature can be seen in Caravaggio, *The Incredulity of St. Thomas*, *ca*. 1602–03. Potsdam–Sanssouci: Bildergalerie staatlicher Schlösser und Gärten.

28. The distancing effect of the forbidden touch is to be seen in Hans Holbein the Younger's early sixteenth-century *Noli me tangere*. London: Hampton Court Palace.

29. Rembrandt places Bathsheba's body in the center of the viewer's gaze, *The Toilet of Bathsheba*, 1632. New York: Metropolitan Museum of Art.

30. Charles Le Brun's, *Repentant Magdalene*, 1656, provides the moment of the prostitute's enlightenment. Paris: Musée du Louvre.

31. Rembrandt, *Susanna Surprised by the Elders*, *ca*. 1630. The Hague: Mauritshuis.

32. The various episodes in the life of Mary Magdalene are represented in this thirteenth-century Italian altarpiece. Florence: Galleria dell'academia.

33. Medallion of Mary Magdalene ascribed to the school of Donatello, *ca*. 1550, represents the hairiness of Mary as a coat of fur. London: Victoria and Albert Museum.

34. Mary Magdalene is represented with her entire body covered with hair by Tilmann Riemenschneider, *Maria Magdalena*, 1490–92. Munich: Bayerisches Nationalmuseum.

35. The skull of Adam as held by Adam in Johann Stephen of Calcar, *Adam*, probably after Titian, from Andreas Vesalius, *Epitome* (Basel: Oporinus, 1543). Ithaca: Howard B. Adelmann Collection, Olin Library, Cornell University.

36. Eve covers her genitalia in Johann Stephen of Calcar, *Eve*, probably after Titian, from Andreas Vesalius, *Epitome* (Basel: Oporinus, 1543). Ithaca: Howard B. Adelmann Collection, Olin Library, Cornell University.

37. Composite plates of the male genitalia from the 1565 edition of Vesalius's anatomical atlas from John Bertrand Saunders and Charles O'Malley, *Illustrations from the Works of Andreas Vesalius* (Cleveland: World Publishing, 1950). Ithaca: Howard B. Adelmann Collection, Olin Library, Cornell University.

38. Composite plates of the female genitalia from the 1565 edition of Vesalius's anatomical atlas from John Bertrand Saunders and Charles O'Malley, *Illustrations from the Works of Andreas Vesalius* (Cleveland: World Publishing, 1950). Ithaca: Howard B. Adelmann Collection, Olin Library, Cornell University.

39. Thomas Geminus, *Comendiosa toitus anatomiae delineatio* (London: J. Herford, 1545), engraving of full-length male and female nudes. London: Wellcome Institute for the History of Medicine.

40. Illustration of the viscera man and the birth of Eve from Bartholomaeus Anglicus, *De proprietatibus rerum* (Lyons: Guilaume L. Roy, 1485). Ithaca: Howard B. Adelmann Collection, Olin Library, Cornell University.

41. Woodcut of male anatomy from Gregor Reisch, *Margarita philosophica* (Freiburg im Breisgau: J. Schott, 1503). London: Wellcome Institute for the History of Medicine.

42. The map of the body from Magnus Hundt, *Anthropologium* (Leipzig: Baccalarius Wolfgang Monacensen, 1501). Ithaca: Howard B. Adelmann Collection, Olin Library, Cornell University.

43. Late medieval ivory anatomical figures used for the teaching of anatomy. London: Wellcome Institute for the History of Medicine.

44. Uncovering the ivory miniatures reveals a fetus in the uterus of the female, as well as the intestines. London: Wellcome Institute for the History of Medicine.

45. The zodiac man/woman with the genitalia masked but indicated by the sign of Scorpio, from Johannes Adelphus, *Mundini de omnibus humani corporis* (Strassbourg: M. Flach, 1513). Ithaca: Howard B. Adelmann Collection, Olin Library, Cornell University.

46. Arterial system of a pregnant woman, from Persian ms. no. 1576. Oxford: Bodleian Library.

47. The earliest image of the uterus (ninth century) from a European source. Brussels: Royal Library.

48. Image of the bicornate uterus from Jacopo da Carpi, *Isagogae breves* (Bonona: Benedictus Hector, 1522). Ithaca: Howard B. Adelmann Collection, Olin Library, Cornell University.

49. Image of the uterus in situ from Jacopo Berengario da Carpi, *Isagogae breves* (Bonona: Benedictus

Hector, 1522). Ithaca: Howard B. Adelmann Collection, Olin Library, Cornell University.

50. A full-length woodcut depicting female sexual anatomy from Johannes Dryander, *Anatomia capitis humani* (Marburg: E. Cervicornus, 1536). London: Wellcome Institute for the History of Medicine.

51. Composite plate from Andreas Vesalius, *De humani corporis fabrica libri sept* (Basel: Johannes Oporini, 1543), depicting the female torso, the bicornate uteruses of the cow and dog, and the penile representation of the human uterus. Ithaca: Howard B. Adelmann Collection, Olin Library, Cornell University.

52. Woodcut of fetuses from Walter Hermann Ryff, *Schwangerer Frauen Rosengarten* (Frankfurt: C. Egenolff, 1569), depicting the seven-chambered uterus. London: Wellcome Institute for the History of Medicine.

53. The seven-chambered uterus from Magnus Hundt, *Anthropologium* (Leipzig: Baccalarius Wolfgang Monacensen, 1501). Ithaca: Howard B. Adelmann Collection, Olin Library, Cornell University.

54. Anatomical fugitive sheets depicting the genitalia and intestines of a female. London: Wellcome Institute for the History of Medicine.

55. A woodcut of a childbirth scene from Gregor Reisch, *Margarita philosophica* (Freiburg im Breisgau: J. Schott, 1503). London: Wellcome Institute for the History of Medicine.

56. Galen discusses the hidden nature of sexuality before two persons in bed. Fourteenth-century Galen Ms. Dresden: University Library.

57. An image of coitus from the late medieval manuscript *Tacuinum sanitatis* of Ububchasym de Baldach. Ms. 4182. Rome: Biblioteca Casanatense.

58. An image of coitus from Marcantonio Riamondi, *I Modi, ca.* 1534. Vienna: Graphische Sammlung Albertina.

59. An image of coitus by Rembrandt, *Le Lit à la française (Ledekant)*, 1646. Hamburg: Kunsthalle.

60. A 1345 image of the opening of the body from Guido da Vigevano, *Liber notabilium . . . anothomia*. Ms. 334, fol. 260v. Chantilly: Musée Condé.

61. Frontispiece from Andreas Vesalius, *De humani corporis fabrica libri sept* (Basel: Johannes Oporini, 1543). Ithaca: Howard B. Adelmann Collection, Olin Library, Cornell University.

62. The boundary-crossing serpent as the figure of death and disease in Hans Baldung Grien, *Eve, the Serpent and Death*, 1515. Ottawa: National Gallery of Canada.

63. The figure of Death as a sign of the loss of feminine beauty through the process of aging in Hans Baldung Grien, *Three Ages of Woman and Death*, 1510. Vienna: Kunsthistorisches Museum.

64. The fourteenth-century image of "Madam World" from the portal of the St. Sebaldus Church in Nuremberg displaying her overt beauty and her hidden corruption. Ithaca: Private collection.

65. The title page of Charles Estienne, *La dissection des parties du corps humain* (Paris: Simon de Colines, 1546). Ithaca: Howard B. Adelmann Collection, Olin Library, Cornell University.

66. The female reproductive system from Charles Estienne, *La dissection des parties du corps humain* (Paris: Simon de Colines, 1546). Ithaca: Howard B. Adelmann Collection, Olin Library, Cornell University.

67. The male reproductive system from Charles Estienne, *La dissection des parties du corps humain* (Paris: Simon de Colines, 1546). Ithaca: Howard B. Adelmann Collection, Olin Library, Cornell University.

68. Albrecht Dürer's image of a syphilitic as fop (1496). Ithaca: Private collection.

69. The illustration of "lapides infigeri," or the fire-darting stones, from an illustrated manuscript, Ashmole 1511. Oxford: Bodleian Library.

70. The title page vignette to Sebastian Brant's 1496 pamphlet on syphilis. Reproduced from Karl Sudhoff, *Zehn Syphilis-Drucke aus den Jahren 1495–1498* (Milan: Lier, 1924).

71. The vignette from Joseph Grünpeck's 1496 commentary on Brant's syphilis pamphlet. Reproduced from Karl Sudhoff, *Zehn Syphilis-Drucke aus den Jahren 1495–1498* (Milan: Lier, 1924).

72. The beautiful temptress in Lucas van Leyden, *Temptation of St. Anthony,* 1506. Ithaca: Herbert F. Johnson Museum of Art.

73. An engraving by J. B. Mauzaisse after a lost image by Lucas Cranach, "Peasant and Whore," depicts the "unequal lovers," unequal in all respects. Ithaca: Herbert F. Johnson Museum of Art.

74. The icon representing the arranged marriage as a sexually transmitted disease from Andrea Alciatus, *Emblemes d'Alciat, de nouveau translates en françois vers pour vers iouxte les latins* (Lyons: Mace Bonhome, 1555). Ithaca: Private collection.

75. The source of the disease that marks the face is to be found in the sexual fantasy of the male in Peter Breughel the Elder's late sixteenth-century *Syphilitic with Couple*. Ithaca: Private collection.

76. Long thought to be a portrait of the German knight Ulrich von Hutten, whose firsthand account of syphilis is one of the most remarkable documents of the sixteenth century, this portrait of a syphilitic ascribed to Hans Holbein the Younger is now simply labeled: *Head of a Young Man, ca.* sixteenth century.

Cambridge, MA: Fogg Art Museum, Harvard University.

77. The syphilitic as leper from Amico Aspertini's *Portrait of St Valerian and His Brother*. Reproduced from Karl Sudhoff, *Zehn Syphilis-Drucke aus den Jahren 1495–1498* (Milan: Lier, 1924).

78. The syphilitic as melancholic from a broadside "On the Pox Called Malafranzosa," *ca.* 1525. Reproduced from *Archiv für die Geschichte der Medizin* 1 (1907).

79. Leonardo's first image of sexuality and disease. Windsor: Queen's Collection.

80. Leonardo da Vinci, *Allegory of Virtue and Envy*. Oxford: Christ Church.

81. A copy of the lost painting by Leonardo da Vinci of *Leda and the Swan*, 1510–15. Rotterdam: Museum Boymans, van Beuningen.

82. Illustration of the image of the "lustful" from a mid-fourteenth-century Italian manuscript of Dante's *Purgatorio XXVI*. Arsenal 8530. Paris: Bibliothèque nationale.

83. The image of sexual exploitation of the black woman in Christiaen van Couwenburgh, *The Rape of the Negress*, 1632. Strasbourg: Musée des Beaux Arts.

84. The chimpanzee as quasi-human with walking stick from Edward Tyson, *Orang-Outang, sive Homo Sylvestris; or, The Anatomy of a Pygmie Compared with That of a Monkey, an Ape, and a Man* (London: T. Bennett & D. Brown, 1699). Ithaca: Howard B. Adelmann Collection, Olin Library, Cornell University.

85. The urinary and reproductive parts of the chimpanzee from Edward Tyson, *Orang-Outang, sive Homo Sylvestris; or, The Anatomy of a Pygmie Compared with That of a Monkey, an Ape, and a Man* (London: T. Bennett & D. Brown, 1699). Ithaca: Howard B. Adelmann Collection, Olin Library, Cornell University.

86. The Vesalian torso of the female from Ambrose Paré, *The Works Translated out of Latin and Compared with the French by Th. Johnson*. (London: M. Clark for J. Clark, 1678). Ithaca: Howard B. Adelmann Collection, Olin Library, Cornell University.

87. The Vesalian torso of the male from Ambrose Paré, *The Works Translated out of Latin and Compared with the French by Th. Johnson* (London: M. Clark for J. Clark, 1678). Ithaca: Howard B. Adelmann Collection, Olin Library, Cornell University.

88. The image of the hermaphrodite from Ambrose Paré, *The Works Translated out of Latin and Compared with the French by Th. Johnson* (London: M. Clark for J. Clark, 1678). Ithaca: Howard B.

Adelmann Collection, Olin Library, Cornell University.

89. The hairy woman and the black child from Ambrose Paré, *The Works Translated out of Latin and Compared with the French by Th. Johnson*. (London: M. Clark for J. Clark, 1678). Ithaca: Howard B. Adelmann Collection, Olin Library, Cornell University.

90. The hairy woman and the black child as the frontispiece of *Aristotle's Compleat Master-piece . . . Displaying the Secrets of Nature in the Generation of Man*, twelfth ed. (London: The Booksellers [rep. in 1752]). Ithaca: Howard B. Adelmann Collection, Olin Library, Cornell University.

91. The woman, no longer hairy, and the black child as the frontispiece of *Aristotle's Master-piece: Displaying the Secrets of Nature in the Generation of Man* (London: The Booksellers, 1776). Ithaca: Howard B. Adelmann Collection, Olin Library, Cornell University.

92. The woman as the image of classical beauty from *The Works of Aristotle, the Famous Philosopher . . .* (Derby: T. Richardson [*ca.* 1820]). Ithaca: Howard B. Adelmann Collection, Olin Library, Cornell University.

93. The fetus in situ from Hieronymus Fabricius, *De formato foetu* (Venice: Franciscus Bolzettam, 1600). Ithaca: Howard B. Adelmann Collection, Olin Library, Cornell University.

94. The female genitalia from Hieronymus Fabricius, *De formato foetu* (Venice: Franciscus Bolzettam, 1600). Ithaca: Howard B. Adelmann Collection, Olin Library, Cornell University.

95. The female genitalia from Jan Swammerdam, *Miraculum naturae, sive uteri muliebris fabrica* (Rotterdam: C. Boutesteyn, 1679). London: Wellcome Institute for the History of Medicine.

96. Adam's anatomy in an engraving attributed to Léonard Gaultier from Jourdain Guibelet, *Trois discours philosophiques* (Evreux: A. Le marie, 1603). London: Wellcome Institute for the History of Medicine.

97. Eve's anatomy in an engraving attributed to Léonard Gaultier from Jourdain Guibelet, *Trois discours philosophiques* (Evreux: A. Le marie, 1603). London: Wellcome Institute for the History of Medicine.

98. The anatomy of the fetus from Jacques-F. Gautier d'Agoty, *Anatomie générale des viscères en situation . . .* (Paris: Gautier, *ca.* 1752). London: Wellcome Institute for the History of Medicine.

99. The breast and the vagina from Jacques-F. Gautier d'Agoty, *Anatomie des parties de la génération* (Paris: J. B. Bruned and Demonville, 1773). Ithaca:

Howard B. Adelmann Collection, Olin Library, Cornell University.

100. Male generative organs with homunculus in glass from Jacques-F. Gautier d'Agoty, *Anatomie générale des viscères en situation . . .* (Paris: Gautier, *ca.* 1752). London: Wellcome Institute for the History of Medicine.

101. Female generative organs from Jacques-F. Gautier d'Agoty, *Anatomie générale des viscères en situation . . .* (Paris: Gautier, *ca.* 1752). London: Wellcome Institute for the History of Medicine.

102. The vascular systems and deep muscles in an oil painting on canvas, by or after Jacques-F. Gautier d'Agoty, eighteenth century. London: Wellcome Institute for the History of Medicine.

103. Gravidae in an oil painting on canvas, by or after Jacques-F. Gautier d'Agoty, eighteenth century. London: Wellcome Institute for the History of Medicine.

104. The Vesalian torso in quite a different context in an illustration by Robert Fludd and Johannes de Bry, from Robert Fludd, *Philosophia sacra* (Frankfurt: Officiana Bryana, 1626). Ithaca: Howard B. Adelmann Collection, Olin Library, Cornell University.

105. The title page illustrated by Robert Fludd and Johannes de Bry, from Robert Fludd, *Philosophia sacra* (Frankfurt: Officiana Bryana, 1626). Ithaca: Howard B. Adelmann Collection, Olin Library, Cornell University.

106. The title page from Robert Fludd, *Utriusque cosmi historia* (Oppenheim: Johannes de Bry, 1617). Ithaca: Howard B. Adelmann Collection, Olin Library, Cornell University.

107. The male generative organs from Adrian Spigelius and Julius Casserius, *De humani corporis fabrica* (Venice: E. Deuchinum, 1627). Ithaca: Howard B. Adelmann Collection, Olin Library, Cornell University.

108. The female generative organs from Adrian Spigelius and Julius Casserius, *De humani corporis fabrica* (Venice: E. Deuchinum, 1627). Ithaca: Howard B. Adelmann Collection, Olin Library, Cornell University.

109. The female reproductive organs in situ from Adrian Spigelius and Julius Casserius, *De humani corporis fabrica* (Venice: E. Deuchinum, 1627). Ithaca: Howard B. Adelmann Collection, Olin Library, Cornell University.

110. The male reproductive organs in situ from Adrian Spigelius and Julius Casserius, *De humani corporis fabrica* (Venice: E. Deuchinum, 1627). Ithaca: Howard B. Adelmann Collection, Olin Library, Cornell University.

111. The male generative organs in an engraving by Gerard Leonardo Blasio from Johann Vesling, *Syntama anatomicum, commentarius* (Amsterdam: Johann Jansson, 1659). Ithaca: Howard B. Adelmann Collection, Olin Library, Cornell University.

112. The female generative organs in an engraving by Gerard Leonardo Blasio from Johann Vesling, *Syntama anatomicum, commentarius* (Amsterdam: Johann Jansson, 1659). Ithaca: Howard B. Adelmann Collection, Olin Library, Cornell University.

113. Homunculi and the placenta from Thomas Bartholin, *Anatome ex omnium veterum recentiorumque observationibus* (Amsterdam: Jacob Hackium, 1686). Ithaca: Howard B. Adelmann Collection, Olin Library, Cornell University.

114. The title page from Thomas Bartholin, *Anatome ex omnium veterum recentiorumque observationibus* (Amsterdam: Jacob Hackium, 1686). Ithaca: Howard B. Adelmann Collection, Olin Library, Cornell University.

115. The title page illustrated by Johannes de Bry and Johannes Theodore from Caspar Bauhinus, *Theatrum anatomicum* (Frankfurt: Matthaei Beckeri, 1605). Ithaca: Howard B. Adelmann Collection, Olin Library, Cornell University.

116. The title page from Adrian Spigelius and Julius Casserius, *De humani corporis fabrica* (Venice: E. Deuchinum, 1627). Ithaca: Howard B. Adelmann Collection, Olin Library, Cornell University.

117. Popular images of the body in the form of anatomical fugitive sheets. London: Wellcome Institute for the History of Medicine.

118. The male body reveals itself [primary level] from Johann Remmelin, *Catoptrum microcosmicum . . .* (Ulm: Sum pt. J. Gorlini, 1660). London: Wellcome Institute for the History of Medicine.

119. The secondary level of the male body from Johann Remmelin, *Catoptrum microcosmicum . . .* (Ulm: Sum pt. J. Gorlini, 1660). London: Wellcome Institute for the History of Medicine.

120. The female body reveals itself [primary level] from Johann Remmelin, *Catoptrum microcosmicum . . .* (Ulm: Sum pt. J. Gorlini, 1660). London: Wellcome Institute for the History of Medicine.

121. The secondary level of the female body from Johann Remmelin, *Catoptrum microcosmicum . . .* (Ulm: Sum pt. J. Gorlini, 1660). London: Wellcome Institute for the History of Medicine.

122. The title page from Johann Remmelin, *Catoptrum microcosmicum . . .* (Ulm: Sum pt. J. Gorlini, 1660). London: Wellcome Institute for the History of Medicine.

123. Engraving of the spring, an anatomical fugitive sheet showing seasons of the year and other scientific or moral matters; anon., n.d. [*ca.* 1620]. London: Wellcome Institute for the History of Medicine.

124. Engraving of the summer, an anatomical fugitive sheet showing seasons of the year and other scientific or moral matters; anon., n.d. [*ca.* 1620]. London: Wellcome Institute for the History of Medicine.

125. Engraving of the autumn, an anatomical fugitive sheet showing seasons of the year and other scientific or moral matters; anon., n.d. [*ca.* 1620]. London: Wellcome Institute for the History of Medicine.

126. Engraving of the winter, an anatomical fugitive sheet showing seasons of the year and other scientific or moral matters; anon., n.d. [*ca.* 1620]. London: Wellcome Institute for the History of Medicine.

127. Hidden oil painting by Sommonte on three layers of panel in box frame. The visible, outmost image is a still life of roses, n.d. [early nineteenth century], outside of first layer: roses. London: Wellcome Institute for the History of Medicine.

128. Hidden oil painting by Sommonte on three layers of panel in box frame. Inside of first layer: man, woman, death, n.d. [early nineteenth century]. London: Wellcome Institute for the History of Medicine.

129. Hidden oil painting by Sommonte on three layers of panel in box frame. Outside of second layer: fruit, n.d. [early nineteenth century]. London: Wellcome Institute for the History of Medicine.

130. Hidden oil painting by Sommonte on three layers of panel in box frame. Inside of second layer: five erotic scenes, n.d. [early nineteenth century]. London: Wellcome Institute for the History of Medicine.

131. Hidden oil painting by Sommonte on three layers of panel in box frame. Inside of second layerpartly removed to show third layer, n.d. [early nineteenth century]. London: Wellcome Institute for the History of Medicine.

132. The title page from Nicolaus Heinsius, *Schmachtende Venus, oder curieuser Trachtat vor spanischen Pocken . . .* (Frankfurt und Leipzig: C. Hülsse, 1700). Ithaca: Howard B. Adelmann Collection, Olin Library, Cornell University.

133. The martyrdom of mercury from Johannes Sintelaer, *The Scourge of Venus and Mercury, Represented in a Treatise of the Venereal Disease* (London: G. Harris, 1709). London: Wellcome Institute for the History of Medicine.

134. The image of the shepherd Syphilis in Luca Giordano, *Allegory of Syphilis*, 1664. Frankfurt: Staedelsches Kunstinstitut.

135. A Flemish copy after an engraving by Johann Sadeler based on a mid-seventeenth-century composition by Christoph Schwartz, *Warning against Venereal Disease*. Potsdam–Sanssouci: Bildergalerie staatliche Schlösser und Gärten.

136. The icon of "The Choice of Hercules," engraved by Crispyn van de Passe the Elder taken from George Wither's *A Collection of Emblems, Ancient and Moderne* (London: R. Allot, 1635). Ithaca: Rare Book Collection, Olin Library, Cornell University.

137. The moment before the contagion spreads in Agnolo Bronzino, *Venus, Love and Jealousy*, 1546. Budapest: Szépmüvészti Museum.

138. The moment of contagion in Agnolo Bronzino, *Venus, Cupid, Folly and Time, ca.* 1545. London: National Gallery.

139. The black musician in Titian, *Venus and the Organ Player, ca.* 1550. Berlin: Staatliche Museen Preußischer Kultur/Dahlem: Gemäldegalerie.

140. Hendrick Goltzius, *Touch*, a copperplate engraving from a series of the five senses, 1587c. Ithaca: Private collection.

141. Frans Floris's image of Touch in an engraving (1561) by H. Cock. Ithaca: Private collection.

142. Cesare Ripa's image of Touch from an early French edition of his emblem book *Iconologie, ou, Explication nouvelle de plusieurs images, emblèmes, et autres figures hyerogliphiques* (Paris: Chez M. Guillemot, 1644). Ithaca: Rare Book Collection, Olin Library, Cornell University.

143. The male responds to the painful touch in Caravaggio, *Boy Bitten by a Lizard*, 1594. Florence: Fonazione Longhi.

144. The erotic touch becomes domesticated in Dirck Hals, *The Five Senses*, 1624. The Hague: Koninklijk Kabinet van Schilderijen.

145. The image of the senses as a social event in Louis Finson, *Happy Party (Allegory of the Five Senses)*, 1737. Braunschweig: Herzog Anton Ulrich-Museum.

146. Food as the context for the senses in David Teniers's mid-seventeenth-century *Merry Company at the Table*. Brussels: Musée des Beaux-Arts d'Ixelles.

147. The social environment becomes the classical stage scene for the image of the senses in Hendrik van Balen's mid-seventeenth-century *Allegory of the Five Senses*. Karlsruhe: Staatliche Kunsthalle.

148. Crispyn van de Passe the Elder, *The Seasons and the Senses*, engraved in Cologne between 1594 and 1610. Ithaca: Private collection.

149. The erotic touch becomes overt in Cornelius Drebbel, *Touch, ca.* 1596. Ithaca: Private collection.

150. The erotic touch in the bedchamber as a seventeenth-century line engraving by Abraham Bosse, *Tactus, le Touche*, an allegory of the sense of touch (Paris: Tauermeier, n.d.). London: Wellcome Institute for the History of Medicine.

151. The erotic touch as satire in Thomas Rowlandson's eighteenth-century *The Five Senses*. Ithaca: Private collection.

152. The world of the monstrous engraved by Cornelis Huyberts from Frederik Ruysch, *Observationum anatomico–chirurgicarum centuria* (Amsterdam: Henricum and Viduam Theodori Boom, 1691). Ithaca: Howard B. Adelmann Collection, Olin Library, Cornell University.

153. The prolapsed uterus from Frederik Ruysch, *Opera omnia anatomica–medica–chirurgica*, Vol. 3 (Amsterdam: Janssonio Waesbergios, 1721–[28?]). Ithaca: Howard B. Adelmann Collection, Olin Library, Cornell University.

154. The penis anatomized from Frederik Ruysch, *Opera omnia anatomica–medica–chirurgica*, Vol. 1 (Amsterdam: Janssonio Waesbergios, 1721–[28?]). Ithaca: Howard B. Adelmann Collection, Olin Library, Cornell University.

155. The female generative organs after Huber by Bernard from Denis Diderot and Jean-Baptiste le Rond d'Alembert, *Encyclopédie* (1751–80). London: Wellcome Institute for the History of Medicine.

156. The penis after Heister, Morgagni, Du Verney, by Bernard from Denis Diderot and Jean-Baptiste le Rond d'Alembert, *Encyclopédie* (1751–80). London: Wellcome Institute for the History of Medicine.

157. The female generative organs by D. Kaltenhofer engraved by Gött, 1748, from Albrecht von Haller, ed., *Disputationum anatomicarum selectarum*, Vol. 5 (Göttingen: Abram Vandenhoeck, 1750). Ithaca: Howard B. Adelmann Collection, Olin Library, Cornell University.

158. The male generative organs from Hermann Boerhaave, *Oecanomia animalis* (Amsterdam: Johann Noon, 1741). Ithaca: Howard B. Adelmann Collection, Olin Library, Cornell University.

159. The female generative organs from Hermann Boerhaave, *Oecanomia animalis* (Amsterdam: Johann Noon, 1741). Ithaca: Howard B. Adelmann Collection, Olin Library, Cornell University.

160. The male body from Govard Bidloo, *Anatomia humani corporis* (Amsterdam: Joannis a Someren, 1685). Ithaca: Howard B. Adelmann Collection, Olin Library, Cornell University.

161. The female body from Govard Bidloo, *Anatomia humani corporis* (Amsterdam: Joannis a Someren, 1685). Ithaca: Howard B. Adelmann Collection, Olin Library, Cornell University.

162. The muscles of the male body from Johann Adam Delsenbach, *Kurtzer Begriff der Anatomie . . .* (Nürnberg: L. Bieling, 1733). Ithaca: Howard B. Adelmann Collection, Olin Library, Cornell University.

163. The male body from B. S. Albinus, *Tabulae sceleti et musculorum corporis humani* (Leiden: Verbeek, 1747). London: Wellcome Insitute for the History of Medicine.

164. The Adamites in Amsterdam as represented by Bernard Picart, an assembly of nudists in Amsterdam accepting a new member to the group, 1723. Ithaca: Howard B. Adelmann Collection, Olin Library, Cornell University.

165. The female torso as flesh from Govard Bidloo, *Anatomia humani corporis* (Amsterdam: Joannis a Someren, 1685). Ithaca: Howard B. Adelmann Collection, Olin Library, Cornell University.

166. The reproductive organs and urinary tract of the female as the object of dissection from Govard Bidloo, *Anatomia humani corporis* (Amsterdam: Joannis a Someren, 1685). Ithaca: Howard B. Adelmann Collection, Olin Library, Cornell University.

167. The penis anatomized from Giovanni Battista Morgagni, *Adveraria anatomica omnia* (Leiden: J. A. Langerak, 1723). Ithaca: Howard B. Adelmann Collection, Olin Libary, Cornell University.

168. The female reproductive system from Giovanni Battista Morgagni, *Adveraria anatomica omnia* (Leiden: J. A. Langerak, 1723). Ithaca: Howard B. Adelmann Collection, Olin Library, Cornell University.

169. The anatomy lesson seen from the physician's point of view from William Cowper, *The Anatomy of Humane Bodies*, revised and published by Christianus Albinus, second edition (Leiden: J. A. Langerak, 1737). Ithaca: Howard B. Adelmann Collection, Olin Library, Cornell University.

170. The fly crawling across the cover of the opened torso points toward the hidden genitalia, the source of corruption and death, in William Cowper, *The Anatomy of Humane Bodies*, revised and published by Christianus Albinus, second edition (Leiden: J. A. Langerak, 1737). Ithaca: Howard B. Adelmann Collection, Olin Library, Cornell University.

171. The male reproductive system and viscera with the testicle removed but the scrotum unopened. From William Cowper, *The Anatomy of Humane Bodies*, revised and published by Christianus Albinus, second edition (Leiden: J. A. Langerak, 1737). Ithaca: Howard B. Adelmann Collection, Olin Library, Cornell University.

172. The female body as revealed in the midwife's handbook as redesigned for the "man mid-wife," the physician from C. N. Jenty, *Demonstration de la matrice d'une femme grosse et de son enfant à terme* (Paris: Charpentier, 1759). London: Wellcome Institute for the History of Medicine.

173. The gravid uterus revealed but the genitalia remaining in the shadows from C. N. Jenty, *Demonstration de la matrice d'une femme grosse et de son enfant à terme* (Paris: Charpentier, 1759). London: Wellcome Institute for the History of Medicine.

174. The fetus in situ from C. N. Jenty, *Demonstration de la matrice d'une femme grosse et de son enfant à terme* (Paris: Charpentier, 1759). London: Wellcome Institute for the History of Medicine.

175. The female torso uncovered and the genitalia exposed but the legs discreetly covered, from William Hunter, *The Anatomy of the Human Gravid Uterus* (Birmingham: John Baskerville, 1774). Ithaca: Howard B. Adelmann Collection, Olin Library, Cornell University.

176. The fetus in situ, the female body reduced to the fleshy torso, from William Hunter, *The Anatomy of the Human Gravid Uterus* (Birmingham: John Baskerville, 1774). Ithaca: Howard B. Adelmann Collection, Olin Library, Cornell University.

177. Hunter's teacher was William Smellie, one of the first "man midwives." His *A Sett of Anatomical Tables* (London: n.p., 1754) revealed the external female parts, including the clitoris. Ithaca: Howard B. Adelmann Collection, Olin Library, Cornell University.

178. A standard reference book of the period, A. D. Burrowes, *The Modern Encyclopaedia; or a General Dictionary of Arts, Sciences, and Literature* (London: S. Richards, 1816–20 [?]), included a line engraving of the uterus as well as one of the gravid uterus by Campbell taken from the obstetrical atlases of the day. London: Wellcome Institute for the History of Medicine.

179. The arteries and cavernous tissues of the penis in a wax cast (Hunterian BB.21). Glasgow: Department of Anatomy of the University of Glasgow.

180. A wax cast of the external genitalia of an adult black woman (Hunterian CC. 16). Glasgow: Department of Anatomy of the University of Glasgow.

181. The "flayed man" with his reproductive parts from Pietro da Cartona and Cajetano Petrioli, *Tabulae anatomicae* (Rome: Antonii de Rubeis, 1741). Ithaca: Howard B. Adelmann Collection, Olin Library, Cornell University.

182. The opening of the female body is made parallel to the opening of a solid wall through which the fetus can be seen. Taken from Pietro da Cortona and Cajetano Petrioli, *Tabulae anatomicae* (Rome: Antonii de Rubeis, 1741). Ithaca: Howard B. Adelmann Collection, Olin Library, Cornell University.

183. The male body from Bartholomeo Eustachi, *Otto tavole anatomiche* (Rome: Antonio de' Rossi, 1750). Ithaca: Howard B. Adelmann Collection, Olin Library, Cornell University.

184. The female body from Bartolomeo Eustachi, *Otto tavole anatomiche* (Rome: Antonio de' Rossi, 1750). Ithaca: Howard B. Adelmann Collection, Olin Library, Cornell University.

185. The title page of Bartolomeo Eustachi, *Otto tavole anatomiche* (Rome: Antonio de' Rossi, 1750). Ithaca: Howard B. Adelmann Collection, Olin Library, Cornell University.

186. The title page of Johann Adam Kulmus, *Tabulae anatomicae* (Amsterdam/Rome: Laurentii Barbiellini, 1748). Ithaca: Howard B. Adelmann Collection, Olin Library, Cornell University.

187. The title page vignette from Félix Vicq d'Azyr, *Traité d'anatomie et de physiologie* (Paris: Francis Ambrose Didot L'Aine, 1786). Ithaca: Howard B. Adelmann Collection, Olin Library, Cornell University.

188–196. The wax anatomical figure of the female from the eighteenth-century anatomical collection at La Specola in Florence. On the surface, with pearls and coiffure, she is the epitome of the classical beauty. As her layers are removed, we move to the center of the male gaze, the fetus. All of this is done in the context of the torsos to be seen in the rear case, which reduce the female to the sum of her sexuality. Florence: Museo Zoologico della Specola.

197. A wax model of the urogenital system of the male. Florence: Museo Zoologico della Specola.

198. A wax model of a double monster with two chest cavities (*Cephalothoracopagus monosymmetros*). Vienna: Aus der Sammlung geburtshilflicher Wachspräparate, Josephinum.

199. (1) A wax cast of the vagina (2) a wax cast of the uterus. Vienna: Aus der Sammlung anatomischer Wachspräparte, Josephinum.

200. A hemisected view of the urogenital system of the male. Vienna: Aus der Sammlung anatomischer Wachspräparate, Josephinum.

201. M. V. Acier's illustration for one of the Marquis de Sade's novels (1797) representing visually the genitalia as depicted verbally by the Marquis de Sade. Ithaca: Rare Book Collection, Cornell University.

202. The image of the female genitalia as the Medusa by Gustave Courbet, *The Origin of the World*, as reproduced in Gerard Zwang's *Le sexe de la femme* (Paris: la Jeune Parque, 1967). Ithaca: Olin Library, Cornell University. The original has recently been rediscovered in Paris.

203. The female torso as seen by Philip Pearlstein,

Seated Female Nude on Black Chair, 1968. Troy, NY: Rensselaer Polytechnic Institute.

204. The erect male genitalia from Philip Verheyen, *Anatomie oder Zerlegung* (Leipzig: Fritschen, 1714). Ithaca: Howard B. Adelmann Collection, Olin Library, Cornell University.

205. The flaccid penis from Carlo Cesi, *Cognitione de muscoli del corpo humano per il disegno* (Rome: Billy, [1730]). London: Wellcome Institute for the History of Medicine.

206. An engraving of the second stage of dissection: the torso of the flayed man and his genitalia from Sir Charles Bell, *A System of Dissections, Explaining the Anatomy of the Human Body* (Edinburgh: Mundell, 1798[–1800]). London: Wellcome Institute for the History of Medicine.

207. The penis dissected from Sir Charles Bell, *Letters concerning the Diseases of the Urethra* (Boston: W. Wells and T. B. Wait; Philadelphia: Edward Earle, 1811). London: Wellcome Institute for the History of Medicine.

208. The male urogenital system from Pierre Dionis, *The Anatomie of Humane Bodies Improv'd* (London: H. Bonwicke, 1703). Ithaca: Howard B. Adelmann Collection, Olin Library, Cornell University.

209. The female reproductive system from Pierre Dionis, *The Anatomie of Humane Bodies Improv'd* (London: H. Bonwicke, 1703). Ithaca: Howard B. Adelmann Collection, Olin Library, Cornell University.

210. The male reproductive system from Alessandro Pascoli, *Il corpo-umani* (Venice: Presso Andrea Poletti, 1712). Ithaca: Howard B. Adelmann Collection, Olin Library, Cornell University.

211. The female reproductive system with fetus from Alessandro Pascoli, *Il corpo-umani* (Venice: Presso Andrea Poletti, 1712). Ithaca: Howard B. Adelmann Collection, Olin Library, Cornell University.

212. Etching of parts of the genitourinary systems of the male and female, after Eustachi, Cheselden, and De Graaf from R. James, *A Medical Dictionary* (London: T. Osborne and J. Roberts, 1743). London: Wellcome Institute for the History of Medicine.

213. The penis from Guichard Joseph Duverney, *Oeuvres anatomiques*, Vol. 2 (Paris: Charles-Antoine Jombert, 1761). Ithaca: Howard B. Adelmann Collection, Olin Library, Cornell University.

214. W. H. Hall, *The New Royal Encyclopaedia; or, Complete Modern Dictionary of Arts and Sciences*, second edition revised by T. A. Lloyd, n.d. [*ca.* 1790], pl. 10, line engraving with etching, male generative organs, by Lodge after Birnie, published 28 August 1789. London: Wellcome Institute for the History of Medicine.

215. The penis as seen from below from Georg Kobelt, *Die männlichen und weiblichen Wollust-Organe der Menschen* (Emmerling: Freiburg i. Br., 1844). Ithaca: Howard B. Adelmann Collection, Olin Library, Cornell University.

216. The clitoris from Georg Kobelt, *Die männlichen und weiblichen Wollust-Organe der Menschen* (Emmerling: Freiburg i. Br., 1844). Ithaca: Howard B. Adelmann Collection, Olin Library, Cornell University.

217. Jean-Jacques Lequeu's early eighteenth-century image of the *Penis Strangulated by Paraphimosis*. Paris: Bibliothèque nationale.

218. Jean-Jacques Lequeu's early eighteenth-century image of the *Vessel of an Adolescent Girl Inflamed with Unseemly Desire*. Paris: Bibliothèque nationale.

219. A painting of the medicalized world of the syphilitic by William Hogarth, *The Luetic Viscount Visiting the Quack*. London: National Gallery.

220. The head of a syphilitic prostitute preserved in wine spirit signified the hidden face of the polluted female in this eighteenth-century engraving. London: Wellcome Institute for the History of Medicine.

221. Hand-colored engraving of the young and healthy patient from Samuel Auguste André David Tissot, *L'onanisme; ou dissertation physique sur les maladies produites par la masturbation*, nouv. éd. annotée d'après les nouvelles observations des docteurs Gottlier, Vogel etc. (Paris: Chez les Marchands de nouveautés, 1836). London: Wellcome Institute for the History of Medicine.

222. The same patient near death from the masturbation marked upon his skin from Samuel Auguste André David Tissot, *L'onanisme; ou dissertation physique sur les maladies produites par la masturbation*, nouv. éd. annotée d'après les nouvelles observations des docteurs Gottlier, Vogel etc. (Paris: Chez les Marchands de nouveautés, 1836). London: Wellcome Institute for the History of Medicine.

223. The pustules as the sign of disease on the skin of the masturbator from Samuel Auguste André David Tissot, *L'onanisme; ou dissertation physique sur les maladies produites par la masturbation*, nouv. éd. annotée d'après les nouvelles observations des docteurs Gottlier, Vogel etc. (Paris: Chez les Marchands de nouveautés, 1836). London: Wellcome Institute for the History of Medicine.

224. Mlle. Ch_____ at the healthy age of 15 from Samuel Auguste André David Tissot, *L'onanisme; ou dissertation physique sur les maladies produites par la masturbation*, nouv. éd. annotée d'après les nouvelles observations des docteurs Gottlier, Vogel etc. (Paris: Chez les Marchands de nouveautés, 1836). London: Wellcome Institute for the History of Medicine.

225. The same patient at the age of 16, during the final stage of her illness, from Samuel Auguste André David Tissot, *L'onanisme; ou dissertation physique sur les maladies produites par la masturbation*, nouv. éd. annotée d'après les nouvelles observations des docteurs Gottlier, Vogel etc. (Paris: Chez les Marchands de nouveautés, 1836). London: Wellcome Institute for the History of Medicine.

226. The "corona veneris" marks the face of the masturbator from Samuel La'mert, *Self-Preservation: A Medical Treatise on Nervous and Physical Debility, Spermatorrhoea, Impotence, and Sterility* (London: n.p., [*ca.* 1860]). London: Wellcome Institute for the History of Medicine.

227. A line engraving of the "varicocele" showing dilated veins marks the hidden disease of the masturbator's genitalia signified by the "corona veneris" on his face from Samuel La'mert, *Self-Preservation: A Medical Treatise on Nervous and Physical Debility, Spermatorrhoea, Impotence, and Sterility* (London: n.p., [*ca.* 1860]). London: Wellcome Institute for the History of Medicine.

228. The senses as a masculine assemblage also representing the ages of man in Theodore Rombouts's early seventeenth-century image of *The Five Senses as Represented by the Ages of Man*. Rombouts studied with Rubens but was greatly influenced by Caravaggio, as can be seen in this image. Brussels: Institut Royal du Patrimoine Artistique.

229. Urinary and genital parts of a man from William Cheselden, *The Anatomy of the Human Body* (London: N. Cliff, D. Jackson, & W. Innys, 1713). London: Wellcome Institute for the History of Medicine.

230. The genital parts of a woman from William Cheselden, *The Anatomy of the Human Body* (London: N. Cliff, D. Jackson, & W. Innys, 1713). London: Wellcome Institute for the History of Medicine.

231. An engraving of the genitalia of a black hermaphrodite from William Cheselden, *The Anatomy of the Human Body* (London: C. Hitch & R. Dodsley, 1750). London: Wellcome Institute for the History of Medicine.

232. A mezzotint, *Feeling*, by Alexander Vanhacken after a lost early eighteenth-century painting by Jacopo Amigoni. London: Wellcome Institute for the History of Medicine.

233. Jacques Louis David's postcoital image of *Cupid and Psyche*, 1817. Leonard C. Hanna, Jr., bequest, Cleveland, OH: Cleveland Museum of Art.

234. The act of seduction represented in William Hogarth's etching and engraving *Before*, 1736. Ithaca: Herbert F. Johnson Museum of Art, Cornell University.

235. Postcoital depression represented in William Hogarth's etching and engraving *After*, 1736. Ithaca: Herbert F. Johnson Museum of Art, Cornell University.

236. Moll Hackabout as the Jew's mistress, the second plate of William Hogarth's *A Harlot's Progress*, 1731. Ithaca: Private collection.

237. The brothel represented in the third plate of William Hogarth's *A Rake's Progress*, 1735. Membership Purchase Fund, Ithaca: Herbert F. Johnson Museum of Art, Cornell University.

238. The title page to G. M. Bossi, *Esposizione delle malattie veneree e della medicazione di esse* (Milan: Mon. S. Amb. Mag., 1793). London: Wellcome Institute for the History of Medicine.

239. *Amatory Mania* from Alexander Morison, *The Physiognomy of Mental Diseases* (London: Longman, 1840). Ithaca: Private collection.

240. *Amatory Mania, Recovered in About Eight Months* from Alexander Morison, *The Physiognomy of Mental Diseases* (London: Longman, 1840). Ithaca: Private collection.

241. From John Singer Sargent, secret notebooks dated from 1890–1915, *Reclining Male Nude*, a charcoal drawing on off-white paper. A gift of Mrs. Francis Ormond. Cambridge, MA: Fogg Art Museum, Harvard University.

242–244. During his trip to Rome in 1787–88, Johann Wolfgang von Goethe made a number of sketches of the nude male, with prominent genitalia, in pencil and ink. Weimar: Nationale Forschungs- und Gedenkstätten der klassichen deutschen Literatur.

245. The female reproductive organs from Justus Christian von Loder, *Tabulae anatomicae* (Weimar: Landes–Industry–Comptoir, 1803). Ithaca: Howard B. Adelmann Collection, Olin Library, Cornell University.

246. Fetal anatomy and reproductive anatomy seen as parallel structures from Justus Christian von Loder, *Tabulae anatomicae* (Weimar: Landes–Industry–Comptoir, 1803). Ithaca: Howard B. Adelmann Collection, Olin Library, Cornell University.

247. The male genitalia from Leopold Mark Antony and Caldani Floriani, *Icones anatomicae ex optimis neotericorum operibus* (Venice: J. Picotti, 1804). Ithaca: Howard B. Adelmann Collection, Olin Library, Cornell University.

248. The female genitalia from Leopold Mark

Antony and Caldani Floriani, *Icones anatomicae ex optimis neotericorum operibus* (Venice: J. Picotti, 1804). Ithaca: Howard B. Adelmann Collection, Olin Library, Cornell University.

249. The viscera and the genitalia from Gerard Sandifort, *Tabulae anatomicae* (Rotterdam: S. and J. Luchtmans, 1804). Ithaca: Howard B. Adelmann Collection, Olin Library, Cornell University.

250. The image of the penis dissected engraved by N. H. Jacobs from Philippe Blawdin, *Traité d'anatomie topographique* (Paris: Auger Mequignon, 1826). Ithaca: Howard B. Adelmann Collection, Olin Library, Cornell University.

251. Spermatazoa in a lithograph by N. H. Jacobs from Marc Jean Bourgery, *Traité complet de l'anatomie de l'homme* (Paris: C. A. Delaunay, 1844). Ithaca: Howard B. Adelmann Collection, Olin Library, Cornell University.

252. The ovum and the initial stages of fertilization in a lithograph by N. H. Jacobs from Marc Jean Bourgery, *Traité complet de l'anatomie de l'homme* (Paris: C. A. Delaunay, 1844). Ithaca: Howard B. Adelmann Collection, Olin Library, Cornell University.

253. The erect penis in a lithograph by N. H. Jacobs from Marc Jean Bourgery, *Traité complet de l'anatomie de l'homme* (Paris: C. A. Delaunay, 1844). Ithaca: Howard B. Adelmann Collection, Olin Library, Cornell University.

254. The female genitalia in a lithograph by N. H. Jacobs from Marc Jean Bourgery, *Traité complet de l'anatomie de l'homme* (Paris: C. A. Delaunay, 1844). Ithaca: Howard B. Adelmann Collection, Olin Library, Cornell University.

255. The bicornate uterus as a pathology from Karl Rokitansky, *Lehrbuch der pathologischen Anatomie* (Vienna: Braumuller, 1861). Ithaca: Howard B. Adelmann Collection, Olin Library, Cornell University.

256. The ovarian cyst from Karl Rokitansky, *Lehrbuch der pathologischen Anatomie* (Vienna: Braumuller, 1861). Ithaca: Howard B. Adelmann Collection, Olin Library, Cornell University.

257. The face of the female syphilitic from Jean Louis Alibert, *Description des maladies de la peau* (Paris: Barrois l'Aine, 1814). London: Royal Society of Medicine.

258. The genitalia of the male syphilitic from Jean-Louis Alibert, *Description des maladies de la peau* (Paris: Barrois l'Aîné, 1814). London: Royal Society of Medicine.

259. The genitalia of the female syphilitic from Jean-Louis Alibert, *Description des maladies de la peau* (Paris: Barrois l'Aîné, 1814). London: Royal Society of Medicine.

260. The title page vignette of the nineteenth-century French translation of Fracastoro's poem *Syphilis* by Auguste Barthélémy, *Syphilis: Poème en deux chants* (Paris: Béchet junior et Labé & Bohaire, 1840). London: Wellcome Institute for the History of Medicine.

261. The moment of seduction from Alfred Elmore, *On the Brink*, 1865. Cambridge: Fitzwilliam Museum, University of Cambridge.

262. The dead prostitute in an engraving after Abraham Solomon, "Drowned! Drowned!" from *Art Journal* (March 1862). Ithaca: Olin Library, Cornell University.

263. The seducer fails in William Holman Hunt, *The Awakening Conscience*, 1853. London: Tate Gallery.

264. An illustration for Alfred de Musset's *Garniani* (1883) by Achulle Deveria. Ithaca: Private collection.

265. The redeemed prostitute from Dante Gabriel Rossetti, *Found*, begun in 1853. Wilmington: Delaware Art Museum.

266. An early erotic photograph by François J. Moulin, *ca.* 1855. Ithaca: Private collection.

267. The fear of penetration trivialized in Adolphe William Bouguereau, *Young Girl Defending Herself against Eros, ca.* 1880. Santa Monica, CA: J. Paul Getty Museum.

268. The woman mad with love as she commits suicide in John Everett Millais, *Ophelia*, 1852. London: Tate Gallery.

269. The beautiful dead woman at the moment before the autopsy begins in Gabriel Max, *Der Anatom*, 1869. Berlin: Gravure Hanfstaengl.

270. The beautiful dead woman during the autopsy in Enrique Simonet, *Tenía corazón*, 1890. Malaga, Spain: Museo de Bellas Artes provincial.

271. The stabbing murder of Martha Tarbram on 7 August 1888, was thought in retrospect not to be by "Jack." But at the time it was seen as the first of the series of Whitechapel murders. From *The Illustrated Police News*. Ithaca: Olin Library, Cornell University.

272. The first of "Jack's" Whitechapel murders was most probably Emma Smith (2 April 1888). From *The Illustrated Police News*. Ithaca: Olin Library, Cornell University.

273. Jack the Ripper as the Jew and the murder of Mary Ann Nichols (31 August 1888). From *The Illustrated Police News*. Ithaca: Olin Library, Cornell University.

274. Jack the Ripper eviscerated Annie Chapman on 8 September 1888. From *The Illustrated Police News*. Ithaca: Olin Library, Cornell University.

275. Annie Chapman's life as a prostitute represented as a reflex of her dead body. From *The Illustrated Police News*. Ithaca: Olin Library, Cornell University.

276. Jack the Ripper murdered Elizabeth Stride in Mitre Square and Catherine Eddowes in Berner Street on 30 September 1888. The prostitute becomes the torso of the anatomical atlases. From *The Illustrated Police News*. Ithaca: Olin Library, Cornell University.

277. The face of Jack the Ripper as the Eastern Jew in juxtaposition with the torso representing the nature of his victims as well as his own sexuality. From *The Illustrated Police News*. Ithaca: Olin Library, Cornell University.

278. The double murder on 30 September 1888. From *The Illustrated Police News*. Ithaca: Olin Library, Cornell University.

279. Jack the Ripper as a well-shaved member of the working class, following the anti-Jewish riot in the East End. From *The Illustrated Police News*. Ithaca: Olin Library, Cornell University.

280. The face of the prostitute. From *The Illustrated Police News*. Ithaca: Olin Library, Cornell University.

281. The bearded Jew in his kaftan flees the scene of the murders. From *The Illustrated Police News*. Ithaca: Olin Library, Cornell University.

282. Jack the Ripper as a well-dressed Death as a physician, carrying his doctor's bag, about to open the prostitute's body. From *The Illustrated Police News*. Ithaca: Olin Library, Cornell University.

283. The masturbating Jew from Gray Joliffe and Peter Mayle, *Man's Best Friend* (London: Pan Books, 1984). Ithaca: Private collection.

284. A six-year-old thumbsucker and masturbator, the daughter of a bookkeeper, from Freud's source, S. Lindner, "Das Saugen an den Fingern, Lippen etc. bei den Kindern (Ludeln.)," *Jahrbuch für Kinderheilkunde und physische Erziehung* 14 (1879). Ithaca: Olin Library, Cornell University.

285. The sensory homunculus from Wilder Penfield, *The Cerebral Cortex of Man* (New York: Macmillan, 1952). The right side of the figure is laid upon a cross-section of the hemisphere, drawn somewhat in proportion to the extent of sensory cortex devoted to it. The length of the underlying block lines indicates more accurately the comparative extent of each representation. Ithaca: Olin Library, Cornell University.

286. The skin of the hysterical child from T. D. Savill, "Hysterical Skin Symptoms and Eruptions," *Lancet* (20 January 1904). Ithaca: Olin Library, Cornell University.

287. A sample sheet of Victorian child pornography, *ca.* 1880. Ithaca: Private collection.

288. Lewis Carroll's nude female child, 25 July 1879. Ithaca: Private collection.

289. Baron Wilhelm von Gloeden, *A Study of a Nude Boy*, early twentieth century. Ithaca: Private collection.

290. Hiram Powers, *The Greek Slave*, 1846. Washington, DC: In the Collection of the Corcoran Gallery of Art, Gift of William Wilson.

291. The young girl Hermine Rosen, from the private photographic collection of Peter Altenberg. Vienna: Österreichische Nationalbibliothek.

292. The black female child as the image of the erotic, from the private photographic collection of Peter Altenberg. Vienna: Stadtbibliothek.

293. "Dementia" from J. É. D. Esquirol, from the atlas to his *Des maladies mentales* (Paris: Baillière, 1838). Ithaca: Private collection. This is the parallel image to that found in William James's representation of his own madness.

294. The prostitute unclothed and the black servant in Édouard Manet, *Olympia*, 1862–63. Paris: Musée du Louvre.

295. The prostitute clothed in Édouard Manet, *Nana*, 1877. Hamburg: Kunsthalle.

296. The erotic representation of the black child in Franz von Bayros, *The Servant, ca.* 1890. Ithaca: Private collection.

297. The black child as the sign of the erotic in Dante Gabriel Rossetti, *The Beloved, or The Bride*, 1865. London: Tate Gallery.

298. Sarah Bartmann, the famed "Hottentot Venus," from Géoffrey Saint-Hilaire and Fréderic Cuvier, *Histoire naturelle des mammifères avec des figures originales* (Paris: A. Belin, 1824). Ithaca: Olin Library, Cornell University.

299. An engraving of a "Hottentot Venus" at *The Ball of the Duchess du Barry*, 1829. Ithaca: Olin Library, Cornell University.

300. Cuvier's gift to the people of France, the preserved genitalia of the "Hottentot Venus." Paris: Musée de l'Homme.

301. The genitalia of the "Hottentot Venus" from Johannes Müller, "Über die äusseren Geschlechtstheile der Buschmänninnen," *Archiv für Anatomie, Physiologie und wissenschaftliche Medizin* (1834). Ithaca: Olin Library, Cornell University.

302. The pelvic angle as a sign of race from Pieter Camper, *Demonstrationum anatomicopathologicarum* (Amsterdam: J. Schreuder & P. Mortier, 1760–62). London: Wellcome Institute for the History of Medicine.

303. Sarah Bartmann's pelvis from René Verneau, *Le bassin dans les sexes et dans les races* (Paris: Baillière, 1875). Ithaca: Olin Library, Cornell University.

304. The "Hottentot Venus," a German caricature

from the beginning of the twentieth century from John Grand-Carteret, *Die Erotik in der französischen Karikatur* (Vienna: C. W. Stern, 1909). Ithaca: Private collection.

305. The scale of racial beauty in Edwin Long, *The Babylonian Marriage Market*, 1882. London: Royal Holloway College Gallery.

306. "Anomalies of the Face and the Ear in Prostitutes," from Pauline Tarnowsky, *Étude anthropométrique sur les prostituées et les voleuses* (Paris: E. Lecrosnier et Bébé, 1889). Ithaca: Private collection.

307. The physiognomy of the Russian prostitute in the work of Pauline Tarnowsky: (25) is the "Russian Helen," (18) the "wild eyes of the insane," (20) "very handsome" from *Archivio di psichiatria, scienze penali ed antropologia criminale* 14 (1893). Ithaca: Private collection.

308. Steatopygia in black females from Cesare Lombroso and Guglielmo Ferrero, *La donna deliquente: La Prostituta e la donna normale* (Turin: L. Roux, 1893). Ithaca: Private collection.

309. "Sexual Anomalies in the Hottentot (a, b) and in the European Woman (c, d, e, f)" from Cesare Lombroso and Guglielmo Ferrero, *La donna deliquente: La Prostituta e la donna normale* (Turin: L. Roux, 1893).

310. The atavistic, tattooed prostitute from I. Callari's study of Sicilian prostitution follows Lombroso's discussion of tattooing in his 1893 study of the criminal woman and the prostitute. *Archivio di psichiatria* 24 (1903). Ithaca: Private collection.

311. Abele De Blasio's image of "Steatopygia in an Italian Prostitute" in the *Archivio di psichiatria* 26 (1905). Ithaca: Private collection.

312. Edgar Degas's monotype of well-endowed prostitutes and *The Client*, ca. 1879. Paris: Musée du Louvre.

313. Pablo Picasso's black *Olympia*, 1901. New York: Private collection.

314. A woman with spiderlike hair, wearing a black cloak, stands among rows of graves. She holds a skull in her hands in this powerful illustration of the evils of syphilis in Louis Raemakers, *L'Hecatombe. La Syphillis, ca.* 1916. Madison: University of Wisconsin Medical School Library Collection.

315. The text of this poster by Théophile-Alexandre Steinlen, "Soldat, la patrie compte sur toi . . .," 1916, is written on a tombstone, and presents a dramatic appeal to French soldiers to keep strong their country and to resist those seductions in the street that risk exposure to an illness as "dangerous as war" leading to a "useless death without honor." New York: Private collection.

316. The beautiful but dangerous female in an anonymous American poster, *She May Look Clean—But, ca.* 1944. Washington, DC: NLM Collection.

317–319. The British public health displays on syphilis from 1945, prepared by James Randal Hutchinson (*ca.* 1880–1955) in connection with his work in the Ministry of Health, 1919–47. London: Wellcome Institute for the History of Medicine.

320. The face of the syphilitic from Norman Haire, ed., *Encyclopaedia of Sexual Knowledge* (London: Francis Aldor, 1934). London: Wellcome Institute for the History of Medicine.

321. The position of melancholy as a sign of syphilis from Lucia Radl, *Illustrated Guide to Sexual Happiness in Marriage* (London: William Heineman, 1953). London: Wellcome Institute for the History of Medicine.

322. The AIDS patient being examined by his physicians, from the *New York Times*, 23 December 1985. Ithaca: Olin Library, Cornell University.

323. Four images of the AIDS patient from *Newsday*, 4 August 1985. Ithaca: Olin Library, Cornell University.

324. The AIDS patient as melancholic from *Discover*, September 1986. Ithaca: Olin Library, Cornell University.

325. AIDS as an American biological weapon. A drawing by D. Agaeva, from *Pravda*, 1 November 1986. Ithaca: Olin Library, Cornell University.

326. The AIDS paitent as black, male, and, by implication, gay, from *Newsweek*, 21 July 1986. Ithaca: Olin Library, Cornell University.

327. The prostitute as the source of AIDS. A political cartoon by J. D. Crowe from the *San Diego Tribune*, March 14, 1987. Ithaca: Olin Library, Cornell University.

328. The face of death in the woman's body as represented by Salvador Dali, *In voluptate mors*, 1944, photograph by Philippe Halsman. New York: Hastings Galleries.

Index

Page numbers in bold type refer to illustrative plates.

Berkeley, Bishop, 210
Béthencourt, Jacques de, 78
Bible: human anatomy and, 49–54, 122–24; models of sexuality in, 13, 31, 44, 48, 54; references to, as warning, 146

  Old Testament, 86; Bathsheba, 44, **44**; creation story, 15, 17, 18, 123; Sodom and Gomorrah, 88, 95, 325; Song of Songs, 227; story of Noah, 29, **30**, **31**, 31; Susanna, 44, **45**; views of sexuality, 14–31. *See also* Adam and Eve; images and themes of sexuality; themes of sexuality

  New Testament: kinds of touch in, 36–44, 48; reading of Old Testament, 48. *See also* Christ; Mary Magdelene; Mary, Virgin

Bidloo, Govard, *Anatomia . . .*, 168–69, 170, **168**, **169**, **171**, 173, 179, 212; influence of, 173–74

Billroth, Theodor, *Handbook of Gynaecological Diseases*, 294, 295, 299

Birnbaum, Nathan, 261

black(s): child, images of, 106, 109, **108–10**, 277, **281**, **291**; emblem of hypersexuality, 29, **30**, 101, 106, 290, 294, 303, 322, 324; exhibited to public, 273–74, 275; female, 100, 212, 276, 290, 295; Jews as, 261, 278; link with bestiality, 101–2, 106, 109, 255, 323, 324; linked to disease, 99–100, 101, 148, 150, 216, 261, 274, 303, 322– 25, 327; medical experiments on, 260, 323; as the Other, 13, 276, 278, 307; as primitive, 277, 291, 302, 303; servant, 44, 216, 287, **288**, **290**, 290, 297, 303, 304; as sexual object, 277, 278–79

Blandin, Philippe, *Traité d'anatomie topographique*, 234, **234**

Blasio, Abele de, 302, **303**

Blasio, Gerard Leonardo, **127**

Blumenbach, Johann Friedrich, 90, 291

Boccaccio, Giovanni, *Decameron*, 240

Bodin, Jean, 101

body, human: anonymous images of, **65**, **133**, **136–38**; changing views of, 99, 170, 233–35; flap models of, 127, 129, 132–38, **133–35**, **137–38**, 175; map of, 48, **54**, 55–58, 181; medieval and Renaissance views of, 49, 52, 55–58; as microcosm, 118–20, 123, 133; opening of, 54, 69–71, 117, 130, **180**, **181**, **196**; perfection of, 49, 170, 225; seen as medical subject, 174–75; as tortured and mutilated, 191, 196, 250; viewed as asymmetrical, 170, 174; viscera figures, **53**, **54**, 55, 58; wax models of, 181, *184–88*, 189–91, 343n32. *See also* anatomy, human

Boerhaave, Hermann, *Oeconomia animalis*, 165, **166**, **167**, 167, 195

Bonaparte, Marie, 249, 339n38

Bosch, Hieronymus
  God Presenting Eve to Adam, 17, **17**
  Last Judgement, 24, **26**, 85

Bosse, Abraham, *Tactus*, 159, **159**

Bossi, Giuseppe Maria, *Esposizione delle malattie veneree*, 216–17, **218**

Bouguereau, Adolph William, *Young Girl . . .*, **246**, 246–47

Bourgery, Marc Jean, *Traité complet . . .*, 234, 235, **235**, **236**

Brant, Sebastian
  pamphlet on syphilis, 79–80, **80**, 83, 88, 318
  Ship of Fools, 321

breasts, images of: bared, 276; classical, as sign of innocence, 27, 46, 60, 247; different meanings of, 27–28, 276; nursing mother, 24, **27**, 119, **144**

Breughel, Peter, the Elder, *Syphlitic with Couple*, **84**, 85

Bronzino, Agnolo
  Venus, Cupid, Folly and Time, 148, **149**
  Venus, Love and Jealousy, 148, **148**

Brown, Tom, "A Letter to Madam ----," 255, 257

Bry, Johannes de, **122**, 131, **131**

Bry, Theodor de, *Grand Voyages*, 27, 276

Bucher, Bernadette, 10, 27–28, 276

Buckley, William, 329

Buffon, Georges Louis Leclerc, comte de, 101, 112, 290–91

Burnett, Frances Hodgson, *Little Lord Fauntleroy*, 270

Burrowes, A. D., *The Modern Encyclopaedia*, 177, **177**

buttocks: of black women, 279, 280, 292–96, 299, 300; of prostitutes, 302, **303**, 304

Bynum, William, 291

Calcar, Johann Stephen of, 49, **50**, 69–71

Calenzuoli, Francesco, 181

Callari, I., **302**, 302

Calvert, Thomas, 42

Campe, Maxime du, 192

Camper, Pieter, *Demonstrationum . . .*, **295**, 295

Cantimpré, Thomas de, 42

Caravaggio
  Boy Bitten by a Lizard, 152, **153**, 156, 210, 247
  Incredulity of St. Thomas, The, 40, **41**, 42–43

Carroll, Lewis, 271, **272**

castration: linked to circumcision, 41; fear of, 193, 247, 249–50, 267; theory of, 193, 266–67

Catapano, Salvatore J., 318, 319

Centers for Disease Control, reports by, 310

Cesi, Carlo, *Cognitione . . .*, **195**, 195

Chadwick, Edwin, 277

Chamberlain, Houston Stewart, 261; *The Foundations of the Nineteenth Century*, 278

Charcot, Jean Martin, 265, 270

Charpy, Adrien, 302

Cheselden, William, 210, 212; *The Anatomy of the Human Body*, 198, **212**, **213**

child, children: diseased, **316**, **317**, **320**, 326; Freud's concept of, 264, 268, 269; hysteria in, 270, 271; images of, **271**, **272**, **280**, 280–81, **281**; masturbating, 264, **265**, 267–68; and the senses, 263; stereotypes of, 269, 270, 273; as victim of sexualized touch, 269. *See also* black(s)

childbirth and pregnancy: associated with the Fall, 31, 52, 66; images of, 55, **59**, 66–67, **66**, 92, **121**, **174**; linked to disease, 66, 92, 247; linked to stones, 161

Choulant, Ludwig, 91

Christ: genitalia of, 36, 37, **38**; as healer and Redeemer, 19, 24, 46, 78, **80**, 240; vs. the Jew, 41–42; linked to the Fall, 18–19, 28, 32, 78, 136; opening the body of, 54; as the Other, 36, 43; sexuality of, 32, 36, 39, 40, 42–43, 157, 209; touching penis of, 32, **32**, **33**, 36, 39, 40

Christian, Christianity: condemnation of masturbation, 36, 206; higher form of sexuality, 157; vs. the Jews, 13, 41, 115, 266, 267, 268; reading of the Old Testament, 18; views on disease, 5, 66, 78–79, 83–84. *See also* Bible; sexuality, views of

Chrysostomus, St. John, 44

Cigoli, Lodovico, 179, 184

circumcision: of Christ, 32, 41; definitions, 32, 41–42; as sign of Jewish difference, 41–42, 79, 157, 255, 258, 265

Clement of Alexandria, 94

clitoris, 199–203, 264; images of, **201**, **202**

Coiter, Volche, 184

coitus: connected with disease, 66, 92, 203; and creation, 66–67, 123–24; fantasy of, 279; images of, 66–67, **68**, 74, **90**, 91, **92**, **141**, **244**; and the observer, 66, 67

Cokely, Steve, 325

Colombo, Matteo Realdo, 199

Comestor, Petrus, 15

conception, theories of, 55, 58–60, 91, 122, 165, 167–68, 340n25; elements of, **235**; preformist, 112, 118–20, 127, 144–45, 169,

Manet, Édouard
  Nana, 287, **289**, 304, 305, 306, 353n54
  Olympia, 287, **288**, 297, 303, 304
Manetho, 86
Marr, Wilhelm, 260
Marx, Karl, 261
Mary Magdalene, 43–44, 46, 48; images of, **43**, **45–48**, 60, 106
Mary, Virgin: images of, **20**, **37**, 44, 60, 124, 126, 144; linked to Eve, 18–19, 28, 36, 169; secularized, 34
Masters, William H., and Virginia E. Johnson, 268
masturbation: by child, 264, **265**, 267–68; Church condemnation of, 36, 206; and homosexuality, 206, 208; by the Jew, 258, **259**, 267; linked to disease, 206–9, 220, 264, 268; mutual, 227, 228; theories of, 264, 268; as unnatural, 203, 208. *See also* masturbatory insanity
masturbatory insanity, 4, 206, 208, 264, 268, 271; fear of, 282, 284, 285; images of, 283–84, **283**
Maudsley, Henry, 284
Maupassant, Guy de, "Boule-de-suif," 298
Mauzaisse, J. B., 82
Max, Gabriel, *Der Anatom*, **249**, 249
Medallion Master, *Temptation*, **22**
medical books: handbooks of obstetrics, 174, 177; title pages of, **70, 74, 123–24, 130–32, 136, 142, 182–83, 218**. *See also* medical illustration
medical illustration: classical influence in, 169; flap pictures, 127, 129, 132–38, 175; vs. "higher" art, 5, 8; history of, 8–9; vs. pornography, 7; in textbooks and atlases, 49–65, 69–71, 74–76, 122–35, 161–78, 180–82, 194–99, 212–13, 231, 233–35, 253, 285
medical studies: fascination with sexualized body, 231; focus on disease, 231; idea of development, 234; obstetrics, 174–75, 177, 213; Vienna school, 234–25
medicine, Western: experiments on blacks, 260, 323; in literature, 177, 203; and spread of AIDS, 325. *See also* medical illustration; medical studies; physician
melancholia, 282; images of, 311, **317**, 319, **321**; linked to masturbation, 282; linked to syphilis, 87–88, 145; treatment for, 88
mental illness: hysteria in children, 270, 271; hysteria in Jews, 260, 265; linked to sexuality, 268; love madness, 190, 217–20, 247; and sexually transmitted disease, 87–88, 311, 319. *See also* masturbatory insanity; melancholia
Meyer, Bernard, 280
Meyer's Encyclopedia, 274, 276, 280
Michelangelo, 49, 339n21
  The Drunkenness of Noah, 29, **30**
Michelet, Jules, 279
microscope: role of, 124, 231, 234; technology of, importance, 112, 122, 124
Millais, John Everett, *Ophelia*, 248–49
Minga, Andrea del, 17
Moll, Albert, 266
Molyneux, William, 210, 224
Mondino (Raimondo de' Luzzi), 91, 95
monsters, 173; anatomical analogy of, 168, 173, 174, 178, 191, 192–93, 197; and disease, 203, 205; images of, **162**, **188**; linked to female sexual fantasies, 162, 165, 200; linked to race, 101, 210; linked to sexual perversion of women, 109–10; origin of, 106, **107–9**, 164–65, 167–68, 197
Montagnana, Bartholomeus, 88
Montagu, Ashley, 333n49
Morgagni, Giovanni, *Adveria anatomica omnia*, 101, **164**, 170, **172**, 173
Morison, Alexander, *The Physiognomy of Mental Diseases*, 218, **219**

Moschion, 60, **61**
Moulin, Francis J., erotic photograph by, **245**, 245
Müller, Johannes, 200; "Über die äusseren Geschlechtstheile . . .," 293, **294**
museums, anatomical: in Florence, 184, 189, 190; for teaching, 183, 184; for tourists, 189–90; wax figures in La Specola, 181, 184, **184–88**, 191
Musset, Alfred de, *Garniani*, **244**, 245

Needham, George, 287
Newsday, AIDS article in, 319, **320**
Newsweek, 6; articles on AIDS, 309, 325, **327**
Nietzsche, Friedrich, 2, 261
  The Genealogy of Morals, 277–78
nineteenth century: fascination with female genitalia, 293, 295, 296–97; link of race and sexuality, 280, 290–92, 296, 297; medical interest in sexuality, 231, 306; and the prostitute, 238–50, 297; shifting view of body, 233–35. *See also* fin de siècle; Victorian age
Nordau, Max, 267
nude(s), 2; children as, **272**, **273**, 273; classical models of, 287; images of, **148**, **149**, **229**; as neutral, 193; reclining, **150**, **214**, **225**, **288**, **305**

Oken, Lorenz, 234, 277
Onania; or, The Heinous Sin of Self-Pollution, 206, 209
orgasm, 3, 58, 264
Origen, 42
Other, the: black as, 276, 278, 307; as diseased, 5, 6, 309, 329; fear of, 31, 306–7; female as, 11, 55, 99, 227, 278, 279, 295, 307; homosexual as, 89–90, 97; Jew as, 216, 251, 278; as observer, 36, 66, 67; sexualized, 3, 4, 99, 100, 247, 295; vs. society, 89–90. *See also* difference

Palazzo Torregiani (Florence), wax casts in, 189, 190
Paracelsus, 86, 112, 142, 337n49
Paré, Ambrose, 102, 161; images of sexual difference, 106, 109–11
  The Works . . ., **104–5, 107, 108**
Parent-Duchatelet, A. J. B., 297–99, 302, 303
Parentino, Bernardo, 24, **27**
Pascoli, Alessandro, *Il corpo-umani*, **198**, 199
Paul, St., 18, 41, 48, 115
Pearlstein, Philip, *Seated Female Nude on Black Chair*, 193, **193**
Penfield, Wilder, *The Cerebral Cortex of Man*, 268, **269**
penis: in anatomy textbooks, **63, 166, 172, 194, 195, 198, 199, 201, 202, 236**; in Christian iconography, 32, 33, 36, 39; dissected, 195, **196**, **234**; imagery of, **90**, 94, 129, 162, **245**, 258; structure of, 63–64, 91, 162, **163, 164, 178**, 194–95, 339n23. *See also* erection, male; genitalia, male
Percy, Walker, 1
phallus: black as, 29, 106; in Christian iconography, 32; in images, **124**, 162, 283, 284; as monster, 197, 258. *See also* penis
Philo, *On the Creation of the World*, 28
photography, 245, 246, 287
physician: as healer, 240, 318; Jew as, 86, 325; in obstetrics, 174–75, 177; as observer of sexuality, 67, 69; as opener of body, 69–71, 74, **130**, 130–31, 249, 250; as scientist, 109, 110; and sexually transmitted diseases, 203, 309, 318; training for, 183. *See also* medicine, Western
Piacenza, Franco da, 42, 268
Picart, Bernhard, image of Adamites, 170, **170**
Picasso, Pablo
  demoiselles d'Avignon, Les, 305
  Olympia, 304–5, **305**
Pico della Mirandola, 99